Great Masters

FROM

CORELLI AND VIVALDI

TO STERN,

ZUKERMAN AND PERLMAN

of the

Violin

BORIS SCHWARZ

Foreword by Yehudi Menuhin

SIMON AND SCHUSTER · NEW YORK

Copyright © 1983 by Boris Schwarz
All rights reserved
including the right of reproduction
in whole or in part in any form
Published by Simon and Schuster
A Division of Simon & Schuster, Inc.
Simon & Schuster Building
Rockefeller Center
1230 Avenue of the Americas
New York, New York 10020
SIMON AND SCHUSTER and colophon
are registered trademarks of Simon & Schuster, Inc.
Designed by Edith Fowler
Manufactured in the United States of America

10 9 8 7 6 5 4 3 2 1

Library of Congress Cataloging in Publication Data

Schwarz, Boris, date
    Great masters of the violin.

    Bibliography: p.
    Includes index.
    1. Violinists, violoncellists, etc.—Biography.
I. Title.
ML398.S4 1983   787.1′092′2 [B]   83-11996
ISBN 0-671-22598-7

ACKNOWLEDGMENTS

This book was a decade in the making during which I received advice from various editors at Simon and Schuster—Strome Lamon, William Steinkraus, Norman Monath, Peter Schwed, until the manuscript finally landed on Bob Bender's desk. I am particularly grateful for Bob's perceptive and circumspect guidance. My text was skillfully edited by Hinda Farber, who understood the musical and violinistic problems involved. I am very grateful to Shirley Fleming, editor of *Musical America*, for permitting me to use its pictorial file. The Research Center for Musical Iconography at the City University of New York was kindly opened to me by Professor Barry S. Brook and his assistant Andrew Green. Thanks for rare pictures to Carl Flesch, Jr., Jacques Francais, Mrs. Ivan Galamian, Neva Garner Greenwood, John Pfeiffer, Sylvia Rabinof, Albi Rosenthal, and Emanuel Winternitz; to Peter Harris for photographic work, and to my son Robert for autographing the musical examples. I am grateful to the Library of Congress and the Stockholm National Museum for their cooperation. Thanks also to the following artists' representatives, publishers, and firms: Herbert Barrett Management, CBS Masterworks, Columbia Artists Management, ICM Artists, Ltd., Jacques Leiser Management, The Juilliard School, Robert Levin Associates, Inc., Macmillan Publishers, RCA Victor, Sheldon Soffer Management, Alix Williamson, Young Concert Artists. And to these photographers: Kenn Duncan, Henry Grossman, Leonid Lubianitsky, Peter Schaaf, Bernard Schaub, Christian Steiner.

*To Patty
and to our sons, Jack and Rob,
with all my love*

CONTENTS

FOREWORD

BORIS SCHWARZ's book comes out at a most apposite and remarkable time historically: in point of fact at a moment when the period of Russian Jewish supremacy among international world violinists seems to have passed its apogee and is possibly reaching its end. This supremacy has lasted three generations, from the time those first pupils of Leopold Auer came to the United States and Western Europe as a result of the Russian Revolution. So wonderful a batch—a clutch— what should be the collective noun for such superb violinists? A pride, as it is for lions?

Being myself of the same stock, I may venture a few reasons for the overwhelming number of Russian Jewish musicians in the roster of violinists. Why, indeed, the Russian Jew, and not the Italian, Hungarian, Austrian, Czech, Scottish? I would suggest it sprang from three eminently marketable things, i.e. the goods, the audiences, and the purveyor—or, if you prefer, the middleman.

To retrace the history of the violin, great violinists already abounded in the Italy of the seventeenth and eighteenth centuries, culminating in the nineteenth with Paganini, who was the first international virtuoso, the first "star" to travel from city to city, astounding audiences with his superb, almost diabolical, mastery of his instrument, playing, moreover, his own compositions in the main. For those were the centuries of the violinist-composer. All the great Italian violinists preceding and including Paganini, from Corelli and Vivaldi through Tartini and Locatelli, Veracini, and a host of others, were composers.

Other great peoples had their violin folk music, added to which they made their own violins, played on them in their villages the music which belonged to their people for dancing, for joy or for sorrow. From the Hebrides and Orkneys, through Norway to Austria and Hungary and Rumania you will find the popular fiddle with its local folk music and its special players. However, it was the Italians who reached the literate stage of composing, owing to the microcosm that was their incredibly evolved city states, principalities, and kingdoms, and aided by that tremendous flowering of the arts which was the Renaissance. In Italy these rustic homemade fiddles gradually evolved in the hands of the master craftsmen, the earliest of whom were probably Maggini and Gaspar da Salò and on into the glorious Amatis, Guarneris, and Stradivari we now cherish. The music of the villages became the sonatas of Corelli, the concertos of Vivaldi, and all the great works which are still the basic heritage of the cultivated violinist. But it was left to the nineteenth century to accumulate that great published repertoire of Romantic compositions reflecting the special emancipation of a large middle class which could support and, indeed, demand the international purveyor. And it was the Russian Jewish community, rooted in a universal philosophy, literate and urban, skilled in commerce, driven by passionate, intense feelings and ambitions for liberation, which became the main interpreter to the world; interpreter of that rich vein of composed repertoire accumulating since the days of Mozart, who heralded the dawn of the Romantic, and on to the great Russian, Tchaikovsky.

One must bear in mind that the Russian Jew of the village ghetto had, as well as the example of the village folk fiddler, that of the gypsy fiddler, whose melodies he also shared, to say nothing of the unique treasure of traditional local heritage from the cantors and the Chassidic rabbis. It was the Jewish fiddler who always played the violin to express the joys and sorrows of the Russian villages; thus he had both played and listened to the Russian folksongs and those of the gypsies. This marvelous heritage suddenly dawned on me with a flash when I saw before me what I had never imagined in my wildest fancies: a vast range of rustic, curiously devised, infinitely varied shapes in the Folk Museum in Moscow. For the Russian Jew, highly motivated, highly literate, and yet ever destined to start life anew, the violin was the passport, purse, and path to the summits of society. From the southern warm-water port of Odessa, that egress to the Mediterranean and the wider world, many of the best Russian violinists came. I well remember my amused amazement when, after the first concert I gave there, the people who flocked backstage made no comment whatsoever on the music, but one and all asked me specifically what fingering I had used in such and such a passage. It was more like being engulfed by a gigantic crowd composed of students, ex-students, and professors than by the heterogeneous audiences of any other city I have ever played in. Indeed, there was barely a Jewish family that did not have its young, budding violinist. And Rabbi de Sola Pool, an old friend of my parents when they first emigrated to New York, told me that following the pogroms of 1905, Jews arrived at that time in Palestine with almost every child carrying a violin case. Today, so it would seem, it is only thanks to the Russian Jews emigrating to Israel from Russia that the string ranks, particularly the violin ranks, of the Israel Philharmonic and the Jerusalem Symphony can be maintained. No wonder that, with the extraordinary teaching of Leopold Auer—equal in its own way to the superb coaching of the czar's Maryinsky Theater Ballet—it should be the great school of Auer which took over the United States and its box office.

While Joseph Joachim, himself a Jew, and Spohr, who preceded him, represented the German school, very highly flavored with Hungarian color, as was the music of Brahms, Marteau and Marsick represented the French school, and Eugène Ysaÿe founded the Belgian school. These European schools actually almost held back their international exponents by virtue of too strong a national style.

The peculiarly intimate association of violinist and violin, springing from the imperative necessity to start taming this most demanding of instruments from a very early age, shared not only on the stage, but, of course, in endless hours of work from childhood on, this close relationship as between Don Quixote and his inseparable steed, as close a relationship as that between a crusader and his trusty sword, is what I lived and knew from over half a century's experience of travel and concerts. The ceaseless search for the better fingering, the more deeply expressive, the more universally understanding, the more directly communicative, the more irresistibly convincing and overwhelming, is what my forebears and I tried to make our music convey, every day beginning anew, dreaming, working, polishing, patiently and impatiently, demanding both of oneself and of one's instrument and forever continuing. It is on this that we have spent a greater part of our lifetime.

This is the whole heart of the matter, and the empathy with which this whole book is informed makes of Boris Schwarz a violinist's prime advocate. There can be no more qualified commentator on the violinist, his soul, his character, his interpretation, and his lifestyle. For this alone we are forever indebted to him, to his scholarship so blessedly free of pretentiousness and for the warm generosity and devotion to his subjects. But history is ever on the move, and since the end of the Second World War other races have attached themselves to this universal violinistic currency, along with the many and various sciences and applied technologies, and are now competing with us in all these fields, in particular the people of the Far East. In this metamorphosis our music has become their lingua franca. They sit in an extraordinarily reverent silence in Tokyo, Peking, and Seoul, listening to Elgar and Beethoven, with which composers, despite the fact that they can share no common heritage whatsoever, they can yet somehow identify themselves, sense, and understand. What does sadden me, however, is the way in which, with unseemly haste, every tribe promptly abandons its own idiom, most people their characteristic musical style and language, to play the admittedly great Western works, but those already written, prepared, packaged, recorded, and televised, thus destroying their ancient, irreplaceable gift of improvisation. One asks oneself what kind of universal musical culture will be likely to evolve under these circumstances? More than ever it is, therefore, important to maintain a very high level of creative musical education, as well as purely instrumental prowess, if our sole ambition is not merely that of turning out talented monkeys. In my own humble way I have attempted to inculcate this synoptic approach to musical grounding in all the young pupils, seven to seventeen, at my Music School.

YEHUDI MENUHIN

PREFACE

THIS BOOK owes its existence to the vision of the late Henry Simon. It was his cherished hope to crown the series *The Great Pianists*, *The Great Conductors*, *The Great Singers* with a corresponding book on violinists. I know that he searched for an author to realize this project before he and I had our first meeting in 1970. For three hours we talked about violins and violinists. We must have found the topic inexhaustible, for we had another meeting, equally long. At the end, I was asked to submit an outline for the book and to write a chapter, which Henry edited and I rewrote. His mind was made up and I had a contract for the violin book. The projected publication date was 1973.

During the next few months, Henry and I met several times and he described how he envisaged the book. It should discuss violinists as performers rather than composers—how they played, how they sounded, by what means they impressed their public. These were the questions uppermost in his mind. "Bring them to life, make them sound!" he urged me. He had the curiosity of an ardent amateur violinist, mine was that of a seasoned professional and historian, but we understood each other. Our friendship was all too short—Henry died unexpectedly within the next six months. I was deeply shocked; for a time I thought that I could not continue the project. When I finally returned to it, I felt that I had a responsibility to complete the book in the spirit in which it had begun.

This was more easily resolved than accomplished. Nothing is more elusive than a musical performance. To reconstruct the sound of a Corelli, a Vivaldi, a Paganini, I had to rely on ear witnesses, printed reports, memoirs, letters, autobiographies. After 1900 the invention of the phonograph made the evaluation more objective, though too much reliance on old recordings is problematic. Whenever possible, I preferred to rely on my personal recollections of violinists I had heard since the 1920s, and I was fortunate indeed to have had direct contact with so many of them.

With the earlier centuries, it was difficult to separate the performers from the composers because the old masters were all composer-performers, playing their own music almost exclusively. The art of "interpreting" the music of other composers emerged slowly. One of the first interpreters was Joseph Joachim in the mid-nineteenth century, who subordinated his ambition as a composer to his overpowering desire to be the interpreter of great music, from Bach to that of his friend Brahms. Interpretation grew in importance during the second half of the nineteenth century and became dominant in the twentieth century, when the "performing" virtuoso completely overshadowed the "composing" virtuoso. Today, if we speak of a great virtuoso, we mean his ability to perform flawlessly, to interpret and communicate great music composed by others. He is the "re-creator" of music, standing between the "creator" (composer) and the listener.

Does the activity of re-creating music deserve the epithet "greatness"? Can there be genius in performance? Can a superb performance be compared to a creative achievement? Yes, under certain ideal conditions, if one does not cheapen one's praise by overemphasis of purely technical perfection. Let me quote the poet Heinrich Heine, who lived during this critical juncture in the nineteenth century when composers and performers began to go their separate ways. He wrote in 1843:

> What is the summit in art? . . . the self-assured freedom of the spirit. Such a summit is not only a composition written in the fullness of that self-expression, but also *its performance*, provided it conveys to the listener that miraculous inspiration which proves the Executant to be on an equal level with the Composer—equal in spiritual freedom, proving that he, too, is a freeman.

In a large sense, this book deals with Executants and Composers. When a violinist happens to be equally great as virtuoso and composer (as for example Vivaldi), his performing achievements are explored more fully than his compositions. However, the technical problems encountered in the compositions permit us to draw conclusions about his playing ability and his performance style.

The more estranged the virtuosos become from the act of composition, the more willing they seem to be to collaborate with composers in the creation of violin works. And composers accept their advice willingly. One intention of mine is to clarify in this book the relations between composers and performers, particularly after 1850. The creative friendships of Joachim with Schumann and Brahms, of Sarasate with Lalo and Saint-Saëns, of Oistrakh with Prokofiev and Shostakovich, of Szigeti and Menuhin with Bartók, of Ysaÿe and Franck, Kreisler and Elgar, Auer and Glazunov, Dushkin and Stravinsky, d'Arányi and Ravel (and many more recent) reveal the mutual stimulation of composers and performers. Truly great violinists do not exist in isolation; they form an integral part of the larger musical canvas.

When it comes to violinists, virtuosity is not entirely the result of mechanical finger velocity and sheer technique, as it is with pianists. The violin is an instrument which has almost human whims—it is attuned to the mood of the player in a sympathetic rapport: a minute discomfort, the tiniest inner imbalance, a whiff of sentiment elicits an immediate resonance . . . probably because the violin, pressed against the chest, can perceive our heart's beat. But this happens only with artists who truly have a heart that beats, who have a soul. The more sober, the more heartless a violinist is, the more uniform will be his performance, and he can count on the obedience of his fiddle, any time, any place. But this much-vaunted assurance is only the result of a spiritual limitation, and some of the greatest masters were often dependent on influences from within and without. I have never heard anyone play better—or, for that matter, play worse—than Paganini. . . .

Thoughts on the Violin and on Violinists
Heinrich Heine (1843)

PART ONE

The Distant Past:
1530-1600

One of the earliest known paintings of a violin, by Gaudenzio Ferrari, 1535

THE EMERGENCE
OF THE VIOLIN
AS A NEW INSTRUMENT

The violin faces us with a problem. . . . It can be said that at a given date it was not at all, and that shortly afterwards it is found full fledged in active life.[1]

THE ORIGIN OF THE VIOLIN is uncertain. No one can claim to have invented it. Suddenly it is present. In 1529–30, the Italian artist Gaudenzio Ferrari painted an angel playing a violin. The shape is unmistakable—the sharp bouts, the f-shaped openings, the fretless fingerboard—though the instrument has only three strings. A few years later, in 1535, the same artist painted violins in three sizes, corresponding to violin, viola, and violoncello. The violin family was born, though the number of strings was still uncertain.

"One picture is worth more than a thousand words," says an old Chinese proverb. We have the pictorial evidence of the violin's existence but the models used by the Italian painter have not survived. Also lacking is any clear-cut description of the new instrument in the theoretical treatises of the time. Occasionally there are vague hints: Italian authors mention "arm viols without frets," while German writers speak of "small fiddles tuned in fifths."[2] A violin with three strings, dated 1542, was attributed to Andrea Amati, ancestor of the famed family of violin makers. Violins were also built outside of Italy, notably in Poland, which attracted the interest of the German theorist Agricola. He wrote in 1545,

> Further, I must tell you that there is another class of geigen which is common in Poland, wherein the strings are tuned in

27

fifths and they are played in a different way. . . . The strings are stopped with the finger-nail . . . not with the soft end of the finger, as that would tend to deaden the sound. . . .* It is much more difficult to learn the fingering without frets, but there is no difficulty on earth that cannot be overcome with practice.[3]

Agricola preferred the sound of the Polish violins to that of the Italian ones. However, the instrument discussed here still had only three strings. A fourth string, the highest, was added about 1550; it expanded the range and enhanced the tonal brilliance.

In 1556 we find at last the first unmistakable description of a genuine violin: an instrument "supported on the arm" (meaning held up), without frets, and with four strings tuned in fifths—g, d', a', e'' (the same tuning used today). This information was provided by the Frenchman Jambe de Fer in his treatise *Epitome musical*:[4] he tells us that the new violin is ordinarily used for dance music because the player can move around freely and because the four strings can be tuned easily. He implies that the violin is a "common" instrument while "gentlemen, merchants, and other virtuous people" prefer the viol, a six-string instrument played while sitting down. This social distinction between viol and violin persisted for almost two centuries, and the violin was often denigrated as loud and somewhat vulgar, a musical upstart. Nevertheless, the violin won the battle.

We do not know the name of the luthier who built the attractive instruments used as models by the painter Gaudenzio. At one time, the lute maker Dieffobrugar was advanced as the "inventor," but that myth has been discarded. Another violin maker, Gasparo da Salò, was born too late—in 1540—to have "invented" the instruments depicted by Gaudenzio. But there is the oldest member of the Amati family, Andrea Amati, who was born not later than 1511, and it is not impossible that he built violins similar to those depicted by Gaudenzio. Curious as the claim for priority is, it makes more sense to accept the fact that the violin is a kind of collective miracle, shaped through patient experiments by skilled artisans until an instrument emerged that satisfied all aesthetic demands as to shape and sound.

Violins were built not only in Italy but also in France, Germany,

---

* Contrary to this advice, the violin is played "with the soft end of the finger" while the fingernails are cut short so as to avoid contact with the string. Violinists who practice daily acquire callused fingertips, which prevents the string from cutting into the flesh.

and Poland. However, the Italian instrument makers established a reputation for superior craftsmanship and exported large numbers of instruments to northern Europe. In the 1560s and '70s, Andrea Amati of Cremona delivered thirty-eight violins, violas, and cellos to the French court of Charles IX. Gasparo da Salò of Brescia also exported violins, especially to France, though he complained that the export business was declining. By 1600, violins were made in many parts of Europe and brought high prices.

At first, violins served a dual purpose—doubling voices and playing dance music. When joining a vocal ensemble, the violinist read the music from a voice part, and no special violin part was needed. Dance music was usually played by ear because dance musicians were hardly expected to be able to read music. Obviously, violins were being widely used before there was any specific violin music. The earliest printed music for violins dates from 1582. As part of the *Ballet comique de la Reine*, played for a royal wedding at the French court, ten musicians performed on stage, elaborately dressed in white satin decorated with gold tinsel and wearing plumed hats. They played dances set for violins of various sizes, probably pairs of violins I and II, violas I and II, and violoncellos or basses. After 1600, a repertoire was developed "apt for voyces or viols" or "*da cantare o suonare*" (to sing or to play), which permitted the interchange of singers and players.

In Italy, violins were used in churches, reinforcing voices in the performance of sacred music; in Verona of 1580, for example, violins and organ accompanied the great Mass. In England and Germany, violins were used for dance, for court entertainments, and as dinner music at important occasions. Yet there is little documentary evidence of early violin music because so much of it was improvised or doubled from vocal parts.

The term *violino* was used loosely at first, embracing a family of similar instruments, including at times the viola. An example is provided in the *Sonata pian e forte* (1597) by Giovanni Gabrieli: it contains a single "*violino*" part (used in combination with trombones) that can be played only on a viola because it goes below the range of a violin. But such ambiguities soon disappeared, and *violino* became the undisputed name for the "soprano" instrument of the violin family.

PART TWO

The Age
of Experimentation:
1600-1700

VIOLINIST-COMPOSERS
AS INNOVATORS:
NEW TECHNIQUES, NEW FORMS

ONCE THE VIOLIN was accepted as a new instrument, the players soon developed a new distinctive technique—quick runs, various bowings, double stops, and the use of higher positions to extend the range. A slower process was the development of new musical forms to display the new instrument to best advantage. We witness the emergence of the *canzon da sonare* (*chanson* to be played) from which the *sonata* branched out. The early sonatas were short pieces, subdivided into contrasting sections, which later grew into movements. There were sonatas composed for use in the church (*da chiesa* in Italian), others for the chamber (*da camera*), with a distinctive style emerging for each of these functions: the sacred style more sustained and polyphonic, the secular style dancelike, with more pronounced rhythms.

Such music was composed to be played by groups of violins—usually two, three, or four—always accompanied by one bass part (usually cello) with chords filled in on a keyboard (harpsichord or organ, the so-called *figured bass**). Eventually, the favorite combination became the *trio sonata*, consisting of two violins and a bass part plus the filled-in chords. For over a century, the trio sonata remained the most popular chamber music ensemble, dominating the Baroque era, until it was displaced by the string quartet after 1750.

More important for the development of violin playing was the sonata for a single violin with figured bass, often called *solo sonata*.

* The figured bass was a shorthand for notating the harmony: the chords were indicated by numbers placed above or below the bass line.

33

This became the preferred vehicle for technical display until the violin concerto took over in the early eighteenth century.

Many masters contributed their share to these developments; their names appear in history books, their music is known mainly to scholars. Italians led the way, experimenting and innovating, culminating finally in Arcangelo Corelli, the first of the "great violinists."

ITALY

Let us briefly survey the development of violin playing leading up to Corelli. At the head stands the eminent Claudio Monteverdi, famous for his operas and vocal works. Monteverdi was trained as a professional string player, so it is not surprising that many innovations in the expressive use of the violin can be found in his compositions. In his opera *L'Orfeo* (performed in Mantua in 1607) Monteverdi used a rich orchestra including a dozen violins in assorted sizes and groupings: divided violins, divided violas, cellos, and two *violini piccoli* tuned an octave above the ordinary violins. In later works Monteverdi employed *tremolo* (quick alternating bow strokes on one note) as an "imitation of passionately excited speech"; he also introduced *pizzicato*, namely plucking the string with the right hand. To add to the expressive range he called for a dying-away bow stroke, which he called *arcata morenda*, and initial bow accents followed by sudden *piano*, marked *fortepiano*.

Associated with Monteverdi, and undoubtedly inspired by him, were several excellent violinists. His concertmaster in Mantua was Salomone Rossi, surnamed *Il Ebreo* (The Hebrew), who was so highly regarded at court that he was exempt from wearing the yellow badge of the Jew. Rossi published four books of instrumental pieces between 1607 and 1623, among them the earliest trio sonatas for two violins and plucked bass lute. Included are also violin variations and pieces with dance titles. Rossi's violin technique was very simple; he was more interested in exploring instrumental forms than in virtuosity.

A real virtuoso, on the other hand, was Biagio Marini, who joined Monteverdi's instrumentalists at St. Mark's Cathedral in Venice in

35

1615. His contemporaries praised him as a "most virtuosic violinist," though he also mastered other instruments. He reached the top of his profession in 1628, publishing as his Opus 8 a volume of sixty-eight instrumental pieces for a variety of instruments—violin, cornet, bassoon, trombone—in various combinations. Included were violin sonatas with figured bass. His technical treatment of the violin was novel and demanding: double stops, triple and quadruple chords, rapid runs, experiments in tuning, and other effects. For the development of violin technique, Marini's collection is of historical significance; it establishes a new level of proficiency. At present, Marini's music is being rediscovered by violinists specializing in Baroque performance, and he certainly deserves more attention for his pioneering contribution to violin technique.

Marini spent much of his adult life at the Wittelsbach court in Bavaria, bringing the Italian art of violin playing across the Alps. Another Italian virtuoso, Carlo Farina, settled in 1625 as concertmaster in Dresden, where the famous German composer Heinrich Schütz was music director. In Dresden Farina published five collections of instrumental pieces, using the violin with great imagination. He invented effects for pictorial purposes: his *Capriccio stravagante* (Extravagant Caprice) of 1627 imitates various barnyard noises by unusual manipulation of fingers and bow. All the effects are carefully explained in the music: hitting the strings with the stick of the bow, plucking the violin in the manner of a Spanish guitar (that is, holding it under the arm), sliding up the string with one finger, scraping the bow very near the bridge. The *Capriccio* is a "fun" piece and there is no use pretending that it had musical value, but the technical devices have survived and were adapted to musical purposes by later composers.

At mid-century, the most advanced violin music was being written by Mario Uccellini, who was active in Modena until 1665 at court and cathedral. He expanded the range of the violin beyond that of the soprano voice, and by 1649 reached the high g''' in the sixth position on the E-string. It gave the violin a total range of three

octaves 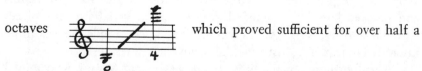 which proved sufficient for over half a

century, until Vivaldi reached for stratospheric heights. Uccellini embellished his cantilena with trills and rich ornamentation, but the rapid passages did not obscure the singing quality of the violin.

In the meantime, the nearby city of Bologna—an intellectual center with its medieval university—underwent a musical regeneration. In 1657, a new music director, Maurizio Cazzati, was appointed at the church of San Petronio. He built a strong musical staff, permanently employing twenty-two singers and thirteen instrumentalists. Among the latter were eight string players: two violins, pairs of alto and tenor violas, one cello and one bass. The cellist was Giovanni Battista Vitali, who was to contribute significantly to the fame of the Bologna school of string players.

A native of Bologna, Vitali joined San Petronio in 1658 to study composition with Cazzati. Though his instrument was the cello, he also played viola and bass, and he knew enough about the violin to teach it to his son Tomaso, who became a prominent musician in his own right. Today, the son is better known than the father: the Chaconne by Tomaso Vitali (or a modernized version thereof) is in the repertoire of virtually every violinist.*

As for the father, Giovanni Battista was a remarkable composer, scholarly as well as imaginative. His fame rested mainly on a large body of chamber music works—fourteen opus numbers, the last of which, edited by his son, appeared in 1692, the year of his death. Not being a performing violinist, Giovanni Battista did not expand the technique of the instrument, but used the violin idiomatically, exploring its songfulness and agility. His main contribution consists of dozens of trio sonatas for two violins and figured bass in both church and chamber style, though the latter prevailed. The chamber sonatas were suites of dances, which undoubtedly were models for the younger generation, not only Corelli but also Henry Purcell, far off in London.

Another prominent member of the San Petronio orchestra in Bologna was Giuseppe Torelli, but he failed to achieve the fame of his contemporary Corelli. The archives of San Petronio bulge with unpublished music by Torelli, all neatly catalogued but rarely performed and known mostly to scholars. His eight published opus numbers consist of chamber music; his most significant achievement is contained in a posthumous volume, Opus 8, brought out in 1709, the year he died. The title "Concerti grossi with a pastorale for Christmas" is actually a misnomer, for among the twelve "concerti grossi" are six genuine *solo* concertos for violin and string orchestra. Historically, the genre of concerto grosso—contrasting a *group* of solo instruments with a string orchestra

---

* Jascha Heifetz opened his memorable debut recital at Carnegie Hall in 1917 with this Chaconne, using an organ accompaniment. The true authorship of this piece is in doubt.

—preceded the solo concerto by several decades. The idea of *one* solo instrument set against a string orchestra was, so to speak, "in the air," but Torelli was the first to give concrete models in print (hiding them behind the better-known designation "concerto grosso"). Torelli's pioneering effort was continued almost immediately by Antonio Vivaldi in Venice, who became the grandmaster of the solo concerto. Modest though Torelli's concertos were, they have historical significance as a new beginning. As for Corelli—enjoying a sheltered career in Rome— he preferred the old ways and adhered to the orthodox form of the concerto grosso as a group effort, ignoring the ambitious solo concerto.

NORTHERN EUROPE

VIOLINS AND VIOLINISTS were among Italy's most valued export assets. Whether in Vienna or Dresden, London or Paris, the Italian influence provided the spark of innovation that activated native talent. However, political or religious events slowed the process in several countries of northern Europe. Germany was ravaged by the Thirty Years' War (1618–48), which was fought mainly on her soil; the only pockets of tranquillity were the neutral Hanseatic cities like Hamburg and Lübeck. Austria, on the other hand, was comparatively unscathed, and Vienna grew in importance, politically and artistically. England experienced political and religious upheavals, and many English musicians took refuge on the Continent, settling particularly in Holland and northern Germany. France enjoyed a stable government, which was so autocratic that it resisted Italian inroads, gallicizing any foreign influences.

English Violinists

The excellent violinist and composer William Brade left his native England around 1590 and held several positions at German courts. He thrived in the free city of Hamburg, where he published several collections; in fact, he is considered the founder of the Hanseatic violin school. As a violinist, Brade excelled in playing "divisions on a ground," that is, extemporizing solo variations on a given bass. English musicians were particularly adept at that art and introduced it to Germany. Traveling in the other direction was the remarkable violinist

39

Thomas Baltzar, who was born in Lübeck and settled in London around 1655. His virtuosity caused a sensation among English connoisseurs, and he was called "the most famous artist for the violin that the world had yet produced." A contemporary reported,

> I saw him run up his fingers to the end of the finger-board of the violin, and run them back insensibly, and all with alacrity and in very good tune, which I nor any in England saw the like before.[1]

Baltzar's wizardry caused one listener to look at his foot as if he expected to see a devil's hoof!

Before Baltzar arrived in London, the English-born Davis Mell was considered the most eminent violinist—he had a "prodigious hand, and they thought that no person . . . could go beyond him." Overshadowed by Baltzar, "Mell was not so admired, yet he played sweeter, was a well-bred gentleman, and not given to excessive drinking as Baltzar was."[2]

Baltzar's premature death in 1663 came at the beginning of a new era in English music, a reorientation toward the French style initiated by the Restoration. The new king, Charles II, who ascended in 1660, had acquired a predilection for French music during the years of his exile. He had "an utter aversion to *fancies* [the traditional English genre] . . . he could bear no music to which he could not beat time."[3] We know that "Charles did not like the viols; preferring the violins as being more airie and brisk than viols."[4] Despite lingering resistance against the "common fiddlers" and their "high-prized noise," the violins took over in England as they did on the Continent. The king established a band of 24 *violins* (actually a string orchestra) after the French model, "and the style of Musick was changed accordingly."

The first Master of the King's Band was Davis Mell, soon replaced by Baltzar. Upon Baltzar's death, John Banister took over, and also led a smaller select group of twelve violins. It was Banister who, in 1672, established the first public concerts in London, every afternoon at four o'clock; the admission was one shilling, which entitled the audience "to call for what they pleased." The musicians performed on an elevated gallery, while the room "was filled with seats and small tables, ale-house fashion." Banister secured "the best hands in London," and there was "very good Musick." After Banister's death in 1679, weekly concerts were sponsored by Thomas Britton, a coal dealer and music patron, which continued until 1714.

In the meantime, an important appointment was made at court:

the eighteen-year-old Henry Purcell was named in 1677 to the post of "composer to the King's violins." It was his duty to write airs and dances for court performances—all of them unfortunately lost—but he was also inspired to compose more artful pieces for string instruments. There are the remarkable String Fantasias of 1680 and the superb twelve Trio Sonatas of 1683 for two violins and figured bass; another ten sonatas were published posthumously in 1697. The first set of sonatas, dedicated to the king, were the first published work of the twenty-four-year-old composer. The volume is adorned by a portrait of Purcell and contains a lengthy Preface attesting to the rising Italian influence:

> Its Author has endeavoured a just imitation of the most famed Italian Masters; principally, to bring the seriousness and gravity of that sort of Music into vogue, and reputation among our Country-men, whose humour, 'tis time now, should begin to loath the levity, and balladry of our neighbours.[5]

Purcell's snickering reference to the French can be explained by the fact that the Italian sonata style had not yet penetrated the French musical defenses. As for the Italian models, Purcell must have known the early church sonatas of Giovanni Battista Vitali or Corelli's Opus 1. Besides, London was saturated with Italian music and musicians; it was said ironically that England had depopulated Italy of violinists. The English connoisseurs received Purcell's sonatas without showing much native pride; so wrote the estimable Roger North of the "Noble set of Sonnatas, which however clog'd with somewhat of an English vein—for which they are unworthily despised—are very artificiall and good Musick."[6] Today we cherish Purcell's trio sonatas, with their slightly archaic and decidedly English flavor, as a delightful addition to the Baroque repertoire.

Purcell's early death in 1695 brought to a close a remarkable era of English chamber music, both for the older viols and the newer violins. The further development of this genre in the British Isles passed into the hands of foreign musicians who settled in London, notably Nicola Matteis, Geminiani, and Handel.

Austria and Germany

Austria and South Germany, as close neighbors of Italy, were always receptive to the blandishments of Italian music. We have mentioned the violinist Biagio Marini, who worked for many years in

Neuburg-on-the-Danube. Another Italian who crossed the Alps was Giovanni Battista Buonamente, who served as chamber musician to the Austrian court in 1626–29 and brought the Italian violin style to Vienna and Prague. Counterbalancing the Italian influence were the many gifted violinists from Bohemia and Moravia who sought to make their fortune in Vienna and at various German courts.

The founder of the old Austrian violin school was Johann Heinrich Schmelzer. In 1649 he was appointed violinist in the court orchestra and rose to director of instrumental music. As such he was in charge at the coronation of Emperor Leopold I in 1658. He was called "the famous and nearly most distinguished violinist in all Europe." His sonatas for violin and figured bass (1664) show him to be technically as advanced as the best Italian contemporaries: adept in runs and arpeggios, higher positions (up to g'''), bouncing staccato, and double stops, his music combines German and Italian traits, and his native tunefulness endeared him to the Viennese public.

The fame of Heinrich von Biber as one of the most accomplished violinists of his generation has endured until today. Born in Bohemia, he entered the services of Prince-Bishop Karl in the mid-1660s, but took French leave in 1670 and settled in Salzburg. It seems that he was sent to Tyrol to select some instruments in the workshop of Stainer and simply absconded, to the fury of his patron, who lost a valuable "chamber valet." In fact, the twenty-six-year-old Biber was already a formidable violin virtuoso who found immediate employment in the court orchestra in Salzburg. Here he rose in rank to Kapellmeister, was ennobled in 1690 (hence the *von* in his name), and died in 1704.

Between 1670 and 1700, Biber had few rivals among Austro-German violinists, and his technique was actually superior to that of his Italian contemporaries, particularly in the mastery of double stops. His achievements can be judged by two collections: the *Rosary Sonatas* of 1676 and the sonatas of 1681, all for violin and figured bass. In addition there is a Passacaglia for unaccompanied violin which can be considered a forerunner of Bach's Chaconne.

When the English historian Charles Burney examined the Biber pieces a century after they were written, he stated with admiration,

> Of all the violin players of the last century, BIBER seems to have been the best, and his solos are the most difficult and the most fanciful of any Music I have seen of the same period. One of the pieces is written on three staves, as if a score for two violins and a bass, but meant to be played in double stops. Others are played in different tunings.[1]

These "different tunings" (called *scordatura* in Italian) make the *Biblical Sonatas* particularly difficult to play. Biber was indeed a composer of great imagination and a violinist of extraordinary skill.

As virtuoso technicians, two German contemporaries can be compared to Biber—Johann Jakob Walther and Johann Paul von Westhoff, both of whom served in Dresden in the late 1670s. Walther is ranked by some reputable historians as the Paganini of his time. The technical arsenal displayed in his two published violin collections (*Scherzi* and *Hortulus*, 1676 and 1688) includes high positions (up to the seventh), firm and bouncing staccato, rapid string crossings, and double stops. He abandoned the musical profession in 1681 to become Italian secretary to the electoral court at Mainz.

Paul von Westhoff, too, divided his career between music and the diplomatic service, which involved extensive traveling. Visiting Paris in 1682, he performed at the royal court of Louis XIV and produced a sensation with his advanced technique, much superior to that of the reigning French violinist Lully. These pieces, which so pleased the king, were immediately published in Paris; they included a suite for unaccompanied violin and a violin sonata with figured bass. For his time, his technique was indeed astounding—elaborate double stops, repeated triple chords, arpeggios, high positions (up to the seventh).

After his return to Dresden (where he occupied the post of court violinist) Westhoff published a few more works: six sonatas for violin and figured bass (1694) and a set of partitas for unaccompanied violin (1696). The latter collection, rediscovered as late as 1974, may have had an indirect influence on Bach. In fact, Bach and Westhoff must have met in Weimar in 1704, where Westhoff died the following year.

Biber, Walther, and Westhoff represented the high point of German violin playing during the seventeenth century. Although they surpassed their Italian contemporaries in technique, the Italians were superior in the cantabile treatment of the violin, as well as in shaping the sonata and concerto forms.

FRANCE

IN FRANCE, the violin led a curious existence. Quite early, the French showed a lively interest in the new instrument, both in theory and in practice. As we have seen, a Frenchman was the first to describe the violin and the French king ordered violins from Italy; but the further development of the art of violin playing was hampered by the restrictive French custom of using violins mainly for dance music. As Pierre Trichet wrote in 1631,

> The violins are principally used for the dance, balls, ballet, masquerades, serenades, *aubades*, feasts, and other joyous pastimes, having been judged more appropriate for these types of recreations than any other instrument.[1]

The music played was simple, limited to first position, and requiring little more than a good sense of rhythm. The range was further constricted by the predilection of French violinists for the upper two strings. The repertoire neither required nor encouraged individual virtuosity, though some adventurous players reached the fourth position.

The violins gained social prestige when Louis XIII granted official status to the 24 *Violons du Roy* in 1626. The 24 *Violons* were actually a string orchestra of instruments belonging to the violin family: violins, violas of various sizes, and large-scale cellos (*"basse de violon"*), distributed as follows:

6 violins
4 viola I*

---

* Only in France was the viola used as second-highest instrument; in Italy and Germany, preference was given to a second violin (violin I and II, viola I and II, violoncello), a practice later adopted in France.

44

4 viola II
4 viola III
6 basse de violon

The sound of this ensemble, according to the learned Marin Mersenne, was "the most ravishing or the most powerful imaginable. . . . The Violin is the King of the Instruments."[2]

In 1653, young King Louis XIV appointed a new court composer for instrumental music, the twenty-nine-year-old Jean-Baptiste Lully. Born in Florence in 1632, he had come to France at the age of barely fourteen as *garçon de chambre* to an aristocratic lady and remained in the household until he was twenty. Here he was given the opportunity of developing his remarkable talent as a musician and dancer, and the violin became his principal instrument. Once at court, he obtained permission to organize a smaller group of string players, the *petits violons* numbering sixteen (later enlarged to twenty-one). Lully enforced a stringent discipline of performance, forbade any kind of individual embellishments, and obtained results that far surpassed the "big" band. Having become a naturalized Frenchman in 1661, he was named superintendent of the Royal Music and soon wielded unlimited power. In 1672 he obtained a monopoly for staged music by seizing control of the Académie Royale de Musique. He now turned to the composition of operas and produced thirteen "lyric tragedies," averaging one a year. Lully was the king's favorite composer and the uncontested master of French music. His death at the age of fifty-four was caused by an accident: while conducting with a heavy oak stick by pounding the floor of the orchestra pit, he hit his foot and died of gangrene.

All the obituaries praised Lully as an incomparable violinist, yet he never composed violin music as such nor was he interested in the technical advances of violinists in Italy or Germany. But for his own type of music—overtures, interludes, ballets, stage music—he created a specific performance style that was imitated at all the courts of Europe: rhythmic bounce, sprightly articulation, short detached bowings, which —so German musicians complained—threatened the sustained singing style. Lully's limited technique (particularly in terms of higher positions and double stops) stunted the growth of French violin playing during the seventeenth century. Having missed the technical progress achieved in Italy and Germany, the French were unprepared to handle the Italian sonata music brought to Paris in the 1680s and '90s—Corelli's sonatas were considered unplayable in Paris. But the French violinists learned fast, as we shall see.

PART THREE

The Classics
of the Violin:
1700-1800

ITALY

Arcangelo Corelli

Corelli is the ancestor of all the great violinists. During his lifetime he was called "master of masters." On each anniversary of his death, his students and admirers gathered at his burial place in the Roman Pantheon to perform his concerti grossi, a ceremony that continued for decades, as long as his students were alive. His reputation spanned Europe, from Rome to Paris and London. His works were to be found everywhere, in prints, reprints, and manuscript copies. Entire families in Italy and England earned their livelihood by hand-copying Corelli's compositions.

Yet his reputation abroad was based entirely on his compositions. He never undertook a major concert tour; in fact, he hardly performed outside of Rome and Bologna. His single trip to Naples was a disappointing experience. Even in Rome, where he spent most of his life, he never faced the broad public: he performed at the palaces of his wealthy patrons for invited guests who were true connoisseurs. Occasionally, he played in a church, usually leading his string ensemble.

Little is known about Corelli's life. He had a quiet, dignified career, sheltered and fulfilled. He was born on February 17, 1653, into a family of wealthy landowners in Fusignano, not far from Bologna. There was no musical tradition in his family, but his love for the violin surfaced very early. A local priest gave him some lessons, and he played well at a young age. In 1666, when he was thirteen, he was sent to Bologna, and his progress was so rapid that—at the age of seventeen—he was elected a member of the exclusive Accademia Filarmonica. (This is the same society to which young Mozart was admitted a century later.)

Corelli's teachers were solid musicians without claim to greatness: first Giovanni Benvenuti, who taught him the technical elements, then Leonardo Brugnoli, who was a more inspiring violinist and composer. But above all, Corelli absorbed the instrumental tradition of Bologna, which flourished at the church of San Petronio. So proud was he of this heritage that he continued to list his name on the title pages of his published compositions as *"il Bolognese."*

After his four years of study in Bologna (1666–70), we lose track of Corelli for some five years. There is an unconfirmed story that he visited Paris and aroused the jealousy of Lully. Eventually he settled in Rome: in 1675 his name is mentioned among the musicians of the Church of St. Louis-des-Français. His was a modest position—the third among four violinists—but the following year he was promoted to second place. In 1679 he directed the opera orchestra at the Teatro Capranica, where he filled the dual role of conductor and leader of the violins.

That same year Corelli entered the service of Christina of Sweden, who, after abdicating her throne and converting to Catholicism, had settled in a sumptuous setting in Rome. The ex-queen was intelligent and artistic; she brought with her a magnificent art collection, surrounded herself with artists and men of letters, and received the social elite of Rome. Her music director, in the years 1679–83, was Alessandro Scarlatti, but there was no rivalry between him and Corelli, since Scarlatti composed primarily for the voice. Corelli directed some of the queen's lavish musical festivities, as in 1687 when he led an orchestra of 150 players, larger than any modern symphony orchestra. In 1681 the queen received the dedication of Corelli's first published opus, a collection of twelve church sonatas for two violins and figured bass.

About that time, a visiting German musician—Georg Muffat—reported having heard "with great pleasure and astonishment" several concertos composed by "the gifted Signor Corelli and beautifully performed with utmost accuracy by a great number of instrumentalists."[1] We must imagine Corelli, violin in hand, leading his massed forces while playing the principal solo part. The players were divided into two groups: a small one (the so-called *concertino*) consisting of two solo violins, a cello, and a harpsichord, and a large body of players called the *ripieno*. The contrast between the solo group and the massive *tutti* was novel and startling. It was the birth of the *concerto grosso*—the "big" concerto—and Muffat's surprise is quite understandable.

Being a favorite in the high society of Rome, Corelli felt no need for a change and refused a flattering offer of the Duke of Modena. In 1687 he accepted the post of music master to Cardinal Panfili and moved into his palace, together with his assistant, the violinist Matteo Fornari. Here he stayed until 1690, when a new patron of the arts arose in Pietro Ottoboni, the young nephew of Pope Alexander VIII. Ottoboni was named cardinal and vice-chancellor and devoted himself to a worldly life—literature, music, the theater. He instituted Monday concerts at the chancellery, which became the favorite meeting place of Rome's high society. Cardinal Ottoboni became Corelli's lifelong patron; he appointed him music master and arranged living quarters for him at his palace. The relationship between the cardinal and Corelli was one of genuine friendship and of "most affectionate and special tenderness," as the cardinal said in one of his letters. Corelli's immediate expression of gratitude was his dedication, to Cardinal Ottoboni, of his Trio Sonatas Op. 4 (1694).

Relieved of all daily worries, Corelli was able to devote himself in a leisurely fashion to his musical activities—performing and composing. We know that he composed slowly and with much circumspection; he kept his manuscripts for years, polishing and perfecting every detail, before entrusting them to a publisher.

In 1700 he reached the pinnacle of his fame with the Sonatas Op. 5 for solo violin and figured bass. They were acclaimed as models of their kind and spread his fame throughout Europe. The success was such that within his lifetime (that is, in the next thirteen years) about fifteen different editions were published. Another twenty editions followed within the eighteenth century, brought out in Rome, Amsterdam, Paris, London, Bologna, and Rouen. At home Corelli was showered with honors. He was elected head of the Assemblage of Musicians of Rome of Santa Cecilia. He conducted the solemn festivities at the Accademia del Disegno, performing his own concertos with a large orchestra. In 1706 he was received into the Accademia dei Arcadi, the most exclusive society of writers and artists in Italy. The praise of his fellow artists was extravagant: he was called the "Columbus in the ocean of music" and the "Orpheus of our time."

But there were occasional disappointments. One of them occurred at one of Cardinal Ottoboni's soirées in 1708 when Georg Friedrich Handel—then a promising young composer from Saxony—presented his overture *The Triumph of Time*. Not pleased with the tame and placid manner in which Corelli played the music, Handel snatched the violin from his hands and began to demonstrate the appropriate interpretation. Annoyed, Corelli replied, "But my dear Saxon, this is music in the French style, which is strange to me."

More embarrassing was another incident in the same year. Corelli was invited by the king of Naples to perform at his court. He traveled with his faithful assistant, the violinist Fornari, and a cellist, in order to be sure of experienced support. In charge of the Royal Music was Alessandro Scarlatti, Corelli's old-time friend. After some persuasion, Corelli led his first concerto grosso and was pleasantly surprised by the expert sight-reading of the Neapolitan musicians. But the king found Corelli's performance of one of his solo sonatas so boring that he left the room during the Adagio. The final humiliation came when Corelli consented to lead the violins in a work by Scarlatti: he was unable to play an exposed passage extending into seventh position—mainly because his own technique rarely required him to reach beyond the modest third position. To his consternation, the well-prepared Neapolitan concertmaster played the passage with ease. Confused by this incident, Corelli started the next piece in a wrong key and had to be corrected in public. He returned to Rome in deep mortification.

Whether or not this hastened his decline, we do not know. At any rate, he retired from public performances in 1710. He spent his last years preparing his twelve concerti grossi for publication. The preface is dated December 3, 1712. A month later he fell ill and dictated his last will and testament, and on January 8, 1713, he died.

In his testament, Corelli entrusted his associate Fornari with supervising the publication of the Concerti grossi Op. 6, for which the preface was already written. In exchange, Fornari was to receive all the proceeds from this work, "if there were any." Fornari faithfully executed the last will of his master, and the following year the Concerti Op. 6 were published. Fornari also received as legacy all of Corelli's instruments and manuscripts.

The instruments left by Corelli consisted of a two-manual harpsichord, a cello, a bass viol, and several violins. One of them is reported to have been a Stradivarius, brought to London soon after the master's death, and was used for a time by the violinist J. P. Salomon, friend and impresario of Haydn; after Salomon's death in 1815, all traces of this violin were lost. According to other information, Corelli actually preferred to play on his Andrea Amati instrument. He also owned a violin made by the Tyrolean master Matthias Albani.

All contemporaries of Corelli stress his benign disposition, his mild temper, and his modest deportment. Yet, his portrait reveals a man of decision; it is an animated face full of character. As leader of large orchestras, his whole countenance had to be decisive. He contributed much to the quality of orchestral playing, and many contemporary composers profited from this improvement. Scarlatti was "extremely struck with the manner in which Corelli played his concertos, and his nice management of the band, the uncommon accuracy of performance gave the concertos an amazing effect, and that even to the eye as well as to the ear." The visual effect must have been enhanced by uniform bowings:

> Corelli regarded it as essential to the ensemble of the band that their bowings should all move exactly together, all up or all down; so that at his rehearsals, which constantly preceded every public performance of his concertos, he would immediately stop the band if he discovered one irregular bow.[2]

Despite his gentleness, Corelli was well aware of his artistic worth. Once, offended by conversation while he was playing at Ottoboni's soirée, he interrupted his performance with the words, "the music might disturb the conversation." When some musicians in Bologna criticized alleged errors in his Trio Sonatas Op. 2, he answered haughtily that "their scruples are born out of ignorance." Yet he proceeded to explain his harmonies for the benefit of "those who are in the dark." The controversy created quite a stir, but Corelli stood his ground.

He was also willing to recognize excellence in others. When the German virtuoso Nicolaus Adam Strungk visited Rome, Corelli admired his technique of using a *scordatura* violin (that is, the strings tuned differently) and exclaimed, "If my first name is Arch-Angel, then yours should be Arch-Devil."

Handel, who knew Corelli personally, is reported to have ridiculed his parsimony:

> He loved paintings for which he did not have to pay; economy was his prime occupation; his clothing was extremely plain, he usually dressed in black and wore a blue cloak as an outer garment. And he was extremely reluctant to pay for a carriage, preferring to go on foot.[3]

There may be some truth in this: Corelli accumulated a collection of 136 paintings, mostly by his friends (Trevisani among them), and he left a modest fortune.

While Corelli's playing may have been too "tame" for Handel's taste, other contemporaries report that he interpreted his own music with much passion. According to Abbé Raguenet,

I never met with any man that suffered his passions to hurry him away so much whilst he was playing on the violin as the famous Corelli, whose eyes will sometimes turn red as fire; his countenance will be distorted, his eyeballs roll as in an agony, and he gives in so much to what he is doing that he doth not look like the same man.

If anyone thinks of classical restraint while interpreting Italian Baroque string music, he should rethink his approach after reading the following eyewitness report:

A symphony of furies shakes the soul . . . the artist himself, whilst he is performing it, is seized with an unavoidable agony; he tortures his violin; he racks his body; he is no longer master of himself, but is agitated like one possessed with an irresistible motion. If, on the other side, the symphony is to express calm and tranquillity . . . they execute it with equal success . . . Every string of the bow is of an infinite length, lingering on a dying sound which decays gradually till at last it absolutely expires.[4]

This type of extroverted playing seems to have been customary among Italians around 1700.

Corelli's impassioned interpretation is all the more remarkable since much of his music is characterized by controlled emotion. In slow movements he heightened the expressiveness by using the *messa di voce*, that is, a swelling and diminishing of the tone on one bow, in imitation of the human voice, probably with a slight vibrato. But he was also a master of the strong sustained bow stroke when his tone could sound as clear as a "sweet trumpet." He gave particular attention to the art of embellishing the melodic line.

As far as technical display was concerned, Corelli was no wizard, nor did he have any ambitions to astound his listeners with stunts. He kept the violin within the range of the soprano voice and disdained the bird imitations so popular in his day. He deliberately limited the range of the violin and rarely exceeded the third position, while other play-ers—fifty years before his time—reached the sixth and even seventh position. Corelli also avoided flashy passages moving rapidly up and down the fingerboard, though he possessed enough agility of fingers and bow. There is nothing in his music to impair the beautiful tone which he considered the aim of every serious violinist. True, his double and triple stops are far from easy, and some passages demand great velocity of bow and fingers, but the music flows comfortably. It was not Corelli's virtuosity but his *style* that conquered Europe: music of balanced beauty, vigorous clarity, noble emotions, and a sense of graceful perfection.

Actually, Corelli composed in two styles—for the church (*da chiesa*) and for the chamber (*da camera*). There is more artfulness and dignity in the church works, more dancelike spirit in the secular pieces. At times the dividing line is blurred, and quite a few of his church movements have a joyous mood. All of his sonatas and concertos for the church have at least one movement that is a fugue, and dances as such were strictly excluded. On the other hand, the music for the chamber consisted almost exclusively of idealized dances such as allemande, gavotte, sarabande, and giga. Shortly after Corelli's death, the distinction between church and chamber became vague, with an intermingling of both styles.

The most famous of Corelli's church works is the so-called *Christmas Concerto* (Op. 6, No. 8), written to be played in church on Christmas Eve, which ends with the lovely *pastorale* movement. Among his secular pieces, the variations for violin, *La Folia* (Op. 5, No. 12), are often played in concerts, though in various modernized arrangements.

Corelli composed no solo violin concertos, the genre with which his younger colleague Antonio Vivaldi dazzled his audiences in Venice. All of Corelli's twelve concertos belong to the concerto grosso type—"group" concertos with occasional solo sections divided between the two leading violins and a cello. Corelli made the soloists emerge from, and recede into, the group; there is little room for individual virtuosity. These concertos can be played by as few as seven players or by any multiple thereof, which expands their usefulness enormously. The technical demands are modest, while the musical rewards are great.

Corelli's concerti grossi, brought out after his death in 1714, were actually composed over a period of several decades. By the time they were published, they appeared almost old-fashioned compared to such "modern" music as Vivaldi's or Albinoni's. It should not surprise us that Johann Sebastian Bach chose Vivaldi, not Corelli, as his model for writing concertos. Vivaldi turned to the solo concerto, to virtuoso display, to wind instruments for added color. But within his self-imposed limitations, Corelli was perfect—and his influence can be traced as late as Handel's concerti grossi of 1740.

Corelli's towering achievement, however, is his twelve Violin Sonatas, Op. 5. They represent the codification of the art of violin playing as practiced in 1700, and they will remain basic for as long as the violin is played. Corelli consolidated all essential achievements and presented them in a musically attractive form, without being particularly innovative. His student Geminiani had said,

> Corelli's merit was not depth of learning nor great fancy or rich invention of melody or harmony; but a nice ear and most delicate taste, which led him to select the most pleasing harmonies and melodies, and to construct the parts so as to produce the most delightful effects upon the ear.[5]

There are respected historians who question Corelli's greatness because he did not break new ground. But greatness does not depend on innovation alone. Just as Bach was a summation in his time, so—in his way—was Corelli: he built a firm plateau on which future generations based the development of violin technique.

Among Corelli's many students, three achieved particular prominence: Francesco Geminiani, who settled in the British Isles and was associated with Handel; Pietro Locatelli, who spent a productive life in Amsterdam; and Giovanni Battista Somis, who founded the Piedmont violin school in Turin and taught several great violinists, foremost Gaetano Pugnani and Jean-Marie Leclair.

Though not his student, the great Tartini felt indebted to Corelli:

> He was so ambitious of being thought a follower of Corelli's precepts and principles, that after his own reputation was at its zenith, he refused to teach any other music to his disciples, till they had studied the *Opus* 5, or Solo's, of Corelli.[6]

Tartini chose Corelli's Gavotte from Op. 5, No. 10 as theme of his variations in *L'arte del arco* (The Art of Bowing); it was a posthumous homage to Corelli.

Corelli, Gavotte

Antonio Vivaldi

Vivaldi was a man of contradictions and contrasts. He was an ordained priest but alleged that he stopped celebrating mass early in life "because of ill health," yet he pursued a far more strenuous life as virtuoso, composer, conductor, and impresario. He was a man of the church, yet he acquired a passion for the world of opera and, incidentally, for a young lady singer who became known in Venice as "the friend of the red-haired priest" (Vivaldi's nickname). He was shrewd in his business dealings, yet he squandered a fortune and died in poverty. So obscure, in fact, were the circumstances of his death that neither date nor place was established until recently. No sooner did he die than the musical world forgot him, and so it remained for two centuries until he was rediscovered in the 1930s. Fifty years ago only scholars remembered Vivaldi's name; today he is recognized as one of the creative giants of his age.

His contemporaries knew and admired him; they were struck by the newness of his invention, the flashes of his imagination, the logic of musical design, the variety of tone color in his orchestral scores. To Johann Sebastian Bach, Vivaldi was a revelation: Bach studied his works by copying and rearranging a number of Vivaldi's concertos until he felt secure in the "modern" Italian style. Bach's own concertos are indebted to Vivaldi, though Bach infused the facile Italian style with a goodly dose of German counterpoint.

Vivaldi's career was checkered and adventurous. He was born in Venice on March 4, 1678, and studied with his father, who had the dual profession of barber and violinist. Frail as a boy, Antonio was destined for the priesthood and ordained in 1703. By then, he was already an accomplished musician—brilliant as a violinist, expert on the organ and the harpsichord. In 1703 he was appointed violin teacher at the Ospedale della Pietà and maintained this connection for thirty-seven years, rising in importance during his tenure.

The Pietà was one of four charitable institutions in Venice which maintained musical establishments. Actually it was a home for illegitimate or orphaned girls where the teaching of music was stressed. One visitor speaks of the "prodigious number of children, amounting to at least six thousand" in these homes. On Sundays and holidays, the Pietà offered public performances of vocal and instrumental music. Thirty to forty girls took part in each concert; they "sang like angels and played the violin, flute, oboe, organ, cello, and bassoon; in short there is no instrument, however unwieldy, that can frighten them."[1]

Although the girls were "cloistered like nuns" and wore nuns' habits, most of them did not take religious vows. In fact, the atmosphere was quite worldly, and contemporary accounts speak of the easygoing manners in these orphan asylums. Malicious tongues wagged, "The stillness of the cloister was broken sometimes by the sound of trumpets and fifes, sometimes by the merry shouts of the young aristocrats as they danced with the nuns, who would go so far as to stay out all night with their lovers."² While the girls performed behind a wrought-iron grille, they were plainly visible to the enraptured audiences and quite coquettish. Some made careers as singers or instrumentalists, others received marriage proposals from well-bred young men.

Vivaldi, who was only twenty-five when he took charge, devoted much time and energy to the education of his talented young students. He not only taught the violin but also composed music and directed the orchestra while playing first violin. The girls' performance was crisp, their orchestral attacks were precise and even superior to what one heard at the Paris Opéra, according to a French observer. The title *maestra* was conferred on the best players among the girls, who served as monitors and assistant teachers. With such a gifted group, Vivaldi had a musical laboratory at his disposal. As composer, he had to supply a quantity of new music, and he produced concertos by the dozen, often being forced into excessive hastiness. He once boasted to an admirer that he could compose a concerto faster than a copyist could copy it.

During the first year, he also celebrated Mass, but his mind was preempted by music. When he had a musical inspiration, he was apt to interrupt the Mass. "One day when he was saying mass, a fugue subject came to his mind. He at once left the altar where he was officiating and repaired to the sacristy to write out his theme; then he returned to finish the mass," says an old report. Years later, Vivaldi rejected such contentions: "I discontinued saying mass, having on three occasions had to leave the altar without completing it because of my ailment."³ (He seems to have suffered from an asthmatic condition.)

Vivaldi had the good fortune of living and working in Venice, a city of immense musical vitality. Whether at the Cathedral of San Marco or the half-dozen opera theaters, the concerts at the orphan homes or the open-air celebrations, music permeated the entire life of the city. Rulers and princes, composers and virtuosos came to Venice from afar to hear and be heard, to perform and study. Among visiting violinists were Francesco Veracini, Tartini, Locatelli, and Johann Pisendel, who came from Dresden in 1716 to study with Vivaldi. Teacher and student became close friends.

Venice also boasted music printers, and it was here that Vivaldi's first works were published: twelve Trio Sonatas for two violins and cello and/or harpsichord, Op. 1 (1705), and twelve Sonatas for violin and figured bass, Op. 2 (1709). In both collections Vivaldi turned away from the church style and concentrated entirely on the secular chamber style. However, it was his Opus 3, the concerto collection known as *L'estro armonico* (The Harmonic Spirit), published in Amsterdam in 1711, that established Vivaldi's European fame; it contained concertos for one, two, and four solo violins with string orchestra. In 1714 came another set of twelve concertos entitled *La stravaganza* (The Extravagance), Op. 4, also published in Amsterdam and equally successful. It was from these two concerto collections that Bach chose his material for transcriptions and elaborations—certainly a high tribute.

Having served the Pietà for ten years, Vivaldi took a brief leave to embark on other musical ventures. During the next five years he composed and staged no fewer than eight operas. In 1716–18, six different Vivaldi operas were played by two Venetian theaters. Another outlet for his interest in vocal music was the composition of two oratorios for the Pietà, of which only one is preserved, *Juditha triumphans* (1716). Nor was the production of concertos neglected, and two more collections, Opp. 6 and 7, were published in 1716–17.

Until then, Vivaldi retained his domicile in Venice, where most of his operas were staged. But his growing reputation made travels necessary. Whenever one of his operas was produced in another city, he was expected to be present to stage and conduct. Without severing his connection with Venice, he accepted a position as music director in Mantua, a city governed by a music-loving German prince, and remained there for three years, probably 1718–20. Here he met a gifted young singer, Anna Giraud (spelled Girò in Italian) who was to become the prima donna in all his future operas. Eventually Anna and her sister followed Vivaldi to Venice and lived in his house. From Mantua Vivaldi traveled to Vicenza and Milan, where several of his operas were staged. In 1723 and 1724 he obtained a remarkable success in Rome, both as opera composer and violin virtuoso. J. J. Quantz, the German flutist who visited Rome in 1724, commented,

> What came most often to my ears was the *Lombard* style.*
> Vivaldi had just imported it to Rome with his operas and had,
> thanks to that style, captivated the Romans to such an extent
> that they would no longer, as it were, endure what was not
> conceived in that style.[4]

---

* The "Lombard" rhythm was a pattern accentuating a short note followed by a longer note, thus ♪♩ , also known as the "Scotch snap." Vivaldi did not invent it but used it freely.

Hearing of Vivaldi's success, the Pope requested to hear him play the violin and expressed much satisfaction.

Vivaldi's activities as opera composer and violinist-conductor were interrelated; his artful accompaniments and violin obbligatos aroused much amazement. He also performed his own concertos between acts of the opera. "Such playing has never been heard before and can never be equalled," observed a German visitor.

Vivaldi worked at a furious pace. He once wrote an opera in five days. In the season 1726–27 he produced "three operas in less than three months, two for Venice and one for Florence . . . which brought in much money." In 1725 he was commissioned to write a *Gloria* for the marriage of King Louis XIV of France. That year, the *Concert spirituel* was established in Paris—vocal and instrumental concerts given during Lent and other religious holidays when the theaters were closed. Very soon, Vivaldi became one of the favorite composers of that establishment, though he never visited Paris. When the French ambassador to Venice wished to honor the birth of a French royal princess, the music was provided by Vivaldi—"a very beautiful instrumental concert which lasted nearly two hours; the music for this as well as for the *Te Deum* was by the famous Vivaldi," reported the *Mercure de France* in October 1727.

In the meantime, the Pietà remembered its errant maestro and drew up a new contract in 1723, obligating him to conduct two concerts a month whenever he was in Venice, and to rehearse with the young musicians so that they would be "in good condition to play properly." It was assumed that he would compose new concertos for these occasions. During his absences, delivery of new concertos was to continue by special messenger "if this could be done without incurring excessive postal expenses." This arrangement worked for a few years, judging by the account books of the Pietà. At that time, he published some of his most famous concertos—*Il Cimento dell'Armonia e dell'Inventione* (Venture of Harmony and Invention), Op. 8 (c. 1725), including the famous set *The Four Seasons*.

In those years, he traveled widely, mainly to produce and conduct his own operas, always with Anna Girò as leading soprano. Though we have little concrete information about his travels, it is known that he stayed in Vienna in 1728 where he enjoyed the patronage of the music-loving emperor Karl VI. It is said that the emperor spent more time with Vivaldi in two weeks than with his cabinet ministers in two years. He may also have visited Munich and other German cities. But somehow he always found time to return to Venice, where he produced eleven of his operas in a ten-year span, 1725–35.

In 1732 the administrators of the Pietà noted with irritation the frequent absences of the maestro and pointed out that his presence was needed to insure good performances of his new works. It was obvious that he could not maintain effective control of the music at the Pietà as an absentee conductor. There was less inclination to be lenient with Vivaldi since he was not without competitors: the Pietà purchased music from other composers, including Tartini, and also imported music from Paris.

In the midst of preparations for an opera premiere in Ferrara in 1737, Vivaldi suffered a humiliating disappointment: the church authorities forbade the performance because his pattern of behavior was considered unbecoming for a priest. (In those days, Ferrara belonged to the Papal States.) His failure to celebrate Mass and his notorious friendship with the singer Girò were found particularly objectionable. In vain, he tried to reverse the decision by writing a long letter in his own defense.

Undaunted, Vivaldi took off for Holland to conduct the musical festivities for the centenary of the Amsterdam theater in January 1738. Being well known in Amsterdam—most of his works were published there—he was received in a manner worthy of his European reputation. His major contribution to the festivities was a concerto for ten instruments: solo violin, string quartet, two oboes, two hunting horns, and timpani. The orchestra consisted of some twenty-five players, and Vivaldi was both soloist and conductor. Near the theater lived another eminent violinist, Pietro Locatelli, who had settled in Amsterdam a few years earlier, but the two maestros seem to have avoided each other.

Upon his return to Venice, Vivaldi reentered the activities of the Pietà. On various festive occasions he played and conducted his own music and received much praise for "the brilliant and very full orchestral accompaniment for which the institution has always been famous." But there were also signs of a decline, as we gather from a letter by de Brosses, whom Vivaldi befriended in order to sell him some "very costly" concertos. De Brosses wrote,

> Vivaldi is a *vecchio* [oldster]* who composes furiously and prodigiously. . . . I found to my great astonishment that he was not as esteemed as he deserves in this country where all is

---

* He was sixty-two at the time.

fashion, where his works have been heard for a long time, and where last year's music no longer brings in receipts.[5]

Vivaldi must have realized that his long association with the Pietà was coming to a close. In 1740 he sold a block of twenty concertos for the small sum of 70 ducats 23 lire, and a few remaining works for one ducat apiece—a mere pittance compared to what he used to receive.

Perhaps Vivaldi needed to raise money for a new journey, for he left Venice for Vienna, where he had once enjoyed the emperor's friendship. But the emperor died in October 1740 and conditions at court changed abruptly. The War of Succession made any appointment or musical commission appear hopeless. Illness, perhaps, kept Vivaldi from continuing his journey to Dresden, where he was well known. He died in Vienna on July 28, 1741, virtually a pauper, and was buried the same day.

No obituary appeared in Venice, his native city—in fact, the circumstances of his death remained a mystery until recently, when an entry was found in the *Totenbuch* (Necrology) of St. Stephen's parish in Vienna. The house where Vivaldi died, near the Kärntner-Tor, has since been demolished, and the cemetery where he was buried was built over in the nineteenth century. A handwritten entry in the Granedigo memorabilia led the search to Vienna; there we read,

> The Abbate Don Antonio Vivaldi, the incomparable violinist, named the Red Priest, highly esteemed for his compositions and concertos, earned in his days more than 50,000 ducats, but because of his exorbitant squandering, he died poor in Vienna.[6]

We have a few contemporary descriptions of Vivaldi's violin playing. A German traveler, Herr von Uffenbach, heard him in 1715 in Venice as the city whirled with the joyous excitement of the carnival season. He saw Vivaldi conduct one of his operas while playing the violin, and found him amazing:

> Vivaldi performed a solo accompaniment admirably, and at the end he added a fantasy [improvisation] that quite confounded me, for such playing has not been heard before and can never be equalled. He placed his fingers but a hair's breadth from the bridge so that there was hardly room for the bow. He played thus on all four strings, with imitations and at unbelievable speed. Everyone was astonished, but I cannot say that it captivated me, because it was more skillfully executed than it was pleasant to hear.[7]

A month later, Uffenbach invited Vivaldi to his home and heard him play some

> very difficult and quite inimitable improvisations. Being close at hand, I had to admire his skill all the more, and I saw quite clearly that he played unusual and lively pieces, to be sure, but in a way that lacked both charm and a cantabile manner.[8]

Uffenbach, an amateur violinist, knew what he was talking about and even engaged Vivaldi for some private lessons. Until recently, Uffenbach's description was taken as rather fanciful, since none of the known concertos by Vivaldi reach such high regions on the fingerboard. While the Vivaldi scholar Pincherle identified the ninth position as the uppermost range used by Vivaldi, another expert, Kolneder, ascribes to Vivaldi the twelfth position, used in a cadenza of 1712 for a concerto written for Padua. The disputed place is marked with a bracket, which Kolneder identifies as an octave transposition (that is, to be played an octave higher).[9] If this reading is correct, then Vivaldi did indeed overreach the accepted violin range of the day; to play the disputed highest

note , Vivaldi must have equipped a violin with a longer

fingerboard, or produced rather unpleasant squeaks.

Even disregarding this extreme, Vivaldi felt very comfortable in the high positions, which he exploited cleverly in elaborate arpeggios (broken chords): while the fingers remained in one position, the bow glided across the four strings, creating the illusion of unheard-of difficulties. Vivaldi was a master in inventing violin passages that sounded much harder than they actually were; his technique was born out of the instrument, idiomatic, "violinistic." His own playing must have had unusual agility and accuracy. He was as much a master of the bow as of the fingerboard, employing a variety of bowings—slurred and detached, hammered strokes and flying staccato, as well as a kind of bouncing bow which resembled our modern spiccato. To indicate these effects, he used colorful language, for example *molto forte e strappato*, meaning, "tear off or wrench the bow stroke." In his well-known Concerto for four solo violins (Op. 3, No. 10), the slow movement assigns a different bowing to each soloist for color effect: (1) staccato detached on one bow, (2) three slurred and one separate note, (3) individual bounced (*sciolto*) bows, (4) two notes to each slur. The result is magic.

Vivaldi's imagination is nowhere as vivid as in his descriptive pieces.

In this so-called "program music," he captured all kinds of situations and moods, yet maintained a formal musical design. The most famous examples are *The Four Seasons*, which form part of his concerto collection Opus 8 (c. 1725). The connection between the program and the music is established by explanatory sonnets printed at the head of the solo violin part. The poetry is provided with guide letters which refer to the music, so that one can follow the descriptive passages in both poetry and music. Certain incidents in the text are pictorialized in the music through realistic means. Thus, the sweet slumber of the shepherd in the *Spring Concerto* is rudely punctuated by a barking dog (sharp accents in the violas). Wind, thunder, and lightning are as graphically rendered as is a walk on slippery ice. So are the joys of wine, the sleep of the drunkards, the noise of the hunt, the fear of the beasts, the song of the birds. The music is full of lighthearted imagery and an exuberant sense of humor. All this is shaped with musical logic and made dramatic by the solo violin's feats of virtuosity, set into the sturdy framework of the string orchestra. If Beethoven called his *Pastorale Symphony* "more feeling than painting," Vivaldi reversed the emphasis: there is definitely more painting than feeling. *The Seasons* belong to Vivaldi's most extrovert compositions—people and beasts communing with nature, in joy and in fear. The mood suited the "back to nature" philosophy of the eighteenth century, and audiences everywhere were enraptured by these musical images. Particularly in Paris, *Les Quatre Saisons*—first performed on February 7, 1728, at the *Concert spirituel*—became an instant favorite, and the popularity lasted throughout the eighteenth century. It can be said that Vivaldi's *The Four Seasons* was the most influential and most widely imitated piece of program music prior to Beethoven's *Pastorale*.

It is a curious aspect of Vivaldi's immense list of works (numbering close to eight hundred) that only a fraction was published during his lifetime.* These were numbered as they appeared, from Opus 1 to Opus 12, and contained sonatas and concertos in sets of six or twelve, altogether 24 sonatas and 78 concertos. After the immense success of his early concerto collections (*L'estro armonico*, Op. 3, and *La stravaganza*, Op. 4),

---

* Vivaldi has been catalogued more often than any other composer. Currently, three catalogues (and three different sets of numbers) are being used to identify his compositions:
RV numbers, after Ryom Verzeichnis (1974–79), the most recent and complete, including instrumental and vocal works;
P numbers, after the Pincherle catalogue (1948), including only instrumental works;
F numbers, after Fanna's Complete Works edition (1947–).
However, the old opus numbers have not outlived their usefulness, though they cover only a fraction of his immense work list.

Vivaldi continued to publish rather selectively, releasing many of his easier concertos while keeping the virtuoso pieces in manuscript for his own use. Perhaps he wanted to prevent his competitors from using them; a century later, Paganini followed the same policy. For this reason, the full extent of Vivaldi's virtuosity was not recognized until after the 1930s, when the manuscript concertos came to light and began to be explored. He was indeed "one of the most astounding violin virtuosos of his time," to quote Pincherle, one of the architects of the Vivaldi revival.[10]

It is possible that Vivaldi's publishers urged him to print comparatively easy-to-play works from his repertoire—in those days, playability and salability went hand in hand. Among Vivaldi's contemporaries there was widespread belief that he declined toward the end. Thus Quantz, an early admirer, wrote,

> He was vivacious, rich in invention, and filled almost half of the world with concertos. . . . At the end, however, due to incessant and daily composing, and particularly when he began to write theatrical music, he fell into a facile and impudent manner, both in composing and playing; for this reason, his last concertos deserve less success than the first ones. . . . It deflected him, in the last years of his life, almost completely from good taste.[11]

Even recently, there are eminent musicians who tend to belittle Vivaldi, as did the late composer Dallapiccola, in his well-known witticism: "Vivaldi did not write six hundred concertos, he wrote the same concerto six hundred times." When questioned, Dallapiccola admitted smilingly that he went too far, though there is a kernel of truth: Vivaldi tends to repeat himself. But this occasional routine is far outweighed by his accomplishments: at his best, Vivaldi is a composer of genius, bursting with inventiveness and imagination, orchestrally far ahead of his time. Nor was he satisfied to compose primarily for the violin, as was the custom among violinist-composers of his time. His restless imagination carried him far beyond such narrow limits. True, he wrote more violin concertos than anyone (over 230!), but he also composed solo concertos for flute, recorder, piccolo, oboe, bassoon, trumpet, and mandolin, as well as for viola d'amore and cello. He combined wind instruments into solo groups, sometimes joined by a dominating solo violin, merging elements of the solo concerto and the concerto grosso.* His

---

* See Concerto in F major (P. 268) for solo violin, two oboes, two horns, bassoon, and string quartet.

student Pisendel brought some of these concerto types to Dresden in 1717 and provided Bach with a model for his *Brandenburg Concertos*. Vivaldi was also innovative in contributing to the creation of the *sinfonia* or *concerto ripieno* (that is, concertos without solo instruments), forerunners of the classical symphony. Being a prolific opera composer (he wrote close to fifty!), Vivaldi was aware of the requirements of the stage—cantilena, colorful orchestration, dramatic tension—elements which can also be found in his instrumental works. On the other hand, his instrumental experience stood him in good stead when writing for the theater. His church music has a joyous, Italianate spirit and is often performed today, in contrast to his operas, which are neglected. But it is as an instrumental composer that Vivaldi is incomparably alive and touched by genius.

Giuseppe Tartini

In the mid-eighteenth century, the name Tartini was known in every part of musical Europe. He was considered the greatest violin master of his time, equally admired as performer and composer for his instrument. His violin concertos served as models not only for violinists but also for harpsichordists. Tartini's fame spread mainly through his compositions and his students, for his few concert trips were limited to northern Italy. He went abroad only once: in 1723 he traveled to Prague and performed with much success at the coronation festivities of Charles VI. But after three years he returned to Italy—disgusted with the foreign climate and the food—and never left again, refusing flattering offers from Paris and London. For almost fifty years he lived and worked in Padua, and visitors came from afar to hear him play solos at the Basilica of San Antonio. He also founded an academy of violin playing and attracted many students from all over Europe. Occasionally he traveled to other Italian cities—to nearby Venice, to Parma (1728), Bologna (1730), Ferrara (1739), and Bergamo (1740). He maintained a large international correspondence and was particularly friendly with the scholarly Padre Martini in Bologna. But the external circumstances of Tartini's life were sedentary and uneventful.

Tartini was essentially self-taught, but he owed much to his older confreres—to Corelli, whose works he greatly admired; to Vivaldi, who furnished the concerto prototype to be expanded and developed; to Veracini, whose virtuosity made such an impact on Tartini. He also

Arcangelo Corelli:
"Master of Masters"

Antonio Vivaldi:
"Genius of the Baroque"

Giuseppe Tartini:
"Master of Nations"

learned from Locatelli, whose *L'arte del violino* was a real technical challenge. Yet, after having absorbed all kinds of influences, Tartini developed his own very personal style, which remained a model for half a century. Historically he represents the essence of "classical" violin playing and violin composition. In truth Tartini was closer to being a "romantic" of the violin; he let himself be inspired by poetic mottoes which he placed at the head of many of his compositions in a secret code; he took liberties in form and content, as for example in the famous *Devil's Trill Sonata*, an astonishing piece of eighteenth-century romanticism; and he filled some of his later concertos with music of nostalgia and sensitivity very characteristic of his time. Too little of his music is heard today. Tartini deserves to be rediscovered.

Tartini was born on April 8, 1692, in Pirano, on the Istrian peninsula (now part of Yugoslavia). His father, a wealthy businessman from Florence, planned a theological career for him. In 1708 young Tartini was sent to Padua, where he matriculated as a law student, but his main interests were fencing and violin playing. His early marriage at the age of eighteen (in 1710) to Elisabetta Premazore (his elder by two years) created a furor in both families, and Tartini had to flee from Padua, temporarily abandoning his young bride. For three years he hid in a monastery in Assisi; here he met a remarkable musician known as Padre Boemo (the "Bohemian Priest," actually the composer Czernohorsky), who encouraged him to make music his career. Tartini's hiding place was discovered by accident: while he was playing the violin at church, a sudden wind raised the curtain that concealed the musicians from the congregation. A visitor from Padua recognized Tartini and passed on this information. By that time, the anger of his wife's family had subsided, and Tartini was able to rejoin her. "From now on he became the most modest, humble, and devout person," we read in an old report of the incident.[1]

We have reasons to doubt that Tartini's marriage was quite that idyllic. Burney remarked dryly, "He married early a wife of the Xantippe sort, and his patience upon the most trying occasions was always truly Socratic."[2] He had an extramarital affair with a Venetian landlady, who threatened him with a paternity suit; this may explain his prolonged stay in Prague.

As for his artistic career, it developed slowly. In 1714 he was active in Ancona as violinist of the opera orchestra. A visit to Venice in 1716 gave him the opportunity to hear the famous violinist Francesco Veracini; so impressed was Tartini by his rival's performance that he went into renewed retirement to perfect his own playing, by practicing eight hours a day. It was particularly Veracini's use of the bow which aroused Tartini's interest (judging by pictorial evidence, Veracini's bow was unusually long); and Tartini began to experiment with different bow sticks and thicker strings. In 1717–18 we find Tartini in Fano as leader of the opera orchestra; during the next few years he lived in Venice and traveled to other cities in northern Italy, building a growing reputation as a violinist.

In 1721 he was invited to become *primo violino* and chief of concerts at the Basilica of San Antonio in Padua, a position he kept—with brief interruptions—until his death in 1770. San Antonio was a place of pilgrimage and had a fine musical establishment: four organs, a choir, and an orchestra consisting of seven violins (including Tartini), four violas, two cellos, two basses, and a trumpet player.*

Tartini was first heard at San Antonio during Easter 1721, and his appointment was confirmed at once. Though his salary was a modest 150 ducats per year (raised to 170 in 1733), he seemed content and remained for almost half a century.

His duties consisted of playing violin solos on certain Sundays and holidays. He used his own concertos, fulfilling the double duty of soloist and conductor of the small orchestra. Occasionally he may have played some of his violin sonatas, with the figured bass realized on the organ. The church fathers knew how to appreciate the artistry of their new *primo violino*: he was praised as *sonatore singolare* (extraordinary performer), he was allowed to appear in academies and in theaters without requesting prior permission, and his travel allowances were liberal.

In 1723 he received a leave of absence to participate in the coronation of Charles VI to be held in Prague. He arrived there in June, though the coronation was not until September. Tartini, competing with some of the best artists of Europe, was much admired, and we have a report of the flutist Quantz, who was present:

> Tartini was indeed one of the greatest violin players. He drew a beautiful tone from his instrument. Fingers and bow were at his command. He executed the greatest difficulties very cleanly without visible effort. He could play trills, even double trills, equally well with all the fingers. In fast as well as in slow movements, he intermingled many double stops and liked to

---

* By 1744 the cello and bass sections were increased to three each, and an oboe replaced the trumpet. By 1770 there were twenty string players and four winds.

play in extremely high positions. But his execution was not
touching, and his taste not noble, actually quite contrary to
the good art of singing.[3]

What Quantz criticized, then, was an excess of virtuosity due, perhaps,
to Tartini's youth at the time. In general, he did not care for Tartini's
compositions—"they are full of dry, simple-minded and quite ordinary
ideas which are better suited to comic than to serious music."[4] Quantz's
harsh judgment reflects his prejudice against the Italian style in music.

Following the coronation, Tartini requested and received permission to prolong his stay in Prague; his patron was Count Kinsky, the
royal chancellor and music-loving aristocrat. Though his earnings were
certainly higher than his church salary, he refused an appeal from his
brother for financial help, explaining that his health was precarious and
the medicines were costly. In 1726 he was ready to return to Padua,
where he was reinstated on the payroll of San Antonio.

In 1727–28 Tartini founded an academy for violinists, which was
to become his main source of income. As many as ten students were
enrolled for the entire school year, a period of ten months. At times
he taught them daily, with ten hours of lessons per day not unusual.
The tuition was two *zecchini** per month for violin lessons, and three
zecchini if the student wished to study counterpoint in addition; there
were always at least two students whom he taught *per carita*, without
pay. Tartini took his teaching very seriously, as evidenced in a letter of
1737 to Padre Martini:

> This year I shall have to teach nine students which makes me
> lose all my composure. Even when I had only four or five, I felt
> like the most worried man on earth.[5]

He maintained a similar schedule for over forty years, and he wrote to
Count Riccati in 1761,

> For months I had to give lessons in the morning and after-
> noon. . . . You can imagine that a 70-year old man has little
> will and strength left after almost seven hours of uninterrupted
> teaching in the mornings and three in the afternoons.[6]

Tartini was a dedicated teacher and developed a paternal involvement
with his students. They came from all over Europe—England, France,
Germany, and, of course, from all parts of Italy. He was called *"maestro
delle nazioni."* Some seventy of his students are known by name, and
they in turn transmitted his method to hosts of other violinists. How

---

* A *zecchino* was a gold coin worth about $2.25 (gold standard!).

deeply attached his students were to him can be judged by Pietro Nardini's devotion: during Tartini's last illness in 1770, Nardini hurried from Livorno to Padua to be with his ailing teacher, though thirty years had passed since Nardini had been his student.

While Tartini taught with undiminished energy until the last years of his life, he curtailed his work as performer and composer somewhat earlier. In 1740 he injured his arm while traveling to Bergamo and from then on limited his playing to Padua. However, there does not seem to have been any permanent impairment of his ability to play. A visitor heard him in December 1760 and was touched to tears. Count Algarotti wrote, "If you had heard him, you would believe that never before in your life you have heard a violin." He performed at the church at the age of seventy, in 1762, "with almost unbelievable art," according to his pupil J. G. Naumann. A less friendly observer, however, noted in 1758 that Tartini "had no fingers left and very little bow."[7] But at the height of his power, he was incomparable, as we see from the report of de Brosses in 1739, who had traveled especially to Padua to hear him:

> He is generally considered the foremost Italian violinist. . . .
> He represents the best I have heard in terms of extreme neat-
> ness of sound, of which no minute detail is ever lost, and the
> perfect purity of intonation. Yet his execution has only little
> brilliance.[8]

De Brosses was also impressed by Tartini's well-bred and unassuming behavior, perhaps in contrast to the shrewd and businesslike Vivaldi, with whom he had to deal in Venice.

The French violinist La Houssaye visited Padua around 1757 and recalled his impression of Tartini's playing:

> Nothing can express the astonishment and admiration which
> I experienced when I listened to the perfection and purity of
> his tone, the charm of his expression, the magic of his bow-
> ing—in short, the total perfection of his performance.[9]

La Houssaye begged Tartini to accept him as a pupil and later became one of France's best violinists.

It appears that Tartini's tone—described as "sweet and miracu-lous"—aimed more at expression than at power. He used a tasteful vibrato which he called *tremolo*, applied not continually but as an occasional ornament. Producing the vibrato with the left wrist, he was able to control its speed—slow, fast, or accelerating on the same note. He also recommended the *messa di voce* (swelling and diminishing the tone on one bow) without vibrato and warned against harsh attacks at the beginning of a bow stroke. Tartini had novel ideas about practicing in various positions and was meticulous about intonation. His command of the bow was legendary, as evidenced in his *L'arte del arco*, consisting of variations on a Gavotte by Corelli. His resourcefulness as a teacher is revealed in his "Rules to play the violin well, fully explained so that the student understands the reasons for everything he does."[10] Shorter, but equally useful, is his instructional letter to his student Maddalena Lombardini, which provides insight into his teaching methods. It was translated into English by Dr. Burney and also appeared in German and French immediately after Tartini's death.

Tartini retired from active duty at the church in 1765, after forty-four years of service, and was pensioned with full salary. His student Giulio Meneghini, a member of the orchestra since 1756, was assigned to assume Tartini's duties, and was named his official successor within a week of Tartini's death in 1770. He inherited Tartini's favorite violin and bow and the scores of 59 concertos by the master.*

A few months later, Dr. Burney arrived in Padua—he was on a continental tour to collect material for his *History of Music*. He was mortified to have come too late:

> But Tartini died a few months ago . . . an event which I regarded as a particular misfortune to myself, as well as a loss to the whole musical world; for he was a professor, whom I was not more desirous to hear perform, than ambitious to converse with.[11]

Burney's opinion about Tartini at that time is summarized in the following words:

> I shall only say that as a composer he was one of the few original geniuses of his age, who constantly drew from his own source; that his melody was full of fire and fancy, and his harmony, though learned, yet simple and pure; and as a performer, that his slow movements evince his taste and expression, and his lively ones his great hand. He was one of the first who knew and taught the power of the bow; and his knowledge of the fingerboard is proved by a thousand beautiful passages, to which that alone could give birth.[12]

---

* Tartini's violin, variously described as a Stradivarius or a Tyrolean instrument, is kept at the Municipal Museum in Pirano, his birth place; two of his bows are at the conservatory in Trieste. Another violin allegedly used by Tartini, a Guarnerius, is in Milan at the instrument museum. The collection of 59 concertos became part of the archives at San Antonio in Padua.

During the next two decades, however, Burney's taste in music changed, and when he came to write his *History of Music*, he somewhat modified his original opinion:

> Tartini . . . seems . . . to have a larger portion of merit as mere instrumental composer than any other author who flourished during the first fifty or sixty years of the present century. . . . And yet, with all my partiality for his style, talents, and abilities . . . it seems as if that energy, fire, and freedom of bow, which modern symphonies and orchestra-playing require, were wanting. It is now [1788] 18 years since I visited Italy. . . . Since that time, the productions of Boccherini, Haydn, Pleyel, Vanhal, and others have occasioned such a revolution in violin-music, and playing, by the fertility and boldness of their invention, that compositions which were then generally thought full of spirit and fire, appear now totally tame and insipid.[13]

Burney stops short of dismissing Tartini entirely, but he says that his music has been "laid aside."

Burney wrote his first opinion in 1770; his revised evaluation appeared in 1788. Much had happened in the meantime. Storm and Stress had come and gone in the 1770s, and a new classicism, elegant yet vigorous and formally perfect, had arisen in the 1780s. Haydn was to visit London in 1791. In comparison, Tartini's ornate style seemed curiously stilted and out of fashion. The audiences of the eighteenth century, avid for novelty, were not historically minded. Tartini's music disappeared from the active concert repertory but was retained as indispensable study material.

Tartini's compositions span almost four decades, from the 1720s to the 1760s, though his productivity slowed down after 1750. He wrote well over four hundred works—sonatas, concertos, sinfonias, trio sonatas, and string quartets. He began to compose while the Baroque style was at its peak but later adopted the current fashion and changed to the *style galant*. It was, in Burney's words, a transformation "from the complex to the graceful," the later works being "more modern, and manifestly composed in his second and best manner, after the year 1744." Actually, the change was gradual and can be traced to the late 1730s. It is most pronounced if one compares the Sonatas Op. 1 of 1734 and the Sonatas Op. 2 of 1745.

Once Tartini had made the stylistic change, he was convinced that it was for the good. He was highly pleased with his new Sonatas

Op. 2 and wrote, "Among my compositions, this work is the best . . . more beautiful than the earlier sonatas," and he was sure that they would be "infinitely more successful." In retrospect, both collections retain intrinsic value.

The twelve Sonatas Op. 1 "for violin and violoncello or harpsichord" represent a late flowering of the Baroque tradition—Tartini's homage to Corelli. They are divided into the customary six for church and six for chamber. While Corelli used a variable number of movements, Tartini established a basic pattern of three movements in the sequence slow–fast–fast. In the church sonatas, the traditional fugue is the centerpiece, flanked by a slow introduction and a sprightly finale. The chamber sonatas are no longer a suite of stylized dances; they follow the same sequence of movements but are composed in a less scholastic style, with richer ornamentation and more affect. One of the chamber sonatas, No. 10 in G minor, is a particularly expressive piece and has achieved fame under the name *Didone abbandonata* (The Abandoned Dido).

In contrast, the twelve Sonatas Op. 2—composed a decade or so later—are entirely in the lighter secular vein of the *style galant*: the technical demands are simplified, the ornaments more abundant, the melodic lines more ingratiating. In keeping with the new concept, the violin is dominant while the bass line is merely supportive and no longer figured. Again the sequence of movements is slow–fast–fast. In the center stands a substantial bipartite Allegro, which foreshadows the later classical sonata-allegro form. The slow movements are no longer solemn, but more fluid and richly ornamented, while the finales are brisk and effective.

We have discussed these two collections at greater length because they are the only publications authorized by the composer. Far longer is the list of sonatas printed against Tartini's wishes, sometimes without his knowledge. Handwritten copies of his works circulated among his students and were appropriated by unscrupulous publishers; in fact, Tartini's own publisher Le Cène abused his confidence. Tartini disapproved of any changes made in his manuscripts. From this point of view, the sonatas published under opus numbers 4, 5, 6, 7, and 9 are particularly suspect: they were brought to Paris in the late 1740s by Tartini's student André Pagin, whose "editing" of the violin parts seems to have been rather free. Two other collections disavowed by Tartini appeared in Amsterdam in 1732 and 1743 under duplicate opus numbers "1" and "2." All in all, some forty-eight sonatas were published without Tartini's approval and must be viewed with caution until the Collected

Works Edition (in progress since 1971) restores the *Urtext* of what Tartini actually wrote.

After Tartini's death, posthumous works came to light, some genuine, some spurious. The most famous posthumous sonata is the *Devil's Trill*, which circulated in manuscript copies during the composer's lifetime (the trill is quoted in Leopold Mozart's violin method of 1756). This remarkable work was not published until 1798, in the Parisian collection *L'Art du violon*, edited by J. B. Cartier, who obtained an anonymous copy from Baillot. No original manuscript of the *Devil's Trill* has survived, which explains the discrepancies in all the existing reprints. Today, the work is usually played with Fritz Kreisler's cadenza, which gives the audience the expected thrill by adding five minutes of assorted trills and tremolos. Cleansed of all additions and alterations, the *Devil's Trill Sonata* emerges as one of the most imaginative and innovative pieces composed in the eighteenth century—or in any century, for that matter. The music is highly romantic, not only because of its unconventional sequence of movements and emotional tension interspersed with technical bravura, but also because of its extramusical connotations. The legend of the *Devil's Trill* originated with Tartini himself, who told it to a visiting Frenchman, Lalande; he in turn published it in 1765–66 (that is, during Tartini's lifetime). It reads like a Tale of Hoffmann and confirms Tartini's known inclination toward mysticism and visionary experiences. Here is the story, somewhat abbreviated, in Tartini's words:

> One night—it was in 1713—I dreamed that I had sold my soul to the Devil. All went well; my new servant fulfilled all my wishes. I gave him my violin out of curiosity; but I was amazed to hear him play a sonata so miraculous and beautiful . . . that it exceeded all flights of imagination. I was enchanted, my breath stopped, and I awoke. I reached for my violin to reproduce some of the sounds I heard in my dream. In vain. The music I composed at that moment is no doubt the best I ever wrote—and I call it the Devil's Sonata—but it is a far cry from what I heard in my dreams.[14]

An Italian saying goes *"se non è vero, è ben trovato"*—if it isn't true, it is well invented. The only exception to be taken is the year 1713—experts now agree that, for stylistic reasons, this sonata could not have been written much before 1745.*

---

* A thematic catalogue of all the published and unpublished violin sonatas by Tartini was compiled and published by Paul Brainard in 1975; the total number is 191, including some works that are incomplete or spurious.

As a concerto composer, Tartini was a dominant figure, standing midway between the old style of Vivaldi and the new classicism of Viotti. From about 1730 to 1760, his violin concertos were considered models, not only for violinists, but also for keyboard players, including the sons of Bach.* As the popularity of Vivaldi and the Baroque concerto declined, Tartini succeeded in fashioning a concerto type that was more attuned to the changing taste of the public. He retained Vivaldi's three-movement form (fast–slow–fast) but increased the importance of the soloist. Tartini was torn between the needs of the church style to satisfy his congregation at San Antonio, and the secular taste of the lighthearted public which expected more brilliant display. Some of his concertos have the solemn dignity fit for the church, others are geared toward virtuosity. In his later concertos, he combined both needs by simplifying his technique and stressing emotion and expression. After 1750 he abandoned technical display and strove toward spiritual beauty. Some of his concertos in the minor mode strike an elegiac, pathetic mood of heartfelt expression, like the one in D minor which Szigeti recorded in a deeply moving performance.

However, Tartini did not recognize the importance of the partnership between soloist and orchestra: he usually limited the accompaniment to string instruments and kept it extremely thin whenever the soloist played.† Gradually, his successors enlarged the accompanying orchestra and introduced elements of the symphony, which made Tartini's concertos sound strangely outmoded and accelerated their oblivion. His sonatas survived better because the combination of violin and keyboard accompaniment retained its validity.

Tartini composed some 135 violin concertos; only eighteen were published during his lifetime in three collections between 1728 and 1734, but many more circulated in handwritten copies.‡ The printed concertos represent the early period of Tartini's style, while his mature and best concertos remained in manuscript because of his reluctance to entrust his works to publishers. (Even the early collections were printed over his protests.) A majority of his concertos still remain in archives, mostly in Padua, and we can look forward to important re-

* Johann Christian Bach wrote a piano concerto "in Tartini's manner" under the supervision of his older brother C. P. E. Bach in the early 1750s. Other pianists transcribed Tartini's concertos for keyboard.
† Often, the soloist is supported by only two orchestral violins.
‡ A complete catalogue of all the Tartini concertos was compiled and published in 1935 by Minos Dounias, who provided each concerto with a "D" number used today for identification.

discoveries. During the 1970s, the Complete Works Edition published six scores of hitherto unknown concertos, but the progress is slow.

Tartini's chief competitor in the concerto was Pietro Locatelli, a formidable virtuoso who settled in Amsterdam and published a volume of twelve violin concertos under the title *L'arte del violino* in 1733. A distinctive feature was the inclusion of twenty-four capriccios (unaccompanied cadenzas) which presented unheard-of technical difficulties. Musically, Tartini had nothing to fear from Locatelli, but as a technician Locatelli was a challenge forcing him to reexamine his own technique. While Locatelli's technical exploits represented a peak to be surpassed only by Paganini, it was Tartini's sterling musicianship combined with tone, taste, and technique that left a lasting imprint.

In the history of violin playing, Tartini is the mighty ancestor whose basic concepts of the instrument are still valid today: variety of bow articulation, sturdy left-hand technique both in double stops and fluent runs, and—above all—a singing cantabile style which he preached to all his students. *Per ben suonare bisogna ben cantare* (to play well one must sing well) was his motto, and it has guided violinists through the centuries. The great violinists of the nineteenth century—notably Vieuxtemps, Wieniawski, and Joachim—were all fervent admirers of Tartini and performed his sonatas.

Italians Abroad: Travelers and Expatriates

Italy was the birthplace of the violin. The first violin makers, performers, and composers were Italians, and they remained the leaders. Italian violinists traveled and settled abroad, exporting their knowledge and talents, teaching in other countries until national schools were formed. They were to be found everywhere—in Austria and Germany, in France and the Lowlands, in London and St. Petersburg. The Italian virtuosos were well paid and admired, envied and imitated, and often subjected to local intrigues and jealousies.

Interestingly, the art of violin building peaked in Italy at about the same time as the art of violin playing. Amati and Stradivari were contemporaries of Corelli and Vivaldi, while Tartini used a Guarneri instrument. The workshops in Cremona and other Italian cities provided the world with violins unmatched in beauty of construction and sonority. With such "tools" in their hands, it is hardly surprising that the Italian violinists emerged as foremost performers; they developed a national affinity for the violin, shaping its graceful appearance and evoking its singing voice.

Among Italian violinist-composers traveling or living abroad, the most prominent were Geminiani, Veracini, and Locatelli in the first half of the eighteenth century, and Nardini, Lolli, and Viotti after 1750.

Francesco Geminiani

Among Corelli's students, Geminiani came closest to the image of his master. Like Corelli, he concentrated his efforts on the composition of instrumental music, continually polishing and revising his limited number of works. Like Corelli, he chose to disregard the brilliant genre of the solo concerto—a field dominated by Vivaldi and Tartini—and devoted himself to concerti grossi and sonatas. In addition, Geminiani had a strong pedagogical interest and wrote an important method for the violin which was widely used in his time.*

As a performer, Geminiani was proficient but lacked the personality of a born virtuoso. Having settled in London early in his career, Geminiani made a name for himself with his solid musicianship and traditional style. His conservative taste and execution were ideally suited to eighteenth-century England, where Corelli's works were considered models of perfection far longer than in continental Europe. And so, the London aristocracy—while neglecting the "flighty" Veracini—lavished its attention on Geminiani, who occupied a place of honor alongside Handel.

Geminiani was born in Lucca in 1687. After some instruction from his father, a professional musician, he was sent around 1700 to Milan to study with Carlo Lonati, nicknamed *il gobbo* (the hunchback). Well prepared, Geminiani turned to Rome for lessons with Corelli on the violin and Alessandro Scarlatti in composition. In 1707 he returned to his native Lucca and played in the municipal orchestra until 1710. The following year he was appointed concertmaster in Naples, but his leadership proved disappointing:

> He was soon discovered to be so wild and unsteady a timist, that instead of regulating and conducting the band, he threw it into confusion; as none of the performers were able to follow him in his *tempo rubato*, and other unexpected accelerations and relaxations of measure.[1]

* See page 83.

Eventually, Geminiani was demoted to the viola section.

Feeling unappreciated in Naples, Geminiani decided in 1714 to try his luck abroad. He received such a warm welcome in London that he remained there. Not wishing to compete with the brilliant Veracini, who had arrived the same year, Geminiani chose a cautious approach. He won the interest of Baron Kilmansegge (an early patron of Handel), who recommended him as an "exquisite performer" to King George I.

Invited to play at a court concert, Geminiani requested to be accompanied by Handel. At that time, Handel was not yet the important figure of later years; in fact, he was a young musician out of favor at court, and it seems that his appearance with Geminiani smoothed the way for a reconciliation. Surprisingly, this successful collaboration did not lead to any future musical association between Handel and Geminiani, although they lived side by side for decades. Geminiani never participated in any of Handel's performances, and there was eventually a certain pique and rivalry between the two.

At the court concert, Geminiani made an excellent impression. In gratitude, he dedicated his Violin Sonatas Op. 1 of 1716 to Baron Kilmansegge. This collection, in style close to Corelli, established Geminiani firmly as a favorite of English music lovers.

Avoiding the challenge of public concerts, Geminiani preferred to perform in select aristocratic circles and to accept students. Burney knew him personally:

> He was seldom heard in public during his long residence in England. His compositions, students and the presents he received from the great, whenever he could be prevailed upon to play at their house, were his chief support.[2]

He also used his wealthy connections to deal in paintings, which brought him near bankruptcy.

Around 1726, Geminiani was music director of concerts sponsored by the masonic society Philo Musicae. This may have given him an incentive to arrange Corelli's Violin Sonatas Op. 5 as concerti grossi for string orchestra. The first six (the church sonatas) met with great success, but the chamber sonatas, consisting mainly of dance movements, "afforded him but little scope for the exercise of his skill and met with but an indifferent reception."[3]

In 1727 Geminiani was offered the post of "composer and master of his Majesty's band in Ireland." He declined when he found out that, as a Roman Catholic, he would have been required to change his faith. He recommended his student Matthew Dubourg, an accomplished violinist, who received the appointment and was grateful to his master throughout his life. It was Dubourg who led the orchestra at the first performance of Handel's *Messiah* in Dublin in 1742.

During the 1730s, Geminiani was very active. In December 1731 he began a series of twenty weekly concerts in London. Here he presented, from manuscript, his new concerti grossi, which were published within the next two years: six of Opus 2 in 1732, six more as Opus 3 in 1733. His prestige soared with the publication of these collections: "Geminiani was now in the highest estimation as a composer for instruments; for, to say the truth, he was in this branch of music without rival. . . ."[4] His success may have stimulated Handel into writing his own Concerti grossi Op. 3 (1734) and Op. 6 (1739); the latter in particular are very much in the Italian tradition.

Despite the public approval, Geminiani's finances did not improve much. The publisher Walsh obtained the manuscript of Opus 2 surreptitiously, and Geminiani went to court to protect his rights. Ultimately, composer and publisher came to terms, but they could not prevent reprints from appearing in Amsterdam within a year.

Undaunted, Geminiani traveled to Ireland in December 1733 and opened a Concert Room in Dublin, with adjoining space for the exhibit and sale of paintings. After two successful concerts in the spring of 1734, he returned to London. In 1737, he revisited Dublin at Dubourg's urgent invitation and stayed for three years, giving concerts and lessons, much to the delight of the music-loving Dubliners.

In the meantime he was also active as composer: a set of twelve violin sonatas was published as Opus 4 in London in 1739 and reprinted the following year in Paris. Nicknamed "the French solos," they did not find favor with the stern Burney: "They were admired more than played, as about this time it became more than ever the fashion for public solo-players to perform only their own compositions, and others were unable to execute them."[5] Geminiani arranged six of these sonatas as concerti grossi in 1743, perhaps in the hope that they would be heard more often. His last set of concerti grossi, published as Opus 7 in 1746, used occasional wind instruments (two flutes and a bassoon) in addition to the customary strings; this work, says Hawkins, "carries with it the evidence of great labour and study, but it is greatly inferior to his former works of the like kind."[6]

Occasionally, Geminiani was heard as conductor and performer. His playing was remarkable, but his conducting was described as inept. Burney heard him in 1749 at a Lenten concert: "The unsteady manner in which he led seemed to confirm the Neapolitan account of his being a bad mental arithmetician or calculator of time."[7]

Between 1749 and 1755, Geminiani paid several visits to Paris, probably to supervise the Parisian reprints of his works. During those years there was a remarkable vogue for his music at the *Concert spirituel*, where his concerti grossi (renamed "symphonies") appeared on fifteen programs between 1749 and 1758. He suddenly became the most often performed orchestral composer in Paris; but he did not participate in any of these performances. He also composed the music for a choreographed piece, *La foresta incantata*, staged at the Tuileries Palace in March 1754. After his return to London, he published the music as a suite in 1756 under the title *The Inchanted Forrest*, "an instrumental composition expressive of the same ideas as the Poem of Tasso of that title." There are twenty-two brief, contrasting movements, corresponding in mood to the danced pantomime on stage without being descriptive. The suite can be enjoyed as absolute music, as a recent recording has shown.[8] The style is a mixture of Lully and Handel, essentially late Baroque and attuned to the prevailing French taste.

In 1759 Geminiani traveled once again to Ireland to accept a post as music master to the Earl of Bellamont. His last years were spent in Dublin, in the company of his devoted Dubourg; he taught and played occasional concerts for the Irish aristocracy. It is said that he was at work on a new theoretical treatise but that the manuscript was stolen by a dishonest servant. This misfortune upset the old master greatly, probably hastening his death, which occurred on September 17, 1762. He was buried with high honors in the churchyard of St. Andrew, the church of the Irish Parliament, near College Green.

Geminiani played until his last years. In 1760 he gave a concert in Dublin, which is described in a letter of Mrs. Delany, one of Handel's friends:

> Geminiani played one of his own solos most wonderfully well for a man of 86 years of age . . . but the sweetness and melody of the tone of his fiddle, his fine and elegant taste, and the perfection of time and tune make full amends for some failure in his playing occasionad by the weakness of his hands.[9]

He was actually seventy-two at the time and died two years later. But how did he play in his youth? Here we have little information, since his public performances were so rare. Tartini once characterized him as *il furibondo* (the violent one), but did he ever hear him play? Burney (never friendly toward Geminiani) mentioned his "overwhelming technical audacity." Hawkins remembered him differently:

> He had none of the fire and spirit of the modern violinists, but [that] all the graces and elegancies of melody, all the powers that can engage attention, or that render the passions of the hearer subservient to the will of the artist, were united in his performance.[10]

By limiting himself deliberately to instrumental music, by teaching and playing the violin in the Corelli tradition, Geminiani contributed immeasurably to raising the standards of violin playing in the British Isles. While Handel was involved in all kinds of operatic ventures, it was Geminiani who satisfied the English taste for concerted string music.

Geminiani was not interested in virtuosity; for that reason he composed no solo concertos and left the field to Locatelli and Tartini. Nevertheless, his Violin Sonatas Opp. 1 and 4 show him to be a solid technician, surpassing his teacher Corelli in matters of high positions, double-stop playing, and general agility. His melodic invention did not flow abundantly, but he was an interesting harmonist and a skillful contrapuntist. In Germany, his fugal writing for instruments was considered exemplary. He enriched the sonority of the concertino (the solo group within a concerto grosso) by adding a viola to the two violins and cello.

While Burney applauds Tartini for changing his style in the 1740s, he reproaches Geminiani for doing the same, a rather ill-tempered judgment:

> After the publication of his Sonatas Opus 4 [1739], his production seems to have been the offspring of whim, caprice, and an unprincipled change of style and taste, which neither pleased the public nor contributed to his own honour or profit.[11]

Being a composer with an active mind but limited creativity, Geminiani liked to revise and rearrange his own compositions. Thus, there are two published editions of his Sonatas Op. 1 (1716 and 1739, the second edition with added ornaments and fingerings) and two editions of his Concerti grossi Op. 2 (1732 and 1755). He also transcribed his Cello Sonatas Op. 5 for violin, and various violin movements for solo harpsichord. He expanded six of his Sonatas Op. 4 into concerti grossi and fashioned trio sonatas out of his Solo Sonatas Op. 1. In the late 1740s he began to produce treatises and instruction books dealing with various aspects of music, of which *The Art of Playing on the Violin* has become most famous.

As a composer of music written for solo violin, Geminiani left a limited number of works—two sets of sonatas for violin and figured bass, Opp. 1 and 4, with twelve sonatas in each set, and another half dozen published singly in various collections. In addition there is a single sonata for unaccompanied violin, preserved in a Dresden manuscript and published as late as 1930. There was no tradition of solo violin playing in Italy, and Geminiani's work stands virtually alone. This excellent piece may belong to a (lost?) set of Geminiani sonatas often mentioned by historians but never identified.

Though Geminiani's scope as violinist-composer is somewhat limited, he represents a vital link between Corelli and the next generation, preserving traditional values yet receptive to moderate innovations. The success of Geminiani's music in Paris in the 1750s demonstrates that his style was not out of step with the sophisticated French taste at mid-century.

By a quirk of history, three violin methods were published within the short span of a decade in various parts of Europe—by Geminiani (London, 1751), Leopold Mozart (Augsburg, 1756), and Abbé le fils (Paris, 1761).[12] Perhaps it was, after all, not mere coincidence but the realization among thoughtful violin teachers that violin playing, long taught empirically, needed a kind of codification, a theoretical and practical manual. The success of Geminiani's and Mozart's publications, in particular, proved that there was a real need for such manuals, and they retained their usefulness into the nineteenth century.

Today, these instruction books are valuable because they teach us how the violin was played during the eighteenth century. They guide our efforts to restore "authentic" performances of early music, from Vivaldi and Bach to Haydn and Mozart, discussing aspects of technique, ornamentation, embellishments, and other points of performance practice.

While earlier instruction books were designed for the amateur, Geminiani's treatise was meant for professionals—a mature, condensed method, not always easy to understand or apply. His was not a "self-tutor," and anyone using it needed a good teacher to amplify the theoretical rules and practical examples. Printed in a large format, it includes nine pages of text, followed by twenty-four etudelike pieces (called "examples") and twelve brief musical compositions for violin and figured bass.[13]

Since Geminiani's *Art* was published without pictorial illustrations, his instructions for holding the violin and bow are a bit vague. However, the French translation, which appeared the following year, has the picture of a violinist (perhaps Geminiani himself) in action (see illustration on page 85). Geminiani's verbal instruction "the violin must be rested just below the collar-bone" is amplified by the picture showing that the violinist presses his head down, holding the violin with his left jawbone (not the chin!) against the tailpiece. It should be remembered that the chinrest did not come into use until about 1820; before that, the chin of the player rested directly on the body of the violin to the *right* of the tailpiece before 1760 and to the *left* (as now) after about 1760. Many old violins still bear perspiration marks on the right side of the tailpiece, attesting to usage according to the "old" method. Leopold Mozart preferred the chin pressure on the right side, while Abbé le fils was the first to advocate, in 1761, the chin position on the left side of the tailpiece, where, of course, it is placed today.

Geminiani recommends the slight tilting of the right side of the violin downward "so that there may be no necessity of raising the bow very high, when the fourth string [i.e. the G-string] is to be struck." This angle is still in use today. Geminiani also admonishes the player not to let the violin droop (as beginners are apt to do): "the head of the violin must be nearly horizontal with that part which rests against the breast, that the hand may be shifted with facility and without any danger of dropping the instrument." The self-confident concert violinist of today holds the violin at a higher angle, sometimes even with exaggeration (as did Heifetz).

As for the bow, Geminiani wants it to be held "at a small distance from the nut, between the thumb and fingers." Judging by the picture in the French edition, the distance was not "small" but apparently one or two inches. In contrast, Leopold Mozart advocated a surprisingly modern grip, to grasp the bowstick "at its lowest extremity" so as to give the tone more robustness. Today, the bow is held right at the nut, not above it. Other of Geminiani's bow rules still apply today: the use of wrist and elbow in playing quick notes, the tilting of the bowstick toward the strings, the involvement of the shoulder joint when the whole bow is employed. "The best performers are least sparing of

Francesco Geminiani,
author of *The Art of
Playing on the Violin*

The label inside the famous
"Betts" Stradivari violin
(1704) now in The Library
of Congress

Francesco Veracini:
"One God
and One Veracini"

their bow, and make use of the whole of it . . ."—an observation applicable today to the unstinting use of bow by Milstein or Heifetz.

Also surprisingly up-to-date are Geminiani's opinions about the use of vibrato. Calling it the "close shake," he not only recommends its use on long sustained notes but more or less continuously: "when it is made on short notes, it only contributes to make the sound more agreeable and for this reason it should be made use of as often as possible." Leopold Mozart, on the other hand, tolerated the vibrato only on long tones but admitted that continuous vibrato was indeed in use: "Performers there are who tremble consistently on each note as if they had the palsy." Yet Mozart, much as he disliked vibrato, explained the mechanics more clearly than either Geminiani or Tartini. Despite Geminiani's encouragement, though, the vibrato remained primarily an ornament in the eighteenth century, used by soloists or advanced players but not in the orchestra.

Geminiani was logical and imaginative in the use of fingerings, which covers the normal seven-position  range of the time. He established the so-called "Geminiani grip" for the four fingers of the left hand (later adopted by Mozart in the second edition of his treatise)— 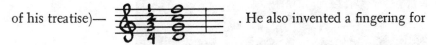 . He also invented a fingering for chromatic scales (using consecutive fingers) which, in our century, was "rediscovered" by Achron and advocated by Flesch.

In certain respects, Leopold Mozart's *Violin School* was more forward looking and modern than Geminiani's, but Mozart belonged to a younger generation (born in 1719) and was thus more attuned to the needs of the approaching classical school. Yet Geminiani's *Art* held its own for fifty years, even reaching the New World in an edition printed in Boston in 1769.

Francesco Veracini

While Geminiani was an expatriate, Veracini was a restless traveler. He was heard in Frankfurt, Venice, Dresden, Prague, and repeatedly in London. At the time of his first appearance in London in

1714, Veracini—according to Burney—was the greatest violinist in Europe. His rivals preferred to withdraw rather than compete with him. His self-confidence was unlimited: "one God and one Veracini," he used to boast. Yet despite his undisputed mastery, his career was checkered and disappointing. Though he held high positions during his lifetime, he was unable to settle permanently in any post—perhaps because of his jealous and overbearing nature. He died in obscurity, so forgotten, in fact, that most biographers set the year of his death in 1750, though he actually lived as late as 1768 in his native city of Florence.

Born on February 1, 1690, Veracini proudly called himself "Fiorentino" throughout his life. He came from a family of excellent musicians; his grandfather enjoyed high esteem as violin teacher, and his uncle Antonio achieved a wide reputation as composer and violinist. It was this uncle who taught Francesco the violin so well that he needed no other instruction. At the age of nine, his grandfather took him to Rome. He remained there for about a year, and though he must have heard Corelli, then at the height of his fame, there is no evidence that he studied with him. But he does seem to have retained a lifelong admiration for Corelli.

Around 1700, Veracini, then only ten years old, returned home to Florence and remained there until 1711, perfecting his violin playing and studying theory with the organist G. M. Casini. In 1711 his first journey abroad took him via Munich to Frankfurt. There he played his own Violin Concerto in D major in honor of the coronation of Charles VI: it is one of his most brilliant though superficial compositions. From there he moved to London in 1714 and made his debut on January 23, playing a concerto between the acts of an opera. His success was such that he was reengaged for a dozen appearances. On April 22 he gave a concert for his own benefit at Hickford's Room and produced his own vocal and instrumental compositions.

However, the British public admired his virtuosity more than his talent as composer, for Burney says, "His compositions were too wild and flighty for the taste of the English at this time when they regarded the sonatas of Corelli as models of simplicity, grace, and elegance. . . ."[1] Veracini soon abandoned London, leaving the field to his compatriot Geminiani, who wrote more traditional music and was hence more adaptable to the English taste.

Veracini appeared briefly at court in Düsseldorf in 1715 and then traveled to Venice where, around 1716, he played first violin at St. Mark's Cathedral. There he met Vivaldi, then at the height of his fame, though no active competition is reported. However, another young rival, Tartini, heard Veracini and was so impressed that he withdrew from a planned contest to perfect his own playing.

At that time, the Elector of Saxony was visiting Venice, accompanied by his own musical staff, including the violinist Pisendel, who was to study with Vivaldi. The elector engaged Veracini to join the musical establishment in Dresden. Here, Veracini occupied an honored post from 1717 to about 1722. While he had a cordial relationship with his princely patron, he was exposed to intrigues by his German colleagues. Particularly Pisendel, then a rising star at the Dresden court, must have felt his position threatened. A plot to humiliate Veracini was hatched: Veracini was asked, in the presence of the king and the court, to sightread a concerto by Pisendel and did it poorly. Immediately Pisendel asked one of the orchestral violinists (whom he had secretly coached) to play the same piece, which he did to much applause. Veracini, his pride deeply wounded, went home and tried to commit suicide by jumping out of a top-floor window. He survived with a broken leg, causing a lifelong limp; as soon as he was able to travel, he left Dresden for Prague and shortly returned to his native Florence.

In 1735, Veracini was back in London, this time as the composer of *Adriano* for the Italian opera. Remarkably successful, it was followed by two more operas in 1737 and 1738. Yet, at least one critical voice was heard, that of Lord Hervey: "I am at this moment returned with the King from yawning four hours at the longest and dullest opera . . . the music [composed] by one Veracini, a madman. . . ."[2]

After his return to Florence, Veracini met the French connoisseur de Brosses, whose evaluations of Vivaldi and Tartini we have already encountered. He spoke highly of Veracini: "the first, or one of the first, among violinists in Europe: his playing is in tune, noble, learned, and precise though somewhat lacking in grace."[3]

In 1741 Veracini reestablished himself in London. On February 28 he played one of his own concertos during the entr'acte of Handel's *Acis and Galatea*. Later that year, Veracini's name appeared along with Handel and Tartini in a concerto collection published by Walsh.

Veracini's success continued into 1742: in the autumn he performed twenty-one times within six weeks, playing concertos during the entr'actes at the Drury Lane Theatre. In 1744 he was again in the limelight as a composer; his opera *Rosalinda* was given ten times, and his *Academic Sonatas* Op. 2 for violin and bass appeared in a resplendent edition. To protect his work against unauthorized piracy, he had obtained a special patent from King George II. An engraving showing

Veracini as performer appears as frontispiece (see illustration on page 85): the maestro is holding the violin boldly on the collarbone without touching it with his chin—obviously posed for the artist. His left- and right-hand position is portrayed with remarkable clarity; the bow is held slightly above the nut, with the little finger held in the air. Interesting is the length of the bow—an Italian "sonata" bow—which was about 2½ inches longer than our present-day bow.

Burney heard Veracini perform in 1745 and his report is full of praise:

> He led the band . . . in such a bold and masterly manner as I had never heard before. . . . The peculiarities in his performance were his bow-hand, his shake [trill], his learned arpeggios, and a tone so loud and clear, that it could be distinctly heard through the most numerous band of a church or theatre.[4]

But regardless of the acclaim as performer and composer, Veracini was unable to shake the prestige of Geminiani, who, at least in England, was the recognized authority on everything pertaining to violin playing.

Veracini left London in mid-1745. On his journey home he was shipwrecked and lost all his belongings, including his two famous Stainer violins which he had named St. Peter and St. Paul. They were considered the finest samples of Stainer's workmanship in existence.*

Veracini's last years were uneventful. He lived quietly in Florence, where he occupied a modest position as director of church music. He was also at work on a treatise, *Il trionfo della pratica musicale* Op. 3 (as yet unpublished), which is highly critical of musical practices in his time. Public appearances became increasingly rare. In 1766, at the age of seventy-six, he played a "spirited concert" in Florence, but the world at large had forgotten him. In October 1768 he dictated his last will and testament and died a few weeks later. The burial took place on November 1, at the family's burial plot at the church d'Ognissanti in Florence.

There are many stories which picture Veracini as arrogant, conceited, and intolerant. One is told by Burney in some detail. As a young man, he wanted to participate in the annual concerto competition held each September in Lucca at the Festa della Croce (a competition

---

* The violins made by the Tyrolean master Jacob Stainer were highly prized in the early eighteenth century and often preferred by professional violinists to the younger Stradivari instruments.

which, incidentally, Paganini was to win in 1801). When Veracini entered the orchestra, advancing boldly toward the first chair, he found it occupied by Padre Laurenti of Bologna. Showing contempt and indignation, Veracini turned his back on Laurenti and sat at the last desk of the orchestra. While Laurenti played his concerto, Veracini sat still and listened. When his turn came, he insisted on playing a sonata—and he played it "in such a manner as to extort an *e viva!* in the public church." Triumphantly, Veracini turned to Laurenti and shouted, "This is the way to play the first fiddle!"[5] Such behavior earned him in Italy the nickname of *capo pazzo* (fool head).

As a musician, Veracini had power, sweep, and boldness—a kind of unbridled imagination that brought him into conflict with traditional trends. However, he became a conservative in later years and failed to move with the times as did Tartini and Locatelli. Nor did his violin technique incorporate any extreme feats comparable to Locatelli's Caprices or Tartini's *Devil's Trill*. But time and again, his music surprises us by flashes of ingenuity and audacity, by unconventional turns, above all by fire and grandeur, a reflection of his imperious temperament.

Veracini's list of violin compositions consists of thirty-six sonatas, published in three collections of twelve each,* and about ten solo concertos (some unpublished). He showed no interest in writing ensemble music such as concerti grossi or trio sonatas. Being a full-blooded soloist, he was eager to display his virtuosity without undue encumbrance by other instruments.

The sonatas of the first set, dated 1716, were actually designed for flute or violin; they are short, unpretentious pieces, musically attractive but not particularly violinistic. In no way do they reveal Veracini's superior standing in the virtuoso profession. He himself did not attach too much importance to his first essay, since he left it unpublished.

By designating his next sonata collection Opus 1, Veracini gave it his personal stamp of approval; it was published in 1721 in Dresden, perhaps at the composer's expense, since there is no publisher's name. In these works Veracini is decidedly the imaginative violinist, with sonorous themes and fiery passages. Reversing the usual order, he opened the set with six chamber sonatas (in six different minor keys), followed by six church sonatas (in six different major keys). He took

---

* Another collection, actually an elaboration of Corelli's Sonatas Op. 5, remained unpublished during his lifetime. All four collections are reprinted in excellent modern editions.

over Corelli's pattern of four or five movements, contrary to the newer trend toward a three-movement sequence. Compared to his earlier sonatas, there is more stress on contrapuntal writing in the Opus 1 set, but his fugal movements are inferior to those of Tartini. One can say that Veracini is more fancy-free and ingenious, Tartini more scholarly and disciplined.

More than two decades elapsed before Veracini turned to the publication of another collection of violin sonatas, which may be considered his crowning achievement: the twelve *Academic Sonatas* Op. 2 (1744). The title indicates that they were meant to be "concert" sonatas, not amateur entertainment. Indeed, the composer overwhelmed the performer with works of such length and complexity as to discourage any casual perusal. Veracini's Opus 2 represents a belated flowering of the Baroque style. Accomplished and artful though these sonatas are, they came at a time when the interest for such involved compositions had all but vanished. Veracini may have composed and collected them over a number of years, but at the time of publication they seemed out of step with the times and aroused little interest.

Veracini's new work preceded by one year the Sonatas Op. 2 by Tartini. But while Tartini had changed to a simpler, less learned, more *galant* style, Veracini was determined to turn back the clock by reverting to the complexities of the past. He paid for his eccentricity by public indifference.

The *Academic Sonatas* are divided into six church and six chamber sonatas, though neither type is strictly preserved. Interspersed are fancy titles such as *Aria Schiavonna* (Slavic), *Scozzese* (Scottish), *Polonese*, *Cotillion*, *Ritornello*. There are a number of *Capriccio* movements where fugal double-stop sections alternate with sweeping passage work. Much thought is given to the sequence and balance of movements. The final sonata begins with a *Passagallo* (Passacaglia) built on a descending chromatic scale of six tones (*d* to *a*) followed by a *Capriccio cromatico* based on the same chromatic motive. The third and last movement opens with an Adagio—again related to the chromatic opening—and ends with a brilliant *Ciaconna*. On the whole, these sonatas are large-scale works, requiring an artist with style and virtuosity to do them full justice.

Veracini provided his *Academic Sonatas* with a preface entitled "Intentions of the Author." They show his concern for a correct performance by giving instructions to the player and explaining various signs and abbreviations. He was also concerned with the length of his sonatas—they are indeed unusually long—and advised,

Since each of these sonatas is provided with four or five movements, be advised that such is done for the enrichment and adornment of the collection, and for the greater diversion of amateurs of music. Otherwise, two or three movements of these, selected as one pleases, suffice to comprise a sonata of just proportions.

Veracini's violin concertos are less challenging than his sonatas. Some ten are known, but only one has recently received wider attention: the *Coronation Concerto* (1711) for solo violin with oboes, trumpets, and strings. It is appropriately extrovert and effective.

More than half of Veracini's compositions consist of vocal works—operas, oratorios, cantatas, church music. From this point of view, he was far more versatile than any of his violinist contemporaries—Corelli, Geminiani, Locatelli, Tartini—who concentrated on instrumental music. Veracini may not have been "the Beethoven of the eighteenth century," as one eminent Italian music historian called him in a fit of national hyperbole;[6] but he certainly was an imposing musician of many talents and an undisputed master of his chosen instrument.

Pietro Locatelli

Locatelli was the greatest violin technician of his century. In fact, he could be called the father of violin virtuosity. He achieved in the eighteenth century what Paganini was to accomplish in the nineteenth—an unprecedented expansion of the violin technique of the time. Their rivals were incredulous when they saw the printed samples of violin acrobatics, but both Locatelli and Paganini could actually play what they wrote down. Locatelli stirred his contemporaries with *L'arte del violino*, which contained twenty-four caprices encapsuled in twelve violin concertos. Paganini's work of 1820 was simply called Twenty-four Caprices, which he dedicated "To the Artists." (In other words—amateurs, beware!) To reinforce the link between the two, Paganini took the cue for his first caprice from Locatelli's seventh caprice.

Locatelli

Paganini

Thus Paganini paid homage to an older master, by then almost forgotten, from whose works he confessed he had learned much.

Locatelli's posthumous reputation was nearly ruined by the intemperate criticism of the nineteenth-century German music historian Wasielewski. That defender of musical virtue branded Locatelli as a technical exhibitionist, a near-charlatan dedicated to "finger heroics," who was apt to lead violin playing down the primrose path. Eventually, voices were raised in defense of Locatelli, and ultimately his artistic reputation was salvaged by two other German musicologists, Arnold Schering and Andreas Moser. The Dutch pitched in, too, since Locatelli had lived in Amsterdam for many years. Municipal archives were combed by the Dutch musicologists Arend Koole and Albert Dunning, who wrote full-length biographies of Locatelli. There emerged a new image of the old master as one of the important innovators in the eighteenth century, not only of violin technique (where he was long recognized as unique), but also in the genres of the concerto, the sonata, and even theater music. The stylistic transformation from Baroque to *style galant* can be clearly traced in his works.

Nothing in Locatelli's early career indicated that he would become one of the great violinists of his generation. He was born on September 3, 1695, in Bergamo, an ancient town in the Alpine foothills. Bergamo had an old musical tradition centered on the twelfth-century Basilica Santa Maria Maggiore, which supported a regular school for singers and instrumentalists. Here young Locatelli received his basic musical training and was appointed third violinist in 1711, at the age of fifteen. The same year he was granted a leave of absence to study in Rome, presumably with Corelli. The study was short, for the ailing master died in January 1713. However, Locatelli remained in Rome for another ten years and it is possible that he had additional violin instruction from Giuseppe Valentini, a highly respected musician. At the same time, Locatelli participated in various musical activities arranged by the Roman aristocracy without gaining much prominence.

Still, the years in Rome were well spent, for Locatelli composed his first large-scale work, the twelve Concerti grossi Op. 1, published in Amsterdam in 1721. Though reflecting the tradition of Corelli, Locatelli's concertos have a personal profile quite remarkable for a composer in his twenties.

In 1723 Locatelli left Rome and began a career as a traveling virtuoso. His peregrinations are sparsely documented. In 1725 he performed in Mantua and was named chamber virtuoso to the reigning

Prince Philipp. He was also heard in Venice with great success; on this occasion he played the premiere of his new violin concertos, supported by a very large orchestra, at the palatial home of a Venetian patron who later received the dedication of the work.* By 1727, Locatelli was in Munich, playing at the Bavarian court. The following year he appeared in Berlin, accompanying the elector of Saxony on a state visit. Locatelli was asked to play for the king of Prussia, who was known for his frugality. Seeing the artist dressed in a blue velvet frock coat embroidered with silver, with diamond-studded rings on his fingers and a ceremonial sword hanging on his side, the king was amused and exclaimed, "That fellow looks like a councilor of war!" After the performance, the king sent Locatelli a gift of twenty thaler, which the artist refused to accept, handing it back to the messenger as a tip. When the king heard the story, he was furious and complained to the elector, who merely said that Locatelli was used to princely gifts. After Locatelli played at the Prussian court a second time, the king personally handed him a gold box filled with ducats. "Since you are so generous with tips," said the king, "I wish I could keep this as a tip." The quick-witted Locatelli replied, "A present from the hand of your majesty has so much weight that I could not part with it."[1]

That same year (1728) Locatelli visited Cassel, where he played at a court concert. It is reported (but not documented) that the eminent French violinist Jean-Marie Leclair was also heard on this occasion. We extract the following from a late-eighteenth-century report:

> When he [Locatelli] and Leclair once were heard together at the court at Cassel, the court-jester said already at the beginning, "That fellow [Locatelli] runs over the violin like a rabbit," and at the conclusion, "That one [Leclair] plays like an angel, and the former [Locatelli] plays like a devil." . . . Leclair, with a little-practiced left hand, knew how to win the hearts with an uncommonly pure and lovely tone, while the other [Locatelli] mainly tried to cause the listener astonishment by performing the most difficult passages while croaking.[2]

During 1729, Locatelli spent some time in Amsterdam to supervise and proofread a new edition of his Concerti grossi Op. 1. Soon thereafter he took up residence in Amsterdam and remained there for the rest of his life, though he never acquired Dutch citizenship.

What induced Locatelli to settle in Amsterdam? Its musical life was far less active than that of Paris or London, and eighteenth-century

---

* Published in 1733 under the title *L'arte del violino*.

travelers complained about the absence of an opera. In the opinion of a
Frenchman, M. de la Barre de Beaumarchais, dated 1738,

> Few among the Dutch have achieved a certain degree of ex-
> cellence [in music]. . . . I don't know if one could not attrib-
> ute this kind of sterility to a lack of brilliant opportunities
> and sufficient remunerations for musicians. From time to time
> there are concerts, some students in the cities, that's about all
> they have and, as for the rest, no opera.[3]

Burney, in visiting Amsterdam in 1772, described it as "a place where
little other music is encouraged or attended to, than the jinging of bells,
and of ducats."[4]

The fact is that the sensible Dutch burghers were more inclined
to support solid instrumental music than spend money on opera, a
flighty entertainment sung in a strange language. Amsterdam also became, early in the eighteenth century, an important center for music
publishing, mainly through the influx of Huguenot refugees from
France. Among them was Estienne Roger, who was joined later by
his daughter Jeanne and his son-in-law Le Cène. The successful enterprise flourished until Le Cène's death in 1743. Another publisher was
the organist Witvogel, active in the years 1730–45, "a busy publisher,
an original good-for-nothing, and a great drunkard," according to one
description.

In terms of business practices, the international publishers of those
days were little more than intellectual pirates. They stole from each
other and they stole from composers. Tartini and Geminiani were vic-
timized, as were many others. Perhaps Locatelli decided to remain in
Amsterdam in order to protect his interests as a composer. In 1731 he
received the privilege of printing his own music. From then on he made
it a practice to publish his chamber music under his own imprint while
entrusting his orchestral music to professional publishers, mainly
Le Cène, who undertook to publish the monumental L'arte del violino
in 1733. The process of music engraving was slow and laborious: it
took a craftsman a week to engrave two pages. Since L'arte consisted
of 295 pages, it is reasonable to assume that the engraving began
around 1730. At the same time, Le Cène was publishing the newest
works by Tartini and Geminiani; the competition was very keen. Being
eminently practical, Locatelli kept a watchful eye on the publication
process and worked closely with Le Cène, often acting as proofreader
on behalf of other composers.

By 1740, Locatelli had established an enviable reputation as a performer and composer. Without seeking the limelight, he led a comfortable bourgeois existence independent of princely or churchly patronage. A circle of Dutch instrumentalists—mostly amateurs—gathered around Locatelli and performed regularly as a collegium musicum. Some of his influential Dutch admirers received dedications of his works. In 1742 he moved to a large house on the fashionable Prinsengracht, and advertised that he had for sale a stock of excellent Italian strings for violins and other stringed instruments. Here he also sold his own music. His house was used for public performances, and for this purpose he had a large collection of instruments, as well as seven music stands, 46 chairs, and 21 footwarmers—indispensable accessories in those days. Among his violins were an Amati of 1618, a David Teckler of 1724, and his concert instrument, a Stainer of 1667 (the same Tyrolean maker also preferred by Veracini).

A visiting Englishman revealed a peculiarity of Locatelli: "Locatelli is so afraid of people's learning from him that he won't admit a [professed] musician into his concert; and he never will play anywhere but with gentlemen. . . ."⁵ Apparently he taught only amateurs, and most certainly he did not share any of his technical secrets with his French colleague and competitor Leclair, who was in Holland around 1740. Locatelli may have avoided meeting Leclair just as he failed to meet Vivaldi during the latter's visit to Amsterdam in 1738. Unlike Tartini, Locatelli did not create a "school" through personal instruction: he exerted his influence through his published *L'arte del violino*, which contained the sum-total of his fabulous technique.

Following this monumental achievement, Locatelli continued to compose and to publish a variety of works in rapid succession. There were theater overtures and concerti grossi, violin sonatas and trio sonatas. At times he acted as intermediary on behalf of the publisher Le Cène, as in the case of the scholarly Padre Martini of Bologna, with whom he had an extensive correspondence. Locatelli was helpful and affable, as well as businesslike. After Le Cène's death in 1743, Locatelli was one of the appraisers of his estate. Locatelli's last published work appeared in 1744 as Opus 8 under his own imprint—a collection of ten sonatas that was reissued in 1752. After many years of silence, Locatelli produced a new work in 1762—six Concerti grossi, Op. 9, which disappeared mysteriously and must be considered lost.

Little is known about the last ten to fifteen years of Locatelli's life. He was not married, perhaps having been widowed at a young age while he lived in Rome: a *Symphony of Mourning* commemorating the death of his wife is tentatively attributed to Locatelli. In Amsterdam he lived the life of a bachelor, though rumors had it that he was under the influence of an avaricious housekeeper. His biographer Koole believes that the woman was actually the widow Aurelli, who dealt in Italian strings and transferred her business to Locatelli's house.

In any event, he died in apparent loneliness on March 30, 1764, without leaving a will. His heirs were sought in Italy, and ultimately two nephews arrived in Amsterdam to collect their share of the profits from the auction sale of his library and art collection. The printed catalogue revealed Locatelli's broad cultural interests—more than a thousand Italian and French volumes, printed and manuscript music, paintings and engravings, musical instruments and *objets d'art*. The obituary in *Nouvelles d'Amsterdam* appeared in French on April 10, 1764:

> The Signor Pietro Antonio Locatelli, native of Bergamo, died in this city to the great regret of all the music lovers on the 30th of last month at the age of 68 years, 7 months, and 26 days, having been born on 4 Sept. 1695. Equally famous by his works and by the manner he performed them, he was rightly regarded as one of the foremost violinists of Europe.[6]

Two English travelers, Dr. Dampier and young Mr. Tate, had visited Amsterdam in 1741 and heard Locatelli play. Their amusing impressions are related in their letters:

> Locatelli must surely be allowed by all to be an earth quake. . . . What bowings! what fire! what rapidity! He plays his "Laby-rinth" . . . with more ease than I can hum the "Black Joke"; and what is still more extraordinary, he never pulls off his coat to play it, as I have observed most great musicians do. . . . He plays with so much fury upon his fiddle that in my humble opinion he must wear out some dozens of them in a year. . . . He never was known to play one note out of tune except once when . . . he thrust his little finger through the bridge of the fiddle and could not get it out again.[7]

Locatelli is known to have played in the uppermost regions of the violin, beyond the support of the fingerboard (which in those days was shorter). To get the little finger caught in the bridge is indeed embarrassing!

Young Mr. Tate, a "gentleman performer" on the violin (obviously not a professional!), added, "Locatelli plays with a short bow, and the reason he gives for doing so, that he believes, no fiddler can play anything with a long bow that he can't play with a short one. . . ." We have seen that Veracini, at about the same time, used an unusually long bow; the length of a violin bow was not standardized in those days.

> Locatelli never sits by to rest, but plays on for three hours together, without being in the least fatigued. I never in my life saw a man play with so much ease. . . . He holds the fiddle always upon his breast, and has the most affected look just before he begins to play, that I ever saw in my life.

Locatelli's facial affectations are also remembered by an observer, the organist Lustig, who was never friendly disposed toward the master: "He who has heard Locatelli improvise 55 years ago, knows what grimaces he produced before coming to his senses and exclaiming, 'Ah, que dîtes-vous de cela?' " Whether this trancelike state was affected or sincere is difficult to tell. Facial contortions were observed with Corelli and others as well.

Locatelli's predilection for playing in excessively high positions may explain such unfavorable comments about his tone quality as, "He once played the violin very harmoniously . . . but at the same time so roughly that tender ears found it unsufferable. . . ."[8]

Burney arrived in Amsterdam a few years after Locatelli had died, and talked to one of his students, the organist Potholt, who remembered the old master fondly. Burney reported,

> Locatelli was possessed of a great deal of both [taste and fancy]; and though he delighted in capricious difficulties, which his hand could as easily execute as his head conceive, yet he had a fund of knowledge, in the principles of harmony that rendered such wild flights agreeable as in less skilled hands would have been unsupportable.[9]

Burney's later judgment is more detached and dry—"The celebrated Locatelli . . . had more hand, caprice, and fancy than any violinist of his time. He was a voluminous composer of music that excites more surprise than pleasure."[10]

Because of Locatelli's formidable reputation as a virtuoso, many violinists—professionals as well as amateurs—avoided his music for fear of its difficulties, though there is nothing terrifying in his ensemble music. Tate tried to persuade his friends and fellow musicians to try Locatelli's concerti grossi, but "they looked upon them as the most extravagant things in the world and not to be played at sight" because of "some passages out of the common road." When Locatelli's music was mentioned to the professional leader, Michael Festing, "he looked as if he had been condemned to be hanged."[11]

Although Locatelli's compositions soon became outmoded, professional violinists remained aware of his technical accomplishments. So said Dittersdorf, the Austrian violinist-composer, in the 1790s:

> Though the Locatelli Sonatas may seem old-fashioned in our time, I must recommend them to every ambitious violin student as material for study, more so than for performance. By learning them, he will make great strides in fingering, in various bowings, arpeggios, double stops, etc.[12]

Leopold Mozart's recognition of Locatelli's importance was posthumous: not until the third edition of his violin method (1787) are there examples of difficult passages culled from several of Locatelli's capriccios, though the author is not named.

Among Parisian violinists, it was Leclair who profited greatly from his contact with Locatelli. Whether this contact was personal or indirect (through studying the published works) is immaterial; but in the late 1730s Leclair's violin technique acquired a higher level of proficiency, evident in Book IV of his Sonatas (Op. 9, published in 1743). For unexplained reasons, Locatelli's music did not enter the repertoire of the *Concert spirituel* as did the concertos of Tartini and Geminiani. The often repeated story that the young Pierre Gaviniès made his brilliant debut in 1741 with a concerto by Locatelli is inaccurate (he chose music by Leclair and Vivaldi on that occasion). Nor did any other French violinist of that generation select Locatelli for public performance, except for André Pagin (a student of Tartini), who is rumored to have played a Locatelli concerto in 1749. That does not mean that French violinists were ignorant of Locatelli's technical achievements: the steep rise of French virtuosity after 1740 is undoubtedly connected with the impact of Locatelli's *L'arte del violino*, which was eagerly reprinted in Paris.

The ultimate tribute came from Paganini, who discovered Locatelli's *Arte* during his student years. "It opened up a world of new ideas and devices that never had the merited success because of excessive difficulties," he confided to Fétis.[13]

Thus, for the history of violin technique, Locatelli must be recognized as the most influential personality and outstanding virtuoso of the pre-Paganini era. This does not necessarily mean that he was the most engaging player: greatness is not measured by technique alone, and among his contemporaries were violinists with more charm and grace. But in his Twenty-four Caprices, Locatelli enriched the technical vocabulary of violin playing, encouraging others to experiment further until a plateau of proficiency was reached from which a genius like Paganini could take off to reach yet greater heights.

Locatelli's caprices are part of his collection of twelve violin concertos, which he proudly called *The Art of the Violin* (*L'arte del violino*). Each concerto consists of the customary three movements; inserted into each corner movement is an unaccompanied "capriccio" to display the soloist's technical skill. In order not to discourage lesser virtuosos, the capriccios were designated "optional"; nevertheless, Locatelli's concertos received very few performances. Eventually, the Twenty-four Caprices were detached from the concertos and published separately for study purposes. While some of them resemble dry etudes, others are musically attractive and technically ingenious, for example No. 23, entitled *Labyrinth*—an imaginative study in arpeggios, which sounds ravishing in the hands of an artist.

There has always been a tendency to downgrade the musical achievement of *L'arte del violino* because of the pyrotechnics of the caprices. Yet the concertos proper contain much beautiful material, not only in the expressive middle movements, but also in the initial Allegros. In fact, some of the concertos (Nos. 2, 3, 7, and 8) start with an Andante movement; others have Largo introductions. Each concerto begins with a tutti whose theme is taken up by the soloist an octave higher, that is, on the luminous E-string. Locatelli was the first to employ this principle consistently.

As a sonata composer, Locatelli has not received deserved recognition. He composed eighteen sonatas for violin and figured bass, published in two collections in 1737 and 1744. Particularly the first set (Opus 6) is of pivotal importance: he added *da camera* to the title to indicate his abandonment of fugal writing and his shift toward the homophonic *galant* style. In this respect he was ahead of Tartini. Locatelli's melodic line is warm and pliant, with tasteful embellishments written out in detail. Technically, these sonatas are very demanding, though less virtuosic than his concertos: double stops, long staccato runs, and intricate passages place them beyond the reach of the average amateur. The number and sequence of movements is varied: seven sonatas are in three movements, four in four movements, and the last, No. 12 in D minor, has five, ending with a Capriccio in D major, subtitled *prova dell' intonazione* (test of intonation). And a test it is, every bit as difficult as the caprices in his concertos. The musical high point of this collection is No. 7 in F minor, called *Le Tombeau* because of its grave character (of the four movements, three are slow). It was a favorite piece of Ysaÿe, who published a free adaptation, and has been beautifully recorded by David Oistrakh. But on the whole, the music of Locatelli still awaits rediscovery.

Gaetano Pugnani

Pugnani owes his posthumous fame to a good-natured hoax of Fritz Kreisler. Eager to expand the violin repertoire, Kreisler composed a number of short pieces imitating the style of older composers. They were published in a manner suggesting that they were genuine classical manuscripts rediscovered by Kreisler. Among them was a Prelude and Allegro ascribed to Pugnani and allegedly "arranged" by Kreisler. The piece proved immensely popular with audiences and performers. Though no one could find Pugnani's "original" manuscript, the Prelude and Allegro continued to be played under the joint name "Pugnani-Kreisler." In 1935 Kreisler casually admitted that the Pugnani piece as well as many similar ones by "old" composers were really his own original compositions. Some people laughed, others were furious at the deception, and the thundering indignation of the British critic Ernest Newman filled many columns. But after a while the furor died down, and today the pieces continue to be popular, though stripped of their borrowed plumes.

The *real* Pugnani, however—a composer of importance in his day—remains forgotten. No attempt has been made to revive his many sonatas, symphonies, and chamber works, not to mention his operas. The oblivion is not undeserved: there is no message of lasting value in his music. One of the many pioneers who prepared the way for the classic masters, Pugnani was but one year older than Haydn and outlived Mozart by seven years, but his music reflects hardly any of the glory of these two great contemporaries.

Nevertheless, Pugnani is important as a link between tradition and innovation in violin playing. The Corelli tradition had been handed down to him by his teacher Giovanni Battista Somis, himself a student of Corelli. This Pugnani transmitted to his best student, Viotti, who is often called the "father of modern violin playing." Through Viotti and his French disciples as intermediaries, a somewhat modernized Italian tradition entered the Paris Conservatoire, which in turn became a bulwark against the inroads of Paganinian virtuosity. The lineage

Corelli–Somis–Pugnani–Viotti–Baillot–Kreutzer–Massart–Wieniawski–
Kreisler is the strongest unbroken link between the violin's past and
present history.

A few words about Pugnani's teacher Somis are in order. Giovanni
Battista Somis (1686–1763) came from a family of musicians in Turin,
who had served for generations in the ducal musical establishment. In
1703, young Somis was sent to Rome to study with Corelli. By 1707
he was back in Turin, and eventually rose to concertmaster and solo
violinist of the ducal orchestra, a post he occupied until his death in
1763. His violin compositions were printed in Amsterdam and Paris,
and he appeared as soloist of the Parisian *Concert spirituel* in 1733;
his playing was described as "utter perfection," but at least one dissenting voice, that of de Brosses, considered Somis "inferior to Tartini
and Veracini."[1] Somis attracted many students to Turin, among them
several gifted Frenchmen—Leclair and Guillemain—who transplanted
his school to Paris. Two of his Italian students—Guignon and Chabran*—moved to Paris, where they became quite prominent. In addition, Somis's younger brother Lorenzo, also a violinist, was active in
Paris for a time. The Somis school of violin playing was certainly well
represented in the French capital.

G. B. Somis's most important student was undoubtedly Gaetano
Pugnani. Also a native of Turin, he owed his entire musical education
to Somis. Born in 1731, young Pugnani was considered advanced
enough at the age of ten to play at the last desk of the Turin orchestra,
and became a full-fledged member in 1748. A royal scholarship enabled
him to go to Rome for further studies in composition; by 1750 he was
back in Turin at his modest orchestral post though he had to wait
until 1763 for a promotion to leader of the second violins. In the
meantime, Pugnani visited Paris in 1754 and played his own concerto
at the *Concert spirituel*. The *Mercure* reported after his debut, "The
connoisseurs who attended the concert, claim that they have never
heard a violinist superior to this virtuoso."[2] Pugnani spent almost a
year in Paris—he had a paid leave from Turin—and found a publisher
for his Opus 1, consisting of six trios for two violins and cello. After
touching London, Holland, and Vienna, Pugnani returned to his position in Turin.

In 1761, Johann Christian Bach (youngest son of Johann Sebastian)
visited Turin and was so impressed by Pugnani's excellence that he

---

* Guignon's original name was Ghignone, Chabran's Chiabrano.

Gaetano Pugnani,
master of
the "grand bow"

Pietro Locatelli:
"The Paganini of the
Eighteenth Century"

Pietro Nardini, Tartini's favorite student

engaged him as opera leader at King's Theater in London. For three consecutive seasons, Pugnani was extremely successful in London, not only as conductor but also as solo performer and opera composer: his opera *Nanetto e Lubino* was the hit of the 1769 spring season.

At long last, the court in Turin realized Pugnani's artistic stature: on May 7, 1770, he was named concertmaster and conductor of the Royal Theater (Teatro Regio), as well as chamber virtuoso of the court. His initiative was felt very soon: an order to the orchestra was issued, instructing the string players to use thicker strings. (Thinner strings were cheaper and produced less tone.) Pugnani is known to have preferred heavy-gauge strings on his Guarnerius del Gesù violin.

In 1773 Pugnani revisited London (for an opera premiere) and Paris; here he must have made the acquaintance of Tourte *père* and his son, François Tourte, who were working on an improved bow model. In some way, Pugnani influenced the evolution of the modern bow; his thicker strings needed a heavier bow, and he was known for his powerful bow stroke. He must have conveyed his experiences to the members of the Tourte family. The first violinist to reap the full benefit of the new Tourte bow was Pugnani's student Viotti.

Young Viotti (born in 1755) had been under Pugnani's musical guidance since the age of eleven. His apprenticeship in Turin was slow and long, but there can be no doubt that he was Pugnani's favorite student. It is not surprising that Pugnani asked Viotti to accompany him on an extended concert tour through Northern Europe. They set out in 1780—Pugnani was close to fifty at the time, Viotti twenty-four. It goes without saying that on this tour Viotti played "second fiddle" to his master, but his talent was recognized. They were heard in Geneva, Berlin, Warsaw, and finally St. Petersburg. There, on February 3, 1781, they played at court before Empress Catherine the Great. In the official statement, only Pugnani is named, while Viotti is identified as "his student." In Pugnani's two public concerts in St. Petersburg on March 11 and 14, Viotti is not mentioned, though he may have participated.

Obviously, such a subordinate role could not please Viotti indefinitely. On their way back, teacher and student separated: Pugnani returned to Turin while Viotti proceeded to Paris, where he became a celebrity overnight.

The last period of Pugnani's life was active: his duties in Turin were expanded to supervise all instrumental music, including military bands. He continued to be in charge of concert and opera performances; he composed and conducted several of his own operas, both in Turin and in Naples, where he traveled several times during the 1780s. After returning from a last trip to Vienna in 1796 for the performance of his *Werther* suite, his health began to deteriorate and he gave up all teaching. He died on July 15, 1798, only a few months before the abdication of the king—enforced by Napoleon—and the dissolution of the royal musical establishment in Turin.

As a teacher, Pugnani's continuation of the Somis tradition reinforced the fame of the Piedmont School. Characteristic for the entire school was a powerful bow stroke. Somis was reported to have possessed "the most majestic and most beautiful bow stroke in Europe." Pugnani was famous for his *arco magno* (grand bow), and his disciples always drew praise for their rich and full tone. He was a performer of eloquence, power, and nobility, of general excellence rather than brilliant virtuosity. A certain reluctance in displaying virtuoso technique is noticeable in Pugnani's compositions: he preferred to write sonatas and duets rather than concertos, and only one concerto of his has survived in manuscript—an undistinguished work, though not easy to play and in the awkward key of E-flat major.

Because of his vanity, Pugnani was often the butt of jokes. His appearance was unattractive, at times he looked grotesque, with a high wig, modish frock coat, and a bouquet of flowers on his chest. His weakness for women was known. He was vain and easily offended if not treated with deference. Once, a certain prince asked him dryly, "Who are you?" Pugnani answered quickly, "Sir, with a violin in my hand I am Caesar!"

Pietro Nardini

Among Tartini's numerous students, Pietro Nardini occupies the most prominent place. He had come to Padua at the age of twelve to study with the master, and remained for six years. Having spent his formative years in daily contact with Tartini, he absorbed the master's style and method to the fullest extent. There was a bond of personal affection between teacher and student which endured through the years. In 1761, Nardini, by then a celebrity, visited Padua, and Tartini referred to him in a letter as his "dearest student. . . . He is a miracle, and I thank God that I was able to hear him so often before my death."[1] When Nardini was informed in 1769 that his old teacher was gravely ill, he hurried from Livorno to Padua and spent months at

Tartini's bedside, caring for him "with true filial affection and tenderness" until the end, as Dr. Burney noted in his diary for 1770. It so happened that Burney arrived in Padua a few months after Tartini had died. Later that year he met Nardini and described his performance:

> Nardini, who played to me many of Tartini's best solos, as I thought, very well, with respect to correctness and expression, assured me that his dear and honored master, as he constantly called him, was as much superior to himself, in the performance of the same solos, both in the Pathetic and brilliant parts, as he was to any of his scholars.[2]

At the time of Tartini's death, Nardini was close to fifty years old and famous in his own right. All the more touching is his modesty in comparing his performance with that of his late teacher.

Nardini was born on April 12, 1722, in the port city of Livorno (Leghorn). Nothing is known about his early music studies, but he must have been quite advanced at the age of twelve to be sent to Padua.

After studying with Tartini from 1734 to 1740, he returned to his native city. In 1760 he traveled to Vienna to perform at the wedding celebrations of the crown prince and also visited Dresden. Two years later, in October 1762, we find Nardini as chamber virtuoso at the ducal court of Stuttgart. The following year he was named concertmaster of the Stuttgart orchestra, whose membership included the "first virtuosos" in Europe. Among Nardini's colleagues was a violinist of rising fame, Antonio Lolli, whom some historians describe as "forerunner" of Paganini. While Lolli amazed his listeners with feats of technique, Nardini became famous for the beauty of his tone and the sensitivity of his phrasing. We have the words of an expert, Leopold Mozart, who passed through Stuttgart in July 1763:

> I have heard a certain Nardini and it would be impossible to hear a finer player for beauty, purity, evenness of tone, and singing quality. But he does not display any difficulties at all.[3]

Mozart's mild objection was that Nardini disdained virtuosity. Another perceptive observer, the Italian Rangoni, compared the styles of three leading violinists of the day, Nardini, Lolli, and Pugnani: "Nardini neglects difficulties, but he creates them without aiming to do so, because it is in the nature of a great master never to create anything easy."[4] We must understand that Nardini was a "nonvirtuoso" by choice, not by inability. His strength was the playing of soulful cantilenas, and his

Adagios were famous. The poet and musician Daniel Schubart left us a flowery description of his impression:

> Nardini is a violinist of love. . . . The tenderness of his playing is indescribable, every comma seems to be a declaration of love. . . . One has seen ice-cold aristocrats cry when he performed an Adagio. While playing, he himself would shed drops of tears which fell on his violin. His magic play expressed every pain felt by his soul, but his melancholy manner was capable of transmuting the most extravagant phantasy into a funereal mood. His bow stroke was slow and solemn; yet, unlike Tartini, he did not tear out the notes by the roots but merely kissed their tips. He detached the notes very slowly, and each seemed like a drop of blood from his tender soul.[5]

Nardini left Stuttgart in March 1765 and returned to his native Livorno. After spending some months in 1769–70 in Padua near his dying master Tartini, Nardini was appointed to an important position, that of music director to the ducal court of Florence. Dr. Burney heard him in 1770 and had high praise:

> Nardini's tone is even and sweet; not very loud but clear and certain; he has a great deal of expression in his slow movements. . . . As to execution, he will satisfy and please more than surprise; in short, he seems the completest player on the violin in all Italy . . . and his style is delicate, judicious, and highly finished.[6]

Once again, the absence of any "surprising" features is noted; nevertheless Burney found Nardini more impressive than Pugnani, whom he had heard in Turin.

That year, the paths of Nardini and Mozart crossed again when father and son Mozart visited Florence in April 1770. Wolfgang, all of fourteen years old, played at a private concert, and a rather dry entry by father Mozart notes, "Nardini, the good violinist, accompanied."

Nardini spent his last twenty-three years in Florence, performing, composing, and teaching. He maintained his playing ability until late in life, according to the composer Adalbert Gyrowetz, who heard him in the 1780s. Calling him "the most famous violinist of his time," Gyrowetz praised "the purity and assurance of his tone, the well-ordered firm guidance of the bow" as Nardini's principal assets, "though he played very difficult passages with great bravura."[7] Among his last compositions were six attractive string quartets, very much in the spirit of Boccherini and young Mozart. Nardini had a large circle of students and maintained his teaching until the end of his days. He died in Florence on May 7, 1793, outliving Mozart by almost two years.

Neither as performer nor as composer did Nardini strive to appeal to the great public, but was best appreciated by connoisseurs in intimate surroundings. This is evident in his compositions: his strength lies in chamber music. His violin sonatas and duets and his string quartets have a quality of nobility and restraint, serenity and elegance. He was a true pre-Classicist; the ornate and embellished *style galant* was his natural musical environment. While Haydn and Mozart outgrew that style, lesser musicians—like Pugnani or Nardini—remained trapped in conventionalism; but it is foolish to reproach Nardini for not being a Mozart. Within the limitations of his talent, he wrote pleasing and often ingratiating music. In an era which saw the rise of shallow virtuosity, Nardini represented musicianship and refined taste.

Only one of Nardini's compositions has become truly popular among violinists: the Concerto in E minor. Paradoxically, the piece is a mild hoax—it is not a concerto at all but consists of three movements stitched together from several of Nardini's sonatas. This musical transformation occurred in 1880, but the hoax was not discovered until 1918. By then the so-called "Nardini Concerto in E minor" was firmly established in all conservatories and among concert violinists. Aside from its doubtful pedigree, the work is enjoyable and effective.[8]

Compared to this pseudo-concerto, the *real* concertos of Nardini are somewhat disappointing. Particularly the Six Concertos Op. 1, published around 1760, seem to lack the flair of brilliance which is an indispensable ingredient of the concerto genre. However, there are four manuscript concertos in Vienna (one, in E flat, is recorded) and six manuscript concertos at Berkeley (California) (one of them, in G major, recently published), which show Nardini as a virtuoso and contradict Mozart's remark about his technical limitations. As these manuscript concertos become available, Nardini's posthumous fame will appreciate accordingly.

Some of Nardini's violin sonatas, too, remained unpublished during his lifetime. Seven of his sonatas were rescued from oblivion by the meritorious Cartier, who included them in his collection *L'Art du violon* (third edition, 1803). Each of these sonatas opens with a slow movement, where the soloist can choose between a simple or an embroidered melodic line; hence, they are called Sonatas *"avec les Adagios brodés."* Each of the Adagios is followed by two fast movements, showing Nardini's familiarity with pre-Classical sonata patterns. In these works Nardini is at his best—a sensitive, imaginative composer with a bold and highly idiomatic violin style, effective in fast movements, deeply felt in Adagios. Of this entire set, the Sonata No. 2 in D major is occasionally played in public. It was in the repertoire of Carl Flesch, who published a new edition with an added slow movement interpolated between the two fast movements. (The added movement is culled from another Nardini sonata and transposed.) It is to be hoped that present-day concert violinists will take an interest in these neglected masterpieces.

Recently, six additional Nardini sonatas for violin and piano were published in New York—a reprint of an eighteenth-century set which contains some lovely movements (including those used in the pseudo-concerto mentioned above). But they do not have the sweep of the "Cartier" sonatas and are better suited for intimate music making.[9] In fact, Nardini's compositions were widely printed and bought in the eighteenth century just because they were easily playable and genteel. Among amateurs there was great demand for such music all through the eighteenth century, and easy sonatas for violin or flute and keyboard were printed in reams. They were as quickly forgotten as they were produced. Accessibility is the key to success, but not to immortality.

GERMANY AND AUSTRIA

DURING THE eighteenth century, the German-speaking countries produced no extraordinary violin virtuosos, but they were well provided
with competent violinists. Famous foreign virtuosos (mainly Italians)
were given preferential treatment, while native violinists were relegated
to the orchestras. In contrast to France, where Paris and the court at
Versailles were the center of the musical universe, German musical life
was totally decentralized. The dozens of reigning courts often patterned their musical establishments after Versailles and needed large
numbers of solid performers. This fragmentation led to a widening of
musical culture in Germany and reached beyond the aristocratic circles
deep into the middle class.

While Germany and Austria may have lacked great virtuosos at
that time, they did have great composers who wrote for the violin.
Johann Sebastian Bach, Handel, Haydn, Mozart, and young Beethoven
produced masterpieces that are in every violinist's repertoire. While all
these composers played the violin, they were not primarily performing
violinists and depended on other violinists to present their works to
the public.

Violinists around Johann Sebastian Bach

Although Bach's instrument was the organ, he played the violin
professionally, for a time even as concertmaster. His violin concertos,
influenced by Vivaldi's, though less flashy, were certainly within his

technical reach. But it is doubtful that he wrote the towering Unaccompanied Sonatas and Partitas for his own use. Who, then, was the violinist within the composer's circle of associates able to cope with these difficult solos?

The name of Johann Georg Pisendel is often mentioned in this connection. He was one of the most versatile and accomplished German violinists of his generation and owned a copy of Bach's solo works. Born in Franconia in 1687 (hence two years younger than Bach), Pisendel studied with Torelli in Ansbach; by the time he was sixteen, he was ready for a professional career. Passing through Weimar in 1709, he had a brief meeting with Bach. They renewed their acquaintance in 1717 in Dresden, by which time Pisendel was firmly settled as a leading member of the court orchestra. He had recently come back from Venice after studying with Vivaldi, who had taken a particular liking to his gifted German disciple. Pisendel received the dedication of six concertos from Vivaldi and returned to Dresden with a rich collection of Vivaldi manuscripts.

It is possible that Bach heard Pisendel play his own unaccompanied violin sonata, perhaps in church where Pisendel often played violin solos during services. This chance meeting with Pisendel may have inspired Bach to plan his own cycle of solo sonatas and partitas, a project he completed in 1720. In writing unaccompanied violin music, Bach continued an old German tradition represented by composers like Biber and Westhoff. Bach's solo works circulated in manuscript copies but were not published until 1802, except for the Fugue in C major, which appeared in 1798.[1]

Among Pisendel's own violin concertos are several in the Baroque style of Vivaldi, others in the pre-Classical style of Tartini. One in particular, in D major, foreshadows the structure of Mozart's Concerto No. 5: after a lively tutti, the soloist enters with a slow cantabile theme which does not return within the movement. The editor, A. Schering, wrote, "There is a combination of perfect form, depth, and Italianate sensuousness which make this Concerto by Pisendel a worthy precursor of Mozart's violin concertos. . . ."[2]

Another violinist for whom Bach had high regard was Franz (or František) Benda. Born in 1709 in Bohemia, Benda had an adventurous youth and studied for a time with Pisendel. In the 1730s, Benda joined the musical entourage of Crown Prince Frederick of Prussia and served as concertmaster of the royal establishment for many years. Bach may have met Benda during his memorable visit to Potsdam in 1747 or even earlier in Dresden. Benda was famous for his soulful playing of slow movements. "More than once one has seen people shed tears when Benda played an Adagio," a contemporary reports.[3] Burney heard him in 1772, at a time when his fingers were enfeebled by gout, and concluded that *"good singing"* was the model for Benda's peculiar style.[4] But his technical skill was considerable, too, if one judges by the caprices (almost one hundred), which show him on a par with Tartini and Nardini. Benda was considered the foremost master of the North German violin school.

Leopold and Wolfgang Mozart

Leopold Mozart was thirty-seven years old when he published his *Violin Method* in 1756—the same year his son Wolfgang was born. Trained as a professional violinist, Leopold Mozart was active in Salzburg's court orchestra beginning in 1743; he rose to court composer in 1757 and to deputy Kapellmeister in 1763.

But it was the publication of his violin method—*Versuch einer gründlichen Violinschule* (A Treatise on the Fundamental Principles of Violin Playing)—that established him as an authority in his field. New and expanded editions appeared in 1769–70 and in 1787, the year he died. The text was translated into Dutch and French during the author's lifetime.

The Mozart *Method* appeared five years later than Geminiani's (London, 1751), but Mozart was unaware of the London publication.* This makes Mozart's text all the more independent and original. He relies much more on verbal explanations than does Geminiani: Mozart's first edition has 264 pages of text, compared to only nine in Geminiani. On the other hand, Geminiani includes examples and complete compositions, while Mozart relies on brief excerpts to illustrate his text, like the remarkable quotation of Tartini's *Devil's Trill*, which was not yet in print. In general, Mozart favored the Classical Italian school, considered the model in the eighteenth century.

In 1762, Leopold Mozart began to devote himself almost exclusively to the education and career of his two prodigies, "Nannerl" (born 1751) and Wolfgang. His diaries and letters are an inexhaustible

---

* By the time of the second edition (1769–70), Mozart had seen Geminiani's treatise and adopted the "Geminiani grip" (see pp. 84 and 86 for comparisons between Geminiani and Mozart).

source of information with regard to European music and musical life of the 1760s and '70s. He was an astute observer and his praise was not given easily. In a letter to his wife, Leopold described a touching encounter of 1770 in Florence, where Wolfgang met a young student of Nardini, Thomas Linley:

> This boy, who plays most beautifully and who is the same age and the same size as Wolfgang, came to the house. . . . The two boys performed one after the other throughout the whole evening, consistently embracing each other. On the following day the little Englishman, a most charming boy, had his violin brought to our rooms and played the whole afternoon, Wolfgang accompanying him on his own. . . . These two boys played in turn the whole afternoon, not like boys but like men![1]

The two boys continued to correspond in Italian; one letter from Wolfgang to Linley has been preserved. Young Linley returned to England in 1771 and was very active as performer and composer. He wrote some twenty violin concertos (recalling his master Nardini), of which only one has survived. Linley's tragic death at the age of twenty-two, in 1778, occurred during a boating excursion with his family; it was "one of the greatest losses that English music has suffered."[2] In later years, Wolfgang spoke of Linley with great affection. According to Michael Kelly, the Irish tenor, who lived in Vienna in the 1780s and knew Mozart well, "He said that Linley was a true genius; and he felt that, had he lived, he would have been one of the greatest ornaments of the musical world."[3]

The encounter with Linley in 1770 indicates that the fourteen-year-old Mozart was already a fine violinist, on a level with the English prodigy. Thus it should not surprise us that Wolfgang, after his return to Salzburg in December 1771, became a salaried violinist in the orchestra, as third concertmaster. In 1774 he moved up to second place, while Michael Haydn (the younger brother of the famous composer) became principal concertmaster.

A year later, we see the nineteen-year-old Mozart composing a series of five violin concertos.* There is no doubt that he intended them for his own use, not (as often reported) for the violinist Antonio

* They are: Concerto No. 1 in B-flat, K. 207; Concerto No. 2 in D, K. 211; Concerto No. 3 in G, K. 216; Concerto No. 4 in D, K. 218; Concerto No. 5 in A, K. 219. All were composed between April and December, 1775. Three additional violin concertos attributed to Mozart are of doubtful authenticity.

Brunetti, who arrived in Salzburg the year after they were completed. Once established in Salzburg, Brunetti showed interest in the talent of his young colleague; at his request, Mozart wrote a new slow movement for the Concerto No. 5 and a new Rondo for the Concerto No. 1. They played together for the last time in April 1781—on the program were the Rondo in C (K. 373) and the Violin Sonata in G (K. 379) especially written for Brunetti. The performance took place at the Viennese palace of Prince Colloredo, the father of Mozart's ill-tempered employer, the Archbishop of Salzburg. A month later Mozart was summarily dismissed by the Archbishop.

We have evidence of Mozart's self-image as a violinist during his journey of 1777–78 to South Germany and Paris. He reported to his father of his performances in Munich and Augsburg in October 1777, "I played as though I were the finest fiddler in all Europe. . . . It went like oil, everybody praised my beautiful pure tone."[4] Among his own pieces he played the Concerto in G major and the Divertimento in B flat (K. 287), technically demanding though not virtuosic. (It should be noted that both Leopold and Wolfgang Mozart disliked empty showmanship, while they valued technical proficiency, a principle Wolfgang adhered to in all his concertos.)

Leopold—always a violinist at heart—was pleased to hear that Wolfgang was not neglecting his violin playing and replied, "I am not surprised—you yourself do not know how well you play the violin." But Wolfgang's mind was made up: "I will no longer be a fiddler."[5] As a performer he turned entirely to the fortepiano though he played the violin occasionally in domestic quartet sessions.

During his six-month stay in Paris in 1778, Mozart became thoroughly acquainted with the French musical scene—and he was disgusted. "I am surrounded by wild beasts as far as music is concerned,"[6] he complained in a letter to his father. The Parisian public was capricious, unpredictable, and hard to please. Nor was he impressed by the famous orchestra of the *Concert spirituel*, often praised as the best in Europe. He ridiculed the legendary unanimity of the orchestra: "That famous first bow attack? what the devil is it? Don't we start together elsewhere?" When he finally obtained a commission to write a symphony for the *Concert spirituel*, he was appalled at the first reading:

> I was very nervous at the rehearsal, for never in my life have I heard a worse performance. You have no idea how they twice scraped and scrambled through it. I was really in a terrible way. . . . I at last made up my mind to go [to the concert], determined that if my symphony went as badly as it did at the

rehearsal, I would certainly make my way into the orchestra, snatch the fiddle out of the hands of La Houssaye, the first violin, and conduct myself.[7]

In fact, Pierre La Houssaye, leader-conductor of the *Concert spirituel* (a former student of Tartini), was one of the best French violinists of his time. Despite Mozart's misgivings, he led a fine premiere performance of the so-called *Paris Symphony* (K. 297) on June 18; it was repeated (with a new slow movement) on August 15. But this success was obscured by many disappointments, and Mozart left Paris on September 26 with a sense of frustration and failure.

Nevertheless, he kept in touch with musical trends in Paris. A French-style violin concerto by Viotti captured his interest around 1786, and he planned to have it performed at one of his subscription concerts in Vienna; for this purpose he provided the Viotti score with additional trumpet and timpani parts.*

Having become an acclaimed keyboard performer, Mozart lost interest in the genre of the violin concerto, but not in the violin as such. He turned to the violin sonata, which had undergone a strange dichotomy. On one hand, the violinist-composers (like Tartini and Nardini) continued to write sonatas with a prominent violin part and a thin bass accompaniment (no longer figured). On the other hand, the keyboard composers (like the sons of Bach or Johann Schobert) appropriated the violin sonata by transforming it into a keyboard piece with violin accompaniment. Mozart "rescued" the violin-piano duo by elevating the violin to an equal partnership with the fortepiano; he diversified and enriched the collaboration of the two instruments so that violinists began to take renewed interest in performing sonatas. Mozart was always willing to join forces with a first-rate violinist. In 1784 a young Italian violinist, Regina Strinasacchi, had come to Vienna for concerts and asked Mozart to compose and perform a sonata with her. He agreed and wrote to his father, ". . . She is a very good violinist and plays with much taste and feeling. I am just writing a sonata which we shall play together on Thursday at her concert."[8] But Mozart was not quite ready to meet the date; the violin part was written out but the piano part was only sketched and Mozart had to improvise. (The Sonata was K. 454 in B-flat major.) The following year, Regina Strinasacchi came to Salzburg for a concert and Leopold Mozart reported in a letter to his daughter,

---

* The performance did not take place, but the extra parts are preserved and catalogued as K. 470a. The Viotti-Mozart version has been recorded.

I am very sorry that you did not hear this attractive young woman, some twenty-three years old, not at all bad looking and very skilled. There is not one note without sentiment, even during the Symphony [tutti] she plays everything with expression, and no one can play the Adagio with more feeling and touching effect than she does. Her whole heart and soul is with the melody, and her tone and its strength is equally beautiful. All in all, I find that·a woman who has talent, plays with more expression than a man.[9]

Leopold's tribute to the potential of female talent must have heartened his daughter Nannerl, whose remarkable talent was totally overshadowed by the genius of her brother Wolfgang and who spent her life in provincial oblivion. Regina Strinasacchi had a better fate: she married a fine cellist in the ducal orchestra of Gotha, and they appeared in concerts together. At the end of her career, in 1822, she sold her Stradivari violin to the eminent Louis Spohr, who described the tone of the instrument as "divine."

THE FRENCH SCHOOL

Leclair and His Time

Leclair was a pivotal figure in the history of French violin playing. Having studied in both France and Italy, he raised the technical level of the native French school to a point where it could compare and compete with the Italians. While learning from his Italian contemporaries, Leclair preserved his French profile: his compositions represent a balanced coexistence of French and Italian elements. He never aspired to the dizzying virtuosity of his contemporary Locatelli, but developed an individual technique that represents a milestone in the evolution of violin playing. Leclair towered over his French peers; even during his lifetime he was called the "French Corelli."

His success in Paris as a young man in his twenties is all the more remarkable since he arrived unknown and unheralded from the provinces, with none of the connections needed for a career. He was not a member of the tight fraternity of the 24 *Violons du Roi* (like Rebel, Duval, Francoeur, Senaillé), where jobs were often handed down from father to son. He did not belong to the Italian clan of musicians (like Mascitti or Piani), who enjoyed much favor with the aristocracy and the public. He was not part of the inner circle around Philidor, who organized the *Concert spirituel* in 1725. One wonders how Leclair acquired the expertise to compose and publish, in 1723, his First Book of Sonatas, which do not reveal the hand of a novice.

At that time, the French violin sonata as a genre was barely two decades old. Preferring vocal music to instrumental music, the French had shown indifference, even hostility, toward the imported Italian violin repertoire. *"Sonate, que me veux-tu!"* exclaimed the littérateur Fontenelle, and his sentiments were echoed by many learned critics. Nor were the French violinists, trained in Lully's orchestral discipline, ready to deal with Italian violin technique. When Corelli's sonatas were received in Paris, the Duc d'Orléans—so the story goes—could not find a single violinist in Paris capable of playing them. The only solution was to have them sung!

But the Parisian composers of the early eighteenth century thought otherwise: they began to cultivate "with a kind of fury" the new sonata style of the Italians. More than two dozen volumes were published within the first two decades. François Duval, a violinist in the service of the Duc d'Orléans, was the first to publish, in 1704, a collection of "sonatas and other pieces," which reveal a knowledge of Corelli while maintaining certain French traditions. Duval continued to produce violin sonatas until 1720. Another violinist-composer was Jean-Féry Rebel, whose sonatas were published in 1712, though composed earlier. A player of moderate technique, he was praised for tempering the "fire and flair of the Italians" by the "wisdom and gentleness of the French." A talented violinist and versatile composer was François Francoeur, whose first book of violin sonatas appeared in 1720. He and Rebel (a close friend and associate) visited Prague in 1723, where many virtuosos were assembled for the coronation festivities; this experience made itself felt in Francoeur's second sonata collection of 1730.

The most prolific and talented sonata composer of that early period was the violinist Jean-Baptiste Senaillé. Between 1710 and 1727, he published no fewer than fifty sonatas, in five collections. Into the framework of the Italian sonata Senaillé injected French elements of spirited dance and bittersweet melody, creating a coexistence of the two styles. His sonatas are among the most attractive of his time, without being technically challenging. As a performer, he aroused less interest, though he performed at the *Concert spirituel* in 1728, the same year Leclair made his remarkable debut.

Rated higher as a performer than Senaillé was Baptiste Anet, who had studied with Corelli in Rome in 1695–96 and had gained his teacher's affection. Anet's first performance at the French court in 1701 attracted the king's attention. It was said that he was more concerned with pleasing and moving his listeners than with astounding them by technical feats. Acclaimed as a performer, Anet was selected as the first French violinist to play at the newly established *Concert spirituel* in

1725, side by side with the Italian Ghignone (Guignon). These "spiritual concerts" were offered on religious holidays when the Opéra and all theaters had to remain closed. The king granted the use of the Tuileries Palace, and the orchestra soon acquired the reputation of being the best in Europe. During the sixty-five years of its existence, the *Concert spirituel* exerted a powerful influence on musical taste in France.* Italian instrumental music made its entrance: Corelli's *Christmas Concerto* was played at the opening concert, Vivaldi's *Four Seasons* followed soon and became one of the most popular program selections. But French music retained its dominance.

In 1723, Jean-Marie Leclair, age twenty-six, stepped into the maze of Parisian music life. He was not inexperienced: trained as a violinist and dancer in his native city of Lyon, he had started to compose in 1721 and had been active as ballet master in Turin in 1722. Here he came into contact with the royal orchestra and its famous leader, G. B. Somis, who encouraged his violin playing.

The following year, Leclair decided to try his luck in Paris. He found a wealthy patron, Monsieur Bonnier, to whom he dedicated his Opus 1, a book of twelve sonatas for violin and figured bass. In 1726 Leclair was back in Turin, this time as violin student of Somis and fully dedicated to the study of music, though he worked intermittently as a choreographer.

In 1728 Leclair returned to Paris, by now an accomplished violinist. After his brilliant debut at the *Concert spirituel* on April 17 and 19, the *Mercure* reported, "Mr. Leclerc, famous violinist, played a Sonata and was generally and vigorously applauded." He was immediately reengaged and appeared eleven times that year—a sure sign of public demand—alternately playing sonatas and concertos of his own composition. A second book of violin sonatas (Op. 2) was published in 1728.

For the next ten years, Leclair remained in Paris. He continued to be heard regularly at the *Concert spirituel* but less often—on an average of twice a year. He composed and published his works under his own imprint, which became a family enterprise; widowed early in life, he had taken in second marriage Louise Roussel, a music engraver, who had done his Sonatas Op. 2. After their marriage in 1730, all of his remaining works, up to the posthumous Opp. 14 and 15, were engraved by "*Madame Leclair, son épouse.*"

By 1733, Leclair's reputation was so well established that King

---

* The *Concert spirituel* closed its doors in 1790, under the impact of the Revolution.

Louis XV appointed him chamber musician of the royal musical establishment. An identical appointment was handed to his archrival Pierre
Guignon. It was left to the two musicians to compete for priority,
which led to endless wrangling. Finally, they arranged an alternation,
but when Leclair's turn came to play second violin, he could not bring
himself to undertake a subordinate role and preferred to resign his position altogether. He left the field to the ambitious Guignon, who remained in the service of the king's music until 1762.

Obviously aggravated, Leclair decided to leave Paris for a time. In
1737 or 1738, he traveled to Holland, where he remained until 1743.
He took with him the first book of his Concertos Op. 7, just published,
and the manuscript of his fourth book of sonatas which was in progress.
Holland, at that time, had many wealthy music lovers, while Amsterdam
was a center for music publishing. It was here that Locatelli had settled
around 1730, enjoying a widespread reputation as a violinist-composer
and formidable virtuoso.

A violinist of such accomplishments was of great interest to Leclair, and it has been suggested that the chief purpose of his trip to
Holland was to establish closer contact with his colleague Locatelli.
Strange as it may seem, there is no evidence that the two had a meeting
while Leclair was in Holland.* But undoubtedly Leclair was impressed
by Locatelli's technical achievements, which must have motivated him
to refine his own technique. Indeed, Leclair's fourth book of sonatas
(Op. 9), which he completed in Holland, shows a greater degree of
difficulty and technical variety.

Leclair secured two patrons in Holland. One was of royal blood—
Princess Anne of Orange, daughter of King George II of England, who
held court at the Château du Loo in a rather remote part of northern
Holland. Before her marriage in 1734, she had been one of Handel's
patrons. A good musician, she organized concerts at her castle, which
became justly famous. Leclair was a regular participant in these concerts.

Leclair's other Dutch patron was the financier François du Liz,
who maintained a lavish musical establishment in The Hague until he
went bankrupt in 1743. However, Leclair was fully reimbursed for his
services and returned to Paris.

Having handed his wife the manuscript of his Sonatas Op. 9 to
engrave, Leclair departed again, this time for Chambéry in Savoy, where
Don Philippe of Spain held court in exile at the head of an army. Don
Philippe loved music passionately and was himself an able cellist. Le-

* An earlier meeting of the two, in 1728 in Cassel, is conjectural (see page 94).

clair had brought with him an incomplete set of concertos, works in progress, which he later dedicated to Don Philippe as Opus 10.

By January 1745 Leclair was back in Paris. His finances were much improved, and he was able to invest his newly earned capital at ten percent interest, which brought him a comfortable annuity. His wife, too, was well off while continuing her profession as music engraver.

A new departure for Leclair was the writing of an opera, *Scylla et Glaucus,* first performed in 1746 at the Académie Royale in Paris by some of the best available singers and dancers. The work received faint praise and held the stage for eighteen performances, after which it disappeared from the repertoire. His hope of a belated career as an opera composer remained unfulfilled.

This marked the end of Leclair's activity in Paris. At the age of fifty, he found himself on the sidelines, while his former competitors enjoyed success as composers and performers. At the *Concert spirituel,* Leclair's works were played very rarely, the last time in 1750, when an otherwise unknown violinist presented one of his concertos, perhaps from the most recent set, Opus 10 of 1745.

Leclair himself found employment in the services of the Duc de Gramont, who maintained a private theater at Puteaux, a suburb of Paris; for this stage, Leclair composed many vocal and instrumental pieces and acted as music director. He enjoyed being involved with the stage, which brought back memories of his youth as ballet master.

Separated from his wife since 1758, Leclair had bought an inexpensive piece of property in a shabby suburb and lived alone in a house surrounded by a stone wall. His patron, the Duc de Gramont, was worried about his safety and had asked him repeatedly to join him at Puteaux. Leclair was on the verge of accepting when, early in the morning of October 23, 1764, his gardener found his body in a pool of blood: he had been stabbed three times with a sharp tool. Although his watch was missing, the house was not ransacked and money was found in a drawer. The motive of the crime was obviously personal vengeance or jealousy, not burglary. Two men were under suspicion: the gardener and Leclair's nephew, a violinist by the name of Vial. The latter had complained publicly about his uncle's avarice and egotism; furthermore, his friendship with the estranged Madame Leclair made him suspect. Ultimately, there was not sufficient evidence and the case was dropped. One modern historian speculates that Madame Leclair killed her husband with her own hand, using her engraver's tool as a murder weapon.[1]

Madame Leclair did not attend the funeral and was in no hurry to claim any property left by her husband. Eventually, she sold Leclair's two violins, of unidentified make and considered of minor value. She also proceeded to engrave and publish two manuscripts, a trio for two violins and bass and a sonata for violin and bass, which she designated as Opp. posthumous 14 and 15. The trio—like the *Ouvertures en trio* Op. 13—seems to be arrangements of incidental music composed for the Duke's private theater.

The obituaries following Leclair's death were generous. They described him as one of the most famous violinists of Europe and compared his style of composition to that of Rameau, the greatest French musician of his time.

The musicians of the *Concert spirituel* honored Leclair's memory with a church concert, performing the master's sonata *Le Tombeau* (Op. 5, No. 6) in an orchestral arrangement and the choral *De Profundis* by Mondonville. Few of the musicians remembered Leclair's playing, since he had not appeared at the *Concert spirituel* for almost thirty years. But indirectly every French violinist of the mid-century was indebted to Leclair: almost singlehandedly he had raised French violin playing to the advanced level of the Italians, adding a French profile to the Italian tradition.

Nothing is known about Leclair's early violin studies in his native Lyons. He was twenty-five when he first met Somis in Turin and twenty-nine when he became his student. By then, he was far advanced as a violinist, and the guidance he received from Somis was probably more concerned with style than with technique. Somis—once a student of Corelli—was a fine player and famous for his powerful bow stroke, but he was no technical wizard. He taught Leclair the Corellian concept of violin playing—a singing style and a certain violinistic discipline. From Somis Leclair acquired a preference for the secular chamber sonata, excelling in elaborate stylized dance movements—not surprising in view of his early career as a dancer.

But we must look beyond Somis to other influences that shaped Leclair's development. Evidently, he studied the works of Vivaldi, Locatelli, and Tartini: they were the technical innovators of the day whom he tried to emulate. But even here he was selective: he seldom played in the extreme high positions that his Italian confreres had made their specialty. His strength was the command of multiple stops. Leclair's technique is not "showy" in the Italian manner: it is just plain difficult, but, when played well, it is effective.

Leclair's progress as violinist and composer is clearly demonstrated in his forty-eight sonatas for violin and figured bass, published in four books of twelve sonatas each. Book I, started in 1721, is still modest in its demands. Book II (1728) shows Leclair's progress under the guidance of Somis. Book III (1734, bearing the opus number 5) represents him at the height of his career: successful soloist of the *Concert spirituel*, newly appointed royal musician. Book IV (begun in 1737 and published in 1743 as Op. 9) is more intricate in technical matters, probably under Locatelli's impact, and makes no concessions to the lighter taste of the 1740s. These sonatas demand a master violinist and occupy an honored place in the violin repertoire.

In addition to these difficult pieces, Leclair also composed lighter sonatas for two violins with and without accompaniment, which are designed for the enjoyment of amateurs and students.

Compared to his sonatas, Leclair's output of concertos is small. He left only two collections of six concertos each (Opp. 7 and 10), which he designated "for three violins, viola, and bass." However, they are clearly dominated by the first (solo) violin, accompanied by string quartet. Here, the model is obviously Vivaldi, with the established three-movement form; the thematic invention is graceful and outgoing, the technique fluid and effective. However, the concerto genre developed so rapidly within the next decades that Leclair's soon became outmoded and forgotten.

Leclair was a masterful performer of his own music. Among the many contemporary evaluations is that of Ancelet: "Everybody agrees that Leclair is exact, precise, and strictly observant of all the rules. All these fine qualities united might contribute to making his playing somewhat cold."[2] Dixmerie also described a certain reserve in Leclair's performance: "His playing was prudent but that prudence was not timidity; it resulted from an excess of taste rather than a lack of audacity and freedom."[3] An anonymous contemporary added,

> Leclair is the first who, in his works, has combined the agreeable with the useful; he is a very knowledgeable composer, and he plays double stops in a manner difficult to equal. His bow and his fingers interacted perfectly, and he had much accuracy. While one could reproach him a bit of coldness in his manner, this is a matter of temperament which ordinarily dominates almost all the people.[4]

Leclair was very demanding in terms of accurate intonation, and he is known to have tuned his strings frequently while performing. This is understandable, since precise tuning is a precondition for playing double stops, which he used generously in his works. He was also concerned about the proper performance of his music: in his prefaces he explained his manner of figuring the bass and cautioned performers against too much ornamentation and rushed tempos. "I do not consider the term Allegro to mean too fast a tempo: it is a gay tempo," he admonished.[5]

His greatest admirer was his friend and eulogist de Rozoi; he called Leclair a

> profound genius who transformed the mechanics of his art into a science. . . . He was the first to disentangle the art of the violin, he unraveled its difficulties and its beauties. . . . He created that brilliant execution that distinguishes our orchestras, and Rameau owes as much to Leclair as he does to his own genius.[6]

The writer credits Leclair with raising the standards of French orchestral playing, which in turn helped Rameau realize the technical difficulties in his scores.

The list of Leclair's immediate students—as far as their names are known—is not large: Dauvergne, L'Abbé le fils, probably Gaviniès, perhaps Saint-Georges and Mademoiselle Hotteterre, the first woman admitted to perform the violin at the *Concert spirituel*, where she played Leclair's sonatas in 1737. Gaviniès and L'Abbé also made their debuts with music by Leclair. There can be no doubt that Leclair laid the foundation for the spectacular rise of the French violin school in the second half of the eighteenth century, leading to the eventual predominance of the French after 1800.

Pierre Gaviniès

Gaviniès continued where Leclair left off. He dominated the second half of the eighteenth century, just as Leclair had dominated the first half. For violinists, Leclair signified the end of the French Baroque, while Gaviniès ushered in the era of pre-Classicism.

Professional violinists remember Gaviniès for his etudes, the difficult 24 *Matinées*, which represent a high point in technique prior to Paganini. But his six violin concertos are historically more important as the early models of the so-called "French violin concerto." Discarding the Vivaldi model that had served Leclair so well, Gaviniès placed the solo violin within the framework of the new pre-Classical symphony, with its innovations of form, melody, rhythm, and harmonic organization, while enriching the accompanying orchestra with oboes and

French horns. True, Gaviniès was somewhat influenced by Tartini and the Mannheim School, but he added a typically French trait—the proud introductory tutti, which gave birth to the *"concerto héroïque."* Gaviniès performed his first concerto at the *Concert spirituel* in 1749, though the entire set of six concertos was not published until 1764. But the Gaviniès concertos were known and played in Paris before publication; they circulated in manuscript and exerted their influence on the younger generation of violinists.

The career of Pierre Gaviniès, though not spectacular, was meritorious. Born in Bordeaux in 1728, he grew up in Paris as son of a violin maker. Young Pierre was ready to perform in public at age eleven and made his debut at the *Concert spirituel* when he was thirteen. Together with another prodigy, L'Abbé le fils (age fourteen), he was heard in a Duo by Leclair (possibly the teacher of the two young performers) and played the *Spring Concerto* by Vivaldi a month later.

After a pause of seven years, Gaviniès was again soloist at the *Concert spirituel* in 1748. His success was so great that he played seven more times that summer. The following year he was heard performing his own concerto as well as music by Tartini and Mondonville, and formed a two-violin team with the famous Guignon. For the next five years, Gaviniès was the violinist most in demand at the *Concert spirituel.*

Suddenly, in mid-1753, Gaviniès disappeared from the stage for half a dozen years. He was rumored to have spent a year in prison because of an amorous adventure with a countess whose irate husband had him incarcerated. When he reappeared in 1759, the critics were ecstatic: "Gaviniès belongs without question to the foremost violinists of Europe."[1] His greatest success was a soulful *Romance*, which he allegedly composed in prison. It became his most popular piece for decades.

Encouraged by his success as a composer, Gaviniès decided to publish some of his works: two collections of violin sonatas (1760 and 1764) and six concertos for violin and orchestra (1764), already familiar to the public through prior performances at the *Concert spirituel.* Also performed were several of his symphonies, but they remained unpublished and are lost.

In 1762, Gaviniès was named concertmaster and conductor of the *Concert spirituel;* at the same time, the post of time-beater (*batteur de mesure*) was abolished. Gaviniès was in full charge of the performances, leading his forces with violin in hand from the first stand. He was the ideal leader: his strong sound carried easily above the orchestra, his technique was faultless, and he was an admirable sightreader.

Late in 1763, Leopold Mozart arrived in Paris with his prodigy children; the name "Mr. Gaviniès, virtuoso on the violin," appears in Leopold's travel log. Gaviniès participated in one of the concerts given by Wolfgang and Nannerl, and father Mozart remembered fifteen years later that Gaviniès, in characteristic generosity, had refused to accept payment.

In 1773 Gaviniès became codirector of the *Concert spirituel,* together with Gossec and Le Duc; they remained in charge until 1777. The directorate was no bed of roses and included responsibilities both financial and artistic. Gaviniès and his associates did very well and expected to have their contract renewed, but they were outbid by the singer Legros—the same Legros who treated young Mozart so cavalierly in 1778.

Gaviniès, hard hit by the sudden end of his directorship, went into retirement; he was only forty-nine at the time and far from being well off. When he lost his pension in 1789, through the events of the Revolution, he had to accept a subordinate place in a theater orchestra. He was rescued by an appointment to the newly founded Conservatoire, where he served as professor "of first class" from November 1795 to his death in 1800. During those years he composed the etudes 24 *Matinées;* it is said that he could play the difficult material to the end of his days.

The choice of Gaviniès as teacher at the Conservatoire was significant and farsighted: he represented a vital link with the past, preserving all that was best in the French violin tradition going back to Leclair. His confreres at the Conservatoire—Rode, Kreutzer, Baillot—were young and gifted, belonging not only to a new generation but a new tradition, that of Viotti. In fact, Viotti, a newcomer to Paris in 1782, recognized the stature of the older master, whom he called "the Tartini of France."

French Contemporaries of Leclair and Gaviniès

Undoubtedly, Leclair and Gaviniès were the most significant violin personalities of their generation, but they were not necessarily the most successful in terms of public recognition or royal favors. Paris was full of ambitious and scheming violinists, vying for patrons, positions, and financial security. Some had mediocre talents which they exploited far beyond their merits; others contributed more modestly to the progress of violin playing. An important factor was the influx of gifted Italian violinists, who found life in cosmopolitan Paris so attractive and re-munerative that they settled permanently, often under French-sounding names.

Most important among them was the Turin-born Jean-Pierre Guignon (1702–74), who outrivaled Leclair. In 1725, Guignon was the first foreign violinist to appear as soloist at the newly established *Concert spirituel*, successfully playing his own works and Vivaldi's *The Four Seasons*, which he introduced to Paris. Guignon also joined forces with French colleagues like Gaviniès and Mondonville in violin duets. In 1734, both Guignon and Leclair were appointed to the king's music; but while Leclair quit in anger in 1737, Guignon remained a favorite at court until 1762. No sooner had he been granted French nationality, in 1741, than he prevailed upon the king to appoint him *"Roi des violons."* This post had not been filled since 1695; now Guignon became "king" of all the dance and music guilds in the country, able to exert control and to collect certain fees from the guild members. He took his responsibilities seriously and instituted new rules, which were met with great resistance by the powerful guild of organists and composers. Forced to retreat, he was stripped of his powers by Parliament in 1750; however, this did not diminish his in-fluence at court. When the Dauphin began studying the violin with Mondonville, Guignon intervened and insisted on his right to be the teacher, despite the fact that Mondonville was his friend and musical associate. That was the end of their friendship. In life as in his play-ing, Guignon was something of a daredevil: his performance had fire and technical facility, he drew a beautiful tone from his instrument, and imposed his mastery on any orchestra he led. He liked to be sur-rounded by young gifted students whom he taught without charge.

Jean Cassanéa de Mondonville (1711–1772) was hardly less clever than Guignon but was endowed with more creativity as a composer. Trained as a violinist, Mondonville must be credited as the first to use harmonics on the violin, namely in his sonata collection *Les Sons harmoniques* (Op. 4, c. 1738). In a carefully worded preface, he illus-trates the position of every natural harmonic on the four strings of the violin by a drawing. Also innovative was his Opus 3, *Pièces de clavecin en sonates, avec accompagnement de violon* (c. 1734), that is, harpsichord sonatas with an accompanying violin. This represents a reversal of roles: the harpsichord, heretofore the accompanist, now becomes the pro-tagonist with a full keyboard part, while the violin is subordinate. To assign the harpsichord a leading role in chamber music was an idea whose time had come. There had been isolated experiments by French and German composers,* but it was Mondonville who gave a firm direction to the new relationship of harpsichord plus violin. Within the next decades, the keyboard sonata with violin accompaniment gained general acceptance (particularly among pianists), while the violin sonata with figured bass withered away. Mondonville handled the new balance between harpsichord and violin with skill and imagination; his approach was adopted by French composers of the 1740s, notably Guillemain and Rameau, and spread abroad. In fact, a direct line of influence can be traced leading to the early violin sonatas of Mozart, still very much centered on the keyboard. Mondonville's dual talent as violinist and composer was recognized as early as 1738 by the *Concert spirituel*, which paid him a yearly stipend "for his motets and for playing the violin," and appointed him codirector in 1755. When he retired from the directorate in 1762, he did so without grudge, but he took all his compositions with him "to give them a rest," to the dismay of both the public and the new directors. Mondonville died, honored and wealthy, in 1772.

Also worthy of mention is Louis-Gabriel Guillemain (1705–70), who succeeded Leclair as member of the royal music in 1737 when the latter resigned abruptly. Like Leclair, he was a student of Somis. As a technician, Guillemain was extraordinary for his time, but was too timid to play solo in public and entrusted the performance of one of his concertos to another violinist, Mangean, who played it at the *Concert spirituel* in 1743. Guillemain's output was considerable—eighteen opus numbers were published between 1734 and 1762—and particularly his symphonies were often played at the *Concert spirituel*. His first book of sonatas for violin and figured bass and his last published opus containing *airs variés* and twelve caprices for violin alone reveal Guillemain as one of the great violin technicians of his generation, in terms of both left hand and bowing. His contemporaries recognized his excellence; as Marpurg wrote in 1764, "He does not know the meaning of the word 'difficult'; his compositions are rather bizarre, and he works every day to make them even more bizarre."[1] It is true that Guillemain's melodic line is often too ornate and his writing burdened with extreme tech-

---

* J. S. Bach's six sonatas for harpsichord obbligato and violin, composed around 1720, were an important innovation, but they followed a different principle, being essentially trios, not duos. It is safe to assume that Bach's music was unknown to Mondonville. In France, Elisabeth Jacquet de la Guerre essayed pieces for harpsichord and violin (1707).

nical difficulties, which discouraged other violinists (not to mention amateurs) from playing them. But "he was a man of fire, genius, and vivacity . . . perhaps the fastest and the most extraordinary violinist one could hear," according to Daquin.[2] His end was tragic: depressed and indebted, he committed suicide, stabbing himself fourteen times with a knife. He was buried hurriedly on October 1, 1770.

L'Abbé le fils (1727–1803) made his debut at the *Concert spirituel* in 1741 at the age of fourteen, playing a Leclair duet with the thirteen-year-old Gaviniès. After a respectable career as violinist and composer, he retired in 1762 to devote himself primarily to teaching. His pedagogical skill is shown in a methods book entitled *Principes du violon* (published in 1761). For its time, it was a remarkably progressive work: it marks, in Boyden's opinion, "the beginning of the leadership of the French school during the following century." Compared to the methods of Geminiani (1751) and Leopold Mozart (1756), L'Abbé was quite modern in his technical approach: he advocated holding the violin with the chin placed on the left side of the tailpiece; he described a bow grip which is not different from that of Baillot in the nineteenth century; and he taught not only natural but also "artificial" harmonics. As a true disciple of Leclair, he paid much attention to double stops and bowings (with emphasis on up-and-down bow staccato), proclaiming the bow to be the "soul" of violin playing. Many French methods, beginning with Cartier's *L'Art du violon* (1798), have borrowed from L'Abbé's *Principes*, which appeared in a second edition in 1772.

A strange fate befell the excellent violinist André-Noël Pagin (1721–after 1785): he was ostracized by his French countrymen for being overly devoted to the music of his teacher Tartini, and to Italian music in general. Pagin had gone to Padua to study with Tartini and, at the age of twenty-six, returned to Paris in 1747. He made his debut at the *Concert spirituel* in one of his own sonatas and was well received. During the next two years he appeared repeatedly but usually chose to play a work by Tartini or occasionally Vivaldi. After a final performance on Easter day 1750, Pagin's name disappeared forever from the announcements of the *Concert spirituel*. Twenty years later, the English scholar Charles Burney met and heard Pagin privately in Paris and reported in his diary, "He had the *honour* of being hissed at the *Concert spirituel* for daring to play in the Italian style, and this was the reason for his quitting the profession."[3] There must be some truth to this story, which cost Pagin the good will of the Parisian audience. A contemporary Frenchman, Daquin, explains,

Among all the students of the famous Tartini who . . . at times is criticized in France though more often admired, Mr Pagin occupies the first place. He owes everything to Tartini; he developed under his eyes; he recognizes no one but him; he plays his music exclusively because it is the only music that—to him—seems touching and sublime. But this young and admirable artist . . . should perhaps lend himself a bit to all the tastes. Is he not equipped to embellish all types of music?[4]

Thanks to Pagin's initiative, Tartini's Sonatas Op. 4 were published in Paris in 1747, followed by the Sonatas Op. 5 and Op. 6 (c. 1748). In the 1750s, Pagin edited a revised edition of Tartini's Sonatas Op. 7. All this was done without Tartini's consent and we do not know to what extent Pagin may have revised the original manuscripts.

Nevertheless, Pagin was considered the legitimate heir of the Tartini tradition in France. His own playing did not strike Burney as remarkable when he heard him in 1770, but Benjamin Franklin, who also heard him play in Paris, described him as "one of the best men possible."[5]

A student of Pagin and Tartini was Pierre La Houssaye (1735–1818). Already a talented violinist when he met Pagin at a private gathering, La Houssaye played Tartini's *Devil's Trill Sonata* (circulating only in manuscript) to everyone's astonishment. Pagin was so impressed that he offered to prepare him for a study trip to Padua, which took place in 1753. Later La Houssaye resumed his studies with Tartini, who thought very highly of him. After many years abroad, La Houssaye returned to his native Paris in 1776 and was appointed conductor and concertmaster of the *Concert spirituel* the following year. We have seen how displeased Mozart was by the slipshod manner in which La Houssaye conducted the rehearsal of his *Paris Symphony* in 1778, but the performance on June 18 was received "with great applause." La Houssaye was a solid orchestra leader, certainly far more competent than the nervous Mozart made him out to be, and he remained in his post for another ten years. When Viotti organized the new Théâtre de Monsieur in 1789, he engaged La Houssaye as concertmaster for the French opera repertoire—a position he retained after Viotti's hurried departure. In 1795, La Houssaye was named violin professor at the newly founded Conservatoire and taught until 1802. His last years were plagued by deafness and poverty.

Among other French contemporaries of Mozart, mention must be made of the violinist-composer Simon Le Duc: "he plays well," noted father Mozart, who heard him in the winter 1763–64. Simon Le Duc (c. 1745–1777) made his brilliant debut at the *Concert spirituel* in 1763 with a work of his teacher Gaviniès. A gifted composer, he curtailed his solo performances to concentrate on composition while his younger brother Pierre, also an excellent violinist, did all the playing. Pierre was entrusted with presenting the first performance of Simon's first violin concerto in 1770, described by a critic as "brilliant and very songful."

Simon Le Duc left three violin concertos, composed between 1770 and 1775, which makes them almost contemporaneous with Mozart's five concertos of 1775. Perhaps Mozart remembered his childhood impressions of French violin playing as practiced by Gaviniès and Le Duc, whom he heard in 1763–66. He was certainly aware of the type of violin concerto fashionable in Paris in the early 1770s, since French influences are intermingled with Austro-German in all of Mozart's concertos.

In turn, Le Duc's concertos are imbued with a charm and gracefulness akin to Mozart. La Laurencie has coined the expression "*Mozartisme avant Mozart*";[6] it could be applied to Le Duc. Indeed there was, during the 1770s, a common musical language among composers of all nations, which was used by Mozart as well as by composers of lesser stature. Le Duc (who died young) showed immense promise, not only in his violin concertos but also in his symphonies, which "can rival with the best in Europe," in the opinion of a modern historian.[7]

One month after Le Duc's premature death, one of his symphonies was to be performed at the *Concert des Amateurs*. During the rehearsal, the leader of the orchestra, Chevalier de Saint-Georges, "moved by the expressiveness of the Adagio and recalling that his friend existed no longer, dropped his bow and began to weep; this emotion communicated itself to all the artists and the rehearsal had to be suspended."[8]

Joseph Boulogne de Saint-Georges (1739–99) was one of the most flamboyant personalities on the Parisian scene. Born in the West Indies of a French aristocratic father and a native mother, he was brought to Paris at the age of ten and received a careful, gentlemanly education including fencing and music, and proved very gifted in both fields. His versatile talents endeared him to French society; in fact, his spectacular exploits as a fencer and sportsman at first surpassed his musical achievements. Whether he studied the violin with Leclair is doubtful, but

Gossec may have been his teacher in composition. His career in Paris is closely connected with the *Concert des Amateurs*, an orchestral association founded in 1769 by Gossec which soon rivaled the old established *Concert spirituel*. Not burdened by a chorus, the *Amateurs* concentrated on an orchestral repertoire, giving twelve concerts from December to May with a formidable orchestra of about eighty players, including twenty violins, twelve cellos, eight double basses, and a full complement of wind players. Not all the members participated at each performance, but it was still the largest orchestra of its time.

Saint-Georges belonged to the inner circle and founding members of the *Concert des Amateurs*; here he made his debut as soloist and composer in two of his own concertos during the season 1772–73. His success was such that he was named leader-conductor in 1773, when Gossec left to become codirector of the *Concert spirituel*. Under the firm leadership of Saint-Georges, the *Amateurs* soon acquired the reputation of being the best symphony orchestra in Paris, perhaps even in Europe. Despite its size, the ensemble was described as perfect, the execution full of nervous energy and subtle dynamics. At the center of activities was Saint-Georges, who functioned as leader-conductor, soloist, and composer; many of his concertos and symphonies were written for these concerts.

The *Concert des Amateurs* disbanded in January 1781, to be replaced by the *Concert de la Loge Olympique*, and again Saint-Georges was called upon to be the leader-conductor. The orchestra—as before a mixture of professional musicians and the best available amateurs—was even more resplendent than the defunct *Amateurs*. Since the queen and members of the royal family attended some of the concerts, audience and performers appeared in court regalia. The musicians played in embroidered frock coats, with lace cuffs, ceremonial swords, and plumed hats, the latter deposited on a bench. It was customary for all players to stand.

The new concert society invited guest conductors and commissioned composers to write special works. Composed for the *Loge Olympique* were the six *Paris Symphonies* of Joseph Haydn, first performed from manuscript during the 1787 season. The orchestra of the *Loge Olympique* was directed, so we assume, by Saint-Georges from the concertmaster's stand, violin in hand. He knew Haydn's style, for he had conducted some of his earlier symphonies at the *Concert des Amateurs*. But these premieres were a special occasion. The best musicians in Paris (including Cherubini and Viotti) were eager to participate, and the public received the new symphonies with enthusiasm. One of them (No. 85) became the favorite of Queen Marie Antoinette and was nicknamed *La Reine*.

The Revolution of 1789 brought this glittering musical life to a halt. The concerts of *La Loge Olympique* were discontinued in December 1789; the *Concert spirituel* gave its last performance on May 13, 1790. Some musicians (among them Viotti) decided to leave France; others remained and made their accommodation with the new regime. One of them was Saint-Georges, who became a captain in the National Guard and organized a black regiment while maintaining some of his musical activities. However, he was relieved of his command and kept under house arrest for eighteen months. After his return to private life, he conducted the concerts of the *Cercle de l'Harmonie* in 1797 and remained musically active until his death two years later.

At the height of his career, Saint-Georges was a brilliant performer, and his twelve violin concertos reflect his bold and effective technique, his easy command of the fingerboard, switching registers with lightning speed. He employed broken octaves and even tenths, and invented idiomatic passages. His slow movements are tinged with melancholy, his finales (usually in rondeau form) sparkling. Lately, the instrumental works of Saint-Georges—his concertos, symphonies, and *symphonies concertantes*—are being rediscovered; some of them are performed, recorded, and republished in facsimile editions. Saint-Georges is hailed as the first black composer in the European tradition.

With the concertos of Le Duc and Saint-Georges, the French violin concerto had reached a certain plateau of achievement but also a certain stagnation. The formal pattern and the balance between soloist and orchestra are genteel and well ordered, but also predictable and formalized. What was needed was the infusion of a creative spark, of deeper human emotion. The regeneration of the French violin concerto came through the genius of an Italian, Viotti.

Jean-Marie Leclair: "The French Corelli"
Below left, Pierre Gaviniès: "The French Tartini"
Below right, Giovanni Battista Viotti: "The father of modern violin playing"

GIOVANNI BATTISTA VIOTTI

On March 17, 1782, Giovanni Battista Viotti, the favorite disciple of Pugnani, made his debut in Paris. Unheralded and unknown when he arrived, Viotti—at the age of twenty-six—became a celebrity overnight. He played one of his own concertos, accompanied by the orchestra of the *Concert spirituel*. Within ten weeks, he was heard twelve times at these prestigious concerts. The public so clamored to hear him that an "extraordinary" concert had to be arranged on April 6. The success was repeated the following year: during 1783, between April and September, Viotti appeared sixteen times as soloist at the *Concert spirituel*, always playing his own concertos. He outshone all his competitors, French and foreign, not only as a masterful virtuoso but also as an effective composer for his instrument.

This brilliant acclaim induced Viotti to settle in Paris, where he remained for ten years. His presence transformed and revitalized the French violin school, and from Paris his influence spread across Europe. Between 1782 and 1791, nineteen of Viotti's violin concertos were published in Paris and served as models of their kind wherever the violin was played. One of his concertos (No. 16) aroused Mozart's interest.* Traces of Viotti's influence can be found in Beethoven's Violin Concerto. Even Paganini did not disdain to play Viotti's concertos in public.

Prior to his arrival in Paris, Viotti's career had been unspectacular. Yet he was a musically precocious child. Born in 1755 in the village of Fontanetto da Po, he learned to play the violin with very little instruction. At the age of eleven, he was brought to Turin, where he astounded

* See p. 115.

135

the professional musicians by his ability to read difficult music at sight. Young Viotti found patrons in the Marchesa di Voghera and her son Alfonso Dal Pozzo, who took charge of his education. He became a pupil of the famous Gaetano Pugnani, music director of the Royal Theater in Turin. "Viotti's education cost me more than twenty thousand francs, but by God I do not regret this money; the existence of such an artist cannot be overpaid," said Dal Pozzo many years later.[1] Pugnani must have taught his young student not only the violin but also the rudiments of composition, for Viotti wrote his first violin concerto at the age of fourteen; it was published a dozen years later, in 1781. Nonetheless, Viotti's talent was permitted to mature slowly. At the age of twenty, he became a supernumerary violinist in the Royal Theater, and for several years he sat at the last stand of the first violins.

In 1780 Viotti accepted Pugnani's flattering offer to join him on a concert tour that led through Switzerland, Germany, and Poland to Russia. They were a strange pair—the handsome, youthful Viotti and the grotesquely ugly (but vain) Pugnani. Their concerts were very successful, yet the older master received most of the attention, while Viotti played a secondary role. Somewhere on their way home they separated: Pugnani returned to Italy, while Viotti decided to seek his fortune in Paris, the musical capital of Europe. He arrived there at the end of 1781 and made his sensational debut a few months later.

Viotti represented the virtuoso-composer to perfection. Standing in front of the orchestra with violin in hand, he was both conductor and soloist in his own work. He was in full charge: his mastery of the violin, his authority of leadership were felt immediately. "Hearing him, our best masters dropped their bows in amazement," wrote a contemporary. Viotti drew extraordinary sounds from his violin, yet his style remained noble and pure.

What was the secret of Viotti's success? Virtuosity alone does not explain it. When he appeared in Paris in the 1780s, the public was ready for a new sound. Formerly, the ideal violin tone was sweet and slightly nasal, like the Amati and Stainer instruments that the previous generation of performers favored. Now Viotti arrived with a powerful Stradivari violin and produced a sound richer and more brilliant than anything heard before. His bow, too, may have contributed to the carrying power of his tone. Viotti must have used the new model developed at that time by François Tourte: the stick was thicker and heavier, the bow hair broader, and the balance had shifted toward the frog, which favored stronger accentuation and attack. At times, Viotti could sound "brusk and hurtful," as one contemporary critic observed; but it was precisely that assertive style that enthralled a public tired of graceful gallantry. He replaced the dainty with the dramatic. Finally, Viotti is known to have used a more pronounced vibrato (the critics called it "tremulando"), which gave his tone a more sensuous, expressive quality.

Viotti's grand manner of playing was reflected in his concertos, conceived on a larger scale than those of his older contemporaries. He applied symphonic principles to the violin concerto, drawing dramatic traits from the French opera, orchestral elements from German symphonies, and fusing them with his Italian heritage of the violin as a cantabile instrument. "To play well one must sing well," was Tartini's motto, to which Viotti fully subscribed. Thus arose a new concerto prototype, the French violin concerto. Why French? Because, under Viotti's impact Paris became the focal point for the art of violin playing. Viotti's French disciples, mainly Rode, Kreutzer, and Baillot, adopted the Viotti concerto as their model, adding a touch of French sophistication and verve.

Viotti's skill as a concerto composer developed gradually. He arrived in Paris with several concertos composed under Pugnani's guidance, which had as yet few attributes of future greatness. Viotti's initial success was a tribute to his brilliant performance rather than to the quality of his music. Once established in Paris, Viotti soon shed all traces of Piedmont provincialism and acquired a Gallic sparkle, which was particularly evident in the frothy, brilliant Rondo-Finales. In 1786, Luigi Cherubini—five years younger than Viotti but already a well-known opera composer—settled in Paris and became a close friend; for about six years, they shared lodgings. Cherubini's powerful sense of musical drama made a strong impression on Viotti and was reflected in his concertos of the late 1780s. Another influence was his growing acquaintance with Haydn's symphonic output.

Around 1786, six new symphonies by Haydn arrived in Paris; they were commissioned by the concert society *La Loge Olympique*, which sponsored the first performances during the 1787 season.* The splendid orchestra was reinforced by some of the best musicians in Paris, who clamored to participate. Among them was Cherubini, who appeared "utterly astounded and enchanted" by the new symphonies; at the end he stood "pale and petrified." Viotti, too, must have participated in some of these premiere performances, and his impression must have been equally strong. Of course, Viotti was familiar with a number of earlier Haydn symphonies which belonged to the indispensable reper-

* See pp. 132–33.

toire of the Parisian orchestras, but Haydn's latest symphonies opened new horizons.

After settling in London a few years later, Viotti had the opportunity of meeting Haydn personally during the 1794–95 seasons, and they had many professional contacts. Their creative work ran parallel: while Haydn wrote his *London Symphonies*, Viotti was composing his London concertos. Haydn's influence is evident in the extended tutti introductions, which Viotti treated on a symphonic scale. Quite often, the public broke into applause after the initial tutti, prior to the entrance of the solo violin. In Viotti's hands, orchestra and solo violin became equal partners in the presentation and elaboration of thematic material.

While living in Paris, Viotti's concert career as a virtuoso was cut short by his own decision. Despite continued success at the *Concert spirituel* in 1782 and 1783, he suddenly withdrew from public performances after a last appearance on September 8, 1783. There is no satisfactory explanation for this decision; it was rumored that he was offended by a cool reception at his last concert. From then on, Viotti restricted his performances to the court concerts of Queen Marie-Antoinette, who became his patroness. Even here, his sensitivities were not spared. Once, while presenting a new concerto before a bejeweled audience, his playing was rudely interrupted by the noisy cries of footmen to "Make room for the Comte d'Artois!" The music stopped, his highness was seated, the orchestra recommenced. But when the count continued to converse loudly, Viotti packed his violin and walked out, leaving the audience stunned and the orchestra in confusion.

Yet he had to make his peace with the aristocracy, since he stubbornly refused to appear in public concerts. For a time, he conducted the private orchestras of the Prince de Soubise and the Prince de Guémenée; occasionally he led the fashionable orchestra of the *Loge Olympique*.

Viotti continued to compose and publish his works, which were played publicly by other violinists. He also assembled a large number of students, whom he taught without remuneration. Every Sunday he gave musical matinees at the lodgings he shared with Cherubini. Here one could hear chamber music or the latest Viotti concerto played by the composer himself. To be admitted to these sessions was considered a privilege, since it was nearly the only opportunity to hear the master. To be asked to play at these sessions was a test of nerves even for experienced performers. Viotti, a man of great modesty, was almost embarrassed to see fine violinists incapacitated in his presence.

But Viotti's true ambition was to run an opera house. In 1788, under the patronage of the Comte de Provence and with the conniving help of the Queen's *coiffeur*, Viotti was appointed director of the new Théâtre de Monsieur. He offered a varied repertoire of French and Italian operas and some interesting premieres, like Cherubini's *Lodoiska*. During Easter Week, when no stage performances were permitted, the excellent orchestra (handpicked by Viotti) gave public concerts. Members of the orchestra appeared as soloists; for example, young Pierre Rode, Viotti's favorite pupil, was entrusted with performances of Viotti's latest concertos in 1791 and 1792.

But the times were not propitious for such fashionable entertainment. The Revolution of 1789 frightened and dispersed the aristocratic audiences. After the arrest of the queen in 1792, her *coiffeur* (who was copartner in this operatic enterprise) fled to Russia, fearing for his life. Viotti tried to shore up the tottering theater with his own means, but bankruptcy seemed inevitable. In late July 1792, he packed his Stradivarius and his music and embarked for London, forced to make a new start.

Musical life in London was no less intense than in Paris, but it had a broader foundation because it enjoyed the support of a prosperous middle class. Interest in music spanned a wide spectrum of English society from the king himself, who sponsored the Concerts of Ancient Music, to the ordinary citizens, who enjoyed their Threepence Concerts in a Hayloft. Invitations to subscribe to the fashionable concerts were sent to the nobility and the gentry. The season usually began in January or February and extended through May. A subscription for twelve concerts could be bought for five guineas, and separate tickets were issued for ladies and for gentlemen which—for some curious reason—were not interchangeable.

In the 1780s and '90s, a lively rivalry developed between the Professional Concerts led by Wilhelm Cramer, and the Hanover Square Concerts directed by Johann Peter Salomon. Cramer and Salomon, both German-born, were excellent violinists who had settled in London and were held in high esteem by English music lovers. Salomon, in addition, proved to be an astute impresario who won general praise for persuading Haydn to come to London. The composer's first visit, in 1791–92, turned into a historic occasion: the premieres of the first six *London Symphonies* were given at the Salomon concerts. Haydn's return visit was planned for 1794.

Just between these two visits, Viotti arrived in London. Salomon, who needed a stellar attraction for his new season, engaged Viotti to make his debut at the Hanover Square Concerts. It took place on February 7, 1793, and the success was spectacular. In the following three months, Viotti made fourteen appearances at Hanover Square. Though he had not played publicly in ten years, it did not take him long to prove his preeminence as a violinist-composer. As usual, his repertoire consisted exclusively of his own works. A correspondent wrote in 1794,

> Viotti is probably the greatest violinist in Europe. A strong, full-bodied tone, incredible agility, accuracy and precision . . . are characteristic, and his concertos surpass all others known to me. . . . He is equally irresistible as composer and performer.[2]

Obviously, there was a close rapport between Viotti and Salomon, the leader of the orchestra, and they appeared several times as joint artists in Viotti's *Symphonie concertante* for two solo violins and orchestra.

The following season of 1794 was no less successful for Viotti, though Haydn's return visit to London understandably absorbed most of the public interest. Throughout that spring season Viotti's name appeared side by side with that of Haydn and he was soloist in ten of the twelve concerts. In addition a concert was given "for the benefit of Mr. Viotti" and one for Mr. Salomon; at the latter, Viotti became "leader of the band" while Salomon was soloist in his own concerto. The critics continued to treat Viotti with admiration and esteem, praising his "grand and impressive style" and hailing him as "a most finished and masterly performer."

> Viotti again produced the rapturous sensations; he indeed possesses not only sweetness, vigour, and every variety that the bow and the finger seem capable of affording, but he adds the grand ingredient, soul.

> His power over the instrument seems unlimited . . . he awakens emotion, gives a soul to sound, and leads the passions captive.[3]

Viotti gave a concerto, simple and affecting, like his genius.[4]

In October 1794, Viotti was named "acting manager" of the King's Theatre in London, where operas were produced; it was an appointment of considerable importance. Haydn was still in England, awaiting the opening of the new season of Salomon's concerts early in

1795. On January 12, a startled public read the announcement that Salomon's concerts were to be discontinued. At the same time Salomon urged support for a new concert series at the King's Theatre, to be known as Opera Concerts, which promised to be the "exclusive union of all talents" in London. Many "eminent masters" joined as performers; the orchestra was increased to sixty players, to be led by Mr. Cramer (formerly the leader of the defunct Professional Concerts). The great Haydn was to present the premieres of his latest three symphonies in the course of the season. "The whole [was] to be under the direction of Mr. Viotti who will also occasionally furnish new Pieces of Music." This placed Viotti at the helm of a prestigious new concert series: in addition to planning the programs, he was expected to perform his own violin concertos, while the job of orchestra leader was delegated to the experienced Cramer. Viotti was at the pinnacle of his fame and influence in London; he obviously enjoyed the confidence and cooperation of all the prominent musicians, including Haydn and Salomon, Dussek and Clementi. Nine concerts were announced for the "Great Room" of King's Theatre, which could accommodate eight hundred people; the series was sold out by subscription, with no single tickets issued. The first concert took place on February 2, 1795, the ninth on May 18, but the popular demand was so great that two additional concerts were given.

In planning the programs, Viotti displayed "happy discrimination," as one reviewer noted. Along with the usual mixture of vocal and instrumental performers, the symphonies of Haydn continued as the mainstay of the orchestral repertoire, including several premieres. Viotti did not push himself unduly into the foreground. He was heard in three performances of his own concertos and fulfilled the highest expectations, as we can read in the *Morning Chronicle* on February 3:

> The new Concerto of VIOTTI, both in composition, execution, and taste, was a capital performance: each movement gave great pleasure, but especially the *adagio*, which, for sweetness of harmony, we have scarcely ever heard surpassed.

And on April 29, the same paper reported,

> . . . a new Violin Concerto by VIOTTI, who played with a degree of power and energy, unexpected even from him (in his hands this little instrument is in itself an Orchestra) . . .

That season, Viotti also played several of his works for two violins, once with Salomon, the other time with his student Philippe Libon. Much as Salomon's playing was praised, there can be no doubt that Viotti was preeminent among the violinists of the day.

Haydn left London on August 15, 1795, to return to Austria, while Viotti remained to enjoy continued success. Named to succeed Cramer as orchestra leader at the King's Theatre, he reappeared in the Opera Concerts of 1797: between February 6 and June 5 his name was listed six times, including several "new" concertos. The Opera Concerts continued in early 1798, and again Viotti's name figured prominently. He played concertos at the first two concerts and a duet with the famous bass player Dragonetti at the third.

Suddenly, an unexpected event shattered Viotti's career: he was expelled from England and ordered to leave the country on March 4, 1798. The London *Times* reported,

> Salomon led the band . . . in the place of Viotti, who has been sent out of the country under the authority of the Alien Bill. . . . Much interest was made to keep him here. . . . He left yesterday.

The charges of revolutionary sympathies were obviously trumped up, but all protestations of innocence under oath were in vain. He was accused of having used "heinous and sanguinary expressions" with regard to the king. Viotti, having fled France as a royalist, was now being expelled as a suspected Jacobin. His parting statement, published in the *Times*, is pathetic:

> I have received an order from the Government to quit a country which is dear to me, and which I consider my own. I obey, but in declaring . . . that I have never interfered in any political affair whatsoever,—that during the six years I have passed in England I have never written a syllable . . . related to its political concerns, or to those of my other country,— that I have never held any conversation to which the smallest degree of blame could attach. . . . The purity of my peaceful conscience assures me that I shall in the end be fully justified.

Viotti's banishment from England lasted three years, which he spent in isolation in a village near Hamburg, Germany. He refused all offers to give public concerts and devoted his time to composition. Here he wrote some of his finest violin duets, which he dedicated to his devoted English friends, Mr. and Mrs. Chinnery, with the words, "Some of these pieces were dictated by pain, others by hope." On February 18, 1801, the expulsion order was lifted and Viotti was free to return to London.

But his ambition as an artist seemed shattered. Though as great a violinist as ever, he played only in small private circles. During a brief visit to Paris in 1802, he was heard at an intimate musicale for his friends and former students. One of them, the faithful Pierre Baillot, wrote, "We were struck by the grand character of his playing. . . . His tone had become so mellow, so sweet, and yet it was so rich and so energetic that one could speak of a 'bow of cotton guided by the arm of Hercules.'"[5] It must have pleased Viotti to see that his foremost disciples—Rode, Kreutzer, and Baillot—were established as professors of the Paris Conservatoire. Thus the continuity of his school was assured.

Perhaps Viotti had come to Paris in the hope of finding a position worthy of his reputation, but no offer was made. The only tangible result was the signing of a publication contract with the newly founded Magasin de Musique, a cooperative venture run by several composers, including his old friend Cherubini. All his concertos composed in London appeared within the next few years in Paris.

When he finally returned to London, Viotti made an attempt at a musical comeback: in November 1803 he gave a "concert particulier" at the New Room of King's Theatre. Some two hundred people attended to hear him play a "new concerto" as well as a trio and two arias of his composition. He was advertised as "the French glory of the violin"—as if his eminent position in London's musical life during the 1790s had been forgotten. The event did not succeed in reestablishing his reputation.

As if disgusted by the vagaries of a music career, Viotti turned to a commercial enterprise—he became a wine merchant. For the next ten years, he led a double existence: while running his import business, he continued to play privately and to compose, and his works, though fewer in numbers, show no decline in creative power. His last two violin concertos (Nos. 28 and 29) date from the early 1800s; they are works of autumnal beauty, but they remained unknown at the time and were not published until the 1820s. Music, for Viotti, became an avocation: he was no longer involved in the mainstream of musical life. When, in 1813, the new Philharmonic Society was launched in London, the leaders were Viotti's old associates, Salomon and Clementi, while he was merely among the "sponsors." "The Philharmonic Society did not choose to give me satisfaction. . . . It pains me very much," wrote Viotti in 1815.[6] That was the year when his old friend Cherubini visited London to be feted by the Philharmonic Society, while Viotti was relegated to a minor role. Viotti's name appears four times on the Philharmonic programs of the first three seasons, but never as soloist in a concerto. He is listed as "leader," that is, concertmaster of the orchestra. In each concert he also appeared as composer-performer, twice in his own string quartet (1813 and 1814) and twice as first violinist in his own *Concertante* for two violins and cello plus orchestra (1815). These were honorable assignments, but not in keeping with his former reputation. When he spoke bitterly about the neglect by the Philharmonic Society, he must have thought about the manuscripts of his last two violin concertos, written a decade earlier and as yet unperformed.

To compound his disappointments, his wine business went bankrupt in 1814, leaving him deeply in debt. Once again, Paris beckoned—the Bourbon monarchy had been restored and Viotti's old patron was on the throne as Louis XVIII. A quick trip to Paris in 1814 turned into a sentimental journey: at an improvised gathering at the Conservatoire, Viotti appeared like "a father among his children."[7] The scene was charged with emotion.

Viotti's last performance for a small circle of his Parisian friends was a memorable occasion. He had returned in 1818 and was given a surprise party, at which a piece composed in his honor was played, a kind of salutatory cantata. The composer Habeneck interspersed the vocal parts with instrumental violin solos based on excerpts from Viotti's concertos, played on this occasion by Baillot. Viotti, deeply moved, consented to play for the small gathering and chose his last Concerto in E minor, as yet unpublished and unknown in Paris. In fact, he had recently added a slow movement to this work. "He played with his customary verve," remembered Baillot, but the effect was unexpectedly emotional when a young student, overcome by the experience of hearing the legendary master, broke out in loud sobs. "Alas, it was his swan song; we heard him for the last time; but this farewell meant a new beginning for most of those present."[8]

Viotti's repeated visits to Paris were undertaken in the hope of finding a professional opening. This time he was lucky—on November 1, 1819, he was named director of the Royal Opera House, which also entailed the directorate of the Théâtre Italien. The appointment almost cost him the friendship of Cherubini, who had aspired to the same post. In fact, both theaters had been badly mismanaged and were on the verge of bankruptcy.

Despite his managerial experience, Viotti could not stem the decline of the once-famous opera house. External misfortunes complicated the situation: a few months after Viotti became director, the Duc de Berry (nephew of the king) was assassinated while attending the opera. As a result, the opera was temporarily closed and ultimately transferred to a private theater. Viotti was harassed from all sides: the old repertoire was unsuited for the small new stage, the deficit was mounting, and there was open criticism of his administration. A second transfer of the opera, to yet another theater, proved catastrophic. The opera remained closed for months during the high season, and the public clamored for Viotti's resignation. On October 22, 1821, he was discharged, with an annual pension of 6000 francs.

For a year he retained the Théâtre Italien, but it led nowhere; at sixty-six, his career was finished. He suffered much but behaved with dignity. For a time he stayed in Paris, where he signed his last will and testament on December 13, 1822, leaving everything, including his Stradivarius, to his devoted English friend Mrs. Chinnery. He still enjoyed playing the violin, as we gather from an affectionate note to his loyal disciple Baillot, inviting him for a good dinner and some violin duets. That was in late July 1823; shortly thereafter he returned to London. He rejoined the Chinnery household and died at their home on March 3, 1824. He was buried in the parish of St. Marylebone, in the presence of a few friends.

Viotti was proud, gentle, and affectionate. He was also self-defeating, strange, almost enigmatic. Though he lived to be sixty-nine, his musical career virtually ended when he was forty-three. He was a superb virtuoso, yet he chose to perform publicly for only six or seven years. He was an inspiring teacher, but limited his teaching to a small group of gifted disciples during the 1780s in Paris; his motivation was purely artistic and he accepted no money for his lessons. He was a composer of natural gifts who wrote with obvious ease, though he had little formal instruction; he left some 160 works. His style is rooted in eighteenth-century Classicism, but is often tinged with early Romantic melancholia or "Storm and Stress."

At the time of Viotti's death, the musical world was in ferment: Classical ideals were shattered, Romanticism and virtuosity were on the rise. Hence it is not surprising that his concertos—so immensely popular before 1800—were soon considered old-fashioned and mainly fit for study purposes. Even the more advanced concertos of his finest disciples, Rode and Kreutzer, had only a comparatively brief life; they were soon overshadowed by the new wave of virtuosity sparked by Paganini and adopted by Bériot and Vieuxtemps. The older masters were relegated to the classroom, where they have indeed become indispensable. Recently we are witnessing the beginnings of a Viotti renaissance through recordings and scholarly publications of scores.[9]

At least one of Viotti's concertos—No. 22 in A minor—was once a favorite of Joachim and Kreisler. Joachim went so far as to rank it above the concertos of Mendelssohn and Brahms and second only to the Beethoven concerto. And Brahms himself, while composing his own violin concerto, had Viotti on his mind; as he wrote to Clara Schumann in 1878,

> The Viotti Concerto [No. 22] is my particular love. . . . It is a glorious piece, of a remarkable freedom of invention, sounding as if improvised, and yet everything so well planned. . . . People in general do not understand nor respect the very best things, such as Mozart's concertos or this one by Viotti—that's how men like us survive and become famous! If people only knew that we give them *in drops* what they could drink there to their heart's delight!

Joachim, recalling that Brahms "did not rave as passionately about the Beethoven Concerto" as he did about Viotti's No. 22, continued,

> During my bachelor years in Hanover, when we played together up in my room, I had to play the Viotti for him two and even three times in a row. With flushed face, raised shoulders, and groans of delight Brahms belabored the keyboard while accompanying me and was happy that "such a thing existed in this world." That is why I always called this piece *his* concerto by Viotti.[10]

Brahms remembered "his" Viotti in his own Violin Concerto, quoting a phrase from Viotti—reshaped yet recognizable:

Viotti, Concerto No. 22 A minor
First movement, measures 168–72

Brahms, Violin Concerto in D
First movement, measures 236–242

Viotti's twenty-nine concertos span twenty-five years of his creative
life, falling into the three stages in his career: he wrote his youthful
works in Turin, reached his early mastery in Paris, and attained the
height of his maturity in London. At a glance, the chronology is:

Turin, up to 1780:   Concertos Nos. 1–3
Paris, 1782–91:   Concertos Nos. 4–19
London, 1792–98:   Concertos Nos. 20–27
London, 1801–04:   Concertos Nos. 28 and 29*
(after return
from exile)

Although essentially Classical in form, Viotti's concertos fore-
shadow the approaching Romanticism in many ways. Most conspicuous
is his preference for minor keys: of his last sixteen concertos (Nos. 14–
29), no fewer than ten are in the minor mode. (For the sake of comparison, Mozart wrote only two concertos in minor keys, Beethoven
only one!) Viotti's concertos in minor keys are at times dramatic and
passionate in character, but more often lyrical and melancholic. The
sinuous theme of his last concerto (E minor, No. 29) points toward
Mendelssohn and Schumann, who were not yet born when Viotti composed it. In other ways, too, Viotti was ahead of his time, as in his
attempts to loosen the rigid three-movement form. In several of his
concertos, he prepares the entrance of the Finale by a transitional
modulation or even a short connecting movement (as did Mendelssohn
decades later). In his Concerto No. 21, Viotti quotes the first movement in the Finale, thus establishing a cyclic unity. He also takes certain liberties in the construction of the opening movements, for example in No. 25. Without being greatly innovative, his mind was certainly
unconventional and could take surprising turns.

In his late Parisian concertos (Nos. 14 to 19), Viotti stressed the
dramatic aspects, and they created a sensation when his young student
Rode played them in 1791–92 at the Théâtre de Monsieur. Undoubtedly the influences of Cherubini and the contemporary French opera
shaped Viotti's style at that time. A fine example of this period is the
Concerto No. 16 in E minor, which aroused Mozart's interest.† Equally
stirring is the Concerto No. 19 in G minor (also available in a version
for piano and orchestra).

Viotti's "London" concertos are more mellow, more expansive;
here Haydn's influence becomes apparent. He also used a larger or-

* Andante of No. 29 added in 1818. Both Nos. 28 and 29 published in 1824.
† See p. 115.

chestration, particularly for the works composed for the Opera Concerts, where an orchestra of sixty players was available. However, he differed from Haydn in his frequent use of minor keys. It was unusual enough to be singled out by a London critic who wrote, "Viotti played a concerto in a minor key, the composition and performance of which were alike masterly. In style it was neither perfectly ancient or modern, though it partook of the beauties of both."[11] He may have referred to the Concerto No. 22 in A minor.

Very little is known about the genesis of the last two concertos (Nos. 28 and 29), written after Viotti's return from exile. The watermarks of the music paper used in the autographs reveal that they were composed in the early 1800s. Perhaps Viotti wrote the works expecting a comeback as a virtuoso, but it never happened. Mystery surrounds his appearance in London on or about November 24, 1803: did it take place? which was the "new" concerto mentioned in the announcement?* No further information can be found in the newspapers of the time. We have mentioned the performance of Concerto No. 29 in Paris in 1818, with an added Andante. It was published in 1824, the year of the composer's death, and we do not know whether he lived to see the publication.

Viotti was a productive composer and left a long list of compositions numbering over 160†—sonatas, trios, quartets, *symphonies concertantes*, and even a few vocal works. Some have genuine charm, particularly his many duos for two unaccompanied violins. But nothing can match the excellence of his violin concertos, which enjoyed such popularity that ten of them were arranged as piano concertos and a few others for flute and orchestra.

Within the history of the violin, Viotti's claim to immortality rests on two achievements: he perfected a type of violin concerto which remained the model for half a century, and he established standards of violin playing which inspired an entire generation of young violinists, thus creating a "school" whose principles are still valid today. His legacy survived the tidal wave of virtuosity brought about by the rise of Paganini, and it proved timeless.

* See p. 143. The silence surrounding the event is such that one doubts that it ever took place.
† A Thematic Catalogue of Viotti's works is appended to the biography of Viotti by Remo Giazotto (Milan, 1956). Each work is given a "G" number for easier identification.

PART FOUR

The Nineteenth Century

FRANCE:
THE HEIRS OF VIOTTI

VIOTTI'S DEPARTURE from Paris in July of 1792 was barely noticed. France was in the throes of a revolution; there were many emigrés, and Viotti was just one of them. His decision to leave France, a country which had received him with so much hospitality and acclaim, was certainly a difficult one, but it was unavoidable. As former court violinist of Marie Antoinette and protégé of the Bourbon family, Viotti was politically suspect. Moreover, as the Parisian musical establishment disintegrated and new forces began to take over, Viotti's personal presence seemed no longer needed nor important. He had left a rich legacy, and his disciples carried forward his ideas. Among them were Pierre Rode, Rodolphe Kreutzer, and Pierre Baillot, who were destined to play a decisive role in making the French violin school the first in Europe.

But there was also deep social significance in this shift. Viotti's career was built on the support of the aristocracy, which was dispersed by the Revolution. His disciples, all young Frenchmen, adjusted themselves quickly to the political changes and built their careers within the new social framework.

One of the new republican institutions was the Conservatoire de Musique, formally established in 1795. It was the outgrowth of a free municipal music school sponsored by the Garde Nationale Parisienne, based on new democratic principles of free education for the qualified. Among the newly appointed faculty members were the three rising young violinists of the Viotti school—Rode, Kreutzer, and Baillot. Their names were further linked as authors of a new violin methods book commissioned by the Conservatoire; it was adopted in 1802 as the official study guide and provided a unified approach. About the same time, Kreutzer made his individual contribution to violin pedagogy with the publication of his Forty Etudes or Caprices, which are considered indispensable to any young violinist's curriculum.

Due to this coordinated approach to teaching, violin playing in France gained an immense advantage over that of other countries: the Viotti tradition became codified. This is how a French critic described it in 1810:

> In the past, the orchestra violinists were individually very good players, but each had a different method of bowing . . . the result was that the ensemble was flawed. Today, these drawbacks no longer exist: while the principal professors at the Conservatoire—Rode, Kreutzer, and Baillot—have certain individualities of bowing, all three resemble very closely the method of their great master, the famous Viotti. The graduates of these three classes all have a broad and energetic playing style: the result is such a unity of execution that one could think of hearing one single violin.[1]

Much later, in 1832, Mendelssohn wrote admiringly about the Paris Conservatoire orchestra:

> . . . this is the best I have ever heard. Baillot's, Rode's, and Kreutzer's schools supply the violinists; it is a joy to see that mass of young people in the orchestra, and how they start with exactly the same bowing, the same style, the same deliberation and ardour.[2]

How strongly entrenched the Viotti style was within the Paris Conservatoire can be gauged by the fact that the performance of a Viotti concerto was obligatory at the annual prize contests of the Conservatoire until 1853 (with a single exception in 1845).

Rode, Kreutzer, and Baillot—the triumvirate of Viotti "heirs"—were very different in temperament and personality. As a performer, Pierre Rode was the most brilliant, and he made an international career. Kreutzer's solid playing was technically accomplished but less elegant, though he was a more versatile composer and enjoyed a certain vogue at the opera, particularly during the 1790s. Baillot, whose talent developed more slowly, was the most intellectual and articulate of the three; he was at his best as a chamber music player and contributed much to the growing appreciation of Beethoven in France. He was personally close to Viotti and published an affectionate memoir after the master's death.

Pierre Rode

Among Viotti's disciples, Pierre Rode deserves first place, as "a perfect reflection of his great master." Born in Bordeaux in 1774, he began to play the violin at an early age and was considered a prodigy by the time he was twelve. Taken to Paris in 1787, the boy aroused the interest of Viotti, who offered to teach him without fee. Soon, young Rode became Viotti's favorite pupil and quickly developed into a superb performer.

At the age of sixteen, Rode made his debut in a Viotti concerto at the *Concert spirituel* on April 5, 1790, just a month before that venerable institution was forced to close its doors. Other concert societies had already gone out of existence. Eager to continue the concert tradition, Viotti arranged his own "spiritual concerts" at the small opera theater he was directing at the time; two such concerts took place during Easter 1791 and nine during Holy Week 1792. Viotti's purpose was twofold: to present his own latest violin concertos before the public, and to give his best pupils—primarily Rode, Kreutzer, and Alday—an opportunity to be heard as soloists with orchestra.* Since Viotti persisted in his refusal to play before Parisian audiences, he entrusted young Rode with the premieres of his two latest concertos (No. 17 in D minor and No. 18 in E minor), in addition to the revival of several of his older concertos. In April 1792, Rode appeared six times within two weeks as soloist in the works of his master and scored a tremendous success. The new concertos aroused as much enthusiasm as the young interpreter. Baillot, a fellow student who played in the orchestra, reminisced.

> In these concertos, Viotti adopted a dramatic manner whose impact was so unexpected and imposing when Rode, his student and his worthy interpreter, played them with all the charm and all the purity that distinguished his talent.[1]

Thus, Rode's solo career was launched. Within a few months he was left on his own, when Viotti emigrated to London.

* Kreutzer and Alday played their own concertos, while Rode played exclusively those of Viotti.

During the next few years, Rode expanded his musical activities in many directions: he composed his first violin concerto, a bold and brilliant piece published in 1794; he undertook concert tours to Holland, Germany, England, and Spain; he was appointed to the faculty of the Conservatoire; and he served briefly as *violon solo* of the Grand Opéra in 1799.

The following year Rode was named solo violinist of Napoleon's private orchestra and soon reached the height of his fame in Paris; the public adored his playing as well as his compositions. A critic wrote in 1800, "Rode made an impression bordering on the miraculous. He is the most accomplished violinist in all of Europe."[2] Most popular were his Concerto No. 7 in A minor and his brilliant *Air varié* Op. 12, the latter performed not only on the violin but also by famous singers to show off their coloratura!

But Rode loved to travel—"the artist has no country, he belongs to the world, and the world belongs to him," he once wrote. He accepted an invitation to visit Russia and began the long journey early in 1803, in the company of the composer Boieldieu. Traveling leisurely through Germany, he gave concerts in Leipzig, Dresden, Berlin, and other cities. The critics were ecstatic: "All who have heard his famous teacher Viotti, confirm without hesitation that he possesses to perfection his teacher's own interesting style, but with more mildness and more refined feeling."[3]

Early in 1804 Rode arrived in St. Petersburg and soon became the darling of the public. Presented to Czar Alexander I, he was named Soloist of the Czar at a fabulous salary of 5000 silver rubles a year. He was heard in concertos and string quartets, as well as in solos at the opera. An extended visit to Moscow proved equally successful. All in all, Rode exerted a very beneficial influence on violin playing in Russia: he established high standards of technique and taste which the indigenous Russian violinists tried to emulate. In the past, the visiting violin virtuosos had been mostly Italians; beginning with Rode, the French influence became dominant and remained so throughout the nineteenth century.

Rode—like his contemporary Beethoven—was obviously much taken by Russian folk music; his Concerto No. 12 (dedicated to Czar Alexander) has a final Rondeau "*mêlés d'airs russes*." The main theme is the well-known folk tune "In the field stood a little birch tree"—the same tune Tchaikovsky later used in his Fourth Symphony.

In the spring of 1808, Rode decided to return to Paris. After an absence of five years, he gave a concert at the Odéon, on December 22. But the reception was cool and disappointing:

> His choice of concerto was not exactly a happy one. He had composed it in St. Petersburg; and it would seem that the cold climate of Russia was not without influence on this composition. . . . Rode aroused little enthusiasm. His talent, though perfectly schooled, leaves much to be desired in terms of fire and inner life. What harmed Rode even more was the fact that, not long ago, we had heard Lafont. He is at present the most popular of all violinists.[4]

The last sentence added insult to injury. In Rode's absence, a new idol had captured the affection of the Parisians: Charles Lafont, a former student of Kreutzer and of Rode himself, who was eventually to challenge Paganini. But for the time being, Lafont disappeared from the Parisian scene, traveling to St. Petersburg as Rode's successor.

But this did not appease Rode: deeply offended by the public's fickleness, he retired to private life. He even declined to return to his old post at the Conservatoire and was put on the inactive list.

In 1811 Rode resumed his concert tours outside of France. In December 1812 we find him in Vienna, where he met Beethoven. It so happened that Beethoven had a half-finished violin sonata, which he now completed at short notice for a performance by Rode and Archduke Rudolph (Beethoven's student and patron). In his letters to the archduke, Beethoven referred several times to Rode in unflattering terms; for example,

> I have not hurried unduly to compose the last movement . . .
> as in view of Rode's playing I have had to give more thought
> to the composition of this movement. In our Finales we like
> to have fairly noisy passages, but R[ode] does not care for
> them—and so I have been rather hampered.[5]

The Sonata (Op. 96 in G major) was finished just in time for a performance at the Lobkowitz Palace on December 29, 1812. A critic praised the archduke's playing, but had reservations about the violinist: "Mr. Rode's greatness does not seem to lie in this type of music, but in the performance of the concerto."[6] Beethoven, obviously dissatisfied with Rode's playing, planned to send him the violin part of the sonata in the hope that he would study it, but hesitated to offend the famous guest. A second performance took place on January 7, 1813, one day after Rode's first public concert in Vienna.

All in all, Rode's appearance in Vienna was not an untarnished success. Louis Spohr, who in his youth had been a fervent admirer of Rode, now wrote,

> In a state of almost feverish excitement I awaited the beginning of Rode's playing which—ten years ago—I considered the highest model. But already after the first solo it seemed to me as if he had lost ground. I found his playing cold and mannered, I missed the previous boldness in vanquishing great difficulties, and was particularly dissatisfied with his treatment of the cantabile.[7]

From 1814 to 1819 Rode lived in Berlin, where he was always well received. He gave occasional concerts and composed much, including the famous Twenty-four Caprices. In 1819 he moved back to France, but refused to play in Paris. Mendelssohn met him in 1825 and reported, "Rode remains firm in his refusal to take the violin in his hand"—he called the Parisian scene "a musical tumble."[8]

Rode composed his thirteenth and last violin concerto for his old-time colleague Baillot, who agreed to give the first performance at the inaugural concert of the Conservatoire Society on March 9, 1828. Feeling indisposed, Baillot asked his best student, Sauzay (a recent first-prize winner at the Conservatoire), to substitute for him. The program also included the Parisian premiere of Beethoven's *Eroica*, which, needless to say, received all the attention, while Rode's mediocre concerto was listened to politely.

Yet Rode felt encouraged to announce a personal appearance as a violinist in Paris. This performance, in the fall of 1828, was a near fiasco and probably shortened his life. He suffered a stroke and died two years later in his native city of Bordeaux on November 25, 1830.

There is a certain tragedy in witnessing the decline of a great artist in the prime of his life. Rode was only thirty-four years old when he returned from Russia to face an indifferent public in Paris, and just thirty-nine when he was found to have deteriorated as a violinist by his former admirer, Spohr. But he tried again and again—in Berlin in 1815, in the French provinces around 1821, and finally in Paris in 1828. As a composer, he faced diminishing acceptance after his initial successes with the Concertos Nos. 7 and 8 and the famous *Air varié*. The only work of his later years to survive is the Twenty-four Caprices, which combine musical invention with technical purpose. Written around 1815, they are still in use, though their technical demands are moderate. Only five years later, Paganini published his incomparable Twenty-four Caprices— a challenge to all violinists who shook their heads in disbelief when they first saw these "unplayable" pieces. A brief comparison of the Rode Caprices with the Paganini Caprices shows the abyss which opened up suddenly between the "classical" school and the new virtuosity.

Whatever Rode's shortcomings in later years, one must realize that from 1795 to 1805—while he was in his twenties—he was recognized as a violinist "only to be compared with himself," as one critic remarked. He was copied and imitated from Paris to Petersburg, leaving his mark wherever he appeared. A generation of violinists learned from his example of flawless, elegant, yet virile violin playing. A perceptive evaluation was written by the German composer Reichardt in 1802:

> Rode played with absolute mastery. One cannot imagine a purer, more perfect intonation, a more penetrating and brighter tone, and as perfect as his tone is his whole playing. His interpretation is occasionally a bit mannered but always in good taste. He acquired the original style of his teacher Viotti—particularly his Adagio has something endearingly naive which well reflects his tender mind and character. He is also a very well-mannered person of high moral standards and an enchanting artist.

While Rode preferred to play his own music in public, he was a fine performer of Mozart quartets which he liked to play in private circles— "Rode played several quartets of Mozart, which are so difficult to interpret, with such clarity and precision, with so much expression and bravura as I have never heard them played before."[9]

One of Rode's idiosyncrasies seems to have been his frequent use of portamento (today called glissando), that is, the expressive slurring and sliding from one note into the other. Spohr used to imitate this peculiarity and was criticized for it by Reichardt as being "an exaggerated imitation of Rode's style."

The carrying power of Rode's tone is stressed repeatedly. He owned two superb Stradivari violins which undoubtedly enhanced the beauty of his cantabile. In later years, however, he seems to have forced the pressure on the strings, lending his tone an occasional stridency.

Rode's musical idiom is reminiscent of the early Viennese classicism; there is a cool, chiseled elegance in his violin writing, with an abundance of ornamentation overlaying his melodic line. A natural-born composer, without much artfulness or intellectual strength, he wrote music for his time rather than for posterity, though he influenced the young generation. The French school would not have been possible without Rode, who transformed Viotti's Italianate concertos into something intensely French, adding brilliance, drama, and sparkle to Viotti's more lyrical style.

Rodolphe Kreutzer

Today, Kreutzer's fame rests mainly on his receiving the dedication of Beethoven's finest violin sonata (Op. 47), now generally known as the *Kreutzer Sonata.** But ironically, Beethoven's dedication was actually an afterthought. The sonata was composed for George Bridgetower, who played the first performance in Vienna in 1803, with Beethoven at the piano; but they later quarreled. Remembering Kreutzer from a meeting in Vienna in 1798, Beethoven changed the dedication "to my friend R. Kreutzer," explaining to his publisher,

> This Kreutzer is a dear kind fellow who during his stay in Vienna gave me a great deal of pleasure. I prefer his modesty and natural behavior to *all the exterior* without *any interior* which is characteristic of most virtuosi. As the sonata was written for a competent violinist [i.e. Bridgetower], the dedication to Kreutzer is all the more appropriate.[1]

And so the engraved sonata was sent to Kreutzer in Paris with a personal note. The response was nil. Not only did Kreutzer neglect to acknowledge the dedication, but he never played the sonata, which he considered "outrageously unintelligible." His lack of affinity for Beethoven's music is strange, for he was a first-rate musician with a reputation as a violinist, conductor, and composer. But Beethoven had his detractors: we need only remember Spohr, whose comments on Beethoven were often negative.

Kreutzer was born in Versailles in 1766, the son of a German musician. His violin teacher was Anton Stamitz, also German-born and son of the famous symphonist Johann Stamitz. Young Kreutzer made such rapid progress that he was engaged as soloist at the *Concert spirituel* in 1780, at the age of thirteen. He played a concerto of his teacher and obtained such applause that he had to repeat the last movement.

Two years later Viotti arrived in Paris and young Kreutzer was

---

* Tolstoy added to the immortality by writing a novella of the same title.

drawn into his circle. It is not known whether there was actually a teacher-student relationship, but Kreutzer gradually absorbed the style of Viotti and is considered one of his foremost disciples. In 1784, Kreutzer attained a mark of distinction at the *Concert spirituel* by playing his own concerto (No. 1 in G major), a youthful work still indebted to Stamitz's influence. The success was considerable and brought Kreutzer several reengagements.

As early as 1785, Kreutzer became a member of the Royal Music in Versailles. Orphaned at the age of eighteen, he had to struggle hard to support four younger brothers and sisters. In 1788 he married the daughter of an affluent courtier and his fortunes took a turn for the better. It was a happy marriage, and eventually his house became a meeting place for artists and intellectuals. The Royal Music was transferred to Paris in 1789, and Kreutzer moved with the establishment. That year he appeared twice at the *Concert spirituel*.

The Revolution did not affect Kreutzer's career; he managed the transition from royal musician to republican office-holder with surprising ease. In 1790 he became solo violinist at the Théâtre Italien, and in 1793 was named violin professor at the Institut National de Musique (later the Conservatoire). He also played a leading role in organizing the massive revolutionary festival in honor of the "Supreme Being." But most of Kreutzer's efforts during the 1790s went into composing for the lyric stage. He became one of the most popular opera composers of the day, competing with Cherubini and Méhul. Kreutzer's activity as opera and ballet composer extended well into the nineteenth century; he wrote over forty works for the stage.

In 1796 Kreutzer—armed with his violin—followed the victorious French armies into Italy and Germany. In November of that year he gave a concert in Genoa and met the fourteen-year-old Paganini; it was said that they were mutually impressed. (In fact, Paganini kept several works of Kreutzer in his repertoire.) In the spring of 1798 Kreutzer reached Vienna—he was attached to the retinue of the French ambassador Bernadotte—and became friendly with Beethoven. Wherever Kreutzer performed, he enjoyed unqualified success.

Unlike Rode, however, Kreutzer did not become a traveling virtuoso: he built a solid career in Paris. For a time, in 1800–1802, Rode and Kreutzer were friendly competitors in Paris; Kreutzer was deemed the only violinist who could be compared to Rode. After Rode left for Russia, Kreutzer filled the void: he was named solo violinist of the Grand Opéra and chamber soloist of Napoleon.

In 1810 Kreutzer had the misfortune of breaking his left arm, putting an end to his concert career. He became a full-time conductor, an art he had practiced since the 1790s as a sideline. Named conductor of the Grand Opéra in 1816, he was in charge of the revived *Concerts spirituels* during the 1820s. Young Berlioz, as yet totally unknown, tried in vain to interest Kreutzer in performing one of his manuscript pieces. He received a rude rebuff: "We have no time to rehearse new music for these concerts." On several occasions, Kreutzer showed his displeasure with the music of Beethoven; he once stormed out of a rehearsal of the Second Symphony, covering his ears with his hands. It took musicians like Baillot and the conductor Habeneck to convince the Parisian public of Beethoven's greatness. By that time, Kreutzer was in retirement. He had relinquished all his posts in 1826, but his parting wish—to see his last opera staged in Paris—remained unfulfilled. Embittered by this humiliation, he spent the last years of his life battling a protracted illness, and died in Geneva in 1831.

Kreutzer was a strong violinist, with a secure technique and a big tone, stressing power rather than subtlety. Contemporary critics often described him as a "copy" of his master Viotti, but the same was said of Rode, who played very differently. One wonders which of the two represented the true manner of Viotti. Probably neither in an exact sense—a creative student superimposes his own personality on that of his teacher. For whatever it is worth, here is one of those comparisons:

> The manner of Viotti is also his. The same strong tone and the same broad bowings in the Allegro; his execution of the most difficult passages is precise and extremely clean. In the Adagio, Kreutzer shows himself to be even more a master of his instrument.[2]

Rode and Kreutzer were friends as well as competitors, and did not hesitate to appear side by side at concerts. It became fashionable in high society around 1800 to take sides, to favor one or the other. Kreutzer composed a double concerto for one of their joint appearances; one critic wrote,

> Mr. Kreutzer courageously entered the arena with Rode, and both artists offered the connoisseurs a most interesting contest. . . . One could clearly observe that Kreutzer's talent was more the fruit of long study and untiring effort, while Rode's art seems to have been born with him.[3]

Though Kreutzer may have lacked Rode's innate charm, his playing was distinguished by grandeur and "instinct," as Fétis said:

This instinct, so rich and full of verve, gave his performance an originality of sentiment and style which created an emotional communication with the audience to a degree which no one has surpassed. Kreutzer had a powerful sonority, correct intonation, and he phrased with infectious warmth.

Fétis added later that "Kreutzer's playing was bold, brilliant, and almost chivalrous."[4]

Kreutzer was a self-taught composer who wrote with facility. While his earliest concertos still bear the imprint of his teacher Stamitz, he quickly acquired the verve and drama of the Viotti style. At the same time, however, he absorbed the techniques of the Viennese masters in terms of form, harmonic idiom, and thematic development. He admired Haydn as a great model and even wrote a violin concerto (No. 16) based entirely on themes of Haydn, under curious circumstances: Early in 1805 a rumor swept through Europe that Haydn had died. His admirers were deeply saddened; the Parisian musicians arranged a memorial concert for February 6, with a program consisting of Mozart's Requiem and a commemorative cantata by Cherubini. In addition, Kreutzer dashed off a concerto based on Haydn themes. Just before the concert, Haydn was reported to be alive and well. The concert was held, with a changed program, but Kreutzer insisted on playing his "Haydn" Concerto. A cleverly designed *pastiche*, it keeps the listener amused as the well-known Haydn themes reappear in the most unexpected disguises and contexts.

With his next concerto (No. 17), Kreutzer returned to his own inspiration and reached his summit with the last two violin concertos, No. 18 in E minor and No. 19 in D minor. Particularly the latter is in the grand French tradition, perhaps the last of its kind. Joseph Joachim thought highly of it:

> In the construction of his first movements, Kreutzer displays that bold decisiveness for which his playing was so much admired by his contemporaries. Above all, the first movement of Concerto No. 19 is a beautiful example of that kind of pathos which expresses itself, among French composers, in the sudden shifts from high to low registers or vice versa, without ever violating the expressive limits of the instrument.[5]

Kreutzer's enduring significance, however, lies not in his compositions, but in violin teaching and methodology. For thirty years he served on the Conservatoire faculty and, unlike Rode, who was mostly "on leave," Kreutzer was always "on the job." He taught a generation of French violinists; he was, in fact, one of the architects of French violin supremacy in the nineteenth century. One of his pupils was Lambert Massart, the most successful violin teacher of his time (a faculty member at the Conservatoire for forty-seven years!), who in turn taught Wieniawski and Fritz Kreisler. By the end of the nineteenth century, there was hardly a French violinist who could not trace his ancestry to the teaching of Kreutzer or Massart.

Kreutzer's pedagogical talent is shown in his incomparable Forty Etudes or Caprices (later editions added two etudes to make a total of forty-two). The earliest known publication is dated 1803, though the collection was advertised as early as 1800. Kreutzer must have written the etudes for his Conservatoire students, at about the same time that he collaborated with Baillot and Rode on the *Méthode de violon*. But in fact, Kreutzer's etudes contain both basic and advanced technical material and are equally useful for students and artists. We know that Joachim and Flesch never gave up playing them to keep their technique flexible. Even a virtuoso like Wieniawski used them regularly and once said, "These etudes are much more difficult than most violinists assume!"

Only those familiar with Kreutzer's concertos know that many of his etudes are mainly elaborations of passages in the concertos. Sometimes it is difficult to tell which came first—the etude or the concerto. Kreutzer's inventiveness in creating idiomatic violin passages did not go unnoticed: a few point directly toward Beethoven's Violin Concerto. Obviously, Beethoven was quite familiar with the French treatment of the violin; and though not above "borrowing" some idiomatic traits from Kreutzer, Viotti, and Rode, Beethoven transformed them from mere "display" material to the embellishments of great musical ideas.[6]

Pierre (Marie François de Sales) Baillot

Pierre Baillot (1771–1842) was the third member of the triumvirate guarding Viotti's tradition. In contrast to Rode and Kreutzer, Baillot had no early plans for a musical career. As a boy he showed talent for the violin, but his father—a lawyer—discouraged music as a profession and preferred to give him a broad education. In 1782, the eleven-year-old Baillot heard Viotti in Paris and carried away a lifelong impression, but there is no evidence that he became his pupil. The following

Pierre Rode,
Viotti's greatest disciple

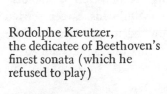

Rodolphe Kreutzer,
the dedicatee of Beethoven's
finest sonata (which he
refused to play)

Pierre (Marie François
de Sales) Baillot
introduced Beethoven's
Violin Concerto in Paris.

year, the Baillot family moved to Italy where Pierre was able to continue his violin studies under the guidance of a Nardini student. The next few years were spent in travel as secretary to an aristocratic patron.

In 1791, Baillot returned to Paris and entered the Viotti circle. Obviously he was a solid violinist, for Viotti placed him in the first violin section of the Théâtre de Monsieur. This was the season when Kreutzer and Rode aroused public attention with their brilliant performances, while Baillot was still an orchestra violinist, a position that may have discouraged him, for he resigned after five months and entered the Ministry of Finance. However, he remained in touch with Viotti and was able to absorb the master's style without actually taking lessons. The personal contact came to a temporary halt when Viotti left for London in 1792, but they remained friends through life and whenever Viotti visited Paris, Baillot was at his side.

After serving twenty months in the army, Baillot turned to music as his chosen profession. He undertook further theory studies, appeared as soloist in a Viotti concerto and, in 1795, was appointed to the newly established Conservatoire. It was to be a long and fruitful career—he remained on the faculty until 1842 and became one of the foremost violin pedagogues of his time. He also won high recognition as a soloist, orchestra leader, and chamber music player. While his career started comparatively late and developed slowly, it proved to be more durable: during the 1820s, when his two colleagues Rode and Kreutzer had already withdrawn from active playing, Baillot was at the height of his fame.

Baillot represented a rather new type of performer—the interpretative violinist. That is, he took interest in interpreting the works of various composers and style periods, in contrast to other virtuosos, who limited their public performances to their own works. Baillot studied the violin classics of the eighteenth century, played the quartets of Haydn and Mozart, and performed the modern music of his time—that of Beethoven, Cherubini, Reicha, Spohr, and Mendelssohn. His much-admired versatility was attested to by Fétis:

> . . . a rare, I should say unique, talent which permitted him to adopt as many manners of playing as there were styles in the music he performed. . . . Baillot as quartet player was more than a violinist: he was a poet.[1]

Likewise, his expressive manner of playing was praised by Karl Amenda, who wrote to his friend Beethoven,

What a mighty instrument is the violin when it speaks through the soul of Baillot. Not since I heard you play at Zmeskall's the last time, was I ever so shaken by a mortal as I was by Baillot.[2]

In 1805 Baillot went to Russia, passing through Vienna on the way. Here he played for Beethoven "in great embarrassment," as he himself admitted. But he carried away a lasting admiration for Beethoven and became his foremost advocate and interpreter in France.

Baillot was forced by the Napoleonic Wars to prolong his stay in Russia until 1808; he spent most of the three years in Moscow as leader of a professional string quartet. He declined to become successor to Rode in St. Petersburg, and the two French violinists (who were old-time friends) returned together to Paris in 1808. On January 17, 1809, Baillot reintroduced himself to the Parisian public and—unlike Rode, who had been criticized upon his return—he was praised as having grown artistically during his absence. A lonely dissent was printed in distant Leipzig, written by a Parisian correspondent:

> Now people try to arouse true fanaticism for him which is ridiculous; some of his students put him even above Viotti and Mestrino. . . . Baillot's bow is excellent and controlled, but his tone is not always agreeable because he tries to give it too much thickness. . . . He has much precision but little nimbleness. . . . He has no more expressivity than most Parisian violinists who play continually on the same dynamic level.[3]

While Baillot was a true representative of Viotti's "bold and emphatic style," he lacked the grace and charm that made Rode's playing so ingratiating. But this was counterbalanced by his serious musicianship, fiery intensity, and exploratory zeal. With Rode in self-imposed retirement, Lafont in far-away Russia, and Kreutzer incapacitated by a broken arm, Baillot had no competitors in Paris and quickly regained his preeminent position.

In 1814 Baillot realized his most ambitious project: he established regular chamber music concerts in Paris. The public response was apathetic, as we can gather from this report, written in 1817:

> Quartets are not popular at all in Paris. Baillot, at present the idol and one of the most finished players, gives a subscription series during the winter for an audience of fifty people; that is all one can gather in this colossal city for this type of music.[4]

Baillot encountered particular resistance when he tried to introduce Beethoven's late quartets. Berlioz tells us about a concert in 1829, when the Baillot Quartet played Beethoven's String Quartet Op. 131:

> About 200 persons were in the hall listening religiously. After a few minutes, the audience grew restless; people began to talk, each telling his neighbor of his increasing discomfort and boredom. Finally, unable to stand such weariness of spirit, nine tenths of the audience got up and left, complaining aloud that the music was unbearable, incomprehensible, ridiculous. . . . Silence was at last restored . . . and the quartet was concluded. Thereupon the voice of condemnation broke out again. Mr Baillot was accused of making fools of the public by presenting extravagant nonsense.[5]

Baillot was philosophical about it—"It is not enough that the performer should be thoroughly prepared for the public's sake. The public should be just as well prepared for what it is about to hear."[6]

We gain a vivid picture of Baillot through the letters of Mendelssohn. In 1825, the sixteen-year-old Mendelssohn visited Paris for the first time and brought his new Piano Quartet Op. 3 to Baillot's soirée, where it was sightread on the spot. The composer wrote home,

> At first, Baillot seemed absent-minded, even negligent, but then he caught fire at a certain place in the first movement, and he played that movement and the following Adagio with great vigor and very well. But then came the Scherzo. Obviously he liked it right away and began to drive the tempo. . . . I could barely follow, it became crazier, faster, and louder. . . . As soon as we finished the movement, he said, *"encore une fois ce morceau."* . . . Finally, in the Finale, all hell broke loose . . . Baillot tore into the strings so that I was frightened by my own quartet.[7]

When Mendelssohn returned to Paris in 1831, Baillot played several of his chamber works—the Octet, the String Quartet Op. 12, among others—and the composer was delighted:

> The man plays beautifully. . . . To hear my E-flat Quartet [Op. 12] performed by Baillot and his Quartet gave me the greatest joy; he attacked it with fire and enthusiasm. . . . Baillot played my Octet in his class, and if there is anyone in the world to play it, it is he. He was so extraordinary as I never heard him before, and also Urhan, Norblin, and the others, they all hit into it with furor and rage.[8]

Mendelssohn also enjoyed playing Bach sonatas with Baillot; he particularly remembered the beautiful rich sound that Baillot drew on the G-string.

More matter-of-fact and objective is the evaluation of the German violinist Spohr, who spent two months in Paris in 1820–21. Praising Lafont as the best French violinist, he found Baillot "almost as perfect" and appreciated the fact that "besides his own compositions he plays almost all those of ancient and modern times." He added,

> Baillot played all these works with the most perfect purity, and with the expression that is peculiar to his manner. His expression, nevertheless, seemed to me more artificial than natural . . . and has the appearance of mannerism. His bow-stroke is skillful and rich in shades of expression, but not so free as Lafont's, and therefore his tone is not as beautiful . . . and the mechanical process of the up- and down-stroke of the bow is too audible.[9]

At the time Spohr wrote those lines, Baillot approached his fiftieth year and was about to enter his most active and successful decade. In 1821 he was named *violon solo* of the Grand Opéra, a post once filled by Rode and Kreutzer, and for a time he directed the revived *Concerts spirituels*. In 1825 he also joined the royal orchestra as solo violinist. Despite his many obligations, he never neglected his class at the Conservatoire.

A high point in Baillot's career was undoubtedly the first Parisian performance of Beethoven's Violin Concerto on March 23, 1828, during the inaugural season of the *Société des Concerts du Conservatoire*. The success was such that the concerto was repeated the same season. One must remember that the Beethoven concerto—after its indifferent Vienna premiere in 1806—had fallen into near-oblivion. The performance was a genuine resurrection.

Baillot performed a similar service for Beethoven's Sonata Op. 47, the one dedicated to and maligned by Kreutzer. Baillot played it on November 24, 1834, with Ferdinand Hiller at the piano, in the presence of Cherubini, Meyerbeer, and Chopin. (Kreutzer had died three years previous.) The *Gazette* musicale printed a letter to the editor, speaking of the "indescribable joy of admiration and enthusiasm" of those present, and adding, "There is only one Baillot in this world . . . the prince of French violinists."[10]

That same year, 1834, saw the publication of the long-awaited *L'Art du violon*, Baillot's monumental violin method. As far back as 1802, he was linked with Rode and Kreutzer as coauthor of a *Méthode de violon*, commissioned by the Conservatoire; actually, Baillot wrote the text while Rode and Kreutzer contributed the exercises. Now, after the death of his two colleagues, Baillot felt justified to bring out his own *Art of the Violin*, which represents the sum-total of French violin playing based on, but not limited to, the Viotti tradition. By coincidence, the German master Louis Spohr published his *Violinschule* about the same time, in 1831. Both works appeared at a juncture—the meteoric rise of Paganini outside of Italy. Neither Baillot nor Spohr was willing to yield to the fascination of that super-virtuoso. In fact, both Baillot and Spohr detested Paganini's "tricks" and made no secret of their contempt. Yet, neither could prevent the young generation of violinists on both sides of the Rhine from succumbing to the witchery of this novel approach to violin technique. Paganini's Twenty-four Caprices were published in 1820, yet it took his personal appearances in central and northern Europe between 1828 and 1834 to convince his confreres that he was no myth.

The French violinists, so carefully trained in the somewhat inbred and sheltered Viotti tradition, were forced to raise their sights after hearing Paganini. It speaks for the strength of the Conservatoire that it survived Paganini's impact. A new generation of Paris-trained violinists emerged, still centered on the Conservatoire, who combined established values with the new technical level of Paganini. For Baillot himself it was too late to adapt, even if he had wanted to; but some of his best students caught and tamed the new spirit of virtuosity. Foremost among them were François Habeneck and Charles de Bériot, who in turn taught Alard and Vieuxtemps.

François Habeneck

François Habeneck was trained as a violinist but rose to prominence as a conductor.[1] He was one of the early violinist-conductors who emerged from the ranks of the orchestra to assume leadership of their fellow players. Though conducting became his main career, Habeneck never abandoned the violin, and taught at the Conservatoire for over twenty years. Among his successful students was the excellent Delphin Alard, who in turn taught the great Pablo de Sarasate.

Habeneck's first teacher was his father, a German-born band musician who played many instruments. In 1800, the nineteen-year-old Habeneck entered Baillot's class at the Conservatoire and was awarded first prize in 1804. He gained his first orchestral experience in the student orchestra of the Conservatoire. Soon he demonstrated his ability to conduct, and in 1806 was put in full charge of that ensemble. It was a youthful, highly skilled group, which gave remarkable concerts under the modest designation of Public Exercises. Under Habeneck, the programs displayed new initiatives: he conducted the first Paris performance of Beethoven's First Symphony in 1807, sightread the Second, and attempted the *Eroica* in 1811. His youthful enthusiasm for Beethoven remained with him throughout, and he was the driving force behind the ultimate recognition of that composer in Paris.

In the meantime, Habeneck earned a living as an orchestral violinist, first in the pit of the Opéra-comique, then at the Grand Opéra, where he had a long and honorable career. Eventually he rose to assistant concertmaster and, in 1818, to principal violinist. He also belonged to the Opéra's conducting staff, subordinate to Kreutzer, the chief conductor. In 1818, Habeneck was put in charge of the revived *Concerts spirituels*, given at the opera house during Easter Week. Here he conducted several works of Beethoven, including the Second Symphony, despite Kreutzer's opposition.

When Viotti's directorship faltered in 1821, Habeneck was called to the rescue. Finally, in 1824, Habeneck was named to the highest post—chief conductor—and served until 1846, presiding during a period of great brilliance. Among his detractors was Berlioz, at the time a rising young composer and sharp-tongued critic, whose *Memoirs* contain some scurrilous tales about Habeneck. They must be taken with a grain of salt; actually, Habeneck volunteered to conduct some of Berlioz's earlier works, but apparently grew disenchanted with him.

Habeneck's most important achievement, however, was the founding of a concert association consisting of prize-winning alumni of the Paris Conservatoire. Named *Société des Concerts du Conservatoire*, this meritorious group was an unsalaried cooperative,* since all the members had paying jobs with opera and theater orchestras. Under Habeneck's direction, the inaugural concert was given on March 9, 1828, opening with Beethoven's *Eroica*. Concerts were given every two weeks, on Sunday afternoons, during the spring season; the success surpassed all expectations. Habeneck's chief objective was to acquaint the Parisians with the works of Beethoven, which was not an easy task. In the words of Berlioz,

---

* At the end of each season, the surplus was divided among the performers.

Not the least of Habeneck's troubles was the steady under-current of opposition from French and Italian composers, who regarded the whole idea with malicious and ill-concealed dis-approval. They had no desire to see official homage paid to a German [Beethoven] whose works seemed to them misbegot-ten monstrosities and yet at the same time a threat to their own style of composition.[2]

Thus, Habeneck laid the foundation for a veritable Beethoven "cult" in Paris. For twenty years he presided over the Conservatoire con-certs; by the time he stepped down on April 10, 1848, he had conducted 186 performances, and there was hardly a program without a Beethoven work. The excellence of the Conservatoire orchestra became famous all over Europe, and particularly the Beethoven interpretations were praised by such exacting musicians as Mendelssohn and Richard Wagner.

A flattering tribute was paid to Habeneck by a fellow violinist— Paganini. The legendary virtuoso had arrived in Paris in February 1831, and went to hear Habeneck conduct at the Conservatoire. He was deeply impressed. During March and April 1831, Paganini gave twelve concerts at the Paris Opéra, and Habeneck conducted the accompany-ing orchestra. Paganini, notoriously difficult to please, sent Habeneck a flattering note of thanks: "Only in Paris did I find the best orchestra in Europe—one that presented my music in the way I imagined it should sound—an orchestra that knew how to accompany me per-fectly."[3] It is said that among the professors of the Conservatoire, Habe-neck was alone in attempting to penetrate Paganini's technique by play-ing his Caprices. In fact, Habeneck was considered a "brilliant violinist" by the severe Spohr, though a bit coarse in tone and bow stroke.

Habeneck summarized his teaching experience in a useful *Méthode théorique et pratique de violon* (published c. 1835), which has a curious feature: it incorporates the facsimile of an extensive sketch for a violin method by none other than Viotti. Judging by the feeble handwriting, Viotti had jotted down these ideas in his last years. After Viotti's death, his heirs entrusted Habeneck to sift through Viotti's posthumous manu-scripts. The projected violin method was a fragment and could not be published separately; to salvage it and bring it to public attention, Habeneck included it in his own work. As it happened, Viotti's fleeting thoughts were no major revelation and attracted no attention until they were rediscovered in the 1920s.[4] It is interesting to note that Viotti at-tached great importance to the study of scales, considering the playing of a perfect scale the most difficult of all achievements. More than a century later, two of the greatest violinists of our time, Ysaÿe and Heifetz, expressed similar ideas.

Despite a career as a conductor, Habeneck remained a violinist at heart. He taught a violin class at the Conservatoire from 1825 to 1846, training such first-rate violinists as Alard and Léonard. He conducted with a violin bow, operas as well as symphonies, the latter from a first-violin part instead of a score. During the early years of the Conservatoire orchestra, he often played along with the violins, especially at rehearsals. As *primus inter pares*, he enforced complete uniformity of bowings among all string players of the orchestra, a "phalanx of bows plying up and down," as one English observer remarked with slight discomfort.[5] As violin soloist, Habeneck performed only rarely at the Conservatoire concerts, for example, during the first season, when he played a Fantasy of his own composition. His Stradivari violin, a late model dated 1736, is now at the Royal Academy of Music in London.

Charles Lafont

Who was this Charles Lafont, who had the temerity to challenge Paganini to a musical contest in 1816? The story of his "defeat" pursued Lafont until he could bear it no longer and published a rebuttal in 1830, giving his own version of the story. It redressed the balance, but it did not change the judgment of history by which Paganini is immortal and Lafont is forgotten.

A few words about Lafont's career. Born in 1781 in Paris, he was a child prodigy and gave successful concerts at the age of eleven. His first teacher was his uncle, the violinist Bertheaume, who prepared him for Kreutzer. But the experience was not altogether a happy one, as Fétis says:

> Dissatisfied with the style of his master [Kreutzer] which did not sympathize with his own, Lafont joined the school of Rode, which seemed appropriate for the development of his own qualities, combining grace, purity, elegance, and charm . . . which rendered him a perfect master of his art.[1]

In 1802 Lafont was acclaimed at the *Concerts français* in Paris. The unbiased Reichardt compared him to his teacher—"Lafont possesses such a rare perfection as one could only expect from Rode."[2] He also developed an attractive voice and was heard occasionally as a singer of French ballads.

While Rode was away in Russia, Lafont endeared himself to the

Parisian public, and by 1808 he was at the height of success. He left for St. Petersburg to succeed Rode at the czarist court, but by 1815 was back in Paris, having somehow survived the Napoleonic invasion of Russia and all the political turmoil. Appointed solo violinist of King Louis XVIII, he left on another concert tour, this time to Italy. In February 1816 Lafont played at La Scala in Milan. This in itself was a challenge to Paganini who, at that time, was immensely popular in his own country, though as yet unknown abroad.

Paganini rushed from Genoa to Milan to hear his famous French colleague. His opinion was, "He plays well, but he does not astonish." A week later, Paganini gave his own concert in Milan to offer—as he put it—his rival a chance to hear him. The next day Lafont invited Paganini to give a joint concert in Milan. This was the historic challenge, actually a highly civilized offer. At first Paganini declined, saying that it would be misinterpreted as a "duel" for supremacy, inflamed by the intensely nationalist public. But Lafont insisted, and Paganini's friends (among them Rossini) persuaded him to accept. What happened at the concert has been told with many embellishments, mostly favoring Paganini's side; Paganini apparently improvised at the concert, adding octaves, thirds, and sixths so that the "poor Frenchman became utterly confused and was unable to play as well as he could."[3] Paganini's own story is somewhat different and actually quite flattering to Lafont:

> I allowed Lafont to arrange the program. In order to fight with equal weapons, I waived the right to play on a single string. I began with one of my concertos,* then Lafont followed with a substantial work, and after this we played Kreutzer's Double Concerto, which Rode and Kreutzer had once played in Paris together. Where the two violins played together, I held strictly note for note to the written text, so that Lafont was ready to wager that we both belonged to the same school. But in the solo passages I gave free rein to my imagination and played in the Italian manner that is really natural to me. True, this did not altogether please my friendly rival, who next played a set of variations [on a Russian theme], and I closed the concert with a similar composition of my own [*Witches' Dance*]. Lafont could perhaps produce a more powerful tone than I, but it was evident from the applause

---

* Here Paganini's memory failed him: he did not play his own concerto, but a Concerto in E major by Kreutzer. Lafont followed with one of his own concertos, after which they played Kreutzer's *Symphonie concertante* in F major for two violins and orchestra.

that I did not suffer in comparison. I do not hesitate to acknowledge Lafont as a great and highly distinguished artist.[4]

This dispassionate account confirmed an eyewitness report by a German
critic, published in 1816:

> A few days ago Paganini and Lafont gave a concert together.
> . . . There was a great rush for seats. Everyone wanted to wit-
> ness the duel between the two artists and, as might have been
> foreseen, the result showed that, when it comes to artificiality,
> to technical mastery, Paganini is without peer, Lafont being
> far behind him in this respect. Both, however, are about equal
> when it comes to beauty of playing, with the odds perhaps on
> the side of Lafont. Both artists received extraordinary ap-
> plause.[5]

Nevertheless, distorted versions describing Lafont's "defeat" continued to circulate until he published his own account in 1830, just as
Paganini was preparing to conquer Paris and London:

> Far from being beaten by him . . . I obtained a success the
> more flattering as I was a stranger in the country and I had
> no other support than my talent. I played with Paganini the
> concerted symphony of Kreutzer in F-major. For several days
> previously to the concert we rehearsed this symphony together
> and with the greatest of care. . . . It was performed by us
> as it had rehearsed and with no change whatsoever; and we
> obtained an equal success in the passages executed together
> or separately. . . . I was not beaten by Paganini, nor he by
> me. On all occasions I have taken pleasure in rendering hom-
> age to his great talent; but I have never said that he was the
> first violinist in the world. I have not done such an injustice
> to the celebrated men, Kreutzer, Rode, Baillot, and Habeneck.
> And I declare now as I have always done, that the French
> school is the first in the world for the violin.[6]

This reaffirmation of his French heritage does honor to Lafont, but
in truth the "celebrated men" he mentioned were no match for Paganini (only Baillot was still active as a violinist), and Lafont himself was
past his prime. It took some time before a new generation—Bériot,
Vieuxtemps, Alard—could face the challenge of Paganini.

The encounter with Paganini did not hamper Lafont's career, nor
did it diminish his self-confidence. Apparently, Lafont and Paganini remained on speaking terms. Their paths crossed occasionally, as in

Baden-Baden in 1830; "Lafont embraced me," Paganini noted in a letter, but added with some malice that Lafont and his family "had to pay for their tickets to hear my concert."

When Spohr heard Lafont in 1821, he placed him above all French violinists of the day, including Baillot and Habeneck:

> In his play, Lafont combines beauty of tone, the greatest purity, power, and grace, and he would be a perfect violinist if, with these qualifications, he possessed depth of feeling. . . . Although he dresses up his slow movements with many elegant and pretty ornaments, yet he remains somewhat cold.[7]

Lafont's habit of practicing a concerto for a year before playing it in public puzzled Spohr—"I cannot imitate him, and cannot even understand how . . . it is to be done without losing every vestige of real art, in such a mechanical mode. . . ."

As a composer, Lafont had no particular profile and his concertos are academic. But in his shorter pieces, notably the *Airs variés*, he shows ingenuity in writing idiomatic and brilliant technical passages for the violin, which prepare the ground for the elegant virtuosity of Bériot. Looking at his runs in thirds and dazzling staccatos, one begins to understand his self-assurance in challenging Paganini, though he lacked the latter's wizardry. Lafont often collaborated with prominent pianists (among them Moscheles, Kalkbrenner, and Herz) in writing joint compositions, so-called *Duos concertants*, where each virtuoso is responsible for his part. In a piece such as the Duo in C minor "composed" with Moscheles, the pianist seems to have contributed the Beethovenian spirit, while Lafont's share must have been minor.

Lafont continued his traveling career until late in life. On a concert tour in southern France in August 1839, he lost his life when the carriage overturned. He was buried in Paris with great solemnity.

NICOLÒ PAGANINI

"Paganini begins where our reason stops."
—*Giacomo Meyerbeer*

BY HIS TECHNICAL WIZARDRY and personal magnetism, Paganini dominates the history of the violin as its foremost virtuoso. His impact was so overpowering that an entire generation of Romantic musicians became aware of the significance of virtuosity as an important element in art.

Paganini's concert career spanned forty-three years, from his first appearance at a church in Genoa in 1794 to his last charity concert in Turin in 1837. Yet he did not venture outside of Italy until the age of forty-five. For decades he was content to give concerts in his native Italy, where he towered above all his competitors. Foreign violinists came to Italy in the hope of hearing that mysterious rival—Spohr and Lafont in 1816, Lipinski in 1818. Reviews of Paganini's successes began to appear in German and English journals, proclaiming, "His method of performance has no equal." The publication, in 1820, of his Twenty-four Caprices (proudly dedicated "To the Artists") aroused a certain incredulous curiosity. Count Metternich, the great Austrian statesman, heard Paganini in 1818 in Rome and urged him to visit Vienna. Yet it took Paganini another ten years to realize this plan: in 1828 he set out to conquer northern Europe. And conquer he did—Vienna, Berlin, Paris, London were at his feet, showering him with acclaim and gold. The apotheosis was as brilliant as it was brief. Within six years he amassed a fortune and established a reputation second to none. Then the decline began: the public grew tired, intrigues flared up, his health deteriorated, the playing began to falter. By the mid-1830s, his performance career had virtually ended. Yet he maintained his interest in the violin until his death.

175

Paganini's life story has received many romanticized treatments. Wild rumors circulated during his lifetime—about years spent in prison because of an amorous affair, with only the violin as companion; as the strings broke one by one, he continued to play on the remaining G-string and acquired that famed virtuosity on one string. His weak rebuttals did nothing to stop the gossip, and perhaps he even welcomed the additional publicity. But after a while, layers of fiction began to obscure his true life as an artist, his remarkable accomplishments as an innovator and a gifted composer. Recently new documentation has come to light, and his compositions—long buried in private collections—have become accessible. A new evaluation of Paganini as a composer has become possible, as well as the verification of Paganini's autobiographical statements.

Nicolò Paganini was born in Genoa on October 27, 1782. His father was a musical amateur ("not without talent," in the words of his famous son) who played the mandolin. The family was poor, but not impoverished, and the father provided for his five children. The two sons, Carlo and Nicolò, were taught music by their father. (Carlo became a mediocre violinist and served in the Lucca orchestra side by side with Nicolò.)

Nicolò began to play the mandolin at age five and the violin at seven. The father was a harsh taskmaster; the boy was forced to practice from morning till night and was deprived of food whenever his diligence faltered. His gentle and pious mother gave him spiritual support and encouragement; in her dreams she saw an angel predicting a great career for little Nicolò. He remained tenderly attached to his mother throughout her life.

When Nicolò outgrew the paternal teaching, he became a student of an orchestral violinist named Cervetto. Soon, the boy aroused the interest of Genoa's leading violinist, Costa. Years later, Paganini remembered "with pleasure the painstaking care of worthy old Costa . . . but his principles often seemed unnatural to me and I showed no inclination to adopt his method of bowing." Nevertheless, Costa was proud of his talented student and presented him to the public: on May 26, 1794, the eleven-year-old Nicolò played at church during mass and aroused "universal admiration." About that time, the violinist Duranowski visited Genoa—a virtuoso of shallow brilliance and master of a multitude of technical tricks. Young Nicolò was impressed and admitted years later that "many of my most brilliant and popular effects were derived to a considerable extent" from Duranowski.

Nicolò's progress was so prodigious that he was taken to Parma, where he could study with Alessandro Rolla. To raise funds for the journey, Nicolò gave a benefit concert on July 31, 1795. On that occasion, he may have played his first composition, the violin variations on "*La Carmagnole*," a French revolutionary song then very timely. (The manuscript, considered lost, has recently been rediscovered.)

When father and son Paganini arrived in Parma, they found Maestro Rolla ill in bed. While waiting, Nicolò noticed a manuscript of Rolla's latest violin concerto; casually, the boy picked up a violin and sightread the music with such perfection that Rolla, rushing out of bed, exclaimed, "I can teach you nothing; in God's name go and see Paer, here you're wasting your time."[1] The implication was that Nicolò had nothing to learn as violinist but should study composition with Ferdinando Paer, then active in Parma. Paer, however, was busy composing an opera, and referred the boy to his own teacher, Maestro Ghiretti, for an intense course in counterpoint. Somewhat later, Paer took charge of Paganini's lessons in composition. During his one-year stay in Parma, young Paganini gave a concert and also played for the sovereigns. Late in 1796 he returned to Genoa, remaining until 1799.

These were years of musical exploration, as he later recalled: he "composed different music and worked continually at different problems of his own invention." He also became interested in the guitar and mastered it completely. A meeting with the eminent Parisian violinist Rodolphe Kreutzer, who played in Genoa in 1796 and 1797, proved stimulating; Nicolò received much encouragement from the older master. Another influence was Paganini's discovery of the half-forgotten *L'arte del violino* by Locatelli, published more than half a century earlier. Locatelli's volume contained twenty-four caprices for solo violin which, in Paganini's words, "opened up a world of new ideas and devices that never had the merited success because of excessive difficulties." Paganini paid tribute to Locatelli's memory by quoting Locatelli's Caprice No. 7 in his own Caprice No. 1.*

In 1801 Paganini—barely nineteen years old—finally succeeded in freeing himself from the oppressive paternal tutelage: he traveled to Lucca to participate in the annual festival, accompanied by his older brother Carlo as chaperon, and simply decided not to return home. For the next eight years, Lucca became his base of operation: he was appointed leader of the new National Orchestra and gave successful concerts in northern Italy. Most of the money he earned he gambled away, even going so far as to pawn his violin. Once he appeared for a concert

* See example on p. 92.

in Livorno without his instrument. A wealthy amateur lent him a Guarnerius and refused to take it back after the concert, exclaiming, "I do not want to profane the instrument after Paganini played on it."

Conditions in Lucca changed drastically in 1805 when Princess Elise, a sister of Napoleon, was installed as ruling sovereign. Soon the sleepy little city was transformed into a glittering capital. The princess was young, art-loving, and attractive; she was also ambitious and headstrong. Before long she discovered Paganini's talent and he was made solo violinist of the court. There are strong indications that he was romantically linked with her. As for his musical duties, he described them dryly:

> I had to conduct the opera whenever the reigning family attended, play three times a week at court, and give a big concert every fortnight at the formal soirees, but Princess Elise did not always attend or else did not remain all through the concert because my harmonics irritated her nerves.[2]

For one of these concerts Paganini prepared a musical novelty which he called *Scena amorosa*. "I entered the salon with only two strings on my violin—the E-string (representing the lady) and the G-string (portraying the man). The novelty was eminently successful." Asked whether he could play on a single string, he composed a sonata for the G-string which he named *Napoleon* in honor of the emperor's birthday. "This was the beginning of my predilection for the G-string. . . . I progressed from day to day until I had completely mastered this style of playing."[3]

As time went on, Paganini grew tired of being a courtier. His behavior became increasingly independent, which annoyed the princess. In 1808 when the government was moved to Florence, the court orchestra was dissolved. Paganini left Lucca in December of 1809 and embarked on the career of a traveling virtuoso.

During the next three years, Paganini was heard in many Italian cities, large and small, and developed his skill in mesmerizing an audience. Quite often he humored his provincial public and engaged in "buffoonery unworthy of his art and his talent," as one French observer wrote in 1810.[4] Even his friends urged him to drop the role of *"grande pagliaccio"* of the violin. By 1813 he felt ready to make his debut in Milan, the cultural center of Italy.

For this occasion he wrote a new piece which was to become a favorite of his repertoire—*Le streghe* (*Witches' Dance*), variations on a popular ballet tune of the day. His first concert at La Scala, on October

29, 1813, was triumphant, and within the next two months he performed eleven more times. A very favorable review appeared in a Leipzig musical journal:

> In a sense, Paganini is without question the foremost and greatest violinist in the world. His playing is truly *inexplicable*. He performs certain passages, leaps, and double stops that have never been heard from *any* violinist.[5]

On the negative side, the critic observed that "in matters of simple beautiful playing, one can find a number of violinists as good as he is" and that he played a concerto by Kreutzer "not at all in the spirit of the composer."

The success in Milan propelled Paganini into national prominence. Yet he felt hesitant to face the connoisseurs abroad. He declined to play for Spohr in Venice in 1816, apologizing that "his style was calculated to impress the mass public." Spohr formed an opinion on the basis of hearsay, writing in his *Autobiography*,* "The very thing by which he fascinates the crowd debases him to a mere charlatan, and does not compensate for that in which he is utterly wanting—a grand tone, a long bow-stroke, and a tasteful execution."[6]

The notion that Paganini's success was based on "charlatanry" was a widespread misconception among foreign violinists. His contest with Lafont in 1816† proved that even the greatest violinist of France was no threat to him.

But in order to succeed in the capitals of Europe, Paganini had to prove that he was more than a technical wizard: he was expected to demonstrate his creativity by playing his own concertos. Until then he had relied mainly on a repertoire of selected concertos by Viotti, Kreutzer, and Rode. Although he had written music since boyhood, little was published until 1820. In fact, he withheld his major works from publication, for fear that his competitors might steal his thunder. All his concertos and virtuoso pieces remained in manuscript during his lifetime, with the exception of the famous Twenty-four Caprices.

Paganini composed his earliest (unnumbered) concerto around 1815, but discarded it soon after. In 1819, he performed what he called Concerto No. 1, which has remained one of his most popular compositions. Two additional concertos followed in 1826—No. 2 in B minor (with the famous *Clochette* rondo) and No. 3 in E major. This gave

---

* See p. 184 for Spohr's later opinion on Paganini.
† See pp. 172–73.

him a solid repertoire to take on his foreign tour. But he was in no hurry. For the time being he preferred to exploit his growing fame in Italy, which he crisscrossed with enormous success. An important stage in his career was Rome, where he appeared for the first time in 1819, followed by Naples and Palermo. He displayed yet another talent in 1821, when his friend Rossini called on him as a last-minute replacement to conduct the premiere of his new opera. In 1822 and again in 1826, Paganini fell seriously ill; each time his recovery was slow and left him looking cadaverous. In fact, his physique was not strong, and his many bouts with serious maladies were aggravated by inept medical treatment.

While concertizing in northern Italy in 1824, Paganini met Antonia Bianchi, a young singer. They had a liaison that lasted until 1828, and in 1825 she bore him a son, Achille, to whom he was deeply attached. Antonia Bianchi was, perhaps, the most lasting relationship in Paganini's stormy and adventurous love life (he blamed his "hot Genovese blood"). Mother and son accompanied him on his first trip abroad. They set out on March 6, 1828, crossing the Alps in a specially built carriage, and arrived in Vienna ten days later.

The focal points of Paganini's European tours were Vienna, Berlin, Paris, and London. His meteoric appearance had an unprecedented impact: he not only obscured every living violinist but threw pianists, composers, and critics into ecstasy. "He forms a class by himself," reported the *Times* of London.

As a rule, Paganini performed with the assistance of an orchestra and one or several guest singers. (The solo recital with piano accompaniment was as yet unknown.) Within a program, Paganini usually appeared three times, playing a concerto and two shorter selections. His debut concert in Vienna can be considered a typical program:*

[March 29, 1928, Grosser Redoutensaal]

1. Beethoven, *Fidelio* Overture
2. Paganini, Concerto No. 2 in B minor
3. Paer, Aria (Miss Bianchi)
4. Paganini, *Sonate militaire* (on the G-string)
5. Rossini, Rondo (Miss Bianchi)
6. Paganini-Rossini, Variations on *Cenerentola*

Every concert required at least one lengthy orchestral rehearsal. The handwritten orchestra parts were distributed just prior to the rehearsal

---

* At times, his solo pieces were placed *between* the movements of a classical symphony.

and collected immediately afterwards to forestall any unauthorized copying. To accompany such a willful artist as Paganini was a difficult task, and many a local conductor must have been driven to despair. Paganini is known to have turned to the orchestra to conduct the first ritornello of his concerto (that is, the introductory tutti), urging the players to play vigorously. During rehearsals he demanded utmost accuracy. Paganini was sensitive to the quality of the accompaniment, as is evident in his letter of thanks to Habeneck and the Paris Opéra orchestra.* In smaller towns it must have been an ordeal.

Paganini was a careful bookkeeper (people called him avaricious) and he kept accurate accounts of his itineraries and concert receipts. Ticket prices were usually doubled for his concerts (to the point where there was a protest action in London) and the receipts were unprecedented. Paganini's success grew like an avalanche; he became a legend in his own day. It was more than technical wizardry that attracted the masses: there was a demoniac quality as well as an enticing poetry in his playing. His repertoire consisted almost exclusively of his own inimitable compositions and even when he performed an occasional concerto by Rode or Kreutzer, he transformed it in his own image. He played everything from memory (unusual for his day), lending his performance an improvisational, devil-may-care quality. Everything was planned to impress the audience: the prolonged wait before he entered ghostlike through the wings, the emaciated—almost cadaverous—figure clad in black, the immobile face framed by long black locks, the awkward bows to acknowledge the applause. "Paganini represents the turning point of virtuosity," wrote Schumann, meaning that his technique was not mere effect but an integral artistic ingredient. As much admired as his technical mastery was his poetic communicativeness; the sensitive Schubert said after hearing Paganini, "I heard an angel sing in the Adagio." When trying to compare him to "conventional" violinists, a perceptive listener was at a loss for words: "He really doesn't play the violin—he doesn't have the tone (or tones) of Rode, of Duranowski, . . . of Giornovicchi—but he actually talks. . . ."[7]

Rich and poor flocked to his concerts, not once but repeatedly, hence the unprecedented number of concerts Paganini gave in the capital cities: fourteen in Vienna, eleven in Berlin, twelve in Paris, fifteen in London—sometimes as often as once or twice a week. His repertoire had to be stretched, certain works had to be repeated, but the public did not tire of hearing him. Toward the end of each concert series the

* See p. 170.

receipts began to fall, and he knew when to stop. Not all his concerts were given at his own risk and expense: sometimes he signed contracts with opera houses (as in Paris or Berlin), guaranteeing him a good orchestra and a large percentage of the receipts. At times he gave "half concerts"—his performance was interpolated between acts of an opera, or between two one-act plays as an intermission attraction. At all times he knew how to extract a maximum of profit and publicity for himself. Calculating though he was, he gave himself fully to his musical performances: he played with utter concentration and abandonment, emerging totally wrung out after each concert. He was not a technical automaton, and he had his nights off when passages could misfire. He was, as Heine said, often subject to moods and influences: "I have never heard anyone play better, or for that matter, play worse than Paganini . . . !"[8]

Vienna was an important milestone in Paganini's career. For the first time in his life—and he was by then forty-five years old—he faced a non-Italian audience, and the boundless enthusiasm of the Viennese was a touchstone of his international stature as an artist. The public idolized him, the emperor named him "chamber virtuoso of the court," the City of Vienna awarded him the medal of Saint Salvador. He tested and expanded his repertoire, played his first three concertos and many shorter pieces, including a new composition, Variations on the Austrian National Anthem. At all his concerts (except the last) his assisting artist was his mistress, Antonia Bianchi, who was also well received by the public. But their personal relationship became untenable and they separated in Vienna. After protracted negotiations, Paganini was awarded full custody of their infant son, in exchange for an annuity for Antonia, and for the next twelve years the boy Achille became his father's inseparable traveling companion.

Socially, Paganini enjoyed himself in Vienna: he played at the palace of Count Metternich, attended operas and concerts, played quartets with Viennese musicians, and heard for the first time Beethoven's Seventh Symphony, which moved him to tears. Despite his immense success, Paganini never returned to Vienna, but he left a lasting imprint on Viennese violin playing, which acquired renewed brilliance and bravura. Its best-known representative is Heinrich Wilhelm Ernst, then a young student of Boehm and Mayseder, who soon became the "heir apparent" of Paganini.

Despite their geographic proximity, Prague and Vienna often differed in musical matters, and Prague liked to assert its artistic independence. This may have been why the Bohemian capital gave Paganini such an unfriendly welcome in October of 1828. Perhaps he was not at his best: barely arrived, he had to undergo two painful jawbone operations and all his teeth were removed, which gave his mouth a sunken appearance. After his recovery he gave six concerts, but the critics were cool, even hostile, and Paganini left the city after four months.

However, Paganini gained one influential friend in Prague, Professor Julius Schottky, who received his permission to write a biography. The book appeared in German in 1830, and despite some inaccuracies it has become a valuable source because much of it is based on personal interviews.

Germany offered richer opportunities because it was divided into many independent smaller states; culture was decentralized and the various sovereigns rivaled with each other in patronizing the arts. There were opera houses and orchestras in every capital city, large and small. For two years, Paganini crisscrossed Germany, reaping artistic and financial success. The high point of the first year was the Prussian capital Berlin. Despite its reputation as a cold and sober city, Berlin's enthusiasm equalled that of Vienna. The learned critics tried to explain the phenomenon of Paganini in ecstatic prose. Curiously enough, they attached less importance to his technical feats than to his emotional appeal. "The external elements of his playing, all the seemingly impossible tours de force . . . all these things are merely vehicles. . . . The inward poetry of his imagination, molding the creations before our eyes— this is what captivated the listeners," wrote A. B. Marx.[9] In a similar vein, H. F. Rellstab said, "Never in my whole life have I heard an instrument weep like that . . . I never knew that music contained such sounds! He spoke, he wept, he sang!" And he added more soberly,

> The mighty Spohr, the sweet Polledro, the fiery Lipinski, the elegant Lafont, merely aroused my admiration. Paganini is not himself; rather he is the incarnation of desire, scorn, madness, and burning pain. . . . He often scratches and scrapes quite unexpectedly, as if he were ashamed of having just yielded to a noble or tender emotion. Yet when you are about to turn away in disgust, he has recaptured your soul with a golden thread.[10]

At the time, German Romanticism was in full bloom, and Paganini's mysterious, almost diabolical appearance seemed straight out of the *Tales of Hoffmann*.

Eventually, Paganini visited Cassel where Spohr reigned as music director. The first concert, in May 1830, was poorly attended, the second was crowded. Spohr was a good host, and Paganini was "in very gay spirits, even boisterously so." But in his evaluation of Paganini, Spohr remained cool:

> Paganini's left hand, the purity of his intonation, and his G-string are admirable. In his compositions and his style of interpretation there is a strange mixture of consummate genius, childishness, and lack of taste, so that one is alternately charmed and repelled. In my own case my total impression . . . was by no means satisfying and I have no desire to hear him again.[11]

While in Germany, Paganini spent some five months in Frankfurt-am-Main, one of Germany's four "free cities," where an enlightened citizenry, rather than a ruler, took care of the practical and artistic needs of the population. Paganini, warmly welcomed by the music-loving public, felt at ease in the more democratic atmosphere. He struck up a friendship with Carl Guhr, the director of the municipal orchestra and an excellent violinist. During months of almost daily contact, Guhr observed Paganini's playing at close range and published a series of articles (later summarized in a book) entitled "Paganini's Art of Playing the Violin" (1829–30). It is the first analysis by a professional, doubly valuable because of the personal observation. Guhr stripped Paganini's art of all "supernatural" attributes and tried to be factual, but he did not succeed in explaining the inexplicable. He also wrote down, from memory, one of Paganini's virtuoso compositions, the variations on *Nel cor più non mi sento*, after having heard them played "some twenty or thirty" times.

The two years of concert tours in Germany had brought Paganini rich rewards but ruined his health. Traveling conditions were atrocious: "We would advise anyone who does not have a chest of iron, intestines of copper, and buttocks of platinum to avoid a journey in the ordinary post chaise . . ." wrote a contemporary. Paganini wrapped himself in furs even during the summer months, for fear of catching cold. He was on a strict diet because of his lack of teeth. Barely arrived in a city, he would rush to an orchestral rehearsal during which he was exacting and irritable. At the hotel, hordes of visitors, curiosity seekers, violin dealers, and prodigies would beleaguer his room. After a concert in the evening he was totally exhausted, looking as though he had suffered an epileptic seizure. His ever-present little son had to be cared for and entertained, which Paganini did with infinite patience.

Early in 1831, Paganini's mind was made up: the next goal was Paris. An Italian friend wrote, "If you feel better now—as we all hope—then go at once to Paris in order to surprise, terrify, annihilate those professors who deny the existence of a Paganini. . . ."[12] Had it not been for the unsettled situation in France—there was a revolution in 1830—he would have gone earlier. By 1831 Paris had calmed down and Paganini was ready to face the critics of the Conservatoire. He was confident of success; after all, as far back as 1816 he had outplayed Lafont, France's best violinist.

Paganini's fate in Paris was varied, ranging from initial triumph to ultimate defeat. Within ten days after his arrival on February 24, he signed a lucrative contract with the Opéra: he was to appear twice a week, on Wednesdays and Sundays, with ticket prices doubled. After each of his performances, a ballet brought the evening to a close.

Paganini's Parisian debut took place on Wednesday, March 9, 1831. After his opening piece, the Concerto No. 1, pandemonium broke loose. "His success exceeded the wildest expectations . . . and the connoisseurs shared the opinion of the public," wrote the critic Escudier. They loved his music as much as his performance—"Their stupefaction turned to enthusiasm when the great artist dazzled all present with the wealth of his melodic inspiration." A German visitor, the poet Boerne, who had heard him previously in Frankfurt, reported, "It was a heavenly and a diabolical enthusiasm, I have never seen or heard its like in my life." Castil-Blaze summarized, "He is not a violinist but an artist in the widest sense of the word. . . . No comparison is possible between him and all who have gone before."[13]

The French violinists were not quite ready to accept this verdict. Baillot, the senior master and last survivor of the Viotti school, said to the famous singer Malibran, "Madame, it is miraculous, inconceivable—there is something in his playing that drives one to distraction."[14] Baillot was impressed but not convinced; he covered his ears when he heard the harmonics. Lafont, somewhat younger, published an open letter in defense of the superiority of the French school,* though recognizing Paganini's excellence. But the young generation—among them Alard, Bériot, and Vieuxtemps—listened carefully and absorbed this new spirit of virtuosity. To them Paganini was a revelation, as he was to a young pianist, Franz Liszt, who vowed to become the "Paganini of the piano."

His repertoire in Paris offered one novelty, the Concerto in D minor,

* See p. 173.

known as No. 4, rediscovered in the 1950s. Paganini had composed it in Germany and intended to introduce it in Paris ("I want to 'deflower' it in Paris," he wrote). He played it there on his second concert on March 13, to great approval. "This work exhibits a most original form and contains several highly picturesque effects," wrote the critic Castil-Blaze.[15]

After the eighth Parisian appearance, Paganini wrote to his friend Germi in Italy, "It is impossible to give you an idea of my triumph in Paris." Altogether he gave twelve concerts between March 9 and April 24, including one for charity, and he earned over 165,000 francs—an unprecedented sum.

The stay in Paris ended with a discord: on April 21 Paganini published an open letter protesting the malicious rumor that he had spent many years in prison for a "crime of jealousy." For fifteen years, he wrote, he had tried to silence this calumny . . . but in vain! The denial served only to increase publicity, and a lithograph by Boulanger, *Paganini en prison*, found many buyers. Less than a week later, he left Paris for London.

Paganini's stay in London began with a hostile press campaign against the inflated ticket prices. Accused once again of being greedy, he canceled his first London concert and a new date was set for the debut, June 3, with reduced ticket prices. It was a resounding success, and the penitent *Times* admitted, "He is not only the finest player that ever has existed on that instrument, but he forms a class by himself." It is interesting to note that here again, as in Berlin and in Paris, his technical feats were not considered crucial. We read in the *Times*,

> The difficulty and complexity of the passages . . . do not, however, form that which is most to be admired in him. His genius is displayed in a far greater degree in his slow movements, in which he develops . . . every shade and gradation of feeling. . . . If the instrument could be said to speak and to feel, it does so in his hands.[16]

Paganini's success in London was overwhelming: between June 3 and August 20 he gave fifteen concerts and collected more than ten thousand pounds. But the success was well deserved: the professional musicians were his strongest boosters. Veterans of the orchestra, including the double bass virtuoso Dragonetti, watched his performance with evident amazement. The concertmaster Mori, in mock despair, offered to sell his violin for eighteen pence. The pianist Cramer joked, "Thank Heavens I am not a violinist." *The Athenaeum* wrote with malice, "The arrival of this magician is enough to make the greater part of the fiddling tribe commit suicide."

Following the concert series in London, Paganini went on tour; he gave twenty-two concerts in Ireland, twenty-three in Scotland, and forty-nine in the English provinces. The number of performances is staggering, if one considers his precarious health and the discomfort of travel by horse-drawn carriage during the autumn and winter months. There was also the drudgery of orchestral rehearsals wherever he appeared. At times he tried a piano accompaniment, but he was immediately chastized as being "too cheap" to engage an orchestra. After about 140 public concerts during this ten-month stay in the British Isles, he embarked on March 9, 1832, for Paris, where he had left his little son in "excellent hands."

He found conditions very unfavorable for entertainment: a cholera epidemic raged in Paris and was reaching across the Channel. The wealthy were fleeing to the country; those who remained in the city were fearful and stayed indoors. Unperturbed, Paganini made arrangements to give ten concerts in Paris in March–June, with one a charity affair for the cholera victims. The receipts were smaller than those of the previous year, yet still considerable. The critic Jules Janin wrote,

> I know nothing more solemn than the concerts Paganini gave during the epidemic. One arrived trembling, one listened, one was astonished, one wept. All pain and sadness was suspended; one forgot both death and the fear that is worse than death.[17]

Returning to London, he gave a dozen concerts at Covent Garden (July–August) followed by more in the south of England. The winter of 1832–33 was inactive; he stayed in Paris and did not touch the violin for months. But another English season was planned and he had to prepare. "Not having played the violin for six months, I can't tell you how difficult it is for me to work up the necessary electricity to play," he wrote. Evidently he was less bothered by stiff fingers than by the lack of tension needed to give an exciting performance.

Nevertheless, he was back in harness in the summer of 1833: eight concerts in London, forty-four in the provinces, traveling to thirty-one cities within ten weeks. It was a cruel exertion, made worse by an unfriendly press and mediocre attendance. There were vile personal attacks on him in the papers, picturing him as a greedy miser, though he donated his services to all sorts of charities.

On his return to Paris in November 1833, Paganini suffered a pulmonary hemorrhage. By December 22 he had recovered sufficiently to attend a concert of works by Berlioz. Highly impressed, he asked the young composer to write a work for viola and orchestra.

Nicolò Paganini: "Paganini begins where our reason stops."

I have a marvelous Stradivari viola and should greatly like to play it in public. But I have no music for it. Would you write me a solo? I have no confidence in anyone but you for such a work.[18]

Berlioz was encouraged to sketch *Harold in Italy*, which includes a prominent solo viola. But the part was not prominent enough for Paganini—when he saw the first movement, he objected to all the rests for the soloist. "That's not at all what I want. I'm silent for too long. I must be playing the whole time," he told the composer. Berlioz saw his point, but felt unable to write a concertolike composition, and *Harold* was completed as originally planned. Nevertheless, Paganini did not forget Berlioz, and a few years later, in 1838, presented him with a generous gift of 20,000 francs, after hearing Berlioz conduct a concert of his works. The unexpected generosity of a man generally regarded as avaricious created a furor in Paris, and some people branded it as a fraud, a publicity stunt. Yet the documents prove that the gesture was genuine.

The year 1834 saw the gradual decline of Paganini's international career. He had signed a contract with the impresario Watson, whose pretty daughter Charlotte had ambitions as a singer. The Paganini-Watson tour through the Lowlands was ill-fated, since Paganini had injured a finger and was not at his best. The critics were disappointed, the receipts poor. There followed a disastrous tour in England, beginning in April. A series of six daily concerts in London was initiated; Paganini appeared twice on each program, with the balance filled by vocal soloists, including Miss Watson. There were many empty seats, and a second series was canceled. Moreover, his debut on the viola was received with misgivings. The provinces showed little interest in hearing Paganini and his vocal entourage; Watson lost money and was imprisoned for his debts. Paganini bailed him out and consented to give a benefit concert for Charlotte. However, when the young singer eloped to join Paganini in France, her father sued Paganini for abduction. Eventually the Watsons sailed for America, where Charlotte became quite successful. They kept in touch with Paganini and encouraged him to visit America. He actually booked passage but felt too ill to go.

In September 1834, Paganini was again the victim of vicious attacks in the Parisian press. Embittered, he departed for Genoa—he wanted to be home again. In his six years abroad he had amassed a fortune, but his health was shattered.

Once back in Italy, he recovered quickly. He performed in Genoa, Piacenza, and Parma, and was showered with honors. He decided to settle in the Villa Gaione, his estate in Parma. No doubt he remembered the pleasant town where he had studied as a boy. Since 1816 Parma had been ruled by Marie Louise of Austria (the second wife of Napoleon), well known for her interest in music and the arts. She had met Paganini in Vienna and was no doubt pleased to acquire such an illustrious citizen, appointing him to the governing board of the court orchestra in November 1835. He began to rehearse with the orchestra, which responded with great zeal, and directed a brilliant concert on December 12, the birthday of Marie Louise. His share of the program consisted of conducting two overtures by Rossini and Beethoven. We can assume that he conducted the orchestra with bow in hand, for there is a satirical drawing (dated 1836) showing the disheveled Paganini swinging a bow.

During his travels through Europe, Paganini had become acquainted with the best—and the worst—orchestras, and he was eager to reorganize the Parma ensemble. Marie Louise ordered him a free hand—"everything that Paganini proposes will be adopted." He submitted a thirty-two-page plan which encompassed everything, from playing ability to disciplinary fines. He proposed a merit system within the violin section so that anyone could be promoted to leader. Everyone in the section should be able to play "the twelve famous quartets of Beethoven." He recommended an increase from thirty-four to fifty players, with alternate players for all wind instruments, and the appointment of probationers in all the sections.

Paganini's work with the orchestra produced immediate improvement. He rehearsed with the string instruments, he changed the reeds of the wind players. On January 5, 1836, he wrote, "The orchestra is fanatical. I am delighted at having obtained everything." He was quick in declaring the Parma orchestra to be the best in Italy, and his new duties occupied him to the fullest.

However, by not waiting for the formal approval of his proposal, Paganini created a crisis by demoting certain players and engaging others, thus exceeding his powers. His efforts were frustrated by court officials jealous of his success. Disillusioned, Paganini preferred to resign in July 1836, rather than fight petty intrigues.

The entire Parma episode, though brief, is important for a balanced evaluation of his personality. Evidently, his musical interests exceeded by far the narrow confines of the violin. Aware of the inadequacies of Italian orchestras (described as "miserable" by musicians like Spohr, Berlioz, and others), Paganini wanted to raise the standards to a symphonic level needed for the modern repertoire, particularly Beethoven.

His planning showed organizational ability and musical acumen. He was moved by idealism, not by ambition, since he did not see himself as the ultimate court conductor—a job for which he recommended a pianist-composer. He failed because his eagerness outpaced the immovable status quo.

On the road again in December 1836, we find him in Nizza (Nice), then still Italian. He wrote to his friend Germi, "My violin is still out of humor with me, but after another six or eight concerts in Marseilles it will go perfectly. I have more courage than strength." He was right; the next concerts in Marseilles, in January 1837, must have been excellent, for he could compete with the phenomenal violinist H. W. Ernst, who appeared in Marseilles at the same time. Ernst wrote, "The consensus of opinion was that I played with more sentiment while he conquers greater difficulties. But I must tell you that Paganini is no longer the same man, he has lost much." [19]

Paganini was really at the end of his career: two benefit concerts in Turin, in June 1837, were his last public appearances before he left for Paris.

A strange interlude in Paganini's adventurous life was his investment in a Parisian entertainment center, to be known as Casino Paganini. Music and gambling were to be the main attractions, but the gambling license was denied, and the music was not distinguished enough to attract the public, since Paganini felt too ill to play. He stayed in Paris from late June 1837 to December 1838 to supervise the venture, but it closed after only two months of operation. Swindled by speculators and would-be friends, he suffered financial losses and the humiliation of a lawsuit. What a sad spectacle—Paganini's name dragged through the courts while Johann Strauss and his Viennese orchestra drew crowds of Parisians.

To make matters worse, Paganini's larynx became paralyzed so that he lost his voice completely; he could communicate only in writing or with the help of his twelve-year-old son, who could read his father's lips. The stay in Paris was prolonged by court order because of various litigations pending against him; finally, on Christmas 1838, father and son left for the south of France. Soon they were in Marseilles, away from the harsh Parisian climate.

Despite his failing health, Paganini remained interested in various projects. "I want to succeed as a dealer in stringed instruments," he wrote to a musician in Milan, asking him to buy instruments "at a price that will leave a margin for a turnover when reselling them." He continued, "I am glad to have the beautiful cello which I always keep with me along with the Stradivari violin which completes the quartet.* . . ."[20] At his death Paganini owned twenty-two Italian instruments, a remarkable collection including seven Stradivari and four Guarneri violins, as well as violas and cellos made by Stradivari and a guitar of Guadagnini's hand.

Another thought occupied Paganini a few months before his death, which he confided to a visitor: "Paganini still speaks of a new method for the violin which he wishes to publish and which will materially shorten the time needed for study."[21] In his conversations with Schottky, Paganini had mentioned certain short-cuts in the study of the violin or, for that matter, of any string instrument—a more rational approach. This led many people to believe that he had a "secret" that he took to his grave. His only pupil was Camillo Sivori, who spoke of him as probably the world's worst teacher, impatient and sarcastic. "However," he recalled, "I carried one great lesson away with me—not to neglect even for a day to practice scales."[22] Sivori's career was built on the fact that he was the only pupil of Paganini. There was a certain affection between teacher and student. Sivori visited Paganini shortly before his death, and Paganini bequeathed to him one of his Stradivaris. Previously Paganini had given Sivori a copy (made by the luthier Vuillaume) of his favorite Guarneri del Gesù violin.†

In November 1839 Paganini returned to Nizza to spend a lonely winter. His hand was trembling, so that he could hardly hold a pen; he was plagued by constant cough and insomnia; he could not speak and could barely swallow. Repeatedly he refused to see a priest until the Church gave him up as a hopeless heretic.

The end came on May 27, 1840, toward five in the afternoon. The bishop of Nizza denied permission for burial, and for several years the coffin with his remains was stored in a cellar. In 1845 the Grand Duchess Marie Louise of Parma authorized his interment at the Villa Gaione, and in 1876 his remains were reinterred in the cemetery in Parma, to be transferred in 1896 to the new cemetery, where his heirs erected an imposing monument.

---

* The quartet of Stradivaris once owned by Paganini was reassembled in the 1940s by the violin dealer E. Herrmann and was used by the Paganini Quartet, (1946–66).
† Paganini's original Guarneri del Gesù is preserved in the Museo Municipale in Genoa. Honoring the bicentennial of Paganini's birth in 1982, it was brought to New York to be played by Salvatore Accardo at Carnegie Hall on November 4.

Paganini's son Achille was not quite fifteen years old at the time of his father's death. He was born out of wedlock, but Paganini succeeded in legitimizing him after much legal wrangling. He was the only heir and took exemplary care of the legacy. In 1851 he arranged for the publication of nine posthumous compositions and continued to preserve the unpublished manuscripts until his death in 1895.

In 1908, the Paganini heirs made an offer to the Italian Government to sell eighty-seven unpublished compositions of Paganini still in the possession of the family. A committee of distinguished musicians was appointed to examine the works. The shortsighted conclusion was that only a few of the compositions represented greater musical values, namely the three unpublished concertos (now known as Nos. 3, 4, and 5) and the Viola Sonata. Manuscripts, documents, and memorabilia were scattered throughout the world. Some private collectors guarded their holdings jealously. Fortunately, the present Italian Government has made up for the neglect of the past: in 1972 the most important collection of Paganiniana was opened to the public in Rome, at the Biblioteca Casanatense, including most of the unpublished musical manuscripts. The Istituto di Studi Paganiniani, established that same year in Genoa, has acquired and published some hitherto lost items, such as the posthumous Concerto in E minor and the Variations on *La Carmagnole* of 1795, Paganini's earliest composition. The Library of Congress in Washington houses a valuable collection acquired in 1940. Here we find four little notebooks of Paganini, including the "Little Red Book," with fascinating entries concerning his concert receipts and other day-by-day minutiae, as well as a number of compositions, letters, posters, and much pictorial material.

The name Paganini has become a synonym for the apex of virtuosity. But it should not be equated with mechanical, automatonlike perfection. Undoubtedly, Paganini's technical wizardry was the chief factor in his unparalleled public success, yet the thoughtful musicians found much more to admire. So said Friedrich Wieck, father and teacher of Clara Schumann: "Never did I hear a singer who touched me as deeply as an *Adagio* played by Paganini. Never was there an artist who was equally great and incomparable in so many genres."[23]

Paganini's demoniac personality and style of playing, his magnetism and mystique were inimitable, but the purely technical aspects of his performance were avidly analyzed and imitated. Among his contemporaries, Heinrich Wilhelm Ernst came closest to reaching Paganini's technique, even surpassing him at times. Others to experience the immediate impact of Paganini were Ole Bull, Bériot, and Vieuxtemps. The technical level of violin playing rose sharply. Particularly the Franco-Belgian school lost no time in assimilating Paganini's technical advances, though they retained the Viotti tradition as their base.

The German violin school reacted more slowly to Paganini's style. Undoubtedly, Spohr's opposition had something to do with it; the tendency prevailed to consider Paganini's technical innovations as "tricks," not worthy of a serious musician and not quite compatible with the noble classical style of Tartini. However, Joseph Joachim, recognized as the greatest musician-violinist of his generation, admired the caprices (as did Schumann and Brahms) and studied them assiduously.

But opposition to Paganini was actually quite futile. Violinists everywhere rushed to expand and refine their technique in line with the famous Twenty-four Caprices, especially after they were republished in Paris in 1831–32. Once Paganini's important compositions (Opus 6 to Opus 14) appeared in print in 1851, they formed a new plateau of violin technique. Among these posthumous compositions were the Concertos Nos. 1 and 2 (with *La Clochette* as finale), the *Moto perpetuo,* and the variation sets *Le streghe, I palpiti, Non più mesta,* and the *Carnival of Venice.* Even today, these works are the touchstone of every great violinist.

Paganini was a truly gifted composer, well schooled by excellent teachers. He did not approach the art of composition lightly; he said to Schottky, "Composition is no easy task for me as you think. My great rule in art is complete unity within diversity, and that is very hard to achieve. . . . It requires much reflection before beginning to write."[24]

All his works are "display" pieces in the best sense of the word, designed to show the violin's idiomatic qualities in terms of dazzling technique and expressive cantabile. From this point of view, Paganini was an innovative and scintillating composer: he developed a new vocabulary of violin effects, incorporating them into his works with remarkable skill. He transformed display into art, thus inaugurating a new era of virtuosity.

Nowhere can this be seen as clearly as in his violin concertos. He worked with the musical language of his Italian contemporaries—Donizetti, Rossini, Bellini—and accepted the traditional form of the French violin concerto. Within this framework he created works of breathtaking bravura and warm intensity.

When he played these concertos, the ending of the first solo invariably caused wild applause. After the substantial first movement follows an expressive Adagio, and then a final Rondo of sparkling charm. Best known is the Rondo of Concerto No. 2, nicknamed *La Clochette* or *La Campanella*, where the soloist matches the sound of a little bell (tuned to F-sharp) with a harmonic of the same pitch. Occasionally, single movements are played, like the Allegro from Concerto No. 1 (in Wilhelmj's adaptation) or *La Clochette* in Kreisler's shortened version. Paganini himself included single movements from his concertos on certain programs; but today's virtuosos take pride in playing Paganini "uncut."

Until the 1950s only two concertos by Paganini were performed— No. 1 in D/E-flat* (Op. 6, premiered by Paganini in 1819), and No. 2 in B minor (Op. 7, first performed in 1827). They were never published during the composer's lifetime and appeared posthumously in 1851.

In the past few decades, the Paganini repertoire has been enriched by four additional concertos (Nos. 3–6), but while they are all recorded, only No. 6 is printed. This situation might soon change, since the manuscripts have been acquired by the Italian government.

Two of the "new" concertos belonged to Paganini's own concert repertoire: he premiered No. 3 in E major in 1828 in Vienna, while No. 4 in D minor was first played in Paris in 1831 (after a preview in Frankfurt). No. 5 in A minor is preserved in an incomplete state: only the original solo violin part has survived, while the accompaniment has had to be reconstructed by others. Finally, No. 6 (published as Opus posthumous) exists in a version for violin and guitar accompaniment; it may well be the long-lost youthful concerto, composed and then discarded in 1815. The rediscovered concertos have been recorded by Szeryng, Ricci, Grumiaux, Accardo, and Gulli, who deserve our gratitude for having revived and enlarged our knowledge of Paganini as a composer of large-scale works.

Paganini's own orchestrations of the violin concertos are rich and colorful, with trombones and various percussion instruments (timpani, bass drum, cymbals, bells). In fact, contemporary critics described his use of the orchestra in the *tutti* sections as "noisy" at times, but he always knew how to thin out the orchestra in the solo sections so that every note of the soloist is audible. Paganini emerges a well-schooled musician, whose accomplishments as a composer become more apparent as new works are rescued from oblivion.

* The double key signature indicates a retuning of the violin one half-step up (*scordatura*); see p. 196.

Paganini's Op. 1, the Twenty-four Caprices for violin solo, were a stroke of genius. Though not published until 1820, the caprices must have been composed much earlier, during his stay in Lucca, probably shortly after he discovered the caprices by Locatelli. Compared to these unrewarding finger twisters, Paganini's collection is colorful and imaginative. He incorporated virtually the entire arsenal of violin technique, but making each caprice musically attractive.

It was left to Paganini to produce that happy combination of technique and music, to mask mechanical problems in an aesthetic guise. Undoubtedly, Paganini's caprices inspired the pianist-composers; Chopin's two sets of etudes (Opp. 10 and 25) and Liszt's *Etudes transcendentales* are direct heirs of Paganini. Liszt and Schumann transcribed a number of Paganini caprices for the keyboard. Brahms and Rachmaninoff, among others, based variation sets on Caprice No. 24. Other musicians provided piano accompaniments for the unaccompanied caprices, among them Schumann, Auer, Kreisler, and Szymanowski. The fascination with Paganini's demonic genius continued.

As early as 1829, the German violinist Guhr analyzed Paganini's technical innovations in these categories:[25] (1) *scordatura*; (2) bowing; (3) left-hand pizzicato; (4) harmonics; (5) performing on the G-string only; (6) fingering. Each of these aspects merits a closer look.

Used as far back as 1680 by Heinrich Biber and even earlier, *scordatura* (mistuning) is an old technique, which Paganini applied to a limited extent. For certain compositions he tuned the violin one half step up, enabling him to play a piece in a "flat" key with an open-string fingering, so that the soloist rang out brilliantly while the orchestra remained subdued. He used this *scordatura* for the Concerto No. 1, *Le streghe*, *I palpiti*, and the *Carnaval de Venise*. In the *Moses Fantasy* (for G-string alone) he pulled the G-string up to B-flat so that the orchestra accompanied in E-flat minor while he played in C minor. Today it is customary to play all the Paganini pieces in normal tuning, though I have heard Menuhin play *I palpiti* on a *scordatura* violin, a very tricky procedure.

Concerning Paganini's bowing, Guhr observed that he took "upbeat" phrases with a downbow and accentuated phrases with an upbow. Such an unorthodox procedure is followed to good effect by some modern violinists, but it breaks the rules. Indeed, Paganini seems to have broken many rules. He manipulated his bow exclusively with forearm and wrist while holding the upper arm close to his body. His arms may have been unusually long, enabling him to immobilize the upper arm. Even in Paganini's time, such a position was considered unusual. Very innovative, on the other hand, was Paganini's reliance on the bouncing bow, at a time when Spohr condemned any such flighty bowings.

One of Paganini's specialties was the *ricochet*, a number of self-bouncing notes on one bow, either up or down. He uses ricochet extensively in his caprices and his Concerto No. 1 (the final rondo). The bowing becomes more complicated if used down and up in succession, as prescribed in the Caprice No. 5 in A minor. Here, modern violinists do a bit of swindling and simply play *sautillé* (single bouncing bows, up and down). Paganini went even further, as Guhr remarked: "In his Moto Perpetuo he plays *whole passages* with one bow stroke and the staccato with incredible perfection." Today the *Moto perpetuo* is played with single strokes in *sautillé*; there is not a living violinist capable of playing the piece as described by Guhr.

Among Paganini's most striking effects were left-hand pizzicato (derived no doubt from his guitar playing) and double-stop harmonics. The left-hand pizzicato works in descending scales and arpeggios if the player tears the fingers off the string sideways instead of lifting them. It is a "machine-gun" effect and quite startling at first. Although harmonics were known and used on the violin since the 1730s, Paganini's double harmonics were totally innovative. It is an extremely risky effect which virtuosos of today like to avoid (see the Kreisler edition of *La Clochette*, which omits the entire section in double harmonics). With the modern steel and aluminum-wound strings, harmonics have become somewhat more reliable and easier to produce. Paganini's writing for harmonics has forced an entire generation of violinists to devote much time to that technique. Guhr noticed that Paganini used rather thin strings, which facilitated the playing of harmonics but produced a smaller tone. Indeed, Paganini's tone was not as full and rich as that of Baillot or Lafont, but it had infinite shadings down to a whispering triple piano. Schumann said, "I expected him to begin with a tone such as had never been heard before. But with how small, how thin a tone did he begin! Bit by bit, imperceptibly at first, he threw his magnetic chains into the audience. . . ."[26]

Another hallmark of Paganini's violin style, the ability to perform entire pieces on the G-string, demands almost acrobatic control of the fingerboard, a kind of daredevil technique moving with lightning speed from the lowest to the highest positions. Exponents of the French violin concerto liked to contrast the silvery register of the E-string with the dark-hued sound of the G-string, but there was none of the exhibition-ism displayed by Paganini. He acquired this peculiar technique through hard work in his early years in Lucca (though not in prison, as his romantic biographers have it). His best-known piece using this device is the Fantasy on themes from Rossini's *Moses*, though he wrote a number of such one-string pieces and always included one on a concert program. He exploits the G-string effect repeatedly in his concertos and in several caprices. What started out as a stunt actually proved very useful to the development of violin technique in general.

Guhr observed that Paganini often used unusual fingerings. It may well be that he changed positions by stretching, rather than by the more conventional shifting. The build of his hand was peculiar, as we learn from his personal physician, Dr. Bennati, who published his findings in 1831:

> Paganini's hand is not larger than normal; but because all its parts are so stretchable, it can double its reach. For example, without changing the position of the hand, he is able to bend the first joints of the left fingers—which touch the strings—sideways, at a right angle to the natural motion of the joint, and he can do it with effortless ease, assurance, and speed. Essentially, Paganini's art is based on physical endowment, increased and developed by ceaseless practicing.[27]

There have been other attempts to link Paganini's "secret" to his peculiar fingerings conditioned by the build of his hand, but the results are mostly speculation and guesswork. The astonishing fact is that Paganini was able to reach four A's on four strings without moving his hand—in other words, he could reach from the lowest to the highest notes on the fingerboard by sheer stretch.

In general, there are many passages in Paganini's compositions that demand great stretching of the left fingers. For this reason, violinists with small hands (like Sarasate and Elman) have avoided the Paganini repertoire altogether.

Such was the fascination with Paganini's dexterity that people were convinced that he had a "secret." But Guhr, observing him at close range, assures us that there was no secret, only a predisposition of the hand to violin playing and ceaseless work from early childhood. We know now that Guhr was right: Heifetz, the greatest violinist-technician of our century, achieved a Paganini-like perfection by the same means.

It is interesting to note that no one heard Paganini practice the violin while he was on tour. Ernst followed Paganini from city to city, always endeavoring to rent a room adjoining his. He later told his young colleague Joachim that his efforts were fruitless. He did hear Paganini play in his room, but apparently with a mute, playing *mezza voce*. Moreover, he seems only to have prepared the pieces that were on the next concert program. Occasionally he practiced one or the other caprice which he liked to play as an encore. Joachim asked, "Did he play them faultlessly?" "Yes, absolutely," answered Ernst, "though even better at home than on the stage. He must have practiced enormously when he was young; if a passage did not succeed the first time, it was sure to succeed the second. He had an iron will. . . ."[28]

Paganini's preoccupation with technique brought him into undeserved disrepute as a musician. In truth, he had a fine musical mind. He was an assiduous quartet player who knew and loved *all* the Beethoven quartets (in contrast to Spohr, who cared only for those of Opus 18). Paganini understood and encouraged Berlioz, the most avant-garde composer of his time. He was a fabulous sight-reader who once offered, as a stunt, to read at sight any composition put before him at the end of a concert. He was an astute judge of music and musicians. It is true that his concert repertoire was limited to his own compositions, aside from a few concertos by Viotti, Rode, and Kreutzer. But this was also the case with Spohr, as well as with other traveling virtuosos. Paganini was aware that he was not at his best when he played the music of other composers; his own personality superseded and overpowered anything he played. Fétis, in fact, wrote that Paganini's interpretations of music by other composers were "mediocre." But as a rule, the Romantic virtuosos were not ideal interpreters of music by other composers; they were too egocentric to submerge themselves. Paganini was the prototype of the Romantic virtuoso. He emerged as a conqueror, achieving limitless mastery of his instrument, and by example showed others what to strive for. He extracted every possible secret from the violin, which he loved beyond anything else.

AFTER PAGANINI:
THE AGE
OF VIRTUOSITY

PAGANINI ECLIPSED all other violinists during his triumphant sweep through Europe; he wiped the slate clean of all competitors. However, as soon as he left the musical stage in the mid-1830s, a resurgence took place among violin virtuosos. Many tried to fill the void that his departure had created. Though no one could hope to surpass him, a new generation of violinists arose eager to emulate him. This collective effort led to a new plateau of excellence. First came those who actually heard Paganini play and tried to imitate him; among them were such exceptional virtuosos as Heinrich Wilhelm Ernst, Charles de Bériot, Henry Vieuxtemps, Ole Bull, Karol Lipinski, and Camillo Sivori (Paganini's only known student). A second wave followed, those who were too young to have heard the great violinist but were caught in the maelstrom of virtuosity. They learned about Paganini's technical wizardry from his compositions. Foremost among them were Henri Wieniawski and Pablo de Sarasate; even Joseph Joachim, the classicist, felt stimulated by the study of Paganini's Caprices. The late nineteenth and early twentieth centuries produced a flowering of "Paganini mania." Many aspired to be called "Paganini redivivus"—Jan Kubelik, Willy Burmester, August Wilhelmj, and countless others who gave the term *virtuoso* a bad name. But in the first flush of enthusiasm the imitation of Paganini's achievements had positive aspects—it raised the general level of violin playing by several notches, affecting even the ranks of orchestral players.

Paganini's Impact on the Viennese School

Vienna has been the traditional gateway between Italy and Germany. Whereas Vienna dominated northern Italy politically for centuries, Italy reciprocated by prevailing in matters of music. The Habsburg court reserved its choicest appointments for Italian musicians. The Viennese public adored Italian music, singers, and virtuosos. But while Vienna easily succumbed to southern charms, a strong homegrown musical tradition persisted in withstanding alien inroads. There was assimilation and absorption, but no surrender.

Permeating Vienna's musical life were not only Italians but also musicians from the adjoining lands of the Habsburg empire. From the north and east came the violinists of Bohemia, Moravia, and Slovakia, from the southeast the gifted Hungarians. Vienna was the magnet, the cosmopolitan capital where talented artists were always welcome.

It is thus not surprising to see a Hungarian-born violinist—Joseph Boehm—appointed first violin professor at the newly founded Vienna Conservatory. Born in Pest in 1795, Boehm was first taught by his father and appeared successfully as a child prodigy. Around 1813 he had a brief encounter with Rode, who visited Austria at that time and consented to give him a few lessons. Though the contact was brief, Boehm acquired many characteristic French traits; he is usually counted among Rode's students.

In 1816, Boehm made his Vienna debut during an entr'acte at the Court Theater, impressing the critics by playing from memory (not customary before Paganini). The success encouraged him to settle in Vienna. His arrival had coincided with the departure, for Russia, of the violinist Ignaz Schuppanzigh, a popular quartet player and longtime associate of Beethoven. Boehm quickly filled the void by announcing a series of six quartet concerts. In 1819 he was named violin professor at the Conservatory, a post he held until 1848. His concerts continued to enjoy success; in 1821 a critic wrote, "This is the way one must hear the quartets of Beethoven and Mozart."[1] When Schuppanzigh returned to Vienna in 1823, he resumed his own quartet concerts, but a certain rivalry lingered between him and Boehm. This became quite obvious in 1825, when Beethoven "dismissed" Schuppanzigh after the lukewarm premiere of the Quartet Op. 127. Beethoven selected Boehm to play first violin in a repeat performance, which turned out far more impressive. Boehm was also a participant in several early Schubert performances, but soon decided to retire from public concerts and devote himself entirely to teaching and playing in the Imperial Orchestra.

One could speculate that Paganini's sensational appearance in Vienna might have induced Boehm to stop concertizing, though he was only in his mid-thirties. Quite a few violinists wanted to quit after hearing Paganini; as we hear from Mayseder, another Austrian violinist, "We never heard anything like it before nor shall we ever hear anything like it again. All of us wanted to smash our violins."[2] But Mayseder continued his career long after Paganini departed, becoming the darling of Vienna. As for Boehm, he maintained his proficiency in private: one of his students was Joseph Joachim, who joined his class in 1838 and reminisced, "Based on a reliable left hand and an ideally smooth bowing, Boehm possessed an art of phrasing that enabled him to realize anything that he envisaged and felt."[3]

Boehm's class was important as the meeting place of fiddling youngsters from all parts of the Habsburg empire—students intuitively gifted for the violin but much in need of traditional culture. Boehm not only disciplined their skills but imparted to them a sense of classical style. His versatility as teacher is remarkable: he shaped some of the greatest virtuosos of his time, for example H. W. Ernst and Miska Hauser, as well as some of the greatest musicians, Joseph Joachim and Georg Hellmesberger. Others, like Jacob Dont and Jakob Grün, became teachers, themselves transmitting the great tradition to another generation of violinists. Out of this background arose the talents of Leopold Auer, Fritz Kreisler, and Carl Flesch, who in turn shaped the violin playing of the twentieth century.

Heinrich Wilhelm Ernst

Among Boehm's students was Heinrich Wilhelm Ernst, born to a middle-class Jewish family in Brünn (Brno) on May 6, 1814. He performed as a child prodigy at the age of nine, and in October 1825 entered Boehm's class at the Vienna Conservatory where he learned "everything that one can learn from a teacher." Paganini's Vienna appearance in March 1828 made a lasting impression on young Ernst, who decided to emulate him. A year later Ernst began his own concert tours; he made it a point to follow Paganini on his travels through Germany, in the hope of hearing him as often as possible, and of copying his peculiar style. In Frankfurt Ernst had the temerity of giving a concert shortly after Paganini had played. To the audience's surprise, Ernst played Paganini's as yet unpublished variations on *Nel cor più*, which he had written down from memory. Even Paganini was amazed, and when Ernst visited him a few days later, he hid an incomplete manuscript under the bed cover, exclaiming, "I must guard myself not only against your ears but even against your eyes!" All in all, Ernst heard Paganini play some twenty times, and came as close to his "secret" as any other living violinist. Now and then he went so far as to secretly rent a room adjoining Paganini's apartments, hiding there day and night hoping to hear Paganini practice, but he could snatch only a few notes here and there. Far from avoiding rivalry with Paganini, Ernst sought to compete with him publicly, as in Marseilles in January 1837, where Paganini gave some of the last concerts of his career. "By that time his previous infallibility had declined so much that I was able—without bragging—to play some of his favorite pieces as well, if not better, than he could," reminisced Ernst twenty years later.[4]

With Paganini no longer a rival (he died in 1840), Ernst was acclaimed as his worthy successor. During the next decade, he traveled incessantly through Europe and as far as Russia. As an accomplished performer on the viola as well, he played the solo in Berlioz's *Harold in Italy* under the composer's direction, in Brussels (1842), St. Petersburg (1847), and London (1855).

Ernst achieved his most enduring success in London, where he was first heard on July 18, 1843. The critic of the *Musical World* called him the "most accomplished living violinist." He repeated his triumphant success in April 1844 at the Philharmonic Society, performing Spohr's *Gesangscene* and his own Fantasy on *Il pirata*. From then on he became a regular visitor to London and settled there in 1855. Memorable were the string quartet sessions at the Beethoven Society, where Ernst led the quartet consisting of Joachim (second violin), Wieniawski (viola), and Piatti (cello). These men, perhaps the four greatest string players of the time, modestly combined their talents to play chamber music. Joachim, much younger than Ernst and still at the beginning of his career, remembered their quartet sessions:

> Never have I heard a more expressive tone than the one he produced in the Adagios of Beethoven's Quartets Op. 59 and 74. More than once did I and my associates want to embrace him or kiss his hand during a rehearsal. . . . In short, Paganini may have been a greater virtuoso, but he could not have played with more warmth, poetry, and esprit than Ernst.[5]

London was overrun with violinists in the 1840s, all eager to assume the mantle of Paganini. The influential critic of the *Musical World* awarded it to Ernst:

> Ernst has certainly established himself unmistakably . . . as one of the most perfect violinists that the history of music can boast, and in many respects greater than any of his predecessors [!] or contemporaries. It takes nothing from such fine artists as Joachim, Vieuxtemps, Ole Bull, Artôt, Sivori and others, to pronounce this opinion. . . . Ernst is our violinist *de coeur*. He plays the fiddle, certainly . . . but he *feels* something far beyond it—and *he expresses what he feels.* . . . Where is his superior? [6]

The victory was not won easily. All through 1843, a fierce controversy raged in London between the Ernstists and the Sivorists. Sivori lost out, and the final judgment of the *Musical World* was, "Sivori is a *fine* player, Ernst is a *great* one." Revealing is the opinion of a young fellow violinist, the sixteen-year-old Joachim, who visited London in 1847 and wrote to his teacher in Leipzig,

> I consider Ernst to be a *very great* violinist and he seems to me incomparably greater than Sivori as virtuoso, artist, and man. The latter plays the most astonishingly difficult things, but he is often out of tune, and is altogether a great charlatan. There is a superfluity of foreign violinists here. [7]

Among Paganini's successors, Ernst was alone in reaching (and occasionally even surpassing) the technical accomplishments of his model. His works represent the pinnacle of violin technique, the ultimate challenge for the virtuoso of today, though attempted by only a few. Time and again, Ernst was compared to Paganini by Schumann, Berlioz, and Heine, among others. But Ernst was not infallible as a technician: though superb at his best, he was subject to moodiness and could lose control.

But there is more to Ernst than mere virtuosity. He earned the admiration of the leading composers of his time for his soulful interpretations and sterling musicianship. Unlike Paganini, he did not limit himself to his own works but was able to do justice to the chamber music repertoire. With Liszt at the piano, he played Beethoven's *Kreutzer Sonata,* and on various occasions was accompanied by Mendelssohn as well. In his colleague Joachim he inspired unrestrained adulation: "Ernst was the greatest violinist I have ever heard; he towered above all others. . . . Who has not heard Ernst in his good days . . . does not know how communicative the cantilena of a violin could be."[8]

Berlioz called Ernst "a great musician as well as a great violinist." Heine, a particular admirer of Ernst, wrote in 1844, "Recently I heard him play a Nocturne which was dissolved in beauty." But at least one observer, Anton Schindler (the friend and biographer of Beethoven), objected to Ernst's sentimental manner: "He is a great violinist with fantasy and feeling though the latter suffers from the mannerism of sliding up and down."[9] This sliding between notes ("portamento" or "glissando") was an entrenched Viennese habit known as *maniera languida*.

Nor was Ernst a purist when he played works of other composers. He lived in an age when it was considered the virtuoso's prerogative to shape a work in his own image. We know that he took certain liberties in Spohr's *Gesangscene*: he modernized the cadenza, added difficult passages, and reshaped the conclusions of each solo. There was no outcry among critics.

Ernst last appeared with the London Philharmonic in 1855, once again playing Spohr's *Gesangscene* under the baton of Richard Wagner. His health—always precarious—gave out after the quartet concerts in 1859, forcing his retirement from concertizing, though he was only forty-five years old. Joachim, his staunch friend, tried to help by arranging a benefit concert in London in 1864 at which Ernst's two string quartets were played. By that time Ernst was dying of consumption; he spent his last years in Nizza, where he died in 1865. His Stradivarius was acquired by the violinist Wilma Neruda (Hallé), his Tourte bow by Joachim.

As a composer, Ernst rode the romantic crest, combining sentiment and brilliance. He published twenty-six opus numbers and a few unnumbered works, all involving the violin; they appeared between 1840 and 1865. Some achieved enormous popularity, for example, the soulful *Elegy* Op. 10, which became the most widely played violin piece of its time and was arranged for all kinds of instruments. A favorite virtuoso piece was his *Othello Fantasy* Op. 11 (on themes by Rossini), full of brash technical display yet put together with such good taste that even Mendelssohn and Joachim enjoyed playing it. (In fact, there is one spot in Mendelssohn's Violin Concerto that is patterned after a bold phrase in the *Othello Fantasy*.*) In frank imitation of Paganini, Ernst wrote the *Carnaval de Venise*, a set of "burlesque variations" on a theme Paganini also used. Ernst's variations are more elaborate and sophisticated

* See p. 209.

than Paganini's; for some time it was thought that he had merely copied Paganini's variations by ear, but this is not the case. Ernst's *Airs hongrois variés* (Variations on Hungarian Tunes) enjoyed some popularity but was eventually displaced by Sarasate's *Zigeunerweisen*. A serious challenge to the most accomplished virtuoso are the *Six Polyphonic Studies* and a transcription of Schubert's *Erlking*, all for unaccompanied violin.* When Ernst first played the *Erlking* in London in 1844, the critics spoke of the "extraordinary feat of executive powers" and of "difficulties which by many had been pronounced unsuperable . . . perhaps the most complete and difficult feat that was ever performed in the violin." Even today there are only a few violinists who dare perform these pieces (among them Ruggiero Ricci and Gidon Kremer). Beyond the technical feat, one must admire the ingenuity with which Ernst transferred the different strands of Schubert's ballad onto the four unaccompanied strings of the violin.

In the *Six Polyphonic Studies* Ernst repaid the affection of his many friends and admirers by dedicating each segment to a different colleague—Laub,† Sainton, Joachim, Vieuxtemps, Hellmesberger, and Bazzini.‡ Ernst's most serious and ambitious work is his *Concerto pathétique* Op. 23 in F-sharp minor, which he premiered in Vienna in 1846. It is a well-constructed piece in one movement, full of romantic passion and soaring melodies, interspersed with finger-breaking bravura sections. Today, few violinists care—or dare—to play it because its difficulties far outweigh its aesthetic values. Even Ernst himself could not always handle this work to perfection, as Joachim remarked:

> Even if Ferdinand Laub, for example, can play the passages in the F-sharp minor Concerto more cleanly than the composer himself—because he had more finger strength—I still preferred Ernst's interpretation which was more elegant and (when he was in the mood) far more characteristic, because he knew how to shape a phrase with plasticity.[10]

In our century, such pedagogues as Leopold Auer and Carl Flesch have stressed the importance of Ernst's works for the development of ultimate violin virtuosity. But his contemporaries saw in him the image of the great melancholy Romantic, with a tone of "bleeding beauty,"[11] a musician who filled virtuosity with soul.

---

* The last of the studies was also published separately as *The Last Rose of Summer*, variations on an Irish tune.
† Ferdinand Laub (1832–75), like Ernst a Bohemian, taught at the Moscow Conservatory, 1866–74; he was a great technician.
‡ Antonio Bazzini (1818–97) composed the famous *Ronde des Lutins* for violin.

Paganini's Impact on the French and Belgian Schools

Paganini's Parisian concerts in the early 1830s came at a critical juncture in French violin playing. The Conservatoire had become stagnant and self-satisfied after having codified the Viotti tradition. His disciples Kreutzer and Baillot were solid teachers but not particularly innovative. Only Lafont seemed interested in technical advances, especially after encountering Paganini as early as 1816, but he underestimated his rival; besides, Lafont did not teach and was too weak a composer to make an impact. In the meantime, the French violinists became complacent and supercilious.

That complacency was stirred up by Paganini's arrival. While Baillot, the grand old master, was too settled in his ways to change his approach, his former student Habeneck was more receptive to the novel style of Paganini, whom he observed at close quarters during rehearsals and performances. Habeneck is known to have studied Paganini's Caprices, just then republished in Paris, and transmitted his interest to his own students at the Conservatoire. Among them was Delphin Alard, who became a leading violinist in Paris as a performer and teacher, and Hubert Léonard, who carried Habeneck's teaching to Belgium. As the century progressed, the Belgian school of violin playing was to grow into a serious competitor to the Parisian Conservatoire.

Charles de Bériot

Before Belgium became an independent kingdom in 1830, it was considered obligatory for a young musician from the Low Countries (especially the French-speaking parts) to study in Paris. One of the last to follow this tradition was Charles de Bériot. He came to Paris in 1821, at the age of nineteen, and played an audition for Viotti. He received encouraging advice: "You have a fine style; endeavor to perfect it. Hear all musicians of talent—profit by all but imitate no one." Indeed, Bériot developed a personal style at an early age without much instruction. While in Paris, he made an attempt to acquire academic discipline by attending Baillot's class, but he was too far advanced to fit in. Baillot, on the other hand, disliked the unorthodox style of the newcomer. Without waiting for professorial approval, Bériot made a successful debut in Paris. He met with equal acclaim in London, where he played his own Concertino at the Philharmonic Society in 1827. After his return to Brussels he was named soloist of King William of the Netherlands, an appointment that was terminated after Belgium seceded in 1830.

In 1829, Bériot's life took a romantic turn: he fell in love with the singer Maria Malibran, then only twenty-one and already an acclaimed star. She was separated from her husband but could not obtain an annulment until 1836, when she married Bériot. In the meantime, they traveled together, giving joint concerts in Belgium, France, England, and Italy. After hearing Paganini in Paris, Bériot worked on developing his own technique, which acquired new brilliance. His Second Concerto, which he presented at the London Philharmonic in 1835, displayed many of Paganini's innovations. The following year, shortly after their marriage, tragedy struck when Madame Malibran collapsed after a concert in Manchester and died. The grief-stricken Bériot returned to Brussels and retired from the stage for almost two years.

He resumed his career in 1838, concertizing jointly in Austria and Italy with his late wife's younger sister, the singer Pauline Garcia (later Madame Viardot). Spohr, who attended one of their concerts, praised Bériot's playing, though he disliked his compositions. In 1840 Bériot was heard in Russia. Offered a professorship at the Paris Conservatoire as successor to Baillot, he declined, preferring to teach at the Brussels Conservatoire. Here he served as head of the violin faculty from 1843 to 1852, when he was forced to retire because of failing eyesight. During his tenure, he established the image of the Belgian violin school, which continued to grow in importance.

Bériot occupies a significant place in the history of the violin. He adapted the technical display of Paganini to the elegance and piquancy of Parisian taste. It was he who modernized the stagnant French Conservatoire style. Not a true disciple of that school, Bériot had no hesitancy in breaking the stranglehold of a faded tradition. He developed a new, essentially Romantic, approach: sweet and sentimental melodies, elegant and elfin playing style, and ingenious and sparkling technique. His encounter with Paganini did not change his basic personality, which was fully developed by then, but stimulated him to enlarge his technical resources. One need only compare Bériot's First Concerto of 1827— effective but technically traditional—with his Second Concerto of 1835, which bristles with such Paganiniana as harmonics, ricochet, left-hand pizzicato, and even *scordatura*. However, he soon retreated from technical extremes and composed pieces of easygoing brilliance, aiming at effect rather than depth. His personal success as a virtuoso was not based on mere technique: he could play with such melting warmth that the poet Heine exclaimed, "It seems as if the soul of his late wife were singing through his violin!"

Bériot published ten violin concertos (of which Nos. 1, 7, and 9 are widely used for study purposes), a dozen *Airs variés*, and shorter pieces (such as the elegant *Scènes de Ballet* Op. 100). His music is characterized by melodies of perfumed sweetness and flashy technical display, ideally suited to prepare budding virtuosos for greater challenges. His most famous student was Henry Vieuxtemps.

Bériot's graceful style, stressing the bouncing bow and the flying staccato, stood in direct contrast to the German school of Spohr, whose bow always adhered to the string. Mendelssohn admired Spohr's solid musical qualities, but realized that the future of violin playing belonged to the daring brilliance of Paganini, Ernst, and Bériot. Mendelssohn's own Violin Concerto of 1844 shows the influence of all three of these virtuosos in technical details, but total independence in musical matters:

Paganini, *Caprice No. 1*

Mendelssohn, first movement, cadenza

Ernst, *Othello Fantasy*

Mendelssohn, Finale

Bériot, Concerto No. 3, excerpts

Mendelssohn Concerto, excerpts

Henry Vieuxtemps

Within the post-Paganini generation, Vieuxtemps occupied a leading position. He embodied all the criteria of a great musician: an accomplished virtuoso, an inventive composer, a versatile interpreter of great music, and a dedicated teacher. Berlioz's statement might seem a bit exaggerated today—"Vieuxtemps is as remarkable a composer as he is an incomparable virtuoso"[1]—but in his time, Vieuxtemps's violin concertos were significant accomplishments.

Vieuxtemps (born in Verviers, Belgium, on February 17, 1820) began to play the violin at the age of four, tutored by his father, an amateur violinist. By the time he was six he performed in public, and in 1828 attracted the attention of Bériot, who obtained a royal scholarship for him. Bériot wasted no time in taking his young prodigy to Paris, where young Henry made his debut in 1829 with Rode's Seventh Concerto. The critical Fétis wrote, "Yesterday we heard a violinist who was scarcely taller than his bow. His assurance, aplomb, and precision are truly remarkable for his age; he is a born musician."[2] The lessons with Bériot came to an end in 1831, when the master left for Italy. In 1833, father Vieuxtemps, a rather fierce taskmaster, took the thirteen-year-old Henry on a tour through Germany, which not only brought success but also served to broaden the boy's musical horizon. He was deeply moved by Beethoven's *Fidelio*; he met older masters like Spohr and Molique, and finally settled in Vienna for the winter of 1833–34. Here he studied counterpoint with the eminent theorist Sechter, and entered a circle of

Music reproduced from *Die Musik in Geschichte und Gegenwart*, Vol. 13, courtesy of Bärenreiter-Verlag, Cassel, 1966.

musicians who had personally known Beethoven and Schubert. When young Vieuxtemps heard Mayseder play the *Kreutzer Sonata*, he approached tears and condemned Kreutzer for rejecting the work dedicated to him: "All the same—Kreutzer, the wretch, though he may have been a great artist and a remarkable violinist, should have made the journey from Paris to Vienna on his knees to see the god, to render homage to him, and then to die."[3]

At that time, the fourteen-year-old Vieuxtemps was asked to learn Beethoven's Violin Concerto, until then sadly neglected by the Viennese violinists.* With only two weeks of preparation, Vieuxtemps mastered the concerto and performed it on March 16, 1834, at a concert conducted by Baron Lannoy, the director of the Vienna Conservatory. The Baron, in a letter written the following day, praised Vieuxtemps's "original, novel, and yet classical manner" of interpretation.

That same year Vieuxtemps performed in Leipzig, earning a noteworthy review from Robert Schumann: "His accomplishment is complete and truly masterful." Even a comparison with Paganini was flattering: while Paganini created a "gradual enchantment," Vieuxtemps drew the listener immediately into a magic circle. Continuing his journey to London, young Vieuxtemps made his debut on June 2, 1834, at the Philharmonic with an *Air varié* by his teacher Bériot; strangely enough, he aroused no attention and received one good notice. His arrival was poorly timed, for London was under Paganini's spell. The two met privately and Paganini is reported to have said, "This little boy will become a great man!" As for the "little boy," he was overwhelmed after having heard Paganini:

> Despite my youth (I was barely fourteen) I knew enough about the art of violin playing to understand the immensity of his talent. . . . Though I could not tell exactly by which means he arrived at the desired effects my impression was not less immense.[4]

For the winter 1835–36, Vieuxtemps settled in Paris and studied composition with Berlioz's teacher, Anton Reicha. He set himself the goal of "combining the pure form of the Viotti Concerto with the technical demands of modern times." The result of his efforts was the Concerto in F-sharp minor (published as No. 2, Op. 19), which clearly shows the influence of Paganini.

By 1837, Vieuxtemps's apprentice years were completed and he re-

---

* The Beethoven concerto was virtually unperformed between 1806, the year of its premiere, and 1828, when Baillot revived it in Paris.

sumed his concert tours, going as far east as Russia. In St. Petersburg, on March 16, 1840, he first performed two of his recently completed compositions, the *Fantaisie caprice* Op. 11 and the monumental Concerto in E major Op. 10 (published as No. 1). The success of the concerto was repeated in Brussels in July, where his former teacher Bériot embraced him in public, and in Paris the following January, where Baillot, the grand old man of the French violin school, rushed to the stage to demonstrate his approval. To appear as soloist-composer at the Conservatoire concerts under Habeneck was a distinct honor for an artist not quite twenty-one. The event was hailed by Berlioz in an enthusiastic review.

That same year—1841—Vieuxtemps returned to London, where his reappearance at the Philharmonic was triumphant. He became a frequent visitor to London and helped launch the first season of the Beethoven Quartet Society in 1845.

In the meantime, he had visited America for the first time in 1843–44, but found the public rather naive. Among other cities he visited New York, Boston, and Albany, and later reminisced,

> At that time the inhabitants of the United States were not yet afflicted with musicomania as they are today [1880]. I went there too early, I was "too classical," and aside from a few connoisseurs, I could not charm and excite the Yankees except with their national theme, "Yankee doodle" which made me popular.*

His second American tour, in 1857–58, was more satisfying artistically:

> Ole Bull, Herz, Sivori, Lind etc. had achieved miracles. The ignorance had disappeared, the musical instincts manifested themselves, the need for harmony and comprehension began to flower. This journey . . . was full of adventures.

His third and last tour of America, from September 1870 to May 1871, was a complete success. He gave no fewer than 120 concerts, and his memories were happy:

> Immense progress had been realized since my last journey. Everywhere were great Philharmonic Societies and musical associations; the taste for serious music was evident and developed. Leaving aside the natural propensity of the Yankee for eccentricity, I have no doubt that with time given for purifica-

---

* During the American Bicentennial, Vieuxtemps's amusing *Yankee Doodle Variations* were revived by the violinist Itzhak Perlman.

tion these new people will become a nation perfectly able to discern, comprehend, and assimilate great art.[5]

Between his first and second American visit, Vieuxtemps lived in St. Petersburg from 1846 to 1851, occupying the honored position of solo violinist of the czar. He also taught the violin at the Theatrical Music School and contributed significantly toward the development of Russian violin playing. As a devotee of chamber music, Vieuxtemps introduced public quartet concerts on a subscription basis in St. Petersburg.

During his Russian years Vieuxtemps composed his finest work, the Concerto No. 4 in D minor. He chose this piece to reintroduce himself to the Parisian public in December 1851. Berlioz called it "a magnificent symphony with a principal violin." Having resigned his position in St. Petersburg, he resumed his worldwide tours, including a second voyage to America, where he played sixty-five concerts in less than three months, with the pianist Thalberg.

In 1861 Vieuxtemps completed his Fifth Concerto in A minor, actually composed as a "contest piece" for the Brussels Conservatory, but immediately acclaimed as an important enrichment of the solo repertoire. It became one of Wieniawski's favorite pieces; in our century Heifetz has been its most brilliant interpreter.

In 1871, after completing his third American tour, Vieuxtemps made an important decision: he returned to his native Belgium to become violin professor at the Brussels Conservatory, a post once held by his teacher Bériot. He devoted all his energies to the new task, which he considered a "sacred mission"; among his students was Eugène Ysaÿe. Unfortunately, after only two years of this work, he was incapacitated by a paralytic stroke. A slight improvement in 1877–78 enabled him to resume some teaching, but in 1879 he was forced to resign, and he died in 1881.

Vieuxtemps was one of the great violin personalities of the nineteenth century, ranking alongside Ernst, Wieniawski, and Joachim. In addition to being virtuosos, composers, quartet players, and teachers, they belonged to the new post-Paganini generation, who expanded their repertoire to include music other than their own. It meant the art of interpretation, of subordinating virtuoso instincts to the personality of the composer. Paganini was criticized whenever he attempted works of other composers (which was rare); he was unable to enter into the spirit of someone else's creative mind. The younger generation was more versatile and flexible.

Vieuxtemps, at the age of fourteen, played and interpreted the Beethoven concerto to the satisfaction of the critical Viennese. Twenty years later, in 1854, when he returned with the same concerto, the critic Hanslick wrote,

> Listening to Vieuxtemps is one of the greatest, most unqualified pleasures music has to offer. His playing is as technically infallible and masterly as it is musically noble, inspired, and compelling. I consider him the first among contemporary violinists. Some may counter with Joachim . . . but for one who has not heard Joachim, the existence of a greater player than Vieuxtemps is hard to imagine.

Seven years later, in 1861, Hanslick did hear Joachim play the Beethoven concerto and made some comparisons:

> This Concerto sounded more brilliant, more lively, when Vieuxtemps played it; Joachim searched it more deeply and surpassed, through a truly ethical force, that which Vieuxtemps had achieved through an irresistible temperament.[6]

Schindler (the same who criticized Ernst's sentimental "slides") was more satisfied with Vieuxtemps's style—"He produces a beautiful, vigorous tone, does not slide up and down the strings à la Paganini, each tone is positive."[7] A detailed evaluation of Vieuxtemps's playing was provided by T. L. Phipson, an aspiring violinist in his youth, who observed the artist at close range. He is admiring but not uncritical:

> Vieuxtemps' execution was truly prodigious; his tone was very fine, and his intonation perfect. He had a splendid staccato. To me he appeared sometimes to lack expression in the cantabile passages; and in his variations on the 4th string [the G-string] almost every note rattled in a most disagreeable manner.* He was very energetic on the 4th string. At that time he played on a fine violin by Storioni of Cremona, which he had himself adjusted and made as perfect as possible. Later in life he parted with it and procured a Guarnerius del Gesù.†

Phipson recalled that

> . . . at his concerts Vieuxtemps appeared to revel in difficulties, and his playing was more or less of the Paganini school, but sobered down by the classical influence of de Bériot. . . . He had a remarkably fine tone: at the slightest touch of his

---

* The rattling on the G-string is caused by too low a bridge and can be adjusted.
† Shortly before his death, Vieuxtemps seemed ready to sell his Guarnerius but backed out at the last moment. It was sold after his death.

bow every fibre of his violin seemed to vibrate, and to produce the fullest and roundest tone of which the instrument was capable.[8]

Bériot's "classical" influence (if there ever was any) did not go very far, and Vieuxtemps's programs strike us as rather lightweight. One program at Ostende (remembered by Phipson) consisted of Tartini's *Devil's Trill Sonata*, his own *Fantaisie caprice*, and his own Fantasy on themes from Bellini's *Norma*, interspersed with arias sung by a tenor. On his tours, Vieuxtemps was often accompanied by his wife, the pianist Josephine Eder.

One German musician who objected strongly to Vieuxtemps's virtuoso mannerisms was Clara Schumann, who could be quite a critical judge. Their paths crossed often on the concert circuit in Germany in the 1850s. She did not like Vieuxtemps, either as musician or as person, and felt that by his virtuoso affectations he created a climate detrimental to serious art. There was a degree of intolerance between those—like Clara—who considered Joachim the true guardian of German musical standards, and others, who admired the fluent and less searching elegance of Vieuxtemps and the French school.

Joachim himself became quite intransigent toward virtuoso music. During his boyhood he had his fill of display pieces (including those by Vieuxtemps). In judging Vieuxtemps's musicianship as quartet player, Joachim seems cool:

> I used to admire Vieuxtemps in former years because of his brilliant playing that was not without grandeur. But as a quartet player he was less impressive because—like so many violinists of the Franco-Belgian school in recent times—he adhered too strictly to the lifeless printed notes when playing the classics, unable to read between the lines.[9]

Contemporary critics, in particular Berlioz, lavished much praise on Vieuxtemps's talent as a composer. If it seems exaggerated today, it must be understood in the context of his time. One must recognize Vieuxtemps's efforts at elevating virtuosity to a higher musical level. His Concerto No. 1 in E major (1840) filled a real void; Spohr's concertos, never popular in France, were fading fast while those of Bériot aimed no higher than elegant entertainment. The old repertoire of Viotti-Rode-Kreutzer was too classical, while Paganini's concertos—not yet published but known—overstressed virtuosity. Vieuxtemps's achievement was to rejuvenate the grand concept of the French violin concerto by using the orchestra in a more symphonic manner and by let-

Members of the much-admired Ernst Quartet, which played in London in 1859: *left to right*, Joseph Joachim, Heinrich Ernst, Henryk Wieniawski

Above left, Heinrich Wilhelm Ernst rivaled Paganini during his lifetime.
Above right, Henryk Wieniawski, famed Polish virtuoso and composer, partner of Anton Rubinstein.
Below left, Charles de Bériot, founder of the Belgian violin school.
Below right, Henry Vieuxtemps, the Belgian violinist-composer admired by Berlioz, made three tours of America. He was the teacher of Eugène Ysaÿe.

ting the solo violin speak with a more eloquent and impassioned voice. In his Fourth Concerto (1849–50) he abandoned the traditional form by inserting a Scherzo and by shaping the opening movement freely, almost like an improvisation of the solo violin; there is also a cyclic connection with the Finale. In contrast, the Fifth Concerto (1861) is built as an integrated one-movement work. In terms of violin virtuosity, he fused elements of Paganini and Bériot in a highly personal manner, creating a violinistic vocabulary that remained valid for the entire nineteenth century. While he knew how to exploit brilliance, he never cheapened a passage for effect; good taste and a certain nobility are always in evidence, as well as a fervent romanticism. Even in his shorter pieces—evidently "crowd pleasers"—Vieuxtemps maintained dignity and impeccable taste; some, like the *Ballade et Polonaise* or the *Fantasia appassionata*, have maintained themselves in the current repertoire; as teaching material, they are indispensable. Vieuxtemps's catalogue of works is large (sixty-one opus numbers) and varied, including compositions for viola, cello, string quartet, orchestra, and chorus, though the violin was foremost. Evidently, he took his creative work very seriously. His cadenzas for Beethoven's Violin Concerto deserve attention as a Gallic approach, though they will hardly displace those by Joachim or Kreisler.

Henryk Wieniawski

Wieniawski's life was short—he died at the age of forty-five, virtually destitute and burned out. But he performed for some thirty-five years, having started as a child prodigy, and was praised throughout life not only by critics and audiences but more importantly by great musicians like Rubinstein, Vieuxtemps, and Joachim.

Wieniawski's life was filled to the brim with music—he shone as virtuoso soloist, chamber music player (equally adept on the viola as on the violin), composer, and teacher. A true Romantic, he poured forth melting melodies, then roused his public with brilliant technical feats, yet always with impeccable taste. The combination of Slavic temperament and French elegance was irresistible. He knew how to fuse Paganini's pyrotechnics with romantic imagination and Polish coloring; he can be compared to Chopin, though his creativity was not on that level of genius. Wieniawski's two large-scale compositions, the Violin Concertos in F-sharp minor and D minor, reveal a firm grasp of compositional technique. His approach to the violin has become an indispensable part of modern playing, even more so than that of Ernst or Vieuxtemps; it is an arsenal of skills that any ambitious violinist must master.

Wieniawski's repertoire was not limited to his own pieces; in fact, he was among the early "modern" virtuosos to play a wide range of compositions, including Bach's Chaconne, Beethoven's *Kreutzer Sonata*, the concertos of Beethoven, Viotti, Mendelssohn, and Vieuxtemps.

Wieniawski was born on July 10, 1835, in Lublin, Poland, then a part of Czarist Russia. He came from a musical milieu: his mother was a professional pianist, as was his uncle, Edouard Wolff, who lived in Paris and counted Chopin among his friends. The Wieniawski home in Lublin was the center for many musical activities and welcomed artists from abroad.

Henryk's exceptional talent for the violin was discovered very early. By the time he was eight he was so far advanced that he was sent to Paris for further studies. After a brilliant audition, he was admitted to the Conservatoire, an unprecedented distinction for such a young child. Soon he was placed in the master class of Lambert Massart, the legendary disciple of Kreutzer. At age eleven, Henryk was awarded the First Violin Prize, but continued studying with Massart for another two years.

Before leaving for a concert tour to Russia (at the request of the czar, it was rumored), the twelve-year-old Henryk gave a concert in Paris. On the program were two of his own compositions, an *Air varié* and a Caprice. The latter was later published as his Opus 1, dedicated to his *maître* Massart as "testimony of gratitude."

Between March and May 1848, Henryk gave five successful concerts in St. Petersburg. In the fall, he returned to Poland and formed a friendship with the Polish nationalist composer, Stanislaw Moniuszko. Feeling the need for further theoretical instruction, Henryk reentered the Paris Conservatoire in 1849 to study harmony and received an honorable mention the following year. His apprentice years completed, he now embarked on a career as a concertizing virtuoso. Together with his younger brother Jozef, a pianist, he traveled through Russia and presented some two hundred concerts during the next two years. The two brothers, ages sixteen and fourteen, formed an attractive duo and received much acclaim. True, there were also dissenting voices, for example the critic-composer A. Serov, who warned against excessive praise for child prodigies and saw nothing but a "gift for virtuosity" in the brothers Wieniawski.

Henryk soon proved him wrong by composing and publishing four-teen opus numbers by the time he was eighteen. Among them were some of his best-known pieces, like the Polonaise No. 1 in D, *Souvenir de Moscou,* several mazurkas, a collection of violin studies (*L'école moderne*), and, most importantly, his First Violin Concerto Op. 14 in F-sharp minor. The concerto, requiring tremendous virtuosity, prompted his first success in Germany in 1853, at the famous Gewand-haus concerts in Leipzig. (Just four years earlier, his older colleague Ernst had played his own Concerto in F-sharp at the same concerts—not an easy act to follow!)

Wieniawski's European fame grew rapidly. His versatility was much admired: he could give an imposing performance of Beethoven's *Kreutzer Sonata* (with the pianist Anton Rubinstein, in Paris in 1858) and then dazzle the public with a rendition of *Carnaval de Venise,* in which he outplayed (so the critics said) all his predecessors and com-petitors, including Paganini and Ernst. The following year he came to London to participate as violist in the memorable quartet concerts of the Beethoven Society, where Ernst played first and Joachim second violin. While in London, Wieniawski married Isabella Hampton, niece of the composer George Osborne; she received the loving dedication of a new composition, *Légende.* (Their youngest daughter Irene became a composer under the pen name Poldowski.)

Rubinstein, the Russian-born pianist, was so impressed by Wie-niawski that he persuaded him to move to St. Petersburg, where a major effort was underway to reorganize musical life along European academic standards. In 1860 Wieniawski settled in St. Petersburg for twelve years of intense activities: he was appointed soloist of the czar and the Im-perial Theatre, leader of the string quartet of the Russian Music So-ciety, and—most importantly—professor at the new St. Petersburg Con-servatory. In 1868 he resigned his teaching post* in sympathy with Rubinstein, who left abruptly because of faculty dissension. But Wieniawski remained active in St. Petersburg until 1872, when he and Rubinstein embarked on a lengthy American concert tour.

The Russian years constituted a period of artistic growth for Wie-niawski both as composer and as performer. He played with eminent colleagues at the Conservatory—the pianists Rubinstein and Lesche-titzky, the cellist Davydoff; he became acquainted with the young group of Russian composers, including Balakirev and Tchaikovsky. Wieniawski

---

* His successor was the twenty-three-year-old Hungarian-born Leopold Auer, often re-garded as the father of the Russian violin school.

enlarged his repertoire, performed extensively, and enjoyed great popularity. "He is without doubt the first violinist of our time—there is no one comparable: his playing produces a tremendous effect," said Rubinstein.[1] Wieniawski entered fully into the artistic life of the czarist capital, which was polarized by the music-loving conservative aristocracy and the liberal literacy circles. He had friends and admirers in both camps. The author Turgeniev, who heard Wieniawski play first violin in Beethoven's Quartet Op. 127 in 1864, wrote to Madame Viardot, "It was played to perfection. . . . Wieniawski has grown enormously since I heard him last: he played Bach's Chaconne in a way that could bear comparison even with the incomparable Joachim."[2]

While in Russia, Wieniawski composed his finest work—the Second Concerto in D minor. The first performance on November 27, 1862, in St. Petersburg, with the composer as soloist and Rubinstein conducting, produced a sensation. César Cui, the composer-critic, wrote to Balakirev two days later, "I still cannot collect myself from the impact of that first *Allegro* of his Concerto."[3] Tchaikovsky, too, thought highly of the work.

At first, comparisons between Wieniawski and his older colleague Vieuxtemps, who had left many admirers in St. Petersburg, were quite frequent in the Russian press. One critic wrote in 1860,

> At present, Wieniawski has in many ways surpassed Vieuxtemps. The latter astounds you with his powerful bow and mastery of performance, but he does not move you; in Wieniawski, however—aside from his mastery—there is that sacred fire that captivates you, at times agitating and exciting all your feelings, at times caressing your ear.[4]

Another critic stressed the "plasticity" of Vieuxtemps's interpretation as compared to the "impetuosity" of Wieniawski, who was advised to temper his emotional style in "classical" music. With every passing year, Wieniawski matured as an artist and grew in the favor of the Russian public until he achieved a position of unrivaled eminence as a master violinist.

On May 23, 1872, Wieniawski performed his farewell concert in Pavlovsk (near St. Petersburg, a favorite spot for summer concerts) to the ovations of both public and critics. His departure was regretted, but he felt that the time had come to be free of official encumbrances and duties. To play at the czarist court meant, as he put it, "to play for people who are as high-born as they are glacial, who are forbidden by eti-

quette to show any signs of satisfaction."[5] He disliked the Russian police state and the constant surveillance; he resented the atmosphere of
repression toward his Polish countrymen (in fact, his brother Julian was
involved in the Polish insurrection of 1863 against the czarist regime).
Yet, on the whole, Wieniawski's parting was friendly; he returned in
1878 for concerts and died in Moscow in 1880.

The first American tour of Rubinstein and Wieniawski extended
from October 1872 to May 1873. We know that Rubinstein gave 215
concerts in 240 days, and Wieniawski participated in most of them. As
the pressures increased, there were frictions between the two high-
strung artists. Wieniawski resented receiving second billing to Rubinstein, and for a time they stopped speaking to each other. As soon as the
tour ended, Rubinstein left for Europe, totally exhausted, branding the
whole experience as "penal servitude." "May Heaven preserve us from
such slavery. Under these circumstances there is no chance for art—one
simply becomes an automaton. . . ." Rubinstein had a few sarcastic
words for Wieniawski:

> He was a man of extreme nervous temperament who, for rea-
> sons of ill health, quite often failed to meet his appointments
> in St. Petersburg at the Opera and the Conservatory; but in
> America he never missed a concert. However ill he might be,
> he always managed to find strength enough to appear on the
> platform with his fairy-like violin. The secret of this punctu-
> ality lay in the fact that he had to forfeit 1000 francs for every
> non-appearance.[6]

Financially, the tour was a huge success; Wieniawski's share was 100,000
francs. Always in need of money, Wieniawski signed up for another
year of concertizing, this time with the celebrated singer Pauline Lucca.
Again the result was a great success, but the effort shattered his frail
health.

In 1874, after his return from America, Wieniawski accepted a
temporary post at the Brussels Conservatory, replacing the ill Vieuxtemps. Here he had some talented students—young Ysaÿe, for one, and
a prodigy from San Francisco, Leopold Lichtenberg. But Wieniawski
was not cut out for a sedentary life, and resumed his travels in 1876.
That spring he played Vieuxtemps's Concerto No. 5 in Paris, then
moved on to Vienna to meet the challenge of a new young rival, the
phenomenal Pablo de Sarasate. Wieniawski conquered the public wherever he went—Prague, Budapest, Scandinavia, London, and of course

his homeland, Poland. In the spring of 1878, he participated in a famous series of Russian music given in Paris under Nicolai Rubinstein (Anton's younger brother, a conductor and pianist).

By that time, Wieniawski's health was very precarious, and a heart condition often made it difficult for him to perform. Well known is an incident of November 1878 in Berlin. Visibly indisposed, Wieniawski began by asking the public's indulgence for his playing seated. However, a few minutes later he had an asthmatic attack and had to be helped off stage. Joachim, who was in the audience, rushed to the wings; a few minutes later, he appeared on stage, apologizing for his street attire, and played Bach's Chaconne, using Wieniawski's violin. After he had finished, the hall broke into tumultuous applause while Wieniawski, still shaky, walked onto the stage to embrace his old friend.

Undaunted, Wieniawski continued his journey east to fulfill engagements in Poland and Russia. On December 15, 1878, he played his Second Concerto in Moscow under Nicolai Rubinstein. The public gasped at the sight of Wieniawski, barely able to walk to the front of the stage. But once his violin was up, he performed beautifully, as in previous years. On the same program was Beethoven's *Kreutzer Sonata* with Sergei Taneyev at the piano; but Wieniawski had an attack during the second movement and left the stage; the work was finished by a young violinist on the Conservatory faculty, Arno Hilf, who later became quite famous.

Wieniawski struggled on. Desperately in need of money, he went on a tour through the south of Russia but was taken ill in Odessa and remained in a hospital for several months. On April 14, 1879, he was well enough to give a farewell concert in Odessa, and eventually returned to Moscow, where he was again taken ill and hospitalized. His friends rallied to him, visiting from as far as St. Petersburg. In February 1880 Tchaikovsky's patroness, Nadezhda von Meck, took the desperately ill Wieniawski into her palatial home to provide him with better care. A benefit concert was organized in St. Petersburg to raise funds for the premium on a life insurance policy which otherwise would have lapsed. It saved his family in London from starvation. After his death on March 31, 1880, a memorial concert was conducted by Nicolai Rubinstein in Moscow on April 3, and his remains were transferred to Warsaw.

In 1885, Wieniawski's widow sold his violin—which he called "my Amati"—to the Hungarian violinist Jenö Hubay, who identified its maker as Petrus Guarnerius.

In 1935, the Polish Government instituted a Wieniawski Competition for violinists. The first was won by the late French violinist Ginette Neveu, while David Oistrakh received the second prize. Interrupted by the war, the contests were resumed in 1952 and take place every five years.

Wieniawski was an emotional and fiery performer, yet capable of great lyricism. His tone was particularly intense* and full of subtle shadings. He could move listeners to tears with his *Légende*, charm them with the graceful rhythms of his mazurkas, or lift them out of their seats with the panache of a polonaise. His virtuosity was not calculated for cold perfection, but was hurled at the audience with daring gusto. With such an approach, a passage could occasionally misfire, but it did not matter. "*Il faut risquer*" (one must take risks) was his motto, which he wrote in red pencil across difficult passages; "I write these words for my own encouragement, for these passages are really dangerous!" Joachim called him "the wildest violinistic daredevil I've ever met. What he can do with his left hand is incredible."[7]

But in Joachim's circles in Berlin, there were reservations about Wieniawski's bow arm, which, as Joachim's assistant Moser contended, was "incredibly stiff. . . . His angular high elbow and inflexible wrist had a ruinous effect on many younger violinists." In truth, Wieniawski did not "ruin" the young violinists but rather freed them from the constricted low right elbow advocated by Joachim and his school. By the time Moser wrote this criticism, many of the leading violinists—including Kreisler, Elman, and Heifetz—had achieved spectacular success with the elevated right arm, which provided more freedom and greater power. Wieniawski apparently used the so-called Russian bow grip, with the index finger pressing on the stick above the second joint. This method puts more weight on the string, and the excessive pressure must be controlled; but among twentieth-century violinists, the Russian bow grip is used as much as the traditional Franco-Belgian grip. Wieniawski was a pioneer, though probably more by instinct than by design.

One of Wieniawski's special effects was a very rapid staccato bowing, which he admitted to achieving by unconventional means. As a boy, he was unable to produce this bowing by Massart's method, namely with a relaxed elbow joint. His inability drove him to despair, since a fine staccato is the hallmark of a great virtuoso. Exhausted by hours of

---

* A comparison with Kreisler's tone is not out of place; see page 296.

practicing, Wieniawski fell asleep, and in a dream he felt a motion in his right arm producing a rapid staccato from his shoulder, not the elbow. He jumped up, grabbed his violin—and it worked: by raising and tensing his right shoulder and stiffening the arm, he was suddenly able to achieve a marvelous staccato at great speed. He learned to control this motion and used the virtuoso staccato bowing in many of his works.

Among the members of the post-Paganini generation, Wieniawski must be ranked at the top, surpassed perhaps only by Ernst. While Ernst, Vieuxtemps, and Bériot actually heard Paganini perform, Wieniawski was too young and could evaluate Paganini only by a few published compositions such as the Caprices and the variations on Nel cor più. By the time Paganini's posthumous works were published in 1853, Wieniawski's mastery was fully developed. Actually, in technical matters, Wieniawski was closer to Ernst than to Paganini, and he far outdistanced Vieuxtemps.

Occasionally, Wieniawski was called "the Chopin of the violin"—a risky comparison. Yet there are some parallels—his ardent Polish nationalism, his writing of polonaises and mazurkas—that can be traced to the influences of Moniuszko and Chopin, whom he had known during his boyhood. Wieniawski's nationalism was subdued: he spent decades in Russia while Chopin chose exile. Nevertheless, it is reflected in his compositions.* He did not have to rely on nationalism to achieve his effects: his Second Concerto, for example, is a glowing example of Romantic inspiration, highly regarded by Joachim, Cui, Tchaikovsky, and others.

Leopold Auer, who heard Wieniawski at the height of his career, was close to him in the years 1868–72, and reminisced some fifty years later:

> Wieniawski was one of the greatest masters of his instrument in any age. He fascinated his audience with an altogether individual talent, and he was as entirely different from any of the other violinists of his day in outward appearance as he was in his manner of playing. Since his death no violinist has ever seemed able to recall him.[8]

Another violinist, Sam Franko, was in Paris in 1878 as a member of the orchestra when Wieniawski played his Second Concerto at the All-Russian Music Festival. Franko, who heard every living violinist of his time and was a sharp critic, wrote many years later,

* Wieniawski's published works comprise 23 opus numbers and several unnumbered works. A complete works edition is in progress in Poland.

I was electrified by Wieniawski's playing. I have never heard
anyone play the violin as he did, either before or since. His
wonderfully warm tone, rich in modulation, his glowing temperament, his perfect technique, his captivating *élan*—all
threw me in a kind of hypnotic trance; when I think of those
days, I can still feel the red-hot intensity of his playing. No
other violinist gave me such a thrill as did Wieniawski.[9]

Wieniawski was the Romantic virtuoso *par excellence,* who gave of
himself unstintingly, who led a life of emotion and excitement, whose
nervous energy sapped his physical strength. Though he died in his mid-
forties, wasted before his time, he lived a singularly fulfilled life.

Ole Bull

The life and career of Ole Bull are embroidered by tales. Some
considered him a Nordic Paganini, others a charlatan. Neither description is justified. He was a highly original artist, musically endowed by
nature but not formally schooled, generous and sincere yet a calculating
showman. His success began while Paganini was still active, and his
name resounded in Europe and America side by side with those of
Bériot, Joachim, Vieuxtemps, Wieniawski, and Sarasate. His appeal was
based primarily on his own, very special repertoire. When he ventured
into the "classics," the results were questionable at best. Playing a Mozart quartet, Ole Bull would stand up on center stage while his three
"accompanists" sat in the pit. He performed Beethoven's *Kreutzer Sonata* with Franz Liszt at the piano "in a manner that should have made
Beethoven rise up in his grave in protest," according to a London critic.
But when he played his own pieces and arrangements, he was incomparable and held thousands spellbound.

On and off stage, Ole Bull was an imposing figure. Six feet tall,
with a broad chest, slim waist, and long, blond (later silvery) hair, he
looked like the incarnation of the "Magnus Apollo." From the stage, he
would survey the multitude of his public as a king looks at his subjects.

The pose of Mr. Bull when playing is a model of manly grace.
He rests his body centrally over the left leg . . . while the
right foot is advanced and the right leg forms an oblique
brace. . . . The figure is singularly erect. . . . Both the head
and the chin are absolutely free and seem to feel no responsibility for the position of the violin.[1]

However, he did use a chinrest of his own invention that fit across the tailpiece. He owned many fine instruments; his favorite was a Gaspar da Salò (one of the oldest known violin makers), which he described as matchless. "The violin is full of joy and bears its virtuoso like an Arab steed," he wrote from Russia in 1867. He also owned another Gaspar da Salò violin, more a showpiece, with an inlaid fingerboard and a scroll allegedly carved by Benvenuto Cellini, which probably dates prior to 1570. The rare instrument is now in the Town Museum in his native Bergen.

Ole Bull fitted his violins with a bridge that was almost flat, enabling him to play three- and four-part chords simultaneously. Further facilitating this feat was an unusually long and heavy bow, also of his own design. In fact, Bull liked to tinker with his violins; whenever he was in Paris he spent long hours in the workshop of the famous Vuillaume, watching and working. The idea for the flat bridge is obviously adapted from the Hardanger fiddle, a Norwegian folk instrument which was used chordally or with a drone bass; in addition to the four strings to be played with a bow, it had four sympathetic wire strings underneath the fingerboard. As an ardent Norwegian nationalist, Bull was interested in the unique sonority of the old folk fiddle, which he played and imitated on his Italian-style violin. In fact, he took a Hardanger fiddle with him to Paris and used it for one piece at his Paris debut in 1833, without arousing much interest. Later he adapted the chordal style of the folk fiddle to the traditional violin and achieved polyphonic effects that were considered unique.

The Bach scholar Albert Schweitzer had his own theory:

> The last representative of chord playing on the violin was the Norwegian, Ole Bull. His bridge was quite flat; he had his bows made in such a way that the stick stood at a considerable distance from the hair.* It is interesting to know that he always maintained that this method was no new invention of his own, but a return to the true violin method of the past. It is quite possible that in Scandinavia the traditions of the 17th century had been retained, along with the old bows, down to Ole Bull's time.[2]

It is improbable that Ole Bull had any knowledge of the curved "Bach bow" as Schweitzer envisaged it, but he certainly achieved the effect of unbroken chords and polyphonic playing that Schweitzer advocated.

---

* His stick was bent downwards considerably at the point.

Ole Bull never played on a violin other than his own, since his style was dependent on the special bridge and bow.

How did Ole Bull, this untutored "nature boy," "*ce jeune sauvage*" (in the words of the Parisian critic Janin), succeed in conquering the public of cultured Europe and ebullient America? He had talent, looks, charm, and a certain eccentric naïveté which he shrewdly exploited. He knew his limitations, especially as a composer, though this did not humble him. The entire catalogue of his works consisted of less than a dozen pieces, among them the Concerto in A, the *Adagio religioso*, the *Quartetto a violino solo*, the *Polacca guerriera*, and a few shorter pieces of Norwegian character, some of them arranged folk songs. He also played, as his classic contribution, a transcribed Adagio by Mozart (originally for clarinet), very rarely a Spohr concerto or a few pieces by Paganini (*Nel cor più, I palpiti*, a concerto, and the *Carnaval de Venise*). In America he added *Yankee Doodle* and one or two other popular tunes. He knew and played a few quartets of Mozart. He did not care for Beethoven, and the *Kreutzer Sonata* seems to have been a one-time performance.

This is the repertoire that he played and replayed for fifty years. His unsophisticated music, performed in a grand yet ingratiating manner, captivated the hearts of multitudes everywhere. At that time, famous virtuosos appeared only two or three times on an evening's program; the balance was filled by several assisting artists and orchestral selections. But Bull certainly made a virtue out of scarcity. Since he often gave a dozen or so concerts in the same town, people obviously came to hear *how* he played, regardless of *what* he played.

As a performer, Ole Bull was not quite as untutored as he claimed to be; he just did not belong to any "school." He was born in 1810 on the west coast of Norway, in Bergen, a Hanseatic city with cultural traditions. Young Ole heard string quartets played at home and took violin lessons from an itinerant Danish violinist. On his ninth birthday he was presented with the Etudes by Fiorillo—a useful study book—but soon his teacher left town and there were no lessons for three years. In 1822, a Swedish violinist schooled by Baillot settled in Bergen and tried to teach Ole according to the rules. But there was an untamable streak of freedom in the boy: he liked to listen to nature, compose his own little tunes, observe the peasant fiddlers. He first heard the name of Paganini in 1824. His grandmother got him some of Paganini's music, and Ole went wild over that treasure. He also tried to play some of

Spohr's music. But he had to fight the resistance of his father, who wanted his son to study theology, not music. By the time Ole was sent to Christiania (now Oslo) to enter the university, in 1828, he already had a reputation as a violinist. He failed the Latin examination, but found acclaim as a musician and was appointed director of the Philharmonic and Dramatic Societies in the capital. He was tall, overgrown, and sickly looking at the time; he composed some music but was unable to shape his crude ideas, though he had a wealth of imagination.

Feeling the need for guidance, he decided to travel to Cassel in May 1829 to consult Spohr. The reception he received from the maestro was very cool, but the disappointment was mutual, since Bull did not care for Spohr's playing. Disillusioned, Bull thought of resuming his academic studies and visited Göttingen; what he learned there was brawling and drinking in the best German student tradition. By September he was back in Christiania.

Having earned some money with concerts, Bull again went on the road in 1831, on his way to Paris in pursuit of Paganini. Fascinated by Paganini's unique style, he tried to emulate him—and with some success, since history considers Ole Bull one of the best among Paganini's numerous imitators. But imitation alone is not enough for a career, and Bull's first concert in Paris in 1833 failed to arouse any attention. In fact, the two years spent in Paris belonged to the most miserable of his life: he was penniless and close to suicide. Nor was he more successful in Milan; his playing of compositions by Spohr, Mayseder, and Paganini at La Scala was criticized, not for lack of talent but for lack of style. So impressed was Bull with the criticism that he stayed in Milan for six months to work on self-improvement. His next concert in Italy launched his career: he substituted at short notice in Bologna for the indisposed Bériot and created a sensation. Even Madame Malibran, the famous diva and Bériot's concert companion, was enchanted by Bull's sweetness of tone. The Italian sojourn transformed Ole Bull: Italy taught him how to "sing" on his instrument. Here he composed most of the works that he continued to play for the rest of his career.

The Italian success opened at last the doors of the Parisian Grand Opéra, where, a few years earlier, he had failed an audition for an orchestra job. Appearing as soloist in June 1835, he achieved a triumph and was singled out by Janin's review of the "young savage" from distant beautiful Norway—"He is a musician who has not had a master . . . who does not belong to any school. There is something naive and inspired in him, something of incredible power. . . ."[3] After having been lionized in Paris, he moved on to London, where he was heard on May 21, 1836. "His command of the instrument is absolutely perfect," wrote the *Times*. True, there were also voices that accused him of being a charlatan and a cheap imitator of Paganini, whose playing was still fresh in people's minds. But Ole Bull prevailed: he played at the London Philharmonic on June 6 and then embarked on a tour of the British Isles, during which he gave more than 250 concerts in little over a year. He filled King's Theatre, Drury Lane, Covent Garden. His success with the public overshadowed even that of Madame Malibran. Critics mentioned the beauty of his tone on the G-string and his chordal playing on three simultaneous-sounding strings while plucking an accompaniment on the fourth string, i.e. pizzicato with the left hand. (This was his famed *Quartetto a violino solo*.)

There followed extended tours through Europe, as far as Russia. Bull's English carriage was equipped with runners for the northern snows. It was large enough for him and his servant to sleep in. In the spring of 1838 he gave two concerts in Cassel, Spohr's stronghold, which elicited this comment from the maestro:

> Bull's double stopping and chord playing and the assurance of his left hand are admirable, but—like Paganini—he sacrifices to his acrobatics too many of the nobler things of the instrument. His tone, with the thin strings he uses, is bad, and with an almost flat bridge he can use the A and D strings only in the lower positions and pianissimo. That makes his playing, when he cannot show off his fireworks, rather monotonous. We noticed this in two Mozart quartets which he played at my house. He plays however with great feeling, but not with refined taste.[4]

It is interesting to compare this evaluation with one by Joachim, made some twenty years later. In December 1860, Ole Bull was invited to Hanover, where Joachim was Royal music director. Bull was soloist at an orchestral concert and played Paganini's Second Concerto, as well as a solo of his own. Joachim wrote in a letter to Clara Schumann,

> The Norwegian interests me more than I expected: he has remarkable power over his instrument, a very fine tone, and plenty of vitality. It is true I have only heard him play, in a room, fragments of some very beautiful little Norwegian folksongs of the simplest description.

A few days later, after Bull played at court together with Clara Schumann, Joachim added, "I like his playing better in a room than in public, because, in private, he often selects very original Norwegian melodies. His tone is pleasantly soft and full of feeling."[5]

Many years later, Joachim confided his private opinion about Bull to his trusted biographer, Moser:

> In some violinistic specialties, for example staccato up-bow and down-bow, bouncing arpeggios over four strings, and pizzicato with the left hand, Bull could be called near-perfect. His intonation was very pure and clean, even in the most difficult runs. But he displayed an almost childish simple-mindedness and awkwardness when confronted with classical music; he was utterly unable to deal with it and had the most outlandish conceptions about its character.[6]

One thing is certain: a violinist of such technical attainments cannot be called charlatan. When playing for large untutored audiences, he stooped—like Paganini and other contemporary virtuosos—to some cheaper "acrobatic" tricks on the violin, but this was showmanship rather than charlatanry. Nor should one doubt Bull's basic musicality, though it may not have conformed to German taste. In general, virtuosos were held in low esteem by musical connoisseurs. Mikhail Glinka, the Russian composer, met and heard Ole Bull in Spain and jotted down in his *Memoirs*, "In the spring [1847] the famous violinist Ole Bull came to Seville. He did, in fact, play powerfully and with great precision, but like most virtuosi, he was weak in music."[7] However, Glinka's compatriots in Moscow and St. Petersburg disagreed and gave Bull a rousing reception; in fact, he visited Russia four times between 1838 and 1867 and was overwhelmed by the warmth and hospitality of the Russian music lovers. The Russian public was fully up to date in terms of violin playing: virtuosos from the West arrived regularly, among them Bériot, Ernst, and particularly Vieuxtemps, who lived in St. Petersburg during the 1840s. All the more remarkable is the article of the leading Russian music authority, Count Odoevsky, who recognized in Bull the new type of Romantic artist:

> When Ole Bull raises his divine violin, we are all conquered by him. . . . My advice to all *young* artists is to leave that old school of Kreutzer and Rode; in our time it serves only to train mediocre musicians for the orchestra. Everything must have its end. . . . They collected justified tributes in their

time—and that is enough. Today we have our virtuosos, spanning a wide gamut, with brilliant passages, with passionate cantilena, with versatile effects. Let our critics call that charlatanry. The public and the connoisseurs who understand the art, will treat their poor judgment with an ironic smile.[8]

To Odoevsky, Bull was the "Nordic bard." Compared to Bull's soaring flight, the passages of the old school—phlegmatic and heavy—seemed like the efforts of a "galloping cow."

Ole Bull's adventures in the New World deserve special mention. He made his New York debut on November 25, 1843, appearing at the Park Theater between two plays. Announced as "the prince of violinists," he did not disappoint the audience. Wrote the New York *Herald*, "We cannot describe Ole Bull's playing—it is beyond the power of language." He had presented himself with his best pieces—Paganini's *Nel cor più* and his own Concerto in A and *Polacca guerriera*; as an encore he played *Yankee Doodle*. Not that he was without competitors: New York, in fact, was overrun by visiting violinists—the Frenchman Artôt was already there and Vieuxtemps was to arrive in December.* The influential French colony supported its countrymen, but Ole Bull had more popular appeal, creating a furor never before produced in America. In one month he gave six concerts in New York, five in Philadelphia, three in Baltimore, two each in Washington and Richmond. In 1844 he began to tour the continent from Canada to Cuba. He travelled 100,000 miles, gave over two hundred concerts and earned close to $100,000. He was the common people's ideal of a great musician; on the day of a concert, the roads into town were crowded with whole families traveling by oxcart to hear him. Bull loved the rough life of the frontier and its people; he joked and drank and brawled, he faced dangers and earned the respect of anyone who ever wrestled with him. He developed an attachment to America second only to his love for Norway.

This explains the eccentric plan Bull conceived in 1852—he wanted to found a colony, a "New Norway" in America. He bought 11,000 acres of land in Pennsylvania and invited impoverished Norwegian farmers to settle. They began to clear land and build a town, to be called Oleana. Only too late did Bull discover that he had been swindled and that he had bought land that was not for sale. The colony collapsed and

---

* On December 16 both Bull and Vieuxtemps were elected first honorary members of the fledgling New York Philharmonic.

the Norwegians moved on toward Minnesota, where they prospered. But the idealism that prompted Bull is to be admired.

Similar idealism motivated him to found a National Theater in his native Bergen. He organized a theater company and an orchestra. A Festival in Bergen in 1851 was a huge success. Bull discovered the playwright Ibsen and appointed him to the theater. (Ibsen stayed for five years; his successor was the writer Bjørnson.) Ole Bull championed Norwegian independence, political and cultural, and his prestige lent much force to the movement, though he also met with domestic opposition.

Bull's ventures in America and Norway involved him in financial losses and legal troubles. Undeterred, he resumed his concert tours and rebuilt his fortune. In 1857–58 he was back in Bergen to prop up his National Theater. At that time he heard the fifteen-year-old Edvard Grieg play some of his juvenile compositions and persuaded his parents to send the boy to Leipzig for training as a musician. Grieg was forever grateful to the older master.

During the 1860s, Bull traveled extensively on the European continent. Critics tried to sink him, but he proved unsinkable. Hanslick wrote a learned article which read more like a dirge:

> Ole Bull exercises little of his old magic. He was always given to a one-sided virtuosity, to a combination of sovereign bravura and bizarre manners which might best be called "Paganinic." Enthusiasm for this kind of thing . . . has decreased astoundingly during the last twenty years. We look for deeper satisfaction even from a virtuoso. . . . We demand of a virtuoso, himself insignificant as a composer, that he place his technical abilities at the service of superior music.[9]

This was written in 1858, when Ole Bull reappeared in Vienna after an absence of eighteen years. True enough, the time of unbridled virtuosity had passed, but Ole Bull still found admirers. Even Joachim considered him interesting when they met in 1860. In 1861, Bull had a successful season in London, where he played twelve times during May and June, facing competition from Vieuxtemps, Wieniawski, and other famous artists. In 1866 and 1867 he again visited Russia, reviving the old enthusiasm. Then he reembarked for America, where his name was still magic. In 1870, his life took a new turn: at the age of sixty and widowed, he met a twenty-year-old American, Sara Thorpe, the daughter of a wealthy Wisconsin state senator. She played the piano very well and fell in love with the glamorous artist. Despite resistance from her businessman-father, they were married. For a time Ole Bull and his young wife lived in Boston, where their baby, Sara Olea, was born. He gave some concerts, though a Boston critic deplored his programs as "barroom trash." But the old wanderlust hit Bull again and he returned alone to Norway. He had lost none of his flamboyance: on his sixty-sixth birthday he climbed Cheops's Pyramid in Egypt while a Bedouin carried his violin. Standing proudly at the top, with a Norwegian flag beside him, he gave an emotional rendition of his favorite Norwegian tune, *Et saetersbesoeg* (1876). That year Sara rejoined her errant husband and took him firmly in hand: she managed his life and his concerts and made his last years happy. During the summers they lived in the magnificent house he built on an island off Bergen, on a 600-acre estate, while the winter months were spent in America, where his magic name still filled the concert halls. His seventieth birthday, on February 5, 1880, was celebrated with a surprise party in Cambridge, Massachusetts, where he had many friends. His last performance took place in Chicago on May 21, and he only played his favorite piece, *Mountains of Norway*. A month later the family sailed for Europe and he arrived home feeling ill. He died on August 17 and was buried in Bergen while the nation mourned.

His young widow guarded his memory. She collected all the documents concerning his romantic life and in 1882 published *Ole Bull: a Memoir*. One of his last projects was to raise money for a memorial in honor of Leif Ericsson, the legendary Norse discoverer of America. Sara Bull saw the project to completion; the memorial statue was erected on Commonwealth Avenue in Boston. Eventually, she returned to live in Cambridge, where she died in 1911. Ole Bull's violin, the famous Gaspar da Salò, was donated by Mrs. Bull to the Town Museum in Bergen, not to be played by anyone.

The life and music of Ole Bull are better seen in the larger framework of Norway's struggle for independence. After centuries of Danish rule, the country was governed, during the nineteenth century, by Sweden and did not gain independence until 1905. Ole Bull's founding of the National Theater in Bergen in 1850 showed his patriotic concern for Norway's language and literature; bringing Ibsen and Bjørnson to work in Bergen was an act of historic significance.

Ole Bull showed similar dedication to Norwegian music. He collected and arranged folk tunes; he gave concerts with Møllarguten, the leading player on the Hardanger fiddle. He inspired and encouraged a generation of younger Norwegian composers—Kjerulf, Nordraak, Grieg, Svendsen—to delve more deeply into the folk sources of their native country. His arrangements of instrumental folk melodies became part of an important repertoire. Grieg's eulogy said it all:

> Because you, like no one else, were the warm and devoted pioneer of our young national music; because you, like no one else, knew how to conquer all the hearts; because you planted the seeds which will bloom in the future and for which future generations will bless you—because of all this and with infinite gratitude on behalf of Norwegian music, I place this laurel wreath on your grave. May you rest in peace![10]

Pablo de Sarasate

Sarasate was the last of the great nineteenth-century virtuosos—suave, elegant, brilliant in a very personal way, idolized by the public in both hemispheres. He did not teach and he left no school, because his art was too subjective. Yet he had a hypnotic effect on young violinists who fell under his magic spell. His caressing style was not adaptable to powerful music, such as the Brahms concerto, which he refused to play. But within his circumscribed personal style he was inimitable, and his perfection was admired not only by audiences but by fellow violinists and composers. Ysaÿe summed it up: "It is he who taught us to play exactly." With Sarasate (according to Flesch) began "the modern striving after technical precision and reliability, whereas before him a somewhat facile fluency and brilliance were considered the most important thing."[1] Composers dedicated a surprising number of works to Sarasate; the list includes Bruch's Concerto No. 2 and *Scottish Fantasy*, Saint-Saëns's Concertos No. 1 and 3 and *Rondo capriccioso*, Lalo's Concerto No. 1 and *Symphonie espagnole*, Dvořák's *Mazurek* Op. 49, Joachim's Variations Op. 11, and Wieniawski's Concerto No. 2. His willingness to study and perform such a varied new repertoire indicates a musicianship much broader than is generally assumed.

Sarasate's artistic image was shaped as much by his playing as by his own compositions. His total output of fifty-four opus numbers is considerable. He became known for his elegant Spanish Dances and brilliant operatic fantasies; even today, his *Carmen Fantasy* is a challenge to any virtuoso. Even when he ventured outside the familiar Spanish idiom, he proved his skill, as in the ever-popular *Zigeunerweisen*.

Pablo de Sarasate,
the fabulous Spanish
virtuoso and composer
whose elegant playing was
internationally admired

Ole Bull,
"The Nordic Paganini,"
played in Europe and
America.

Sarasate was born in 1844 in the old city of Pamplona, in northern Spain. His father, a bandmaster, began to teach him the violin when he was five. He was ready to perform in public at eight and was awarded a scholarship to study at the conservatory in Madrid. At age ten, he received the gift of a Stradivari violin from Queen Isabella of Spain. In 1856, the twelve-year-old Pablo, already known in Spain as a prodigy, was sent to Paris to study at the Conservatoire with the eminent Delphin Alard, but he was so far advanced that he was awarded a first prize in less than a year. He remained at the Conservatoire as a theory student and received a second prize in harmony in 1859, completing his formal education when he was fifteen years old.

For the next four decades, Sarasate enjoyed great acclaim wherever he appeared. For years he played in North and South America and visited the Orient. But his true success on the European continent dated from his sensational debut in Vienna in 1876. At the time, there was certainly no dearth of violinists—Wieniawski, Joachim, Auer, to mention but a few. Yet Sarasate carved a place for himself with his elegant and immaculate playing: he conquered Germany, where Joachim was king; he scored a huge success in Russia, where Wieniawski and Auer reigned; he became a welcome guest in England. London was slow to acclaim him: he attracted little attention in 1861, but returned in 1874 to play at the Philharmonic Society. He was heard at the Crystal Palace in 1877 and again at the Philharmonic in 1878. At the Birmingham Festival in 1885 he gave the premiere of the concerto composed for him by Alexander Mackenzie.

Basically, Sarasate's chiseled style was not ideally suited for large-scale compositions, and when he played the Beethoven concerto in Berlin in the early 1880s, the critics compared him unfavorably with Joachim. Sarasate was quite angered about it and did not hide his indignation from Moser: "Of course, in Germany one obviously believes that whoever plays the Concerto by Beethoven must perspire as much as your stout teacher." Flesch, generally an admirer of Sarasate, stated bluntly, "As an interpreter of the Beethoven Concerto, Sarasate was impossible."

As for the Brahms concerto, Sarasate delivered his negative opinion to Moser:

Leave me alone with your symphonic concertos like the Brahms. I won't deny that it is pretty good music, but do you really think I'll be so insipid as to stand there on the stage, violin in hand, to listen while the oboe plays the only melody in the Adagio?![2]

This judgment was, in fact, not directed against Brahms, whose string quartets Sarasate loved to play, but against the concept of a concerto in which the soloist is not the dominating force. It ran counter to the aesthetic beliefs of Sarasate and many other virtuoso violinists of the day; and the Brahms concerto, in fact, was slow in gaining acceptance among performers.

Nevertheless, Sarasate was a discerning musician, though his ideas of interpreting the classics may not have conformed to the German ideal. He approached classical music with scrupulous attention to details, but without imagination (if we are to believe Moser and Flesch). He played sonatas by Bach and Beethoven, and his favorite quartets were Brahms's, Schumann's, and Beethoven's *Razumovsky*. Much admired was his interpretation of the Mendelssohn concerto, with the last movement a pyrotechnic display. Sir George Henschel, the first conductor of the Boston Symphony Orchestra, reports on Sarasate's performance in 1877,

> His interpretation of the Mendelssohn Concerto came to German ears like something of a revelation, creating a veritable furore, and indeed I doubt if in lusciousness of tone, crystalline clearness of execution, refinement and grace that performance has been, or ever will be, surpassed.[3]

The same Mendelssohn concerto produced quite another effect on George Bernard Shaw, active as a music critic in London in 1888–89:

> He played Mendelssohn's Concerto last night. But I had as lief hear him play "Pop goes the Wiesel" as any classic masterpiece; and what is more, I believe he would himself just as soon play one as the other. . . . He never interprets anything; he plays it beautifully, and that is all. He is always alert, swift, clear, refined, certain, scrupulously attentive and quite unaffected.[4]

A detail mainly of interest to violinists is Henschel's observation that Sarasate used a harmonic on the fifth note of the Andante—an exposed A—which gave him a "thrill of artistic joy never to be forgotten."

No violinist today would play this note as a harmonic—that is, without vibrato—because it is the high point of an expressive phrase. However, we know from Joseph Szigeti that when *he* studied the concerto with Hubay around 1900, the "living tradition" required a harmonic on that note! The changing taste of players and public is particularly evident in the changeover from an unexpressive "white" harmonic to a warmly vibrated note, especially in expressive phrases.

Szigeti himself heard Sarasate play in 1906 or 1907, and recalls Sarasate's "fixed gaze beyond the heads of the audience and a feeling that he was somewhat absent from and not deeply involved in the music."[5] That "fixed gaze" seems to indicate that Sarasate turned his face toward the audience while playing, a stance also used by Kreisler. In contradiction, Auer observed that Sarasate often looked at his fingers while playing, which means that his profile was toward the audience. Either way, Sarasate used little chin pressure to hold the violin and was able to turn his head while playing.

Auer made his observations during Sarasate's frequent visits to Russia, where the public adored him. He later wrote:

> Sarasate was a small man, very slender, and at the same time very elegant; his face framed in a fine head of black hair, parted in the middle, according to the fashion of the day. . . . From the very first notes he drew from his Stradivari . . . I was impressed by the beauty and crystalline purity of his tone. The master of a perfected technique for both hands, he played without any effort at all, touching the strings with a magic bow in a manner which had no hint of the terrestrial. . . . In the midst of his St. Petersburg triumphs, Sarasate remained a good comrade. He spent the evenings with the cellist Davydoff, the pianist Leschetitzky, or myself, always merry, always smiling and in good spirits.

Auer provided a few technical details about Sarasate:

> Sarasate used only the *staccato volant* [i.e. flying staccato], not very rapid but infinitely graceful. In fact, gracefulness illuminated his whole playing and complemented his extraordinarily singing tone which, however, was none too powerful. He held his bow with all his fingers* which did not prevent

---

* Many violinists have the habit of lifting the little finger of the right hand from the bow stick, especially when playing at the tip, including quite a few of Auer's students! Ysaÿe, the great Belgian violinist, almost never put his "pinky" down. The little finger, however, serves a definite purpose by controlling the balance of the bow.

him from producing a free-swinging tone and ethereal lightness in passages. He also had a very precise, rapid, and even trill.[6]

Flesch made an additional observation with regard to the "flying staccato":

> Sarasate was the only violinist whom I ever heard play the flying staccato in the Finale of the Mendelssohn Concerto at the extreme tip of the bow. . . . The fingertips of his left hand were quite smooth and ungrooved; they hit the fingerboard in a normal fashion, without raising or hammering. His vibrato was rather broader than had hitherto been customary.[7]

This last remark is particularly revealing: we know that in general the vibrato (which gives the violin tone the touch of the human voice) became gradually broader during the nineteenth century. Joachim, for example, still advocated a narrow vibrato like a *tremblement*. The broader the vibrato, the more sensuous the tone quality. Sarasate's broader vibrato seems to have given his tone an unusual quality. In his later years, his ability to vibrate suffered (as it does quite often with aging violinists), and he also began to play sharp.

Flesch thought of having discovered the secret of Sarasate's frictionless tone production, the "continually mild, passionless, smooth, eely tone": he drew his bow invariably in the exact middle between bridge and fingerboard, hardly ever approaching the bridge with more pressure for higher intensity. He simply did not wish to "dig in," and all the "scraping" often associated with fiddle playing was abhorrent to him. It was said that he never played louder than mezzo-forte. He was "the ideal embodiment of the salon virtuoso of the greatest style; the history of modern violin playing cannot be imagined without him."[8]

His unforced approach to bowing was also reflected in his left-hand technique: no undue finger pressure on the strings. His hands were comparatively small; for this reason he avoided any pieces that demanded large stretches and extensions for the left hand, as for example Paganini or Ernst. Nevertheless, his hands were well suited for violin playing, and he had no need for much practicing. In fact, he never practiced during the off-season summer months. (Kreisler, too, never touched the violin during his summer vacations.)

Albert Spalding, the noted American violinist, depicted Sarasate as

> a bewitching violinist. His prodigious facility was coupled with an elegance of style difficult to describe. His tone had a silvery

sheen and a piercing sweetness. . . . The paradox of a player who made trivial music sound important and deep music sound trivial. He played Beethoven with the perfumed polish of a courtier who doesn't quite believe what he is saying to Majesty. But when he reached . . . his own Spanish Dances, he was completely in his element. The violin sang like a thrush, and his incomparable ease tossed aside difficulties with a grace and insouciance that affected even his gestures. . . . I don't think I ever heard a *forte* passage from his bow; his palette held pastel shades only.[9]

Flesch described his appearance:

His features were regular, only the lower jaw was rather long in relation to the upper part of his face. It was a unique experience to see this little man stride onto the platform with genuine Spanish *grandezza*, superficially calm, even phlegmatic, to witness how . . . he began to play with unheard-of sovereignty and, in a rapid climax, put his audience into astonishment, admiration, and highest rapture.[10]

Wasielewski remembers that "one would have welcomed occasionally a more forceful and energetic treatment of the instrument. Sarasate's manner of handling the violin had something feminine and gracefully sinuous, without being sentimental."[11]

Sarasate represented the Apollonian ideal of violin playing—a tone of unsurpassed beauty, a technique of effortless perfection, an interpretation of elegant objectivity. His style marked an epoch in modern violin playing.

Sarasate was one of the first violinists to make recordings. They date from 1904—four years before his death—but show no decline in technical mastery: astounding agility of left and right hand, impeccable intonation into the highest positions, and a devil-may-care handling of virtuoso matters. Only his tone quality is disappointing—the sound is thin and "white"—but this may be due to imperfect recording techniques. He is at his best in his own pieces; the recording of Bach's Prelude in E suffers from excessive speed—it was rerecorded too fast, which also caused the pitch to be raised by almost a third.

During his long and successful career, Sarasate amassed a considerable fortune, which he willed mainly to charitable institutions. His native town of Pamplona received all his collections and mementos, for which a museum was built. During his lifetime he returned regularly to Pamplona and he was feted like a king.

He owned two Stradivari violins, which he left in his will to the two institutions where he had studied. His favorite instrument, a golden-yellow Strad built in 1724, was given to the Paris Conservatoire, while the reddish "Boissier" Strad of 1713 went to the Madrid Conservatory. The tone of his favorite violin was not large, but responded with great ease and had surprising carrying power—obviously the ideal instrument for Sarasate's unpressed tone production. It is interesting to note that he liked to practice on a modern violin—a copy of a Stradivari made by Gand in Paris*—which required more effort and pressure to respond. Switching back to his genuine Stradivari made playing appear easy and effortless. A Gand violin was given to every winner of a first prize at the Paris Conservatoire; this is how Sarasate acquired his. The name of the winner was usually inlaid in the ribs of the violin; and I have known quite a few first-prize winners who, like Sarasate, have kept and used their well-made Gand violins as workaday companions throughout their career.

---

* The Gands were a family of expert violin makers who became the official luthiers of the Conservatoire. Charles Gand *père* was succeeded by his two sons; later the firm became "Gand et Bernardel."

COUNTERCURRENTS

Louis Spohr

Louis Spohr represented the German countercurrent to the influence of Paganini. He stood for solid musicianship and opposed the inroads of virtuosity; to him, Paganini represented a kind of charlatanry.* But as time went on, Spohr witnessed not only the rise of Paganini's imitators but another generation of Austro-German violinists who—with all due respect for their old master—evolved a modernized approach to the violin. Among them were his own student Ferdinand David, the Viennese Ignaz Mayseder, and even the young Joseph Joachim, all of whom outgrew Spohr's dominant influence.

Spohr's performance and his treatment of the violin reflected his physical appearance. Tall and of athletic build, he was endowed with long arms, large hands, and strong fingers. Standing almost immobile while performing, he could produce a robust tone, well modulated in all dynamic shadings; he controlled his bow as a fine singer controlled his breath, starting a tone in pianissimo and swelling to a forte while gradually adding a left-hand vibrato—a *bel canto* technique which he used in the true Italian singing style. Indeed, his Concerto No. 8 is subtitled *Gesangscene*, that is, a vocal scene. His bow always adhered to the string, and he belittled all bouncing bowings as "windbag style." In other words, he rejected such bowings as spiccato, *sautillé*, flying staccato, and ricochet—bowings that were used not only by Paganini but also by Romantic composers like Cherubini and Mendelssohn. In his own way,

* See his opinion on pp. 179 and 184.

Spohr's bow control was supreme, shown in his effective use of staccato runs—rapidly detached notes on one bow stroke without leaving the string. When Spohr played for Mendelssohn in 1834, the composer especially admired such a staccato passage and, turning to his sister, said, "See, this is the famous Spohr staccato that no violinist can imitate." (Spohr conceded in his Diary that the perfect mastery of this bowing is a matter more of inborn gift than of study.) Mendelssohn, in his own Violin Concerto written in the 1840s, decided not to use the Spohr staccato, but plenty of flying staccato and *sautillé* (particularly in the Finale, with its elfin style). It marked a break with the Spohr tradition.

Other hallmarks of Spohr's playing (and composing) style are the frequent use of double stops and wide-reaching tenths, facilitated by his strong left hand. He also had a masterful trill, and he liked to play chromatic scales, a technique rarely used today. Earlier in our century, the study of Spohr's concertos was considered indispensable by teachers like Auer and Flesch, but today they have gone out of fashion even in the conservatories. Heifetz and Erica Morini used to play the *Gesangscene*, and Heifetz's masterful recording is still in circulation. It is hard to believe that, between 1810 and 1840, Spohr's violin concertos dominated the German scene to such a degree that they delayed the acceptance of a work like the Beethoven Violin Concerto. He was also very popular in England, while the French received him with respectful coolness.

Though Spohr was German-trained (mainly by Franz Eck of Mannheim), he was influenced decisively by the violinist Rode and his peculiarly French style. Spohr met and heard Rode for the first time in 1803 in Brunswick. At that time, Spohr was only nineteen, but already an advanced violinist, while Rode enjoyed an international reputation. Awaiting Rode's appearance with impatience, Spohr prepared himself by studying the works of the great master. "Up to the time when I had by degree formed a style of playing of my own, I had become the most faithful imitator of Rode among all the young violinists of that day," he recalled. Once he heard Rode play, he was captivated by his style. His infatuation with Rode became such that he discarded his own older works "because they no longer pleased me after I had adopted Rode's style of execution."[1] Soon he had absorbed all there was to learn from the French master and developed his own brand of musicality. In 1804 Spohr appeared in Leipzig with his Violin Concerto No. 2 in D minor and was praised to the sky by the critic Rochlitz, both for his playing and his composition:

He afforded us a treat such as . . . no violinist with the exception of Rode ever gave us. Herr Spohr may without doubt
take rank among the most eminent violinists of the present
day. . . . His Concerto [in D minor] ranks with the finest in
existence. . . . Its peculiarity inclines mostly to the grand and
to a soft dreamy melancholy. And so it is with his brilliant
play.

A more laudatory evaluation could not be imagined—the young artist
was barely twenty—and it opened the doors for a fine career. After his
marriage to an accomplished young harpist, the pair set out on extensive concert tours in a carriage especially built to accommodate the harp.
For a time, compositions for violin and harp became Spohr's preferred
genre.

In the years 1812–15, Spohr lived in Vienna. His arrival, in late
1812, coincided with the visit of Rode, the idol of Spohr's youth. To
compete with such a celebrity was no easy task, but ten years had passed
and Spohr had grown into a supremely self-confident artist. He hastened
to announce his debut for December 17, which attracted many connoisseurs, including Rode, who had just arrived. Spohr showed his gifts as
performer and composer in his Concerto No. 5, his Sonata for Violin
and Harp, and a brilliant *Potpourri,* and was warmly applauded. Rode,
on the other hand, disappointed the large audience at his own concert
on January 6, nor did he please Beethoven with his performance of the
master's newest sonata (Op. 96). During the month of January Rode
and Spohr met often at private soirées and Spohr noticed the decline of
Rode's virtuosity. In Spohr's words,

I had the rudeness to . . . ask him if he no longer remembered the way in which he played his compositions ten years
ago. Yes! I carried my impertinence so far as to lay the Variations in G major before him and said that I would play them
exactly as I had heard him play them so frequently ten years
before. After I had finished playing, the company broke out
into rapturous applause, and Rode, for decency's sake, was
obliged to add a "bravo," but one could plainly see that he felt
offended by my indelicacy. And with good reason. I was soon
ashamed of it.[2]

As one contemporary, the poet Körner, wrote, "Spohr has won a
brilliant victory over Rode and he is considered the hero of the day
which—God only knows—he fully deserves."
Each of the artists gave one additional concert, after which Rode

departed. Spohr, as a result of his success, was offered the position of orchestra leader at the Theater-an-der-Wien. Here he acquired experience in the opera, which stood him in good stead later in life.

Living in Vienna, Spohr came to know Beethoven personally and had a few unflattering things to say about him—"His rough and even repulsive manners at that time arose partly from his deafness, which he had not learned to bear with resignation." Nevertheless they became friendly and Beethoven visited Spohr and his wife—"He could then be very friendly with the children." Spohr described Beethoven's conducting as "uncertain and frequently laughable." In general, he made many harsh evaluations, belittling the Fifth Symphony, ignoring the Violin Concerto, and despising the Ninth Symphony:

> I have never been able to relish the last works of Beethoven. Yes! I must even reckon the much admired Ninth Symphony among them. . . . I cannot understand how a genius like Beethoven could have written it. I find in it another proof of what I already remarked in Vienna, that Beethoven was wanting in aesthetical feeling and in a sense of the beautiful.[3]

However, this did not keep him from conducting Beethoven's symphonies on various occasions, for example a cycle of five in 1818–19 including the *Eroica*, the *Pastorale*, Nos. 4 and 8, and in later years the Ninth and the *Missa solemnis*. He also played Beethoven's Quartets Op. 18.

Late in life, Spohr expanded (almost grudgingly) his appreciation of Beethoven. In 1855, he heard the twenty-four-year-old Joachim play the Violin Concerto. After listening attentively, Spohr said, "Well, that's all very nice, but now let me hear a *real* violin piece!" * The following day, Joachim and his quartet played Beethoven's Op. 59, No. 1, and Op. 131 for Spohr. Pensively scratching his ear, he expressed his reaction: "Well, dear Joachim, if one has lived with these bedeviled things as you have, and play them as you do, they certainly touch your heart and soul. . . ."[4]

On the other hand, Spohr was one of the first to champion young Richard Wagner. He conducted *The Flying Dutchman* in Cassel as early as 1843 and insisted on mounting *Tannhäuser* in 1853, despite official opposition. He wrote in 1843, "I consider Wagner as the most gifted of all our dramatic composers of the present time." Spohr's anti-Beethoven and pro-Wagner attitude might seem puzzling at first unless one realizes that Wagner's early operas represented the Romanticism of

---

* But he did not like Joachim's Cadenzas—"superfluously long, very difficult and ungrateful."

their day, while Beethoven's late abstract style was far ahead of its time.

Spohr, while in Vienna, did not have the courage to show Beethoven his own compositions since "Beethoven took not the least interest in the compositions of others." But at some time or other, Beethoven saw works by Spohr and told a visitor in 1825, "Spohr is too rich in dissonances, pleasure in his music is marred by his chromatic melody."[5]

In the years 1816–17 Spohr had some success in Italy, though he had to compete with Paganini, the "Inimitable." The two virtuosos met in Venice in 1816 and exchanged pleasantries, but Spohr did not hear Paganini until 1830 in Cassel. He formed a prejudiced opinion of Paganini on the basis of hearsay.

Spohr's debut in Milan—the most critical of all Italian cities—took place on September 27, 1818, at La Scala. He found the immense size of the theater and the physical arrangement disconcerting: the orchestra sat in the pit while he, the soloist, stood alone on the stage in front of the lowered curtain. The conductor was Rolla, at one time teacher of Paganini, who attended to his job with great care. The audience was sparse, but the applause was generous; it was meant for Spohr not only as performer but also as composer. But he was annoyed by the habit of the public of breaking into applause during the performance: "Gratifying and encouraging as this noisy approbation may be to the solo-player, it is nevertheless exceedingly annoying to the composer. By it, all connection is completely disturbed. . . ."[6]

Though he did not draw any crowds, Spohr had the satisfaction of being compared favorably to Paganini. The review, by a German correspondent, appeared in Leipzig:

> One could not praise Mr Spohr highly enough and at the least one did not hesitate to set him side by side with the famous Paganini who charms everybody. I say "at the least": for in fact, in beauty of playing Mr Spohr certainly surpasses him.[7]

Paganini himself is reported to have called Spohr "the foremost singer on his instrument."

In his autobiography, Spohr describes his concerts, and musical conditions in general, in Venice, Florence, Rome, and Naples. He has quite a few unflattering things to say about Italian orchestras, nor was he impressed by the vocal performances he heard. As for the students at the Naples conservatory, "the violinists have no school at all; they know neither how they should hold the bow nor the violin, and play neither purely nor distinctly."

In the spring of 1820, Spohr made his memorable debut in London with the Philharmonic Society. The season consisted of eight concerts, and Spohr participated in six of them, as composer, soloist, chamber music player, and leader of the orchestra.

At his debut on March 6, he played the well-tested *Gesangscene,* but he was nervous and not at his best. He was made uncomfortable by the hall, overheated by the new gas illumination. But there were also psychological reasons—"I can explain it only through the presence of Viotti and other distinguished artists, whose possibly over-excited anticipation I had to satisfy."[8] But the critics, though noticing his discomfort, were very laudatory and called him "one of the most accomplished and delightful players we ever heard." As for the *Gesangscene* (listed as a "Concerto in the dramatic style"), "he imported so much sentiment to it that his violin, if it did not exactly speak a language, 'discoursed most eloquent music' and was more passionate than many singers we hear."

At his second appearance, Spohr won unanimous admiration with a performance of his own String Quartet in E, Op. 43, supported by three English string players. The only criticism raised was the excessive brilliance of the first violin part "so as to injure its effect as a concerted piece."[9]

Finally, on April 10, Spohr faced the Philharmonic Society for the first time as leader and made conducting history. In London, the orchestral concerts were traditionally directed by two musicians: one (called the leader) was the concertmaster, whose task it was to play the first violin part forcefully and to keep the tempo with violin and bow in hand; the second, called conductor, had his place at the pianoforte, in front of him a full score from which he played occasionally. Spohr, well aware of what he called the "defective system," startled the orchestra at the first rehearsal: instead of raising his violin, he drew a conducting baton out of his coat pocket and gave the signal to begin. There were immediate protests from the players, but Spohr asked at least for a trial. To make clear who was in charge, Spohr persuaded his friend Ries to give up his place at the piano and hand over the full score to him. The first piece went so well that the orchestra "expressed aloud its collective assent to the new mode of conducting." And Spohr adds with pride, "The triumph of the baton as a time-giver was decisive, and no one was seen any more seated at the piano during the performance of symphonies and overtures."[10]

Actually, the "triumph" was short-lived: leader and conductor continued to coexist in London for at least a decade. In fact, we are not even sure whether or not Spohr conducted the evening concert with a baton as he had done at the rehearsal. None of the contemporary London newspapers mentions a baton conductor in reviewing the concert, but they write admiringly that "Mr Spohr led the band in a very novel and superior manner." Yet there can be no doubt that Spohr's innovative action in asserting the single directorship with baton in hand eventually modernized the art of conducting.

The musical novelty at that concert was Spohr's new Second Symphony, "which places him among instrumental composers of the highest class," in the words of one critic. At the last concert of the season, he also introduced his First Symphony to London, as well as his Nonet for strings and winds. His was a triple victory—as violinist, composer, and orchestra leader. The London public remained faithful to him throughout his life. At the end of his stay in London, he wrote home with undisguised pride,

> We can be very satisfied with the results of our visit, since we earned more money than any other artist since Haydn. More than that, I was happy with the applause that all our public and private concerts have received, and which was so stormy at our own benefit concert as one may never hear in London from an English public.[11]

The "we" included his wife Dorette, whose harp playing earned her a share of the success.

A few months after returning from the strenuous London season, the Spohrs set out for Paris, where they arrived in mid-December 1820. At that time, Paris had no concert tradition comparable to the London Philharmonic Society, and Spohr had to bother with planning every step, every appearance. Provided with many letters of introduction, Spohr began the rounds of personal visits. Among the first he saw was Cherubini, whom he had admired since his youth. It was Spohr's plan to make himself known to musicians and connoisseurs at private musicales; one of them took place at the home of his eminent colleague Kreutzer, in the presence of such celebrities as Viotti, Baillot, Habeneck, and Lafont. (Rode was out of town at the time.) Spohr performed several of his own quartets and quintets and praised the ability of the French musicians to play his music at sight. His colleagues were kind to him: "The composers present expressed to me in very laudatory terms upon my compositions, and the violinists upon my play." But soon Spohr was made to understand that his type of music was not exactly fashionable in Paris. Just like Mendelssohn a few years later, Spohr decried the shallowness of musical taste:

> It is very singular how all here, young and old, strive only to shine by mechanical execution, and individuals . . . devote whole years and every energy to the study and practice of one single piece of music, frequently of the most worthless kind, in order to create a sensation before the public.

Spohr's plan to give a public concert met with so many difficulties that he agreed to present an evening of entertainment, equally divided between a concert and a ballet. The event took place on January 10, 1821, at the Théâtre Favart; the hall was well filled, and the audience gave Spohr what he considered a "brilliant reception." But the critics, though friendly, were not overwhelmed. His playing was praised for its "*pureté et justesse*," but his compositions were found full of "Germanic enharmonic." One paper advised him to remain in Paris for a while to perfect his taste, after which he could return to Germany and in turn improve the taste of the "*bons allemands*." Spohr adds sarcastically, "If the good man only knew what this '*bon allemand*' thinks of the musical taste of the French?!" He blamed the lukewarm reviews on the arrogance of the French:

> It is always a hazardous undertaking for a foreign violinist to make a public appearance in Paris, as the Parisians are possessed with the notion that they have the finest violinists in the world, and consider it almost in the light of arrogant presumption when a foreigner considers he has talent sufficient to challenge a comparison with them.[12]

There is a grain of truth in this observation; and yet—only ten years later—the "foreigner" Paganini arrived in Paris and conquered the city overnight.

After two months in Paris, Spohr departed with a rather low opinion of musical conditions there, though he had high respect for some individual musicians like Baillot and Lafont.*

In 1822 Spohr was appointed court conductor at the newly built theater in Cassel. At the time, he lived in Dresden without firm appointment; and having traveled and concertized extensively during the past years, he was obviously glad to settle down, at the age of thirty-seven. He remained in Cassel for the rest of his life; he celebrated the twenty-fifth anniversary of his appointment in 1847, and he was pensioned,

---

* In July 1844 Spohr revisited Paris and was well received by Habeneck and his Conservatoire orchestra; they sightread his Fourth Symphony in his honor, and excerpts were played in 1846 and 1847, but his music was never accepted in Paris.

much against his will, in 1857. He died in Cassel two years later, disgusted with the political intrigues. He had been a liberal all his life and became quite outspoken during the revolutionary year 1848; it contributed to his eventual removal. At one time, he toyed with the idea of emigrating to America but felt too old to start a new life.

In 1822 Cassel was a city of some 20,000 inhabitants, ruled by an elector who liked music but meddled in artistic affairs. Spohr's control was subject to the whims and vetoes of the elector. Still, he had enough power to shape and develop the musical life of the city and he took full advantage of it. In addition to the opera, he conducted the symphony concerts (about six a year) and was in charge of a newly founded choral society; he also performed as soloist and in chamber music. He liked to be in the public eye and gave the public of Cassel a full measure of his art; for example, in the years 1822–57, his compositions received 238 performances at the subscription concerts, and he appeared forty-six times as soloist between his debut in 1822 and his retirement as soloist in 1850. Eight of his operas were given premieres in Cassel between 1822 and 1845, and his *Faust* was restaged in a new version in 1854. Members of Spohr's family performed, too: his wife Dorette as harpist and his daughter Emilia as singer. Obviously, the public of Cassel was satisfied with his musical leadership, though he had frequent quarrels with the court bureaucrats and suffered under petty chicanery. Several times he was denied permission to travel, though he had flattering offers from England; once he was fined for taking a vacation without waiting for approval, and lost his case in court.

Nowhere was Spohr more admired and beloved than in England. Ever since his memorable debut in 1820, his compositions were played regularly, even in his absence. Between 1839 and 1853 he visited England five times. "He was received like a Prince, the whole company rising spontaneously from their seats to salute him," reported the *Spectator* about Spohr's reappearance at the London Philharmonic on July 3, 1843. A week later, Spohr was honored by a "Command Performance" for Queen Victoria and Prince Albert: the program (no doubt selected by Prince Albert) included works by Mendelssohn, Beethoven, Mozart, and Weber, as well as several works by Spohr, who conducted the entire concert. The English music lovers could not get enough of his music: one Sunday at the Queen Square Select Society a Musical Festival in honour of Spohr began at two o'clock, was interrupted for a meal at five and resumed at seven o'clock.

No less admired was Spohr as composer of sacred-style oratorios, and there were opinions that nothing as beautiful had been heard since Handel. London also acclaimed him as opera composer when he conducted the premiere of his *Faust* in 1852. His farewell appearances in London took place in 1853: he conducted Beethoven's Ninth Symphony and his own Seventh Symphony.

Shortly after Spohr's forced retirement from his position in Cassel in 1857, he fell and broke his left arm. Though the break healed well, he was unable to play the violin to his own satisfaction, much as he tried. He still filled some conducting engagements in 1858 and 1859, but soon thereafter his Herculean strength began to ebb. He died peacefully on October 22, 1859, at the age of seventy-four, surrounded by family and friends.

As a composer, Spohr belonged to the Romantic generation of Weber and Mendelssohn (both of whom he admired), but his creative talent did not reach the genius level and his music—despite much excellence—faded fast. One need not be as sarcastic as George Bernard Shaw, who, only thirty years after Spohr's death, described his Septet as "a shining river of commonplaces, plagiarisms, and reminiscences" or the once so popular *Gesangscene* as "lifeless and artificial, in spite of its shapely plausibility." Even earlier, while Spohr was still alive, Brahms wrote to Clara Schumann about a "very dull Concerto by Spohr." Spohr's own students tended to avoid his violin works once they had left the master's tutelage: there was so much of his own inimitable playing in his compositions that they were feared and neglected by other players. Some German historians stress Spohr's "Germanism" which was displaced by "French" shallowness,

> The elegant and brilliant mannerisms of the newer French school found acceptance while Spohr's style was pushed to the side and soon became a historic memory. The bouncing bow replaced the full tone, and German soulfulness, despised by many as too "heavy," had to yield regrettably to French superficiality.[13]

This is an oversimplification. The trivialization of musical taste was initiated as much by Paganini as by the French, who adapted and embellished the new trend in their own glittering way. Spohr's technique was heavy-handed and difficult but not very effective, while French technique was less difficult but much more effective. (Paganini is both difficult *and* effective!)

Spohr knew precisely what he was doing; he deliberately swam against the stream, he openly challenged the popular trend—and he paid the price. In 1839, he wrote a Concertino with the subtitle "Then and Now," in which he tried to juxtapose old and new styles of violin playing. He commented,

> Listening to Ole Bull, as previously to de Bériot, I noticed with how little these violinists manage to arouse the enthusiasm of the great masses. It gave me the idea of writing a piece under the title "Then and Now" [*Sonst und jetzt*] in which the "Now" aims at mocking the new style. . . . Without being more difficult than my other Concertino, it is infinitely more brilliant and produces an effect on the public such as I have never observed before.[14]

But his mockery did not go far: he could not bring himself to using "tricks" like harmonics and pizzicato, and merely added a military drum to the "Now" section to poke fun at the *Polacca guerriera* of Ole Bull. Even when trying, Spohr could not really change his skin and remained true to himself.

Spohr's stage presence was imposing, tall and dignified:

> The small instrument, which he mastered so admirably, seemed in his hand like a toy in the hand of a giant. It is hard to describe with what nonchalance and freedom, elegance and mastery Spohr treated that little thing. Calmly, like a bronze statue, he stood before his music stand. The softness and gracefulness of his movements, the playful ease . . . were inimitable.[15]

The reference to the "music stand" indicates that Spohr performed from music, unlike Paganini.

Spohr was the inventor of a chin rest that straddled the tail piece; thus his eyes faced straight across the bridge toward the fingers of the left hand. He held his violin rather flat and more forward to the right, while other violinists preferred to tilt the violin at an angle. His bow grip was that of the German school, with all fingers close together and the "pinky" not placed on the stick with its end. The hand position was not fixed, and changed at the frog and at the tip. His bow stick was slightly tilted (away from the face of the player). The bow had to move in a right angle to the string. Close attention was paid to the even division of the bow, as well as to the ability of increasing and diminishing the tone on one bow, in the tradition of a singer. Most of the time he produced a full-bodied yet mellow tone, which corresponded to his noble and large interpretation of the cantabile. For this purpose he also liked to use strings of a heavier gauge. Yet he was sensitive to dynamic shadings and could play with much tenderness. Spohr was opposed to the use of artificial harmonics; he considered it a "degradation" of the noble instrument to play whole melodies with these "infantile sounds." He even disclaimed the *flautato* sound (produced by a light bow stroke skimming the surface of the string) and went so far as to dislike using the mute.

The vibrato was to Spohr a "trembling motion of the left hand in the direction from saddle to bridge," raising and lowering the pitch very slightly. He differentiated between fast vibrato on *marcato* notes and slow vibrato in cantabile passages of a passionate nature; he also knew how to increase vibrato speed from slow to fast in crescendo, and vice versa. But he used the vibrato only on single notes, never on several legato notes on one bow, and he used it sparingly, as was the custom of the time.

Spohr was very specific and selective in the choice of fingering. He often prescribed playing an entire phrase or melody on one string in order to achieve a certain timbre. He also showed a preference for slides, not only when changing remote positions but also between neighboring positions where slides could have been avoided. He must have aimed at a dreamy, blurred, or exalted expression. Slides with the same finger covering a half step or a whole step are common in his violin parts. As early as 1805, a Berlin critic took exception to Spohr's frequent slides, describing them as an imitation of Rode, who used them first and to perfection.* In 1808, a Prague critic wrote,

> Spohr's Adagio would be called unsurpassed if he did not destroy our pleasure rather disagreeably by a manner too often used—the up-and-down sliding with the same finger covering all sorts of intervals, creating an artificial meow if this expression does not sound too joking.[16]

Spohr's aversion to the rapid bouncing bow (*sautillé* or ricochet) was not an isolated case; there was an opinion that the short bounce led to a neglect of the long melting bow stroke. During the first decade

---

* We have mentioned this so-called *"maniera languida"* (languid manner) in connection with the playing of Ernst (see p. 205). Rode is said to have been influenced by the vocal style of the contralto Giuseppa Grassini.

Louis Spohr, the greatest German violin master of his time, opposed Paganini.

of the 1800s there were frequent discussions in the pages of the Leipzig *Music Journal* about the pros and cons of the bouncing bow: Cramer used it, while Rode and Kreutzer apparently did not. This prejudice disappeared gradually, simply because much of the solo and chamber music of the Romantic age demanded the flighty, light spiccato or *sautillé*.* One of Spohr's students, Alexander Malibran, relates that Spohr was horrified to find violinists use *sautillé* in chamber music of Haydn and Beethoven; he thought this countered tradition. Only in a few Scherzo movements of Mendelssohn, Onslow, and Beethoven was Spohr willing (according to Malibran) to tolerate bouncing bow; certainly never in his own works. The French school differed: the eminent Baillot permitted and even required bouncing bowings to obtain *leggiero* effects, and his student Bériot used it almost to excess. Under Mendelssohn's gentle influence, young Joachim dropped the taboo against bouncing bow.

Spohr no longer used free ornamentation of the melodic line, which was still practiced by Viotti, Rode, and Kreutzer. He also rejected improvised cadenzas. Essentially he was a Romantic artist, yet his feelings were classically disciplined. In later years, the soft and sensitive element in his playing became more pronounced. After he returned from his Italian journey in 1818, one critic said,

> This critic had the opportunity of hearing this great artist before; but it seems that the Italian journey gave his playing an even greater degree of tenderness than previously when we admired the audacious giant-like performer.[17]

Spohr attached great importance to the quality of the instrument used by a performer, and he believed that the idiosyncrasies of the violin could influence the style of the player. "One tries to cover up the weakness and bring out the best traits of the instrument," he said, "the instrument influences the method of the player as much as the voice influences the singer." After the loss of a Guarnerius early in his career, he had to struggle with inferior instruments and experimented with ways to improve the sound. He then acquired a contemporary French violin made by Lupot, which had a powerful, somewhat inflexible, tone. Using this instrument in the large halls of La Scala and San Carlo, he

---

* In orchestral playing, however, some twentieth-century conductors forbid the use of *sautillé* by an entire violin section as being "imprecise." For example, Toscanini wanted the violins to play "on the string" in a piece like the *Moto perpetuo* by Paganini, which requires *sautillé* when played by a soloist.

was forced to omit finer nuances. Shortly before assuming his post in Cassel, he came into possession of a fine Stradivari formerly used by Regina Strinasacchi, Mozart's sonata partner. After his debut in Cassel he wrote, "The violin sounded divine, and after every solo I had applause, both clapped and shouted. With this violin I really enjoy playing publicly."[18]

Spohr attracted many students, though he was not attached to any conservatory. They came from afar to study with him; the list of his private pupils in Cassel alone numbers 145, and another forty are known in other cities. He charged only one thaler per lesson (one guinea in London), and poor students were accepted without charge. In midnineteenth century, there was hardly an orchestra in Germany without one or several of Spohr's students as members. As a teacher, Spohr was rather doctrinaire, and his students tended to become mirror images of their master. In 1831 Spohr published a violin method (*Violinschule*), which shows him as a moderately progressive technician, but his technical characteristics were soon overshadowed by the innovations of the Franco-Belgian school centered on the Paris Conservatoire. Here, Baillot published his own *L'Art du violon* in 1834, which treats technical advances more liberally.

The German school of violin playing was too personality-centered: first Spohr, then Joachim—both superb artists, but highly individualized players whose method and style could not be easily applied to a "school" of aspirants. In Paris, on the other hand, there was a wide spectrum of teachers who agreed on certain basic tenets of the Viotti tradition, but granted their students more individual freedom. Nobody in Paris cared to imitate "*maître* Massart," but from his class emerged some of the greatest violin geniuses, like Wieniawski and Kreisler.

The list of Spohr's compositions is long and varied: there are 154 opus numbers as well as selected unnumbered works. He wrote in all genres—operas, oratorios, symphonies, songs, concertos, and a great variety of chamber music, from violin duets and sonatas to octets and nonets. His preferred ensemble was, of course, the string quartet, of which he wrote thirty-four; in addition there are several double quartets and a Concerto for String Quartet and Orchestra. Often the first violin part is set in a virtuoso style in the manner of the popular *quatuor brillant*.

Spohr's fifteen violin concertos (1803–44) bridge the gap between Beethoven's concerto of 1806 and Mendelssohn's of 1845; it almost seems that no one in Germany wrote violin concertos during those intervening years except Spohr! Spohr obtained his first major success with his Concerto No. 2 in D minor (1804), which, in form and technique, is strongly influenced by Rode and the French violin concerto. In his next concertos he grew increasingly independent of French models, mainly by stressing symphonic elements and by thematic developments. Only the final movements retain such French favorites as *"alla polacca"* or *"alla spagnola."*

While in Vienna, Spohr wrote one of his most personal concertos, the Seventh in E minor (1814)—the melodic invention is warm and romantic, the harmonic treatment richly modulating, the thematic workmanship skillful and inventive. While indifferent to Beethoven, Spohr adored Mozart, which is evident through the mixture of lyricism and brilliance. With his next violin concerto, No. 8 in A minor (*Gesangscene*, 1816), Spohr succeeded in writing a masterpiece. The idea of an instrumental work in a vocal style occurred to him while he prepared for a concert tour of Italy. Knowing the preference of the Italian public for operatic music, he put the solo violin into the role of a solo singer, with recitatives and arias. Though clearly subdivided into movements, the entire work runs without interruption and is well integrated and concise. Spohr kept the orchestral accompaniment sonorous but "very simple and easy," since he had heard that the Italian orchestras were "worse than those of the provincial towns in France." This concerto became one of the most popular repertoire pieces of the nineteenth century, played by many prominent violinists like Ernst, Wieniawski, and Joachim; it is the only concerto of Spohr to have survived into our time. It is a pity, in a way, that it has overshadowed the Ninth Concerto in D minor (1820), which is a work of major importance. Here Spohr returned to the classical three-movement form but filled it with romantic content; particularly the slow movement is a gem. The Ninth Concerto is brilliantly orchestrated for a full orchestra, including trumpets and trombones, and the solo violin part makes great technical demands. In fact, it can be considered the technical summit of the pre-Paganini era. The remaining six concertos offer little new, except that some are written in the more concise *concertino* form.

Spohr was not merely a great violinist: as composer, conductor, and teacher he was a forceful influence for over a quarter of a century, from 1820 to 1860. His influence was felt mainly in Germany and England, but he was admired throughout Europe as a musician of integrity and a man of steadfast character, a bulwark against the rising tide of shallow virtuosity.

Joseph Joachim

Joachim inaugurated a new era—that of the art of interpretation. Prior to Joachim, the great violinists rarely, if ever, performed the music of other composers; they concentrated on playing their own works, tailored to fit their own technical ability, designed to highlight their personal style. Whether Tartini or Viotti, Paganini or Spohr, their repertoire consisted of their own compositions almost exclusively; only in this manner could they display their full individuality.

The nineteenth century brought a gradual change: the egocentric virtuosos began to take interest in the music of other composers, but often with little respect for the integrity of the original version. Joachim represented a new type of artist, willing to submerge his own personality into the work of another composer, eager to serve the cause of great music through his own musicianship. He became the ideal interpreter of great masterworks. Although he had creative talent as a composer, he derived greater satisfaction by probing the depths of the great classical masters, or by associating his art with that of important contemporary composers like Mendelssohn, Schumann, and Brahms. In his search for greatness in music, he became uncompromising, and even as a teenager—with technique to burn—he discarded the repertoire of virtuoso pieces by Vieuxtemps, Bériot, or Ernst. "That stuff revolts me," he wrote as early as 1848.

Thus Joachim became a kind of missionary, a prophet of beauty in music, regardless of the fact that the concertgoing public was not ready for that sort of puritanism. Only in German-speaking countries and in England did he find a wholehearted response. Even the Viennese were a bit disconcerted by his unbending "Roman earnestness." Joachim's few appearances in Paris and Russia aroused more respect than enthusiasm. His immediate competitors were Wieniawski and Sarasate— great artists in their own rights, but more attuned to the public taste of their time. In fact, Joachim was full of admiration for the virtuosity of Ernst, Wieniawski, Laub, Ysaÿe—an admiration without envy, but also without any desire to emulate the virtuoso style. His was an art totally his own; his goal was not the public's acclaim but the public's ennoblement. He felt ill at ease in glamorous settings and played his best when surrounded by devotees, by his own audiences in Berlin and London, to whom he was a musical oracle, the prophet of the great composers of the past.

Clara Schumann, the wife
of Robert Schumann,
accompanying their
favorite violinist,
Joseph Joachim.
Drawing by
Adolph von Menzel, 1854.

Johannes Brahms (sitting)
with his friend Joseph Joachim
in 1867. Both were in their
mid-thirties and often concertized together.

Joseph Joachim, photographed in his Berlin studio, about 1905

As for the present, Joachim linked his beliefs to Mendelssohn, Schumann, and Brahms, deliberately estranging himself from the other direction, the so-called New German School of Wagner, Liszt, and Berlioz. He became embroiled in the polemics between the two groups, almost against his will, for he had admiration and affection for Liszt and no ill will toward Wagner. But it was Brahms, his junior by two years, who became his closest associate.

Joachim, admired as the personification of German classicism, was no German at all. He was born the son of a Jewish merchant of modest means in Kitsee, Hungary, a town mainly inhabited by Swabian immigrants who, through generations, continued to speak German. Joseph, the seventh of eight children, was born in 1831. When "Pepi" was two years old, the family moved to Pest to give the children a better education. A toy violin given to Pepi on his fourth birthday proved such a fascination that the father decided to let him have violin lessons. After a public performance at the age of eight, it was decided to take Joseph to Vienna, where he studied for the next five years.

He was entrusted to Joseph Boehm, the Hungarian-born professor of the Vienna Conservatory and former teacher of the famous virtuoso Ernst. In fact, it was Ernst who heard young Joachim and insisted that he study with Boehm. The boy lived in the professor's house, subject to strict but well-meaning supervision, and with the opportunity of participating in chamber music sessions.

By the time he was twelve, Joachim was sent to Leipzig to enter the conservatory. Mendelssohn himself examined him, accompanying him in Beethoven's *Kreutzer Sonata* and asking him to do some harmony exercises. The verdict was, "This boy needs no conservatory. Let him play occasionally for concertmaster David; I myself will endeavor to play with him. He should study composition with Hauptmann and, above all, get a good general education."[1]

For the next three years, Joachim followed Mendelssohn's plan. He coached some repertoire with Ferdinand David,* though he never called himself David's student, out of loyalty to his old teacher Boehm. He studied Spohr, Bach, Ernst, and much Paganini. The strongest influence was undoubtedly Mendelssohn, who played sonatas and chamber music with the boy every Sunday, and insisted that "An artist should only play

---

* Ferdinand David (1810–73), concertmaster of the Leipzig Gewandhaus orchestra, also had ambitions as composer. Mendelssohn, who thought highly of David, entrusted him with the premiere of his Violin Concerto. Robert Schumann remarked dryly to David, "You see, this is the concerto *you* always wanted to write!"

the best." And he always admonished the boy never to change a single note in the work of a great master; he called such changes "inartistic, even barbarous." Mendelssohn also freed Joachim from Spohr's prejudice against *sautillé*, the bouncing bow—"Why not, if it sounds good and if it is appropriate for that particular spot?"[2]

Mendelssohn was very much taken with Joachim's playing, with his sight-reading ability, and with his intelligence. As conductor of the Leipzig Gewandhaus Orchestra, he gave the twelve-year-old Joachim the opportunity to play as soloist at one of the concerts: the piece was the difficult *Othello Fantasy* by Ernst. The date was November 16, 1843; the success was complete.

In March of the following year, Joachim traveled to London with warm letters of recommendation from Mendelssohn. He made his debut in the same *Othello Fantasy* and was also heard in Spohr's *Gesangscene*. One critic wrote that the thirteen-year-old played it better than Ernst! The real triumph came on May 27, 1844, when he performed the Beethoven concerto from memory at a Philharmonic Concert under Mendelssohn's baton. He was invited to play at Windsor Castle for Queen Victoria and Prince Albert. For the rest of Joachim's life, England, where he was fully appreciated, became his second artistic homeland.

Soon Joachim had the opportunity to prove that he was equal to any challenge: on his return to Leipzig he participated in a performance of Maurer's *Concertante* for four violins. Ernst played first, Bazzini second, Joachim third, concertmaster David fourth violin. Each of the soloists is given a spot for his own cadenza; when Joachim played his, it was so clever that Ernst exclaimed "bravo," while David dropped his cadenza altogether. In 1846 he was invited to play Spohr's Seventh Concerto at a concert honoring the old master, and Spohr described the playing of the fifteen-year-old Joachim as "quite masterful."

While visiting Vienna in 1846, Joachim was introduced to Liszt and played the new Mendelssohn concerto for him. Liszt sightread the accompaniment with great brilliance, as Joachim later recalled, without relinquishing the lit cigar he held between the fingers of his right hand!

Mendelssohn's unexpected death in 1847 was a heavy blow for Joachim, the most serious of his young life. He later wondered, "What would have become of me if I had not lost Mendelssohn so early!"[3]

While living in Leipzig, Joachim had been permitted to play in the violin section of the Gewandhaus Orchestra for the sake of experience. Eventually he moved up to associate concertmaster, sitting next to David, and occasionally substituting for him. As such he was involved in the preparation of Schumann's opera *Genoveva* in Leipzig in 1850, and he renewed his previously casual acquaintance with Robert and Clara Schumann. Clara's judgment of Joachim's playing was cool at first—"His playing is perfect, yet . . . there is neither soul nor fire in him. . . ." Six weeks later, she reversed herself: "Joachim played Robert's Second Quartet most beautifully, with ravishing tone and extraordinary ease, and today I regret what I said about him the other day."[4] His friendship with the Schumanns deepened; he became Robert's favorite violinist and remained Clara's trusted friend after Robert died in 1856.

After Mendelssohn's death there was nothing to keep Joachim in Leipzig. He accepted Liszt's invitation in 1850 to become concertmaster in Weimar. The pay was modest but the challenge was enormous, for Liszt was beginning to build Weimar into the citadel of new music. Just before starting his work as concertmaster, Joachim heard Wagner's *Lohengrin* as conducted by Liszt and was deeply moved; in fact, he temporarily turned into a Wagnerian!

Liszt's magnetic personality attracted a circle of gifted musicians, young and old. Joachim befriended the composer Raff and the pianist von Bülow (later Liszt's hapless son-in-law); soon the composer Peter Cornelius joined the circle of friends. Joachim also came in contact with Berlioz and was on the way to becoming engulfed by Liszt's modernistic trend. But he also maintained his contacts with Leipzig and with the Schumanns, who in the meantime had moved to Düsseldorf. He revisited London in May 1852, but felt dissatisfied with the results because his efforts on behalf of Schubert's string quartets found no response. This was counterbalanced by the enormous success of his debut in Berlin on December 13, 1852, when he played the Beethoven concerto. Eventually, Berlin was to become the center of his activity.

Joachim gradually became disenchanted with his life in Weimar, mainly because he was irritated by the constant disparagement of Mendelssohn and the Leipzig "academicism." He could not pretend that he loved the music produced in Weimar, and there was a gradual estrangement between him and Liszt, though outwardly everything seemed smooth. Not until 1860 did Joachim publicly break with the Liszt circle.

Eighteen fifty-three was an important year for Joachim: he accepted the post of royal music director in Hanover; he intensified his relationship with the Schumanns; and he met Johannes Brahms, who was to become a lifelong friend.

Professionally, the position in Hanover was a step forward because, in addition to his concertmaster duties, Joachim conducted the symphony concerts. His nominal superior was the opera director Heinrich Marschner, an amiable composer whom Joachim considered "a phlegmatic Northerner with a Restoration mentality." The King of Hanover, extremely musical, soon recognized the sterling qualities of his new concertmaster and drew him into the musical activities at court. His duties left him enough time to expand his concert travels. An important occasion was Joachim's performance, in May 1853, at the Rhenish Music Festival in Düsseldorf, where Schumann was active as music director. He played the Beethoven concerto under Schumann's baton and Clara noted in her diary,

> Joachim was the crown of the evening . . . he celebrated a victory greater than any of us. But he played with such poetry, such perfection, with so much soul in every note—really ideal—I have never heard violin playing like it. Never before did I receive such an unforgettable impression from a virtuoso.[5]

The following day Clara and Joachim played Schumann's Violin Sonata in A minor and he performed with such beauty that, according to Clara, "only then did I fully understand the work."

It was the last creative year of Schumann's life, and the deepening friendship with Joachim played an important role. With Joachim in mind, Schumann had composed a Fantasy for violin and orchestra and modestly asked for Joachim's opinion:

> During my work I have often thought of you. . . . This is my first effort of this type for the violin. . . . Write and tell me what may not be practical in it. I also ask you to mark the bowings in arpeggios and elsewhere. . . . The cadenza is not the final one, I plan to replace it some time later with a weightier one.[6]

Joachim played the first performance of the Fantasy in Düsseldorf under Schumann's direction on October 27, 1853, and received the dedication of the printed score. However, another late work by Schumann, the Violin Concerto in D minor, written for Joachim, remained unpublished. Schumann's mental collapse on February 27, 1854, prevented him from carrying out some planned revisions. After his death in 1856 Joachim advised strongly against a posthumous publication; the original manuscript remained in Joachim's possession. The decision not to include the Violin Concerto in the Complete Works Edition was taken jointly by Clara Schumann, Joachim, and Brahms; it was a difficult and, for Clara, an emotional decision. Joachim, too, was upset but remained firm in refusing to rework the last movement, which was the stumbling block; he was convinced that the publication would be detrimental to Schumann's memory. However, while Schumann was alive, he had spared no effort to be helpful. During Schumann's visit to Hanover in January 1854, Joachim had given the concerto two readings with orchestra, which convinced the disappointed composer that a radical revision was needed. There were several references to the concerto in letters exchanged between Joachim and Schumann. In 1858, Joachim gave the concerto another trial, at the Leipzig Gewandhaus, with negative results. It reinforced the decision to withhold the work from publication. As late as 1898, Joachim summarized his reservations about the concerto in a letter to Moser, repeating that the decision was taken "with a bleeding heart."

Nevertheless, many people now believe that the decision to "bury" the Schumann concerto was unjustified.* Szigeti called it a "beautiful, romantic piece." Tovey considered it "richer and more attractive" than Schumann's published Fantasy Op. 131. But the most convincing case is made by Menuhin; he studied the concerto, brought it before the American public in 1937, and wrote,

> The Schumann Concerto is the historically missing link of the violin literature; it is the bridge between the Beethoven and the Brahms concertos, though leaning more toward the Brahms. Indeed, one finds in both the same human warmth, caressing softness, bold manly rhythms, the same lovely arabesque treatment of the violin, the same noble themes and harmonies. There is also a great thematic resemblance. One is struck by the fact that Brahms could never have been what he was without Schumann.[7]

Joachim's refusal to revise the posthumous Schumann concerto is evidence of his scrupulous respect for the original concept of a composition, which he considered inviolable *under all circumstances*. He once said to his younger colleague Marteau,

---

* The long-delayed premiere took place on November 26, 1937, played by Georg Kulenkampff and the Berlin Philharmonic, closely followed by Menuhin's performance with the St. Louis Orchestra on December 23. In England it was presented by Jelly d'Arányi and the BBC Orchestra on February 16, 1938.

If Schumann really erred, he must account for it with his own name. If *we* loosen one tone in such an edifice, others will feel entitled to follow our example; people less qualified will start similar experiments, and before we know it, the whole edifice will collapse.[8]

Joachim had first encountered Brahms in 1853, when Joachim was twenty-two, Brahms barely twenty. They met in Hanover, where Brahms had arrived as accompanist of the Hungarian violinist Remenyi. It did not escape Joachim's attention that the pair was ill-matched, and indeed the partnership soon broke up. Brahms returned to Hanover alone, and proceeded from there to Düsseldorf to meet Schumann, with an introduction from Joachim. The rest is history. Schumann was overwhelmed by Brahms's talent; he wrote in his diary, "Brahms a visitor (a genius!)." That same month Schumann wrote his famous article *New Paths*, announcing Johannes Brahms as the new musical Messiah.

It was at that time that the interesting Violin Sonata F–A–E* was composed, meant as a surprise for Joachim: one movement was by Albert Dietrich (a young composer friend), another by Brahms (the Scherzo in C minor, now known as *Sonatensatz*), the remaining two movements by Schumann. Joachim arrived in Düsseldorf in the last days of October and sightread the new sonata with Clara at the piano; he guessed easily who the author of each movement was. Schumann and Dietrich used the notes F–A–E as motto; Brahms did not, but he incorporated it into the opening theme of his String Quartet in A minor.

During the twelve years spent at Hanover (1853–65), Joachim rose to international prominence. His visits to London became more and more frequent—1858, 1859, 1862—and soon became annual events. It was peculiar to the London music scene that visiting virtuosos were expected not only to appear with orchestra but to participate in chamber-music concerts. The Beethoven Quartet Society played host to the visiting virtuosos, and in 1859 the string quartet consisted of Ernst and Joachim (violins), Wieniawski (viola), and Piatti (cello). Joachim did not mind playing second violin to the admired Ernst and was generous in his praise of Ernst as well as of Wieniawski.

Remarkable was Joachim's 1861 debut in Vienna, a city he had left as a boy of twelve. He gave six concerts, beginning with a performance of the Beethoven concerto. The critic Hanslick registered his immediate reaction: "Here was no mere stunning virtuoso but rather a significant and individual personality." Joachim surpassed Vieuxtemps's per-

* "Frei Aber Einsam" (Free But Alone) was Joachim's motto.

formance "through a truly ethical force." Hanslick mentions Joachim's "modest, unadorned greatness," but also his "unbending, Roman earnestness."⁹

Joachim showed himself also as a composer: he presented his own *Concerto in the Hungarian Style*, written in Hanover in the years 1857–60. It is without doubt Joachim's finest composition and his claim to immortality: though immensely difficult technically, it is no mere virtuoso piece, but a noble work of Brahmsian density suffused with the national spirit of his native country. Hanslick found it "too expansive and complicated" to be judged at first hearing. All in all, Joachim's unbending classicism was perhaps more than the Viennese public could bear, and even Hanslick had to admit that the truly Viennese violinist Hellmesberger "played more directly to our hearts" than Joachim.

While in Hanover, Joachim attracted a small but select group of students, among them young Leopold Auer, a fellow Hungarian who, though already a concertizing artist, felt the need to absorb Joachim's unique approach to music. Through Auer, it eventually entered the Russian school. Joachim later visited Russia twice, in 1872 and 1884. There was Auer, now famous in his own right, conducting the orchestra for his old master.

Joachim's success in Russia was not undisputed; critics like Cui called him "cold." Certainly his classically pure style contrasted to the playing of Wieniawski, whom the Russians had adopted as their own. Tchaikovsky, comparing Joachim and Ferdinand Laub (the Czech violin professor in Moscow), noticed that Joachim was superior in extracting from the violin a "touching tender melody," while Laub was superior "in power of tone, in passion and well-directed energy." Joachim (who greatly admired Laub) played a Spohr duet with Laub at a Moscow concert in 1872, eliciting this review: ". . . a competition of two heroes. In this duet we could perceive the calm classicism of Joachim and the fiery temperament of Laub. We can still hear the bell-like sound of Joachim and the fiery cantilena of Laub."¹⁰

Joachim resigned his post in Hanover in 1865 in protest against anti-Jewish discrimination against one of his colleagues, Jakob Grün. The following year, Prussia annexed the Kingdom of Hanover, the royal family went into exile, and the city became a provincial capital. In 1868 Joachim moved to Berlin—soon to be the capital of a united German Reich—and in 1869 he was named director and violin professor at the newly established Hochschule für Musik, a post he held until his death in 1907.

Culturally, Berlin lacked the tradition of such capitals as Munich or Dresden. But there was money and ambition behind Berlin's drive to achieve cultural status, and once it became the imperial capital, musical life grew rapidly. For the next four decades, Joachim became part of that growth. He had much influence, though he was not involved in the intrigues of the operatic world. His field was concert and chamber music: he was quite active as orchestral conductor, and with his newly founded string quartet he established a great tradition. Under his guidance, the Hochschule grew from nineteen students in its first year to 250 students in 1890. Joachim did not want to expand beyond this number, because he disliked the "factory" aspects of music schools: he wanted to control quantity as well as quality.

As principal violin professor he created a distinct Berlin violin school. He relied on the help of assistants, since he took no interest in teaching technical details. His class accepted only advanced and technically secure students. (This was true even in his younger years in Hanover). His method (if indeed there was any) is described by Leopold Auer:*

> We hardly ever played any scales or etudes for him, with the single exception of some of the Paganini Caprices. Anything which had to do with the technique of the two hands we were supposed to attend to at home. Joachim very rarely entered into technical details, and never made any suggestions to his pupils as to what they were to do to gain technical facility. . . . Throughout the lesson he kept his violin and bow in his hands, and whenever he was dissatisfied . . . the master would draw his bow and play the passage or phrase. . . . The only remark which he would utter at times, after having demonstrated a point, would be, "So müssen Sie es spielen" [That's the way you must play it].[11]

In the 1890s, the Russian violinist I. Nalbandyan came to Berlin on Auer's advice to profit from the personal contact with Joachim. (Nalbandyan later became one of Auer's most trusted assistants.) Once Nalbandyan entered Joachim's class, he was amazed to see that all the students held their instruments and bows in different ways, just as they pleased. Such technical matters simply did not interest Joachim; he left

---

* Despite the implied criticism of this method, Auer himself never taught technique, nor did he demonstrate in class.

the mechanics to Emanuel Wirth, a thorough teacher known among colleagues as "the wristler." *

Was Joachim really a poor teacher? He admitted that much in a letter to the American violinist Sam Franko. Franko studied with Joachim in the 1870s at the Hochschule and left the following comment:

> Fascinated by Joachim's overwhelming personality and the genius of his playing, I tried to imitate him, as did everyone else in the class, and in so doing I lost my own individuality. Joachim the teacher was quite another being than Joachim the violinist. When teaching, he paid scarcely any attention to the technical side of violin-playing, made only general remarks about position, bowing, fingering etc. and devoted his attention principally to interpretation. But even there it was impossible to follow him unconditionally, for he would play a piece differently every time, following the inspiration of the moment. . . . A genius is rarely fitted to be a great teacher. . . . Of all his hundreds of pupils not one has become world-famous. They became skilled musicians . . . but none of them really made a career as a solo violinist.[12]

Joseph Szigeti had a promising audition with Joachim in 1905 when he was thirteen, but declined the offer to become his student. He later described the classroom scene:

> I saw the master seated alone on a little platform in the middle of the room, no violin in his hands, listening, criticizing—but not demonstrating. This lack of interplay, this lack of kindling the pupils' enthusiasm through actual example, made for a certain remoteness in their relationship, or so I thought. It was as if the little platform symbolized the absence of flow between the two.[13]

In over forty years of teaching, Joachim had about four hundred students. Yet only a few great violinists emerged from his classroom, and those who did were finished technicians before they came to him, needing only some last polish. Among the virtuosi were Franz von Vecsey and Bronislaw Huberman, both child prodigies whose contact with Joachim was minimal. Leopold Auer, Willi Hess, Jenö Hubay, and Bram Eldering became primarily teachers, while Karl Klinger made his reputation as quartet player.

* The German word is *Handgelenkler*, a coined expression meaning "wrist manipulator."

Was there a "Joachim School"? Andreas Moser, Joachim's assistant and collaborator, denies it, seeing Joachim as descendant of the Italo-French school of Viotti and Rode. In truth, however, Joachim's teacher Boehm had only a passing acquaintance with Rode, and Joachim's bowing differed from that of the French school. Actually it was closer to the method used by Spohr, which Joachim knew well through Ferdinand David.

Characteristic for Joachim's bow position was a very low upper right arm pressed against the body, which necessitated a highly angled wrist. He gripped the bow stick with his fingertips; the fingers were kept close together, the index finger touching the stick at the first joint (counted from the nail), while the little finger remained on the stick at all times. The change of bow at the frog was accomplished by a rotary wrist movement and stiff fingers.

This bowing method fitted Joachim's personal needs, but it proved cramped and unnatural when transmitted to students by mediocre assistants. Flesch, an opponent of this method, asserted that "a majority of the students thus maltreated contracted arm troubles and, as violinists, became cripples for life." Only the few who "succeeded in casting off the straight jacket into which they had been thrust" were able to reach a higher plateau of achievement.[14] Actually, Joachim himself had an unsteady bow arm when he was nervous, and gave up solo playing in his sixties, concentrating on quartet and chamber music.

As a performer, Joachim considered himself a servant of music. It was his task to recreate the works of great composers. There was no personal vanity in his playing, no effort to dazzle the public with technical display or tonal sensuousness. His interpretation was spiritualized, rhythmic yet free, and totally involved in the stream of music. He had dignity and nobility, yet he was modest and unassuming. His tone was not large, but extremely pure and capable of infinite shadings. He used vibrato very sparingly and avoided sentimental slides. His aim was objectivity, and the composer's manuscript was his law; to change a composer's directive was unthinkable. Joachim lived in a period dominated by virtuosos—Vieuxtemps, Ernst, Wieniawski, Sarasate, Ysaÿe—whose talents he praised without envy. But somehow he towered above them all because of the purity and sincerity of his musical concepts, and in turn he was much admired by his colleagues.

But there were also occasional dissenting voices. One of them was George Bernard Shaw, who was irritated by the uncritical adulation of the London public toward Joachim, at the expense of other artists whom

Shaw valued more highly. In a review of 1889 he seemed to be bent on toppling the graven image of Joachim:

> Joachim was never to me an Orpheus. . . . Now that he is on the verge of sixty he keeps up the speed at the cost of quality of tone and accuracy of pitch; and the results are sometimes, to say the least, incongruous. For instance, [in] Bach's Solo Sonata in C major . . . Joachim scraped away frantically, making a sound after which an attempt to grate a nutmeg effectively on a boot sole would have been as the strain of an Aeolian harp. The notes which were musical enough to have any discernible pitch at all were mostly out of tune. It was horrible—damnable! Had he been an unknown player, introducing an unknown composer, he would not have escaped with his life. Yet we all—I no less than the others—were interested and enthusiastic. We applauded like anything: and he bowed to us with unimpaired gravity. The dignified artistic career of Joachim and the grandeur of Bach's reputation has so hypnotized us that we took an abominable noise for the music of the spheres.[15]

Here and there, however, Shaw was forced to admit that he had heard Joachim play "very finely" and that he was "in excellent form."

In 1904 Joachim's diamond jubilee was celebrated in London, in remembrance of his British debut in 1844. The list of the committee and subscribers numbered 603 and included all great names in music, literature, painting, and politics. Joachim was prevailed upon to play the Beethoven concerto with his own cadenzas and his arrangement of Schumann's *Abendlied* for violin. He also conducted his own Overture to Shakespeare's *Henry IV* and Brahms's *Academic Festival Overture*. Sir Henry Wood reminisced,

> Of Joachim I always felt that one was in the presence of a Hungarian gentleman of great intellect, and although his playing lacked the emotional depth of dear Ysaÿe, his was a quiet classical serenity free from any trace of exaggeration and always musical and scholarly. Joachim was always conscious of his dignity; one could never have the fun out of him that was possible with Ysaÿe.[16]

Joachim's last visit to England took place late in 1906: between November 21 and December 7 he participated in a monumental Brahms Cycle of seven concerts, presenting most of Brahms's chamber music works. The performers were, of course, the Joachim String Quartet; among the pianists was young Donald Francis Tovey.

Joachim remained active to the end: he played a cycle of the complete Beethoven quartets in Vienna in the spring of 1907, and gave his last chamber music concert in Berlin on April 6. During the summer he worked with Moser on the edition of the Bach solo sonatas, but when they had reached the Chaconne he fell ill. On June 28, he observed his seventy-sixth birthday sitting in an armchair. In mid-July he underwent an operation and was hopeful that he would be able to play the violin again soon. But the abscess was malignant, and he died in Berlin on August 15.

Joachim was not only a great performer but also a composer of considerable gifts. As such he had a particular affinity to fellow composers who often consulted him on problems of string writing and dedicated their works to him. Among them were Schumann, Dvořák, Bruch, Niels Gade, and above all Brahms.

The Joachim-Brahms friendship spanned over forty years, beginning with their casual meeting in Hanover in 1853 and ending with Brahms's death in 1897. One must realize that the two friends never lived in the same city for any length of time, so that their contact was limited to letters and a few meetings each year. The intensity of their friendship underwent changes and fluctuations over the years. At the beginning they were "comrades-in-arms," sharing their musical ideals, encouraging each other's compositorial development, learning from each other. Joachim's criticism—invited by Brahms—was not limited to violinistic problems, but often touched on questions of form and orchestration. Virtually every one of Brahms's works involving the violin, be it solo or chamber music, was planned for Joachim as performer.

Their musical collaboration was never closer than during the genesis of Brahms's Violin Concerto. It began with a casual note, dated August 21, 1878, in which Brahms informed Joachim that he was working on a concerto in four (!) movements. At the same time he sent him the violin part of the virtually completed first movement and the first two pages of the Finale with some passages he called "awkward." Joachim reacted with enthusiasm, though he had a few minor reservations. There followed more than a dozen written exchanges and one or two personal meetings. Brahms encountered some creative difficulties, dropping one movement and rewriting another; but within the short span of four months, the concerto was completed, including the orchestration.

With Joachim applying much pressure on Brahms (who did not like to be hurried in his composing), the premiere was set for January 1,

1879, at the Leipzig Gewandhaus. The performance, hastily prepared, left much to be desired: Brahms's conducting was as insecure as Joachim's nervous rendition of the difficult solo part and his own barely completed cadenza. The reception by the staid Leipzig public was cool, the reviews mediocre.

Disgruntled by the reaction in Leipzig, Brahms did not conduct the first performance in Vienna set for January 14, but yielded the baton to Hellmesberger, the well-known violinist-conductor. Soon a witticism made the rounds: Brahms (said Hellmesberger) had composed a concerto not *for*, but *against* the violin!

More disconcerting was the criticism of Hanslick, usually so well disposed toward Brahms: he found the new work masterful in workmanship but somewhat dry in invention and imagination. Even Joachim's initial reaction to the concerto appears a bit guarded, but he admitted that his affection grew with each succeeding performance. Brahms was generally pleased, as he wrote to a friend: "Joachim plays my piece more beautifully with every rehearsal, and his Cadenza has become so beautiful by concert time that the public applauded into my Coda."[17]

In the spring of 1879, Joachim took the concerto to England and played it several times with growing success. At the London Philharmonic on March 5, it was so well received that a repeat performance was announced for the same season—"something unheard of since Mendelssohn played his own G minor Piano Concerto," reported Joachim. With disarming modesty, Brahms asked, "Is the piece really good and practical enough to be printed?" The exchange of letters goes into June; by that time the manuscript was in the hands of the publisher, ready to go to print.* Brahms and Joachim joined forces in reading the proofs; the published score was dedicated to Joachim.

Ultimately, though Brahms asked persistently for suggestions, he accepted few of Joachim's recommendations, but he needed Joachim's ideas for clarifying his own thoughts. The following excerpt from a letter is revealing:

> Now, once you see our concerto in print, I don't want you to consider it hypocritical if I urgently ask you for your opinion and then—persist in my own views. . . . For your own use you can change it again, and I shall prefer by far to hear it from you in *your* version than from someone else in mine.[18]

* The score, in Brahms's own hand, bears visible evidence of all the corrections entered by Brahms and Joachim with colored pencils and red ink. It is in the possession of the Library of Congress (a gift of Fritz Kreisler) and has recently been published in facsimile with a preface by Yehudi Menuhin—a fascinating document.

Brahms found his close collaboration with Joachim so stimulating that he offered to join him in a concert tour through Transylvania in the fall of 1879. Though no longer a concertizing pianist, Brahms did not wish to be a mere accompanist, and the programs were carefully balanced to include sonatas, piano solos, and a violin concerto like the Mendelssohn, the Bruch, or even the new Brahms concerto! The tour went well, though the provincial public was often overwhelmed by the weighty programs of the two celebrities. In one little town there was only a single listener, and Joachim suggested that his money be refunded and no concert given. But Brahms said, "Our only admirer does not deserve such lack of consideration" and he insisted on playing the entire program, including some encores! This, incidentally, was the year when Joachim arranged Brahms's popular *Hungarian Dances* for violin and piano. These are exemplary transcriptions, still widely played today.

In 1880, the long-time friendship between Joachim and Brahms suffered a severe strain and nearly collapsed. The reason was personal: Joachim's marriage to the singer Amalie Weiss was breaking up, after many happy years and six children. Joachim, very jealous by nature, accused his wife of infidelity and sued for divorce, contesting the legitimacy of their youngest daughter. Brahms, who admired Mrs. Joachim as an artist, was convinced that she was unjustly accused: he sent her a compassionate letter, expressing criticism of Joachim's behavior. Joachim was indignant, all the more since Clara Schumann had taken his side. At the divorce trial, the Brahms letter served as character reference for Mrs. Joachim, who was declared innocent.[19]

For several years, the correspondence between Brahms and Joachim was interrupted, though Joachim continued to perform Brahms's music. In October 1883 Brahms made the first step toward a reconciliation without retracting any of his actions, and Joachim accepted the outstretched hand of his old friend. Yet the old intimacy was never fully reestablished, though they worked together on the editing of the Double Concerto for violin and cello; Joachim was soloist with the cellist Robert Hausmann at the premiere in 1887. Brahms's death in 1897, preceding that of Joachim by ten years, brought this beautiful friendship to a close.

While Joachim took infinite trouble with Brahms's Violin Concerto and indeed with all of Brahms's compositions, he showed much less concern for the Violin Concerto of Antonin Dvořák. He received the manuscript late in 1879 but put it aside for two years without giving it any attention. Finally, in September 1882, he had a private rehearsal with the composer. As Dvořák wrote to his publisher, Joachim was "kind enough to make alterations in the solo part." However, Joachim never played the Dvořák concerto publicly. It was the Czech virtuoso Franz Ondřiček who gave the premiere in Prague in 1883.

Joachim's finest composition was the *Concerto in Hungarian Style*. It was part of a growing movement of national concert music—the Spanish, Russian, and Norwegian violin works by Lalo, the *Scottish Phantasy* by Bruch, the Rhapsodies by Liszt. Contrary to the method of incorporating national or folk tunes, Joachim's themes in his *Hungarian Concerto* are all freely invented, though in the spirit of Hungarian music. Joachim wrote two other violin concertos, but they have disappeared from the repertoire. The *Hungarian Concerto*, once a favorite display piece despite its length and difficulty, is being rediscovered by violinists seeking a Romantic revival, among them Aaron Rosand and Charles Treger. Undeservedly neglected are Joachim's Variations in E minor, dedicated to Sarasate. For viola Joachim wrote the *Hebrew Melodies* (after Byron) Op. 9 and Variations Op. 10. Masterful are his cadenzas to various violin concertos. During his concertmaster years at Hanover, Joachim played on a Guadagnini violin built in Milan in the 1750s. Later he bought a Stradivarius made in 1714, which he played until 1885, when he exchanged it for another Stradivarius of 1713. After Joachim's death, the violin was acquired by Robert von Mendelssohn, and it was lent for life to Joachim's student Karl Klingler, who formed an excellent string quartet, continuing the Joachim tradition in Berlin.

With the death of Joseph Joachim, the nineteenth century came to an end. It had opened with Paganini, the greatest virtuoso of all times, and closed with Joachim, the greatest musician of his generation. As Joachim grew old, a new generation of violinists arose which combined technique and musicianship and brought new glory to the art of violin playing.

PART FIVE

The
Twentieth Century

A NEW BREED OF VIRTUOSO

Around the turn of the century, a new type of violin virtuoso emerged. He belonged to a generation that had absorbed Paganini's technique and Joachim's musicianship and proceeded to modernize the violinistic vocabulary for the twentieth century.

The foremost representatives of this new breed of virtuoso were Eugène Ysaÿe and Fritz Kreisler. They were superb technicians and sensitive musicians with creative talents, combining instinct and intellect, and determined to take the stigma off the tarnished concept of virtuoso. Around them were many violinists who leaned more in one or the other direction—such Paganinians as Kubelik and Burmester, and such purists as Marteau and Flesch.

Further into the twentieth century, one violinist alone reached that exalted level—Jascha Heifetz—though he lacked the creativity of either Ysaÿe or Kreisler. But Heifetz, with his absolute perfection of technique, his controlled intensity, and his enormous repertoire, came to represent the ideal of twentieth-century violin playing. He was not a "Paganini redivivus" as so many claimed; he was truly a new breed of virtuoso-musician. Now that he has left the center stage that he occupied for so long, the musical world searches in vain for a successor.

Eugène Ysaÿe

At the height of his career, between 1895 and 1912, Ysaÿe was idolized by the young generation of rising virtuosos. His leonine power displaced the suave Sarasate, who, until then, had been the model of perfection. Ysaÿe stood between Joachim's classicism and Sarasate's elegance. He represented a "synthesis between technical perfection and the greatest intensity of expression," according to Flesch.[1] Violinists like Kreisler, Thibaud, Szigeti, Enesco (and later Elman and Milstein) looked up to Ysaÿe as *notre maître à tous*, the master of us all. Having inherited the great Romantic tradition of Vieuxtemps and Wieniawski (both were his teachers), Ysaÿe carried the grand style into the twentieth century—the personification of post-Romanticism.

Born in the Belgian city of Liège, in 1858, Ysaÿe started the violin at the age of four under the tutelage of his father, a violinist-conductor and a strict teacher. At seven he played in his father's orchestra. Vieuxtemps happened to hear the boy and urged him to enter the Liège Conservatoire. Here he completed the course of study, though with some interruptions, by the time he was sixteen, and was rewarded with the silver medal. His violin teacher was Rodolphe Massart (nephew of the famous Parisian professor Lambert Massart), who knew how to handle the volatile temperament of his student. Ysaÿe's hope to study with the revered Vieuxtemps at the Brussels Conservatoire was thwarted by the master's illness; fortunately, Wieniawski agreed to take over the class temporarily, and Ysaÿe learned much from him. As soon as Vieuxtemps was able to resume his teaching on a limited scale in 1876, Ysaÿe hurried to work with him—"he showed me the way, he opened my eyes and my heart," he reminisced many years later.[2] But Vieuxtemps's playing days were past—his left hand was paralyzed, and all he could offer was aesthetic advice. This period of benevolent guidance lasted three years (spent mostly in Paris) and deepened Ysaÿe's grasp of the Franco-Belgian tradition, which he was to represent all his life.

In 1879 Ysaÿe accepted an offer to become concertmaster in Berlin, to lead the Bilse Kapelle, recognized as Berlin's best concert orchestra (it later became the Berlin Philharmonic). The performances were given outdoors, in an establishment named Flora. At the time, Ysaÿe, barely twenty-one, was unknown outside of Belgium and Paris. Once arrived in Berlin, he paid a courtesy visit to Joachim, the musical oracle of Berlin. Asked to play something, Ysaÿe casually picked up Joachim's Stradivari and played Vieuxtemps's *Fantasia appassionata*, followed by Wieniawski's Concerto in D minor. Joachim was overwhelmed by this new young genius. A few days later, he brought a group of his students to the Flora to admire "that splendid fellow."

Thus, Ysaÿe's career was launched, but it was to be a slow rise. His arrival on the musical scene came at a propitious time: Vieuxtemps was gone; Wieniawski stood at the end of a brilliant career; Joachim, though not quite fifty, preferred quartet playing to solo performances. The only competitor was Sarasate, whose graceful suavity was quite different from the emotional power of young Ysaÿe. Soon, Ysaÿe gained an admirer in Anton Rubinstein, the pianist famous for his grand style, and the two artists went on concert tours through Scandinavia and Russia beginning in 1882. "Of all living violinists, only Ysaÿe reminds me of Wieniawski," said Rubinstein. Ysaÿe, in turn, gratefully admitted that Rubinstein (his senior by twenty-nine years) had been "his true master of interpretation."[3] Yet it was not easy to follow in Wieniawski's footsteps, and the first Russian criticism, in 1882, made some unfavorable comparisons: "The young artist . . . recalls Wieniawski in many ways; he has much elegance but he still lacks a large tone, a certain gracefulness and finish which were developed so perfectly in the playing of the late Wieniawski."[4]

In 1883 Ysaÿe settled in Paris and became actively involved in the revival of French chamber music. Among his friends were the composers Franck, Debussy, Saint-Saëns, d'Indy, Fauré, Chausson, and Lekeu. They saw in Ysaÿe the ideal interpreter of French music and honored him with dedications, including such important works as the Violin Sonata by Franck (1886), the String Quartet by Debussy (1893), and the *Poème* by Chausson (1896).

Ysaÿe's Parisian debut as a soloist took place in 1885, when he played Lalo's *Symphonie espagnole* and Saint-Saëns's *Rondo capriccioso* with the Colonne orchestra. The following year he accepted a post in his native Belgium: he was named violin professor at the Brussels Conservatory (a position once occupied by his master Vieuxtemps), and he remained here until 1898. He initiated concerts of contemporary music (mostly French and Belgian) in which he appeared as conductor, soloist, and chamber music player. Gradually, his fame spread through Europe. He made a memorable debut in London in 1889, playing the Beethoven concerto at the Royal Philharmonic Society; in 1901 the Society awarded him the Gold Medal, a distinction given only once before to a violinist, Joachim. He became a frequent visitor to Britain, much admired as a soloist and in sonata evenings with the pianist Raoul Pugno. Russia was another country where Ysaÿe was acclaimed: between 1882 and 1912 he made a dozen visits and formed strong friendships with Russian musicians. He performed works by Tchaikovsky, Glazunov, Taneyev, and Cui, played chamber music with Rubinstein, Rachmaninoff, and Siloti, and became close to his colleagues Auer and Besekirsky. He conquered the Russian critics as well; one of them wrote in 1903, "This is simply a kind of giant who, with his powerful broad tone, conquers the listener from the first note."[5]

The French pianist Pugno was Ysaÿe's favorite sonata partner. "It was like the dialogue of titans," wrote Spalding, who heard the two artists play a three-concert cycle of all the Beethoven violin sonatas in London; it was

> electrifying . . . it gave me gooseflesh . . . Ysaÿe was at his leonine best. His tone was not large but it had an expressive quality impossible to describe. His famous Guarnerius tucked under his chin looked like a half-sized fiddle.[6]

Both Pugno and Ysaÿe were massive men, with a legendary appetite for food and wine, women and music. Ysaÿe was almost constantly on the road and spent only the summer months in Belgium with his family, his wife and five children. Despite his vast experience as a performer, Ysaÿe was invariably nervous, especially before important concerts. Early in life he became a victim of *"le trac,"* the fear of not being able to control his hands; sometimes it affected the fingers of his left hand, which became almost paralyzed, but more often it caused a trembling of the bow. Perhaps it was a physiological weakness which was activated by nervous tension. In fact, an unsteady bow is the curse of many gifted violinists. In Ysaÿe's case, there may also have been a technical defect. He used to hold his bow with an iron-tight grip between the thumb and three fingers while the little finger was always lifted off the stick, instead of balancing the bow. This faulty bow grip, so Flesch believes, led to a loss of stability. The fear of tremor, which had to be masked, often affected his interpretation. Ysaÿe looked with envy at violinists who were blessed with steady hands. In a letter of 1909 he complained, "The fingers are weak and the bow unsteady. . . . I am going through one of those pessimistic crises, nerve-racking and terribly sad. . . . I battle the crisis, I preach to myself, but until now the crisis overcomes me."[7] But overcome he did—the season 1911–12 shows him at the height of his powers, culminating in the memorable performance of the Elgar concerto in Berlin under Arthur Nikisch in 1912. After that, the decline set in.

This unhappiness with his playing induced Ysaÿe to think of a switch in career, from violinist to conductor. He had conducted before, in Brussels and in London; at one time, in 1898, he was invited to succeed Anton Seidl as conductor of the New York Philharmonic. It was in America that he made the definite transition: from 1918 to 1922, he was conductor of the Cincinnati Orchestra. His popularity in the United States was well established since his debut as a violinist in 1894, and his success grew with every return visit. When his native Belgium was overrun by the German armies in 1914, Ysaÿe and his wife fled to England and from there to the United States, where he gladly accepted the opportunity of leading a distinguished orchestra. Cincinnati was a German-oriented community with a Germanic musical tradition; but with Ysaÿe's arrival, the repertoire shifted markedly toward French and Belgian music. On the whole, his experience in Cincinnati was enjoyable, but the public was not always with him: he was a great musical personality but not necessarily a great conductor.

Returning to Brussels in 1922, he revived the "Concerts Ysaÿe" but he felt out of touch with the latest postwar developments in music. He resumed his career as a violinist, though on a limited scale, and despite his waning powers he was received everywhere with affection.

I remember hearing a concert by Ysaÿe early in October 1924 in Copenhagen. At the time I was a teenage violinist scheduled to make my debut in the Danish capital. Arriving a few days earlier, I saw enormous placards all over the city announcing the return of the legendary Ysaÿe. Needless to say, I attended in breathless anticipation. At last he walked slowly, majestically, onto the stage—a titanesque figure with the stance of a conqueror. Before he began the first number on the program, the Sonata in A major by César Franck, he made a charming curtain speech in French. "This work," he said, "was given to me by the composer as a wedding present almost forty years ago, and whenever I play it, I do so *avec amour*, with love." Ysaÿe's playing at that time showed signs of past greatness—the sweep, the *élan*, the grand line were all there, but the technical assurance was shaky. He carried the evening on the strength of his personality.

Two years later, in the summer of 1926, Ysaÿe announced a master course for violin in Paris, at the École Normale, and again I was there, drinking in his every word. It seemed that all of Paris was present— every violinist, every musician of note sat at Ysaÿe's feet. Thibaud, Enesco, the young Milstein—a galaxy of great names, all crowded into the smallish auditorium. Selected young violinists, screened through auditions, were permitted to play for the *maître*, who would give his public comments. Ysaÿe's remarks did not concern themselves with technical details—technique was taken for granted—but with the interpretation of the music, the style of performance, the artistic stance of the player. The violinist Brunschwig reminisced,

> I still see him sitting, violin in hand, scrutinizing attentively the playing of the student. And the advice . . . "Play big . . . extend the bow . . . no petty nuances, give it life and élan . . . give sound . . . Enlarge your playing, make the instrument sing and don't just play 'notes.' Virtuosity without music is nothing. Every note, every sound must live, sing, express pain or joy. Become painters, even in the 'runs' which are actually a series of notes which sing rapidly. . . . Music above all! Always breathe with full lungs. Don't encase your violin inside you, liberate yourself with it and speak through it."[8]

One amusing incident has remained in my memory. A young would-be virtuoso gave a rapid and mechanical account of the *Double* from Bach's Partita in B minor. Ysaÿe nodded and asked, "And what else do you have, my good fellow?" "*Maître*, I'd like to play Paganini's *Moto perpetuo*." "What, another *moto perpetuo*," exclaimed Ysaÿe with mock surprise, "you just played us one," evidently referring to the mechanical rendition of Bach. And turning to the illustrious audience, he remarked, "You want to flabbergast us, don't you? Well, we are flabbergasted, aren't we, Thibaud?!"* The irony was not lost on the audience, which broke out in laughter.

At the end of the master course, Georges Enesco came modestly to play Ysaÿe's Solo Sonata in D minor dedicated to him—a moving experience!

A year later in Barcelona, Ysaÿe made his last appearance as a violinist, playing Beethoven's Violin and Triple Concertos and conducting the *Eroica Symphony*, with the assistance of his friend Pablo Casals. Soon thereafter, Ysaÿe's health declined (he was suffering from diabetes) and in 1929 his right foot had to be amputated. Undeterred, he conducted several concerts in November 1930 in Brussels, the last on the 13th with Casals as soloist. His supreme wish—to conduct the premiere of his Walloon opera—remained unfulfilled; he collapsed at the first rehearsal. Yet he saw it staged a few weeks before his death on April 25, 1931.

Flesch described Ysaÿe as "the most outstanding and individual violinist I ever heard in all my life. . . . His tone was big and noble . . . his vibrato was the spontaneous expression of his feeling . . . his

---

* "*Vous voulez-nous épater? Eh bien, nous sommes épatés, n'est-ce-pas, Thibaud?*"

portamentos were novel and entrancing. . . ." He also spoke of the perfection of technique, the "impulsive romantic" style of interpretation.[9]

Curiously, Ysaÿe was not born with the great tonal power that he displayed later in life. Sam Franko, an American violinist living in Paris at the time, tells that in 1877, when the nineteen-year-old Ysaÿe played an audition for the conductor Pasdeloup, he arrived at the hall accompanied by his *maître*, the renowned Vieuxtemps, who took pride in his student's accomplishments. Using Vieuxtemps's Amati violin, Ysaÿe played the Mendelssohn concerto. Pasdeloup, known for his rudeness, turned to Vieuxtemps and said, "No, I can't let him play, he has no tone!"[10]

In 1882 and again in 1895, Russian critics found a certain lack of power and plasticity of tone, while praising Ysaÿe's tender songfulness and lyricism. The "titanesque" element seems to have entered Ysaÿe's playing gradually. Somehow, it fitted his changing physical appearance: tall and slim in his youth, he became massive and heavy-set with advancing age. A change of violin may have contributed: until the mid-1890s, he played on a Guadagnini (a good but not outstanding instrument) until he acquired a magnificent Guarnerius del Gesù of 1740 which remained his favorite.* For an artist to change his tone quality in mid-career is not as unusual as it may seem. David Oistrakh, for example, began to produce a larger, "fatter" tone in the 1940s. For Ysaÿe, a changing repertoire may have induced him to employ a more forceful bow stroke. He expanded his programs by including the powerful concertos of Brahms and Elgar, demanding a big tone to counterbalance a large orchestra.

Ysaÿe's vibrato, which lent his tone its inimitable color, was described by Kreisler (who revered Ysaÿe):

> Wieniawski intensified the vibrato and brought it to heights never before achieved, so that it became known as the "French vibrato." Vieuxtemps also took it up, and after him Ysaÿe, *who became its greatest exponent*, and I. Joseph Joachim . . . disdained it.[11]

Joachim (and the German school in general) advocated "the incidental, thin-flowing quiver only on espressivo notes"—in other words, a very

---

* Ysaÿe also owned the "Hercules" Stradivarius, which was stolen from the artists' room in St. Petersburg in January 1908; at the time it was not recovered. The violin reappeared briefly in occupied Berlin in 1947, though, according to Menuhin, who saw the instrument, there are doubts whether the recovered violin was actually the "Hercules" Stradivarius.

sparing use of vibrato. The French vibrato of the later nineteenth century, pioneered by Ysaÿe and then Kreisler, became wider and was used more abundantly. The violin became a much more sensuous-sounding instrument, and the public loved it. Soon, a violinist with the old-style vibrato had no chance of being successful. Yet Ysaÿe warned of excessive use, of goatlike bleating: "There are a thousand sounds of '*a*' but only one is perfectly in tune. Open your ears, search it out. And then, don't alter it by a nauseating vibrato that is to the violinist what the quaver [*chevrotement*] is to the singer."[12] A sound warning against the hysterical vibrato of some modern violinists!

Another expressive means of Ysaÿe was the portamento (also called glissando or slide). This technique was widely used and misused in the earlier nineteenth century, condemned by critics as catlike meowing (Ernst was accused of overdoing such "expressive" slides). Ysaÿe perfected a technique by which a finger moved subtly into a tone from below—not as much a shift from one position to another as a sensuous expressive device, similar to the method of a fine singer in reaching a high expressive note. Thibaud used this type of slide and it became the hallmark of Heifetz. This "French portamento" became typical of modern violin playing and made the old German-type shift obsolete. Stylish violinists, however, use both types of portamento, the "German" for classical music, the "French" for the Romantic and post-Romantic repertoire. Vibrato, too, is used selectively today, with more restraint for Baroque and Classical music.

Flesch stressed the originality of style in Ysaÿe's playing. It was a free and often willful interpretation, not adhering pedantically to the written note values, but extracting a maximum of expressiveness from every phrase. "Tempo rubato" was Ysaÿe's credo; yet while he took rhythmic liberties, he urged his accompanists to keep time without following each of his slight deviations in tempo. "Have no fear, we'll always find each other," he reassured the pianist Jacques Dalcroze, "for whenever I accelerate certain notes, I reestablish the equilibrium immediately by slowing down the following notes or broadening one of them." Nevertheless, Ysaÿe was criticized by purists for errors in judgment and taste. What was fit for Franck or Saint-Saëns was not suitable for Mozart and Beethoven. Strange irregularities occurred in Bach. His way with the Beethoven concerto "suffered from an imaginative remodelling of the original into a personal experience."[13] He simply could not subordinate his own personality to that of the composer, but ultimately played with so much conviction that even his extravagances were forgiven.

It is interesting to observe Ysaÿe's growth as an interpretative musician as mirrored in his repertoire. He began as an exponent of the virtuoso music of Vieuxtemps and Wieniawski, in which he excelled; he absorbed the new repertoire (mainly French) of the 1880s and '90s by his personal contact with the Parisian circle of composers. He added the concertos of Max Bruch, who found his interpretations ideal. Finally, he emerged as a masterful, though very subjective, interpreter of the classics. He rediscovered two neglected violin concertos by Mozart, No. 3 in G and No. 6 in E flat. His Bach was memorable, particularly the E-major Concerto and the Chaconne. He first played the Beethoven concerto when he was thirty-one and approached the Brahms concerto when he was in his forties. He branched out into the repertoire of the modern Russians and Germans; he played Max Reger's *Suite in the Olden Style*, Op. 93, in St. Petersburg with the composer at the piano, and the two got along very well. Late in life—he was in his mid-fifties by then—he studied and memorized Elgar's Violin Concerto and gave it a wonderful performance in Berlin in 1912 under the baton of Arthur Nikisch.

Ysaÿe arrived in Berlin from Bremen, where he had played the Elgar with great success. He felt fairly confident, having had no slips of memory or technique. Just before the public dress rehearsal in Berlin, his impresario Wolff came to tell him that the hall was filled with a galaxy of violinists—Kreisler, Elman, Flesch, Marteau, among others. Ysaÿe exploded angrily against Wolff, "Oh, that animal! . . . it was a terrible blow. My blood stopped running. I told myself—surely I'm lost, and I was resigned like a victim led to the execution. . . ." But once he conquered his initial nervousness, he gave a splendid performance. "I never played better in my entire artistic life! It was a victory for the work and a great joy for the interpreter. I was in full command of my technical and intellectual means. I played 'happily.'"[14] Kreisler put the general admiration into words:* "No one has yet heard the Elgar Concerto to ultimate advantage who was not present when Ysaÿe introduced it in Berlin. It was one of the noblest specimens of violin playing in recent years."[15]

Following the performance, Flesch invited Ysaÿe, Kreisler, and Elman to his home. After a hearty meal, Kreisler and Elman played the Bach Double Concerto and Flesch performed Nardini's Sonata in D

---

* Elgar had composed his Violin Concerto for Kreisler, who had given the world premiere in London in 1910. All the more significant was the praise that Kreisler lavished on Ysaÿe's performance.

major "very beautifully," as Ysaÿe remembered. Next came Elman, whom Ysaÿe asked to play a movement of the Tchaikovsky concerto. Finally everybody insisted that Ysaÿe take the violin.

> They forced me to play the Fourth Concerto of Vieuxtemps which Kreisler accompanied *from memory* at the piano, including the Scherzo, without missing one harmony! I was very touched by the attitude of these dear children, and if I love them for their talent, I love them as much for their attitude toward me whom they call *"notre maître à tous,"* without intending to make me appear old![16]

At that time, the "dear children" Flesch and Kreisler were in their thirties, Elman a mere twenty, while Ysaÿe was fifty-three. This whole scene was typical of the admiration for Ysaÿe among the younger generation; he was a mesmerizing influence. In fact, Flesch once admitted having refused an invitation to visit Ysaÿe during the summer months because he feared that the master's influence would be too overwhelming. Others, like Enesco and Thibaud, had no such fears and learned much from Ysaÿe without sacrificing their own personality.

Amidst all this adulation, Ysaÿe also had a few detractors. One of them was George Bernard Shaw, who was not easily overawed by reputation or fame. He was an admirer of the easygoing grace of Sarasate, and he was not overwhelmed by the newly arrived Belgian fiddler. In an early review (May 24, 1889), Shaw wrote,

> Ysaye disappointed me. His technical skill is prodigious, his tone strong and steady, his effect on the public unquestionable. But he is an unsympathetic player. In the cadenza of the Concerto he played every phrase so as to make a point; and the audience whispered, "How clever, and how difficult it must be." . . . Now when Sarasate played the same cadenza on Saturday, everybody recognized the reference and nobody had the feat of execution obtruded on them. The spirit of the composition was always missed, and the wonders of the fiddling always insisted on.

Gradually Shaw's reserve began to melt:

> Ysaye was on his mettle: he had probably heard that London is under the impression that Joachim can play Bach; and he accordingly gave us the Prelude and Gavotte in E, just to show us what real Bach playing meant. . . . Of course he overdid it.

. . . He dashed into a speed impossible to himself; but what he succeeded in doing without sacrificing the accuracy of his intonation or the quality of his tone was astonishing.

A year or two later, Shaw finally admitted, "Ysaye, the Belgian violinist, played Mendelssohn's Concerto lately better than any other living violinist could have played it, as far as London knows."[17]

A fervent admirer of Ysaÿe was the conductor Sir Henry Wood, founder of the famed Promenade Concerts, who reminisced about Ysaÿe's first appearance as soloist with him, in 1899:

Words utterly fail me when I think of Ysaye's performances. The quality of his tone was so ravishingly beautiful, and it is no exaggeration to say that, having accompanied all the great violinists in the world during the past 50 years, of *all* of them Ysaye impressed me most. He seemed to get more color out of a violin than any of his contemporaries and he was certainly unique as a concerto player, especially . . . his intensity of tone when playing with the full hairs of the bow near the bridge. I remember his *flautando*-playing, particularly, in a work by Rimsky-Korsakov, and still treasure the memories of this most lovable man.[18]

It was not always easy to work with Ysaÿe. To have him select a program presented problems; he left letters unanswered, and Wood had to go to Brussels to talk it over with him. Ysaÿe did not see why it mattered *what* he played. Perhaps he was right, for Sir Henry adds wistfully, "All we need to tell London was that *Ysaye was playing.*"

At times Ysaÿe arrived unprepared, as in 1911 for the Norwich Festival when he whispered to the manager, "Don't tell Henry, but I've been fishing for the past two months and haven't taken the fiddle out of the case." True enough, his performance of the Beethoven concerto (as Sir Henry remembers) "was easily the worst I ever directed. In the slow movement his memory went to pieces—indeed I do not know what he would have done had not Maurice Sons [the concertmaster] prompted him as he went along, playing the solo part on his own violin. . . ."

Sir Henry's first encounter with Ysaÿe is revealing:

The instant he began to rehearse I sensed his master mind and had sufficient tact to subjugate my will to his. There was nothing else to do. . . .

We began with Bach's E major Concerto. . . . Ysaye

stopped us every few bars. He turned to the strings, showed them his bowing, and gently insisted on their copying it. . . . What impressed me more than anything was his marvelous singing quality and his perfect rubato. . . . I remember so clearly the long G sharp in the slow movement of the Bach Concerto as played by Ysaye. His control was absolute perfection, his vibrato sensitive and refined. . . . His rhythmic energy in the rondo was electrifying. The rondo tune comes over three times; he gave it with three different weights of tone.[19]

Interestingly enough, Ysaÿe was "deadly opposed" to the continuo part performed on a piano or harpsichord: he felt that the sound did not blend with the solo violin. "It irritates me . . . they spoil my *cantilena*." For the continuo part in the Bach concerto—which is indispensable—he preferred the organ, a rather odd choice. He used a part especially worked out by his composer-friend Gevaert, which Wood found "beautifully conceived." Wood described his collaboration with Ysaÿe as enjoyable as well as enriching:

It was an absolute inspiration to accompany him. . . . I learned more in these early days from this great man than from all other [soloists] put together. . . . Ysaye was the first to convince me that nearly all orchestral accompaniments are too heavy, and we went over some of the more fully-orchestrated passages three or four times.[20]

This is an interesting point: Ysaÿe, though the possessor of a "big" tone, did not want to force in order to be heard. "Gentlemen, I am not a trombone—*only a solo violin*," he used to say to the orchestra.

Ysaÿe advocated women's playing in the orchestra, at a time when orchestras were a man's sole domain—"I find their work equal to that of the men," he said. On his advice, Wood accepted six women in his own orchestra in 1913, later admitting that he never regretted his decision.

Ysaÿe was a virtuoso in the best sense of the word. He considered virtuosity essential to musical expression, just as music is essential to virtuosity. It is precisely the marriage of technique and music, in the spirit of the old Italian violin masters, that is characteristic of Ysaÿe's profile as a master violinist. He said,

The compositions of the virtuosos are necessary for the instrumental art, because the composer (alone) cannot conceive that such effects are possible unless he has before him a model, a guide—such as Paganini or our dear Vieuxtemps, or even second-rank virtuosos.[21]

Ysaÿe cherished his ability to communicate his emotions and musical thoughts to the listeners. He did not disdain the violinistic effect, but put it to musical use. In this respect, he considered the virtuoso, the violinist, the interpreter intertwined:

Without the interpreter, a score is but a voice in the wilderness. The interpreter without work, the work without interpreter—two powers without breath, twin souls condemned to die when separated. The interpreter is the blood that circulates, he is the lifeline of music.[22]

Ysaÿe divided the violin repertoire into works *pour le violon* (*for* the violin) and works *par le violon* (*by means* of the violin). It is a precarious distinction: the first category includes compositions "born" out of the instrument, fully idiomatic, whether by Tartini or Sarasate; the second category embraces works where the musical content expresses itself *through* the violin, is—as it were—entrusted to the instrument. It is not a foregone conclusion, at least not by Ysaÿe's standards, that the first category is "cheap" and the second "deep"; to him, a work like Vieuxtemps's Fourth Concerto was a musical *and* violinistic masterpiece. His reasoning becomes clearer when he speaks of the Beethoven concerto: "It addresses itself to the violin, but it is not born out of the violin. . . . Its true greatness lies, not in the technique, but in the *cantilena*."[23] He admits that it was Joachim's interpretation of the Beethoven that made him recognize the greatness of the work. Still, one can be sure that Ysaÿe's Beethoven was very different from Joachim's concept. Whatever Ysaÿe played, his style was grand, eloquent, expressive, but also willful and subjective. He never played passages, he sang them; his technique was always expressive. Ysaÿe belonged to a generation which considered textual fidelity secondary to interpretative greatness. To take liberties meant to bring music to life. Ysaÿe was, perhaps, the last descendant of the Liszt-Rubinstein tradition of interpreter as king. He owed much to Rubinstein's influence and summarized his admiration for him in the words, "Genius—the word is not too strong: he 'genialized' the talent." Ysaÿe, too, was on that borderline between talent and genius.

There are hundreds of violinists who claim to have studied with Ysaÿe. Actually, he never taught regularly after having left the Brussels

Conservatory in 1898; he was constantly on the road. But in the summer months, violinists used to assemble wherever he spent his vacation, usually in Belgium, and there he dispensed musical and violinistic advice to many in an informal manner. He did not bother giving technical suggestions. Asked about a fingering in a difficult passage, he answered with derision, "Use the toes as long as it sounds!" His method was simple: play scales and arpeggios, stressing perfect evenness, inaudible shifts, quiet string crossings. What he tried to teach was the interpretative sweep, the expressive eloquence, but he had no illusions about what was teachable: "To play the violin is rather easy, it is even banal. . . . But to feel, to palpitate, to make vibrate—not the instrument, but the *soul* of the instrument . . . that power cannot be acquired, it is a gift of God!"[24] He passed on this "gift of God" to violinists who were not his students but who came under his influence—Enesco, Thibaud, Milstein, and, indirectly, Menuhin.

Ysaÿe was a musician of many gifts. He played the viola as well as he played the violin; in his youth he used Vieuxtemps's oversized viola and produced an enormous tone ("like an ox," said someone sarcastically). As well as conducting extensively, he was a composer of considerable accomplishments; in fact, he composed much more than he permitted to be published. Yet he never studied composition in a formal way. His creative profile is post-Romantic and influenced by the French Impressionist idiom. He is at his best when writing for the violin; a few of his shorter compositions, like *Rêve d'enfant, Chant d'hiver,* and *Poème élégiaque,* enjoyed some popularity among violinists. (The last-named work inspired Chausson to write his well-known *Poème* for violin and orchestra, which in turn became one of Ysaÿe's favorite pieces; it is said that he helped shape the violin part.)* One of Ysaÿe's transcriptions is a widely played virtuoso piece: *Caprice en forme de valse,* after Saint-Saëns. But his most enduring contribution to the violin repertoire is a collection of Six Sonatas for unaccompanied violin, Op. 27, published in 1924. They reveal a searching mind in terms of harmonic originality and novel violin technique. Ysaÿe dedicated each to a younger violinist, the first four to Szigeti, Thibaud, Enesco, and Kreisler, each a celebrity in his own right. The dedicatee of No. 5 is Crickboom, a former student and member of the old Ysaÿe Quartet,

---

* In his interpretation of the Chausson *Poème,* Ysaÿe made numerous changes, particularly in the first cadenza. He avoided teaching the piece. Chausson died shortly after the premiere of the *Poème,* which was a kind of legacy entrusted to Ysaÿe.

Bravo à Mr Boris Schwarz
avec mes vœux d'artiste pour
que ta carrière soit grande,

E. Ysaÿe
Paris Juin
1926.

Eugène Ysaÿe, the great
Belgian violinist, composer,
and conductor, in a photo
inscribed to the author.
Ysaÿe opened a new era in
modern violin playing.

Fritz Kreisler, whose unsurpassed charm and tonal
beauty served as a model for
a whole generation. His compositions are still in the violin
repertoire.

and of No. 6 the Spaniard Manuel Quiroga, a superb violinist later in-capacitated by an accident. After lying dormant for decades, the Solo Sonatas have lately been rediscovered and appear on concert programs with increasing frequency.

There have been many attempts to summarize Ysaÿe's significance in the history of violin playing. In some ways, he was the French counter-part to Joachim: the sum-total of age-old musical traditions and con-temporary national influences. Coming a quarter-century later, Ysaÿe strikes us as more contemporary, and indeed his influence reaches deep into the twentieth century. In terms of violin playing, Joachim was the last classicist, Ysaÿe the first modernist. While the post-Joachim Ger-man school withered, the post-Ysaÿe Franco-Belgian school prospered until all were overshadowed by a "blitz" from the east, the newly emerg-ing Russian school.

In 1937, Queen Elisabeth of Belgium—an amateur violinist and a long-time admirer and friend of Ysaÿe—established an international competition for violinists and pianists, to be named after Eugène Ysaÿe. The first violin contest (1937) produced a winner who later acquired world fame—David Oistrakh of Moscow. The second prize winner was Ricardo Odnoposoff of Argentina, at that time active in Vienna. The next four prizes were all won by Soviet violinists, which created a minor sensation. Among the obligatory pieces to be played by all contestants was the Solo Sonata No. 4 by Ysaÿe. In 1951 the competition was re-named after Queen Elisabeth, but among connoisseurs it will always re-main the Prix Ysaÿe, honoring the memory of a truly great master.

Fritz Kreisler

Kreisler's slow rise to fame coincided with the reign of Eugène Ysaÿe. It takes time to displace an artistic idol. Just as Ysaÿe's career de-veloped slowly because of the dominance of Joachim and Sarasate, so Kreisler's recognition came slowly because the public was enamored of Ysaÿe's titanesque power. Kreisler's style was quite different from that of Ysaÿe: what he lacked in grandeur, he made up with sweetness and charm. His playing was elegant and chiseled, imbued with high-strung brilliance, irresistible verve, and rhythmic incisiveness. Eventually, Kreis-ler ascended the throne previously held by Ysaÿe as the model for a generation of violinists. Sooner than expected, his triumph was threatened by a phenomenal violinist of a different school—Jascha Heifetz.

Ysaÿe had great fondness for Kreisler. In the early years, he helped the struggling young colleague. When Kreisler made his debut with the Berlin Philharmonic in 1899, Ysaÿe was in the audience and applauded ostentatiously. When Ysaÿe, suddenly indisposed, canceled an appearance with the Berlin Philharmonic in November 1901, Kreisler substituted on short notice and performed on a borrowed instrument. At that time, Ysaÿe said, "I have arrived at the top, and from now on there will be a steady decline of my prowess. . . . But Kreisler is on the ascendancy, and in a short time he will be the greater artist."[1] Kreisler admitted that, though he greatly admired Joachim, it was Ysaÿe who was his idol. But the admiration was mutual: one of Ysaÿe's solo sonatas is dedicated to Kreisler, a tangible expression of affection. In 1931, the last year of Ysaÿe's life, Kreisler participated in a benefit concert for the ailing master. In gratitude, Ysaÿe presented him with the manuscript of Chausson's Poème, one of the works Kreisler had played on that occasion.*

Kreisler's genealogy as a violinist is unusual. One could describe him as a Frenchified Viennese. Born in Vienna in 1875, he began to play the violin at the age of four. His father, a physician and an ardent amateur string player, gave him his first lessons. By some subterfuge, little Fritz was admitted to the Vienna Conservatory when he was only seven (the minimum age was ten). His teacher was Joseph Hellmesberger, Jr., the youngest member of the Hellmesberger clan and a typical representative of the suave Viennese school; Kreisler remembered him as an excellent teacher with a fondness for ballerinas. The Viennese lilt in Kreisler's playing can certainly be traced to those early years under Hellmesberger's tutelage. There were also some theory courses taught by the great Anton Bruckner, a guileless artist little equipped to teach a group of unruly youngsters. It seems that Fritz did more mischief than counterpoint. But he also taught himself the piano and soon was able to accompany most violin pieces from memory. By 1885, Fritz was graduated, winning a first prize in violin playing.

With commendable foresight, Fritz's father decided to take the boy to Paris for further study. Here, the ten-year-old was admitted to the Conservatoire and entered the class of the venerable Lambert Massart (at that time seventy-four), who had been Wieniawski's teacher.

* The manuscript is now at the Library of Congress, a gift of Kreisler.

Much later Kreisler said, "I believe Massart liked me because I played in the style of Wieniawski." But Massart knew a talent when he saw one, and he is said to have written to Fritz's father, "I have been the teacher of Wieniawski and many others, but little Fritz will be the greatest of them all."[2]

Kreisler later recalled his studies in Paris, "Massart laid stress on emotion, not technique. . . . He was passionately devoted to the violin." Nevertheless, both Wieniawski and Kreisler acquired formidable techniques but also a few unorthodox playing habits. Wieniawski's bowing was considered "incredibly stiff" by the standards of the Joachim school. Kreisler, too, had an unconventional bow arm: he disregarded the traditional *sons filés*, the spun-out long bow, considered an important tool in a violinist's technique; instead, he preferred short, intense bow strokes, changing the bow frequently and holding his right elbow rather high. He also tightened the bow hair far more than customary.

Whether Massart was capable of teaching Kreisler the "French vibrato," the intensely sensuous tone color first produced by Wieniawski, is a moot question. Kreisler was too young to have heard Wieniawski, but perhaps he acquired it through Ysaÿe, who had studied with Wieniawski.

Be this as it may, the twelve-year-old Fritz finished the Conservatoire in 1887 with a First Prize in violin, competing against violinists almost twice his age. (Wieniawski was eleven when he received the same distinction.)

A year later, Fritz was sent on a concert tour through the United States. He was not the main attraction, but merely assisting artist during a tour arranged for the celebrated pianist Moriz Rosenthal. He received a set salary of $50 per concert and a guarantee of fifty performances.

The thirteen-year-old Kreisler made his debut in Boston on November 9, 1888, and in New York the following day. In Boston he played the Mendelssohn concerto and the difficult *Hungarian Airs* by Ernst, in New York only the Mendelssohn. The critics were divided; some found him very gifted, others saw nothing extraordinary in his performance. The *Tribune* judged his intonation faultless, but his tone "exceedingly small." At that time, Kreisler played a smallish Grancino violin, and his tone may not have been strong enough to cut through the orchestra, for he was more successful when playing with piano. Several reviews found his left-hand technique superior to his bowing; perhaps the critics reacted to his unorthodox bow arm. We must guard ourselves against thinking that the American critics were provincial; in fact, New York had recently heard such virtuosos as Vieuxtemps, Wieniawski, Ole

Bull, and Franz Kneisel; and Fritz's playing impressed some as that of a "nice studious boy who has a rather musical nature." Only Louis Elson was more positive, "He is, I think, destined to become a very great artist if he does not disdain further study."[3] In general, American public opinion was prejudiced against prodigies, and the appearance of chubby Fritz in a short-panted velvet outfit with flowing cravat and high Hessian boots was not reassuring.

All in all, Kreisler's first American tour led nowhere, both financially and artistically. Back in Vienna, his father decided that the boy's general education had to be given some attention. During the next six years, Fritz finished his secondary education and entered a premedical course. While going to school, the erstwhile prodigy never touched the violin—it was a complete musical hiatus. Then came army service (1895–96), during which he occasionally picked up the fiddle to entertain fellow soldiers. But there was no question of any regular practicing.

The army service completed, Kreisler decided to return to the violin. He applied for the position of assistant concertmaster of the Vienna Opera, but failed the audition. The verdict of the concertmaster, Arnold Rosé, was, "He can't sightread." Foolish as this judgment may seem in retrospect, it must be conceded that Kreisler, with his highly individual style, would have made a bad orchestra player. Particularly his tone could not possibly have blended with the orchestral sound, since he used a very intense vibrato. We have a vivid description of Kreisler's sound in the mid-1890s by his colleague and friend Flesch: "Kreisler's cantilena was an unrestrained orgy of sinfully seductive sounds, depravedly fascinating, whose sole driving force appeared to be a sensuality intensified to the point of frenzy."[4] Many years later, Flesch told me privately, "Young Kreisler's tone was the 'personification of sin.'" To a public used to the "purity" of Joachim or Rosé, this type of sensuousness must have been rather distracting and may help explain his comparatively slow rise.

Two years after failing the audition, Kreisler had the satisfaction of performing as soloist with the same Vienna Orchestra under the baton of Hans Richter, displaying brilliant virtuosity in Max Bruch's Second Concerto. Otherwise, he led a rather bohemian life in the artist circles of Vienna, gambling away the little money he had and at times pawning his clothes and even his violin. But he also met Brahms and Joachim and retained vivid memories of occasional chamber-music readings with Brahms. He gave some concerts in Russia and in Poland, but his career did not advance.

In those days, Berlin was the key to success for a young artist, and

Kreisler's friends arranged a small concert for him in March 1899. It aroused the interest of Arthur Nikisch, the famous conductor, who invited Kreisler as soloist with the Berlin Philharmonic. On December 1, 1899, Kreisler played the Mendelssohn concerto, with Ysaÿe applauding in the audience. It was the beginning of a great friendship.

The following year Kreisler returned for a concert tour in the United States, this time as a mature artist. On December 7 he made his debut at Carnegie Hall with the Philharmonic Orchestra, followed by concerts in Philadelphia, Pittsburgh, Chicago, and other cities. He was reengaged for the following season, but he faced stiff competition from a younger Bohemian violinist, Jan Kubelik, who was hailed as the "second Paganini." The same happened in London, where Kubelik received the gold medal of the Philharmonic Society in 1902, while Kreisler's debut that year at a concert conducted by Hans Richter was given little attention. But his success grew, and two years later, he too was awarded the Philharmonic gold medal. Within a few years, he was in such demand in Europe and America that he played as many as 260 concerts a year.

Contributing to the practical aspects of Kreisler's career was his marriage, in 1902, to the New York–born Harriet Lies. They had met the year before on an eastbound Atlantic crossing. Harriet was a divorcée—strong-willed, with an independent mind and a somewhat abrasive personality, just the opposite of the affable, easygoing Fritz. Once they were married, she decreed an end to his bohemian-style life. She ran his career, put order into his life, and forced him to practice (which he greatly disliked!) and to discipline himself. She also estranged him from many of his former friends. Though often criticized for her almost ruthless domination of his life, she certainly helped build his image as a world figure in music, as a humanitarian and philanthropist. Friends had to admit, "Harriet saved Fritz." He endured, and even enjoyed, being "managed." As for Harriet, she met all criticism with self-assurance: "I know Fritz best. I have made him. The entire world acclaims the result. I knew what was good for him."[5] While his was primarily a virtuoso career, Kreisler was always willing and eager to join other artists in chamber-music programs. In 1901–2 he formed a trio with the pianist Josef Hofmann and the cellist Jean Gérardy, two young artists on the rise, and their performances were highly acclaimed in America. Some ten years later in England, he joined a trio with Harold Bauer and Pablo Casals. Kreisler also formed a sonata team with the eminent Busoni, and though their personalities were rather different, they produced performances of "noble, masculine intellectuality." Most noteworthy was his association with Sergei Rachmaninoff; they recorded sonatas by Beethoven, Schubert, and Grieg around 1930. Thus the breadth of Kreisler's musicianship extended far beyond the narrow confines of a mere virtuoso.

Memorable was Kreisler's premiere of Elgar's Violin Concerto, composed for and dedicated to him. The composer conducted the London Royal Philharmonic on November 10, 1910. Queen's Hall was packed and many were turned away. One listener, Dora Powell (the "Dorabella" in the *Enigma Variations*), reminisced,

> Kreisler came on looking as white as a sheet—even for a player
> of his great experience it must have been a nervous moment—
> but he played superbly. Elgar was also, obviously, very much
> strung up; but all went well, and the ovation at the end was
> tremendous.[6]

Kreisler took pride in having played a part in the genesis of the Elgar concerto, which (he predicted in 1930) "will in fifty years be standing out radiantly as one of the peaks of classical concertos." His prophecy is being realized as more and more young violinists rediscover this neglected masterpiece.

By the eve of World War I, Kreisler was the dominant figure in the violin world. Ysaÿe was on the decline; among younger rivals there were the virtuoso Kubelik, the charming Thibaud, the intense Enesco, the fabulous Russians, Zimbalist and Elman, with a style all their own. But Kreisler's playing had a magnetism unmatched by anyone else. His popularity was enhanced by his growing catalogue of recordings* and by his skill as arranger of short pieces for the violin which graced the programs of many of his rivals.

The outbreak of the war halted Kreisler's career temporarily. He was called to active duty in the Austrian army. A photo of that time pictures a morose-looking Kreisler in uniform with Harriet next to him in a dirndl outfit, a droll sight. But there was nothing droll about his involvement in the war: on September 4, 1914, he was wounded at the Russian front and declared unfit for further military duty. By the end of 1914 he returned to the United States (still a neutral country) and resumed giving concerts. His war experiences left him with a slight limp, but he played as beautifully as ever, with even more maturity and

* Between 1910 and 1950, he recorded well over two hundred titles for RCA Victor and its European affiliates.

depth. He also began to give charity concerts to help the war children of Europe. However, once the United States joined the fighting in 1917, public sentiment turned against anything reminiscent of Germany, and Kreisler, keenly aware of the general animosity, curtailed his public appearances. In fact, he was forced to withdraw because there were massive demonstrations against him, fanned by various "patriotic" groups.

Even after the war was ended, a chauvinist animosity against him lingered on for some time. Though he dismissed these "little pinpricks," he felt hurt. On October 27, 1919, he reappeared in New York's Carnegie Hall—it was a benefit for the Vienna Children's Milk Relief—and received a triumphant ovation. His return to the London stage came on May 4, 1921; it was, as he said, "the tensest moment of my career," for there was agitation against him. But "Kreisler came, he played, and he conquered." As one critic wrote, "He gave us such violin playing as we have not heard for years. . . . The audience's reception for him was something to restore much of the idealism and the belief in human nature that we have lost during the last few years."[7] And the severe Ernest Newman said, "Kreisler is greater than ever. There is not a violinist in the world who can approach him."

Paris took longer to "forgive" Kreisler: not until 1924 did he reappear in a concert given at the Grand Opéra. But personal feelings could transcend political animosity: Jacques Thibaud, the French violinist, served in his country's army and, like Kreisler, was wounded and honorably discharged. In 1917 he came to America (where he was well known) to perform. He and Kreisler had been friends before the war, but now they were technically enemies. Once, when they happened to meet on a New York street, both limping from their war injuries, they looked at each other and saluted without speaking. A few days later they met again, in a hotel lobby, after a concert. As described by the critic Bercovici, "The two men hesitated for a moment, then rushed at each other with outstretched hands. The war was ended as far as they were concerned."[8]

Kreisler used his enforced leisure to compose his operetta *Apple Blossoms*, which was premiered in New York in October 1919, with Adele and Fred Astaire in major roles. In fact, during a summer party, he and Efrem Zimbalist cooked up the idea of each writing a musical comedy. Zimbalist's *Honeydew* was produced a year later, in 1920. Both shows were successful—Kreisler's, in fact, ran for a year on Broadway.

For the next two decades Kreisler was the most beloved violinist of his time. He played everywhere—in Europe and the Americas, in the

Orient and Australia. His appearances were no longer concerts—they were musical events. His public idolized him; his younger colleagues admired and imitated him. Szigeti and Oistrakh, Thibaud and Milstein—they all admitted having been influenced by him. There was something particularly endearing about Kreisler's personality which aroused only adulation, not envy. Even the flaws in his playing were greeted with indulgent smiles. He was not the greatest technician of his time, but simply the strongest musical personality expressing himself through the violin. Grace, vitality, rhythm, taste, the ability to turn an unforgettable phrase—these were the characteristics of a Kreisler performance. His tone quality was absolutely unique, no matter on what violin he played. His technical equipment, very commanding in his youth, declined over the years, but it was of secondary importance. In the words of the Berlin critic Adolf Weissmann, "Kreisler . . . has developed a new type of virtuosity to the highest perfection. He . . . has imbued his playing with a human feeling that no one else attains."[9]

When the Nazis assumed power in Germany in 1933, Kreisler was a resident of Berlin, where he had built a palatial home around 1924.* To what extent Kreisler tried to placate the Nazis is unclear. His tolerance of Nazism has been described by the West German writer Hartnack as "naiveté bordering on stupidity." His colleague Huberman called it "treason on behalf of humanism."[10] However, the fact remains that in a letter addressed to the conductor Wilhelm Furtwängler, Kreisler declined an invitation to appear as soloist with the Berlin Philharmonic during the 1933–34 season (following the lead of Schnabel, Huberman, and others). He declared that only the recall of such men as Bruno Walter, Otto Klemperer, and Adolf Busch could demonstrate the German willingness to keep racial politics out of art. Of course, Furtwängler could not give such assurance. Kreisler was an Austrian citizen devoted to his country, but when Chancellor Dollfuss was murdered in 1938 and Austria overrun by Hitler, Kreisler accepted an offer of the French Government to become a French citizen. However, when the treacherous Vichy Government took over in 1940, Kreisler felt no allegiance to this regime. In May 1943 he became a citizen of the United States.

On April 27, 1941, Kreisler had a near-fatal accident: while crossing New York's Madison Avenue at 57th Street, he was hit by a truck. He fell to the street bleeding and unconscious, not recognized at first;

* I can still remember the handsome villa in the Grunewald, near the church, protected by a high fence. Nothing but charred ruins remained after the war.

rushed to a hospital, he lay in a coma for days with a fractured skull and concussion. Miraculously he recovered; his skillful hands were not injured and his mind emerged unscathed. Late in May, his violin was brought to his hospital room: he picked it up and began to play. On June 16 he was released from the hospital. In January 1942 he made some recordings—his own pieces—and on October 31 he reappeared on the stage of Carnegie Hall, with his musical powers unimpaired. It was a miraculous recovery for the sixty-seven-year-old artist.

On July 17, 1944, Kreisler was heard for the first time on the radio. His performance was transmitted over 118 stations of the NBC network and reached into the farthest corners of America and abroad. He was a late convert to the radio—Heifetz, for example, had played on a network as early as 1931. Kreisler resisted, saying in jest, "I avoid the radio because I don't like the idea of being turned on and off like an electric light or hot water." [11] (The pianist Schnabel resisted making records with the same reasoning.) But he became convinced that the miracle of radio could carry his violin to remote parts of the world while he had to restrict his travel because of wartime conditions, not to mention his health. Accompanied by an orchestra, he played the first movement of the Mendelssohn concerto, his arrangement of Albeniz's *Tango*, and his own *Caprice viennois*. The idea that he could be heard by millions without traveling appealed to him. (A Kreisler broadcast was heard in French Equatorial Africa by Dr. Albert Schweitzer.) Public concerts continued on a limited scale. In June 1944 he played for the first time at the famed Lewisohn Stadium in New York and attracted more than 16,000 listeners.

Kreisler gave his last Carnegie Hall recital on November 1, 1947, and continued to accept some engagements well past his seventieth birthday, during the season 1949–50. His seventy-fifth birthday was observed in New York by a distinguished gathering of artists and friends, at which Kreisler reminisced about his long and fulfilling life in music. Though he lived another twelve years, he gradually lost interest in violin playing and sold his priceless collection of instruments, keeping only his 1860 Vuillaume violin.

During the winter of 1960–61, Kreisler (then about eighty-five) was visited by David Oistrakh, the leading Soviet violinist. Oistrakh, a lifelong admirer of Kreisler, reminisced somewhat sadly about this last meeting:

His vision and his hearing were already much impaired. I brought him the announcement of a concert given by my students in Moscow in honor of his 80th birthday with a program made up entirely of Kreisler's works. He was very much touched. He said, "I've been forgotten. I belong to the past. Wieniawski and Joachim are also forgotten . . . Ysaÿe was the first to play the violin with a really beautiful sound . . ." He began to reminisce about the people he knew in Russia and with whom he was friends: Rachmaninov, Kussewitzky, Safonoff, Conus. We began to speak about Odessa: "I was there"—he said "—a beautiful city. I remember I wanted to play something new for the musical public of that city, and then and there I composed *Schoen Rosmarin*." [12]

Kreisler died in New York on January 29, 1962, four days before his eighty-seventh birthday.

No one who ever saw Kreisler on the stage can forget his appearance—broad-shouldered, proudly erect, acknowledging the applause not with a bow but with a slight inclination of the head. He did not use a shoulder pad but liked to bend back the collar of his jacket to give slight support to the violin. Most violinists offer their profile to the public, with their eyes closed or looking at the fingerboard. Not so Kreisler— he barely touched the chinrest with his jaw, but turned his full face to the public, eyes alert and flashing, a magical and irresistible contact, sharing his delight in the music.

When appearing with orchestra, Kreisler had his own idiosyncrasies:

> While the orchestra played the opening tutti he stood as if at attention, arms at his sides, the violin almost touching the ground, with the scroll hooked over the index finger of his left hand. When it was time to start, he indulged in a bit of show-manship by bringing it to his shoulder with a gesture so rapid that the instrument seemed to have been snapped up between his chin and shoulder blade.[13]

Without any visible physical exertion, Kreisler achieved results that seemed entirely effortless. The listener was never conscious of technical display because, to Kreisler, technique was secondary. One marveled at the elegance of his bowing, the subtlety and charm of his phrasing, the vitality and boldness of his rhythm, but most of all his tone of inde-scribable sweetness and intensity. Though not very large, his tone had unique carrying power because his bow did not choke the natural vibra-tions of the strings; there was a resilience to his bow pressure. The coloration was achieved by the left-hand vibrato, which, he said, originated with Wieniawski and Ysaÿe but was more nervous and high-strung in his own case. He vibrated not only sustained notes but also faster passing notes, even passages, which lost all dryness under his magic touch. His choice of fingering was highly idiomatic and often unusual, but always carefully thought out and quite modern in the use of specific fingers for expressive notes; all his published violin parts are meticulously fingered and allow us insight into his workshop.

He used innate intelligence and musical intuition to make the best of his violinistic gifts. In his youth he had acquired an excellent technique, and he managed to maintain it with a minimum of practice. In fact, he was a determined foe of practicing:

> I never practice. In the accepted sense of the term, in the formal use of the word, I have never practiced in my whole life. I practice only as I feel the need. I believe that everything is in the brain. You think of a passage and you know exactly how you want it.

Excessive practicing, so Kreisler believed, "benumbs the brain, renders the imagination less acute, and deadens the alertness"; for that reason, "I never practice before a concert." He cited the example of the great virtuoso Kubelik, who practiced twelve hours on the day of a concert until his fingertips were bleeding. Kreisler asked him wonderingly, "But why did you?"[14] In the evening, Kubelik gave a technically perfect performance but it was "a blank!" It is true, as Kreisler remarked, that Sarasate was known to walk out on the stage without practicing, and that Paganini was never heard to practice. But one can also point to other artists who admitted the need to practice—Joachim, Auer, Szigeti, among others.

The need to practice has various roots—physiological, psychological, and musical. Muscular coordination, once acquired, must be maintained. An athlete or a dancer needs daily exercise as much as a violinist or a pianist. The physiological build of a hand is a determining factor. Kreisler said, "I have never been troubled with stiff fingers," and indeed he could play impeccably after months of inactivity. Other artists wake up with stiff fingers after only a night's sleep, and the Sisyphean labor of getting the hands into shape starts every morning. In addition to the physiological need there is also the psychological reassurance an artist derives from the knowledge that he is well prepared when stepping onto the stage. As for the musical need to practice, there is the need to refresh one's memory (if one plays without music as most recitalists do), but this did not trouble Kreisler: once memorized, the music was "engraved" in his mind. Learning new music also involves practicing, but here again Kreisler could learn new repertoire by simply studying the score with his eyes, away from the instrument. Such a procedure is unusual; normally, a violinist, faced with a new work, will proceed to absorb it by playing and practicing it with violin in hand. Kreisler's theories about practicing are very personal and may not have general validity; but certainly they are a warning against the mindless, mechanical, day-long drilling of fingers.

Kreisler had a "divine carelessness for all matters technical," remarked Flesch. This is in keeping with his belief that "technique is decidedly not the main essential of the concert violinist's equipment. Sincerity and personality are the main essentials."[15] This is no longer the case—today the highest degree of technical proficiency is expected as a precondition for a career.

Kreisler's technique was never his strongest asset, though it was abundant in his youth. His recordings (made in the old manner, that is, direct to disc with no corrections or splicings possible) testify to his command of the violin. In later years his intonation became unreliable, but this was partly due to his impaired hearing. He retained a manual dexterity until late in life, which aroused the admiration of much younger colleagues. "He is still superb," remarked Spalding in 1948.

Kreisler was active as composer, arranger, and editor. His editorial work ranged from a fingered edition of the complete Beethoven violin sonatas to a revision of a number of Paganini works (published in 1905), and a reshaping of Corelli's *La Folia*, Schumann's Fantasy Op. 131, Tchaikovsky's Violin Concerto (with a new cadenza!), and a few similar projects. He also wrote skillful piano accompaniments to several solo movements of Bach and to various caprices of Paganini and Wieniawski. Kreisler's edition of Tartini's *Devil's Trill Sonata* provides a new piano accompaniment and a "devilish" cadenza, which has become an integral part of most modern performances.

Kreisler's cadenzas composed for the Beethoven and Brahms concertos are used more often than any other cadenzas and have virtually displaced those composed by Joachim. Though published in the 1920s, the Beethoven cadenzas were composed when Kreisler was nineteen. They are fantastically clever, yet much less virtuosic than other cadenzas. Kreisler's cadenza to Beethoven's first movement culminates in a simultaneous sounding of two Beethovenian themes which makes perfect musical sense: "three minutes of miracle, bewilderment, wonder, surprise, and emotion," as the violinist Francescatti once wrote.

The list of original compositions also includes such well-known display pieces as *Caprice viennois, Tambourin chinois,* and the unaccompanied *Recitativo and Scherzo-Caprice.* Of a more serious nature is his String Quartet in A minor.

Kreisler was a very clever arranger; he had an uncanny gift for adapting all kinds of music for the violin and providing an enriched piano accompaniment. So successful were his arrangements that he opened the floodgates for similar transcriptions, though none as good as his. After he left the stage, public taste turned against "arranged" music, and his once-popular short pieces disappeared from the concert programs. In 1975, on the hundredth anniversary of Kreisler's birthday, many of his pieces were revived, all-Kreisler programs were given, and entire recordings containing his violin pieces were released. This might be a passing fad, yet Kreisler's contribution to the violin repertoire is a lasting one.

Finally, we come to a *cause célèbre,* the so-called hoax he perpetrated in mislabeling some of his compositions as works of old masters while, in truth, they were his own. In 1905, the respected publishing house of Schott brought out a collection of Classical Manuscripts, naming Kreisler as purported discoverer and editor-arranger of these musical "gems." Listed as composers were such minor masters as Pugnani, Francoeur, Padre Martini, Cartier, Friedemann Bach, and others. Only one piece was identifiable, the Tartini Variations on a Theme of Corelli, though treated very freely by Kreisler. In addition there were three lilting waltz tunes, supposedly Viennese folk melodies, named *Liebesfreud, Liebesleid,* and *Schön Rosmarin*—altogether seventeen selections. Each bore the following warning in three languages:

> The original manuscripts used for these transcriptions are the private property of Mr. Fritz Kreisler and are now published for the first time; they are moreover so freely treated that they constitute, in fact, original works. . . . When played in public, Mr. Kreisler's name must be mentioned on the programme.
>   The Publishers.

And so, the programs of violinists filled up rapidly with those hyphenated compositorial names—Pugnani-Kreisler, Francoeur-Kreisler, etc.

The publishers' statement was clever double-talk: the original manuscripts were indeed in the possession of Kreisler, since he had composed them himself; no originals other than those in Kreisler's handwriting existed. Emboldened by the fabulous success of these "classical manuscripts," Kreisler composed a Concerto in C, which he ascribed to Vivaldi. This, too, was widely played.

In 1935 Kreisler admitted almost casually that he had fooled the experts for decades; it was the New York *Times* critic, Olin Downes, who made Kreisler's admission public. Hurriedly, the disputed works were newly listed as composed by Kreisler "in the style of Pugnani," or whoever the purported author had been.

The discovery made a few critics very angry, most of all the esteemed Ernest Newman of London, actually an old admirer of Kreisler. He wrote two lengthy articles in the Sunday *Times*, accusing Kreisler of unethical conduct. Kreisler defended himself cleverly and challenged Newman to produce some pieces "in the olden style" if he thought it was so easy. Critics took sides pro and con, but finally the controversy simmered down and many people laughed good-humoredly. Kreisler's popularity did not suffer, and he himself later thought that it was a tempest in a teapot.

Of all the contemporary accounts of Kreisler's playing, the one by his colleague Carl Flesch is the most lucid and objective. Flesch was two years older than Kreisler; both came from the same Viennese-Parisian background, their careers ran parallel, and they were on friendly terms for over forty years.

When Flesch heard the ten-year-old Fritz in 1885, he was overwhelmed—"I sat gaping, for such fiddling I had never heard before." His impression ten years later was equally unforgettable, particularly the sensuousness of Kreisler's tone.* At that time, Kreisler was "a big, strong, broad-shouldered fellow whose facial expression showed a lively temperament with a touch of brutality, and who was amiably superficial and dashing in character." He also sported a twirled-up martial moustache like Kaiser Wilhelm.

Flesch pondered the question of why Kreisler's career took so much time to unfold, why his rise to fame was so slow, even after his Berlin success in 1899, while violinists inferior to him won quick popularity. His answer is perceptive: he maintains that Kreisler's manner of playing was ahead of his era and that the public needed time to accept him. Kreisler's style, at first, was felt to be "exaggerated, overwrought, unrhythmic, even unmusical, and so it was rejected." Particularly his con-

* See p. 308.

stant use of vibrato alienated the conservative listener. In order to appreciate Kreisler, a change in the public's aesthetic judgment was needed. Kreisler followed in the footsteps of Ysaÿe, who already used a broader vibrato; "he not only resorted to a still broader and more intensive vibrato, but even tried to ennoble faster passages by means of a vibrato. . . ." It was this "continuous vibrato" which Flesch considered Kreisler's "most important technical attribute."[16]

Kreisler's bowing also challenged tradition. He avoided the extremities of the bow, explaining that he did not use the tip because his arm was too short, nor the frog because he was afraid of damaging one of the corners of the violin. He played mostly in the middle, using short bow strokes and characteristic accents, lending life to each note with a mixture of bow pressure and vibrato. He rarely, if ever, used a floating stroke (*flautando*), but preferred the tight bow hair to adhere to the string with a certain solidity (the time-tested French method called *à la corde*). His bow strokes had great variety, from graceful ricochet to sharply dotted staccato, all of which lend a high-strung vitality to his playing. Tone and rhythm were his strongest assets.

Among contemporary violinists, Kreisler had hardly any detractors; even his competitors admitted that they could learn from him. There was an incredible outpouring of praise and adulation for him at his seventy-fifth birthday, and deservedly so, for he made a lasting impact on twentieth-century violin playing.

Bronislaw Huberman

Among the great violinists of the twentieth century, Huberman is a controversial figure. Some remember him fondly as one of the truly inspired interpreters of great music; others belittle his technical shortcomings and unconventional ideas. Great conductors, like Toscanini or Bruno Walter, admired and enjoyed playing with him, but fellow violinists were usually harsh in their evaluation. Flesch's judgment was so unfriendly that his translator, Hans Keller, felt compelled to contradict him in an appendix. Yehudi Menuhin remarked perceptively, "Just as there are composers who do not travel well, there are also artists who belong to a particular corner of the world. One such . . . was the violinist Huberman."[1]

He began as a child prodigy whose talent was praised by such eminent musicians as Joachim and Brahms, known for their reserve toward

As a boy of thirteen, Bronislaw
Huberman's playing of the Brahms
Concerto brought tears to the
composer's eyes.

Bronislaw Huberman was an inspired interpreter of the classics. In
1936 he founded the Palestine
Symphony Orchestra.

child performers. His admirers were concentrated in central Europe (particularly Germany and Austria), his native Poland, and Palestine. The American public, attuned to the Apollonian beauty of Kreisler's or Heifetz's violin style, could not fully approve of Huberman's uneven playing. But in Berlin, Vienna, or Paris, Huberman exerted a hypnotic hold on the most sophisticated audiences, who considered his interpretations of Beethoven or Brahms to be ultimate musical revelations.

My own recollections of his playing are quite vivid. I still remember his interpretations of Beethoven's concerto and Sonata Op. 96, Brahms's Sonata in G major, and Bruch's Concerto No. 2, all of which he played with transcendental intensity. He was a master of the most ethereal pianissimo, an incredibly soft tone produced by barely touching the strings with his bow, yet this tone carried into the farthest corners of a large hall. His slow movements had a visionary quality, at times ecstatic, at times introverted. All the more disturbing were his outbursts of strength or passion, when he could indeed produce brusque sounds. His left-hand intonation was faultless, his vibrato intense, but he occasionally misjudged his bow attacks which, in turn, resulted in tonal impurities. Ultimately, his artistry and integrity won out over these momentary lapses, which his admirers were willing to accept as part of his explosive temperament. There can be no doubt that Huberman was one of the most sensitive and probing musicians of his day. The quality of his violin playing depended on psychological and physiological conditions he could not always control. In his happy moods, he could be a superlative artist; under less favorable conditions, he could be disappointing. He needed a sympathetic public which would respond instinctively to his artistic message; under such circumstances, his communicativeness rose to unprecedented heights.

Born in 1882 in a provincial Polish town, Czestochowa, Huberman began to study with the respected violinist Mihalowicz, and performed Spohr's Concerto No. 2 at the age of seven. There followed a three-month course of lessons with Isidore Lotto, professor at the Warsaw Conservatory and himself a former prizewinning student of Massart in Paris. In May 1892, the nine-year-old boy was taken to Berlin where his father, using a subterfuge, gained admission to Joachim's studio. At first disgruntled, the old master became enchanted when he heard the boy and gave him a written testimonial:

I state with pleasure that the 9-year-old Hubermann from Warsaw possesses a truly remarkable musical talent. In all my

life I have hardly ever encountered such a promising, precocious musical development on the violin.

Berlin, June 24, 1892. Joseph Joachim

Nevertheless, he refused to teach him and referred him to an assistant,
Markees. The lessons were not to Huberman's liking, and he worked
secretly with Carl Grigorovich, a Russian-born violinist who had been
a student of Besekirsky and later Joachim. Grigorovich was a superb
violinist; Sarasate counted him among the six leading violinists of his
generation. Huberman remembered him fondly, saying that he learned
from Grigorovich "everything that could be learned from a teacher."
Otherwise, the pedantic academicism of Berlin proved too stifling, and
Huberman left after eight months. He took a few additional lessons
with Hugo Heermann in Frankfurt and with Marsick in Paris; these
concluded his formal studies.

He played successfully in the Netherlands (1893) and in London
(1894). Here he attracted the attention of the famous prima donna
Adelina Patti, who was about to embark on a farewell tour of the continent; she promised him a place on her program in Vienna. This memorable event took place on January 21, 1895. The twelve-year-old Huberman, as assisting artist, played the first movement of Mendelssohn's
concerto, with Hellmesberger, Jr., conducting the orchestra. The success was "thunderous, a hurricane." The boy had to play an encore,
Bach's Prelude in E for violin solo. Madame Patti was furious and
threatened to leave the hall if the boy were permitted to play any more!
The following day, one of Vienna's most respected critics wrote, "We
had come to say farewell to a setting star—and we had the joy to greet a
rising star."[2] A week later, young Huberman gave his own concert, followed by nine additional sold-out appearances. The success continued
the following season, when he opened a series of four concerts in
Vienna in January 1896. The program began with the Brahms concerto,
in the composer's presence. Brahms was prepared for a studentlike performance by the *"Knirps"* (little fellow). The biographer Max Kalbeck
described the scene:

> As soon as Brahms heard the sound of the violin, he pricked
> up his ears, during the Andante he wiped his eyes, and after
> the Finale he went into the green room, embraced the young
> fellow, and stroked his cheeks. When Huberman complained
> that the public applauded after the cadenza, breaking into the
> lovely Cantilena, Brahms replied, "You should not have
> played the cadenza so beautifully." . . . Brahms brought him

a photo of his, inscribed, "In friendly memory of Vienna and your grateful listener J. Brahms." [3]

Brahms is reported to have promised Huberman to compose a fantasy for him, adding in jest "if I have any fantasy left"; but he died the following year without realizing the project.

Critics as strict as Hanslick wrote, "In the face of such transcendent genius, criticism as such ceases." [4] The composer Carl Goldmark entered in Huberman's album, "Now I begin to believe in the wonders of the Bible."

In 1896, Huberman made his New York debut at Carnegie Hall. Reflecting the prejudice against child prodigies, the criticisms were mixed. One called him "the sadly over-advertised young violinist" and advised him to study for a year or two with a "fine master." His tone seems to have been small: "There is not, perhaps, the force of a full grown man in his touch or tone, but no lack is felt, for everything in his playing is homogeneous and in proportion." A headline in the *Times* proclaimed, "The boy violinist proves to be an artist of the first rank." [5]

By the choice of repertoire, we can see that young Huberman had technique to burn; he played the concertos of Mendelssohn, Beethoven, Brahms, and Wieniawski, Bach's Chaconne and Prelude in E major, and virtuoso pieces by Sarasate and Wieniawski. But he was at his best and most inspiring in slow introspective pieces like Schumann's *Träumerei* or Schubert's *Ave Maria*.

Following the American tour (1896–97), Huberman withdrew for four years. In 1902 he reappeared, playing with ever increasing success in Europe and America. After touring Italy, he was invited by the city of Genoa to play on Paganini's famous violin, the Guarnerius del Gesù. This special concert took place on May 16, 1903, at the Civic Palace; the last violinist to have played the instrument was Paganini's only student Sivori, who died in 1894. Ordinarily, the Paganini violin was kept in a glass showcase at the Municipal Museum in Genoa, and the fact that it was not used regularly affected its sound. The violin sounded husky and "dead" on the G- and D-strings, when Huberman first tried it; replacing the strings improved the G but not the D. The two upper strings sounded brilliant. The bridge of the violin was cut rather low and round, with the strings lying close to the fingerboard, inhibiting the vibration, and Huberman, who played with his own bow, took time to get used to it. Nevertheless, the enthusiasm of the invited audience was boundless.

In 1907 and again in 1911, Huberman appeared in Russia, where his interpretation of the Tchaikovsky concerto aroused much interest, though not undivided approval. His technique and tone were admired, but the occasional brusque attacks of the bow were noted. In 1926, when he reappeared in the Soviet Union, his success was enormous.

The First World War interrupted his career. When he resumed his travels, the public response was enthusiastic: fourteen consecutive concerts in Paris in 1920, ten in Vienna in 1924, eight in Berlin in 1926. The city of Vienna offered him the Palace of Hetzendorf (former residence of Emperor Karl) as a permanent domicile. He also taught intermittently at the Vienna State Academy until 1936. During the 1920s he became interested in a political movement called Pan-Europa, publishing articles and delivering lectures on this topic.

When the Nazis came to power in Germany in 1933, Huberman canceled all engagements there and wrote an open letter (dated July 10, 1933) to the conductor Furtwängler, explaining his position:

> The question of a more or less inspired interpretation of a violin concerto is only one of many aspects . . . which obscures the essential problem. . . . The issues are the most basic preconditions of our European culture: the freedom of the personality and its unconditional self-responsibility, liberated of all chains of caste and race.[6]

As the Nazi power expanded, he wrote another open protest, which appeared in *The Manchester Guardian* on March 7, 1936. Discouraged by the indifference of world opinion to the plight of the victims of Nazism, Huberman initiated a private rescue effort: he organized the Palestine Symphony Orchestra and invited persecuted musicians from central Europe to join. Staking his entire artistic prestige on the success of this project, he raised the funds, overcame political obstacles, auditioned the instrumentalists, and created the physical means for the functioning of the new ensemble. No detail escaped his attention. Ultimately he persuaded Arturo Toscanini, long known as foe of Fascism and Nazism, to conduct the inaugural concerts: on December 26, 1936, in Tel Aviv, on December 30 in Jerusalem, on December 31 in Haifa. The new orchestra also paid a visit to Cairo, and Toscanini, who had been a friend of Verdi, was particularly interested in seeing the opera theater where *Aïda* had received its world premiere. Huberman did not appear as soloist with the orchestra until 1938, keeping modestly in the background. Ultimately, his faith and vision were fully vindicated: today, the Israel Philharmonic Orchestra is considered one of the finest ensembles in the world.

Continuing his world travels, Huberman suffered a near-fatal accident on October 6, 1937, in a plane crash on Sumatra (Dutch East Indies). His hands and arms were injured; for a time the doctors thought that he would never play again. The recovery was slow, but he was able to retrain his hands, using the violin as an "orthopedic rather than a musical instrument" (as he wrote to George Szell). His first reappearance in a public concert took place, significantly, as soloist with "his" Palestine Orchestra in December 1938. After revisiting the Middle East in 1940, he spent the years of World War II in the United States. As soon as the war ended, Huberman resumed his concerts in Europe, but was unable to return to Palestine because of failing health. He died in Switzerland on June 15, 1947, less than a year before the State of Israel was established. His library was transferred to the Central Music Library in Tel Aviv, where a street is named after him.

Huberman made comparatively few recordings, and they convey an incomplete picture of his art. Most characteristic (if not most perfect) is his recording, with the Polish pianist Ignaz Friedman, of Beethoven's *Kreutzer Sonata*. The explosive character of this work is ideally suited to Huberman's temperament, and Friedman is a superb partner.

In many ways, Huberman's recordings are out of date and only serve to demonstrate the changing taste in musical interpretation. Most were made in the 1920s, some in the 1930s, but his style of playing was based on the aesthetics of an earlier time. The dated qualities of Huberman's records are not unique; one may have similar reactions to some early recordings of Kreisler or Thibaud, Ysaÿe or Elman. In all such cases one must listen selectively, with an "inner filter," disregarding old-fashioned mannerisms in order to penetrate to the musical core of these venerable artists. There is much to be learned from them.

Flesch's negative evaluation of Huberman has been challenged repeatedly. Hartnack, a German biographer of violinists and a warm admirer of Huberman, rejected Flesch's judgment as a "distortion without objective value." Having known both Flesch and Huberman, I can only guess that it was a clash of two contrasting personalities—Flesch, the most objective, versus Huberman, the most subjective violinist of their generation. There was no personal antipathy; on the contrary, they were on good terms throughout their lives. It was a musical and violinistic chasm that separated them.

Keller, in refuting Flesch's criticism of Huberman, makes an interesting observation: "Since Huberman's was a strongly developing personality, Flesch and I may at times be talking, as it were, about different artists." Flesch formed his opinion about Huberman at a rather early date (he first heard him in Bucharest around 1901 or 1902), while Keller, a much younger man, came to know Huberman as an artist more than a quarter of a century later. Huberman, a highly self-critical musician, worked incessantly on perfecting his performance ability and interpretative art. Certain characteristics of Huberman's playing, criticized by Flesch, were no longer in evidence when Keller heard him. For example, Flesch asserted that Huberman held the bow "in the old manner" (that is, Joachim-style); Keller denies it. Both observers may be right; Flesch himself changed his bow grip late in life, and the same must have been true of Huberman.* Flesch criticized Huberman's "pure finger vibrato," and again Keller contradicts. In his youth, Huberman may well have employed Joachim's finger vibrato and adjusted it later under the impact of the Ysaÿe-Kreisler "new" vibrato technique. I recall Huberman's vibrato as unobtrusive, at times imperceptible (when he produced "white" tones), and his sound chaste as compared to Kreisler's sensuousness. I also remember Huberman's German-style portamentos (in the manner of Joachim), rather than the more modern "French" slide of Kreisler. In fact, Keller's observation that Huberman's style seemed to have much in common with that of Joachim (judging by old recordings of Joachim still in existence) should not be surprising: as a boy, while studying in Berlin (in 1892), he must have heard and absorbed much of Joachim's playing, and as late as 1912, Huberman wrote a glowing testimonial to Joachim and his art.[7] It was the purity of Joachim's musical concept that fascinated Huberman, running counter to the more modern earthy and sensuous style of the younger generation.

Yet Huberman was basically a much more explosive personality than Joachim; in his interpretations he liked to juxtapose strong contrasts, from the most ethereal pianissimo to heavy, passionate, even rough accentuation. Flesch called it "extravagant"—he either "scraped" or "whispered." But even Flesch had to admit (and rightly so) the "extraordinary power of artistic conviction" that emanated from Huberman's playing when he was at his best, a "hypnotic suggestion" that enveloped the "receptive listener." Keller states unequivocally, "Huberman was one of the greatest musicians I have ever come across."[8] Serving this musicality was a brilliant technique, rivaling the greatest virtuosos of his time, but always as a means to a musical end.

* A photo taken in December 1938 shows Huberman's bow grip clearly as that of the modern Franco-Belgian method. See photograph.

GERMAN ANTIPODES
TO JOACHIM

FOR FOUR DECADES Joachim was installed in Berlin and exerted a powerful influence in all matters pertaining to the violin and to musical taste in general. His personal views were conservative. He himself was not narrowminded, but his adherents were. While he personally welcomed such virtuosos as Ole Bull, Wieniawski, Sarasate, and Ysaÿe, his followers and disciples snarled contemptuously at any manifestation of "shallow virtuosity."

Nevertheless, there were some German violinists who disagreed with the straightlaced views of the Joachim camp. A few succeeded in challenging the trend, and they made careers despite Joachim's animosity. Less purist than the entrenched Berlin school, they believed that Paganini's heritage deserved cultivation. Two of them, Wilhelmj and Burmester, were particularly successful, and each was acclaimed by credulous critics as "Paganini redivivus." Their success was short-lived, but had a certain impact on the staid German scene.

August Wilhelmj

Wilhelmj, born in 1845, was a student of Ferdinand David, who also coached the teenage Joachim. David, a worthy disciple of Spohr and friend of Mendelssohn, served as violin professor at the Leipzig Conservatory from its inception in 1843; for many years he was concertmaster of the Leipzig Gewandhaus Orchestra.*

* David is also remembered as the editor of old violin music, reviving an almost forgotten repertoire, though his treatment is considered too free for present-day standards.

Wilhelmj entered David's class in 1861 with a warm recommendation from Franz Liszt. He was already far advanced, having played publicly since the age of nine. At the conservatory, young Wilhelmj played Ernst's virtuosic Concerto in F sharp, and he made his debut at the Gewandhaus concerts with the monumental *Hungarian Concerto* by Joachim. His tours through Europe began in 1865, and he was particularly successful in England. In 1876, Richard Wagner invited him to be concertmaster in Bayreuth for the production of the *Ring des Nibelungen*, where he led the select orchestra. The following year, Wilhelmj induced Wagner to conduct some concerts at the Albert Hall in London, with Wilhelmj leading the violins. In 1878 Wilhelmj embarked on a four-year tour around the world, including, of course, America. After his return to Germany, he founded a Master Academy for Violin Study, but it did not succeed; obviously he could not overcome Joachim's hegemony. In 1894 he decided to settle in London, where he was appointed violin professor at the Guildhall School of Music. There he died, highly respected, in 1908.

Wilhelmj was famous for his powerful tone and his strong left-hand technique, particularly in double stops. His violin sounded like a cello when he played his famous arrangement of Bach's Air on the G String. Moser, always protective of Joachim, attributed Wilhelmj's tonal strength to his habit of changing the bow very often, regardless of phrasing (a procedure strictly unacceptable to Joachim). Joachim himself was disappointed when he heard Wilhelmj's Berlin debut in 1872; he found a "pomade-like sensuous revelry in beautiful violin sound . . . but much inner emptiness."[1] This unkind judgment is not surprising, for Wilhelmj was the antithesis of the purist Joachim. Interested in exploring the technical and sonorous potentials of the violin, Wilhelmj made a special study of Paganini's posthumous works, which he edited and published in practical editions. For a time, his edition of Paganini's Concerto No. 1 in D major was widely used—actually a truncated version consisting of the first movement (Allegro) only, which he provided with a new pseudo-heroic orchestral introduction and enriched orchestration. Known as the Paganini-Wilhelmj Concerto, it effectively displaced the original three-movement version, which was revived in the 1930s. He also perpetuated the separate performance of Paganini's *La campanella* (originally the finale of Concerto No. 2), which he published in a special edition.

Being an ardent Wagnerian, Wilhelmj arranged selections from Wagner's operas for violin and piano, for example Walther's Prize Song from *Die Meistersinger*, and concert paraphrases on *Siegfried* and *Parsi-*

fal, as well as an arrangement of the song *Träume* for violin and small orchestra.

Joachim abhorred Wilhelmj's transcription of Bach's Air on the G String. No less objectionable is his treatment of Schubert's *Ave Maria,* first on the G string, then in luscious double stops. Wilhelmj was a clever but ruthless arranger; he did not hesitate to transpose compositions to other keys in order to increase the resonance of the violin. Thus we have two nocturnes by Chopin (in E flat and D flat) appear in D major in Wilhelmj's version. He went so far as to transpose the middle part of Schubert's Violin Fantasy Op. 159 from A-flat major to A major to make it sound more brilliant; this bowdlerized version actually appeared in print. Such arbitrary liberties were condoned in virtuoso circles of the nineteenth century; nevertheless, Wilhelmj a century later remains an imposing violin personality.

Willy Burmester

Willy Burmester, born in 1869, was a student of Joachim who struggled to escape the shadow of the master. A child prodigy in his native city of Hamburg, young Willy was brought to the attention of Joachim, who promised his admission to the Berlin Hochschule. The boy entered in 1881, at the age of twelve, but was far too young for the advanced courses offered there. After four years of study, his report card read, "Burmester is unsatisfactory in all subjects except the violin." Such a verdict—so Burmester reminisced with bitterness—was more like a "warrant of arrest for an escaped music criminal" than a letter of recommendation for a young artist in search of a career. Apparently, Joachim had not developed any friendly feelings for Willy; perhaps he was disappointed by his obsession with technique. Joachim did little to help young Burmester in his struggle for recognition.

Two eminent musicians influenced Burmester's artistic growth—Tchaikovsky and Hans von Bülow. Burmester played Tchaikovsky's Violin Concerto for the composer when he visited Hamburg as guest conductor in 1887. The work was comparatively new and Tchaikovsky was very pleased with Burmester's performance; in fact, they became good friends. On the strength of Tchaikovsky's recommendation, Burmester was invited to appear in Pavlovsk, the famous summer resort near St. Petersburg. The success was such that he was reengaged for the summer of 1888, and again in 1892.

In the meantime, Bülow was engaged to conduct a series of concerts in Hamburg. Among the local members of the orchestra was Burmester; he sat in the first violin section, though not in a leading position. Despite the busy season, Bülow found time to coach Burmester in the sonata repertoire, certainly a sign of musical esteem.

An important step forward was a two-year stay in Helsingfors as concertmaster of the Philharmonic Orchestra (1892–94). Determined to present himself in Berlin with an unusual program, he hit on the idea of an all-Paganini concert. In preparation, he practiced up to fifteen hours a day during the five summer months preceding this debut. He admits with a certain pride that he repeated a certain caprice by Paganini 4276 times during those months until he could play the runs in thirds as fast as any other violinist played single-note scales. By that time, his musical mind must have been paralyzed! But he was determined—*aut Caesar, aut nihil!*

The Burmester debut in Berlin, late in October 1894, stands as an historic landmark: it was termed "a violinistic sensation" even by Moser, who had no liking for the artist. The Paganini program consisted of the Concerto No. 1, the variations on *Nel cor più*, and *Witches' Dance*, as well as several caprices (Nos. 17, 18, 13). The critics hailed him as "Paganini redivivus" and as the greatest violin technician alive, not excepting Sarasate. It was pointed out that, in addition to a fabulous technique, Burmester also possessed a large and firm tone.

A second concert, sold out after the sensation created by the first, brought the Tchaikovsky concerto, Spohr's Concerto No. 7, and the *Faust Fantasy* by Wieniawski. As soloist in the Philharmonic Concerts under Nikisch, he chose to play the Concerto Op. 206 by Joachim Raff, a difficult but unimportant work. At any rate, Burmester proved that he was not "only" a Paganini specialist but could hold his own in a general repertoire (though he wisely avoided the Beethoven concerto, considered Joachim's domain).

For the next decades, Burmester was—particularly in Germany—a magic name: sold-out houses everywhere. He was successful in London, too, but not in Paris, where the public of the Colonne Concerts lost patience with the Spohr concerto: he could not finish the Finale because of catcalls.

Burmester had another specialty besides Paganini—small violin pieces in his own arrangements, "classic miniatures" which delighted the audiences and were extremely popular with amateur players, too. The *Burmester-Stücke* became an indispensable musical staple, even more so than the Kreisler pieces, because they were simpler to play. Long after Burmester's acrobatic technique declined, he still entertained the public with his musical confections. After World War I he tried to resume his career, but his days were past. He died in near poverty in 1933.

Flesch had nothing good to say about him; he found his prolonged success inexplicable, his style unmusical, and a "harmful influence in every respect." In his autobiography *Fifty Years of an Artist's Life,* Burmester reveals himself as vain and arrogant, but clever and at times witty.

BERLIN
AFTER THE DEATH
OF JOACHIM

WHEN JOACHIM DIED in August 1907, Berlin's musical scene lost its major figure. He had lived there since 1868, becoming a kind of musical conscience for the burgeoning city. In the second half of the nineteenth century, Berlin had grown from a somewhat provincial royal residence with few cultural traditions to the self-confident capital of the new German Empire, and Joachim was one of the architects of a cultural growth that kept pace with rising political importance.

At the center of Berlin's musical life was the Philharmonic Orchestra, which, under Hans von Bülow's brief but creative tenure, had acquired a national reputation. Arthur Nikisch took over as chief conductor in 1895 and led it until 1922. Soon the Nikisch concerts became the most prestigious in Europe, and they could make or break the career of a soloist. Even the most experienced virtuosi trembled before their debut under Nikisch, and the appearance at the Sunday noon public "dress rehearsal" and the Monday night concert was an ordeal challenging the steadiest nerves.*

After Joachim retired as soloist, he exerted his musical influence mainly through the subscription concerts of his string quartet. Here he gathered a large and adoring public of true connoisseurs. In performing the great classics, particularly Beethoven's late quartets, Joachim was unsurpassed, despite the fact that his coplayers were not of the first rank. As primarius he lent the performances an aura of near-prophecy.

Equally important was Joachim's position as director of the Hochschule für Musik and principal violin professor. Since the founding of

* The Philharmonic Hall was a converted roller coaster rink with fabulous acoustics and uncomfortable wooden chairs; it was destroyed during World War II.

the school in 1869 he occupied both posts and retained them until his death. Academically, the Hochschule (a state-supported institution) enjoyed high prestige, though there was criticism of its staunch conservatism in all branches.

The violin department in particular was patterned in Joachim's image. He himself admitted that he was not a good teacher. The violin faculty—Wirth, Halir, Markees, Moser, Klingler, later Hess—were carbon copies of the master without having his genius; no other approach was tolerated. A few of them (Wirth, Halir, also briefly Klingler) were members of the Joachim Quartet. After Joachim's death, Karl Klingler formed his own string quartet and retained some of the devoted following of the master.

Among the violin teachers, Andreas Moser was closest to Joachim. The two collaborated closely on the Joachim-Moser *Violin Method*, as well as on classical editions of the Bach solo sonatas and the Beethoven string quartets. Much of the paperwork was done by the diligent Moser, who no longer played because of a hand ailment and turned increasingly to writing and editing. He sat at Joachim's elbow, urging him to commit his interpretative ideas to paper.* We owe Moser a basic biography of Joachim and an equally basic *Geschichte des Violinspiels*, both enlivened by personal anecdotes; he was also the overly protective editor of the Joachim correspondence.

As soon as Joachim died, there was speculation about his successor as chief violin professor. The logical choice would have been Carl Flesch, who enjoyed a growing reputation in Berlin as performer and teacher, but he did not belong to the Joachim circle and was often critical of the old master. An outsider was considered unthinkable. Yet to everyone's surprise the appointment went to Henri Marteau, a violinist of the French school, who had never studied with Joachim. In his *Memoirs*, Flesch states outright, "Moser had decided to make Marteau, then at the height of his career, the successor of Joachim."[1] But Moser denied having played any sinister role in that choice. He described how Joachim met Marteau in 1906 and took a great liking to his young French colleague (who, incidentally, was half German). Marteau had endeared himself to both Joachim and Moser by volunteering to translate the *Violin Method* into French. At that time, Joachim considered the idea of having Marteau join the violin staff of the Hochschule to infuse some new blood, but there was no suitable vacancy. Moser makes it appear that Marteau's appointment in 1908 was made in fulfillment of the late

* See Joachim's introductory essays in Vol. 3 of the Joachim-Moser *Violinschule*.

master's wish. Be this as it may, Marteau received a ten-year contract, which was abrogated by the outbreak of the First World War in 1914. Eventually, the post went to Adolf Busch in 1918.

Henri Marteau

Joachim's confidence in Marteau was not misplaced. At the height of his career, he was considered by Flesch and others as "one of the finest violinists of his time . . . an exemplary interpreter of Mozart."[1] However, he could also perform such a tricky piece as Sarasate's *Carmen Fantasy* with perfect technique and engaging charm. He used an exceptional violin—the Maggini of his late teacher Léonard*—and produced a tone of "purity, fullness, timbre and modulation," though his vibrato was "somewhat slow and slack." Marteau's style was a judicious mixture of French and German elements, but his schooling was entirely French— he was a first-prize winner at the Paris Conservatoire in 1892.

Marteau used his exceptional technique in the service of great music. He was opposed to the general trend toward virtuosity, at a time when the term "Paganini redivivus" was attached to various virtuosos, and was in complete agreement with the anti-virtuoso theories of Joachim and Moser, as expressed in their *Violinschule*.

Marteau was born in 1874 in Rheims of a French father and a German mother. This explains his lifelong ambivalence in terms of national allegiance; his career was in fact destroyed by the epic struggle between France and Germany during the First World War. At the outbreak of the war, in 1914, he was well established in his position at the Berlin Hochschule, and he chose to remain in Germany as an enemy alien. Unfortunately, he became embroiled in a messy espionage case and was arrested. Eventually he moved to neutral Sweden and became a Swedish citizen in 1920. Having declined as a performer, he concentrated on teaching and was active in Prague, Leipzig, and Dresden during the 1920s, though without notable success. His disloyalty to France was neither forgotten nor forgiven, and he died in 1934 in Germany, his old reputation a mere shadow.

Marteau's musical mind was inquisitive: he was equally interested in the past and the present. He contributed notably to the revival of the Mozart concertos, particularly No. 3 in G major, which he brought to

* The violins of Maggini of Brescia predate those of Stradivari by a century. His large-model violins have a dark-hued, rich tone approaching the viola timbre. Maggini violins are extremely rare.

Joachim's attention.* (There are exemplary Marteau editions, with cadenzas, of Mozart violin concertos.) In the 1900s he became interested in a revival of the music of the all-but-forgotten Swedish composer Franz Berwald (1796–1868); he founded the Berwald Society in Stockholm in 1909 and revived the Berwald Violin Concerto (composed 1820)† at an orchestral concert in Berlin on October 5, 1909; he played the work repeatedly in Germany, Sweden, and Russia.

At the same time, Marteau befriended various contemporary composers. Among them was the eminent Max Reger, who dedicated several violin works to him, including the monumental Violin Concerto Op. 101, which Marteau premiered at the Leipzig Gewandhaus in October 1908. It was a labor of love; the work never entered the active repertoire because of its complexity and length. Flesch (who played some of Reger's music, but not the concerto) suggested a few cuts, but the composer declined: "The work is, and will remain, a monster." Nevertheless, Reger believed that he had created a violin concerto worthy to join those of Beethoven and Brahms.

In 1908, at the time of his appointment to the Berlin Hochschule, Marteau was at the peak of his career. Whether his premature decline as a performer is due, as Flesch surmises, to his effort to "Germanize" his violin style is a moot question. "Marteau was thrown out of his natural course, disoriented; he had aided and abetted a falsification of his own personality," according to Flesch, who observed him at close range.[2] Instead of bringing new blood to the German school, as Joachim had hoped, Marteau succumbed to the Berlin environment. His is the tragedy of an uprooted artist, buffeted by divided loyalties and unable to establish a balance.

Adolf Busch

Joseph Szigeti recalls a story he heard in Cologne around 1909: There was "a young man of extraordinary musical and violinistic attainments who had amazed a recent visitor, the composer Max Reger, by playing to him from memory the then much-discussed Reger Violin Concerto. . . . He was Adolf Busch."[1]

At that time, Busch was barely eighteen, just completing his studies

---

* Joachim played only the Violin Concertos Nos. 4 and 5 by Mozart (K. 218 and 219).
† Berwald's Violin Concerto was republished in 1974 (Bärenreiter-Verlag) as part of a Complete Works edition.

at the Cologne Conservatory under Willy Hess and Bram Eldering. Hess was an old Joachim disciple, but Eldering had a more modern background in violinistic matters, particularly through his work under Hubay. Having completed his violin studies, Busch continued studying composition in Bonn with Hugo Grüters.* In 1912 he moved to Vienna to become concertmaster of the Konzertverein Orchestra, but found time to make extensive concert tours. His debut in London in the spring of 1912 was very well received; and one critic remarked that "no one short of Kreisler could approach Busch for purity of style and intense beauty of phrasing,"[2] though he lacked the polish of some of the great violinists then before the public. Considering the abundance of violinistic competition at that time, this was high praise indeed.

In 1918, Busch, barely twenty-seven, was appointed violin professor at the Berlin Hochschule, replacing Marteau and succeeding to the chair once held by Joachim. For the second time, Flesch was passed over as the logical candidate for this important post. But Busch seemed the ideal answer to the Germans' prayers: a true German, a musician in the classical mold of Joachim dedicated to German music from Bach to Reger. As soon as he was settled in Berlin, Busch founded his own string quartet, which soon established its preeminence in the classical repertoire. In fact, Flesch wrote that he preferred Busch as quartet player "since in that role he can give himself over to his sentiment unencumbered by technical worries,"[3] while his solo performances were often marred by a lack of self-control. True, Busch had no ambitions as a virtuoso (a word that, among Germans, has a pejorative meaning): he was the servant of great music, a dedicated, pure musician—serious, honest, with warmth and inner intensity, persuasive in his sincerity, though one could disagree with his solid and at times rigid approach. His musical vision guided his hands and enabled him to conquer the mechanical problems; his technique was adequate for the task but neither excessive nor flawless. Nevertheless, his debut in 1931 with the New York Philharmonic under Toscanini (playing the Beethoven Violin Concerto) was very impressive and led to a lasting friendship between the two musicians.

As early as 1926 Busch left his post in Berlin and settled in Switzerland. When the Nazis came to power in 1933, Hitler spared no effort to lure "the greatest German violinist" back into his homeland. Not only did Adolf Busch refuse, but his brother, the conductor Fritz Busch, left

* Busch married Grüters's daughter; one of their children, Irene, became the wife of the pianist Rudolf Serkin. Peter Serkin is their son.

his post in Dresden and emigrated of his own free will. In 1934, replying to a letter from a German publisher signed "Heil Hitler," Adolf Busch wrote, "We live in Switzerland, which means that we consider your greeting an insult."[4] The letter was cosigned by the pianist Rudolf Serkin, his young partner who was to become his son-in-law.

Busch settled in the United States in 1940 and dedicated his activity primarily to chamber music. In particular, the Busch Chamber Players—actually a Baroque chamber orchestra—acquired a wide reputation and recorded, among others, the concerti grossi of Handel and Bach. Busch made no fetish of "authentic instruments" and did not hesitate, for example, to have the solo harpsichord part in Bach's Brandenburg Concerto No. 5 executed on the modern piano by Rudolf Serkin; the result was a thrilling performance full of natural exuberance. Since Busch's death in 1952, his spirit of musical dedication lives on at the Marlboro Music Center in Vermont, which Serkin has been guiding for the past three decades.

Busch was not a teacher in the accepted sense of the word; one could take him as a model, but he himself could not develop a tender talent. We owe much perceptive information about him to Yehudi Menuhin, who worked under Busch's guidance for two summers. At the time, in 1929, Menuhin was thirteen but already a world-renowned violinist; he had studied with Persinger and Enesco, and his stay with Busch was meant as a kind of initiation into the mysteries of German classicism. Menuhin pays tribute to Busch, who "contributed enormously toward my musical knowledge and growth, towards an achievement of a pure classical style. . . . [He] developed in me a sense of discipline, precision, and authority, particularly in the playing of Bach. . . . Busch was unbending in following the letter of the composer's intent . . . one can give a satisfying performance of a classical composition only within a strict rhythmic framework."[5] In this connection, Busch insisted on the use of a metronome during practice, something that did not sit too well with Menuhin's free-wheeling imagination. Busch had certain preconceived notions, for example, that all fugal themes in Bach must be presented *forte*. This rigid concept, shared by some Baroque experts, ran counter to what Enesco had taught—namely, that some themes, especially in the minor mode, are "evocative, not affirmative." Busch's printed edition of the sonatas and partitas for violin solo by Bach is virtually an *Urtext* edition—not a single bowing changed, with a minimum of added indications.

In his teaching, Busch "tended to emphasize and supervise the execution of the minutest detail . . . [his] unbending insistence on the letter, rather than the spirit, marks him as a musician in the very German tradition," in Menuhin's opinion. "Busch's vision of the bond between teacher and pupil was almost religious; like a disciple with his guru, or a medieval apprentice with his master, a student should live with his teacher, making music morning, noon and night, sharing his life and thought as he shared his roof and his dinner." Menuhin tells us that "Busch's teaching was . . . musical rather than violinistic. If he didn't have Enesco's flair or glamour, as a musician he was extremely serious and deep, a passionate fundamentalist who ate, breathed, and slept Bach and Beethoven." He played "the violin cleanly and beautifully, if with no Russian or Gypsy touch. . . ."[6]

All these qualities can be observed in a recently reissued set of recordings played by Busch with Serkin and with his Chamber Players,* performances of extraordinary musicianship and depth, but also of technical adroitness and tonal beauty. They display an art which is probably as close to the great Joachim as anything in our time, perhaps an art lost forever.

Georg Kulenkampff

Of all the German violinists I have known, Georg Kulenkampff (1898–1948) was the most un-German. He was head and shoulders above the mediocrities peopling the Berlin Hochschule. Even measured by his older contemporary Adolf Busch—the ideal of a German violinist—Kulenkampff was very different: his tone was sensuous, his technique brilliant, and his affinity with French and Slavic music remarkable. Such works as the Debussy sonata, the concertos by Tchaikovsky and Szymanowski (all works outside of Busch's repertoire) received memorable performances by Kulenkampff. Circumstances prevented him from becoming well known outside of Germany, and after World War II, his illness and early death cut short his career.

Kulenkampff was born and raised in the old Hanseatic city of Bremen, whose citizens have the reputation of being aloof, reserved, and clannish. Some of that reserve was noticeable in Kulenkampff, but it melted away as soon as he began to play. His principal violin teacher was Willy Hess, with whom he studied from 1912 to 1915 at the Berlin Hochschule. Professor Hess had been a pupil of Joachim; before being appointed to the faculty of the Hochschule in 1910,† he had served as

* Columbia/Odyssey Y3 34639.
† Hess retired in 1928 and Flesch succeeded him at the Hochschule.

concertmaster of the Boston Symphony from 1904 to 1910. Flesch described him as "a passionate and inexhaustible teacher with solid, if obsolete, principles and a profound musicality."[1]

In keeping with the German tradition, Kulenkampff began his career as a concertmaster and served with the Bremen Philharmonic from 1916 to 1919. His solo career moved slowly until 1923, when he obtained a resounding success at the Cassel Music Festival, playing a modern concerto by Emil Bohnke. He executed the complex solo part with unsurpassable ease, and earned the admiration of the critics with his "virile, audacious and yet sensuous performance." The same could be said about his performance of Szymanowski's Concerto No. 1, which I heard in the mid-twenties: there was a suave elegance and vibrant tension in his interpretation that belied his north-German origin. Soon, Kulenkampff was recognized as the leading German violinist, especially after Busch had left Germany and denounced the Nazi regime. However, it must be said that Kulenkampff kept his distance from the Nazis, despite the fact that he remained in Germany until 1943.* That year, he moved to Switzerland and became Flesch's successor as professor at the Lucerne Conservatory in 1944. His last years were a period of introversion; he gave up virtuoso travels and concentrated on chamber music, particularly with the pianist Edwin Fischer. He also formed his own string quartet and was a thoughtful teacher.

Kulenkampff's ideas on music and teaching were collected and published posthumously in 1952 under the title *Geigerische Betrachtungen* (Violinistic Reflections). He speaks out against the "motoric, factual interpretative style of our time." While he played much modern music, he knew how to imbue it with warmth and conviction.

A high point of his career was the world premiere of the rediscovered concerto by Robert Schumann on November 26, 1937, with the Berlin Philharmonic. The chauvinistic Nazi government did not permit the premiere to be played outside of Germany, and so Kulenkampff was officially chosen to do the honors.

Carl Flesch

As a student of Carl Flesch for a number of years, I have many recollections of him as both man and musician. Though I had other eminent teachers (like Thibaud and Capet), it was Flesch who was the decisive influence and who shaped my concept of violin playing. As a

* Kulenkampff taught at the Berlin Hochschule from 1923 to 1926 and after 1931.

The great German violinist Adolf Busch
with his piano partner, Rudolf Serkin, who
later became his son-in-law

Carl Flesch, the eminent violinist, pedagogue, and theorist who influenced an
entire generation of violinists

Three prominent former students of Martin
Marsick—Carl Flesch, Jacques Thibaud,
and Georges Enesco—playing at a memorial
concert for their late teacher

teenage student, I was overwhelmed by his personality and barely dared to open my mouth. Later, in 1929 at Baden-Baden, I was able to meet him on more equal terms, and began to appreciate his human qualities of humor and charm behind the somewhat stern facade.

Flesch was a complex individual. He himself recognized a conflict between emotion and intellect in his nature, which inhibited the spontaneous unfolding of his artistic personality. In appearance he resembled more an academician or a bank executive than an artist. His manner was controlled and cultured without any temperamental mannerisms. As a performer, he was a consummate master, but somewhat lacking in spontaneity. As a teacher, his approach was decidedly analytical, not inspirational. It was teaching on the highest, most mature level. He appealed to the student's intellect; he taught the fundamental concepts of technique and interpretation, showing how to deal rationally with problems as they arose. "Use your head for your technique and your heart for your music," was one of Flesch's principles. He taught how to make the best of one's talent and how to minimize one's limitations, speaking from experience as one who had struggled along the road of self-analysis and self-improvement himself.

As a violinist, Flesch grew slowly. At a time when his contemporaries Kreisler and Thibaud were conquering the world, Flesch was still polishing his style, improving his technique, and searching for the best means to express his musical thoughts. His hands were poorly equipped for the violin—fleshy and flabby, with broad fingertips, and a little finger that was too weak and too short to be of much use; it forced him to employ fingerings favoring the three strong fingers. He worked all his life to minimize his innate weaknesses, while developing certain natural skills which lay well in his hands. Thus he played fingered octaves with legendary speed (once Ysaÿe visited him for the express purpose of hearing him play Paganini's Caprice No. 17, which employs rapid octaves), and his octave runs in his own cadenzas made the experts gasp. He had developed this skill in his student days in Paris, using the fingered octaves as a device to warm up his hands in an unheated room. While his bowing may have lacked elegance, it was wonderfully steady and controlled, the envy of artists like Ysaÿe, who suffered all his life from a "trembling" bow arm. Another specialty was his harmonics; the German word for harmonic is *flageolett*, which punsters transformed to "Flescholetts."

Everything Flesch did as a musician was governed by intellect. His technique was planned with such care that only a total nervous collapse could produce a mishap on stage. Nor was his interpretation left to momentary inspiration; he did not "let go" of himself easily. The impression was one of magisterial command.

Flesch belongs to the "Berlin circle": he lived and worked there for over twenty years, beginning in 1908, and his fame spread from there. He himself remarked on the paradox that he—a Hungarian of Jewish parentage, a violinist schooled in Vienna and Paris—should have become the epitome of German violin playing (somewhat similar to Joachim). Those who knew and admired Flesch must concede that neither Hungary nor Vienna nor Paris left a distinctive mark on his style. His dominant quality seemed German, marked by a classical approach to music based on scholarly study, purity of style devoid of showmanship, a sturdy sense of rhythm tending toward slow tempos, and a deliberate objectivity of interpretation. Flesch also had a preference for the German repertoire from Bach to Brahms, though he liked to teach French and Slavic music, for he was thoroughly familiar with the requirements of those styles. In fact, I heard him play Dvořák, Saint-Saëns, and Glazunov with polished perfection, but without the ultimate affinity. Though I also heard him play the Paganini Concerto in D major with astounding virtuosity, he was not a virtuoso by temperament, and his true kinship was to Bach, Beethoven, and Brahms.

In his *Memoirs*, Flesch told his life story so well that one need only summarize. He was born in 1873 in Moson, in a region of Hungary which has produced such prominent musicians as Liszt, Nikisch, and Joachim. At the age of six, Flesch started the violin with a local, rather incompetent teacher. By the time he was ten he was taken to Vienna, where he eventually joined the conservatory class of Jakob Grün, a dedicated but oldfashioned teacher. Searching for a more modern approach to violin playing, the seventeen-year-old Flesch decided to continue his studies in Paris, following the example of his fellow student Kreisler. Admission of foreign students was strictly limited at the Paris Conservatoire, and Flesch considered himself lucky to be accepted by Professor Sauzay. Eighty-one and obviously past his prime, Sauzay struck Flesch as antediluvial in his method. In fact, the four violin professors at the Conservatoire were patriarchs with a combined age of some three hundred years, as Flesch soon discovered. Fortunately, he found another teacher in Martin Marsick, then in his forties: "it was he who taught me to think logically without endangering the spirit of the living work of art," Flesch recalled in gratitude.[1] In 1892, Sauzay finally retired and

Marsick took his place on the Conservatoire faculty. Flesch happily joined his class and improved enormously. In 1893 he received a second prize (he was outplayed by Lucien Capet), and graduated the following year with the first prize. In retrospect, Flesch was quite critical of the "fusty" Conservatoire, its "mummified" violin repertoire, and its limited curriculum.

During his Conservatoire years, Flesch acquired orchestral experience by playing in the Lamoureux orchestra, whose conductor was a champion of Wagner's music. In order to enforce attention, Lamoureux made his string players sit on stools without backs to prevent them from leaning back and relaxing. Nevertheless, Flesch found the orchestral discipline very useful and recommended an orchestral apprenticeship to each of his students, even the most gifted. Experience in chamber music playing was another skill that Flesch acquired in Paris and urged upon all his students.

Despite successful debut recitals in Vienna and Berlin with a demanding program (including the Bach Chaconne and the Paganini D-major Concerto), Flesch's career did not move forward. After spending the year 1896 in Berlin (which brought "much honor but little cash"), Flesch decided to accept a post in Bucharest. His varied duties included regular performances at the court concerts of the Rumanian queen (a German princess by birth, who wrote poetry under the pen name "Carmen Sylva"); he was also leader of a string quartet and professor at the conservatory. Despite the somewhat provincial atmosphere, Flesch made great strides in his artistic development. Among famous violinists who visited Bucharest at that time were Kubelik, Marteau, Huberman, and the Rumanian-born Enesco.

After five years in the Rumanian capital, however, Flesch felt the need to rejoin the musical mainstream of Central Europe. He accepted a professorship at the conservatory of Amsterdam, where he remained from 1903 to 1908, combining teaching and concertizing. It was a time when Amsterdam, a city of traditional music lovers, developed into a musical center of prime importance. Responsible for this growth was the Concertgebouw Orchestra under Willem Mengelberg, which became one of the best ensembles of Europe. Flesch's presence in Amsterdam contributed to its musical development.

At that time, Flesch, who had mastered a large repertoire, conceived the idea of five violin recitals as a historical cycle, showing the development of the violin as a solo instrument from Corelli to the contemporary Max Reger. Altogether fifty composers were listed on the five programs. Flesch presented his monumental cycle in 1905 in Berlin, the most critical of all musical capitals; he noted with pride that Joachim attended one of the concerts and congratulated him afterwards. The success was such that Flesch decided to settle in Berlin in 1908, this time as a freelance artist and private violin teacher. Secretly he may have hoped to succeed Joachim at the Hochschule, but that position, through various manipulations already described, went to Marteau. Flesch had to wait until 1921 to be offered a "special course" at the Hochschule, though it was not part of the regular curriculum.

In the meantime, Flesch built his reputation as a soloist and chamber-music player. He formed a violin–piano duo with Artur Schnabel and a trio with the cellist Gérardy.* Flesch never wanted to form a string quartet, though urged to do so, because he felt that quartet playing was a full-time profession and not compatible with solo work. His musical versatility was much admired: he could play the Beethoven and Paganini concertos with equal proficiency, and proved that the terms *musician* and *virtuoso* were not mutually exclusive. Flesch had contempt for the violinists emerging from the Berlin Hochschule—a "rare collection of violinistic cripples" who "scratched and scraped and thrashed on the violin," much inferior to the graduates of the Paris Conservatoire.[2]

Early in 1913, Flesch made his first appearance in New York. He was not a sensational success, but slowly acquired a reputation as a sterling musician. The First World War, which he spent in Berlin as a Hungarian citizen, interrupted his international career. Having lost most of his modest fortune in the German inflation, Flesch embarked again on an American tour, arriving in New York in December 1923. By that time he was famous, not only as a solid performer, but also as an outstanding teacher. He had written the first volume of his monumental *Kunst des Violinspiels* which was soon to be translated into English.

Through a lucky coincidence, Flesch was in America when a new conservatory was established in Philadelphia, the Curtis Institute of Music. Endowed by Mrs. Louise Curtis Bok, the school had a huge budget and charged no tuition; in fact, needy students received weekly stipends. A faculty of world-renowned artists was assembled, at fabulous salaries. Flesch was appointed head of the violin classes and received $25,000 for three-and-a-half months of work, an unheard-of fee for a teacher. He held this position for four years, until 1928, when he decided to return permanently to Europe.†

* Gérardy was later replaced by Hugo Becker and eventually by Gregor Piatigorsky; in 1921, Schnabel's place was taken over by Carl Friedberg.
† His successor was Leopold Auer, who died in 1930; after that, Efrem Zimbalist took over, eventually becoming director.

After his return from America, Flesch divided his time between Berlin, where he taught during the winter months at the Hochschule, beginning in 1928, and Baden-Baden, where he gave private summer courses at his lovely villa. Each summer saw a growing number of students assembling in Baden-Baden, many of them already concertizing artists, others at the beginning of a promising career. I myself spent the summer of 1929 with Flesch in Baden-Baden and remember such present and future celebrities as Kulenkampff, Odnoposoff, Szeryng, Alma Moodie, Ginette Neveu, and many more, some to take lessons, others just to visit the old master. All lessons were given publicly, with all students and auditors in attendance. The compositions to be played were announced in advance, so that one could bring the music. Playing at those master classes and being "analyzed" by the professor was a rather agonizing experience. But it must be said that Flesch's criticism was always expressed in a very civilized way, politely though searchingly, and always on a level from which not only the student playing but everyone present would profit and learn. Sundays included group excursions and friendly gatherings, when Flesch "unbuttoned" and entertained us with a stream of anecdotes.

The rise of Nazism forced Flesch to leave Germany. In 1934 he settled in London and continued his activity as teacher and performer. The outbreak of World War II found him in Holland, at that time still neutral, and he decided to stay. For a while he was in danger of being arrested by the invading Germans, but he succeeded in having his Hungarian citizenship restored and was permitted to return to Hungary. An offer to teach at the newly established Conservatoire in Lucerne came just at the right time, and Flesch settled happily in hospitable Switzerland in 1943. He was delighted by the new surroundings and began to work with great success. But his health had been shattered by the trying experiences of the last few years, and on November 15, 1944, he succumbed to a heart attack.

Flesch was a teacher by choice and conviction, though he continued to perform publicly to much acclaim until late in life. "Teaching is the noblest of artistic activities," is a statement to be found in his *Memoirs*. There was, in his nature, a conflict between calculation and impulse, and he admitted,

> As a performer, I never succeeded in welding these opposite talents into a unity. It was only in the teaching activities of my later years that I found my vocation completely fulfilled,

for there I was able simultaneously to enlist my intellect and my emotions.[3]

How many students did Flesch have during a lifetime of teaching? No one kept track of either the number or the names. But since he instituted the concept of "master class" in the 1920s, their number grew by leaps and bounds. Even those who were only auditors in these courses felt the impact of his teaching. Yehudi Menuhin—*not* one of his students—wrote in his preface to Flesch's posthumous volume *Violin Fingering*, "The massive living evidence of his great teaching represented by his numerous family of violinists and teachers spread throughout the world—perhaps the most important body of executant-pedagogues in existence."

But Flesch reached an even wider circle of violinists through his published works: the *Urstudien* (Basic Studies), the two-volume *Art of Violin Playing*, the *Problems of Tone Production*, the *Scale System*, and the vast repertoire of violin music he edited. They address themselves primarily to the thinking musician who strives to understand the finer points of violin playing and interpretation without relying on intuition or blind imitation. "Study should be governed by intellect, performance by emotion," was one of Flesch's sayings. He taught his students the art of self-analysis and self-help: To diagnose a problem is already part of its solution. A student acquired a life's worth of prescriptions to overcome violinistic failures; he learned how to choose a fingering that was rational, dependable, and artistic, how to deal with intricate passages, how to diagnose his own weaknesses.

When Flesch began his career as a teacher around 1900, violin teaching lagged behind the art of performance. At the conservatories, the violin was taught according to outdated principles, while the great performers of the day—Sarasate, Ysaÿe, and Kreisler—freely discarded many time-worn conventions. Flesch's own development as a violinist had been hampered by poor teaching at the prestigious conservatories of Vienna and Paris, and he had to learn mostly through trial and error, by observation and self-analysis. When he published his monumental *Art of Violin Playing* in the 1920s, he offered the sum-total of his twenty-five-year experience as teacher and performer. It is an exhaustive presentation of all branches of violinistic knowledge—"violin playing as a craft, as a science, and as an art," in the author's words. Kreisler called it "the most significant work in this field" and recommended it to every violinist. Sevčik, himself a great teacher, wrote, "With your work you have provided violinists with a bible to which teachers and players will continue to refer as long as there is violin playing in the world."[4]

No doubt Flesch's work is as significant for our time as Leopold Mozart's *Violinschule* was for the eighteenth century or Baillot's *Art du Violon* for the nineteenth. Yet the comparison must be used with caution, for Flesch's *Art* is not a conventional violin method for beginners: it is a treatise embracing all aspects of violin technique (in Volume I) and interpretation (in Volume II). It is not a teaching manual, though it offers much specific advice on how to improve one's playing. Discarding all meaningless finger acrobatics, Flesch expects from the player a new mental attitude, rational and analytical.

So advanced were some of Flesch's ideas that they seemed unnatural to some conventionally trained violinists. His theories on fingering and bowing, on intonation, on vibrato (to mention but a few points) can be quite bewildering at first. It takes time to grasp the logic of his thoughts, and there are violinists who refuse to accept it. Flesch restructured the violin technique, abolishing old taboos, such as the low right elbow, the avoidance of second and fourth positions, the tale of the "unteachable" vibrato. It was he who analyzed the various bow grips—the old German, the Franco-Belgian, the Russian—and who, in fact, popularized the so-called Russian grip. He named it Russian because he observed the playing style of Elman and Heifetz and assumed that Auer taught that particular grip.* Convinced that this grip was superior to his own Franco-Belgian method, Flesch changed late in his career and recommended it to his students. What he did not realize was that Auer did not teach the Russian bow grip and did not use it himself:† Auer was quite permissive in letting the student choose a grip that seemed most comfortable to his build and the length of his arm. The Russian grip advocated by Flesch has certain advantages and drawbacks: it produces a bigger tone with less exertion, but it is a bit heavy and inflexible. Some of Flesch's students abandoned the Russian grip in later years and returned to the more conservative Franco-Belgian method. Few of the present-day Soviet violinists use the Russian grip. At any rate, Flesch's innovative step freed a generation of inhibited "low elbow" players and wrist wigglers from violinistic straitjackets.

The first lesson with a new student was a diagnostic one. Flesch made a complete list of his technical or musical shortcomings; then a

---

* It is said that Wieniawski held the bow in this manner, with a high elbow, and introduced this method to Russia.

† The photos in Auer's *Violin Method* show that he did not use the Russian grip. Flesch must have changed over rather late, for in his *Urstudien* (1910) he still uses the Franco-Belgian grip.

"diet" of appropriate exercises was set up to eliminate those weaknesses. Only when the shortcomings were overcome did the study of repertoire begin. That preparatory period could take months, but it was worth the investment in time and effort.

A lesson with Flesch was logically planned. At the piano sat a professional accompanist. The student was expected to give an uninterrupted performance of a major segment of the piece to be studied. He was also expected to use the fingerings and bowings recommended by Flesch; if he wanted to make changes, he had to explain his reasons.

While the student was playing, Flesch listened silently with the music in front of him. During the performance, he would jot down his criticisms on the margin of the violin part, using a shorthand familiar to the student. The playing finished, he would approach the student with the marked copy and explain his criticism point by point. (The student took the annotated copy home as an aid in correcting the mistakes and reworking the piece.) Flesch demonstrated all corrections not on his own Stradivarius, but on the student's instrument. At the end, he would perform the entire piece, or at least important sections, for the student. One such lesson, well digested, could keep the student busy for a full two weeks. Rarely, if ever, did Flesch listen to a piece again; it was up to the student to understand him the first time, to absorb the criticism, and to make the necessary corrections. Such a method assumed a certain maturity on the student's part. It was certainly not geared to the mentality of a "wunderkind," and, in fact, Flesch produced very few, though some of his students started with him quite young (for example, Ida Haendel, Szymon Goldberg, and Max Rostal).

While Flesch was rather stern during his private lessons, he displayed a marvelous sense of humor in his master classes, where he had a captive audience. Once he discoursed about the temperament (or the lack thereof) of a performing student and said, "Of course, a violinist who likes to wear red ties will play differently from one who . . ." Suddenly his eye fell on a well-known violinist sitting in the first row who turned purple . . . he was wearing a red tie! Everyone broke out in laughter. Red ties were quite in demand for the next few days.

During the summer of 1929, I kept a diary of proceedings at the master course. In one incident, a student played the Mozart Concerto in G major (No. 3) in a rather graceless and heavy-handed manner. Flesch asked, "What do you imagine if you play a piece like that?" Embarrassed silence. Flesch, insisting, "But you must have some concept of the piece." Still silence. Flesch helped along—"the first movement has something knightly; the second movement—intense, yet pure, expression; the third—a winged dance. . . . If someone wants to be a good Mozart performer, he must not only possess all the technical and stylistic means, but his whole appearance must be harmonious, his posture, his motions. . . ."

At this point a question was raised about Flesch's cadenza, which is rather modern: "You seem to believe that it is not necessary to limit a cadenza to the technical means available to the composer at that time." Flesch: "A cadenza serves the purpose to display the technique of the performer; hence, one can allow oneself all freedom in technical matters, but not in matters of harmony."

At another session, a student gave a tame and placid performance of Joachim's *Hungarian Concerto*. Flesch commented,

> This Concerto is a piece aglow with temperament, really wild. . . . It is rarely played now, it was neglected even during Joachim's lifetime. He himself had no longer the technique, in his later years, to perform it. Some of his students played it so poorly that it acquired a "bad" reputation. A very unfair judgment, for it is one of the most beautiful pieces ever written for the violin. One must not make the mistake of playing it "classically"—it is a gypsy piece. Brahms thought highly of it and learned quite a bit for his own Concerto.

About the Beethoven concerto:

> One of the most difficult works because it is built on introspection. The first movement consists almost entirely of embellishments, of passing notes into which one must put expression and life. Most of the time one hears it played like an etude—there are not three or four violinists in existence who play it well.

Flesch himself played the passages with a certain rhythmic freedom. About the *Spanish Dances* by Sarasate (*Malagueña, Habanera*):

> One needs a very secure, well-balanced technique to play these pieces well. As for interpretation, the generation of today has no conception as to how they should be played. Their playing is not Spanish but Russian. Only when one has heard Sarasate play these dances can one understand how they should sound. It is erroneous to believe that Spanish music must glow with temperament and eroticism. On the contrary, Spanish music is very refined, almost reticent, but very rhythmical—more inner than outer temperament.

Flesch was opposed to excessive practicing: "If you can't learn to become a violinist in four hours of daily practice, you never will." But those four hours had to be spent intelligently, carefully divided between technique, repertoire study, and interpretative playing. Continuous slow practicing of a piece was bad, it took the "wings" off the music, so a period of slow practice had to be followed by playing the piece through in tempo to restore the "brio." The use of the metronome was discouraged, for this artificial time restraint weakened the player's natural rhythmic impulses.

Flesch thought highly of the vocation of an artist. I remember him saying, "It isn't enough to have talent to become somebody; one needs *character*. . . . One can lack character in life and get away with it, but not in *art*."

Among Flesch's posthumous writings are his *Memoirs*, a scrupulously honest account of his own career, interspersed with astute observations on the musical scene and realistic vignettes of fellow violinists. He recommended that the volume be published twenty-five years after his wife's death ("otherwise she would lose all her friends!"), but he was overridden by Mrs. Flesch, though the first edition of 1957 was somewhat edited to avoid offending fellow artists who were still alive.

His unpublished papers also included a completed German manuscript, on the art of fingering, which was entrusted to me for adaptation and translation into English; it was published in 1966 under the title *Violin Fingering: Its Theory and Practice*. In addition to the text, it contains 1753 musical examples—a dictionary of problem spots with recommended fingerings from the entire violin repertoire. Flesch was a fingering "fiend" and had very definite ideas about "good" and "bad" fingerings. His fingerings are not always the easiest, but always the most logical or the most musical. (A certain concert violinist once said, "There are two fingerings: the one which is good and the one which you take on stage when you panic.") Flesch must have collected his fingering examples for a number of years, and he kept a card file. The story is told of a session between Flesch and Kulenkampff, comparing fingerings in the Brahms concerto. Suddenly, Flesch remarked, "That's interesting; I must look and see whether I have this fingering in my file."[5]

Flesch was a true connoisseur of fine violins and bows. Early in his career, in 1898, he acquired a Gofriller, but soon exchanged it for a Joseph Guarnerius filius Andreae (actually made by Guadagnini, as he found out later). In 1907 he bought a Stradivarius, the "Brancaccio," made in 1725, and used it at the height of his career. Forced to sell it in 1931, he then played on a fine Petrus Guarnerius. In fact, he had an interesting collection of nineteenth-century Italian and French instruments (makers like Pressenda, Lupot, Vuillaume), for he believed that the Cremona violins would eventually be "played out," to be replaced by the more modern, vigorous-sounding nineteenth-century instruments. That point has not yet been reached; the Cremona instruments of Stradivarius and Guarnerius are still considered the best, but by now they are so high-priced that many rising virtuosos are forced to use violins of "minor" Italian masters. Flesch's theory may yet prove right.

It is unfortunate that Flesch's playing has not been preserved more fully through recordings. He made a number of special records for Thomas Edison, mostly short pieces, some of which are excellent, but they have not been reissued. Some private recordings, made from radio transmissions, show his impeccable technique, noble style, and grand concept of works like the Beethoven and Brahms concertos. To have known him, to have heard him, to have worked with him, is a privilege to cherish forever.

The Flesch School

Carl Flesch taught for almost half a century, from 1897 to 1944, in individual lessons, class lessons, and master classes. He taught students of all nationalities and ethnic backgrounds in Bucharest, Amsterdam, Berlin, Philadelphia, Baden-Baden, London, and Lucerne. His subject was the mastery of violin playing, which, to him, was the precondition of artistic interpretation. Most of his students were in need of technical help; but the problems were not always technical—they could be also caused by emotional inhibitions, a lack of projection, or excessive nervousness. Whatever it was, Flesch knew the cure, but the student had to trust him implicitly. There was but one salvation: follow the master's precepts to the letter! Those who did, improved; those who could not, drifted away and sought advice elsewhere, only to find out that Flesch had been right.

The successful Flesch student is a specific breed: technically secure, intellectually arrogant, emotionally restrained. He was not the right teacher for high-strung players or impressionable children. But those who understood and absorbed his intellectual approach remained forever grateful for the firm foundation built by Flesch.

There is no reliable register of Flesch students—there were simply too many of them—and I shall limit myself to those who have achieved great renown or whom I have known and heard personally.

Josef Wolfsthal (1899–1931) studied with Flesch prior to World War I. Flesch wrote,

> Wolfsthal was ten years old when I took over his training. When he was sixteen, I released him and let him play a few times in public, but thought it wiser to put him into an orchestra for the time being in order to widen his musical horizon. In quick succession, he sat at the first desk in Bremen, Stockholm, and Berlin, and became a teacher at the Berlin Hochschule at the early age of twenty-six, but died at thirty-one from the after-effects of influenza. He was already considered one of the finest violinists of Germany; his bowing particularly was near absolute perfection.[1]

In the late 1920s, Wolfsthal was concertmaster under Otto Klemperer at the Kroll Opera in Berlin, an institution dedicated to modern ideas in music and staging. Wolfsthal was called upon quite often to perform as soloist, particularly premieres of new works, as for example the *Kammermusik No. 4* by Hindemith, actually a violin concerto with chamber orchestra. He was also the violinist in a string trio with the composer-violist Hindemith and the cellist Feuermann; it was a virtuoso ensemble specializing in modern music.

The Australian-born Alma Moodie (1900–43) had studied in Brussels with César Thomson before coming to Flesch around 1919. He called her "the most outstanding female violinist of her time, a worthy successor of Norman-Neruda."[2] Miss Moodie's special trait was her affinity with modern music. As early as 1914 she had played music by Max Reger to the composer's great satisfaction; she received the dedications of the violin concertos by Hans Pfitzner (1923) and Ernst Krenek (1924), and played Igor Stravinsky's *Suite after Pergolesi* with the composer at the piano in its premiere in 1925.

During the 1920s, Flesch's most brilliant student was undoubtedly Max Rostal. Born in 1905 in Teschen, Austria, he concertized as a child prodigy before he was ten. Until his thirteenth year he was a student of Arnold Rosé in Vienna, but the subsequent four years with Flesch in Berlin were decisive for his development. I heard him privately in Flesch's studio in 1923 and found the finish and panache of his performance truly amazing. In 1925 he was awarded the Mendelssohn Prize; nevertheless, Flesch insisted that he acquire orchestral experience and so he became concertmaster of the Oslo Philharmonic. In 1928 he returned to Berlin as Flesch's assistant at the Hochschule and was given his own class in 1930. When the Nazis assumed power, he emigrated to England in 1934, where he became extremely successful as soloist and teacher. He continued to live in London throughout the blitz, giving concerts for the Allied armed forces; eventually he became a naturalized British subject. In 1943 he was appointed professor at the Guildhall School of Music. Especially after Flesch's departure from London in 1939, Rostal became the most sought-after teacher in England, and his studio in Hampstead attracted students from all parts of the Continent. Donald Brook writes,

> It has been said by some that Rostal is establishing an English "school" of violin-playing. . . . His influence in this country is of the utmost significance to the art of violin-playing, for he has pupils, or ex-pupils, in every symphony orchestra of any importance in England.[3]

To everyone's surprise, Rostal decided to return to the Continent; in 1957 he accepted a master course at the Academy in Cologne, and in 1958 was named professor of violin at the Conservatory of Bern. At present, he lives and teaches in Bern.

Despite his success in Britain and on the Continent, Rostal has not made an outstanding solo career. This is surprising, for he has all the necessary qualities—a vibrant tone, technical mastery, and excellent musicianship. His initially fiery and sensuous temperament has given way to a more intellectual, detached approach, as is clearly discernible on his excellent recordings.

Rostal is a thinking violinist, and he expects the same of his students. He insists on stylistic differentiation in performing various composers; he distrusts all "edited" music and urges the use of an *Urtext* wherever possible. "The majority of editions are not to be trusted," he has said (which does not prevent him from publishing his own heavily edited editions!). He urges his students to delve into the life and background of a composer while trying to interpret his work, to acquire a knowledge of his total output. He requires the study of a full concerto score, not only the piano reduction. All these are admirable principles which, however, presuppose a certain maturity on the student's part. Spontaneity and inspiration seem to have been expunged from such a cerebral approach, but also shallowness.

Of all Flesch's students, Rostal is—in his manner of thinking and teaching—most like his late master, and yet he was understandably eager to establish his independent profile. I remember a small incident that goes back to the early 1920s, when he and I were students of Flesch. I was under pressure to find Flesch's fingerings for the Tchaikovsky concerto and finally turned to Max, who had recently studied the piece with the maestro. "Sure, you can have my violin part," he said with an ironic smile, "but the fingerings are mostly mine, not Flesch's." When I arrived in Flesch's studio with the carefully copied fingerings, Flesch asked with a trace of irritation, "Where did you get the fingerings?" "From Max," I replied meekly, fearing the worst. But Flesch merely shook his head and remarked, "You couldn't have found a more unlikely source for my fingerings." Obviously, he was aware of Rostal's independent thinking, even as a teenager, but he respected such signs of independence if they were logical—and he certainly thought highly of Rostal's talent, despite his cockiness.

Rostal's fingerings may be different from those of Flesch, but they are equally complex. He also continues to use and teach the so-called Russian bow grip as defined by Flesch, though it has been abandoned by many violinists. But it works well for Rostal and his prominent students, among them Norbert Brainin (leader of the Amadeus Quartet) and Edith Peinemann. Today, Rostal's studio enjoys a deserved reputation for excellence.

After World War I Berlin became a mecca for the arts, especially for modernism and experimentation. There was a considerable immigration from eastern Europe. Particularly noticeable was an influx of gifted young Polish violinists, most of whom were poor and needed scholarships. Their idol was their compatriot Huberman, who recommended Flesch as a teacher, and so they wound up in Flesch's studio in Berlin.

Initially, the climate in Berlin was not ideally suited for those young Poles: they had to contend with a foreign language, a sophisticated culture, German haughtiness, and latent anti-Semitism. As for Flesch, his intellectual approach to the violin was diametrically opposed to their "gutsy" concept of fiddling. But they survived and learned; they became remarkably well acclimatized to the Germanic surroundings; and most of them prospered during the years of the Weimar Republic. All dispersed when the Nazis came to power in 1933.

The young Polish group in Flesch's studio included Szymon Goldberg, Stefan Frenkel, Bronislaw Gimpel, Roman Totenberg, Henryk Szeryng, and Ida Haendel. All had played the violin since early childhood and had concertized as prodigies; some had studied in Warsaw with Mihalowicz, a fine teacher. But by Flesch's standards, all had to be reschooled, and retrained. Not every remodeling process went smoothly, there were personality clashes between teacher and student, but on the whole Flesch's iron discipline was beneficial.

The oldest of the group was Stefan Frenkel (1902–79). Born in Warsaw, he arrived in Berlin in 1919 and, after a short stay with Adolf Busch, joined Flesch's class in 1921. He was a versatile musician and composer. While his violinistic talent was not of the very first order, he staked out a field in which he became unique: the interpretation of modern music. There was not a piece too dissonant, atonal, or allegedly unplayable that Frenkel could not handle successfully; he played literally dozens of important premieres in the 1920s and early '30s. He also served as concertmaster of the Dresden Philharmonic (1924–27), the Orchestre de la Suisse Romande (1935), and the Metropolitan Opera in New York (1936–40). However, his career in the New World did not develop, though he continued to be active as performer and teacher.

Of all of Flesch's students, Szymon Goldberg came the closest to the perfect balance between technique and interpretation. On this level he can be compared to Szigeti.

Born in 1909 in central Poland, Goldberg first studied with Mihalowicz in Warsaw and came to Berlin in 1917. After a brief stay with Madame Joachim-Chaigneau, he became Flesch's student at the age of ten. What distinguished Goldberg's playing even at an early age was his sterling musicianship based on impeccable technique. In 1921 he returned to Warsaw to make his debut. In 1924 he was considered ready by Flesch to present himself in Berlin, playing three of the most demanding concertos in one evening: Bach's E major, Joachim's *Hungarian*, and Paganini's First. Young Szymon resisted all attempts to be presented as a prodigy: he wanted to be judged as an adult. The success was remarkable, and a concert tour through Germany was equally successful. Nevertheless, Flesch urged him to acquire orchestral experience, and so the sixteen-year-old Goldberg was installed in 1925 as concertmaster of the Dresden Philharmonic. This experience proved valuable when Furtwängler chose Goldberg as one of the concertmasters of the Berlin Philharmonic, a prestigious post which he held from 1929 to 1934. During that time he also joined Hindemith and Feuermann in a string trio (replacing Wolfsthal, who had suddenly died). With the Nazis in power, the Berlin Philharmonic dismissed all its Jewish members, although Furtwängler made every effort to protect Goldberg and other leading players.

This forced Goldberg to concentrate on a concert career. In the years 1934–40 he played in Europe, Japan, China, and the Dutch Indies, as both soloist and sonata partner with Lili Kraus, the pianist known as a Mozart expert. In 1938 Goldberg made his New York debut. In 1942, while on a concert tour of the Dutch East Indies, he was interned by the Japanese. In 1946 he resumed his career and played in Australia, South Africa, and the Americas. For fifteen summers, from 1951 to 1966, he was a faculty member of the Aspen Festival, where he formed the highly successful Festival Piano Quartet with pianist Babin, violist Primrose, and cellist Graudan.

A new career opened up for Goldberg in 1955, when he was appointed music director of the newly founded Netherlands Chamber Orchestra. He achieved international success as soloist-conductor in a repertory of violin concertos and concerti grossi, symphonies by Haydn and Mozart, and a select modern repertoire, particularly Bartók and Hindemith.

In the 1970s Goldberg was on the move again. For a time he lived in London, and in 1978 he returned to the United States to teach at the Juilliard School, Yale University, and the Curtis Institute.

Goldberg is a masterful violinist whose sole concern is the interpretation of great music, to the exclusion of all virtuoso frills. His technique is flawless, his tone warm and pure, his sense of style and his musical taste exquisite. His performance style stresses refinement, intimacy, and noble intensity, equally evident in the classical repertoire and modern works. Outstanding among his recordings are the six *Brandenburg Concertos* and his recent Mozart sonatas with the pianist Radu Lupu. I also remember a performance of Goldberg with the New York Philharmonic in 1950 playing the Beethoven concerto, in which he attempted to restore the *Urtext* of the violin part, but the results were unexpected. Every time Goldberg played a passage somewhat different from the established version a shudder went through the audience because it seemed as if the soloist had gone astray. Soon thereafter Goldberg gave up these puritanical attempts, which brought him more criticism than gratitude.

Bronislaw Gimpel (1911–79) was a fiery violin talent whom even Flesch could not fully tame. His early studies were done in Vienna at the Conservatory from 1922 to 1926. By that time he was sufficiently

The Polish-born Szymon Goldberg, sensitive performer of classical music.

Henryk Szeryng, born in Poland and now living in Mexico, is considered **one** of the leading violinists of today.

accomplished to play in Italy with much acclaim: he was invited to perform on Paganini's famed Guarnerius del Gesù violin, kept in a museum in Genoa, followed by a command performance for the Italian king and Pope Pius XI. In 1928 he joined Flesch's class at the Hochschule in Berlin, but that lasted only one year; Flesch thought of Gimpel as talented but undisciplined. In such cases Flesch always recommended orchestral posts, and so Gimpel served as concertmaster in Königsberg, Göteborg, and (from 1937 to 1942) Los Angeles. While in California, he founded and conducted the Hollywood Youth Orchestra. After three years in the U.S. Army, Gimpel resumed his career, dividing his time between America and Europe. Chamber music absorbed much of his energies: he was a member of the New Friends of Music Quartet, the Mannes Piano Trio, and the Warsaw Quintet. Returning to the United States, he accepted a professorship at the University of Connecticut (1967–73) but felt constricted in an academic framework: his main interest was still performance.

Gimpel played with virtuoso flair and effortless technique. His driving temperament matured and mellowed over the years. His vibrato was intense, his interpretations authoritative. For a time he performed large-scale concertos (such as Beethoven and Mendelssohn) without a conductor, leading the orchestra while playing the solo part, but the performances did not gain by it. He has made many excellent recordings.

The career of Polish-born Roman Totenberg (born Lodz, 1913) did not fulfill the early promise of his bright talent, but he is a highly respected musician and at present director of the Longy Music School in Boston. He studied with Mihalowicz in Warsaw before coming to Flesch in the late 1920s. Awarded the Mendelssohn Prize in 1932, he concertized with the Polish composer Szymanowski in 1935–36; he emigrated to the United States in the late 1930s. Totenberg's teaching appointments included the Music Academy of Santa Barbara, the Aspen Institute in Colorado (1950–60), and Boston University, where for many years he was head of the string department.

Henryk Szeryng is undoubtedly the star pupil of Flesch's career as a teacher. Szeryng developed in an unhurried, unpressured way. He was born in Warsaw in 1918, the son of an affluent industrialist and a mother trained as a pianist. His first instrument was the piano, but he soon switched to the violin by his own choice. By age nine, he progressed far enough to play the Mendelssohn concerto for Huberman, who was a friend of the family. Huberman recommended that the boy be sent to Berlin to study with Flesch. "I studied with Flesch until I was thirteen," Szeryng reminisced, "and everything I know, violinistically speaking, I learned from him." When asked whether he found Flesch too strict, Szeryng replied, "Yes, he was a disciplinarian, a technician, but he had one overriding tenet—not to impress his own personality on pupils who had a personality of their own." In 1933, Szeryng undertook his first major concert tour—a debut in Warsaw under Bruno Walter with the Beethoven concerto, and concerts in Bucharest, Vienna, and Paris.

However, he settled in Paris for further studies. Here he acquired a profound admiration for the French violin school. "They don't attack the violin, they don't rape it, they treat it like a human being. And it isn't greasy or oversweet." He was befriended by Enesco and Thibaud and admits having learned from both musically without having studied with either of them. At that time Szeryng must have switched to the Franco-Belgian school; obviously he no longer uses the Flesch bow grip. Szeryng also studied theory and composition with Nadia Boulanger and thought seriously about becoming a composer.

When World War II broke out, Szeryng enlisted with the Polish army in exile. Being a linguist, he was assigned as translator to General Sikorski and was involved in placing four thousand Polish refugees in Mexico. In 1943, while giving concerts in Mexico, he was invited to reorganize the string department at the University of Mexico. He accepted and spent the next ten years teaching and performing on a limited scale. Apparently the great world had forgotten him. He became an honored citizen of Mexico and seemed happy with his activities.

By sheer accident, he was rediscovered by none other than the pianist Arthur Rubinstein. Surprised to find a fellow Pole in Mexico City, Rubinstein asked to hear Szeryng play and was so impressed that he persuaded his impresario Hurok to bring Szeryng back from oblivion into the international world of music.

Thus, in the mid-1950s, Szeryng reentered the concert scene. His debut in New York in 1956 established him as one of the great violinists of our day. Since then, he has played in sixty-five countries on five continents. He has also made a number of superb recordings, including two complete sets of all the solo sonatas and partitas of Bach, the great concertos from Bach to Bartók, the Mozart sonatas with Ingrid Haebler, and Beethoven sonatas with Arthur Rubinstein. His second set of the Bach solo sonatas is particularly accomplished. Szeryng plays with a normal bow and does not pretend to revive any Baroque practices; yet the polyphonic movements sound rich and the chords give the illusion of being played almost simultaneously. He adheres scrupulously to the original text—every embellishment, every bowing is chiseled to perfection. Special mention should be made of his premier recording of Paganini's Concerto No. 3 in E major, a work he resurrected by persuading Paganini's heirs to let him reconstruct and perform the forgotten work.

When hearing Szeryng in live performances, one is always struck by the nobility and aristocracy of his concept; occasionally there is almost too much restraint. Nevertheless, he can give superlative performances even of an emotional piece like the Sibelius concerto, as he recently did with the New York Philharmonic.

Szeryng is often cast in the role of a goodwill ambassador—he travels with a diplomatic Mexican passport and takes an interest in various cultural projects of the United Nations. He recently presented the city of Jerusalem with a Stradivari violin, and he is always willing to contribute his art to charitable causes. His idealistic belief in the unifying "miracle of music" seems genuine.

The youngest of Flesch's "Polish prodigies" was Ida Haendel, born in 1923 in Khelm. Her precocious talent was developed by a number of teachers; the most influential was Flesch, with whom she had a somewhat troubled relationship. She came to him as a child and played with childlike instinct; Flesch wanted her to play with an intellect she did not possess at that time.

Ida was dominated by an ambitious father (a painter and an amateur cellist) who pushed her career aggressively and made many enemies on the way. When he took her to Paris to consult Enesco, Flesch became very angry and dismissed her from his class, and though they were later reconciled, there was never much warmth.

Despite her adolescent problems, Haendel had some early successes, winning a special prize for Polish contestants at the 1935 Wieniawski Contest, quite an accomplishment for a twelve-year-old girl. Two years later, she played the Beethoven concerto in London under Sir Henry Wood and drew this enthusiastic comment in *The Observer*: "No prodigy since Menuhin has shown such a sense of fitness, or played with such glow, such dignity."

Her American debut was planned for 1940, but delayed by the war until 1946. Hurok advertised her as "The New Violin Sensation," but the critics chose to have a different view when she appeared at Carnegie Hall in December 1946.

Somehow, Haendel never achieved recognition in New York.

While she was treated condescendingly by the critics, her chief rival, Ginette Neveu,* received accolades. But elsewhere she was acclaimed warmly—England, South America, Israel, and particularly Italy and Holland. Her musicianship matured, she expanded her repertoire into the modern field, and learned from great conductors like Kubelik and Celibidache. The German author Hartnack is particularly impressed by her stylistic fidelity, the manner in which she differentiates between Bach and Mozart, Beethoven and Brahms. Unfortunately, her recordings are no longer easily available.

In 1982, Ida Haendel was among the great violinists invited to perform at the Huberman Centenary in Tel Aviv—a singular honor.

Henri Temianka's career has had kaleidoscopic aspects—he has lived in so many places and accomplished so much in various fields. Born in Scotland of Polish parents in 1906, he was educated on the Continent—in Holland, Berlin, and Paris—before joining Flesch's master class in Philadelphia in 1926. His previous teachers had been the solid Willy Hess and the elegant Jules Boucherit, and this background of German and French schooling stood him in good stead to absorb Flesch's artistic guidance. Not spending his childhood as a prodigy explains, perhaps, the sanity and balance of Temianka's musicianship.

In 1928 he made his New York recital debut, but continued to be enrolled at the Curtis Institute until 1930, mainly as a conducting student of Rodzinski. From 1932 to 1939 he made his home in London; one of the highlights of that period was winning the third prize at the 1935 Wieniawski Competition, ranking immediately after Ginette Neveu and David Oistrakh, distinguished competitors indeed. Temianka's success led to an invitation to visit the Soviet Union, where he played repeatedly. Eager to expand his musical experience, he accepted the post of concertmaster of the Scottish Orchestra under George Szell; in 1941–42 he occupied a similar position in Pittsburgh under Fritz Reiner.

After the war, Temianka faced yet another change in his career, becoming first violinist of the newly founded Paganini String Quartet. The name was selected because the players were to use four Stradivari instruments once in Paganini's possession.† Led by Temianka, the Paganini Quartet made its debut in 1946 with an all-Beethoven program consisting of the three Opus 59 (*Razumovsky*) quartets. To play such a

* Neveu, one of Flesch's greatest students, will be discussed in the French chapter (see pp. 378–80).
† See p. 192.

program with only a brief rehearsal period was a bold undertaking, but it succeeded magnificently. I remember that debut concert—the sound was rich and burnished, the interpretation spirited. What made Temianka's quartet playing so remarkable was his past experience as a soloist: he knew how to project and how to handle technical problems with aplomb, though always maintaining a homogeneous chamber style. His outstanding partner was the cellist Robert Maas. During the next twenty years, the Paganini Quartet maintained an international reputation as a leading ensemble while Temianka guided it through various crises of changing membership. In 1966 the quartet disbanded, and the four Stradivari instruments (which were on loan) were passed on to another quartet; at present, they are used by the Cleveland Quartet.

In 1960, Temianka founded the California Chamber Symphony. Alternating as conductor and soloist, he arranges interesting programs, including many premieres, and tours every year with the symphony. He has also been active in narrating and demonstrating educational films, for example *Basic Violin Technique* and *A Story of Chamber Music*. He became known as the author of many articles dealing with music and the violin; in 1973 he published a witty autobiographical book, *Face the Music*, which touches on many problems connected with music as a career. He continues to travel as soloist, conductor, lecturer, and teacher of master classes. His student Nina Bodnar-Horton, a twenty-year-old Californian, has won the 1981 Long-Thibaud violin competition in Paris.

One of Flesch's top-flight students was Ricardo Odnoposoff, born in Argentina in 1914, whose career remained strangely limited despite Flesch's enthusiastic assessment of his talent. Perhaps it was the misfortune of being a runner-up: Odnoposoff was awarded second prize at the 1937 Ysaÿe Contest in Brussels, while Oistrakh was ranked first. Actually, this near-victory was very honorable, but it did not lead to a worldwide career. Odnoposoff's fame is centered on his adoptive city of Vienna, where for many years he was active as concertmaster of the State Opera Orchestra (Philharmonic) and professor at the Academy. In 1944–45 he played in New York to excellent reviews, but was not invited to return, due to some managerial intrigues. He has made a number of recordings which show utmost technical polish and fine musicianship.

A few words about Emanuel Zetlin (born 1900 in St. Petersburg), who was Flesch's assistant at the Curtis Institute during the 1920s.

Trained in the tradition of the Auer school, Zetlin arrived in Flesch's class in Berlin after World War I and faced a period of readjustment. In 1920 he became concertmaster in Frankfurt and joined the Rebner-Hindemith String Quartet. His tenure at Curtis came to an end when Flesch left in 1928; but Zetlin, a violinist of great sensitivity and intelligence, established his own reputation as a first-rate teacher. In 1947 he was appointed violin professor at the University of Washington in Seattle, where he served with great distinction until his retirement in 1971. His students remember him with gratitude and affection.

THE PARIS CONSERVATOIRE
AFTER 100 YEARS

By THE 1890s, when the Paris Conservatoire observed its first centenary, it was a musty, tradition-ridden institution led by patriarchs according to an antiquated curriculum. There was no mandatory retirement age for the faculty, and French musicians are noted for their longevity; the result was a rather superannuated teaching staff. Among the violin professors, Massart retired at eighty, Sauzay at eighty-four, and Dancla unwillingly at seventy-five. The post of *professeur* carried great prestige, though it was poorly paid; as Flesch said, "once a teacher had succeeded in getting on the staff he clung firmly to his post until he had one foot in the grave." [1] Despite all criticism, the Conservatoire produced, in the later nineteenth century alone, such extraordinary violinists as Wieniawski, Sarasate, and Kreisler.

With the appointment of Martin Marsick as successor to Sauzay in 1892, a new spirit entered the violin faculty. Marsick, a Belgian like so many "French" violinists of the time, studied with Massart and also briefly with Joachim. He was comparatively young, in his forties, when he joined the Conservatoire; he was an accomplished violinist as well as a teacher of rare insight. Within five years he had produced three first-prize winners—Flesch, Thibaud, and Enesco. After only eight years on the faculty, Marsick left the Conservatoire. Moser remembers him as one of the finest violinists of his time; Flesch and Thibaud never ceased to praise their old teacher, though Enesco was cooler. Marsick died in Paris in 1924 in rather impoverished conditions. In 1933, his three most famous disciples were reunited for a memorial concert at his birthplace, to perform Vivaldi's Concerto for three violins.* It is hard to imagine

* See photograph p. 329.

three more dissimilar musical personalities than Flesch, Enesco, and Thibaud, but each carried the imprint of Marsick's exemplary teaching.

Jacques Thibaud

Of all of Marsick's students, Thibaud (1880–1953) seems to have been closest to his teacher. He came to Marsick's attention as a boy of thirteen, freshly arrived from the provinces, penniless and naive, eager to enter the Paris Conservatoire. In his native city of Bordeaux, however, Jacques was already a celebrity, having made his debut at age twelve in Wieniawski's Concerto in D minor. Ysaÿe, visiting Bordeaux, heard young Jacques play and commented to Jacques's father, a fellow musician, "You know, your son plays better than I." Even if said half in jest, it indicates the level of Thibaud's accomplishment at a young age. Thibaud, remembering his youthful impression of Ysaÿe—not only his immense playing but also his immense appetite at the table—wrote many years later, "I owe to Ysaÿe what I am."[1] But that decisive influence came much later.

In the meantime, the thirteen-year-old Jacques passed the entrance examinations to the Conservatoire with flying colors—he was first among two hundred applicants! But he faced a hard time, having to support himself with odd jobs playing in cafés and music halls.

Marsick had a particular fondness for this gifted provincial boy and worked with him not only at the Conservatoire but also privately. His paternal interest included some painful blows with the bow across Jacques's fingers and a few well-aimed kicks in the pants whenever the professor was displeased with the student's performance; but this did not diminish Jacques's adoration for his teacher. His progress at the Conservatoire was not spectacular. His ambition was, of course, the first violin prize, but he failed to place in 1894 and received only an honorable mention the following year. He finally won the *premier prix* in 1896, but without glamor, for he placed fourth among four winners, which hurt his pride.* Thibaud was not in top form when he competed; his extreme nervousness at performances could rob him—so he said— of eighty percent of his playing ability! In later years, he joked, "I was fourth because there was no fifth place!"

Whatever the prestige attached to the First Prize, it did not open the doors to a career for Thibaud: he continued to play violin in the

---

* One of the other winners was Pierre Monteux, who later became a famous conductor.

Café Rouge orchestra, where he performed occasional solos. At one such session, the famous conductor Edouard Colonne heard him play Saint-Saëns's *Rondo capriccioso* and invited him to join the violin section of his orchestra. Obviously, the conductor had his eye on the gifted young newcomer, for when the occasion arose, in 1898, Thibaud was asked to play the violin solo in Saint-Saëns's *Le Déluge*, substituting for the concertmaster. He was so nervous that he had several crying fits during the day and approached the hall like one condemned to death. But orchestra and chorus gave him an ovation at the rehearsal and again at the performance. As an encore he played Beethoven's Romance in F. He was famous overnight, and soon was acclaimed in Europe and America as *the* French violinist. Eventually he was ranked with Ysaÿe and Kreisler.

Thibaud's career in America began auspiciously in 1903 with a fifty-concert tour and high earnings. He finally reappeared in 1913 and repeated his success, but the outbreak of World War I prevented his return the following year. After serving in the French Army (he was discharged with an injury) he reintroduced himself to New York at a concert on November 16, 1916, at the old Aeolian Hall. The concert began with an oddity: Saint-Saëns's Concerto No. 1 in A, to which the well-known *Rondo capriccioso* was attached. In a program note the public was informed that this was done at the composer's request, thus restoring the original form of the First Concerto. The connection between the concerto and the *Rondo* was unknown until then, and the critics wondered about it. Although Thibaud was obviously not in top form—the concert had to be interrupted after the Chausson *Poème* to let him regain his composure—the critics were friendly. By 1917 he had overcome the experiences of the war and emerged as an artist "of loftier stature and larger vision." He became a regular visitor to America during the 1920s and '30s. After the Second World War he made a last appearance with the New York Philharmonic in January 1947 under Stokowski, playing Lalo's *Symphonie espagnole*, his old specialty. At that time, Thibaud was sixty-seven and obviously past his prime. Shortly thereafter he gave a violin recital and opened with the Franck sonata, a staple of the French repertoire. The critic Irving Kolodin observed perceptively that Thibaud's interpretation came straight from Ysaÿe and was "much more moderate in pace and accent than we usually hear from Russian hands."[2] This remark pinpoints the revolutionary change in musical taste caused by the ascent of artists like Heifetz, Elman, and the "Russian wave." The French style of violin playing—refined and elegant—had lost out in public favor to the impassioned and incisive style of the Auer disciples; it never regained its once dominant position.

Thibaud met with a sudden and tragic death: the airplane that was to take him on a concert tour to Indochina crashed in the French Alps on September 1, 1953. He was not quite seventy-three years old.

Thibaud's recognized preeminence as the premier French violinist of his time accompanied him through life. There is a facetious anecdote told by Elman: "Twenty years ago I came to Paris and I asked, 'Who is the greatest French violinist?' The answer was 'Thibaud.' Now I come back, I ask again, and the answer is still, 'Thibaud!' What happened to France?"

What really happened to France was that Thibaud represented French taste and style in such an inimitable way that no need was felt to replace him as an idol. When I heard him for the first time in Paris in 1925, he made an indelible impression on me. His tone was of incredible sweetness, a kind of chaste sensuality, warm yet not cloying or overvibrated. His phrasing was subtle, graceful, and elegant; his bowing sparkled. To hear him play Mozart's G-major Concerto was an experience to be cherished, particularly the slow movement. Pieces like Beethoven's F-major Romance or the Adagio from the Sonata Op. 30, No. 1 showed Thibaud's interpretative subtlety at its best. He had particular affinity for the Spanish rhythms of Saint-Saëns (*Havanaise, Rondo capriccioso*) or Lalo's *Symphonie espagnole*, as well as Chausson's *Poème*, with its sultry sensuality, and Milhaud's Brazilian *Saudades*, which he played with wit and elan. His whole appearance on stage created an image of refinement and elegance: slim and erect, feet together, the torso bent slightly forward, manipulating his bow like a magic wand, without involving much body motion. His technique was not overwhelming, but entirely adequate for his special repertoire. Because of his nervousness, his bow control became unsteady when he was under stress—the feared *"trac"* that plagued Ysaÿe, too. He did not slave in order to keep in top shape, for he loved life in all its aspects— he was irresistible to women and took full advantage of it. He left students but no successor, because his art was an extension of his personality. His teaching was limited to master courses at the École Normale in Paris in the 1920s, and his critical observations were always perceptive and constructive. I attended his course in 1925 and remember him as a strong advocate of the traditional Franco-Belgian method of bowing and *à la corde* tone production.*

---

* Literally "on the string," meaning a penetration of bow hair into string.

Even in his teens Thibaud's playing was distinctly personal. Enesco, a fellow student, heard him in the 1890s and reports,

> I was fifteen when I heard him for the first time [Thibaud was one year older]. I honestly admit that it took my breath away. I was beside myself with enthusiasm. It was so new, so unusual. . . . Thibaud was the first among violinists to reveal to the public an entirely new sound—the result of a complete union between hand and string. His playing was marvelously tender and passionate. Compared to him, Sarasate was just a cold perfectionist. To quote Viardot, "Sarasate was a mechanical nightingale while Thibaud—when he was in good form—was a real live nightingale." . . . I pity all young violinists who have not heard Thibaud: in their book of memories an irreplaceable image is lacking.[3]

The mutual admiration of Ysaÿe, Kreisler, and Thibaud was notable. Ysaÿe once said, "There are two violinists from whose playing I can always be certain of learning something—Kreisler and Thibaud." Thibaud, who had boundless admiration for Ysaÿe, always maintained that among his young colleagues "Fritz" would make the greatest career of all. In turn Kreisler is reported as having named Thibaud as "the greatest violinist in the world."[4]

Another of Thibaud's admirers was Pablo Casals. Together with the pianist Alfred Cortot they formed the Trio Cortot-Thibaud-Casals in 1905, perhaps the greatest ensemble of three independently famous artists. Despite a strong dissimilarity of tone quality and style between the two string players, the total musical impression was unified.

Flesch, who knew Thibaud since boyhood (they were classmates in the 1890s), had obvious affection for him as artist and person but offered some criticism. He traced Thibaud's "technical unreliability" to lack of solid practice, which made him vulnerable to accidents; his technique was adequate but there were insufficient reserves against indisposition or nerves. As in the case of Kreisler, Flesch was struck by the "unadulterated eroticism" of Thibaud's sweet and seductive tone. Thibaud had adopted the mannerism of sliding into a note from below. (Vocalists use this technique occasionally, as do gypsy violinists.) Wherever Thibaud learned this device, he used it sparingly and with refinement. But ultimately, Thibaud's artistry was "innate" rather than "acquired" and hence inimitable. "I acknowledged his artistic superiority without envy," admitted Flesch with rare candor; "you could not compare him to any other violinist."[5]

There was a lovable quality about Thibaud; everyone who met him was enchanted. He was urbane, witty, approachable, and utterly unpretentious. Flesch added, "With his natural charm went an unusual talent for story-telling. A typical imaginative Frenchman, he had a masterly way of adorning trivial events with droll trimmings, and delighted his audiences with his Southern vitality."

Thibaud was much beloved in Russia, where he played often before and after the Revolution. His first visit was in 1901–2, and the critic Kashkin praised his lack of virtuoso affectation. In 1936 he returned to Moscow with his piano partner Cortot, and we have an enthusiastic review written by a famous pianist turned critic, Genrikh Neuhaus:

> Thibaud is complete master of the violin. There is not a single reproach one can make as far as his technique is concerned. Thibaud is "sweet-sounding" in the best sense of the word, he never becomes sentimental or sweetish. From this point of view, the violin sonatas of Franck and Fauré were particularly interesting. . . . Thibaud is a romantic . . . his temperament is genuine, sincere, infectious, his soulful playing, the charm of his personal style envelop the listener.[6]

It was David Oistrakh who wrote the obituary for *Sovietskaya Muzyka* in 1953, and there is something very moving and genuine about his tribute to the older master:

> Thibaud was not only an inspired artist. He was a man of crystalline honesty, quick-witted, charming—a real Frenchman. His performance was of heartfelt sincerity, optimistic in the best sense of the word, shaped by the fingers of an artist feeling the joy of communion with the audience. . . . His interpretations of the classics were not hemmed in by dry academicism, and when he played French music he was incomparable . . . models for future generations of violinists.[7]

Indeed, the lack of "dry academicism" was Thibaud's outstanding trait in approaching the classics. Coming to Paris in 1925 with the sound of Russian and German violinists in my ear, I found Thibaud's Mozart and Beethoven a musical revelation—a limpid clarity of sound, rhythmic verve and steadiness, emphasis without overaccentuation, sentiment but no *Weltschmerz*. Could this be the same Beethoven I had heard all my life? Yes, but the grimness was gone and the joy of music came to the surface.

As Thibaud grew older, he apparently realized that no young

French generation was following in his footsteps. His occasional teaching at the École Normale was not sufficient to create a genuine "school." International competitions became *en vogue* to stimulate the ambitions of young performers. In 1943, in the midst of the Second World War,* Thibaud organized, in collaboration with the pianist Marguerite Long, a Parisian contest for pianists and violinists, to be held every three years, after 1949 every two years. The Long-Thibaud contest did not develop into one of the top events, but it certainly stimulated the interest of French violinists. Thibaud was genuinely concerned about the young generation of French violinists; the Wieniawski Prize awarded to young Ginette Neveu in 1935 made him happy, and he was devastated when she perished in an airplane crash. Four years later he was to suffer the same fate.

Georges Enesco

Enesco† is the third and youngest of the triumvirate of great violinists—following Flesch and Thibaud—to have been taught by Marsick at the Conservatoire in the 1890s. In terms of musical versatility, he was probably the most gifted of the three: he was equally accomplished as violinist, pianist, composer, and conductor. Preferring to be considered a composer, he begrudged the time given to violin practice. Conducting seemed a minor sideline, yet so successful was he as guest conductor of the New York Philharmonic in 1937 that he was reengaged for two more seasons. His ability as a pianist aroused the good-natured envy of Arthur Rubinstein; he could accompany any violin work from memory. In fact, his musical memory was legendary; he could remember an entire composition after one perusal of the score. He was an inspiring teacher, according to his erstwhile student Yehudi Menuhin, who remained gratefully devoted to him to the last day.

Altogether, Enesco was one of those rare elemental forces in music, spilling his talent in all directions. His own aspirations as a composer remained largely unfulfilled, which must have been a source of disillusionment for him. Today, among his thirty-two opus numbers, including an opera, several symphonies, and much ensemble music, only his two

---

* Thibaud lived in Paris during the Second World War. On June 10, 1940, the day the Germans moved into Holland, he was making a recording of the Fauré Piano Quartet in Paris. The next day his son was killed at the front.
† In Rumania and eastern Europe the name is spelled with a final "u."

Rumanian Rhapsodies have remained in the orchestral repertoire, youthful works of which he was not very proud. His Sonatas No. 2 and 3 for violin and piano are played by Menuhin and Stern, and some of his chamber music is occasionally revived.

One could call Enesco a violinist against his better judgment. The career of a violinist seemed to him a curse. He once remarked about virtuosos, "Poor devils! They are just like convicts (condemned to hard labor), martyrs . . . sometimes saints."[1] Yet "far from despising the violin, I loved its tone—when someone else was playing! What spells Thibaud's fingers could weave." He called the violin "his intimate enemy"; "I have so often looked at my fiddle in the case and said to myself: You are too small, my friend, much too small!"[2] Although possessing an innate talent for the violin, he hated the daily drudgery of maintaining his technique:

> We live under the motto of perfection. One demands every evening a perfect sonata, without a single wrong note. . . . Well, perfection does not interest me. What is important for an artist is—to vibrate oneself, and to make others vibrate. In fact, it seems to me impossible for a performer to practice eight hours a day, conscientiously, and then to be able, in the evening on the stage, to produce the élan and the desire which transfigure the music. I notice a real incompatibility between the servitude of forced labor and the need to evade all servitude. Between the two one must choose: I have chosen.[3]

On the other hand, he noted, "I like very much to conduct. . . . How marvelous to make music without being obliged to occupy yourself beforehand with fastidious scales which spoil your pleasure."

Such slavery was not for Enesco's free spirit. He earned his living as a violinist, but he satisfied his soul as a composer and conductor.

Enesco was born in 1881 in Liveni-Virnav,* a village in Rumanian Moldavia. A gypsy fiddler showed the four-year-old boy how to play the violin. Demonstrating unusual talent, Georges was taken to Iaşi, the nearest cultural center, and had lessons with Eduard Caudella, once a student of Vieuxtemps and now director of the Iaşi Conservatory. The next step was Vienna, where Georges spent the years 1888–94, studying at the conservatory and absorbing a broad musical curriculum, including violin, piano, chamber music, and composition. He lived at the home of his violin teacher, Joseph Hellmesberger, Jr., who provided him

* Now renamed "George Enescu."

with additional opportunities for orchestral playing. By the time Georges completed the Conservatory in 1894, he was considered an accomplished performer; yet he transferred to the Paris Conservatoire, following in the footsteps of his fellow students Kreisler and Flesch. Assigned to Marsick's class, he did not feel inspired: "He taught me how to play the violin better, and I learned a few pieces."[4] More enjoyable were the theory and composition courses with Gédalge, Massenet, and Fauré. (One of his fellow students was Maurice Ravel.) When he failed to win the first violin prize in 1898, Enesco was ready to give up; he knew that he had not played too well, but the obligatory piece was Viotti's Concerto No. 29 "and who could work up enthusiasm for such a tedious piece?" he asked. Saint-Saëns encouraged the young man to stay on, to try again, and indeed Enesco won the first prize the next year—with the Saint-Saëns Concerto No. 3, which happened to be chosen as contest piece for that year. By that time Enesco had begun to build his own reputation as a composer, and an orchestral work, *Poème roumain*, was conducted by Colonne in 1898. In 1900 he appeared as soloist with Colonne's orchestra; that same year, Thibaud gave the premiere of Enesco's Second Violin Sonata, with the composer at the piano.

Soon Enesco became known as an unusual violinist, combining technical virtuosity with an intensely personal style, improvisational yet disciplined. Flesch remembered him as a "highly attractive combination of gypsy daredevilry and cultivated artistry, based on an extraordinary talent for the instrument."[5] Enesco was also unusual in refusing to shine only as a virtuoso: he gave sonata recitals, he founded a piano trio in 1902 and a string quartet in 1904, he gave all-Brahms programs of chamber music at a time when Brahms was not yet accepted in Paris. While living in Paris, Enesco kept in touch with his homeland; he was appointed court violinist of the queen of Rumania. In 1912 he established a prize for Rumanian composers.

By that time he was known all over Europe: he had made his debut in Berlin in 1902, in London in 1903, in Russia in 1910. That year he played a cycle of the ten Beethoven violin sonatas in Paris with Edouard Risler as partner. He spent the years of World War I in Rumania serving in a hospital; in 1915-16 he gave two cycles of eight concerts each in Bucharest under the title "History of the Violin."

Enesco's first visit to America took place in 1923—he appeared as violinist, composer, and conductor with the Philadelphia Orchestra. That year he also played in San Francisco and made an indelible impression on a seven-year-old prodigy, Yehudi Menuhin, who decided then and there that some day he would study with the great man. This is Menuhin's recollection of his first musical encounter with Enesco:

> He came to San Francisco . . . to conduct his own symphony and to play the Brahms Concerto, and before a note was sounded he had me in thrall. His countenance, his stance, his wonderful mane of black hair—everything about him proclaimed the free man, the man who is strong with the freedom of gypsies, of spontaneity, of creative genius, of fire. And the music he then began to play had an incandescence surpassing anything in my experience. In afteryears . . . I never had the least cause to qualify this first judgment—if judgment isn't too cold a word for my wholehearted response.[6]

Three years later, in 1926, young Yehudi—by then well on his way to world fame—came to Paris to study with Enesco, beginning a long and mutually rewarding relationship.

Enesco became a frequent visitor to the United States—in fact, he returned fourteen times between 1923 and 1946. Most successful were his three seasons (1937–39) as guest composer-conductor of the New York Philharmonic.

During World War II Enesco was again in Rumania. In 1941 he performed a cycle of all the Beethoven string quartets in Bucharest. When the war ended in 1945, he welcomed to Bucharest his eminent Soviet colleague David Oistrakh, who played the Tchaikovsky Violin Concerto under Enesco's baton. That year, Enesco also conducted the Rumanian premiere of Shostakovich's famed *Leningrad Symphony*. In 1946 he paid a return visit to the Soviet Union, playing Bach's Double Concerto with Oistrakh, conducting symphonies by Beethoven and Tchaikovsky, even performing as pianist in a Grieg sonata with Oistrakh. He was given an enthusiastic reception. But then he left for the West and declined all invitations from the Communist regime in Rumania to return. He preferred to end his days in near-poverty in Paris, having lost nearly everything through war and revolution.

Enesco's last visit to America came in 1949: he conducted in Washington, appeared as soloist in New York, and held a master course at the Mannes College. On January 21, 1950, he played a farewell concert in New York. Once again, and for the last time, the program was to show the range of his talents: he played Bach's Double Concerto with Menuhin, he partnered Menuhin at the piano in one of his violin sonatas, and he conducted his *Rumanian Rhapsody*.

The remaining years of his life were plagued by ill health. The once so erect and proud figure was bent and shrunken. He lived in Paris in one room, described by Menuhin: "Enesco lived rather like a monk. All he needed, and all he had was a narrow iron bedstead in a narrow white-washed room, a desk, pen and paper, and, as a luxury, a piano."[7] He continued to compose, though the world showed no interest in his creative output. In 1954 he agreed to teach a course at the Chigi Academy in Siena, but was so weak that he had to spend the day in bed in order to be able to appear at five in the afternoon. He looked exhausted and emaciated, and only his eyes reflected his indomitable spirit. But his memory was not affected: shortly before his death he could still play an entire act of *Götterdämmerung* at the piano without music. Yet the end was near: he became paralyzed on the left side and was virtually crippled. He died in Paris on May 4, 1955, at the age of seventy-four.

Enesco's art as a violinist was unorthodox, both in technique and interpretation, but it was imbued with that intangible ingredient of all truly great artists—magnetism, a quality not acquired or learned but innate. The noted critic Pincherle, himself a violinist, said:

> His technique . . . was absolutely original. Scorning academic principle, he held his right arm away from the body, the elbow raised, the wrist overhanging the violin; and he used a loosely strung bow from which he nevertheless obtained a tone that carried to the farthest reaches of the hall. The strength of the fingers of his left hand was such that in the bravura passages one heard the percussion of each note; he had a dry, almost electric trill. No other tone resembled his—warm, expressive, with sometimes a slight hoarseness in the background, something sad and singularly moving.[8]

While he may have "hammered" his fingers in virtuoso passages, he put them down rather flat in expressive cantilena, according to Flesch— "His fingers touched the strings at an acute angle which resulted in a kind of smooth, velvety tone without any admixture of metallic color."[9] Enesco's tone quality and trill are described by Menuhin:

> He had the most expressively varied vibrato and the most wonderful trills of any violinist I have ever known. Depending on the speed and lightness of a trill, his trilling finger struck the fingerboard higher than the actual note, thus keeping in tune although the light, fast motion of the finger did not push the string to its full depth on the fingerboard.[10]

One of Enesco's expressive devices was to start a sustained note a shade flat and to pull the pitch up by the vibrating finger; it produced, as Flesch observed, a "strange, ambiguous, somewhat lascivious tinge."

(A similar technique was used, as we have seen, by Thibaud; they may have copied it from each other during their student years, though it is essentially a gypsy device; since Enesco's first teacher was a gypsy fiddler, we may seek its origin there.) Flesch noted that Enesco was also inclined to use "over-refined, almost inaudible pianissimos" to create a mystical impression.

Enesco put all of his technical equipment at the service of musical aims—his goals were eloquence and communication, not brilliance and perfection. There was, in Pincherle's words, "a melange . . . of intellectuality and sensual emotion, with a noble amplitude, and especially with that musical eloquence . . . which gives to each melodic line a sense and a form and transforms passages into living phrases. . . ."[11] Flesch, however, had certain reservations; he observed in Enesco's personality a strange cleavage, alternating

> between a capricious and shallow virtuoso attitude on the one hand and a deliberately dry and scholastic pseudo-classicism on the other. In those days he was unable to weld together the individual elements of his artistic character. Personally, too, he was often very difficult to understand. It was as though an inner rift prevented the full development of his capacities.[12]

But when Flesch heard Enesco again in 1935, he was "enchanted from beginning to end," and his playing struck him as "far more mature, balanced, and perfect technically than before."

Above all, it is young Menuhin who experienced intuitively the full impact of Enesco's personality—

> the profundity, the sensitivity, the richness of his musicianship. . . . It was the expressive side of his temperament which most fired me, to the neglect of his discipline. . . . He carried me on the wave of his conception of music. . . . Everything I do carries his imprint yet.[13]

This hints at Enesco's impact as a teacher. Actually he gave no private lessons (Menuhin was the only one so privileged), and his teaching was done in public master classes. Even here he seems to have aimed above the heads of many of his students, as one participant, the French violinist Dany Brunschwig, described: "Often it was difficult for us to follow Enesco's thoughts which he expressed so beautifully and eloquently, because we were, after all, only violinists—and exclusively violinists."[14]

Menuhin put it succinctly: "As a teacher, he had great insight, the sure touch, and at the same time an extraordinary humility." Elsewhere Menuhin described the teaching sessions in greater detail:

> A lesson was an inspiration, not a stage reached in the course of instruction. It was the making of music. . . . He accompanied me at the piano. . . . There were few interruptions. Sometimes he took up his own violin to illustrate a point of, say, vibrato or glissando; very, very rarely would he give me a dissertation on violin theory. . . . What I received from him . . . was the note transformed into vital message, the phrase given shape and meaning, the structure of music made vivid.[15]

In the case of Enesco and Menuhin, there was obviously a mysterious rapport, an affinity of sense and sensibility, that brought Menuhin's talent to the fullest fruition. Enesco's method (if, in fact, there was any) was not geared to instruct mediocrities, but it could inspire artists—or better, it could awaken the latent artist in a gifted student. His method was a kind of musical coaching, which he did while accompanying at the piano. In principle, Flesch, the ever methodical teacher, called such a procedure "not only useless but even harmful," because "it endangers the independence and inviolability of the student's personality by forcing a way of feeling upon him that is foreign to his nature."

I remember vividly one of Enesco's violin recitals in Paris around 1926. On the program was Bach's Solo Sonata in G minor, played in a manner quite different from the German tradition. I was overwhelmed by what seemed to me a novel approach—free, rhapsodic, almost improvisational, yet disciplined and intensely musical. The tone was unforgettable—intense without cloying, using a vibrato that seemed ideal for Bach because it narrowly centered on the note, thus providing perfect pitch, purity, and warmth.

Strange as it may seem, Casals found Enesco's Bach concept "not fully alive," meaning too constricted. Enesco answered that "in Bach's time one did not do that sort of thing." Casals elaborated his point of view:

> In spite of the admiration I have for this very great artist [Enesco] . . . I was sorry to find him tied up with this idea, which I consider as a traditionalist prejudice. In Bach's time people did not use *spiccato* bowing of course; but why not use it now if the music demands it? To my mind no expressive accent in music should be excluded.[16]

Even so, Enesco himself was opposed to an academic approach to Bach; he warned against the theories of the "old bow" and maintained that Bach could, and should, be played with the present equipment.

Aside from the reservations mentioned, Casals thought of Enesco as "a great interpreter for whom my admiration was limitless." He also considered him "one of the most important composers of our generation" and backed this conviction by playing the premiere of Enesco's Cello Sonata in 1907.

Concerning Enesco's choice of fingerings, the Rumanian Manoliu writes, "Enesco liquidated the traditional positions, and by using extensions* as much as possible, he avoids the unnecessary 'glissando' shifts." [17]

As for his bowing, Enesco avoided long legato bowings with many notes on one bow and preferred to subdivide the phrases into smaller units, changing the bow more often and making certain notes more expressive. "This simple procedure, seemingly harmless, gave the bow new breadth and vitalized the phrase with new life," observed Manoliu.†

Oistrakh, too, remarked on the exceptional articulation of Enesco's bowing, which lent each note, or each group of notes, a declamatory, speechlike expressivity. Oistrakh discovered the same quality in Menuhin's playing as well.

With all his lofty ideas about music, Enesco never lost himself in pure speculation. As Menuhin points out,

> At home in all schools, Enesco was sensitive to the need of an appropriate style for each composition. He rarely indulged in theorizing about music, directing my attention instead to the passage or phrase at hand. He invariably found the right word, image, or symbol to help me understand. . . . No matter how rarefied the music he played, it became in his hands earthy, full of vitality and vigor.[18]

Enesco's repertoire was extremely varied, though he avoided the virtuoso literature. He was, according to Pincherle, authoritative in Bach and Beethoven. He also had a deep affinity for Schumann, Brahms, and Fauré, whose late Second Violin Sonata with its "interior drama he

---

* The "extension" fingering was used by Casals for the cello; many modern violinists prefer it to avoid audible shifts.
† Nathan Milstein has adopted similar principles of bowing.

Jacques Thibaud

Above left, for almost a half century, Jacques Thibaud was the model French violinist.

Above right, Georges Enesco, Rumania's greatest violinist and composer (also the teacher of Menuhin), an inspired musician and conductor.

Below, Lucian Capet, *left*, whose Capet Quartet was the foremost French string quartet during the first decades of this century.

alone seemed to be able to penetrate."[19] Mozart, however, "suited him less well" because the needed "transparency of style was not Enesco's forte." Nevertheless, thanks to Enesco's initiative, a newly discovered Mozart Concerto—No. 7 in D major*—received a number of performances. By now, Mozart experts have legitimate doubts about the work, but Enesco was convinced of its quality, provided it with cadenzas, and performed it in various cities. When he first presented it in Russia in 1909, the critics commented that his "lovely, tender, insinuating tone" responded beautifully to the character of the new Mozart concerto.

Also in Enesco's repertoire was Ravel's *Tzigane*, composed for the Hungarian-born violinist Jelly d'Arányi. This Gypsy-style rhapsody, which Flesch heard him play in a "supreme performance," suited Enesco's temperament exactly.

Ravel and Enesco were lifelong friends and fellow composition students at the Conservatoire. In 1897 Ravel completed a sonata in one movement for violin and piano, which he played at the Conservatoire with Enesco. However, Ravel decided against publishing it, and it remained forgotten until 1975.† There is no connection between this early work and Ravel's well-known Violin Sonata in F, first performed by Enesco and the composer in Paris in 1927. Menuhin tells a revealing story about the F-major Sonata. During a lesson Ravel suddenly burst into Enesco's studio with the newly completed manuscript. They had to play it the same day for the publisher Durand. Enesco sightread the difficult piece, with Ravel at the piano, and after a second run-through he "laid the manuscript to one side and played the entire work from memory."

Yehudi Menuhin has left a fitting tribute to Enesco, reflecting a depth of gratitude and adulation rarely encountered:

> The radiance he emanated, his deep humanity, integrity, and tolerance—it all came out in the music he made, and in his teaching. I loved to watch his face, the most beautiful and expressive I have ever known, reflecting the mood of the music we were playing, quietly lyrical or alive with ecstasy and suffering, and always retaining its characteristic gentle manliness. . . . Enesco will always remain the Absolute by which I judge others.[20]

---

* Köechel No. 271i. It was published in 1907, after a copy that seems to have been "modernized" in the solo part, possibly by Baillot's son-in-law Sauzay, c. 1840.
† It was rediscovered by the young American Ravel scholar Arbie Orenstein—an attractive youthful composition without marked originality.

Lucien Capet

Just as the suave Thibaud appears to be the archetype of a French violinist, so the severe Capet strikes us as rather atypically French. But this is a rash judgment, for Capet merely represents the reverse image of the French heritage—logic, reflection, rational thought, Cartesian philosophy. Capet was methodical and painstaking in his attention to detail; he left nothing to chance. But he also had a streak of mysticism and saw himself as the apostle of Beethoven. Once before a concert, the easygoing Thibaud sauntered into the artist room to greet his old colleague, but Capet stopped him in his tracks: "Don't bother me now, I am in communion with the spirit of Beethoven!"[1]

Capet had a miserable childhood. Born into a Parisian working-class family in 1873, he had no encouragement for his musical aspirations. His parents merely exploited his ability to play the violin, and he was forced from childhood to work at menial jobs, playing in cabarets, theaters, cafés, even in the streets. Nevertheless, at the age of fifteen he succeeded in entering the Conservatoire. By instinct or design, he became a student of J. P. Maurin, the cofounder of the Society for the Last Quartets of Beethoven. Maurin and his string quartet contributed significantly to the growing understanding in Paris of Beethoven's late works. Richard Wagner, a severe critic, heard the Maurin Quartet in 1861 in Paris and described the performance as "most perfect." Undoubtedly, Maurin nurtured Capet's incipient interest in quartet playing; eventually, the Capet Quartet became France's leading string quartet, famed throughout Europe.

At the Conservatoire, Capet progressed slowly but steadily, winning four prizes as he ascended the academic ladder. Finally, in 1893, he was awarded the coveted first prize. (This was the year when Flesch had to be satisfied with a second prize.) In the meantime, Capet had joined the Lamoureux Orchestra and was elected concertmaster in 1896. As soon as he graduated from the Conservatoire, he formed his own string quartet, which was active until 1899. That year he accepted a professorship at the Conservatoire in Bordeaux, mainly to have more time, away from the pressures of Paris, to perfect his playing. For the next three years, he practiced eight hours a day, in addition to his teaching duties. He was meticulous and patient; he once told me that he spent three years on the preparation of the Beethoven concerto, and seven years on the Brahms concerto before playing them in public.

Capet's return to Paris, in 1902, was a great success; he was also well received in Berlin, Joachim's domain. A meeting between Joachim and the much younger Capet was not an unqualified success, however, since Joachim sought in vain certain French qualities in Capet's playing, while Capet tried (equally in vain) to impress Joachim with his classically oriented musicality. As Flesch relates,

> Capet was hypnotically influenced by the old Joachim; as a thirty-year-old man, he played the wise and dignified patriarch, wore square boots, polished his spectacles ceremoniously, and stuck his beard into his vest opening before he began to play.[2]

When I met Capet in 1926, he was clean-shaven, having abandoned his biblical beard after an incident on the stage: it seems that his beard had become inextricably entangled in the E-tuner of his violin, and the more he turned the screw, the more firmly the violin became attached to his beard, to the public's understandable amusement.

Moser—Joachim's alter ego—was somewhat critical of Capet's musicianship: "Unfortunately, nature has not endowed Capet with the ability to read between the lines in classical music, and so his interpretations lack on the whole the *brio*, despite the most conscientious execution of all details."[3] Flesch believed that Capet wanted it that way: "His dry style was deliberate—it conformed to the Romance concept of German classicism."[4]

But no such criticism was heard in Paris, where the Capet Quartet was to set standards of excellence valid for an entire generation. Capet assembled his second quartet in 1903 and made a debut a year later with a complete Beethoven cycle in Paris. This cycle became a tradition, attended religiously each year by a devoted public as faithful as the devotees of the Joachim Quartet in Berlin. The Capet Quartet toured the French provinces and traveled to Italy, Germany, and England with ever-growing success. In 1907, Capet—still relatively young—was entrusted with a chamber-music class at the Conservatoire. In 1910 he reorganized his quartet and rehearsed for a year to achieve a minute coordination of playing technique, a total homogeneity of bowing method and tone production according to his particular views. The following year, the Capet Quartet represented France at the Beethoven Festival in Bonn, earning tremendous acclaim. In 1912, the Quartet traveled to Russia with the composer Gabriel Fauré as pianist, specializing in all-French programs (Franck, Debussy, the Fauré Piano Quartet).

After a temporary suspension during World War I, Capet resumed his quartet concerts and taught extensively during the 1920s. He died quite unexpectedly in 1928, after only one day of an illness which no one considered serious. With him died the idealism of the old school.

I came to know Capet in 1926. I heard his Quartet in an all-French program and found the execution, the ensemble technique, and the almost religious devotion of the players overwhelming. The strongest impression of the program was the Franck String Quartet, which was filled with organlike richness and mystic passion.

Wishing to study with Capet, I requested an audition. He listened to my rendition of the Bach Chaconne in silence, without interrupting me, and at the end looked at me as if lost in thought. Finally he raised both hands and outlining an immense square in the air he said gravely, "Il faut jouer comme ça, mon petit gars!" (That's the way one must play it, my young fellow). The gesture was meant to convey the monumentality of the work—a lesson I never forgot.

In order to qualify as a student, one had to acquire a preliminary knowledge of his peculiar method of bowing. I bought his big volume, La technique supérieure de l'archet and started to absorb the theoretical part as well as the minute practical exercises. It was Capet's credo that the technique of the left hand was "impregnated with a certain sterility," while the command of the bow was bound to reveal the most subtle and profound elements of an artistic interpretation. In other words, the left hand was the "body," the bow the "soul" of violin art. With this in mind, he devoted a lifetime to the mastery of bow technique.

From his teacher Maurin, Capet had learned a peculiar method of holding and manipulating the bow: the bow stick was held between thumb and middle finger which formed, as it were, a ring or a central axis. Each of the other fingers had a definite role; in fact, an important part of the Capet method was the highly developed sensitivity of the right-hand fingers, those that hold the bow. The player had to be able to roll and twist the bow stick between thumb and third finger while sustaining a long note; in this way, Capet believed, the hair of the bow would penetrate more deeply into the string. This rolling of the bow could produce a kind of "bow vibrato," a coloring of the tone without any left-hand vibrato. The timbre produced was eerie and not to everyone's liking. Young Menuhin—when he was ten—had the following impression,

When I was first in Paris, in 1926–27, I attended a concert by the Capet Quartet, whose devotion to correctness led them to play without vibrato. . . . So intolerable did my ears find it in performance that I left the hall. (I have regretted my flight ever since; the Capet Quartet were superb musicians from whom I could have learned much.)[5]

Such stretches of *senza vibrato* playing were actually rare; and I did hear the Capet Quartet give "vibrant" performances of the Romantic repertoire.

Capet insisted on the strictest observation of the subdivisions of the bow; for practice purposes, he divided the bow into halves, quarters, eighths, and thirds, and every bow stroke had to be mastered in every part of the bow. He himself practiced with infinite patience and achieved the most fantastic bow control imaginable, but it did not come easily. I heard the following anecdote:

One morning, an unannounced visitor arrived at Capet's home and was told that the *Maître* was not available. For an hour the visitor sat patiently in the anteroom, listening to endless, nerve-racking bow exercises behind closed doors. At last, Capet emerged, and the visitor greeted him with relief. "Poor *Maître*, why must you waste your time on such an untalented student!" "You are mistaken, *cher ami*," replied Capet, "you just heard me play my morning exercises."

Capet had a strong preference for the hammered *martelé* stroke, which sounded neat and precise. The same tidiness extended to his bouncing bows, which had to be studied with a clear-cut attack on each note. He had an infinite variety of staccato bowings at his disposal. But all this mastery was put into the service of Art—"a vast and noble battle of the Spirit over Matter"—so that we may "place all the technical elements into the service of the Ideal."[6]

With Capet died one of the last visionaries to whom Art and the communion with great music was a religion. Through him—so he believed—the message of Beethoven was conveyed.

The secret of the Capet Quartet was that each member had fully absorbed Capet's technical and musical approach. Their unanimity of technique, sound, and musical concept was unsurpassed. They spoke through one voice—that of Capet. As soon as he died, the Quartet fell apart, though the second violinist, the excellent Maurice Hewitt, tried to keep the tradition alive.

Capet's method was perpetuated not only through his book on bow technique, but also through various music publications which he edited with meticulous care. Even those who are not convinced of Capet's infallibility can learn much from his approach to bowing problems. He restored the classical belief in the preeminence of the bow as the ultimate tool of expressivity on the violin. Ideally, *both* hands of a violinist should contribute in equal measure to produce a maximum of expression. The left hand controls the timbre of the tone through vibrato; the right hand is responsible for dynamics, for accentuation and phrasing. Capet's expressive language was bow-oriented, similar to the art of Joachim, whom he so admired. At the time, he ran counter to a trend which favored left-hand virtuosity.

Capet's battle on behalf of the bow was not wasted. True, those of his students who copied him blindly achieved little. But those who gleaned from his teaching the most valuable, enduring elements profited greatly. Many of Capet's principles are in fact applicable to any school of bowing, whether French, German, or Russian. This is most evident in the case of Ivan Galamian—the most successful violin teacher of our time—who studied with Capet during the 1920s. Galamian was a finished artist when he joined Capet, and for this reason he was able to learn from him selectively without abandoning his Russian heritage. There are shades of Capet traceable in every one of Galamian's eminent students.* Thus the name of Lucien Capet endures with respect and admiration.

* In his own book, *Principles of Violin Playing and Teaching* (Englewood Cliffs, N.J., 1962), Galamian recommends some of Capet's special bow exercises.

THE NEW FRENCH SCHOOL

AFTER THE First World War, French violin playing declined from its once-dominant international position. Gradually, Paris lost its attraction as the mecca of violinists. After Ysaÿe left the concert stage, Thibaud alone remained to uphold the French fame, though he was past his prime. Among the new crop of violinists, there were only a few who came from Paris—Francescatti, Neveu, Grumiaux, Ferras—fine players all, but not destined for the summit of stardom. The fact is that the French style of violin playing, with its elegance, refinement, and charm, was being displaced in public favor by the Russian style, stressing sweep, brilliance, and sensuality. Heifetz became king, and every newcomer was measured by his towering standards. Milstein fitted into this framework, and later Oistrakh. The first Ysaÿe competition of 1937 was swept by Soviet violinists. At the same time, a powerful American school made its impact before World War II—Menuhin, Ricci, and Stern. In terms of violin instruction, New York and Philadelphia, Moscow and Leningrad became the centers of gravity. By mid-century, the Paris Conservatoire was but a faded memory.

Zino Francescatti

Zino Francescatti was born in 1902 in Marseilles. His name reveals Italian ancestry, but his musical education was entirely French. His parents, both professional musicians, taught Zino the violin in early childhood, and he became a prodigy at the age of ten. In 1924 he settled in

Paris and attracted the attention of Thibaud, who furthered his career. As so often in France (as elsewhere), a native artist needs to be recognized abroad before he is taken seriously at home. While Paris greeted Zino's debut at the venerable Conservatoire concerts with restrained approval, he had his first resounding success abroad, in Vienna. For a time he had to earn a living as orchestral musician in Paris. In 1926 he accompanied Ravel to England, where he played the composer's *Tzigane* and *Berceuse*. In the 1930s his career expanded to the Americas: Buenos Aires acclaimed him in 1938, New York in 1939. That year he settled in New York, and also bought a house near Tanglewood, which he named "Fiddletop."

Francescatti does not like to travel and prefers a quieter career, accepting engagements that can be met without resorting to airplanes. His favorite partner at the piano was the late Robert Casadesus; their interpretation of the French sonata repertoire—Franck, Fauré, Debussy, Ravel—had the stamp of authenticity. They played with refined musicianship, graceful limpidity, and innate affinity for the peculiar Gallic style. However, these qualities transferred to the Beethoven sonatas also resulted in remarkably balanced performances. In fact, Francescatti's interpretations of the concertos of Mozart, Beethoven, and Brahms are particularly attractive, because they eschew all Germanic ponderousness and add a "Latin" ingredient of resilient rhythm and ingratiating cantilena, an absence of all affectation, and impeccable taste. His recording of the Brahms concerto with Leonard Bernstein may lack the ultimate incisiveness, but it is more than made up by noble grandeur and lyricism.

In a class by themselves were Francescatti's performances of concerto pieces by Lalo, Saint-Saëns, and Ravel, and the virtuoso repertoires of Paganini and Kreisler. Francescatti's aim was not to overimpress with flashiness, but to charm with exquisite precision. His early recording of the *complete* Concerto in D by Paganini was a model of perfection; it was done at a time when violinists preferred to limit themselves to the first movement in the Wilhelmj arrangement. As for Kreisler, he was Francescatti's constant idol, and every one of the Kreisler pieces sparkled with new life when played the French way.

Just as Francescatti's technique was finely honed, so his tone was fine-spun and slender. Later in his career, he began to apply more pressure and produced a richer, fuller tone without loss in timbre or quality. This may have been related to a change in violin: in 1942 he acquired the "Hart" Stradivarius, built in 1727. Perhaps he felt the need to pro-

Before his retirement
some ten years ago,
Zino Francescatti
was considered an
admirable exponent
of the French style.

TWO PHOTOS: MUSICAL AMERICA

The Belgian master
Arthur Grumiaux,
who lives and teaches
in Brussels,
continues the great
Belgian tradition
of violin playing.

Ginette Neveu,
the prize-winning
French violinist
who perished
in an airplane crash
on the eve of
a brilliant career.

duce a bigger sound in the large concert halls of America and to compete successfully with the overrich accompaniments provided by American orchestras. (In Europe, orchestras are usually reduced for concerto accompaniments.)

Francescatti represents civilized musical culture at its best. His playing has no mannerisms, eccentricities, or heaven-storming flights. Everything flows in a seemingly uninhibited yet controlled manner. There is warmth and sentiment without emotionalism, a cultured expressivity that shuns ostentatiousness.

Arthur Grumiaux

Many of the same qualities that distinguish Francescatti are also evident in Arthur Grumiaux. Good taste, valued by the French school above all, abounds in his playing, in addition to an incredibly polished technique and a beautiful sound. His versatility is proven in performances of Mozart and Paganini, which are among his best. His Mozart is in the best French tradition, with lean sweetness of tone and fine-grained articulation. His recording of the rediscovered Paganini Fourth Concerto is admirable in its technical accuracy. But Grumiaux is also an excellent chamber-music player, particularly in string trio repertory.

Born in 1921 near Charleroi, Belgium, he represents the proud lineage of the Belgian school leading from Bériot and Vieuxtemps to Ysaÿe. He came from a musical family and his violin instruction began at the age of five. From the Conservatoire of Charleroi the twelve-year-old Arthur transferred to the Conservatoire in Brussels. After two years in the class of Alfred Dubois he won the first prize. Further prizes included the Prix Vieuxtemps and the Prix de Virtuosité. In the late 1930s he went to Paris for a brief period of study with Enesco. His debut with the Brussels Philharmonic took place just before the outbreak of World War II, which interrupted his career. In 1945 he made his first appearance in London with the BBC Orchestra, and in 1953 he introduced himself to New York with the Philharmonic Orchestra. While continuing his concert career, he accepted a professorship at the Brussels Conservatoire in 1949, succeeding his teacher Dubois.

Grumiaux does not wish to become an eternal traveler and deliberately limits his concert tours. Nevertheless, it is hard to understand why he is so undervalued among great violinists. He has virtually disappeared from the American scene and is remembered mainly through his highly polished recordings. Outstanding are his Bach cycle of the six solo sonatas and partitas and his Beethoven cycle of the ten sonatas with the late pianist Clara Haskil, a finely balanced collaboration; he re-recorded them with Claudio Arrau.

Over the years, Grumiaux's playing underwent a marked development. He began as an intellectually cool player, with a tone of limited volume and restrained vibrato. As he grew in years and maturity, his interpretations acquired more sensuous warmth and fire without losing any of the former noble qualities. Perhaps it is the nobility and uncompromising musicianship that keeps Grumiaux's career within certain limits, as if marked "for connoisseurs only."

Ginette Neveu

Ginette Neveu's death at the age of thirty, in an airplane crash en route to the United States, was a tragic loss. She was on her way to becoming the most widely acclaimed woman violinist of her day. Born in 1919 in Paris, she started the violin at the age of five, and for the next twenty-five years pursued her goal of mastering the instrument with unflagging determination. No one who saw or heard her could forget that impression—the serious concentration, the complete immersion in her task, the burning yet controlled intensity. To speak of technique is pointless because it never served for display—it was always subordinate to a musical goal. Her trademark was the brooding Sibelius concerto, though she realized that no one in her native country cared for that Nordic genius. "In France, they don't know Sibelius, and they don't want to know him," she once said in mock despair.

After starting violin lessons at the age of five with her mother, Ginette played the Mendelssohn concerto with the Colonne Orchestra when she was seven. In 1929 she entered the Paris Conservatoire (class of Jules Boucherit) and won a first prize nine months later, at the age of eleven, an accomplishment reminiscent of young Wieniawski and Kreisler. Yet, nothing happened in terms of a career. Winning a fourth prize in a competition in Vienna, she so impressed Carl Flesch, who was on the jury, that he offered her a full scholarship in Berlin. For four years she remained with Flesch, who was just the right teacher for her—methodical, analytical, intellectual. Many things that she had done instinctively now became part of her conscious technical equipment; in fact, she overdid the analytical approach for a time. Flesch made it financially possible for Ginette to attend the 1935 Wieniawski competition in Warsaw. And the incredible happened: the fifteen-year-old girl emerged the winner, twenty-six points ahead of her nearest competitor, who was none other than David Oistrakh. (He was eleven years older and already a well-known virtuoso.) Altogether she placed at the head of 180 contestants. The victory was all the more remarkable, since the required pieces by Wieniawski were not her strong side. But there was also a Bach solo sonata and her free choice, Ravel's *Tzigane*. It was clearly a triumph. Only at this point did official France become aware of her as a national asset, as an *ambassadrice* of French music who deserved wholehearted support.

However, her 1937 recital debut in New York was disappointing: though she was recognized as "one of the most interesting new violinists of the younger generation,"[1] the critics found a "lack of power" in her rendition of the Strauss sonata and the Bach Chaconne.

In contrast, the audiences of Europe (including Soviet Russia) were enchanted by her classical concept of violin playing. The British critic Ferruccio Bonavia, himself a violinist and once a Joachim student, attributed her sensational success to her reversion to an older style which suddenly appeared as a *novelty*: she "vindicated theories to which all the great players of the last generation—Joachim, Sarasate, Ysaÿe— would have subscribed." Bonavia explained,

> It is a lamentable but undeniable fact that the raising of the average technical standards has been accomplished by a curious reduction in other values. . . . Tone especially, in other days so true an index of character, has lost both power and variety since it came to be an accepted rule that vibrato is more important than bowing in the production of a warm, pleasing sound. No doubt the new system led to easy successes, but now Mlle Neveu has won greater success by ignoring them.[2]

Her success in London in 1946 was immense and she filled Albert Hall. The following year she visited the Americas; her Brahms concerto performances in Boston and New York were sensational. She returned the next year and was booked for an extensive tour in 1949, when the tragedy occurred (on October 28, 1949). A week before leaving Paris, she had given a farewell recital at the Salle Pleyel with her brother Jean at the piano; they died together.

On stage, Ginette Neveu was an impressive figure. Slim, dark-haired, and dark-eyed, she had the stance and the temperament of a conqueror. To her, music was not a profession, but a mission. She was extremely self-critical and made demands upon herself that were almost unreasonable. She was in constant search of improvement; every fine performance was but another step toward the unattainable goal of total perfection. It has been said that her style was overly assertive and lacked femininity, but such arguments make no musical sense; good music making has no gender. It is true that she excelled in works of a "virile" character—the Bach Chaconne, the Brahms concerto, for example. To these works she brought a depth of understanding, a new dimension which combined both "masculine" and "feminine" elements to perfection.

Among the few recordings she made during her brief career are the concertos of Brahms and Sibelius, the sonatas by Richard Strauss and Debussy, and the two Ravel pieces—*Habanera* and *Tzigane*—posthumously awarded a Grand Prix du Disque in 1950.

When the shocking news of her death became known, many great musicians expressed their grief. Thibaud called her "the priestess" of music. Casals wrote,

> For me her playing has always been one of the greatest revelations of the instruments and of music. To the impression of perfection, balance, and artistic taste, she added in her interpretation, fire and abandon which filled her playing with richness.[3]

To which Ormandy added, "The greatest woman violinist—and I'll go so far as to say, one of the greatest interpreters on the violin of our time."

One is reminded of Grillparzer's words at the grave of Schubert, who died at the same age as Ginette Neveu: "The art of music here entombed a rich possession, but even far fairer hopes."

THE HUNGARIAN SCHOOL

THE ART OF violin playing has century-old roots in Hungary, which, after all, is the country of gypsy fiddlers. Surprising, therefore, is the assessment of Flesch, himself a native Hungarian: "Only since Hubay's appointment to the Budapest Academy can one speak of a specifically Hungarian school."[1] Hubay held this post for half a century, beginning in 1886; among his students were Vecsey, Szigeti, Telmányi, Stefi Geyer, Zoltán Székely, Jelly d'Arányi, Oedoen Partos, Erna Rubinstein, Sándor Végh, Eugene Ormandy, and Bram Eldering. This partial list demonstrates the extent and versatility of Hubay's teaching; himself a versatile musician, he guided soloists, quartet players, teachers, conductors, and composers.

Jenö Hubay

Hubay was born in Budapest in 1858, son of the violinist and conductor Karl Huber. After a thorough preparation by his father, Jenö was sent to Berlin to study with Joachim, and remained there from 1873 to 1876. Franz Liszt recommended him to the conductor Pasdeloup in Paris. After a successful debut in 1878, Hubay stayed in Paris and formed a close friendship with the ailing Vieuxtemps. Hubay accepted Vieuxtemps's invitation to join him in Algiers in April 1881 and had "the signal honor of having received the last lessons of the master."[1] At Vieuxtemps's death in June of that year, Hubay was put in charge of the remaining manuscripts, which included two completed violin concertos in piano score. He prepared them for posthumous publication and referred to Vieuxtemps as "my adored master and benefactor."

Vieuxtemps's decisive influence on Hubay is very significant: it brought a French orientation to his playing—elegance, brilliance, warmth of tone—which overshadowed his earlier German training. It is this cross-fertilization between the approaches of Joachim and Vieuxtemps which lent Hubay and the Hungarian school a specific coloration. Still, Hubay retained much affection and admiration for his old master Joachim.

In 1882, shortly after Vieuxtemps's death, Hubay was appointed violin professor at the Brussels Conservatory, which he left, in 1886, for a similar post at the Academy in his native Budapest. The success of his Hungarian violin class was legendary, as can be gathered from the names of his prominent students. Aside from teaching, Hubay was a prolific composer of violin concertos, symphonies, operas, and short pieces in Hungarian style. He also led a successful string quartet with the famous David Popper as cellist. In 1908 Hubay appeared in London with his favorite pupil, the gifted young Vecsey, under Sir Henry Wood:

> A concert which gave me extreme pleasure . . . Franz von Vecsey played a beautiful concerto by Jenö Hubay [Concerto No. 3 dedicated to Vecsey]. Hubay's success as a violinist lay less in his solo playing than in his quartet leadership; at least that was Brahms's opinion. He thought most highly of Hubay's power as a chamber music artist. In addition he was a very great teacher, Vecsey being one of his pupils. Thus it was particularly interesting to me to hear both master and pupil in the Double Concerto of Bach which they played to perfection.[2]

In 1919 Hubay was promoted to director of the Academy and served until 1934. His musical conservatism led to considerable tension with progressive faculty members, particularly Béla Bartók. Hubay died in 1937.

Szigeti remembers with affection the celebration in Budapest in honor of Hubay's fiftieth birthday. Among Hubay's compositions played on this occasion were his four violin concertos, each performed by one of his prominent students—Vecsey chose No. 3 in G minor, Stefi Geyer the Concerto all'antica; Szigeti the second in E major, while Hubay himself played his first, the Concerto romantique, "with youthful mettle."

Franz von Vecsey

Born in 1893 in Budapest, Vecsey received his first lessons from his father, a professional violinist. At the age of eight, he became Hubay's pupil; by the time he was ten he went on his first concert tour. In October 1903 he played in Berlin; Joachim heard him privately and became so fond of the gifted boy that he agreed to conduct the orchestra for Franz's performance of the Beethoven concerto in the autumn of 1904. Meanwhile, Joachim gave him some guidance, but no regular lessons. Yet he helped in every possible way, including a letter recommending him to Leopold Auer in St. Petersburg, which father Vecsey presented prior to Franz's Russian debut. Auer tried to be fair to the young visitor (though his class was full of prodigies) and discouraged any rivalry between Vecsey and his own student Mischa Elman. Soon Joachim had an opportunity to reciprocate, for Elman arrived in Berlin with a letter from Auer.* For a time, the careers of Vecsey and Elman ran parallel; they even joined to play duos in private. Vecsey's style was polished but pallid, while Elman played with verve and vitality. It may well be that Vecsey tried to imitate Elman's warmly vibrant tone, for he was warned by Joachim in 1904, "Get rid of the excessive vibrato and slow wobble with the fingers in cantilena; it is really caused by a weakness of the fingers and reminds me of a dirge of old women."[1]

After playing in London in 1904 and in New York in January 1905, young Vecsey returned to Russia; Elman was never far behind. While America did not receive Vecsey too hospitably, his success in Europe continued to be strong. He retained his old attachment to Hubay, especially valuing his guidance after Joachim's death in 1907; we have mentioned the joint performance in London of Hubay and the fifteen-year-old Vecsey in 1908.

An unusual tribute to Vecsey's precocious talent was the dedication by Sibelius of his new Violin Concerto. Originally intended for Willy Burmester, who withdrew prior to the premiere, the concerto was first performed by Karl Halir, concertmaster of the Berlin Philharmonic, under the baton of Richard Strauss in 1905. The critics were divided, and the famous violinists showed no eagerness to perform it. Joachim heard the concerto and called it *"scheusslich und langweilig"* (abominable and boring); Ysaÿe tried it out and put it aside; Auer was preoccupied with the new Glazunov concerto. At this point, Sibelius must

* See pp. 425–26.

have decided to dedicate his concerto to the prodigious young Vecsey, to whom the future seemed to belong. In 1910, the seventeen-year-old Vecsey was ready to perform it in public: he played it in Berlin and Vienna and remained its most brilliant early protagonist.

Vecsey's career was interrupted by the First World War, in which he served in the Austro-Hungarian armed forces. I remember his reappearance in the early 1920s in Berlin's Philharmonic Hall. The performance was sold out, the audience demonstrative and adoring. Vecsey, looking pale and aristocratic, played a comparatively short program with long intermissions. It was rumored that he still suffered from the aftermath of his war injuries; but nothing of this kind could be detected in his playing, which was utterly perfect and icy cold. He performed with classical purity and inner detachment, letting the music speak for itself, as it were, without interjecting his own personality. His technique was absolutely perfect and effortless. He used a very narrow vibrato, and that sparingly; the unadulterated silvery sound of his beautiful Stradivarius seemed to be drawn by a magic bow. He held his elbow rather low, in the old manner of Joachim. Though his musical taste was pure and noble, his interpretation lacked individuality, unless that seemingly "impersonal" touch was what he intended.

In Berlin, Vecsey's concerts always drew full houses, but his appearances became more and more rare. "It was not quite known how he spent his time," remarked Flesch. Vecsey did some composing, and a *Study in Thirds*, of tremendous difficulty, proved his continued mastery of the fingerboard. After years of absence and silence, his playing became a legend. He died comparatively young, at the age of forty-two, following an operation.

Flesch's evaluation of Vecsey as he played in 1910, at the age of seventeen, does not differ much from the impression I gained in the 1920s. Flesch observed,

> Purely as a violinist, Vecsey made a spotless impression: his tone production was brilliant, his movements were correct, and his technical ability altogether was of high order. But his playing did not seem to contain much: it was primitive and undistinguished musically. . . . His musical and ethical education was left to chance—to the vagaries of concert life. The outcome was an impoverishment of his personality which prevented his full artistic development.[2]

Above left, Franz von Vecsey, who died young, was one of the most accomplished Hungarian violinists. Sibelius dedicated his Violin Concerto to him.
Above right, a pioneer of modern music, the Hungarian master Joseph Szigeti was equally famous for his Bach and Beethoven interpretations.
Below, Joseph Szigeti and Béla Bartók concertized and recorded together. Bartók dedicated several of his works to Szigeti.

It is an ever-recurrent problem: the child prodigy growing up on the concert stage, without time or firm guidance to mature in a normal way. But again there are many who negotiated that difficult transition with success. Ultimately it depends on the inner resources of an individual talent. In Vecsey's case, there was, perhaps, not enough musical substance to fill that impeccable technical framework.

Joseph Szigeti

The careers of Vecsey and Szigeti bear comparison. Both were child prodigies and students of Hubay; both came to Berlin at an early age and played for Joachim. But though Vecsey remained under Joachim's guidance, Szigeti decided to chart his own course. While Vecsey began to reap success, Szigeti continued to work on his own development as a person and musician. In the 1920s, when Vecsey seemed "played out," Szigeti began his belated ascent to the top, purely on the strength of his musical personality.

Szigeti's rise to world fame was a victory of mind over matter. He made a career of a virtuoso without being one; his technique was reliable but labored, his tone expressive but not sensuous, his bowing energetic but angular under stress. What stamped Szigeti with greatness was his sterling musicianship, his searching depth of interpretation, his intensity and rhythmic vitality, his masterful grasp of form and structure. His playing had noble grandeur and convincing communicativeness: he carried a musical message. This sincerity served him in the classical repertoire, but even more so in contemporary music. Composers loved to dedicate their music to him because he had a unique affinity for the modern idiom. Certain works owe their present popularity to his championship, for example Prokofiev's Concerto No. 1, which Szigeti took under his wing after an indifferent premiere by another violinist.

An intellectual among violinists, Szigeti commanded respect. His playing and approach were always so interesting that he earned the admiration of critical colleagues like Ysaÿe and Kreisler. He was also the favorite of conductors: eschewing interpretative extravagances and undue liberties, he was "easy" to accompany; yet even an experienced conductor could still learn from him—there was always a new insight, an unexpected subtlety to enliven a well-known work.

Szigeti's repertoire was another source of interest and enjoyment; his programs were imaginative, unhackneyed, exploring new or neglected aspects of the violin literature. He liked cyclic series such as "Survey of Three Centuries of Violin Music," the Complete Violin Sonatas of Bach, Mozart, and Beethoven, or "Eleven Masterpieces of the Twentieth Century." He displayed much initiative on behalf of contemporary music and performed works by Bartók, Bloch, Milhaud, Roussel, Prokofiev, Ravel, Stravinsky, and Honegger; world premieres given by Szigeti included the violin concertos of Ernest Bloch (1938) and Frank Martin (1952). He also persuaded reluctant record companies to issue many of these works on discs. As a classical interpreter, Szigeti was justly famous for his towering performances of the solo sonatas of Bach and the violin concertos of Beethoven and Brahms.

Szigeti was born in 1892 in Budapest. His father and uncles were professional musicians. Showing talent as a boy, he was transferred from a private music school to Hubay's advanced class at the Academy. By 1905 young Szigeti had completed the violin course at the Academy and was forced by his father to embark on a "child prodigy" career. He remembered those years with pain and embarrassment: he was extremely shy and hated to be "exhibited" at various charity concerts, casinos, and summer resorts. In retrospect, Szigeti was very critical of his student years at the Budapest Academy. He considered the work in Hubay's class shallow and aimed at acquiring technical brilliance. The very young students (Szigeti among them) were exempt from all chamber-music classes: "the younger group was automatically set apart—even by our more mature fellow students—as . . . a genus vaguely freakish."[1] There prevailed, in Hubay's class, "an atmosphere of such puerile technical rivalry, we were so completely absorbed by the externals of our craft [i.e. technique]" that Szigeti shuddered at the mere memory of it. He blamed in part the unhealthy impatience of the parents who wanted their prodigies to be ready for a career as soon as possible.

When Szigeti, at age thirteen, set out to make his debut in Berlin, he admitted to "a lack of solid musical foundation." His limited repertoire consisted of the concertos by Ernst and Wieniawski (both show pieces) and those of Mendelssohn and Viotti; in addition he played the Bach Chaconne, Tartini's *Devil's Trill Sonata,* and a bevy of display pieces by Paganini, Sarasate, and his teacher Hubay. He was ignorant of the sonata repertory and of newer composers like Franck or Chausson. His Berlin debut did not create any sensation, though his program was ambitious. He picked up a few small engagements, even at a circus in Frankfurt, where he appeared under a pseudonym, competing with a trained-dog act for the public's attention. He seemed to be "the young boy who never smiled. . . . It was only when he played that his face lit up."

While in Berlin, Szigeti played for Joachim, but did not accept the invitation to join the master's class.* Was it a missed opportunity? In retrospect, Szigeti did not think so; he always preferred to search for himself. Perhaps he felt instinctively that the aging Joachim was not going to unlock new horizons for him. On the other hand, young Szigeti became painfully aware of his own "provincialism" when he first heard such violinists as Ysaÿe, Kreisler, and the boy Elman. It was a kind of playing he had neither heard nor imagined—virtually a new era in violin playing, a new vibrant tone quality, a new style of "fire, elegance, and rhythmic incisiveness." Suddenly much of what he had learned and heard in Budapest was outdated, many of the violinists he had once admired seemed oldfashioned. Young Szigeti began to rethink and retool his own playing.

But Szigeti, despite his sudden awareness of the "new" style of violin playing, never quite succeeded in acquiring it. His fundamental training had been too oldfashioned; he retained through life the outmoded low bow arm clinging to his body, the bow pressed too close to the bridge, the vibrato which was pleasing but not memorable. All this, however, was counterbalanced by his musical insight.

In the meantime, Szigeti, always under his father's tutelage, crossed the Channel for a debut in London in 1907. He played the concertos of Mendelssohn and Ernst with a small orchestra, followed by virtuoso pieces with piano. It was a moderate success which led to various small engagements in the provinces. For a time he lived in Surrey and found time to make up for his sketchy education through assiduous reading. The boy—who had been forced to shave his legs in order to perform as a prodigy in short pants—grew into a cultured young man. Much later, Szigeti wrote perceptively about the "reluctance to grow up that seems to be inbred in prematurely exhibited virtuosi . . . a vicious circle." His contact with musicians like Busoni, Hamilton Harty, and Myra Hess helped this growth. "What worlds Busoni opened up for me," he remembered. They went together on concert tours in England, and the daily contact with a man so profoundly cultured influenced young Szigeti immensely. He restudied the Bach Chaconne with Busoni, who played it in his own piano transcription.

Little by little, Szigeti freed himself from the "fossilized repertoire" of his prodigy years. One of his rediscoveries was Busoni's neglected Vio-

* See p. 270.

lin Concerto. He added works by Harty, Dohnányi, and Szymanowski to his repertoire, charting his future course as a champion of modern violin music.

In 1913 Szigeti's health forced him to live in Switzerland. During the First World War, he had to limit his concerts to Germany and Austro-Hungary. In 1917 he accepted a professorship in Geneva and remained there until his career suddenly exploded in 1925, the year of his triumphant debut in Philadelphia under Stokowski. He became a regular visitor to the United States.

By designing serious programs, Szigeti raised the concert standards in America's heartland, but he also met with some resistance among small-town concert managers. One such letter of complaint read, "Your *Krewtser* sonata bores the pants off my audiences!" But Szigeti stuck to his guns: he insisted on mixing serious classical music with contemporary works. Only rarely did he play virtuoso pieces, choosing some by his old master Hubay—the *Zephyr* and the czardas *Hejre Kati*.

Some of Szigeti's concepts of programming, freely accepted today, seemed daring and even revolutionary in the 1920s and 1930s. He broke the conventional mold of the recital program by the inclusion of chamber music, by uncompromisingly serious choices of the classical repertoire, by the participation of composers in their own works, in fact, by the whole idea of mixed-media concerts. Szigeti pursued a similar policy in making recordings: he insisted on an offbeat repertoire and on contemporary music, recording many premieres. The microphone flattered Szigeti's tone, and his sound on recordings was superior to that in concerts; his extensive discography contains a number of memorable performances.

In addition to his annual tours of the United States, Szigeti became a regular guest in the Soviet Union; between 1924 and 1929 he made eleven tours of Soviet Russia, an average of two a year, and returned in 1931 and 1937. He brought back indelible impressions of the country, the people and their reaction to music, and he observed the steady improvement in living conditions. In return, he left equally indelible impressions on the Russians through his purely musical (as opposed to technical) approach and the novelty of his repertoire. The Soviet enthusiasm ran so high that he was offered a professorship at the Leningrad Conservatory as successor to Auer—a flattering proposal which he had to decline. His impact was a lasting one, as can be seen from a letter written in 1943 by the Soviet violinist Leonid Kogan:[*]

* At the time Kogan was only nineteen and a promising artist; eventually he became the leading Soviet violinist until his death in 1982.

Your last visit [1937] left a deep impression on me; I was so enormously impressed by your personality of a thinking musician that I resolved to follow in your footsteps, a difficult undertaking indeed. But I was obviously too young to realize this, and I had to abandon this desire in the end. But I still keep studying and analyzing your transcriptions as before.[2]

Shortly before the Second World War, Szigeti had the joy of welcoming his old friend and colleague Béla Bartók to New York. They had played together in the late 1920s—in London, Berlin, Rome, Paris, and above all in Budapest, where they gave the premiere of Bartók's Rhapsody No. 1 on November 22, 1929. (The work is dedicated to Szigeti.) They also appeared together during Bartók's first visit to the United States in 1928, and they chose to perform the problematic Second Violin Sonata in New York.

When Bartók arrived in New York on April 11, 1940 (having left Fascist-dominated Hungary as a sign of protest), he was confused by the new surroundings, and it was reassuring for him to have an old friend and associate like Szigeti nearby. Two days after his arrival Bartók joined Szigeti in a concert at the Library of Congress in Washington; they played sonatas by Beethoven, Debussy, and Bartók, as well as Bartók's First Rhapsody.* A week later, on April 21, Bartók appeared with Szigeti and the clarinetist Benny Goodman playing his new *Contrasts* (for violin, clarinet, and piano) at Carnegie Hall, a performance that was also recorded. Szigeti and Bartók performed for the last time together in February 1942, in Boston and Denver, but the two friends remained in contact. Szigeti had an uncanny affinity for Bartók's music, and one can understand the composer's regret expressed in a letter to Szigeti dated January 30, 1944, "I am really very sorry that it was not you who gave the premiere of my Violin Concerto."[3] Bartók referred here to his Violin Concerto No. 2, commissioned and premiered in 1939 by Zoltán Székely, another Hungarian violinist. In his autobiography, Szigeti devotes many moving pages to Bartók, who died all too soon in 1945.

During the Second World War, Szigeti made his home in California, where he came to know Stravinsky as a neighbor, though they had first met many years ago; now in 1945 they made some excellent recordings of Stravinsky's violin music. Soon Szigeti resumed his worldwide tours—Europe, South America, Japan, Australia and New Zea-

---

* The historic event was recorded and released on two discs twenty-five years later, showing both artists in superb form.

land. He played chamber music with Artur Schnabel in Edinburgh and with Casals at the Prades Festival.

In 1960 Szigeti and his wife moved to Switzerland to be near their only daughter, but he returned to the United States in 1965 to participate in various musical activities on university campuses, including Harvard and Dartmouth.

During his last years in Switzerland, Szigeti did some teaching; among those who sought his advice were Arnold Steinhardt, Nell Gotkovsky, and Masuko Ushioda. He served as member of the jury of the most prestigious competitions in Moscow, Brussels, and London. As a member of a jury, he was hard to please and inclined to be "pernickety" (to quote Menuhin). Otherwise, he was universally beloved and admired for his artistic integrity, his sharp intellect, and his personal charm. Tall and slim, he had an aristocratic bearing on and off stage, yet he was approachable and warm in personal conversation. He was an idealist with a practical mind, an artist who combined spontaneity and intellectualism. This is noticeable in his books dealing with violin problems, which are full of interesting observations but at times overrationalized.

Szigeti died at the age of eighty on February 19, 1973, in Lucerne.*

My own recollections of Szigeti's playing are somewhat mixed. I admired his power of musical communication, his intensity and involvement; but I found that his peculiar style did not easily adapt itself to certain kinds of music. For example, I always felt that his Mozart lacked charm and repose; it seemed overly accented and tonally not always attractive. On the other hand, his interpretations of Bach, Beethoven, and Brahms, as well as of modern composers, were superb. His intonation was exact, his tone chaste and pure, without sensuousness.

Much has been written about Szigeti's oldfashioned bowing method, with the right elbow clinging to the body. He once remarked that he was taught this method as a child, even before joining Hubay's class. He had long arms and looked rather cramped when he played. Some artists have an innate playing stance that reflects their physical relationship with the instrument; it cannot be changed. No great artist is schoolbook-perfect; only mediocrities can fully conform to methods, while strong personalities, though breaking rules, must find their own way.

Szigeti was one of the great violin personalities of his generation.

* The Tenth Anniversary of his death was commemorated on February 19, 1983, at Carnegie Hall, with the participation of Yehudi Menuhin, Isaac Stern, Gyorgy Sandor, David Singer, the Guarneri Quartet, and Nikita Magaloff, the pianist and Szigeti's son-in-law.

Just because he was not a "virtuoso" in the accepted sense, he had a salutary effect on public taste by counterbalancing the trend toward ever-increasing technical brilliance.

The great Ysaÿe wrote,

> I have found in Szigeti that quality rare in our days: to be at the same time a virtuoso and a musician. One senses the artist aware of his mission—like a prophet—and one appreciates the violinist placing technique in the service of expression.[4]

After hearing Szigeti, Ysaÿe felt inspired to write his own solo sonatas and dedicated one to him. No greater tribute could have been imagined.

Emil Telmányi

An impressive representative of the Hubay school was Emil Telmányi (born 1892). In 1906, he won the Remenyi Prize at the Budapest Academy, and made his Berlin debut in 1911 with the first German performance of the Elgar concerto. He settled in Copenhagen, where he married a daughter of the composer Carl Nielsen, and was active for a time both as violinist and conductor. His research in the performance practice of Baroque music led him to endorse the so-called "Vega" bow. This is a newly designed bow with a very high convex arch and hair with adjustable tension. When the hair is loosened, the player can touch four strings at the same time and perform Bach's chords without arpeggiating them; when the hair is tightened, it operates like a modern bow. The use of such a bow results in a new concept of Bach playing—*not* as Bach envisaged it (because there never was a bow similar to the "Vega") but as organlike three- and four-part chords played without attack in all dynamic shadings. Telmányi gave two Bach recitals in London in 1955 showing the practical use of the "Vega" bow, with which he recorded the six solo works by Bach. The initial enthusiasm of historians (as for example Albert Schweitzer) who believed in the authenticity of such Bach performances has been discredited by later research. Today's famous violinists prefer to play Bach's polyphony with the modern Tourte bow; others specialize in handling the old "Baroque" bow, neither of which is ideally suited for the task. No one really knows how Bach expected his solo violin music to sound or what kind of bow he would have preferred; we can only approximate. But one thing is certain: Telmányi's "Vega" bow does not conform to any historically accurate reconstruction of a "Bach" bow. Nevertheless, one must admit that it is very pleasant to hear the theme of the Chaconne sounding sustained and organlike rather than broken and sharply attacked.

No account of the Hungarian School would be complete without mentioning the Budapest String Quartet. The original members were all Hungarians: Emil Hauser, the excellent leader, with Imre Poganyi, Istvan Ipolyi, and Harry Son. They made their debut in 1917 and appeared in London in 1925, playing Bartók's First Quartet. The "Russification" of the group began two years later, when Joseph Roisman joined, eventually becoming first violinist. By 1936 all four members were Russian. The riddle was posed, "What is one Russian? A thinker. Two Russians? Chess players. Three Russians? Conspirators. Four Russians? The Budapest String Quartet."

From 1938 to 1962, the Budapest Quartet had the distinction of being the quartet-in-residence at the Library of Congress in Washington, performing on the Library's priceless Stradivari instruments.

Two other Hungarian ensembles maintained their national identity: the Hungarian Quartet under Zoltán Székely, active in Europe and the United States in 1935–70, and the Végh Quartet, founded by Sándor Végh in 1940.

THE BOHEMIAN SCHOOL

BOHEMIA IS ONE of Europe's most musical regions. For centuries, its strongest export was musical talent, and musicians from Bohemia were active all over Europe. Often their national identity was hidden behind German-sounding names: thus, Jan Stamič became Johann Stamitz, famous as the founder of the Mannheim School; František Benda became Franz Benda, concertmaster to King Frederick II of Prussia. Because of Austria's political domination, many Bohemian musicians migrated to Vienna: the celebrated Heinrich Wilhelm Ernst was trained in Vienna; the gifted Josef Slawjk settled in Vienna in 1825, and became the first to play Schubert's violin compositions.

For centuries the proud capital city of Prague competed with the more glamorous imperial city of Vienna. At all times, Prague retained its own independent judgment in musical matters. Mozart wrote his *Don Giovanni* for Prague, and he was feted there far more than in Vienna. On the other hand, Paganini, who had triumphed in Vienna, received a cool reception in Prague.

Perhaps it should come as no surprise that the Prague Conservatory, founded in 1811, is actually six years older than the one in Vienna. Despite the talent that gravitated toward Vienna, Prague became the center for an excellent school of violin playing with its own profile. The first professor of violin at the newly established Prague Conservatory was a German violinist from Mannheim, Friedrich Wilhelm Pixis. In 1842 he was succeeded by his best student, Moritz Mildner, who trained many fine players.

Mildner's most celebrated student was Ferdinand Laub (1832–75), who earned Joachim's wholehearted admiration. A fiery interpreter with a stupendous technique, he reached the height of his career in 1866 when he was appointed first violin professor of the newly established Moscow Conservatory.* (Four years earlier, Wieniawski had accepted a similar post at the new Conservatory of St. Petersburg.)

In 1869, Laub was joined by another Czech violinist and fellow student of Mildner, Jan Hřimaly. After Laub left Moscow for reasons of health in 1874, Hřimaly assumed all of his performing and teaching responsibilities. While less brilliant a performer than Laub, Hřimaly was an excellent teacher. He remained in Moscow until his death in 1915.

Among other Bohemian violinists of the older generation, one of the most accomplished was Franz (František) Ondříček, who played the premiere of the Dvořák Violin Concerto in 1883 in Prague. In 1892, the Bohemian String Quartet created a sensation with its intense, full-blooded performances, which marked "a turning point in the history of quartet playing."[1] They were particularly brilliant in their native repertoire of Smetana and Dvořák. The second violinist, Josef Suk, later made a name for himself as a fine composer; he married Dvořák's daughter Ottilie. Suk's grandson (also named Josef Suk), born in 1929, is known today as a concertizing violinist.

Otakar Sevčik

For violinists, especially young students, the name Sevčik is synonymous with endless drudgery, with mechanical drills of fingers and bow. Almost forgotten is the inventor of all this self-inflicted pain, the author of a multivolume *School of Violin Technique*. These method books have made, as well as destroyed, many violinists. Flesch once compared Sevčik's method to a strong medicine which can cure or kill, depending on the dosage. In his own teaching, Flesch recommended a limited use of Sevčik's exercises—a "daily dose," as it were. Other teachers, like Auer and Hubay, were opposed to Sevčik's method. But there were also factions among violin teachers who defended the Sevčik method as the most rational way to achieve mastery on the violin.

Sevčik's approach was based on the principle of separating the mechanical from the artistic aspect of performance. He was primarily interested in the technical problems, and developed special exercises to strengthen finger and arm muscles and to achieve coordination of mo-

* See pp. 412–13.

tions. The exercises were designed exclusively for efficiency; they were not meant to be musical; in fact, they were antimusical. Everything was calculated to increase the effectiveness of practicing, to rationalize the process of acquiring technical proficiency. Like acrobats preparing for a circus career, the Sevčik students went through ten hours of daily drudgery. Many students took lessons from Sevčik as a kind of technical medicine, but then moved on to other teachers in order to preserve their musical sanity. True, the list of his students is endless, but (as Moser says) there is no list of those who have been crushed by Sevčik's method. Wolfgang Schneiderhan, the distinguished Viennese violinist, wrote a personal memoir about Sevčik which is almost grotesque but revealing:

> Sevčik was like a man obsessed, when it came to effective and technically polished violin playing. He was of medium height, very active, with a pointed beard and blinded in one eye by a breaking steel string. I spent many summers in the little town of Pisek where I was drilled to have my fingers run and my bow bounce. . . . Sevčik got up very early and took a walk, making the rounds of all the little houses where he knew the students were lodgers. He went from window to window, knocking energetically and calling without bidding "good morning," "Get up. Practice!" When I entered his studio, I had to tune to a very high "a" which I found painful because of my absolute pitch. . . . Sevčik was a fanatic; he would have liked to make a Paganini out of every one of his students. His aim was—brilliance of effect (often at the expense of fidelity to the work), impressive violin position, unfailing technique, and the achievement of an international career.[1]

This tyrant of the violin was born in 1852 in a small Bohemian town and studied violin with Bennewitz in Prague. During the early 1870s he occupied several concertmaster positions in Salzburg and Vienna, but settled as a violin professor in Kiev in 1875 at the Imperial Music School. Kiev, the ancient capital of the Ukraine, was proud of its own cultural tradition. Sevčik remained here until 1892, evolving his system of technical training. He had a large class of Russian and Ukrainian students and strengthened the Czech influence exerted by Laub and Hřimaly in Moscow. The Sevčik method also reached the Russian school through his student Josef Karbulka, who in turn taught P. Stolyarsky, the head of the Odessa school.

In 1892 Sevčik returned to Prague to teach at the Academy; from 1909 to 1918 he was professor at the Vienna Academy, but returned to Prague in 1919 when the Czechoslovak Republic was established.

Sevčik gave master classes in the United States in 1921–23 and in London in 1933. But his main teaching was done in the small Bohemian town of Pisek, which became a kind of mecca for ambitious violinists from all over the world. He died there in 1934.

Sevčik was no mere theoretician—he himself played extremely well and he created quite a stir in London around 1908, when he appeared publicly with his students. But his all-consuming ambition was to teach the technique for violin playing, and this he achieved with an inquisitive mind and a rational approach.

Jan Kubelik

The most famous of Sevčik's students was undoubtedly Jan Kubelik (1880–1940). He was a fantastic technician, particularly in terms of left-hand technique, but his virtuosity did not come easy. He practiced long and hard, up to twelve hours a day, until his fingertips bled. Practicing was an obsession with him, probably instilled by his teacher Sevčik. He burst onto the concert scene with his 1898 debut in Vienna, and was acclaimed as "Paganini redivivus." His international career began in 1900 in London, where he was particularly feted. He received the Beethoven Medal of the Royal Philharmonic Society, bestowed before him only on Joachim and Ysaÿe.

Even at the height of his career—between 1900 and 1910—Kubelik was mainly interesting as a virtuoso. His best pieces were the Paganini Concerto in D and the *Ronde des Lutins* by Bazzini. When it came to a Mozart concerto or a Beethoven romance, Kubelik had much less to communicate. Moser heard Kubelik give a lifeless performance of the Vieuxtemps Concerto in D minor, which left him totally cold. But his crystal-clear runs purled with clockwork precision, his crackling pizzicatos and flutelike harmonics left the audience breathless. His tone, according to Flesch, had a certain "astringent and chaste grandeur."[1] In his youth he played with uninhibited gusto, and everything about him conveyed the perfect image of the Romantic virtuoso.

Kubelik practiced slowly, patiently, and accurately. He never rushed his tempos; his runs were precisely timed and actually seemed faster because of this control. He reached an almost automatic perfection, which was absolutely reliable and unfailing.

Despite this solid base, Kubelik began to decline by the time he was thirty. His technique showed signs of faltering occasionally, his tone became dry and cold; but it was particularly the lack of musical com-

Jan Kubelik, the Czech "Paganini redivivus"

Erica Morini, the finest woman violinist of her generation, shown as a prodigy and later in her career

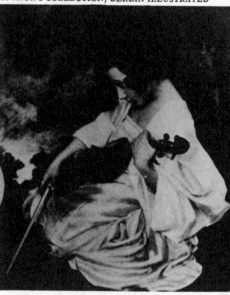

Below, Váša Příhoda, a virtuoso Czech violinist successful between the two World Wars

Below right, Salvatore Accardo, known as a master of the Paganini repertoire, performed on Paganini's violin in New York's Carnegie Hall.

munication that made the public turn to violinists who were warmer but no less accomplished. The fad of neo-Paganinism had run its course. Flesch blames Kubelik's early decline on the stultifying impact of the Sevčik method—prolonged mechanical study which stunted musical feeling. But his countrymen thought otherwise: he concluded his career with a festive season of ten concerts in Prague during 1939–40, showing himself in command of a vast repertoire.

Jaroslav Kocián

Next to Kubelik, Jaroslav Kocián (1883–1950) was considered the most accomplished and characteristic exponent of the Sevčik school. He studied with Sevčik from 1896 to 1901 at the Prague Conservatory, after which he began his international concert career. While he could not match the sensational acclaim that greeted Kubelik, he played with more warmth and expression, though with less technical wizardry. After concerts in western Europe and the United States, Kocián settled in Russia: from 1907 to 1910 he was active in Odessa as professor at the conservatory and leader of a string quartet; in 1910–11 he was first violinist of the Mecklenburg Quartet in St. Petersburg. Kocián's stay in Russia further reinforced the influence of the Czech school on Russian violin playing. From 1924 to 1943 he was violin professor at the Prague Conservatory; one of his best students was the young Josef Suk.

Erica Morini

Listening to Erica Morini, one would hardly believe that she went through the purgatory of Sevčik's workshop. Undoubtedly he polished her technique to a high degree of perfection, but she never lost the musical communicativeness, the controlled intensity which made her interpretations so memorable. Despite her smoldering temperament, her body barely moved when she played; her right arm (held low in the classical manner) was a model of smoothness, yet it was incisive when energy was required; her left hand was a miracle of pure intonation, using a narrow vibrato that never obscured the core of the note, producing a tone of bell-like clarity. Watching Morini play, one felt that she was completely oblivious to the outside world: she seemed mesmerized by her own sounds. Her interpretations of the concertos of Mozart,

Beethoven, and Brahms were truly memorable; to the essentially masculine Brahms she added a delightful touch of femininity. Her particular specialty was the Spohr concertos, now considered antiquated; she brought them back to life with the patina intact.

Morini was born in 1904 in Vienna and had lessons with her father, a professional musician, until she was seven. She entered Sevčik's class at the Vienna Academy and made her concert debut in Vienna in 1916. Her success was such that she was engaged to play with Nikisch at the Leipzig Gewandhaus and the Berlin Philharmonic. After her New York debut in 1921, Miss Morini spent most of her concert seasons in the United States and finally settled in New York. She retired from the concert stage in the mid-1970s, much to everyone's regret.

Váša Příhoda

The career of Váša Příhoda (1900–1960) was brief but brilliant. Between the two world wars, he was highly acclaimed in Europe and America. He had lessons with his father and with Marak, a student of Sevčik, and made his official debut in Prague at the age of thirteen. In 1919 he found himself in Italy, but instead of the dreamed-of concert career he had to earn a living as a café player in Milan. By chance, Arturo Toscanini heard him play and was so impressed that he organized a national collection for the young fiddler. Toscanini was convinced that Příhoda was to be another Paganini. For a time, this prediction seemed to come true: Příhoda played with stupendous technique, a tone of great warmth, and with natural but limited musicianship. In 1921 he appeared briefly in the United States; though unable to compete with established artists like Kreisler and Heifetz, he made a number of recordings on the Edison label which became widely known. Příhoda's sweet tone and scintillating technique sound particularly well on records. During World War II he was active in Germany and Austria, which made him suspect of Nazi sympathies. For a time he taught at the Munich Academy, at the Salzburg Mozarteum, and finally, from 1950 to 1960, at the Vienna Academy. He returned to his native Czechoslovakia in 1956 after a ten-year absence and concertized again, but he was past his prime. His Stradivarius of 1710 (the "Camposelice") was bought by the Czech State.*

---

* Now played by Josef Suk.

Josef Suk

After World War II, only one Czech violinist succeeded in achieving an international reputation—Josef Suk, born 1929 in Prague. He has a distinguished musical ancestry: he is the great-grandson of Dvořák and the grandson of his namesake, the composer Josef Suk. Young Suk was a student of Kocián at the Prague Conservatory. In the mid-1950s, his interpretation of Dvořák's Violin Concerto—played on the Stradivarius once owned by his compatriot Příhoda—established Suk as the leading Czech violinist of his generation. At the same time he was active in chamber music, especially with the Suk Trio, which concertized widely from 1952 on. He also formed sonata partnerships with various pianists, including the late Julius Katchen. In 1964 Suk made his British debut at the Promenade Concerts and his American debut with the Cleveland Orchestra, earning critical acclaim. Since then he has been a regular visitor; in 1979 he played twice with the Chamber Music Society of Lincoln Center in New York. He is recognized as a solid and musicianly violinist, admired for his style and taste rather than brilliance. He uses his accomplished technique for musical purposes. His many recordings of Czech music are particularly attractive. During the winter of 1979–80, Suk was visiting professor at the Vienna Academy, which continues the tradition of close exchange between Prague and Vienna.

The city of Prague, well aware of its rich violinistic heritage, has sponsored various contests for violinists, usually held during the Prague Spring Festival. There have been several contests named after Kubelik (1947, 1949) and one named jointly after Josef Slawjk and Franz Ondriček in 1956. The prizes have usually been won by Soviet violinists, and no major Czech talent seems to have emerged.

THE NEW VIENNESE SCHOOL

THE VIENNA CONSERVATORY, founded privately in 1817, underwent many crises before it became a state-supported academy in 1909. But any institution that can count among its alumni such artists as Ernst, Joachim, Kreisler, Flesch, and Enesco must be considered one of the world's best. The Viennese tradition of violin teaching had a somewhat inbred character: beginning with the first professor, Boehm, through the Hellmesberger dynasty and the pedagogues Dont and Grün, a single method was represented, resulting in a certain stagnation. Perhaps it is not surprising that around 1890 the three most gifted graduates—Kreisler, Flesch, and Enesco—chose to continue their studies at the Paris Conservatoire.

In 1893, Arnold Rosé joined the Vienna faculty and taught with some interruptions until 1924. Rosé was born in Rumania in 1863, but received his education at the Vienna Conservatory. Appointed concertmaster of the Vienna Opera in 1881, he retained this post until 1938 and wielded enormous power during the fifty-seven (!) years of his tenure. Best known as a chamber-music player, he was founder and leader of the Rosé Quartet, established in 1883. In his last years, Brahms preferred the Rosé Quartet to the Hellmesberger Quartet and entrusted Rosé with important Viennese premieres. With the demise of the Joachim Quartet in 1907, the Rosé Quartet was internationally recognized as the heir to the classical tradition; but in addition, Rosé was willing to play some contemporary music by Reger, Pfitzner, and Schoenberg. In 1938, Rosé was forced to emigrate and settled in London, where he died in 1946. "He will live in our memory as the most perfect and versatile type of

Viennese musician," wrote his friend and colleague Flesch, though he considered him "ungifted" as a teacher.[1]

Sevčik's decade as professor at the Vienna Academy (1908–18) brought some fresh ideas to the venerable institution, and even after his move to Prague he continued to attract Austrian students. Among them was Ernst Moravec, who taught at the Vienna Academy from 1930 to 1966 and is considered one of Vienna's best teachers. Another Sevčik student was Rudolf Kolisch (1896–1978), founder of the world-famous Kolisch Quartet, who was dedicated to the music of Schoenberg and his followers. Due to a childhood accident, Kolisch's left-hand fingers became stiff, so that he had to switch hands, drawing the bow with his left hand. Kolisch was a musician of unusual intellectual power; his quartet was probably the first to play the most complex music from memory. Also "drilled" in the Sevčik studio was Austria's most distinguished violinist, Wolfgang Schneiderhan (born 1915).* As a counterbalance, he later studied with Julius Winkler, who opened to him a world of spiritual and musical beauty. Perhaps as a reaction to his early experience with Sevčik, Schneiderhan has become the most classical of all Austrian violinists, an antivirtuoso who specializes in the great repertoire of the past. There is something magisterial in his playing and appearance. He has an uncommon sense of style, at his best in Beethoven and Brahms, perhaps a bit inflexible in Mozart. Schneiderhan has been active as soloist, concertmaster, and quartet leader. From 1939 to 1951 he was professor at the Vienna Academy; in 1949 he took over the master courses at the Conservatory of Lucerne, where he also conducts the Lucerne Festival Strings. Schneiderhan's career is one of solid accomplishment, perhaps not spectacular, but all the more valuable for its high musical standards.

The Viennese spirit can be discerned in Eduard Melkus (born 1928). A natural fiddler, he plays Baroque pieces as well as a Schubert *Ländler* or a Beethoven sonata. His main teacher was Moravec; he also studied musicology at Vienna University under Schenk for several semesters, which proved useful when he decided to explore Baroque performance practice on string instruments. Through his own concerts and recordings, Melkus has become one of the leaders in reviving both a neglected repertoire of string music and the forgotten art of playing on Baroque violins with period bows. He has made a thorough study of ornamentation and plays the music of Corelli, Handel, and their contemporaries

* See p. 396.

with interesting embellishments. As leader of the Vienna Capella Aca-
demica (founded 1965), Melkus aims at using instruments with authentic fittings and has taught the science of Baroque performance practice
at various universities of Europe and the United States. Despite all authenticity, Melkus has preserved a natural, sweet-sounding violin style.
Since 1958 he has been on the faculty of the Vienna Academy; he divides his time between Europe and the United States.

THE NEW ITALIAN SCHOOL

IT IS STRANGE to realize that Italy—the birthplace of the violin and the guardian of the classic violin tradition—produced very few outstanding violinists after Paganini's death in 1840. Paganini's only student, Camillo Sivori, enjoyed some popularity in the nineteenth century. Antonio Bazzini, a rival of Ernst and Joachim in his youth, turned mainly to composition in later years. His compositions are largely forgotten except for the scintillating *Ronde des Lutins* (composed for Ernst), which adorns the repertoire of most virtuoso violinists.

In the twentieth century, the level of violin teaching in the Italian conservatories remained high, but the harvest of great violinists was sparse. A few became internationally known, such as Arrigo Serato (1877–1948), who for many years was considered the official exponent of Italian violin playing. He was quite successful in Berlin, where he was active until 1915; later he taught for many years at Santa Cecilia in Rome, but was also known as a soloist and chamber-music player of distinction. Alfredo Campoli, born in 1906 in Rome, has spent most of his life in London, where he is much admired not only for his interpretations of the great masters, but also as an exponent of high-class entertainment music. Gioconda de Vito (born 1907) studied at Pesaro and Rome. Her first success in Vienna as winner of a violin competition led to concerts and a professorship at Santa Cecilia in Rome. She made her successful debut in London in 1948 and settled in England. Her recordings with Yehudi Menuhin, who praises her highly, have become well known. Pina Carmirelli (born 1914) studied with Abbado and Serato and won the Paganini Prize in 1940. She founded the Boccherini String

Quintet in 1949 and her own quartet in 1954, devoting much effort to a rediscovery of Boccherini's chamber music. In 1970, her complete cycles of Beethoven sonatas with the pianist Rudolf Serkin attracted much attention.

With Salvatore Accardo, Italy has at last acquired a violinist of international stature. Born in Turin in 1941, Accardo began to "fiddle" at three, but did not start regular lessons until he was six. Studying with Luigi D'Ambrosio at the Conservatory in Naples, Accardo received a diploma in 1956. He did some additional work at the Accademia Chigiana in Siena with Yvonne Astruc, a French disciple of Enesco. His early career is studded with first prizes of various European competitions: in 1955 at Vercelli, in 1956 at Geneva, in 1957 at Siena. Winning first prize at the Paganini Competition in 1958, he became a celebrity and was typed as a Paganini specialist. This was reinforced when he made an integral recording of Paganini's six violin concertos, including the rediscovered Nos. 3, 4, and 5, as well as the somewhat spurious No. 6. These are masterful recordings of forgotten works, partly reconstructed from sketchy scores which were held back for over a century by Paganini's heirs. Accardo, in fact, was not the first to bring these concertos to light; there are earlier recordings by Ricci, Grumiaux, Gulli, and Szeryng. But the total impression of Accardo's Paganini is one of effortless beauty, which belies the enormous technical mastery required for performing the six-concerto cycle. Equally impressive is his recording of the Paganini caprices.

Actually, Accardo has a vast repertoire, ranging from the classical Italian masters (which he often performs with the ensemble I Musici) to the present. He has appeared as soloist with many of today's great conductors—Karajan, Mehta, Haitink, Muti—and is now becoming better known in America. His debut recital in New York in January 1980, with a program made up entirely of unaccompanied violin music, was a feast for connoisseurs. Two major solo works by Bach framed a group of nine caprices by Paganini. All were played with impeccable mastery, unfailing technique, and stylish musicianship. For once, there was no schism between virtuosity and musicianship: he played Bach like a virtuoso and Paganini like a musician, and to the enhancement of both composers. While Accardo lacks a fiery temperament, he infuses everything with a kind of inner intensity, always under control, and exuding unruffled calm and confidence. The beauty of his tone is intensified by two rare violins he owns—a Guarnerius del Gesù of 1733 and the "Firebird" Stradivarius of 1718.

During the Paganini Bicentenary in 1982, Accardo was singled out as Italy's representative: he was entrusted to take Paganini's famous Guarnerius violin to New York for an all-Paganini program at Carnegie Hall. The undertaking was doubly risky: the violin had never been exposed to the different climatic conditions overseas, and Accardo had little time to become used to the intractable instrument. Accardo chose to perform the Twenty-four Caprices for unaccompanied violin, and he did it with an almost reckless abandon. His technical mastery was unquestionable, and the few mishaps were undoubtedly due to his unfamiliarity with the instrument; the tone was rich and carried easily through the vast hall. One had wished that Accardo had taken a more poetic view of the caprices, exploring their musical values rather than stressing the technical challenge to be conquered at top speed.

A violinist of remarkable attainment is Franco Gulli, born in 1926 in Trieste, where he attended the Conservatory. He later studied with Serato in Rome. Beginning in 1947 he gave duo recitals with the pianist Enrica Cavallo (later his wife). He attracted international attention in 1959 by playing and recording Paganini's long-forgotten Concerto No. 5 in A minor, in an elegant and accomplished performance. In 1960 Gulli formed the Italian String Trio. He taught at the Chigi Academy in Siena, at the Lucerne Conservatory, and is now professor at Indiana University (since 1972). His recent New York performances with the Santa Fe Chamber Group were highly successful.

An account of twentieth-century Italian string playing would not be complete without mentioning the extraordinary Quartetto Italiano, founded in 1945 with Paolo Borciani as leader, performing with unusual sensitivity. Characteristic is also the Italian revival of the Baroque string repertoire, initiated by such groups as I Musici and the Virtuosi di Roma, exquisite ensembles representing the best in Italian tradition.

THE RUSSIAN SCHOOL

Early History

The Russian violin school enjoyed an unparalleled growth in the early twentieth century. From Leopold Auer's classroom at the St. Petersburg Conservatory emerged some of the greatest violinists of our time. By 1917, when Auer left war-torn Russia, he was recognized as the foremost living violin teacher.

During the 1920s, the Auer tradition was carried forward by violinists who had studied with him or who had grown up under his influence. It was then that the center of gravity shifted to the Moscow Conservatory, though Leningrad still saw some excellent teaching. A third center arose in Odessa, where Stolyarsky taught a group of incredibly gifted child prodigies. Ultimately, Moscow attracted the greatest number of talented students. Beginning with the 1930s, we can speak of a "new" Russian or—better—a Soviet school of violin playing, which earned as much international recognition as did the Auer School in its time. Evidently, the initial success of the Russian school was not entirely due to the teaching of one man but the result of a variety of favorable circumstances, such as a vast reservoir of native talent (especially among the Jewish population), unified teaching methods, generous public support of the arts, and an unbroken tradition of excellence and high standards. This leads to a consideration of what the Russian school was like before Auer took over the violin class in St. Petersburg in 1868.

In the eighteenth and nineteenth centuries, the czarist court at St. Petersburg established the custom of inviting prominent foreign violinists to serve as Soloist of the Czar. Duties included solo and quartet performances, both at court and in public concerts, as well as the playing of violin solos at opera and ballet galas. Wealthy Russian music lovers followed the czar's example and invited foreign musicians to spend prolonged periods of time in St. Petersburg or Moscow and on their summer estates. Here, the guests played chamber music and conducted private orchestras; they also gave lessons to selected students. In return, some gifted Russian musicians were sent abroad by their patrons or masters to study music in Italy, Vienna, and Paris. In this manner, Russian violin playing was never out of touch with the latest developments in western Europe.

Among European musicians of the eighteenth and nineteenth centuries, Russia was a favorite destination: there was much wealth among the aristocrats and landowners and a great hunger for Western culture because of the geographic isolation of the country. Once virtuosos were willing to undertake the long and perilous journey, they were often rewarded by earnings far beyond their expectations—provided they pleased the Russian music lovers, who were a critical lot. Some musicians came for a brief visit and settled for life; others accumulated a fortune and returned to their native land. Among them were opera composers, pianists and violinists, conductors and singers, who contributed their share to the growth of Russian music.

A bird's-eye view of Russian violin history reveals that it passed through three phases of foreign influences before it found its own voice. The first was Italian and belonged to the eighteenth century. At the czarist court served the excellent violinist Dall'Oglio, who had studied with Tartini, and such famous virtuosos as Antonio Lolli and Giovanni Giornovicchi; Maestro Pugnani and his student Viotti visited briefly. Most minor orchestra posts were occupied by Italian musicians.

Phase two was French and began in 1803 with the prolonged stay in St. Petersburg of Pierre Rode, succeeded by Charles Lafont, while Pierre Baillot was active in Moscow; this period came to a temporary halt through the Napoleonic invasion in 1812. But the French influence remained alive, passed on to gifted Russian players. In 1838 Henry Vieuxtemps visited for the first time and returned in 1845 for a seven-year appointment. In 1860 Henry Wieniawski settled in St. Petersburg and remained until 1872. Both Vieuxtemps and Wieniawski taught extensively in the Parisian Conservatoire tradition.

The third phase began with the last third of the nineteenth century and brought central European influences to bear—Vienna, Budapest, Prague, and some German academicism. Leopold Auer, Ferdinand Laub, Otakar Sevčik were the new names that entered St. Petersburg and Moscow in the late 1860s and '70s, making their influence felt. Finally, in the twentieth century, we see an increasing number of Russian-born teachers at various conservatories, rising to important positions.

How did the native Russian violinists survive in the midst of that foreign invasion? At first not too well. The father of Russian violin playing, Ivan Khandoshkin (1744–1804), lived in an age when foreign musicians dominated music in Russia, particularly at the czarist court, while native musicians were assigned secondary posts. Much talent was discovered among the peasant population, living in serfdom and grouped into so-called serf orchestras. Wealthy landowners sought out talented peasant boys among their serfs and had them learn an instrument; occasionally they were sent abroad to study. Some of these musicians spent a life in servitude, others bought their freedom or were freed. Aside from the human misery, the serf orchestras contributed significantly to the evolution of Russian musical culture well beyond 1850.

Ivan Khandoshkin (also spelled Handochkine) may have been of serf origin. Very little is known about his life. He studied with an Italian violinist employed at the czarist court and soon reached such a level of excellence that he could compete with foreign virtuosos like Lolli and Giornovicchi. Khandoshkin's violin compositions were printed and copied during his lifetime in Amsterdam and Moscow, but fell into oblivion shortly after 1800; they are now being rediscovered as important examples of early native Russian violin art. Khandoshkin could and did write sonatas, but he preferred to be inspired by Russian folksongs, which he set for solo violin, for two violins, and for violin and bass. The technical demands were very high, almost on a level with those of Tartini, whose method Khandoshkin obviously knew well. He used all kinds of virtuoso devices—high positions, wide leaps, double stops, fast runs, pizzicato and harmonics, staccato and spiccato—a remarkable variety of techniques. Khandoshkin was the first to turn to Russian folksongs as basis for variations; he collected the original material himself, disregarding the collections already in print. He occupies a place of honor in the history of Russian music by seeking inspiration from native folk tunes. He also led the way in the popularization of the variation genre. However, he found little recognition during his lifetime and died a pensioner, leaving a wife and son in poverty.

An important figure in Russian music was Alexei Lvov (1798–1870). Though trained as a military engineer, he studied violin with the best available teacher, Lafont. Lvov was active as violinist, composer, conductor, and director of the Imperial Chapel Choir, a post he assumed in 1837, succeeding his father. He organized instrumental classes as an adjunct to the court chapel, founded a concert society for orchestral performances, and published a violin method (1859). Between 1830 and 1860, Lvov was considered the best Russian violinist. String quartet playing was his passion. Every week, he and his quartet performed in his salon, where the aristocracy mingled with literary figures and artists. When Robert and Clara Schumann visited St. Petersburg in 1844, Lvov assembled the music lovers to perform Schumann's Piano Quintet for the celebrated guests.

In 1840 Lvov appeared as visiting soloist at the Leipzig Gewandhaus concerts, playing his own Violin Concerto under Mendelssohn's baton. The concerto was an unabashed imitation of Spohr's *Gesangscene*, but his playing found many admirers, among them Mendelssohn, who described Lvov as "one of the finest and most inspired violinists" he had ever heard.[1] Schumann's printed review said, "Lvov is such a singular, rare player that he can be compared to first-rate artists anywhere. . . . If there are any more such 'dilettantes' in the Russian capital, then many artists—visiting there—can learn more than teach."[2] Apparently, everybody was impressed that an "amateur" with the rank of general could compete in Germany's most musical city.*

Lvov was a fiery player with emotion and brilliance, yet disdainful of Paganini's virtuoso tricks. His quartet playing centered around the prominent first-violin part, and his improvisational style often left his partners in disarray. In the 1860s Lvov gradually retired from active playing because his hearing failed. The violin he used was a rare Maggini, once owned by Giornovicchi.

An event of historic importance was the founding, in 1859, of the Russian Music Society (RMS), which was to dominate Russian musical life until 1917. The purpose of the RMS was stated simply, "to make good music available to the broad masses of the public." The RMS sponsored subscription concerts of orchestral and chamber music, and also took charge of music education in Russia by organizing the first conservatories—in St. Petersburg in 1862, in Moscow in 1866. These were the first Russian institutions where young musicians could be trained according to academic standards valid in western Europe. The initiator

* Anton Rubinstein explained the difference: "A dilettante occupies himself with art for his own enjoyment whereas an artist does it for the enjoyment of others. This is the immense difference with regard to the demands put on them, and the evaluation of their performance."

of the RMS was the eminent pianist-composer Anton Rubinstein; the Moscow branch was directed by his younger brother Nicolai, also a pianist and conductor. The young conservatories had enemies on all sides. Conservatives, including the influential Alexei Lvov, were fearful of a hotbed of progressive ideas, while liberals, among them the composer-critic Serov, the author-librarian Stassov, and the composer Balakirev, flatly denied the usefulness of academic instruction for the musician.

At the St. Petersburg Conservatory, Rubinstein assembled a faculty not only of excellent teachers, but also of performing artists able to enrich the musical life of the capital and of Russia in general. Among them was the violinist Henri Wieniawski, then only twenty-five, who settled in St. Petersburg in 1860 and remained for twelve years. Wieniawski was Polish-born (hence technically a subject of the czar) and Paris-trained, truly an ideal choice for the manifold demands of the new job. Rubinstein and Wieniawski had been sonata partners even before the latter was persuaded to settle in St. Petersburg, and they continued to perform together. Wieniawski's superb playing set the standards of excellence for Russians; every other violinist, whether it be Auer or Ysaÿe, was compared to him—and found wanting.

Wieniawski was also a dedicated and inspiring teacher, though better suited for the advanced student. Each semester he had as many as twelve students, whom he met twice a week; he also coached chamber music, usually a string quartet. He was always ready to demonstrate, violin in hand. By 1868, when he resigned his professorship, Wieniawski had trained a number of respectable Russian violinists who assumed important roles in Russia's musical life. For a few years, Wieniawski kept his court duties until, in 1872, he and Rubinstein departed for a lengthy tour of the United States.

Wieniawski's successor was another protégé of Rubinstein, the Hungarian-born Leopold Auer, then only twenty-three years old. The relations between Wieniawski and young Auer were cordial; we know, for example, that both artists participated in a chamber-music program on December 7, 1869. The program included two double quartets by Spohr and Mendelssohn, Wieniawski and Auer each leading his own quartet.

Shortly before Auer joined the St. Petersburg Conservatory, a sister institution was established in Moscow (1866). Here, the first violin professor to be appointed was Ferdinand Laub, then thirty-four, born and trained in Prague. Laub was "one of the greatest violinists of the nineteenth century, in some ways perhaps the grandest," according to the critical Moser.[3] Tchaikovsky, a fellow teacher at the Moscow Conservatory, called Laub a "titanesque violinist" and dedicated his Third String Quartet to the memory of Laub, who died in 1875 at the early age of forty-three. During his eight years in Moscow (1866–74), Laub became extremely popular as soloist, quartet player, and teacher; he laid the foundation for the distinct style of the Moscow violin school. Laub's work was continued by another Czech violinist, Jan Hřimaly, who joined the Moscow faculty as Laub's assistant in 1869 and remained as principal teacher until 1915. Hřimaly taught some of Russia's best violinists: Michael Press, Léa Luboshutz, Alexander Petchnikoff, Jules Conus, Issay Barmas, Alexander Moguilevsky. The Moscow school was less spectacular than the Auer school in St. Petersburg, but hardly less accomplished.

For a comparatively brief time, from 1874 to 1878, the violinist Adolph Brodsky taught at the Moscow Conservatory. The Russian-born Brodsky studied in Vienna with Hellmesberger and added an Austrian touch to the faculty. Brodsky's name has become enshrined as the first performer of the Tchaikovsky Violin Concerto; in fact, the concerto was dedicated to him after Auer refused to play it. Brodsky—who spent most of his life outside of Russia—was a friend not only of Tchaikovsky but also of Brahms; the two composers met at Brodsky's home and behaved in a civilized manner, though they loathed each other's music.

Competing with the Moscow Conservatory was the Moscow Philharmonic Music School, established in 1883. Here, the principal violin professor was Vassily Bezekirsky, an excellent violinist schooled in Brussels by H. Léonard. Bezekirsky held the position of violin soloist at the Bolshoi Theater in 1861–90 and gained an international reputation through his European concert tours in 1868–71; he died in Moscow in 1919. Among Besekirsky's many students was Carl Grigorovich, who later came to Berlin to coach with Joachim. Young Bronislaw Huberman had lessons with Grigorovich and greatly admired him.

An excellent teacher was Konstantin Mostras (1886–1965), who was active at the Moscow Philharmonic School and (after 1922) at the Conservatory. One of Mostras's early students was Ivan Galamian, who emigrated in 1922, first to Paris and then to New York. Mostras is Galamian's "Russian connection," though he also worked with Capet. Galamian's phenomenal success in building his own "school" is well known; we shall speak about it later.

The Czech influence was strongly felt in the Ukraine, through Sevčik in Kiev and through Sevčik's student Karbulka in Odessa. Karbulka in turn taught Stolyarsky, head of the Odessa school and teacher of Milstein and Oistrakh.

Leopold Auer

It is useful to realize that Auer was not the "personification" of the Russian school. He had predecessors, competitors, and successors. Nevertheless, the greatest violinists of our century emerged from his classroom in St. Petersburg. Auer and his students put Russian violin playing on the map and made the world aware of a new approach to violin playing, equidistant from the German gravity and the French levity.

Leopold Auer was born in 1845 in that part of Hungary that also produced Joachim and Flesch. His father was a house painter, well liked by the local citizenry, yet too poor to give Leopold an adequate musical education. The gifted boy was taken to Budapest when he was eight and studied a few years at the conservatory with Ridley Kohne. A debut with the Mendelssohn concerto aroused the interest of some wealthy patrons, who sent him to Vienna for further study. He lived at the home of Jacob Dont, a remarkable teacher; "it was he who gave me the foundation of my violin technique," wrote Auer in his memoirs. He also attended quartet classes with Josef Hellmesberger. By the time Auer was thirteen, the scholarship had run out, and his father decided to launch his prodigy career. The income from provincial concerts was barely enough to keep father and son afloat. An audition with Vieuxtemps in Graz produced no results, nor did a visit to Paris. The years of wandering came to an end when Auer decided to seek the advice of Joachim, then royal concertmaster at Hanover. The two years (1861–63) spent in Hanover proved a turning point. Not that the lessons with Joachim were very regular; the half-dozen or so students were summoned whenever the busy "Herr Konzertmeister" had time. More than through lessons, Auer learned through observation and association. Well prepared as a violinist, Auer discovered a new world, the world of German music making without virtuoso glitter, stressing musical values.

> Joachim was an inspiration for me and opened before my eyes horizons of that greater art of which until then I had lived in ignorance. With him I worked not only with my hands but with my head, studying the scores of the great masters and endeavoring to penetrate the very heart of their works. . . . I [also] played a great deal of chamber music with my fellow students.[1]

Returning to the concert stage in 1864, Auer appeared as soloist with the Leipzig Gewandhaus Orchestra. The respectable success brought him his first job—concertmaster in Düsseldorf. In 1866 he assumed the same duties in Hamburg, in addition to leading a string quartet. On a visit to London in 1868, Auer was invited to play Beethoven's *Archduke Trio* with Anton Rubinstein and the cellist Piatti. In search of a successor to Wieniawski, Rubinstein recommended Auer for the vacant position at the St. Petersburg Conservatory. A three-year contract was signed; little did Auer anticipate that he would remain for forty-nine years.

At the age of only twenty-three, Auer stepped into a difficult situation. Professionally he was well equipped, yet to compete with a violin genius like Wieniawski was more than he had bargained for. Comparisons were unavoidable and put Auer at a disadvantage. The Russian critics were cruel. The Mendelssohn concerto, as played by Auer, was "simply bad" and well below the standards set by Wieniawski. The Beethoven concerto was "out of tune, not to mention technical imperfections . . . and the trivial cadenza of his own composition." Worst of all, Auer played only the first movement "like a student at the final examination."[2] On the same program Auer gave the first performance of Tchaikovsky's *Sérénade mélancolique* (dedicated to him), and the critic Cui wrote, "The lusterless performance was worthy of the insignificant composition."

Tchaikovsky, on the other hand, was very taken by Auer's playing. He had heard him in Moscow in 1874 and wrote a warm review, praising Auer's "great expressivity, the thoughtful finesse and poetry of the interpretation." A warm rapport developed between composer and performer. When Tchaikovsky set out to write a violin concerto, it was only natural that he thought of Auer as its interpreter; but things worked out differently.

The story of the "rejected dedication" has been told many times, usually without being quite fair to either side. Tchaikovsky composed the Violin Concerto in March–April 1878, in Switzerland. It was completed, orchestration and all, in twenty-six days. A visitor from Moscow, the gifted young violinist Josef Kotek, arrived just in time to give some technical advice and to try out the new work with the composer at the piano. When Tchaikovsky returned to St. Petersburg in the fall of 1878, he visited Auer, bringing the printed copy of the concerto, dedicated to Auer. It was a *fait accompli*—he had never consulted Auer, he had never asked his permission about the dedication. Though Auer may have been surprised and even piqued at the lack of consultation, he was polite. Here is Auer's description of the visit:

> I thanked him warmly [for the dedication] and at once had
> him sit down at the piano while I . . . followed with feverish
> interest his somewhat awkward piano rendering of the score.
> . . . When I went over the score in detail, however, I felt that,
> in spite of its great intrinsic value, it called for a thorough
> revision, since in various portions it was quite unviolinistic and
> not at all written in the idiom of the strings. I regretted deeply
> that the composer had not shown me the score before having
> sent it to the engraver, and I determined to subject it to a
> revision which would make it more suited to the nature of the
> violin, and then submit it to the composer.[3]

Auer took his time, however, and a premiere planned for March 1879 was canceled because the concerto was found "too difficult." For several years the work languished, unperformed though published. Tchaikovsky was annoyed, all the more since rumors had reached him that Auer had "intrigued" against the concerto by proclaiming it "unplayable." He suspected that Auer had dissuaded Kotek, and later Emile Sauret, from performing it in Russia. The angry composer blamed Kotek for being a "coward"—he felt that Kotek had a moral obligation to play the concerto because *he* was responsible for the playability of the solo part!

Three years passed after the completion of the concerto, and Tchaikovsky despaired of hearing it. Suddenly, the work found a new champion in Adolph Brodsky, who persuaded the conductor Hans Richter and the Vienna Philharmonic to let him play the world premiere, which took place on December 4, 1881. Hanslick's offensive criticism buried the work: "Tchaikovsky's Violin Concerto brings us face to face for the first time with the revolting idea: may there not also be musical compositions which we can hear stink?"[4]

Nevertheless convinced of the concerto's worth, Brodsky brought it to London on May 8, 1882, and to Moscow on August 8 of the same year; but even on home ground the concerto was criticized as "somnolent and wearisome." Tchaikovsky's gratitude toward Brodsky for having adopted his "unhappy concerto" was boundless: he inscribed his photograph "To the recreator of the concerto deemed impossible, from the grateful Peter Tchaikovsky," and he insisted that the printed dedication be changed to read "Adolphe Brodsky," expunging the name "Auer."

It took Auer fifteen years to admit his mistake: not until 1893 did he play the Tchaikovsky concerto in public, five months before the composer's death. Auer prepared his own edition of the violin part, which he taught to all his students, incorporating a few changes and cuts, none very good or necessary. Today the great performers have returned to the original version as Tchaikovsky wrote it. In time, Auer and Tchaikovsky reestablished a good relationship. In later years, Auer received quite a few dedications from Russian composers—Glazunov, Arensky, Taneyev—but none caused anything comparable to the unhappy incident with Tchaikovsky.

As a performer, Auer was constantly in the public eye. Among his duties were the violin solos for special performances of the Imperial Ballet; in fact, many of the elaborate violin solos in *Swan Lake, Raymonda*, and other famous ballets were composed with him in mind. Until 1906 he was leader of the string quartet of the Russian Music Society, and the regular quartet soirees were as much an integral part of the St. Petersburg scene as those of Joachim in Berlin. In later years there was criticism of less than perfect ensemble and insufficient attention to the contemporary Russian repertoire. Nevertheless, Auer's group did perform the quartets of Tchaikovsky, Borodin, Glazunov, and Rimsky-Korsakov. He championed the music of Brahms and loved to play Schumann. Auer's interest in Spohr, Raff, and other secondary German masters was not shared by the Russian audiences. Eventually, attendance began to fall off, and in 1906 the quartet disbanded.

Undiminished, however, was Auer's interest in the sonata repertoire. He performed with many great pianists—Anton Rubinstein, Leschetitzky, Pugno, Taneyev, d'Albert—but his most cherished partner was Annette Essipova, with whom he performed until her death in 1913. In the 1890s, he gave cycles of the ten Beethoven violin sonatas; later on, he introduced the sonatas for violin and piano by Brahms.

Auer was also active as orchestral conductor; he was in charge of the RMS orchestral concerts at various intervals in the 1880s and '90s. He was always willing to take the baton when a famous foreign soloist arrived (as for Joachim, his old master), and he did the same for his concertizing students abroad. But conducting was not one of his major talents.

As a performing violinist, Auer was handicapped by poorly built hands. He had to practice incessantly to keep himself in playing condition, and he kept his daily routine with an iron discipline. He wrote, "My hands are so weak and their conformation is so poor that when I have not played the violin for several successive days, and then take up the instrument, I feel as if I had altogether lost the faculty of playing."[5]

Despite this handicap, Auer achieved much through tireless work:

Leopold Auer, head of the famous Russian violin school. The inscription is to the author's father, Auer's piano partner.

his tone, though small, was ingratiating, his technique was polished and elegant, his intonation impeccable. His classic nobility made up for his lack of fire; his musical taste was conservative and refined. He liked the virtuoso pieces of Vieuxtemps and Ernst and used them in his teaching, while he cared less for Wieniawski and Paganini. Once a student objected to Ernst's *Othello Fantasy* as "bad music"; angrily Auer retorted, "You'll play it until it sounds like good music, and you'll play nothing else." He played comparatively little Bach and never assigned one of Bach's solo concertos to a student, though the Double Concerto was one of his favorites. Among performers he admired above all Joachim for his classicism and Sarasate for his elegant perfection. He also spoke highly of Vieuxtemps and Wieniawski, of Ysaÿe and Kreisler.

Auer's position in the history of violin playing is based on his teaching. He gave his imprint to the Russian school, and his influence is reflected through today, several generations removed.

What kind of a teacher was he? In technical matters, he was no teacher at all; he left the technical preparation of his students to his assistants. Nor did he try to be helpful if the student ran into a technical problem. Nevertheless he was a stickler for technical accuracy. It is reported that before 1900—during the first thirty years of his teaching—he paid more personal attention to technical details; paradoxically, he did not turn out any significant students during those thirty years. But it would be fallacious to conclude that this kind of nonattention to technical instruction is an ideal method. Far from it. The advice of a teacher to "go home and practice!" is simply inadequate. All Auer students—except Heifetz—struggled sooner or later with technical problems; even natural talents like Poliakin or Elman worked for years to overcome basic deficiencies. Many students, in near despair, turned to each other for help because they were afraid to ask Auer. Clearly, Auer had no "method" of general validity; his greatness lay in sizing up the potential of each student and developing his peculiar individuality. He seemed to be deliberately vague as to how to grip the bow; he relied on the physical structure of the student's arm. Nor was he ever inclined to pick up a violin in class and demonstrate.

Auer's procedure was one of near-hypnosis. One of his students, Kathleen Parlow, said that after having played beautifully in class under Auer's exhortations, she came home and was helpless, not being able to duplicate what she did under his mesmerizing eye. Auer's teaching began where technique ended: he guided the students' interpretation and concept of music, he shaped their personalities, he gave them style, taste, musical breeding. He also broadened their horizons, made them read books, guided their behavior, career, and social graces.

Though he valued talent, he also demanded punctual attendance, intelligent work habits, and attention to detail. He hated absenteeism. He demanded discipline of behavior and appearance; no sloppiness was tolerated. He even told them when to speak and when not to. "Remember, you are a nitwit: don't talk, just play," he admonished one of his gifted but simple-minded students. He insisted that his students learn a foreign language if an international career was in the offing.

Auer was also solicitous of the material needs of his students; he helped to obtain scholarships, to enlist patrons, to get better instruments. He made every effort to obtain residence permits for his Jewish students, using his influence in high government circles. Even after a student had started a career, he followed his path with a fatherly eye. He wrote countless letters of recommendation to conductors and concert agents. When little Mischa Elman was about to make his London debut, Auer traveled there to coach him. He continued to work with Zimbalist and Parlow after their debuts.

To be admitted to Auer's class was a privilege won by talent; to remain there was a test of endurance and hard work. The students revered and feared the master. To say that his word was law is an understatement; a law can be broken, but the professor could not be contradicted. Auer was stern, severe, even harsh. One luckless student was ejected regularly, with the music thrown after him. Others felt Auer's bow poked into their ribs to elicit more "*krov*" (literally "blood," but connoting fire). Auer hated anemic, lifeless playing; he valued musical vitality and enthusiasm. He himself was untiring and his energy was infectious.

A lesson was like a ritual, as demanding as a concert performance. "We did not dare cross the threshold of the classroom with a half-ready performance," a student reminisced. Students did not have weekly lessons; they were required to bring a complete movement of a major work, which usually needed more than a week for preparation. Once a student felt ready to play for the master, he had to inscribe his name ten days prior to the class meeting, which heightened the tension. Before the big day, everything had to be checked—strings, pegs, bow. The student had to dress appropriately. An accompanist was provided, usually a fellow student from a piano class. There was an audience, not only of students but often including distinguished guests and prominent musicians. Outside the classroom, people stood with their ears glued to the heavy double door, trying to catch a few sounds. The professor arrived punctually for the lesson; everyone had to be in place. There was one intermission during the lengthy session to air out the room. During the lesson, Auer would walk around the classroom, observing, correcting, exhorting, scolding, shaping the interpretation. Obviously, such lessons were not geared to everybody. The most gifted became great artists, the less gifted struggled, but many fell by the wayside. It was a survival of the fittest.

Was there an Auer "method"? Some deny it; even Heifetz, when questioned about his bowing, had to admit, "I was never able to say what the so-called 'Auer method' was though I studied with him."[6] Auer's book *Violin Playing as I Teach It* is often in contradiction to the way his best students used to play. For example, his views on vibrato seem totally oldfashioned: while he limits its use to expressive notes, his prize students used a continual vibrato of extreme intensity, something Auer called "pitifully misguided." In his words, "Only the most sparing use of the vibrato is desirable. . . . I always fight it when I observe it in my pupils—though often, I must admit, without success."[7] This was written in 1920, at the time when the continuous vibrato of Kreisler (not an Auer student!) and Heifetz were accepted as norm. And the bow position? "There can be no exact and unalterable rule . . . it is a purely individual matter based on physical and mental laws which it is impossible to analyze." Thus, every Auer student was virtually free to choose his own posture: some played with a high elbow, others kept it low, some pressed the index finger above the second joint, others below. What is certain is that Auer freed his students from the tyranny of the unnaturally low "Joachim elbow" and the wrist wiggling. Judging by the photos of Auer himself, he seems to have used the conventional Franco-Belgian grip. A majority of the present-day Soviet violinists (as far as I can observe) have also returned to the traditional bow grip as taught in Paris. Paradoxical though it may sound, it was Carl Flesch in Berlin who codified the so-called Russian bow grip after careful observation of prominent Auer students.* Auer himself paid no attention, as long as the bow was drawn parallel to the bridge.

Auer's success as a teacher began after 1900, with the influx of students from the Jewish Pale—the parts of Russia where Jews were per-

* See p. 336.

mitted to live, cities like Odessa, Berdichev, Minsk, and small towns in the Ukraine and Byelorussia. On his concert tours through Russia, Auer was always willing to listen to gifted youngsters brought to his hotel by anxious (usually impoverished) Jewish parents; he said that he discovered little Mischa Elman virtually "on the road." Once the talent was established, ways had to be found to bring the child to St. Petersburg and to have him admitted to the Conservatory, which in turn would entitle him to a residence permit in the capital. An additional complication was to obtain a permit for at least one parent to stay nearby. More than once Auer battled with high-placed officials of the czar to bend the anti-Jewish laws.

The first two prodigies to come to Auer in this manner were Efrem Zimbalist (age eleven) in 1901 and Mischa Elman (age twelve) in 1903. In principle, Auer, like Joachim, was opposed to concertizing prodigies. But facing so much precocious talent, he made exceptions. Little Mischa Elman made his Berlin debut in 1904, at the age of thirteen. In the meantime, a new cadre of gifted young fiddlers grew up under Auer's guidance between 1906 and 1917—Kathleen Parlow, Cecilia Hansen, Toscha Seidel, Mishel Piastro, Richard Burgin, Eddy Brown, Max Rosen, Miron Poliakin, and Jascha Heifetz. Each in his or her way became a celebrity, though the crown belongs to Heifetz. (Nathan Milstein is not mentioned in the annals of the conservatory; he may have been a nonmatriculated student around 1915–17.)

Auer established studios outside of St. Petersburg, where he taught during the summer months. He had a studio in London in 1906–11, then moved it to a suburb of Dresden in 1912. He was overwhelmed with requests for lessons, but accepted only a limited number of promising students. The outbreak of World War I trapped Auer and his foreign students in enemy country. Among them was Jascha Heifetz (then thirteen) with his family. My parents and I were there, too, since my father, a pianist, was a former concert partner of Auer. I have a childhood memory of walking down a deserted village street near Dresden hearing sounds of violin concertos coming out of every farmhouse. But this idyllic situation came to an abrupt end in August 1914: the local gendarme saw a spy in every fiddler and put them all under house arrest. By October, Auer was allowed to return to St. Petersburg, and classes were resumed at the conservatory. The summers of 1915–17 were spent in Norway, a neutral country which proved very hospitable to Auer and his students. In the fall of 1917, Auer decided not to return to Russia, which was in the throes of a revolution. He spent the winter in Scandinavia and embarked for the United States on February 7, 1918. He was seventy-three years old and ready to start a new life.

Auer received a warm welcome in New York. Many colleagues, among them the eminent Franz Kneisel, came to greet him. His former students gathered around him, some already celebrities in America, like Elman, Zimbalist, and Heifetz. The old maestro played at Carnegie Hall on March 23, 1918, and was also heard in Boston, Chicago, and Philadelphia. Recordings made at that time show his playing on a high level—impeccable intonation, incisive rhythm, tasteful phrasing aside from a few oldfashioned slides. He established residence on Manhattan's West Side, where he taught a select number of students who were willing to pay a high price for the honorary title of "Auer pupil." He also joined the Institute of Musical Art (now the Juilliard School) in 1926 and the Curtis Institute in Philadelphia in 1928, succeeding Flesch. That same year, Zimbalist joined the Curtis faculty and remained until 1968, continuing the Auer tradition.* Though Auer's ability to teach was somewhat impaired by increasing deafness and old age, he formed a few excellent violinists.† During the 1920s, Auer published several instruction books—*Violin Playing as I Teach It*, *Violin Master Works and Their Interpretation*, and a *Graded Violin Course* (with Maia Bang); he also edited a number of violin repertoire works. His memoirs appeared under the title *My Long Life in Music*. He died on July 15, 1930, at the age of eighty-five, during a vacation trip to his old summer place in Loschwitz near Dresden. He was buried in New York.

Toward the end of his memoirs, Auer lists his star pupils—Mischa Elman and Efrem Zimbalist, then Eddy Brown, "closely followed by Jascha Heifetz who made his sensational debut in New York in the autumn of 1917. A few months later came the appearance of Toscha Seidel and Mishel Piastro. These six artists are the representatives of the new Russian School of St. Petersburg."[8] In the following pages we shall discuss the individual accomplishments of these leaders of the "New School."

---

* One of Auer's oldest associates, Sergei Korgueff (born 1863), who had been violin professor at the St. Petersburg Conservatory from 1900 to 1925, suddenly turned up in New York and taught at the Institute of Musical Art from 1927 until 1933, when he died.
† See Rabinof (pp. 511–13) and Shumsky (pp. 513–14).

THE GREAT AUER DISCIPLES

Mischa Elman

Mischa Elman was born on January 20, 1891, in Talnoye, about half-way between Kiev and Odessa. There was a large Jewish population in that part of the Ukraine—"We Elmans are children of the ghetto," said his father.[1] The grandfather was a musician, a self-taught fiddler, socially at a rather low position. To raise the family standing, the father was brought up as a Hebrew scholar and teacher, but he was passionately fond of music. His little son Mischa showed fondness for music at the age of three. By the time he was five he was permitted to play a small violin. His progress was so rapid that he was talked about as a little wonder. In the meantime, their small town was ravaged by a pogrom, and the Elman family moved to Odessa in 1897.

Six-year-old Mischa was given a scholarship at the conservatory to study with Alexander Fiedemann, a former pupil of Brodsky. The family lived in utter poverty, always mindful that Mischa's future was worth every sacrifice. Whenever a celebrity came to Odessa, Mischa was present to perform, and everyone was enchanted by his talent; but there was no money for him to study elsewhere. The father decided to let Mischa give a few concerts around the Ukraine. His success exceeded all expectations, and a wealthy patron agreed to send the boy to St. Petersburg should Auer accept him. By a happy coincidence, Auer was scheduled to give a concert some 150 miles north of Odessa, in Elisavetgrad. Father and son took the next train and knocked timidly at the professor's hotel door. Auer was packing his trunk but agreed to listen. Auer wrote,

The boy, who was about eleven years old and very small for his age, with tiny hands, played a concerto for me. In the difficult passages he skipped about in the positions as an acrobat does on his ladder. The Concerto finished, I knew at once what my decision must be.[2]

In a letter to the conservatory in St. Petersburg, Auer recommended a full scholarship for Mischa, who was to enter his class.

In January 1903 father and son Elman arrived in St. Petersburg. At the conservatory, Mischa was a sensation. He played Paganini's Twenty-fourth Caprice without having ever studied any of the preliminary etudes. Auer was perplexed. He decided to drop the preparatory training and to treat the boy like a senior student. With his incredible manual and musical gifts, Mischa could grasp anything. Yet the lack of a thorough technical foundation caused Elman considerable difficulties in later years.

In the meantime, Mischa worked on his repertoire under Auer's personal guidance. Though opposed to concerts by child prodigies, Auer encouraged the boy's occasional performances: his talent cried out for public approval. The sudden appearance of another violin prodigy two years younger than Mischa may have forced Auer's hand. It was the ten-year-old Hungarian Franz von Vecsey, who arrived in St. Petersburg with a warm recommendation from Joachim. The young visitor had a very striking success, and Auer decided to risk sending his own prodigy, Mischa, for a debut concert to Berlin.

All through the summer of 1904, while Auer was vacationing in Finland, Mischa had weekly lessons. In September 1904, father and son Elman set out for Berlin, two innocents abroad. Settled at the hotel, the father left the gas jet open after blowing out the light, and little Mischa almost died of asphyxiation. Barely revived and still shaky, Mischa appeared with delay before the impatient audience. But he played like "one possessed" (as his father recalled)—first the Tchaikovsky concerto with piano, then the Bach Chaconne. The invited audience of critics and connoisseurs sat spellbound in the small Bechstein Hall. For his official debut on October 14, 1904, a rather showy program was selected, which "lacked musical significance" (as one critic wrote), but the reviews were superlative. Comparisons with Vecsey were unavoidable. Said the Lokal-Anzeiger, "We are forced to admit that Mischa Elman is a more startling phenomenon than his young rival." Another critic found Elman's "full, beautiful tone . . . vastly superior."[3] There was indeed a personal poignancy in Elman's tone that went straight to the heart of the listener, and people were seen to cry when he played.

Despite professional rivalry, the two boys—Mischa and Franz—were quite friendly toward each other. In Berlin, at the mansion of the music patron Mendelssohn, they played Bach's Double Concerto. It was said that Mischa's tone overshadowed that of Franz.

Mischa had to overcome one hurdle—to win over the great Joachim. The boy visited Joachim's class and, at his request, played the Tchaikovsky concerto. Joachim promised to attend Mischa's second concert (he had missed the debut) but his not going backstage upset the young artist greatly. Rumors began flying that Joachim preferred Vecsey to Elman, and he admitted that much—"after all, he is my countryman" (meaning a fellow Hungarian). But Joachim tried to be impartial: he invited Mischa to his home where the boy played the Bach Chaconne. "You are a brave boy," said the professor, "at your age, too, I played the same." Father Elman said, "We parted the best of friends."[4]

The rivalry between Elman and Vecsey remained alive for years. Technically, both boys were near-perfect, but Elman had more warmth and vitality, more spontaneous communication. Internationally, the public rendered its verdict in favor of Elman, though Vecsey enjoyed much success, especially in Central Europe.

After the Berlin debut, Elman's career grew like a torrent. His London success at Queen's Hall on March 21, 1905, was sensational. He was invited to play at Buckingham Palace for King Edward VII and the king of Spain. Auer kept an eye on Mischa: during the summer of 1905 they spent three months together working on new repertoire. In June 1906, London heard a concert at which Auer (then sixty-one) and Elman (then fifteen) appeared together in Bach's Double Concerto. "The concert was the most memorable in Mischa's entire career," reminisced his father. "Never before have I seen a more enthusiastic audience." Auer seemed very happy and wrote to a friend with modesty, "Probably because of Mischa, the public gave me a special ovation when I appeared on the stage."[5]

Despite the fierce competition among first-rate violinists—Ysaÿe and Kreisler, Kubelik and Thibaud—the teenage Elman was in the front rank. A new period in his career began with his debut in New York on December 10, 1908. He played the Tchaikovsky concerto with the Russian Symphony under Altschuler. He wore a new dress suit to emphasize his "coming of age" and was the proud owner of a newly acquired Stradivarius. The orchestra rehearsal was crammed with musicians eager to hear the new "boy wonder," and they were not disappointed. He gave a memorable performance, perhaps the best of his life. Within three seasons, he beat all records: he appeared with all the major orchestras from coast to coast. At seventeen, he was acclaimed as "king of the violinists" and remained unchallenged until Heifetz's arrival in 1917.

Elman's career in New York was managed by the famous impresario Oscar Hammerstein, who engaged him for a series of Sunday evening concerts at his immense Manhattan Opera House, an unprecedented venture crowned with success. Elman toured all over the world—Australia, the Far East, South Africa. He also became one of the most popular recording artists; during his career, more than two million Elman records were sold. His luscious tone reproduced most beautifully on discs, and in recordings with Caruso he rivaled the great tenor.

As Elman grew older, he had to rethink and retool his technique, which was less infallible than that of his competitor Heifetz. In fact, Elman's chief asset was not his technique, but his uniquely rich tone and his fiery vitality, his communication with the listener. He had rhythmic verve but did not play strictly in time, and occasionally conductors found it difficult to accompany him. As years went by, Heifetz and Kreisler moved to center stage while Elman slipped in popularity. Yet he retained a devoted audience, who adored his burnished tone and warm intensity.

Elman was short and stocky, with short arms, which necessitated a specific bow grip to let the bow reach the tip; even then his bow was not entirely parallel to the bridge. He played with loose bow hair. The fingers of his left hand were set down rather flat, that is, he touched the string with the fleshy part rather than the tip; the fingernails of his left hand were a bit long. He was very fussy about the adjustment of his violin and was apt to experiment with his bridge or soundpost just before a concert. While he was choosy about the violin he played (invariably a Stradivarius), he attached less importance to the quality of the bow he used—it was not essential to his tone production. His vibrato was intense but not broad, produced mainly by the wrist, not the arm; because of his fleshy fingertips, the effect was sensuous, but never "wobbly." His intonation was perfect, his ear infallible. In later years, he played the technical passages more deliberately, in a controlled, accurate manner, every note clearly articulated. He had an excellent musical memory until late in life.

It was his custom to select one or two recital programs for the sea-

son and repeat the pieces again and again with unflagging enthusiasm.*
Among his favorite compositions were the Handel D-major Sonata, the
Poème by Chausson, the sonatas of Franck, Brahms, and Fauré, Beethoven's *Kreutzer*. The Tchaikovsky concerto became his hallmark. He
had little liking for modern music; the most advanced pieces he played
were the concertos of Martinů and Khachaturian.

Elman always had a full-time pianist with whom he rehearsed every
day—usually good musicians but not outstanding personalities. He was
not one to share the limelight easily. For a time, during the 1920s, he
played sonatas with his sister Liza, an excellent pianist.

Elman never aspired to a teaching career. I was lucky enough to
have four or five lessons with him in my teens (my father had been a
childhood friend of Mischa's in Odessa). I recall playing Vivaldi, Tchaikovsky, and Lalo for him. He was always ready to demonstrate but unable to explain exactly how he did a certain difficult passage. His idea
of a good lesson was when the student was able to imitate him as closely
as possible. But I have a very fond memory of those hours in a Berlin
hotel suite.

Elman's outstanding personal trait was his strong family sense: he
was deeply devoted to his parents, particularly his father, who had
guided his every step for decades and who remained his most perceptive
critic, and was also a loving brother to his sisters, Mina, Liza, and
Esther, all musicians. At his parents' apartment on the Upper West Side
of New York, Mischa would come regularly to play his program or to
share chamber music with devoted friends. Like all great artists, he had
an entourage of hangers-on and flatterers who extolled everything he
did. He did not take criticism gracefully and was willing to argue with
Olin Downes, the New York *Times* critic, if need be. He liked to talk
politics and was quite argumentative; I can still hear his high-pitched
voice. But the main topic of conversation was music, the playing of
other violinists and his own. To him, all younger violinists played like
students—that is, without the artistic freedom that he valued; he had
grudging respect only for Kreisler and Heifetz. The famous story about
Heifetz's debut bears repeating. Elman and the pianist Godovsky sat in
a box at Carnegie Hall. Suddenly Elman turned around, tugged at his
collar, and remarked, "Isn't it awfully hot in this hall?" "Not for pianists," replied Godovsky with a sly smile.

Elman's decline in popularity hurt his ego, but he fought on with

---

* Actually, he had a large repertoire. In 1936–37 he played fifteen concertos with
orchestra in five evenings; the cycle was entitled "The Development of Violin Literature" (New York, Carnegie Hall, with the National Orchestral Association).

Efrem Zimbalist, one of the earliest and most famous Auer students, later became director of the Curtis Institute in Philadelphia.
Mischa Elman, the first Auer student to achieve world fame; the "Elman tone"
became legendary. His success established the fame of Auer as a teacher.

undiminished energy. He played concerts until the year he died, at the age of seventy-six.

Though Elman never had time to study musical composition, he composed with charm and ease, without aspiring to depth. He wrote original violin pieces and arrangements, as well as a musical comedy, following Kreisler's example but with less success. He played the piano quite well, was a good sightreader on the violin, and an excellent, though self-centered, quartet leader. He founded the Elman Quartet in the 1920s and the ensemble gave concerts for several years.

One of Elman's greatest admirers and strictest critics was the incorruptible Carl Flesch. After noting his "rhythmic unruliness" and declamatory style, he assigned to Elman "one of the most honored places in the history of contemporary violin playing."[6] Another colleague, Szigeti, compares the impact of young Elman in 1905 to a new era in violin playing. Ysaÿe was a true admirer of Elman, who was his junior by thirty-three years, and they performed together.

In 1964, sixty years after his memorable Berlin debut, Elman returned to play the Mendelssohn concerto with the Berlin Philharmonic. The German violin historian Hartnack reports, "It was one of the most musical performances I ever heard. . . . The inner warmth, the tender lyricism, the masterful shaping of form, the unique *bel canto* gave the performance the stamp of unrepeatable grandeur."[7]

Efrem Zimbalist

Efrem Zimbalist belongs, like Elman, to the early phalanx of Auer students who made a career before World War I. Born in Rostov-on-Don in 1890, he received his early training from his father, a violinist and conductor at the Rostov Opera. In 1901, young Efrem arrived in St. Petersburg and was admitted to the conservatory. After a preparatory period under Auer's assistant I. Nalbandyan, he was promoted to Auer's class, where he remained until 1907. This seems like slow progress for someone so gifted, but Zimbalist was irregular in attendance and rather unruly, particularly during the revolutionary year 1905, when he was one of the leaders of the student strike. He picketed Auer's class, trying to prevent students from taking their lessons, and was once ejected from the classroom for wearing a red shirt! When he was finally ready to graduate in 1907, the director—the composer Glazunov—wrote with enthusiasm about his graduation performance, "A colossal talent.

His interpretation is inspired, full of mood. A shattering impression, beyond comparison."[1] To which his teacher Auer added with irony, "I share the opinion of the director, but I must add that for the past two years he very rarely attended classes, which may have contributed to his progress." This did not prevent Zimbalist from graduating with highest honors, the Gold Medal and the Rubinstein Prize. A few months later, on November 7, 1907, he made his debut with the Berlin Philharmonic, playing the Brahms concerto with enormous success; equally acclaimed was his London debut on December 9 of that year.

Zimbalist was seventeen years old when he first appeared in western Europe—older and more mature than Elman. His appearance was less of a sensation, since he was not judged by prodigy standards, but was appreciated on his artistic merits. On January 1, 1910, he was deemed worthy to perform as soloist at the New Year's Day concert of the Leipzig Gewandhaus Orchestra, an invitation considered a singular honor.

With a solid reputation in Europe, Zimbalist came to the United States in 1911 and made his debut on October 27 with the Boston Symphony under Max Fiedler. Characteristically, he chose the unfamiliar Glazunov concerto (composed in 1905), not yet heard in America. Zimbalist's success was not sensational, but substantial and steadily growing. He decided to settle in the United States. In 1914, he married the famous singer Alma Gluck and appeared with her in joint recitals, not only as a violinist but also as her piano accompanist. (One is reminded of the current Vishnevskaya-Rostropovich team.)

Among the Auer students, Zimbalist was always admired for his musicality, in contrast to his virtuoso-type colleagues. His interpretations were tasteful and refined, technically polished and tonally ingratiating. Less emotional than Elman, less perfectionist than Heifetz, Zimbalist's performances derived their strength from a searching penetration into the essence of the music he played. His quiet temperament was reflected in his preference for unhurried tempos. In general, he avoided virtuoso exhibitionism, yet he was capable of playing Paganini with much flair and was one of the first to use Sauret's intricate cadenza for the Concerto in D major. His style was fine-grained and noble, and he played with great dignity.

In Flesch's opinion, Zimbalist's playing showed "no evidence of a significant personality"[2] and he considered him the least interesting among the elite of Auer students. My own recollection—I heard him in Berlin in the 1920s—was that of a somewhat stolid performer with superb violinistic qualities (he produced some of the fastest spiccato bowing I've ever heard in the final page of Sarasate's *Habanera*).

In 1928 Zimbalist joined the Curtis Institute in Philadelphia, the same year as his old master Auer. After Auer's death in 1930 Zimbalist continued the Auer tradition and taught a number of excellent violinists, among them Oscar Shumsky, Norman Carol, S. Ashkenazi, and H. Suzuki. In 1941 he assumed the directorship of the Curtis Institute, which he held until 1968. After Alma Gluck's death in 1938, he married Marie Louise Curtis Bok in 1943. She died in 1970, after which Zimbalist moved to the West Coast.

In addition to his activities as a widely traveled soloist and teacher, Zimbalist was a composer—not only for his own instrument but also of several stage works, orchestral music, and chamber music. He was also an active editor of violin music. His inquisitive mind was evident in the presentation of a cycle of five violin recitals, spanning the entire violin repertoire from the earliest time to the present.

After having reaped acclaim in all parts of the world, he gave a farewell concert in New York on November 14, 1949, but returned to the stage in 1952 to play the world premiere of the Violin Concerto by Gian Carlo Menotti dedicated to him. He was still heard in 1955 with the Philadelphia Orchestra in the Beethoven concerto. In 1962, 1966, and 1970, Zimbalist was invited to Moscow to serve as member of the jury of the Tchaikovsky Competition; the return to his homeland moved him deeply.

Zimbalist was a man of the world and cut a fine figure in high society. He was also very well liked by his colleagues and had many friends. Among them was Fritz Kreisler; they played the Bach Double Concerto in public as early as 1915 and made a superb recording of the work somewhat later. In fact, of all the innumerable recordings Kreisler made during his career, he singled out the Bach recording with Zimbalist as one of his favorites. Kreisler and Zimbalist also concocted the idea of writing an operetta back in 1917. Kreisler's *Apple Blossoms* reached the stage first, in 1919, while Zimbalist's *Honeydew* followed in 1920; both had excellent runs on Broadway.

Jascha Heifetz

"There has probably never been a violinist who has approached the summit of perfection more closely than Heifetz."[1] Indeed, the name

Heifetz has become synonymous with violinistic perfection. For more than half a century, he has set standards of performance by which all present-day violinists are measured.

Heifetz was born on February 2, 1901, in Vilna, then part of Russian Poland. His father Rubin was a violinist of moderate achievements, but perspicacious enough to recognize and guide his son's prodigious talent. At the age of three, Jascha began playing the violin with his father, who soon entrusted him to Ilya Malkin, a former student of Auer and a teacher at the Vilna Music School. Jascha played publicly at the age of five, and a year later performed the Mendelssohn concerto in Kovno.

Jascha's studies with Auer began in 1910 or 1911; the records of the St. Petersburg Conservatory show that he was enrolled from 1911 to 1916. In order to enable father Heifetz to reside in St. Petersburg (a city closed to Jews), he too was enrolled as a conservatory student in Auer's class, a formality which gave the family a residence permit. In fact, father Heifetz had considerable ability as a teacher, a profession he exercised after his son became famous. But at this time, he devoted every ounce of energy to his son, in whose talent he believed implicitly. "There will be a plaque on the house where Jascha lived," he once remarked quite seriously.

Barely settled at the conservatory, Jascha played a concert in St. Petersburg on April 30, 1911.

About that time, the American violinist Spalding, visiting St. Petersburg, was invited by Auer to listen to a class lesson. He reported,

> I remembered that some weeks earlier Kreisler had been full of praise for a small boy he had heard there. . . . A small boy stood up to play. He had only recently graduated to a full-sized violin; and it made him look even smaller than he was. . . . He played the Ernst Concerto . . . its technical difficulties tax the most seasoned veteran. What a cruel test, I thought, for a child!
>
> But I quickly found out that there was no need for apprehension. The first flourish of fingered octaves was attacked with a kind of nonchalant aplomb; the tone was firm, flowing and edgeless, the intonation of feckless purity. A kind of inner grace made itself felt in the shaping of the phrase. . . . Elegance and distinction . . . I had never heard such perfect technique from a child. Jascha, they called him. . . . While the boy was playing, Auer strode nervously about the room, glancing at me now and then to appraise my reaction.[2]

Auer was well aware that Jascha was a unique phenomenon. No one had ever played with that angelic perfection and technical daredevilry. Once, at an examination, Jascha attacked Paganini's *Moto perpetuo* at such a fast tempo that Auer winced, saying under his breath, "He doesn't even realize that it cannot be played that fast." But play he did.

After hardly more than a year of study at the conservatory, Auer decided to let Jascha make his Berlin debut at the Hall of the Hochschule where Joachim had been king for so long. The old master had died in 1907 and now the Hochschule was peopled by violinistic dwarfs draped in the false mantle of tradition. On May 24, 1912, the eleven-year-old Jascha, with blond curls and a cherubic expression, played a program (with piano) including the Mendelssohn concerto, Wieniawski's *Souvenir de Moscou*, and a few shorter pieces. Impressed by the immaculate performance, a critic placed Jascha "behind Mischa Elman and in front of Franz von Vecsey." [3] But the critics were not kind when little Jascha appeared in the large Philharmonic Hall under Nikisch at a subscription concert in 1912 replacing the indisposed Casals:

> With his 3/4 violin he is not able to float above the orchestra though the accompaniment was as discreet as possible, and his tone which sounds so admirably expressive in smaller halls, became lost in the big space almost to the point of being inaudible. . . . It does him damage. [4]

Another critic was even blunter:

> Though the boy prodigy played the Tchaikovsky Concerto in a virtuoso manner, the painful question remains—does a mere child belong in the framework of such a concert? Here at least one is entitled to expect a personality as soloist. [5]

Jascha resumed his studies with Auer, either at the St. Petersburg Conservatory or at Auer's summer studio in Loschwitz near Dresden. Here, musicians as well as impresarios gathered to hear the latest prodigy. At one of his musical matinees, Auer presented two of his favorites in Bach's Double Concerto—Jascha Heifetz and Toscha Seidel, age eleven and thirteen. Auer reminisced, "Not only I but all the guests were deeply moved by the purity and unity of style, and the profound sincerity, to say nothing of the technical perfection, with which the two children in blue sailor suits played that masterwork." [6]

The whole Auer clan—including the Heifetz family as well as my own—was summering near Dresden when World War I broke out.

After a few anxious weeks, the Heifetz family and mine were permitted to return to Berlin. As enemy aliens, we were obligated to visit the police precinct twice a day. Our families became rather close in the face of common problems. Jascha, who played the piano remarkably well, had lessons with my father, while I was taught the rudiments of the violin by father Heifetz. I can still remember Jascha in our music room, playing the finale of the Mendelssohn concerto at breakneck speed while jumping around and mocking the difficulties that were nonexistent for him. In December 1914 the Heifetz family returned to St. Petersburg; we remained in Berlin.

In the summer of 1916, Jascha joined Auer in Norway, where a small group of his students (including the friendly competitor Toscha Seidel) had assembled. Auer remarked, "These two boys were not regarded as rivals, but shared equally the general favor accorded them. Their numerous concerts . . . were always filled by an enthusiastic audience." [7] In fact, Jascha and Toscha were invited to play for the king and queen of Norway and they performed, once again, the Bach Double Concerto.

In 1917, Jascha was engaged to play in the United States. The family made the long journey via Siberia and Japan. His official debut took place at Carnegie Hall in New York on October 27, 1917. He was seventeen and played a recital program accompanied by A. Benoist: *Chaconne* by Vitali (with organ), Concerto No. 2 by Wieniawski, a half-dozen shorter pieces (mostly transcriptions), and, as a blazing finish, Paganini's Twenty-fourth Caprice in Auer's edition. The program was neither better nor worse than was the custom in those days: short on musical depth, long on showmanship. Yet "It was an occasion never to be forgotten, this sweeping triumph of a boy who, without pose or affectation, cast a spell of utter amazement over every professional listener." [8] And these professionals came in droves—"every violinist of note within radius of 200 miles" was present. With one concert young Heifetz obliterated every rival before the public; only Kreisler held his own. More than that: Heifetz effectively barred the rise of any competitor for a good decade, and all those who arrived after him, gifted though they may have been, were considered "also-rans." Heifetz was king; the public needed no one else. At an early age, his personality was already sharply etched: he was the image of flawless perfection. He seemed calm and unpretentious, he did not sway, he did not smile, he barely bowed. "He wins victory without flourish or appeal," said one critic. Some diagnosed it wrongly as coldness; while Heifetz was not the bubbling volcano of, say, Elman, he had an inborn aristocracy, a nobility of demeanor and expressivity all his own. Technique alone could not have captivated the world—it was a new approach to music, objective, unadorned, and impeccable.

The only criticism that seemed justified was one of repertoire choice. "This phenomenal young violinist can probably not improve his playing, but he can and indeed must better his programs. . . . He has limited himself, in the last analysis, to superficialities."⁹

This criticism was overcome in the next few years: Heifetz included the sonatas of Grieg, Brahms, and Franck. Now the critics began to find fault with his interpretation, especially with the Franck. "There are considerably more things in heaven and earth but technic and tone." Even these two attributes were questioned: the tone was found "not very large," * and cracks began to show in his technical armor. Heifetz himself admitted that he had become at times less fastidious about his technique:

> There came a time when my disinclination to practice caught up with me. . . . Henderson, the music critic of the *Sun*, hinted in his review that I was letting the public and him down, and that I had better watch my step. . . . The warning came in the nick of time. I began to practice seriously. . . . I shall always be grateful to Henderson. He jolted me out of my complacency.

The period was 1919–20, when several critics pointed out technical imperfections. But the pressures on the young artist were enormous. He had broken away from his father's control, and there was no one but himself to "curb his youthful extravagance." Another pressure was to expand his repertoire as rapidly as possible: the public was insatiable, he had to give as many as five Carnegie Hall recitals each season, and the programs showed little duplication. The repertoire learned under Auer's guidance was soon exhausted; new works had to be studied. The pattern of his programs in those days was standardized: two major works, a sonata or pre-Classical piece followed by a concerto with piano accompaniment; after intermission came shorter pieces and a bravura ending. Actually, he played what his public expected; the applause was always cool after the classics, it warmed up after a concerto, and it became delirious during the short selections. In those days, encores were

---

* Heifetz made his New York debut on a violin made by Tononi, a minor eighteenth-century master. He soon changed to a Stradivarius and eventually acquired a Guarnerius del Gesù of 1742.

given freely, even in the middle of a program. On demand, pieces were repeated. But in all fairness, Heifetz did not play down to the public. He included some Bach for solo violin, he played unfamiliar music by Enesco and Joseph Achron, though nothing "experimental." In later years he commissioned and performed more new music than either Elman or Kreisler, for example the concertos by Castelnuovo-Tedesco (No. 2, 1933), Walton (1939), Louis Gruenberg (1944), Erich W. Korngold (1947), Miklós Rózsa (1956). (However, he declined to learn the Schoenberg concerto of 1936.) He also played the underrated concertos of Glazunov and Elgar and popularized the Sibelius concerto. Even when doing the virtuoso repertoire, he did not take the easy way, but played the trickiest works by Paganini (*Witches' Dance, I palpiti, Caprices, Moto perpetuo*), Ernst, and Wieniawski. Needless to say, Heifetz also played every Classic and Romantic concerto, so that his repertoire was truly enormous. And much of it fortunately exists on records, some works recorded several times (like the *Kreutzer Sonata*). These recordings reveal the greater vibrancy and intensity that he acquired during the 1930s.

But his image on the stage never changed: the immobile stance, the unsmiling face showing his profile to the public, the violin held high and pushed far back, the bow arm with the elbow angled up, a minimum of fuss which disguised a maximum of self-discipline. His preference for fast tempos was always in evidence, as was the use of expressive glissandi; the critics called them "Auer slides," but Heifetz actually preferred the more sophisticated French slide established by Ysaÿe and Thibaud, approaching the note from below like a great singer.

After three years of unparalleled success in the United States, it was time, in 1920, to think of a world career. After all, Heifetz's fame was American-made, in contrast to Elman and Zimbalist, who had arrived with European credentials. It almost seems that Heifetz's American image made the Europeans suspicious; there was too much "gloss," too little depth. In Paris, Prunières called him a "miraculous automaton" and criticized his programs. Indeed, Heifetz had to make concessions to appease the traditional European taste: fewer "tidbits," more weighty music. He began his tour in London (Queen's Hall) in May 1920; he proceeded to Paris and Berlin; he toured Australia in 1921, the Orient in 1923, Palestine in 1926. He finally made a glorious return to his native Russia in 1934, after twenty years. He collected many triumphs and a few rebuffs, but the audiences loved him. In America he remained unchallenged: when Toscanini conducted his farewell con-

Jascha Heifetz, the legendary violinist who dominated the music scene from 1917 to 1970. Auer never produced another prodigy like Jascha. Here he is at the time of his Berlin debut (in a photo inscribed to the author's father). The Heifetz family and the Schwarz family, in Berlin-Grunewald, 1914, *left to right*: Jascha, his father, sister, mother, and the Schwarzes with the author at far right.

Heifetz as a mature artist

Heifetz's bow arm and his bow grip, a model of the Russian school

cert with the New York Philharmonic in 1936, he asked Heifetz to be soloist.

Supporting his continued popularity was his activity as a recording artist. He began to record for the Victor Talking Machine on November 9, 1917, playing five of his most popular encore pieces, and he finished on October 23, 1972, with a recital program performed in Los Angeles at the Chandler Pavilion. In the intervening years he recorded virtually the entire violin literature plus much chamber music. When RCA released the "Heifetz collection" in 1971, in celebration of his seventieth birthday, it was a revelation to the young generation. Certain of his recordings (for example, the Sibelius concerto) remain unsurpassed. For the first fifteen years, his recorded repertoire consisted mainly of short pieces or single movements. In 1934 began the great cycle of violin concertos and sonatas. In 1941 he turned to chamber music and recorded piano trios with Arthur Rubinstein and Emanuel Feuermann; additional trio records were made in 1950, with Piatigorsky replacing the late Feuermann. Memorable are also the recordings for string trio (violin, viola, and cello) made in 1941 with Feuermann and William Primrose; these three superb artists achieved an incredible fusion of their instruments.

With these chamber music recordings, Heifetz proved that, while still the supreme virtuoso, he was willing and able to blend his tone and style with instrumentalists he respected as his equals.

After Feuermann's sudden death in 1942, Heifetz formed a close partnership with Gregor Piatigorsky, a marvelous Russian cellist, whose effusive personality was actually quite different from the reserved Heifetz. But they felt so comfortable playing together that they established the Heifetz-Piatigorsky Concerts in California, where they both lived. These programs of mixed chamber music, from duos to octets, began to be recorded around 1960. In 1964, Heifetz and Piatigorsky brought the whole ensemble to New York's Carnegie Hall for three chamber-music concerts. The performances were vibrant and filled with tensile strength, characterized by fast tempos and much brilliance. Occasionally one wished for a bit more repose; nevertheless, the ensemble playing was impeccable and bore the imprint of Heifetz's personality.

Very revealing are the duo recordings of Heifetz and Piatigorsky. They combine two of the most glorious string tones ever recorded. They do not melt, they highlight each other. Heifetz's bowstroke is more decisive, Piatigorsky's more expansive. The violin vibrato is more intense, the cello vibrato more sensuous. Despite differences in technique and temperament, the ensemble is flawless.

In 1971, Heifetz made a television film in Paris, performing an hour's music with unimpaired mastery. Watching him at the age of seventy, one realized that his manner of playing the violin has barely changed: the same imperial stance, the same impassive, yet highly concentrated, facial expression. There were no ecstatic gestures, not a single superfluous move. What a lesson for the young generation, many of whom seem to act out all the emotions.

Again the recording of 1972, made at a concert in Los Angeles, shows his mastery—perhaps a bit more effortful, but nothing autumnal in his interpretation: virility in every stroke, an impatient pressing forward of the tempo, and fearlessness in taking technical risks. With advancing age he seems to press harder with the bow, at times producing harsh sounds, but that is certainly intentional: one can hear emphatic accents even in his early *Kreutzer Sonata* recording.

The beneficiary of this 1972 concert was the scholarship fund of the University of Southern California at Los Angeles, and thereby hangs a tale. In 1962 Heifetz decided to accept a violin master class at USC. It was a momentous decision, in keeping with the tradition of great virtuosos, most of whom taught at some time in their lives. Heifetz said, "My old Professor Auer put a finger on me. He said that some day I would be good enough to teach. . . . Violin playing is a perishable art; it must be passed on as a personal skill—otherwise it is lost." [10]

Heifetz did not become an ideal teacher—he was too authoritarian and lacked personal communication. But he took his new vocation very seriously, set the admission standards to his class extremely high, and made great demands. He stressed technical preparation, as was to be expected of a perfectionist, and he urged the study of scales. Artists who studied with him, like Erick Friedman, Beverly Somach, and Eugene Fodor, testify to his influence. Though Heifetz was intuitively gifted, he acquired his superlative mastery through the discipline of hard practice. His students exhibit the same concern for technical perfection; the danger is that the perfectionism becomes a goal in itself, not a means to express great music.

Some of Heifetz's class lessons were filmed and shown on television. One could admire his concentration, his attention to detail, and his constructive criticism often enlivened by dry wit. Occasionally he demonstrated difficult passages on the violin or accompanied expertly on the piano. Over a ten-year period, more than 150 students attended Heifetz's classes at USC.

Occasionally, Heifetz was willing to learn from his students. Fodor, a Silver Medal winner at the Tchaikovsky Competition in 1974, tells us that Heifetz "made him play staccato for fifteen minutes while the Maestro slowly circled him while studying his method for down-bow staccato carefully so that he could teach it to others." Surprising for anyone who knows Heifetz's near-perfect bow technique is Heifetz's own admission, "I had trouble playing staccato. . . . Really, at one time I had a very poor staccato. . . . The right way of playing staccato came to me quite suddenly while practicing Wieniawski's Concerto in F sharp minor."[11] That must have been when Heifetz was in his teens. He observed Fodor's very natural way of playing the staccato, not because his own needed improvement but because Fodor's method of production interested him.

To critics who dare describe Heifetz as an "automaton," one wishes to point out his innate musicianship: his perfect ear, his facile piano playing, his ability to adjust and assimilate himself in chamber music without giving up leadership, and, last but not least, his expert transcriptions for violin and piano. In fact, Heifetz had a good feeling for jazz rhythms and encouraged composers to write in that idiom (Louis Gruenberg, Robert Russell Bennett).

On February 2, 1981, Heifetz observed his eightieth birthday. Refusing to take part in any celebration, he asked to be left alone, a reaction typical of this very private man and artist. Recently he underwent an unsuccessful shoulder operation, and he plays the violin with effort. He plans to continue teaching, but students are few because he is so intimidating.

On that February evening, a concert took place at Alice Tully Hall in New York, one of the Lincoln Center chamber series. The first violinist, the extraordinary Itzhak Perlman, suddenly turned to the audience and said, "Ladies and gentlemen, today is the eightieth birthday of the greatest violinist that ever lived, Jascha Heifetz, and all of us, I'm sure, would like to wish you, Mr. Heifetz, a very healthy and happy birthday and many many more." Perlman was the spokesman for a generation of violinists who know Heifetz only through recordings, but who look up to him as the paragon of perfection to be emulated.

Nathan Milstein

Nathan Milstein (born 1904) is the last of the great Russian violinists to have had personal contact with Auer. This contact was slight and short. He himself rarely mentions it, and Auer did not name Milstein in his memoirs. He merely referred to "two boys from Odessa . . . both of whom disappeared after I left St. Petersburg in June 1917." [1] One of these boys could have been Milstein, although his name does not appear in the registry of the St. Petersburg Conservatory.

Milstein's first and principal teacher was Stolyarsky in Odessa, with whom he studied until the summer of 1914. (One of his fellow students was six-year-old David Oistrakh.) Milstein remembers his teacher without affection: "Stolyarsky never taught anything. When you played, he said 'Bad' or 'Good.'" [2] This is in contrast to the warm testimony of Oistrakh, who remembers his only teacher with fondness.

Young Milstein's arrival in St. Petersburg around 1915, during the first year of World War I, could not have been auspicious. The war mood, the defeats at the front, affected the general spirit. Milstein reminisced,

> Every little boy who had the dream of playing better than the other boy wanted to go to Auer. He was a very gifted man and a good teacher. I used to go to the Conservatory twice a week for classes. I played every lesson with forty or fifty people sitting and listening. Two pianos were in the classroom and a pianist accompanied us. When Auer was sick, he would ask me to come to his home.

All this came to an end when Auer left for Norway in 1917. A few students accompanied him; Nathan was not among them. He went back to his native Odessa trying to eke out a living as a violinist. These were hard times—a lost war, a revolution followed by civil strife, little food, no clothing, and insecurity. In 1921 young Milstein made his way to Kiev and gave a concert that was attended by Vladimir Horowitz and his sister Regina, also a pianist. They invited him for tea at their parents' home; "I came for tea and stayed three years." Vladimir, Regina, and Nathan became fast friends and soon went on a joint concert tour. Kogan, a concert manager, describes his first impression of Milstein in 1922: "I saw him first in a rather disheveled way: he wore an overcoat obviously borrowed from someone, a sort of lady-like collar, and his hands were wrapped in some rags." Compared to the elegant Horowitz (who came from a sheltered home), Milstein seemed oddly out of place. Yet the difference did not affect their friendship. According to Kogan:

> One [Horowitz] was tall, light-haired, often silent and serious, the other [Milstein] dark-haired, shorter, with broader shoul-

ders, of a lively temperament and not inclined toward pessi-
mism. Milstein liked to talk and to laugh, showing all his
white teeth. He was curious and eager to know things, interested in many subjects; he read a great deal, hoping to make
up by self-study what he had missed in formal education.[3]

Already then, Kogan remembers, Milstein's technique, tone, and
temperament were phenomenal. In his youthful exuberance he attacked
the strings so that one feared for the survival of the instrument. With
the years he learned how to discipline his excess technique. Horowitz
and Milstein became famous in their native land. There was one very
special concert in St. Petersburg on December 2, 1923, when the Philharmonic Orchestra was conducted by the venerable composer Glazunov. Milstein gave an impressive performance of Glazunov's concerto,
but his success was almost obscured by Horowitz's incredible rendition
of the Liszt and Rachmaninoff concertos.

Horowitz and Milstein left for a concert tour of western Europe in
1925, and they never returned to Russia. While Horowitz was an instant success, Milstein's career developed more slowly. In 1926 he spent
a brief time coaching with Ysaÿe, a towering artist though past his
prime. Milstein belittles the importance of this association—"After I
was thirteen, I never had a teacher. I went to Ysaÿe in 1926 but he
never paid any attention to me. I think it may have been better this
way. I had to think for myself."[4]

Milstein quickly outgrew a certain provincialism of repertoire and
style that afflicts many Soviet musicians reared in isolation. He came
to the United States in 1928 and made his debut with the Philadelphia
Orchestra under Stokowski on October 17, 1929, followed by a concert
with the New York Philharmonic on January 23, 1930. Eventually he
settled in New York and became an American citizen. Following World
War II, Milstein reestablished his European reputation and moved back
to the Continent, maintaining residences in Paris and London. Lately
he has become interested in teaching; he has given master courses at the
Juilliard School in New York and continues to give annual courses in
Zurich. His playing ability is unimpaired; today, in his late seventies, he
performs with the same intensity, the same virtuosity of past decades. It
is a phenomenal achievement and quite unusual for a violinist whose
instrument demands a greater physical agility and responsiveness than
the piano. Violin playing, to Milstein, is second nature; as long as he
is healthy, he will play to perfection.

Of all the great Russian violinists, Milstein is perhaps the least

Nathan Milstein, one of the great exponents of Russian violin art

"Russian"—he is not throbbing, he is not emotional in the accepted sense of the word. His violinistic instincts are controlled by musical intellect. He began his career as a dazzling virtuoso, and that epithet "virtuoso" clung to him particularly in Germany, where it has a pejorative meaning. (He defines virtuosity as the highest degree of professional excellence on every level of artistic achievement.) Over the years, Milstein matured into one of the most individualistic interpreters of great music. Whatever he plays—the Bach Chaconne or a Paganini piece—everything bears his personal imprint. Nor does he repeat himself; he rethinks and reinterprets works he has played for decades. His tone is warm, yet not sensuous, because he controls his vibrato to the point where it does not obscure the pure "core" of the note. He does not produce a large sound, because he avoids too much pressure on the string; he allows the string to resonate and to vibrate. Instead of pressing on the string, he achieves sound through sweep, by using a lot of bow, by changing his bow frequently. He even breaks phrases, but the breaks are inaudible because of his seamless bow changes. In his fingerings, he makes free use of open strings and natural harmonics (actually "white" tones), thus extracting from the violin all the natural resonance, all the overtones. This lends his intonation something incomparably pure, combined with his sparing use of vibrato, which is kept narrow.

Equally pure is Milstein's classical conception of the great concertos or of the Bach solo sonatas: they emerge full of nobility and restrained temperament, all the more admirable because his natural inclination is to be fiery and impetuous. But he has learned to discipline himself, revealing at the same time an original mind at work. His playing is a rare combination of classical taste and technical perfection. Yet he can be a dazzling technician when he tosses off his own *Paganiniana* or his new transcription of Liszt's *Mephisto Waltz*. The effortless nonchalance with which he achieves sophisticated technical feats is amazing. Milstein's greatest admirers are his fellow violinists, who understand the underlying intricacy of his flawless mechanism—and that included Kreisler, who considered himself an old friend and admirer. That Milstein did not achieve the world renown of Heifetz is a strange quirk of fate: certainly Heifetz is the only one to whom he can be compared. There is even some similarity in the appearance on the stage—the impeccable stance, the elegant motions, the effortless handling of the violin, which seems an integral part of the player. Attending a Milstein performance is an aesthetic as well as a musical experience.

More Auer Students and a Few Muscovites

So far we have discussed the most famous Auer disciples: Elman, Zimbalist, Heifetz, and Milstein. Others will be treated more briefly—there are simply too many. From 1868 to 1917, two hundred seventy students were registered in Auer's class at the St. Petersburg Conservatory. In addition, he had summer studios in London, Dresden, and Oslo; during the 1920s he taught classes in New York and Philadelphia. All in all, Auer may have taught as many as five hundred students. They became soloists, concertmasters, orchestral players, chamber musicians, teachers; some switched to conducting, others to composition. Those who taught passed on the Auer tradition to another generation, "Auer grandchildren" so to speak.

The Russian Revolution of 1917 caused a migration of musicians from east to west. Emigration was legal during the 1920s, and many Auer students followed the example of their master and headed for America; others had preceded him. The influx of Russian violinists only reinforced the legendary fame established by the triumvirate Elman-Zimbalist-Heifetz. The public was hypnotized by that new breed of fiddlers, though not *all* Russian violinists were geniuses! But the legend persisted. It was then that Arthur Francis and George Gershwin wrote the song "Mischa, Jascha, Toscha, Sascha":

> When we were three years old or so
> We all began to play the fiddle,
> In darkest Russia.
>
> When we began, our notes were sour,
> Until a man, Professor Auer,
> Set out to show us, one and all,
> How we shall pack them in—in Carnegie Hall.
>
> Names like Sammy, Max, or Moe,
> Never bring the heavy dough—Just
> Mischa, Jascha, Toscha, Sascha,
> Fiddle, fiddle dee.*

The public waited for another miracle like Heifetz, and almost ten years later one appeared, though from unexpected quarters—the incomparable Yehudi Menuhin, a true prodigy who arrived from San Francisco on the New York scene in 1926. At the debut recital, three elderly gentlemen sat in the front row to take measure of the new "competition"—the fathers of Elman, Heifetz, and Rosen, whose son Max was among the rising violinists. But that is a new chapter. . . .

First a look at the careers of the other Auer students. The failure of Toscha Seidel (1899–1962) to achieve equal status with Elman and Heifetz is puzzling. A few years older than Heifetz, he arrived in New York on the same boat as his teacher Auer and made his debut on April 14, 1918, about six months after Heifetz. But by that time Heifetz had bewitched the American public and no one could displace him. Seidel had a personality different from Heifetz's; his playing was vibrant and impassioned. In fact, some experts thought that Seidel combined the best qualities of Elman and Heifetz, namely temperament *and* virtuosity. Auer himself thought very highly of Seidel. Flesch wrote in his memoirs,

> Unjustly, Seidel is not often included in the front rank of the Auer school. I do not know the deeper reasons for this underestimation, but one thing I do know—that the quality of his tone is one of the most beautiful I have heard in my career. Technically, too, he is excellently equipped, whence I regard it as an injustice of fate that he is not considered the third in a triumvirate with Heifetz and Elman.[1]

Seidel toured the United States and Europe. After his performance of the Brahms concerto in London in 1925, the *Daily Mail* compared his interpretation to that of Kreisler in its warmth and intensity. But his career did not unfold; eventually he moved to California, where he became a successful studio soloist for films.

An intense performer was also the Canadian-born Kathleen Parlow (1890–1963). She joined Auer's class in St. Petersburg in 1906 and began to concertize in 1908. Auer had the highest regard for her and called her "Elman in a skirt." She worshiped her teacher and always carried his photo in her violin case. In 1908 Auer conducted the orchestra for one of Parlow's appearances. I heard her in Berlin in the 1920s; she impressed me with her sweep and power, but her tone lacked the melting quality of the Russian school. Tall and slim, she played with imposing conviction; I particularly recall her intense interpretation of Pizzetti's Violin Sonata. After many successful years in Europe, she returned to North America in 1926, taught at Mills College from 1929 to 1936, and joined the Royal Conservatory in Toronto in 1941, where she taught and performed with her own string quartet.

The career of Eddy Brown (1895–1974) started auspiciously, but foundered in the 1930s. Born in Chicago, he appeared as child prodigy before being taken to Budapest to study with Hubay around 1904. Eventually he became a student of Auer, who thought highly of him. Brown had much verve and an accomplished technique, but lacked the ultimate refinement. He made his Berlin debut in 1910 and concertized in Germany as late as 1915, being a neutral American. After his return to his native America, he was very well received and appeared frequently with the New York Philharmonic and other orchestras. But the influx of the Russian violinists proved too heavy a competition. He founded a string quartet in 1922 and gradually switched to a career in radio, first with WOR, then with WQXR. He was one of the first to stress serious classical music on the air and exerted a beneficial influence. His later positions, at the Cincinnati Conservatory of Music and at Butler University in Indianapolis, were not really commensurate with his artistic potential.

Three of Auer's best pupils achieved high recognition as concertmasters of America's leading orchestras—Piastro, Burgin, and Hilsberg. To this triumvirate one could add Mischakoff, who was not a direct pupil of Auer but studied with Auer's student, Sergei Korguyev.

Mishel Piastro (1891–1970) was recognized by Auer as one of his very best students. He attended Auer's class in the years 1906–10 and was the first winner of the Auer Competition in 1911. He arrived in California via the Far East in 1920 and was concertmaster of the San Francisco Orchestra from 1925 to 1931. That year, Toscanini engaged him as concertmaster of the New York Philharmonic, and he advanced to assistant conductor during Barbirolli's tenure (1941–43). Suddenly, the ax fell: the newly appointed music director of the Philharmonic, Artur Rodzinski, fired Piastro and thirteen other players, among them six first-desk men. The unprecedented action caused a scandal; eventually, five of the fourteen players were rehired, but not Piastro (who was replaced by the assistant concertmaster, John Corigliano). Piastro turned increasingly to conducting and made a reputation as leader of the Longines Symphonette, which became popular on radio and records. Piastro conducted the orchestra and appeared as violin soloist, but his artistic potential was not fulfilled.

Richard Burgin's (1892–1981) long and distinguished career centered on Boston, where he was concertmaster from 1920 to 1967. Particularly during the tenure of Koussevitzky, Burgin (elevated to assistant conductor in 1927) enjoyed great prestige as performer and teacher.

Born in Warsaw in 1892, he studied with Auer in the years 1908–12; he served as concertmaster in Helsinki and Oslo before coming to the United States. He was a fine performer, though not quite on the level of the finest Auer students. His all-round musicianship contributed much to strengthen the Auer tradition in the United States; he taught at the New England Conservatory of Music, at Harvard University, and at Tanglewood. After 1967 he lived in Florida, where he continued to be active until his death. He married the violinist Ruth Posselt in 1940.

Comparable to Burgin's career was that of Alexander Hilsberg (1897–1961). Though Hilsberg had studied only briefly with Auer (1911–12), he had absorbed enough of the method to transmit it to his students. After his arrival in the United States in 1923, he joined the Philadelphia Orchestra in 1926 and became concertmaster, moving up to associate conductor in 1945. Both Stokowski and Ormandy thought very highly of Hilsberg's ability. He remained with the Philadelphia Orchestra until 1952 and also taught at the Curtis Institute. In 1952 he was engaged as conductor of the New Orleans Symphony and developed the orchestra considerably.

In this context, a few words about Mischa Mischakoff (1895–1981) are in order. A student of Auer's assistant Korguyev at the St. Petersburg Conservatory, Mischakoff landed in New York in 1921 like so many of his fellow violinists. But he had a clear concept of his own potential, and instead of pursuing an illusory solo career, he accepted a succession of concertmaster posts, a profession in which he excelled. His ability earned him the praise and affection of such conductors as Stokowski, Frederick Stock, and Toscanini; particularly the latter relied very much on Mischakoff's experience in shaping the strings of the newly created NBC Symphony Orchestra.

Mischakoff's style of playing was ideally suited for his career as orchestra leader: his tone was strong but always beautiful, his rhythm robust, his technical command most reliable and unaffected by nerves. Despite the many years as orchestral player, Mischakoff never lost the refinement necessary for solo and chamber-music performances; in fact, the Mischakoff String Quartet was active for many years. Mischakoff was a connoisseur and collector of fine violins and at one time owned two Stradivaris and a Guarnerius del Gesù.

A few other Auer students who settled in America deserve mention. Joseph Achron (1886–1943) became known primarily as a composer, though he was an expert violinist. He made his American debut in 1925 and taught mainly in California. Paul Stassevich, violinist and conductor, came to America in 1919 and taught at the Mannes School in New York; he was active as a violinist and conductor.

Several Auer students made reputations as teachers. Vladimir Graffman was connected with the Mannes School in New York; at one time he taught Joseph Gingold, now professor of music at Indiana University and one of the noted violin teachers of America. Raphael Bronstein, at the Manhattan School of Music, recently gained fame through his student Elmar Oliveira, who won a Gold Medal at the 1979 Tchaikovsky Competition.

Indirect students of Auer were Paul Kochanski, a superb violinist and collaborator of Karol Szymanowski; and Boris Koutzen, noted composer and teacher.

Not all the Russian violinists who immigrated to the United States in the 1920s were Auer students, though all profited from the "Auer mystique." Several of the newcomers had a Moscow background. Among them was Léa Luboshutz (1885–1965), who received her early education in her native city of Odessa. She continued in Moscow at the Conservatory under Hřimaly, where she earned a Gold Medal upon graduation in 1903. She came to the United States in 1925 and made her debut with the American premiere of Prokofiev's Violin Concerto No. 1. In 1927 she joined the faculty of the Curtis Institute in Philadelphia, where she taught for twenty years. She gave some sonata recitals with the pianist Josef Hofmann, but did not concertize extensively.

Another Hřimaly student was Michael Press (1871–1938), who graduated from the Moscow Conservatory in 1900 and belonged to the faculty from 1915 to 1918. He emigrated after the Revolution, lived in Germany and Scandinavia, and came to the United States in 1922. For a few years he taught at the Curtis Institute, then accepted an academic teaching post in Michigan. Press was a superior musician, an accomplished violinist, conductor, and teacher. He also became known for his expert transcriptions for violin and piano.

Of great significance was the activity of Naum Blinder in San Francisco. Born in 1889 in the Crimea, Blinder studied at the Moscow Conservatory with Adolph Brodsky. From about 1910 on he was active in Odessa as a violin teacher and leader of the RMS Quartet. In the early 1920s, young David Oistrakh heard Blinder perform in Odessa and was very much impressed by his broad, singing bowing and poetic interpretation. In 1923–25 Blinder was on the faculty of the Moscow Conservatory, but decided to emigrate to America. He settled in San Francisco, where he became concertmaster of the San Francisco Symphony. He also taught a number of students, among them a prodigy named Isaac Stern. Stern was Blinder's pupil from 1932 to 1937 and remembers his teacher with great fondness; he calls him his "principal teacher." It was Blinder who prepared Stern for his successful New York debut in October 1937.

It is important to realize that during the 1920s the Russian school of violin playing—its style of performance and its method of teaching—had all but conquered the American musical scene. The Russian virtuosos of the Elman-Heifetz type had displaced the French virtuosos of the Ysaÿe-Thibaud tradition in the favor of the American public. At the same time, Auer disciples spread the gospel of their method at the expense of the established Franco-German teaching of pedagogues like Kneisel and Déthier. Among the few survivors of the Russian influx were Fritz Kreisler, whose reputation as master violinist remained supreme, and Louis Persinger, a teacher who upheld Ysaÿe's ideals and produced some spectacular violinists like Menuhin, Ruggiero Ricci, and Guila Bustabo. They, as well as Isaac Stern, will be discussed as the American School.

THE SOVIET SCHOOL

Leopold Auer left the St. Petersburg Conservatory in 1917, the year of the Revolution. He spent his summer vacation in Norway, as he had done in the previous two years, and simply did not report back for the opening of the fall semester. The decision to abandon the city and his work at the conservatory after an affiliation of forty-nine years must have been very difficult. But he was seventy-two, and the decision was inevitable. He had been a monarchist all his life and, aloof from all the "liberalizing" trends at the conservatory, he had no desire to witness the dismantling of Russian culture as he had always known it.

The conservatories were shaken to the core by the October Revolution. The Russian Music Society, patron of all music schools, was dissolved and its institutions nationalized. During the interim, subsidies were suspended and salaries remained unpaid for months. The buildings could not be heated—group instruction had to stop, with individual lessons given at the homes of the instructors. Hunger and cold reigned in the cities; public transportation was virtually at a standstill during the winter months. And yet theaters remained open, opera and concerts functioned, though the orchestral players had to play wearing gloves.

Glazunov, the venerated director of the St. Petersburg Conservatory, kept the channels of communication open with the Bolshevik leaders, and the conservatories were treated with consideration. Inevitably there were many changes: faculty and students were socialized, the curriculum was revised, new goals were set. For a time, the quality of instruction suffered.

Yet the tradition of the past was not entirely broken. After Auer's departure, several of his former students on the faculty kept a watchful eye: I. Nalbandyan, Auer's trusted assistant since 1895, retained his professorship until 1942; Sergei Korguyev, appointed in 1900, taught until 1925; Maria Gamovetskaya, a former Auer assistant, had a class from 1912 to 1931. They bridged the gap after the master's departure. In 1928, their ranks were strengthened by the return to Leningrad (previously St. Petersburg) of Miron Poliakin (1895–1941), one of Auer's star pupils before the war.

Leningrad and Moscow: Miron Poliakin

Poliakin had come to Auer in 1908, at the age of thirteen. By that time he was already far advanced, playing the concertos of Mendelssohn and Tchaikovsky. Nevertheless, he had to undergo the usual "conditioning" by an assistant, in his case Nalbandyan. He was sensitive, proud, and arrogant, and he resented Nalbandyan's tutoring. At the examinations of 1910, Auer simply entered three exclamation marks after Poliakin's name while director Glazunov wrote, "Highly artistic interpretation. Marvelous technique. Enchanting tone. Sensitive phrasing. Temperament and atmosphere in his playing. A finished artist."[1] (Poliakin was fifteen at the time!) In 1911 Auer commented, "Outstanding," while Glazunov added, "An exciting impression." In 1912 Poliakin performed at the fiftieth anniversary of the St. Petersburg Conservatory. While still nominally a student, Poliakin received Auer's reluctant permission to concertize in the provinces. For some reason (perhaps to escape the military draft), Poliakin retained a student status until 1918 and left without graduating. Once abroad, he played in Scandinavia and Germany and embarked for America in 1922. He was well received at his New York debut on February 27, but the competition among violinists was fierce. Though he won first prize in a 1925 World Violinists contest, his career did not develop as he had hoped, and in 1927 he decided to return to Leningrad, where he was greeted with open arms.

After his return, Poliakin grew as an artist. In his earlier days he had been primarily a miniaturist, a master of the brilliant or sentimental repertory. Now he showed strength in concertos and sonatas. He communicated with his Russian audiences, throwing himself wholeheartedly into the task of winning the public, and they responded to him with warmth, whether at the Philharmonic or at a workers' club.

In 1936 Poliakin moved to Moscow, which led to a certain rivalry with Oistrakh, who was thirteen years younger and a rising star. Two parties formed among listeners, one favoring Poliakin, the other the more contemporary Oistrakh. Poliakin's playing is described as closer to his teacher Auer in style and taste than any of the other disciples. He was an uneven player, often afflicted by nervousness, which he overcame after a shaky start.

Though Poliakin's presence was important and fruitful for the development of post-Auer violin playing in Soviet Russia, his tense disposition prevented him from being a patient and methodical teacher. He relied primarily on his own demonstrations, preferring to play rather than to discuss. Students learned from observing and hearing him. In moments of inspiration, Poliakin's demonstrations in class grew to full recitals, and here he gave his best as an artist. Like his master Auer, Poliakin required the presence of every student at every class session; they began at three in the afternoon and were attended not only by students but by fellow musicians, with people assembled outside to listen through half-opened doors. While Poliakin did not discuss specific techniques, he required students to play scales and etudes, at times in class. He put great stress on a free-swinging right arm with motions from the shoulder, putting weight into the bow stick, yet with an elastic wrist. The fingers of the left hand had to function with precision. But it was mostly his accomplished playing that fired the imagination of his students. An amusing description of Poliakin's class is given by the violinist Jelagin:

> Poliakin's class consisted of only two or three students. He could not bear to hear them play. After listening for a few seconds to a violin concerto played by a good young violinist, he interrupted him and criticized the performance in violent terms. Then he picked up the violin and no matter how well the student had played, Poliakin always played better.[2]

Poliakin's transfer in 1936 from Leningrad to Moscow was merely a final confirmation of a gradual shift in prestige: the Leningrad Conservatory had become of secondary importance, while the Moscow Conservatory attracted the most talented teachers and students of the entire country. It was part of a general trend, political as well as cultural, to make Moscow preeminent in all fields since it was proclaimed the capital of the Soviet state in 1918.

With Auer's departure, the St. Petersburg Conservatory lost its most prestigious name and waited for ten years to appoint a worthy successor, Poliakin. In the meantime, the Moscow Conservatory had built a vigorous new violin faculty, mostly former Auer students or those influenced by him: Lev Zeitlin, Abram Yampolsky, Boris Sibor, and Konstantin Mostras, followed after 1930 by Dmitry Tsyganov, David Oistrakh, and finally Poliakin. At the same time, cultural officials paid more attention to an important source of violin talent—the Odessa Conservatory, where Stolyarsky continued his unique "talent factory." Graduates of his class were encouraged to come to Moscow to receive postgraduate training at the conservatory.

All this planning paid off handsomely: in 1937 the Soviet school of violin playing won a spectacular victory by placing five winners (among the first six) at the Ysaÿe Contest in Brussels. (The contestants had to be under thirty years of age; the winner Oistrakh was twenty-nine.) Members of the jury included Flesch and Szigeti, who were frankly amazed. Some attributed it to the unique support given to promising young artists by the Soviet government, the early selection of talented children trained in special schools. This was certainly a contributing factor. Here is a list of the Brussels winners:

NAME	TEACHERS
1. David Oistrakh	Stolyarsky
2. Ricardo Odnoposoff	Flesch
3. Elizabeth Gilels	Stolyarsky, Yampolsky
4. Boris Goldstein	Stolyarsky, Yampolsky
5. Marina Kozolupova	Mostras and Poliakin
6. Mikhail Fikhtengolts	Stolyarsky, Yampolsky

Four of the six winners had studied since childhood with Stolyarsky. By the time they were considered ready to go to Moscow, they were accomplished technicians merely in need of polishing. But essentially, the talent came from the same reservoir of Jewish children in the former ghettoes of the Ukraine—mainly Odessa—where Auer's little geniuses used to come from. They were welcomed with open arms at the Moscow Conservatory:

Stolyarsky's pupils arrived in Moscow with the highest available technical equipment but usually they were uneducated musicians with no artistic taste. . . . They rendered complex passages with ease, but they could not, verbally or in their playing, interpret the difference between Mozart and Brahms, or between Bach and Tchaikovsky. . . . The Moscow Conservatory polished a stone that had already been cut. After a few years at the Conservatory the blank spots in the young virtuoso were filled and he was ready to enter any international competition.[3]

Most of the polishing was done in the class of Abram Yampolsky, who, until his death in 1956, was among the most successful teachers on the Moscow faculty. It must be remembered that Soviet conservatories are not concerned with children: they are college-level institutions, where highly qualified students are admitted at the age of seventeen or eighteen. The basic technical training is done in the preparatory special music schools. Some of the conservatory professors also teach in the prep schools, which is particularly beneficial to the youngsters; from the very beginning they receive a solid foundation and there is never any need to relearn.

The startling result of the 1937 Brussels Competition caused some of the judges to speak out against "too much concentration on the mechanical aspects of music."[4] Flesch remarked that technique had taken the place of spirituality. Although the mechanical work is unsurpassed, the warmth and the mystery of music have departed. There is the deadening effect of grim, joyless, technically flawless playing, which makes a Mozart concerto sound like a Kreutzer study. "Is it possible that the new schools have given a technical endowment to a generation of violinists who cannot use it to any purpose?" Flesch's question is overly pessimistic: there are young violinists before the public today who combine technique and spirituality—they are not mutually exclusive.

Odessa: Piotr Stolyarsky

Odessa is a jewel of a city, beautifully planned with broad streets, boulevards, and parks, descending in terraces toward the Black Sea. The climate is mild and the streets lively. With its harbor, it is a bustling city, but also one with a cultural tradition. Opera and ballet have flourished since the beginning of the nineteenth century. Famous soloists visited Odessa, among them Vieuxtemps, Liszt, Wieniawski, and Sarasate. A Philharmonic Society, established in the 1850s, was taken over by the Russian Music Society in 1884; a music school was founded in 1870, which eventually came under the patronage of the RMS and was elevated to a conservatory in 1913.

Independent of the conservatory, the violinist Piotr Stolyarsky established in 1911 a private violin school for children in Odessa; his detractors called it a "talent factory." Until recently, very little was known about his background, but the latest Soviet encyclopedia provides a surprisingly detailed and somewhat fanciful biography, not only of Stolyarsky but also of his obscure teacher Josef Karbulka. The purpose is obviously to reconstruct the violinistic ancestry of the Odessa violin school, which has assumed an important place in the framework of Soviet violin performance.

Stolyarsky was born in 1871 in a village near Kiev. As a child he started the violin with his father, continued with Stanislaw Barcewicz in Warsaw, and completed his studies at the Odessa Music School with Emil Mlynarski and finally with Karbulka in 1898. That year he found employment in the orchestra of the Odessa Opera and remained there until 1919. But his true vocation was to discover musical children, to stimulate their interest, to teach them the violin. "One of the fundamentals of his method was to instill confidence in the young pupil by assuring him that he had extraordinary talent. . . . The child worked with enthusiasm."[1] His explanations were geared to the child's mentality, but he also knew how to deal with ambitious mothers and fathers. His studio consisted of a large flat, which was crawling with small children five years or less. While lessons were given, the small ones played on the floor with tin soldiers or dolls, later with toy violins imitating their elders. However, Stolyarsky was perfectly capable of guiding his advanced students through the concerto repertoire, as he proved in the case of Oistrakh and other contest winners.

Stolyarsky was "an odd, almost fantastic figure—but a teaching genius," recalls the emigré violinist Jelagin, who came to the United States in the 1940s. His report continues,

> Almost all the best violinists in the Soviet Union began their studies under Stolyarsky. . . . He was a very bad violinist. . . . He was not an educated man and at times he seemed illiterate. . . . Unquestionably he had the intuition of genius and his method of placing both hands was perfect, though it had nothing in common with the standard methods used by violin teachers. His pupil Oistrakh held his elbow very low, as if it were dangling; Liza Gilels held her right arm very high; Mischa Fikhtengoltz had a very special way of holding his left arm. . . . Stolyarsky demanded that his pupil take his violin out of the case immediately after breakfast and put it away just before he went to sleep at night. . . . All other activities, including general education, were expected to be cut to a minimum. The child's entire life had to be given to the violin.[2]

This slightly ironic account must be taken with a grain of salt. In the early 1920s, Stolyarsky's studio was incorporated into the Odessa Conservatory, where he was named professor. In 1933 his merits were recognized when a newly established special music school was named after him. In 1939 he received the title "People's Artist of the Soviet Ukraine." During World War II he was evacuated to Sverdlovsk, where he had the joy of meeting his old star pupil, David Oistrakh, and of teaching Oistrakh's son Igor the violin. Stolyarsky died in Sverdlovsk in 1944. His all-important contribution to the formation of an Odessa school of violin playing is belatedly recognized by Soviet historians.

David Oistrakh

Between 1937, when he won the first prize in Brussels, and 1974, at the time of his sudden death, David Oistrakh was the reigning Soviet violinist. He proved that the preeminence of Russian violin art was not based on a single teacher—Auer—but that it was the sum total of many factors. Oistrakh reached the top without having studied directly with Auer; he was exclusively a student of Stolyarsky, though indirectly he absorbed some of the Auer tradition.

David Oistrakh was born (in 1908) and raised in Odessa, the mecca of fiddlers. Odessa was within the Jewish Pale of czarist Russia, and that oppressed segment of the population continued to be an inexhaustible source of musical talent. Most of the budding violinists found their way to the studio of Piotr Stolyarsky.

David was five when he began working with Stolyarsky, and six when he first played in public. In 1923, Oistrakh, then fifteen, entered Stolyarsky's class at the conservatory and remained for three years. As a member of the student orchestra, he played violin as well as viola. He also organized his own string quartet. In 1926, he graduated with Prokofiev's Concerto No. 1 (a comparative novelty), Tartini's *Devil's Trill Sonata*, and the Viola Sonata by Anton Rubinstein. He reminisced, "I must admit that I played rather freely at that time, fluently and with pure intonation. But I still had much to learn in terms of tone, rhythm, and musical depth."[1]

And learn he did, by self-study or by listening to other musicians. He played with Milstein, he admired Szigeti, he learned from Prokofiev. At a banquet given in Prokofiev's honor in 1927, young Oistrakh performed the Scherzo from the Violin Concerto. Prokofiev, listening intently, did not applaud but went to the piano and said, "Young man, you don't play this at all as it should be played," whereupon he gave him a lesson on the stage. Many years later, Oistrakh—by then a close friend of the composer—reminded Prokofiev of the incident. Oh yes, he remembered the occasion and that "unlucky young man" whom he gave a piece of his mind. "And do you realize who that 'unlucky' violinist was?" asked Oistrakh. Prokofiev was not aware of it and for once he was embarrassed when Oistrakh told him. "You don't say!" he mumbled.[2]

At that time, Oistrakh heard recordings made by Kreisler and was so enchanted that he began to copy his style as well as certain technical procedures. Years later, in 1937, when he first heard Kreisler perform in person, he realized that he had copied only external attributes, that Kreisler was an artist of a different dimension. In the meantime, however, Oistrakh endeavored to stress elegance and brilliance at the expense of emotional involvement. He became known as a specialist in miniatures. When he met the conductor Nikolai Malko, who was visiting Odessa, Oistrakh played for him an arrangement of Debussy's A Doll's Serenade. Malko quipped, "Young man, you've outgrown the age to play with dolls, and not old enough to sing serenades."[3] Nevertheless, Malko invited the unknown young violinist to perform with him in Leningrad.

Before that, in 1927, Oistrakh had had the opportunity of playing Glazunov's Violin Concerto under the composer's baton in Kiev and Odessa. It was a profound experience. Oistrakh reminisced, "He conducted sitting down. The tempos were somewhat slower than those I was used to. But it was very convincing. In the complex polyphonic texture of the concerto every detail 'sang,' the orchestral sound was songful; not only in cantilena but also in rapid passages, all the instruments sang. The entire work acquired a new, fresh profile."[4]

Oistrakh's Leningrad debut under Malko took place on October 10, 1928. The orchestral players were at first rather unfriendly, but changed their minds after the first rehearsal of the Tchaikovsky concerto. He played on a cheap violin; nevertheless, it was a success.

That year Oistrakh moved from Odessa to Moscow. As an outsider, a newcomer, he was met with indifference. Some advised him to become a postgraduate student at the conservatory, others recommended a job with the Bolshoi orchestra. He did neither. He made contact with the senior professors at the conservatory, widened his musical horizon, heard visiting artists, and became aware of the provincial aspects of his playing and repertoire. On January 22, 1929, he gave his first formal recital in

Moscow. The program was a curious mixture of serious music and tidbits. He fared better in his next major appearance in Moscow in 1933,
when he played the concertos of Mozart, Mendelssohn, and Tchaikovsky; here he truly proved his growing maturity. The following year he
was appointed to a junior teaching position at the conservatory and rose
to professor in 1939.

The Soviet government encouraged all kinds of contests—it was a
very competitive young society—and music contests were popular.
Oistrakh performed well under pressure and won several first prizes, at
the All-Ukrainian violin contest in 1930 and the All-Soviet contest in
1933. A setback was the Wieniawski Competition in 1935, where he had
to be satisfied with a second prize, while the Gold Medal went to the
fifteen-year-old Ginette Neveu. But he made up for it by winning the
first prize at the 1937 Ysaÿe Contest in Brussels, outplaying a field of
eighty contestants of international caliber. The contest was grueling, the
participants exhausted beyond endurance. The nervous tension caused
hysterics and collapses. Even as experienced a performer as Oistrakh
spoke of the intolerable pressure, the constant practice, the sagging confidence when listening to a rival's performance. Oistrakh's position was
especially vulnerable: he was the oldest and most experienced among
the brigade of young Soviet contestants, and the responsibility to win
was on his shoulders. That four additional prizes went to Soviet violinists was a pleasant surprise but not undeserved: they entered the contest
as a matter of national pride, with the full material support of their
government, while other countries displayed indifference. Speaking as a
member of the jury, Flesch said,

> While other governments gave their candidates good wishes,
> the Russian team was granted support as generous as though
> the Olympic Games were in question. Moscow provided its
> children with superb instruments to play upon; it sent them to
> Brussels long before the competition opened so that they
> could accustom themselves to the atmosphere and come to the
> trial fresh. The player who obtained the second prize [Od-
> noposoff] . . . had been leading the orchestra of the Vienna
> Opera the night he left for Brussels.[5]

The Soviets recognized early that the physical and psychological
preparation of contestants is as important as the musical aspect. Soviet
performers are contest-conditioned: they have trial runs, their resilience
and self-confidence are built up. They do not enter contests, they are
entered as a team by a solicitous committee of experts, some of whom

serve as judges on the jury. Having been preselected, they enter the arena with confidence. All this does not guarantee winners, but it is helpful.

The Brussels experience matured Oistrakh: he expanded his repertoire, acquiring breadth and grandeur. He began to collaborate with Soviet composers on new works: the Miaskovsky concerto in 1939, the Khachaturian concerto in 1940, followed by the Prokofiev sonatas in F minor and D major (the latter, Oistrakh transcribed from the Flute Sonata at the composer's request). He became a close friend of Shostakovich, who later wrote two concertos and a sonata for him.

During World War II, Oistrakh played at the front, in hospitals and factories, in blockaded Leningrad. In May 1945, he met Menuhin, who was the first foreign artist to visit Moscow after the war, but they did not perform together until 1947, at the Prague Musical Spring. Here they came to know each other as musicians and felt enriched by the experience. Over the years, their friendship deepened and they played together, as Menuhin said, "in half the capitals of the developed world," though, strangely enough, never in Moscow.

In 1946–47, Oistrakh presented an impressive cycle of five concerts in Moscow, entitled "The Development of the Violin Concerto." He had enlarged his repertoire by several newer concertos—Sibelius, Elgar, and Walton—and the entire series was a proud achievement. Now he was the uncontested grandmaster of Soviet violin art. Such monumental playing had not been heard in Moscow for decades, if ever.

Oistrakh's international career, delayed by the war, began in earnest in the 1950s. He returned to Brussels in 1951, this time as a member of the jury of the contest he had won fourteen years earlier. Again there was a Soviet winner—Leonid Kogan. While in Brussels, Oistrakh gave a concert with orchestra playing the concertos of Bach, Mozart, and Beethoven.

Finally, in November 1955, Oistrakh made his long-awaited debut in New York. His first recital at Carnegie Hall was followed by his appearance with the New York Philharmonic under Mitropoulos on December 29, 1955; he played the American premiere of Shostakovich's First Concerto, dedicated to him. Carnegie Hall was seething with excitement. In response to the ovation, Mitropoulos raised the score toward the audience, but it was Oistrakh who stood at the center of the enthusiasm. The historic performance was recorded. During the 1960s, Oistrakh returned six times to the United States with ever growing success, though there was competition from other Soviet violinists, mainly Kogan.

Late in life, Oistrakh fulfilled a long-standing ambition: he made his debut as orchestral conductor in 1962, accompanying his son Igor in three violin concertos. Oistrakh's repertoire as conductor expanded, though his career as violinist always took precedence.

When Oistrakh died on October 24, 1974, he was at the height of his career. Death came suddenly, during a concert cycle in Amsterdam devoted to Brahms. He had conducted six concerts and had been soloist in three of them. Though he had once before suffered a heart attack, no one thought that the end was so near. He was a father figure to a generation of Soviet violinists, and there was no one in terms of musical authority and pure humanism to take his place.

Oistrakh was universally loved and admired, not only for his artistry but also for his human qualities. His colleagues were his greatest friends. "I feel as if I had lost a brother," said Isaac Stern; "in all the years I knew him I never heard him say an evil word about anyone."[6] And Menuhin wrote,

> I loved him immediately. Not only was he the gentlest, staunchest, most warm-hearted of men, but he was also simple and ingenuous. He never felt the need to appear other than he was . . . but presented himself candidly, without second thoughts or self-consciousness or doubts about his reception, a complete human being.[7]

Sincerity was also an important part of his musical personality: one could sense it in every phrase, every gesture. His stance on the podium was simple and unaffected. There was no external exhibitionism, no artificial temperament, but an inner warmth that came from a full heart. His playing combined highest technical proficiency and deep intellectual grasp with inner lyricism in a rare balance. None of these ingredients was permitted to dominate. The technique, brilliant though it was, was not self-serving. The intellectual power was intense—he worked and reworked his repertoire, always seeking to improve; he listened to his own tapes while work was in progress and approached his own playing with acute self-criticism. But when it came to interpreting a work in public, everything was overshadowed by his emotional involvement. There may have been violinists who played certain works with greater thrust, with a more biting attack; his playing had a mellifluous quality, avoiding harsh accents. Even thorny scores sounded as if all the corners were smoothed out—every note, every passage sang. Kreisler praised the fact that Oistrakh played more slowly than other violinists. It was not so much slow as it was totally relaxed and natural, as if the instrument were an extension of his body. Though not an exhibitionist, he enjoyed playing in public. Not a "martyr" of the podium like Huberman or Poliakin, fretting before every performance, he was always ready and able to give his best before an audience. He never wanted to reduce the number of his concerts, because he felt that the artist was likely to lose his touch when staying away too long from audiences. He needed that constant reassurance of his ability to hold the public's attention. He was one of the most reliable performers; even when he was not in the mood, his playing was note-perfect. He worked intensely, not always with the violin in hand but in his mind. His energy and ability to work were inexhaustible.

Oistrakh had a model technique. Both left and right hands functioned with effortless precision and total reliability. For this, his only teacher, Stolyarsky, deserves much credit; all his students have basically excellent hand positions. Oistrakh's concept of violin mastery was centered on a cultivated sound which, he felt, depended on the mastery of the bow rather than on vibrato. This, in fact, was the classical viewpoint espoused by, among others, Joachim and Capet. He compared bowing to breathing, an innate gift, though certain elements can be taught. A beautiful sound should pervade not only the cantilena, but also the technical passages; everything must "sound." The student must develop an inner ear for the sound he wants to produce and must acquire the ability to "prehear" a phrase before he actually plays it.

Oistrakh's bow arm was of classic perfection, producing a variety of articulations by use of the arm for power or the wrist for elasticity, seamless cantilena, or sparkling bow strokes. While he seemed to deprecate the role of the vibrato, he himself used it with great subtlety, ranging from a "white" tone to sensuous passion. His fingerings were rational and rather modern in their avoidance of unnecessary slides and the use of extensions.

Oistrakh's art of violin playing is perpetuated by a great many recordings—virtually the entire literature from Bach to Bartók, though avoiding extreme modernism—and by his edited violin parts, all published in Moscow. It goes without saying that he edited all the concertos and concert pieces dedicated to him, but there are, in addition, many works of the classical repertoire. It is interesting to note that his edition of the Tchaikovsky Violin Concerto, done in collaboration with K. Mostras, abandons the Auer revisions and restores the original text with only one or two exceptions.

A violinist with so much mental and musical discipline was predestined to be a good teacher. Yet when Oistrakh was appointed to the faculty of the Moscow Conservatory at the age of twenty-six, he had no teaching experience whatsoever, nor had he reached full maturity as an artist. That year, Heifetz had come to visit his native Russia, and Oistrakh was overwhelmed by the imperious playing of that legendary Auer disciple. He also learned by observing the senior classes at the Moscow Conservatory, taught in a far more sophisticated way than what he had experienced in Odessa. But he was a quick and perceptive learner. The appointment of Oistrakh to the Moscow faculty was a well-calculated move: he represented a different school, that of Odessa, and would counterbalance the domination of the Auer tradition. What resulted was a confluence of the best ingredients of the St. Petersburg, Moscow, and Odessa traditions into the present-day Soviet school of violin playing centered at the Moscow Conservatory. Within this framework, Oistrakh, who taught there from 1934 to 1974, was a key figure.

Oistrakh was a dedicated teacher, convinced of the importance and obligation of insuring continuity of tradition by teaching a young generation. He considered his class a creative laboratory which influenced his own artistic growth.

> The level of our young violinists is so high that constant contact with them somehow raises the teacher. Youth is very sensitive. They eagerly watch the work of their teachers, and if one does not wish to fall behind, one must constantly strive forward.[8]

Behind that modesty hides a great deal of pedagogical insight. One would assume that a teacher-performer of Oistrakh's caliber would teach primarily by playing and demonstrating in class, as Poliakin did. On the contrary: he demonstrated only while the student did the initial work on a new piece, helping him to solve specific problems. Once the work was learned, however, Oistrakh did not play, in order to let the student develop his own approach. "It is my task to help the student find *his* solutions of technical and musical problems," he remarked; "sometimes a very young player might receive my advice guardedly . . . it means that he already has his own profile, which pleases me."[9]

In fact, the students were often left to their own devices simply because Oistrakh had such a busy concert schedule. Here is what a conservatory student of the late 1930s wrote (and it did not change in later years):

> Oistrakh, one of the finest violinists of our time, went constantly on concert tours . . . and held his classes irregularly. During one scholastic year he had time to give only four les-

The violin masters Isaac Stern and David Oistrakh, shown with the famous
conductor Eugene Ormandy during a recording session of the Vivaldi Double
Concerto with the Philadelphia Orchestra.
David Oistrakh with the conductor Dimitri Mitropoulos, listening to a play-
back. "Out of tune," they seem to be saying.

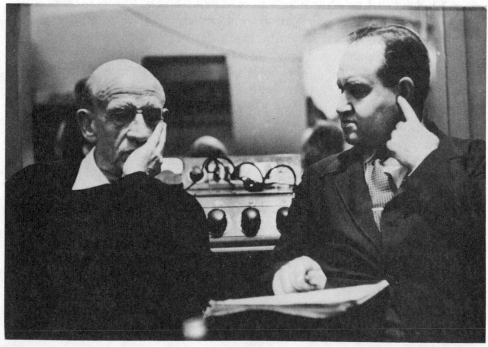

David Oistrakh and his son, Igor, performing together—a remarkable team.

Leonid Kogan followed in David Oistrakh's footsteps as head of the Soviet school, but he died young.

sons to his students. In the classroom he was always extremely willing and polite. He was considerate and not too demanding, but he never enjoyed playing for his students and took his violin out of the case only when it was absolutely necessary.[10]

In later years, Oistrakh had capable assistants to take over his class while he was away. Among them was Piotr Bondarenko, now living in Israel, and Oistrakh's son Igor, about whom we shall speak later in greater detail.

The collaboration of father and son Oistrakh ("King David" and "Prince Igor," as some quipped) was effective on several levels. Most remarkable was their revival of an almost forgotten repertoire of music for two violins. They performed and recorded a variety of violin duets from Leclair to Prokofiev, models of perfect coordination in terms of articulation, tone quality, and interpretation.* Oistrakh *père* liked to record the same work more than once, with different orchestras and at different stages of his career. When listening to his earlier recordings, he was often amazed at the changes in his own interpretation.

Oistrakh's willingness to expand his repertoire at a mature stage of his life is truly astounding. He learned and performed the concertos of Sibelius, Elgar, Walton, Hindemith, Bartók (No. 1), Stravinsky, Szymanowski, and Ernst Meyer. He studied, premiered, and often recorded countless pieces of Soviet compatriots, some successful, others forgotten. He received the dedications of the concertos by Khachaturian, Miaskovsky, and Shostakovich (Nos. 1 and 2), as well as the sonatas by Prokofiev (in F minor) and by Shostakovich (Op. 134); the latter was the composer's present for Oistrakh's sixtieth birthday. Oistrakh's sympathetic and helpful attitude toward Soviet composers, his willingness to try out new works, served as encouragement to his fellow composers and contributed to the expansion of the violin repertoire in his native country. It also set an example for younger violinists to follow.

Leonid Kogan

When Oistrakh died in 1974, Leonid Kogan inherited the unofficial title of reigning Soviet violinist. This was not unexpected: in the

---

* Oistrakh *père* performed the Double Concerto of Bach not only with his son but also with Isaac Stern under Ormandy. For those who like comparisons, there are also the "classic" pairings of Kreisler with Zimbalist, Flesch with Szigeti, Heifetz with himself, Menuhin with Enesco, and many others. The Bach Double Concerto depends as much on the quality and concept of the orchestral playing as it does on the greatness of the soloists.

1950s, Kogan had already reached the high standards set by Oistrakh; some prominent musicians in Russia thought that he had even surpassed the older master.

Whether one preferred Oistrakh or Kogan was a matter of personal judgment. Both were great, yet very different from each other. There was a generation gap—Kogan (born 1924) was sixteen years younger, which made itself felt. Kogan represented a more modern approach to the violin, and to music in general, while Oistrakh was the last great representative of a Romantic past. Oistrakh's playing was bathed in mellifluous beauty; Kogan's playing was leaner, more angular, more aggressive. It was also more rhythmic and propulsive than Oistrakh's meditative approach. Revealing was their preferred choice of repertoire: Oistrakh considered the Tchaikovsky concerto his best piece, while Kogan preferred to make his entree with the more austere Brahms concerto. Oistrakh shied away from the modern idiom of the Berg concerto, which Kogan played with incandescent beauty. Kogan tackled the knotty problems of unadulterated Paganini—the complete Twenty-four Caprices, the entire First Concerto with all three movements and the tricky Sauret cadenza. Oistrakh preferred to show off his technique in the more ingratiating showpieces of Sarasate. Tonally, Oistrakh was more opulent, Kogan more restrained and "purer" in terms of vibrato. Kogan was more akin to the harsher postwar reality, while Oistrakh represented the prewar nostalgia.

In comparing the violinistic ancestry of the two, one finds an interesting difference. Oistrakh, schooled entirely in Odessa, had only a fleeting contact with the Auer tradition, while Kogan, through his teacher Yampolsky, was a direct recipient of that mysterious influence.

Leonid Kogan was born in the industrial city of Ekaterinoslav in the Ukraine. At the age of seven he began playing the violin in the local elementary school. His talent was so pronounced that in 1934 he was sent to Moscow after only three years of study to enter a select children's group within the Moscow Conservatory, which became the nucleus of the now famous Central Music School.* The special curriculum combined intense music study and a standard general education, all designed for particularly gifted children. Leonid Kogan was assigned to the class of Abram Yampolsky, who became so interested in the gifted boy that he arranged for him to live at his home. There was daily guidance in addition to the classroom work, and Leonid progressed rapidly. He

---

* By now, this school boasts of such graduates as Rostropovich, Maxim Shostakovich, and Kogan's own son Pavel, a violinist and conductor.

aroused general attention at a student concert in 1937, and three years later—barely sixteen—he was heard in the Brahms concerto. Though he was still in the high-school division and did not enter the conservatory proper until 1943, he was already a well-known young performer. At the time he professed to be an admirer of Joseph Szigeti, a frequent visitor to Russia, whose austere approach was quite different from the routine Russian style, and to whom he wrote, "I resolved to follow in your footsteps, a difficult undertaking indeed." Kogan enclosed one of his recital programs and added apologetically, "I know that this program will seem to you top-heavy, but we are used to this type of program; it is almost a tradition with us."[1] Indeed the program was very shallow, with only one classical piece, the Tartini *Devil's Trill Sonata*, followed by six arrangements (including Szigeti's transcription of Scriabin's *Etude in Thirds*) and ending with Paganini's *Witches' Dance*. If nothing else, the program showed Kogan's immense technical accomplishment at the time he was just *entering* the conservatory. His talent was quickly recognized, and though officially a student, he was sent on extensive concert tours through Russia, as far as Siberia, Mongolia, and the Far East.

In the fall of 1947 Kogan won first prize at the First Festival of Democratic Youth in Prague. After his graduation from the conservatory the following year, he decided to remain as a postgraduate student beginning in 1949. That year he not only worked on his dissertation on Wieniawski, but astonished everybody with an integral performance of the Twenty-four Caprices of Paganini.

With such a wealth of experience, Kogan was ready to sweep every competition, and indeed he won first prize in the Queen Elisabeth Contest in Brussels* in 1951. The second prize went to Mikhail Vaiman, an excellent violinist schooled in Leningrad, later professor at the Leningrad Conservatory. At the time, Kogan was twenty-six, Vaiman twenty-four—still young, but far removed from the prodigy age. The Soviet educational system does not push to get quick results; though instruction is started young, gifted children are given time to mature at a normal pace.

When Kogan made his first appearance in Paris in 1955, the public at the Palais de Chaillot went wild, the critics were ecstatic. He played three concertos with orchestra—Mozart No. 3, Brahms, and Paganini No. 1. Curiously, no Russian composer was included, breaking a Soviet precedent. Those three concertos remained his favorites, but he expanded his repertoire incessantly. In 1956–57 he gave a grand cycle of six evenings with orchestra, playing eighteen concertos under the title

* Previously known as the Ysaÿe Contest.

"Development of the Violin Concerto." This was exactly ten years after Oistrakh had given a similar cycle, though of only five concerts. In fact, Kogan likes to give cyclic programs—the six Bach sonatas, the twenty-four Paganini caprices, the ten Beethoven sonatas; he obviously enjoys the challenge inherent in such programming.

During the 1957–58 season Kogan came to the United States and made his debut at Carnegie Hall under Pierre Monteux with the Brahms concerto. His excellence was recognized, though he did not receive the same rapturous welcome as Oistrakh. There was something remote and distant about Kogan's playing: it lacked the ultimate impact of a great musical personality, though it was beautifully chiseled and impeccably controlled. This objective approach may be his personal imprint: literal rather than emotional. This was also the impression created at his last New York appearance in February 1979: with his daughter Nina as a capable piano partner, he played an all-Beethoven program in a rather bland manner. His death in 1982 came as a shock.

From 1952, Kogan was on the faculty of the Moscow Conservatory. I was permitted to attend one of his classes and heard him teach a young Japanese violinist* who was about to make her debut with orchestra. She played extremely well, but I was surprised and, in a way, disappointed at Kogan's stone-faced behavior: he listened in silence and his comments were minimal. The impression of Kogan in a classroom was one of non-involvement. Nevertheless, he has trained some successful students.

Kogan showed interest in new music, which encouraged Soviet composers to dedicate works to him; among them are the concertos by Khrennikov, Karayev, Knipper, and Bunin, the sonatas by Vainberg and Levitin, and the Concerto-Rhapsody by Aram Khachaturian. He was the first Soviet violinist to play and record the Berg concerto.

At the height of his career, Kogan interpreted the great classical concertos (notably Beethoven and Brahms) with power, nobility, and an admirable feeling for stylistic purity. He always avoided flamboyant effects, and was rather reticent on stage. His tone was lean, with a tight and sparse vibrato, his intonation infallibly pure, his technical command superb. All these qualities can be heard on the many recordings he made between 1950 and 1970. But in contrast to Oistrakh, who was so universally beloved, there seemed to be a dark shadow over Kogan's personality: his colleagues spoke of him with guarded caution and without affection, though with respect for his violinistic achievements.

Kogan was awarded many honors in his country—he received the

* Ekko Sato, one of the prizewinners at the 1966 Tchaikovsky Competition.

Lenin Prize in 1965 and was named People's Artist of the USSR in 1966. His comparatively early death at the age of fifty-eight came unexpectedly and leaves the Soviet violin school without a dominant reigning personality.

Younger Soviet Violinists

While Oistrakh and Kogan were firmly established as grandmasters, it was not easy for a younger generation of Soviet violinists to gain recognition. One avenue to success was by way of violin contests. Trained to perform under pressure, Soviet violinists entered various competitions, both in eastern Europe—Moscow, Prague, Warsaw, Helsinki, Leipzig—or in the western world—Brussels, Paris, Vienna, Montreal, Genoa. The Soviet contestants continued to win prizes, but the rewards in terms of international careers were less spectacular than in the past. Somehow the public discovered that a contest-winning violinist is not necessarily an inspired artist, and that a glossy technique does not guarantee a great musical performance. On the contrary, artists with sensitive nerves often fail under the grueling conditions of a competition. But the adherents of the competition system argue that the ability to perform under extreme pressure is a precondition for success in our world, and that reliability must rank high among the attributes of a concert artist.

Among the postwar prizewinners are several Soviet violinists who have achieved a measure of international recognition, but only a few have shown a memorable personal style.

Igor Oistrakh, born 1931 in Odessa, found his family name both an advantage and a hindrance. As so often happens with sons of great musicians, Igor was always measured against the supreme standards of his father David—and found wanting. In fact, his violinistic start was not promising: as a child he showed no particular liking for the violin and gave it up for several years. But when the family was evacuated to Sverdlovsk in 1942, he met Stolyarsky, his father's old professor, who succeeded in rekindling Igor's interest in the violin. As soon as the family returned to Moscow in 1943, Igor was accepted as student of the special Central Music School. By 1949 he was ready to enter the conservatory and his father's class. While still a student at the conservatory, he won the first prize at the Wieniawski Competition in 1952.

He began his teaching career in 1958, first as his father's assistant, then with his own class. Over the years, he has been able to establish his personal profile, though he lacks his father's magnetism. His playing is leaner and less emotional, his interpretations more detached and objective. His style lends itself well to modern music, and his performance of Bartók's Concerto No. 2 is among the best one is likely to hear. In classical music, his interpretations are somewhat stolid and not truly moving, but very polished. Lately, he has assumed responsibilities previously held by his father, for example, chairing the violin jury at the Tchaikovsky Competition.

Another son of a famous father is Leonid Kogan's son Pavel (born 1952), an accomplished violinist and aspiring conductor, who won the first prize in the 1970 Sibelius Competition in Helsinki. He was well received when he visited Philadelphia for a guest appearance with the Philadelphia Orchestra in 1976 (sharing the program with his father and the conductor Svetlanov); the question is whether he will choose the violin or the baton for a future career.

Not to be confused with Pavel Kogan is Oleg Kagan, who made a single appearance in New York in December 1979 and departed with a rather favorable review. In the Soviet Union he is highly regarded for his active interest in avant-garde music. In fact, he too is a Sibelius Prize winner (1965). He bears watching.

Great hopes were aroused by Viktor Tretyakov, who won first prize at the Tchaikovsky Competition in 1966. At the time he was only twenty years old, a first-year student at the conservatory. From early youth he had studied with only one teacher, Professor Yankelevich, who guided him through the Central Music School and the conservatory. David Oistrakh, chairman at the competition, had high praise for the winner:

> He became the leader in the contest from the very first round, fascinating everyone with the universality of his style and the virtuosity of his performance. He played the most difficult parts of the Paganini Concerto with ease. At the same time he proved a capable performer of Tchaikovsky's romantic music. I should also like to call attention to the temperament and energy which are characteristic of Tretyakov's manner of playing.[1]

Tretyakov came to the United States in 1969: he made his debut with the Philadelphia Orchestra under Ormandy and with a recital at Carnegie Hall; the acclaim was most impressive. He became the Soviet "violin ambassador" and served as soloist whenever an important Russian orchestra visited New York, as when the Moscow State Symphony performed under Maxim Shostakovich in 1969, the Leningrad Philharmonic under Rozhdestvensky in 1973, the Leningrad Symphony under Temirkanov in 1977. At the same time he was heard in solo recitals and with many American and European orchestras.

Tretyakov is an engaging artist: handsome and elegant on stage, he plays with unruffled perfection, a sweet and silken tone, and excellent taste. Whenever I heard him at Carnegie Hall, I was impressed by his flawless execution. But I also found his tone somewhat small and often overpowered by either orchestra or piano, and his playing was not gripping. Harold Schonberg wrote in the New York *Times*, "He seldom displayed an outburst of temperament or individuality. Indeed, he played like a super-competition winner. . . . After a while, it was something like being smothered in silk."[2] Tretyakov's most convincing interpretation was the Shostakovich concerto, with the orchestra conducted by the composer's son—soloist and orchestra beautifully integrated and attuned to each other and to the composer's work.

Much curiosity was aroused by the Carnegie Hall debut, in January 1979, of Ilya Grubert, who had won a gold medal at the 1978 Tchaikovsky Competition, sharing the prize with the American Elmar Oliveira. Appearing with the visiting Moscow Philharmonic Orchestra, Grubert gave an accurate but small-scaled and uninspired performance of the Tchaikovsky concerto. Unless he develops a stronger personality, Grubert is unlikely to achieve a major career, despite his polished technique.

Remarkable is the almost total absence of virtuoso display in programs offered by recent Soviet visitors, a complete turnabout from typical Russian programs of the past, which were predominantly brilliant. Now Soviet violinists play sonatas and music of substance, while virtuoso pieces are used only as encores. Obviously, the Soviet artists have adjusted themselves to the changing tastes of London and New York, where the typical recital program is considered outmoded.

The new, intellectualized type of Soviet artist is best represented by two violinists who have recently made their debuts in western Europe and New York: Vladimir Spivakov (born 1944) and Gidon Kremer (born 1947). Both represent a new breed: more cerebral, always in search of new repertoire, be it rediscoveries of forgotten works or newly composed music. Both are masters of their instrument and have all the virtuoso equipment needed, but use their virtuosity mainly for musical purposes.

I heard Spivakov at his Vienna debut on June 4, 1975, and I was impressed by his cultivated, noble presentation of the Haydn Violin

Concerto in C major, an unusual choice for a debut. There was a complete absence of showmanship which, in Haydn, would have been misplaced. The slow movement was sung with great simplicity and warmth. A few days later he played the Tchaikovsky concerto, showing temperament and virtuoso flair. Yet Spivakov is essentially a withdrawn player, preferring introspective meditation to extrovert display. He is at his best in Mozart and Haydn, and his choice of repertoire, both in concert and on recording, emphasizes nobility, purity, lyricism. He performs chamber music beautifully, but I have also heard him play Bartók and Prokofiev with much conviction, though lacking the ultimate "bite." His programs are models of modern thinking: avoidance of the hackneyed repertoire, a balance of the classics and of twentieth-century music, and everything played with technical mastery and musical nobility.

Spivakov is not really a "contest" player—he is too reticent to sparkle in all kinds of music. But he has won his share of competitions, though not always first prizes: second prizes at the Paganini Contest in Genoa and the Tchaikovsky Competition in Moscow, first prize in Montreal. When he first came to New York, he attracted immediate attention, and since his 1975 debut he has played from coast to coast with ever-growing success. One could call him the "quiet violinist," but behind that modest, unassuming appearance is a great deal of depth and enormous potential for musical achievement. He is also interested in conducting, and recently formed a new group called the Moscow Virtuosi: twenty-seven musicians, including the reconstituted Borodin Quartet. It will be interesting to watch the further direction of Spivakov's career. He is an extraordinary artist with a strong profile.

Out of the ordinary is also Gidon Kremer, the latest violin sensation from Moscow. Herbert von Karajan's declaration of Kremer as "the greatest violinist of his generation" propelled him into immediate prominence in western Europe. He is a highly subjective artist with his own ideas on interpretation and repertoire. I was in Salzburg in 1976 when he played an uncompromising program for a fun-loving festival public. Kremer startled a half-filled hall with works by such modern composers as Schoenberg, Webern, and Shnitke, a fellow-Russian avant-gardist. As a "tranquilizer" he offered the Richard Strauss sonata and Beethoven's Sonata Op. 96. This is an example of what he considers a good and substantial program: a mixture of the new, the unusual, and the classical. At his debut in New York on January 14, 1977, he opened with Stravinsky's *Elegy* for unaccompanied violin and Charles Ives's Sonata No. 4, for which he did not earn any plaudits from the critics.

Viktor Tretyakov, outstanding young Soviet violinist

Vladimir Spivakov, a sensitive Soviet performer and rising star

Boris Belkin, a highly accomplished emigré Soviet violinist

The prize-winning Soviet violinist Gidon Kremer, now living in the West.
Nina Beilina, a wonderful emigré Soviet violinist, now in New York.

But on the whole he made a very strong impression. His tone is not sensuous, but highly expressive and full of shadings; some of Kremer's idiosyncrasies are reminiscent of Szigeti at his best. He has long arms, long fingers, an elongated body frame, and looks angular and gaunt. While playing he contorts his body. He avoids show pieces on the program, but plays them as encores or on recordings (for example "Romantic Miniatures"). Here he displays a technique second to none; his performances of Ernst's *Last Rose of Summer* or *Erlking* are hair-raising. But Kremer, aside from his virtuosity, is an interesting musician: his interpretation of Beethoven's last sonata (Op. 96) is filled with intimate insight. His recording of the Beethoven concerto, however, is rather mannered, particularly with Shnitke's outlandish cadenzas. He has an enormous repertoire, which runs in cycles: the six Bach solo sonatas, the six Ysaÿe solo sonatas, any concerto from Bach to Elgar and Shnitke. His inquisitive mind finds entirely forgotten music, and he builds excellent recital programs. Particularly committed to the music of Alfred Shnitke, he recently premiered and recorded Shnitke's *Concerto grosso* for two violins and orchestra; in this venture (as in other two-violin recordings) his partner was his ex-wife Tatiana Grindenko, an excellent violinist.

Kremer's background is interesting. Both his parents as well as his grandfather were professional violinists, and "my fate was decided before I came to this globe," as he remarked to an interviewer.[3] In fact, his violin, an eighteenth-century Guadagnini, is a family heirloom, though he now plays a Stradivarius. Well prepared as a violinist, Kremer entered the Moscow Conservatory, where he worked with David Oistrakh for eight years. In 1970, at the age of twenty-three, he won first prize at the Tchaikovsky Competition, though his unconventional style cost him some votes. He is as atypical a Soviet violinist as they come: his ethereal tone, austere musical taste, and independent way of thinking all set him apart. On the way to becoming a world name, he has decided to leave the Soviet Union and has established residence in Paris as of 1978, but spends much time in New York, where he is very successful. To all intents and purposes, he is now an emigré violinist.

Soviet Emigré Violinists

Since 1970, many musicians have joined the flow of emigration from the Soviet Union. Some, like Rostropovich, Kondrashin, and, most lately, Maxim Shostakovich, were already famous; others were well-known concert artists who were tired of being manipulated and exploited by GOSKONTSERT, the Soviet state concert agency. Among the newcomers are also orchestral players, chamber musicians, teachers, or recent conservatory graduates. Enough string players have arrived in New York to form the successful Soviet Emigré Orchestra, led by the expert violinist Lazar Gosman. Other string players have joined existing orchestras—the Boston, Pittsburgh, and Baltimore Symphonies, the Israel Philharmonic, the Jerusalem Symphony, to mention but a few. Some have formed new chamber groups; Rostislav Dubinsky, former leader of the Borodin Quartet, organized the new Borodin Trio in the West. Most Soviet emigré artists have settled in the United States and Canada, in western Europe (particularly Holland and West Germany), and in Israel. Their integration is not easy; while they are usually excellent technicians, their views on methods and repertoire are often a bit rigid, in keeping with the Soviet educational system. But they are learning and adjusting fast.[1]

Here, only a few of the outstanding violin soloists will be mentioned; it is by no means a complete list.

"Russia's loss is our gain," was one of the headlines that greeted Nina Beilina's debut in New York in January 1978. She established herself immediately as one of the important violinists of today, reminiscent of the great Erica Morini: a smoldering intensity controlled by musical discipline, purity of style without purism, effortless technique, and a natural communicativeness that speaks directly to the listener.

Nina Beilina had a distinguished career before coming to the United States. Born in Moscow, educated at the conservatories of Moscow and Leningrad, she absorbed the best of both traditions, to which a postgraduate course with David Oistrakh added a final polish. Beilina placed as finalist in several major international contests, including the Long-Thibaud in Paris in 1963. In her native country she combined extensive concert tours with a professorship at the Gorky Conservatory. Here she has specialized in Bach, offering his complete violin music (fifteen major works) in five programs. Her Bach interpretations are pure and resilient without being austere; she brings the same qualities to Brahms and plays the Romantic repertoire with elegance and verve. Particularly poignant is her interpretation of Shostakovich's late Violin Sonata. Music making of such nobility and distinction is rare, and Beilina's artistry is gaining recognition in America and western Europe.

Albert Markov (born 1933 in Kharkov) studied with both Stolyarsky and Yankelevich. In 1959 he was a prize winner at the Queen Elisabeth Competition in Brussels, but this did not lead to an international career. In Moscow, he divided his activities between concertizing and teaching at the Gnessin Institute. Having emigrated, he presented himself in a New York recital in November 1976, followed by other appearances. The critics had more praise for his virtuoso technique than for his musicianship. The old-style Russian showmanship still needs to be tempered a bit. His eighteen-year-old son Alexander has just won first prize in the 1982 Paganini Contest in Genoa and is said to be extraordinary.

Also remarkable is Boris Belkin. Born around 1948 in Sverdlovsk (Ural), he was rebellious even as a child. He studied the violin from age six to eleven, but then gave it up "because I hated the violin." At seventeen he started again, working very seriously and long hours—seven to eight hours a day. "I practiced like mad." Professor Yankelevich helped him enter the Moscow Conservatory. Here he found the spirit of competition all-consuming; everything seemed to be geared "to win," as he said, "a very bad system—it kills all individuality." Nevertheless, Belkin submitted to the system—he trained for the Paganini Competition in Genoa in 1971, but at the last moment was forbidden to go. The shock was such that he developed a numbness in his hand. After six months in a psychiatric clinic he was cured and began preparing for the 1973 Paganini Competition—again in vain: no visa. That year he won a national Soviet contest and was scheduled for the 1974 Tchaikovsky Competition when he decided to apply for emigration to Israel. By that time he was known as a troublemaker, and in May 1974 he left for the West.

Belkin quickly adjusted. "In my playing, everything changed. Because I was free. It's a completely new feeling about life." He attracted the attention of conductors Zubin Mehta and Leonard Bernstein. I heard his performance at the New York Philharmonic under Bernstein and a recording session for Columbia, playing the Tchaikovsky concerto. Belkin is undoubtedly a big talent, but he sounded a bit unsettled and not quite sure of himself. The critical reception in New York was divided, but since then his career in Europe has flourished and expanded. His future development is worth watching.

An interesting case is that of Dmitri Sitkovetsky. Son of famous parents, the late violinist Julian Sitkovetsky and the pianist Bella Davidovich, Dmitri was born in Armenia in 1954 but was brought to

Moscow in early childhood. Left fatherless at four, Dmitri's gifts as a violinist developed quickly, and he won a prize in Prague at the age of twelve. For some reason, young Sitkovetsky does not like to speak about his studies in Moscow, but attributes his success to the teachings of the Armenian composer-philosopher Josef Andriasian who became his mentor in 1972. Both came to the United States as emigrés in the mid-1970s. In New York, Sitkovetsky entered the Juilliard School, where Galamian and Dorothy DeLay taught him for a time. He served briefly as concertmaster of the National Orchestral Association and played a Prokofiev concerto as soloist with that orchestra at Carnegie Hall in 1979. In September of that year, Sitkovetsky won first prize in the Fritz Kreisler Competition, a new contest sponsored by the City of Vienna. Among the judges was Yehudi Menuhin, who praised the interpretative maturity of the young winner. At an early age, Sitkovetsky finds himself propelled into fame, but he will have to prove himself in the competitive arena of the musical world.

The latest defector from Moscow is the twenty-three-year-old violinist Victoria Mullova, the first-prize winner of the 1982 Tchaikovsky Competition. After a concert in northern Finland, she escaped by taxi across the border into Sweden, leaving behind a government-owned Stradivarius. Once in Stockholm, she asked for political asylum in the United States, and arrived in Washington on July 10, 1983. She expressed her reason for defection as the repressive controls over her career: "My concerts were limited and I was not given an opportunity to show my art." She explained that she had been politically inactive during her Conservatory days and for this reason her career was being stifled. Miss Mullova is no newcomer to success: among previous prizes she has won are the 1976 Wieniawsky Competition and the 1980 Sibelius Contest; but she is virtually unknown in the West. No doubt there will soon be ample opportunity to evaluate this young Soviet artist, who studied with the late Leonid Kogan.

THE BRITISH SCHOOL

TRADITIONALLY, FOREIGN VIOLINISTS have always been received in England with great hospitality and warmth, but little encouragement was given to gifted British young men and women to pursue music as a profession. True, the Royal Academy of Music (founded in 1822) appointed the London-born Nicholas Mori as first violin professor, but he was succeeded in 1845 by the Frenchman Prosper Sainton, a fine violinist trained by Habeneck at the Paris Conservatoire. Another French violinist succeeded Sainton in 1890, Emile Sauret, who taught at the RAM until 1903. Bernhard Molique, an excellent musician of the German school, lived and taught in London from 1849 to 1866; his best student was John Carrodus (1836–95), who contributed much to raising the level of string playing in Victorian England. He divided his energies between solo work, orchestral playing, and teaching; his experience as concertmaster was unexcelled.

In 1880 the Guildhall School of Music was established in London. Viotti Collins was one of the first violin teachers engaged. In 1894, the eminent August Wilhelmj was named principal professor of violin; he died in London in 1908. It was at the Guildhall School that the Flesch Competition was established in 1945 and was administered until 1967.

In 1883, the Royal College of Music was founded in London. Henry Holmes (1839–1905) was appointed violin professor and served until 1893. Two excellent foreign masters were engaged in the 1890s: Enrique Arbos and Achille Rivarde. Later, Albert Sammons was on the faculty, as were Henry Holst and Isolde Menges.

From 1906 to 1911, Leopold Auer maintained a summer studio in

London to fulfill the many demands for lessons since his students Elman, Zimbalist, and Kathleen Parlow had scored such sensational successes in western Europe. During the winter, anyone wishing to study
with Auer had to travel to St. Petersburg, as did Isolde Menges when
she was about sixteen. Born in 1893 in Hove, she played pieces on a
tiny fiddle at age three and a half. Later she studied with Sametini before
going to St. Petersburg in 1909. Her London debut took place in 1913,
and her American debut in 1916. She found much acclaim in the United
States and Canada, where she remained until 1919. She specialized in
giving concerts for schoolchildren, with verbal explanations charmingly
adjusted to a child's receptivity. In the 1920s, she concertized on the European continent. In 1931 she founded a string quartet and also joined
the faculty of the Royal College of Music. For decades, she was a favorite of the British public, which admired the classical expressivity of her
style; she died in 1976.

May Harrison (1891–1959) also traveled to St. Petersburg to study
with Auer shortly after her London debut in 1904. Her earlier teachers
were Arbos and Rivarde at the Royal College of Music, who guided her
precocious talent: she won a Gold Medal at the RCM at the age of ten.
May Harrison became well known on the continent and in England,
playing as soloist and in joint appearances with her sister Beatrice, an
equally accomplished cellist. Their performance of Brahms's Double
Concerto was justly famous, and they gave the premiere of the Delius
Concerto for Violin and Cello in London in 1920; the work is dedicated
to them. Delius also dedicated his Violin Sonata No. 3 to May Harrison; she played it for the first time in 1930, with Arnold Bax at the
piano. May and Beatrice Harrison were lifelong champions of Delius's
music.

In contrast to the Auer pilgrimages of Harrison and Menges, Marie
Hall (1884–1956) chose to complete her studies under Sevčik in Prague
from 1901 to 1903. Before that, she had a variety of teachers, some local,
some famous (including Wilhelmj), but it was the advice of Kubelik
that sent her off to Sevčik. She made successful debuts in Prague,
Vienna, and London, and toured extensively in Britain and the United
States. In 1921 she played the premiere of *The Lark Ascending* for violin and orchestra by Vaughan Williams, a piece composed for and dedicated to her. During the height of her career, Marie Hall enjoyed an excellent reputation.

In 1913, the Hungarian-born sisters Adila Fachiri (1886–1962) and
Jelly d'Arányi (1895–1966), both violinists, settled in London and at-

tracted much admiration, particularly Jelly. The Holst Double Concerto was composed for the two sisters (1930), the *Concerto Accademico* by Vaughan Williams for d'Arányi. Other of d'Arányi's premieres include Ravel's *Tzigane*, both Bartók sonatas, and the rediscovered Robert Schumann Violin Concerto which she introduced to London in 1938.* Memorable were d'Arányi's sonata performances with Myra Hess.

Strictly speaking, Wilma Neruda, born in 1838 in Brünn and trained in Vienna by Leopold Jansa, belongs to the Moravian or Viennese school. But she spent many of her most successful and productive years in England, where she was highly honored and respected. First taught by her father, she was heard publicly at the age of seven. The Nerudas concertized as a family unit: a girl pianist, two girl violinists, and a boy cellist, in addition to the father. They played quartets and solos and traveled all over central Europe and Russia. In 1849 Wilma had a particular success with a Bériot concerto at the London Philharmonic. At the end of a triumphant Scandinavian tour, Wilma was married (in 1864) to the Swedish composer-conductor Ludvig Norman and remained in Stockholm until their separation in 1869. That year she began visiting London regularly, and enjoyed enormous popularity. In 1876 she was presented with a superb Stradivarius by several aristocratic admirers. Her appearances in Charles Hallé's recitals began in 1877; at the same time she was heard in many European countries. She married Hallé in 1888, but was widowed in 1895. She settled in Berlin in 1900, taught at the Stern Conservatory, and was heard with Joachim in Bach's Double Concerto at the Philharmonic. She died in Berlin in 1911.[1]

At the height of her career, Wilma Neruda was considered one of the most accomplished violinists, and certainly the most famous one of her sex. Moser praised her admirable left-hand technique, her faultless intonation, and her beautifully pure tone, although he found her bow arm a bit stiff, "like that of Wieniawski." Far more important was Vieuxtemps's enthusiastic endorsement:

Mme Norman-Neruda . . . for me is the ideal of a woman violinist. I have never heard the violin played with so much soul, passion, and purity. At the same time she is classical, poetic, and possesses all the qualities of a great artist. You regret that her sound is not larger? but that would no longer be like *her*, it would no longer be the *violin-fairy* personified.[1]

* See pp. 265–67.

Vieuxtemps, who died the year after writing this, left his posthumous Concerto No. 6 with a dedication to Wilma Neruda.

Joachim, too, had a very high opinion of her playing and wrote to his wife in 1870, "I like her very much, and I think you would, too. Her playing is more to my taste than that of any other contemporary—unspoiled, pure and musical."[2]

There are a few sour remarks in the criticisms of George Bernard Shaw about Lady Hallé, whom he considered past her prime around 1889, just as he prematurely belittled Joachim or failed to recognize the early greatness of Ysaÿe. But there is no doubt that the playing of Wilma Neruda was an adornment of the London musical scene for almost three decades.

It is remarkable how many of England's finest violinists pursued multiple careers as concertmasters, soloists, teachers, and chamber musicians. True, the strict scheduling of orchestral work makes extensive touring almost impossible; on the other hand, the concertmaster has many solo opportunities with his own orchestra and he is constantly in the public eye. There is no better school to acquire musical discipline than orchestral playing, particularly in a leading chair. But it is this same discipline that limits a virtuoso's fancy. None of the great virtuosos of the recent past—Elman, Heifetz, Kreisler, Huberman, Kubelik—would have made good concertmasters: to subordinate themselves to a conductor's beat was not their style. On the other hand, Joachim, Auer, Ysaÿe, Thibaud, Busch, and Flesch did orchestral service without detriment to their artistic individuality. It is a matter of personality: the self-willed virtuoso versus the disciplined musician.

The British violinists discussed in the following pages were obviously able to combine their ambitions as soloists with the orchestral work. Some tired of assigned duties and tried a freelance career; others preferred the scheduled life of a salaried musician. A compromise chosen by quite a few was to belong to a chamber orchestra, with fewer onerous duties and a repertoire more geared to the individual accomplishments of the leading players, particularly the rich literature of the Baroque and pre-Classical eras.

Arthur Catterall (1883–1943) studied at the newly founded Royal Manchester College of Music, first with Willy Hess, then with Adolph Brodsky,* both excellent artists with a continental tradition. Catterall's

---

* Brodsky, remembered as the first interpreter of the Tchaikovsky concerto, remained on the faculty of the RMCM until his death in 1929, succeeding Hallé as director.

career as concertmaster included the Hallé Orchestra in Manchester, the Promenade Concerts, and the BBC Symphony Orchestra from its inception in 1929 to 1936. He was also active as teacher at the Royal College in Manchester and the Royal Academy of Music. Highly regarded was the Catterall String Quartet, which he founded in 1910 and maintained up to World War II, though with a changing membership. Catterall was described as a "persuasive player in the slightly reserved English classical style,"[3] and was at his best in chamber music.

His successor at the BBC Orchestra was Paul Beard (born 1901), who was the concertmaster of that orchestra from 1936 to 1962. Before that he was the concertmaster of the City of Birmingham Orchestra (1922–32) and the London Philharmonic Orchestra under Sir Thomas Beecham (1932–36). He was schooled by his father, a professional violist in Birmingham. Young Beard played in public when he was six and became known as a boy violinist, touring England. In 1914 he was accepted as a scholarship student at the Royal Academy of Music, where he studied with R. Woof. The career of a concertmaster appealed to Beard, who believed in the systematic training of fine orchestral players. It is refreshing to see a violinist of unquestioned quality look to orchestral playing as a desirable vocation, not as a retreat from career failures. Part of his teaching at the RAM consisted in coaching students in the orchestral repertory. He also extended the benefit of his rich experience to the junior members of whatever string section he was leading. In his own way, Beard disproved Beecham's remark that all orchestral players are disappointed soloists.

A career of wider scope was that of Albert Sammons (1886–1957). He did his share of orchestral duties as leader of the Beecham Orchestra, the Philharmonic Society Orchestra, and the Diaghilev Ballet, but eventually his ambition as soloist gained the upper hand, and his consistently superior performances earned him a reputation as the leading English violinist of his generation.

I heard Sammons for the first time in 1932, and deemed him comparable to the best continental virtuosos—technically impeccable, eloquent yet controlled, and deeply musical without ostentation. I began to wonder why I had not heard of Sammons before. Here was an artist obviously beloved and admired in his own country, yet the outside world did not clamor to hear him. There was nothing particularly "insular" in his interpretations, though they seemed attuned to English taste in music, similar to Adolf Busch being German or Thibaud typically French. Sammons's playing was totally honest and sincere, lyrical but not sentimental, and stressing a wholesome, nobly virile style. Hearing Sammons in a Delius sonata was a particularly fortunate experience, since he had made this composer's work so much his own. Also much admired was an interpretation of the Elgar concerto that he recorded in 1929 (the first recording in its entirety).

Sammons was a self-taught, self-reliant musician. He was given basic violin instruction by his father, a competent amateur violinist. All the rest was done on his own, through constant study and observation. He began to play in a professional orchestra at the age of eleven and continued to do so in various entertainment ensembles, sometimes dressed as a Hungarian and instructed not to open his mouth! He acquired valuable experience playing all kinds of repertory, but was always alert to a lucky opportunity. It came in 1908, when he played the Mendelssohn Concerto at the Waldorf Hotel. Thomas Beecham happened to be present and was so impressed that he engaged Sammons as concertmaster of his newly formed orchestra. (Thibaud and Přihoda, among others, were discovered by famous conductors under similar circumstances—picked out from an entertainment band.) Sammons worked with Beecham for five years.

At the same time he was first violinist of the original London String Quartet, which he led for ten years, until 1919. Then he decided to give all his time to a solo career that had actually begun auspiciously before the First World War. While wartime conditions prevented foreign artists from visiting the British Isles, Sammons acquired the reputation of being England's foremost violinist. After hearing Sammons, Ysaÿe is reported to have said, "At last England has a great violinist!" Kreisler, too, spoke highly of him. In fact, Sammons followed in Kreisler's footsteps by espousing Elgar's Violin Concerto, which Kreisler had introduced in 1910. Elgar himself felt that Sammons was particularly attuned to his concerto. The same was said by Delius, who entrusted his Violin Concerto to Sammons; he became its ideal interpreter. In general, Sammons's name is closely connected with the various British composers whose works he championed with great conviction. It is not surprising that musical Britain called Sammons "our own Albert." Sammons was also a fine teacher (on the faculty of the Royal College of Music). After 1946, his career was curtailed by a muscular ailment which became progressively worse and removed him prematurely from musical activities. He died in 1957.

One of Sammons's best students was Thomas Matthews (1907–69). He began his orchestral apprenticeship with the Liverpool Orchestra at the age of fourteen and with the Hallé Orchestra a year later; eventually he rose to deputy leader. His studies with Sammons ran concurrently; he also took summer master classes with Flesch. For a time, in 1936, Matthews concentrated on solo work and was much admired for his performances of music by Elgar and Delius. Appointed concertmaster of the London Philharmonic Orchestra in 1939, he gave the English premiere of the Britten Violin Concerto with that orchestra in 1941 and repeated it with the BBC Orchestra shortly afterward.* During the 1940s and '50s Matthews continued to take an active interest in contemporary British violin music. Beginning in 1946 he taught both in London and Manchester; he was also concertmaster of the London Symphony Orchestra in the 1950s. His solo career was mostly limited to the British Isles, though he was heard occasionally on the continent. During the 1960s he was active as conductor of the Tasmania Symphony Orchestra.

Among the British chamber orchestras led by first-rate violinists are the London Mozart Players, founded in 1949 by Harry Blech, a violinist of wide experience in orchestral and chamber-music playing. Emanuel Hurwitz has gained considerable fame as the admirable concertmaster of the English Chamber Orchestra (1948–68), the Hurwitz Chamber Orchestra (since 1968; later known as the Serenata of London), the Melos Ensemble, and the Aeolian String Quartet, which recently recorded the complete Haydn string quartets. Hurwitz plays an extremely active role in the musical life of London.

The Canadian-born Frederick Grinke was far advanced as a violinist when he won, at the age of sixteen, a scholarship to study at the Royal Academy of Music in London, where R. Woof became his teacher. At twenty-one he did additional studies with Busch in Basel and with Flesch at his master classes in Spa and in London. Declining the leadership of symphony orchestras, Grinke became concertmaster in 1937 of the Boyd Neel Orchestra, a select group of eighteen string players. For ten years he participated in the successful work of this ensemble, which toured Europe as well as Australia and New Zealand and acquired an international reputation for performances of Baroque music. Such a repertoire offers rich opportunities for the leading first violinist, which Grinke exploited to the fullest. But he is not limited to that repertoire: he has played and recorded a number of contemporary works

---

* The world premiere was given in New York by Antonio Brosa and the Philharmonic in March 1940 under the baton of Sir John Barbirolli.

by British composers, including Britten, Bax, Berkeley, Bridge, and Vaughan Williams, both solos and chamber music. In 1944 he joined the faculty of the Royal Academy of Music. During World War II he was a member of the Royal Air Force Orchestra, whose string section played at the Potsdam conference for Churchill, Truman, and Stalin. Grinke's sound judgment is valued on the jury of various violin competitions, including the Flesch contest.

Alan Loveday, born in New Zealand in 1928, also found his greatest satisfaction in participating in and leading chamber-sized groups. Prepared by his father, he was able to perform at the age of four. From 1939 to 1948 he studied on a scholarship with Albert Sammons at the Royal College of Music. While still nominally a student, he made his London debut in 1947 with pronounced success. After a brief period as concertmaster of the Royal Philharmonic Orchestra, he found his true vocation with chamber-sized orchestras, where his innate sense of style was fully developed. He was heard regularly with such groups as the Academy of St. Martin-in-the-Fields (founded by another violinist, Neville Marriner, in 1959), and with Philomusica of London. Loveday has made it his specialty to play Baroque works (including unaccompanied Bach) on violins with eighteenth-century fittings and appropriate bows. His adaptability to styles of different eras is shown in his recordings for David Boyden's book *History of Violin Playing from the Origins to 1761*, where he skillfully executes the differences between old and modern approaches to Baroque bowing, articulation, pitch, and related problems. Loveday's musicianship and technique are highly praised by critics.

The first winner of the Flesch Contest, in 1945, was Raymond Cohen. Born in Manchester in 1919, at age fifteen he won the Brodsky scholarship to the Royal Manchester College of Music, where the distinguished Henry Holst became his teacher. At the age of twenty, he played three concertos at one session (Bach E major, Mendelssohn, and Brahms). However, his career was interrupted by army service and it was not easy to keep in trim as a violinist. Winning the Flesch Award was a welcome boost for his career and he received numerous engagements as soloist with British orchestras. From 1959 to 1965 he was leader of the Royal Philharmonic Orchestra under Sir Thomas Beecham.

The next year of the Flesch competition, 1946, produced a significant winner in Norbert Brainin. Born in Vienna in 1923, he studied the violin with Rosa Hochmann and R. Odnoposoff before settling in

London in the late 1930s. Here he became a student of Max Rostal, and also briefly with Flesch. The year after winning the Flesch medal, Brainin joined with the cellist Lovett and the violinists Nissel and Schidlof (both Rostal students) in forming the Amadeus String Quartet (Schidlof switched to viola). Since their successful debut in 1948, the Amadeus Quartet has deservedly acquired world renown. Brainin is a strong leader, but does not dominate unduly. The fact that there is a kinship of musicality and that the three top instruments were trained by the same teacher facilitates the homogeneity of approach; nevertheless, a lasting success such as the Amadeus Quartet enjoys would not have been possible without an outstanding primarius. In previous days, the leader gave the quartet his name and his imprint—Joachim, Capet, Busch, Rosé, Kolisch. Lately, quartets are more discreet and seemingly more democratic: names of countries, cities, composers, instrument makers are preferred. But the end result is the same, and the indispensable condition remains the strong leader, a personality a shade above the other players.

The following year, 1947, the Carl Flesch Medal was won by another young emigré from Vienna, Erich Gruenberg (born 1924). He studied the violin in Vienna and was rescued from the Nazi terror at the age of fourteen by a scholarship to the Jerusalem Conservatory. After having worked as the leader of the Palestine Broadcasting Orchestra, he came to London in 1946 and became a British subject in 1950. His success at the Flesch Competition led to engagements as soloist and chamber-music player. Over the years, he has also held various concertmaster positions, including the London Symphony Orchestra and the Royal Philharmonic. He was also leader of the New London String Quartet for some ten years and is known as a violinist in trio and sonata teams. He has a strong interest in contemporary music, and his recorded performance of Messiaen's *Quatuor pour la fin du temps* is highly praised.

Ralph Holmes, born in Kent in 1937, learned to play the violin so that he could surprise his father on his return from the war. Four years later he played surprisingly well for his age. When he was ten, he received a scholarship to the Royal Academy of Music, where he studied with David Martin. From then on, progress was rapid. Two summers spent in Paris with Enesco gave him a concept of interpretation, particularly of Bach. At the age of sixteen, Holmes made his debut with orchestra, followed by his recital debut the following year in London. The critics predicted a great future for this young artist. Though his career developed well, he experienced a crisis of self-confidence in 1964 and sought the help of Ivan Galamian in New York. Experimenting with a new approach to bowing, Holmes finally solved his problems, and his debut at Carnegie Hall in 1966 was very well reviewed. At present he enjoys an enviable reputation in his country and on the Continent. He had an enormous repertoire—over fifty concertos, including many modern works like the knotty Schoenberg concerto, as well as new or neglected compositions of the English repertoire.

When Max Rostal left London in 1958 after twenty-five years of fruitful activity,* the void was partially filled by his former student Yfrah Neaman, who took over for Rostal at the Guildhall School of Music. Born in Palestine in 1922, trained at the Paris Conservatoire where he won a first prize at the age of fifteen, Neaman came to London in 1937 to continue his studies with Flesch and Rostal. His concert debut in 1944 aroused much attention when he substituted for Rostal at short notice, playing the Beethoven concerto with the London Symphony. Since then, Neaman has played successfully in many parts of the world, though London remains the focus of his activities. Aside from teaching an advanced solo class at the Guildhall School, he is director of the Carl Flesch Competition and much in demand as adjudicator at international violin contests. His stimulating ideas on contests were recently published in *The Strad*.[4]

The establishment of the Menuhin School at Stoke d'Abernon in Surrey in 1963 opened new vistas for music education in Britain. The underlying idea is the development of a child's musical gifts concurrent with a general education. Clearly, this is a problem to be approached in a sensitive way, without overburdening a child's receptivity, yet requiring a certain degree of work discipline. Menuhin was aware that the Soviets had experimented with such schools since the 1930s; he had visited the Moscow Central Music School and admired certain aspects while being critical of others. When Stoke d'Abernon came into being, it was a far cry from the Muscovite actuality. Menuhin's school achieves more than teaching: it *conditions* children to the enjoyment of music. The learning process is imperceptible but ever-present. While Moscow aims at producing solo performers, Stoke d'Abernon trains versatile musicians able to function on various levels.† While technical proficiency is expected, it is musical sensitivity that is valued most highly. Never-

---

* See p. 342.
† The head violin teacher at Stoke d'Abernon is the excellent Robert Masters, Menuhin's long-time musical associate, equally experienced as performer, teacher, and orchestral leader. Prior to joining the Menuhin Schcool at its inception, he was for seventeen years on the faculty of the Royal Academy of Music and concertized widely with the Masters Pianoforte Quartet.

theless, the performance standards of the senior students and graduates are very high, and many professional avenues are open to them. Among former violin students who are now making successful careers are Nigel Kennedy and Andrew Watkinson. The school has also produced some outstanding cellists and pianists. But ultimately it is immaterial whether they become virtuosos, ensemble players, or teachers—"their influence must be for good and they will have earned the privilege of sharing an experience unique in English musical education."[5]

H. WRIGHTSON

Albert Sammons, master of the British school in the first half of the century.
Below left, Albert Spalding, foremost American violinist between the two
World Wars.
Below right, Maud Powell, a remarkably accomplished American violinist, successful at home and in Europe.

MUSICAL AMERICA

NEVA GARNER GREENWOOD COLLECTION

VIOLIN PLAYING
IN AMERICA:
THE OLDER GENERATION

ONE HEARS LITTLE about native American violinists of the nineteenth century. All the public attention was focused on the visiting virtuosos from Europe—Vieuxtemps, Ole Bull, Wieniawski, Sarasate, Ysaÿe. A few European violinists, like Franz Kneisel and Edouard Déthier, settled in the United States and became fountainheads of an indigenous American school. Before the First World War, it was fashionable for American violinists to study abroad and receive the stamp of approval from a European master, as did Maud Powell, Albert Spalding, and others.

American conservatories have a venerable history: the Peabody in Baltimore founded in 1857, the Oberlin Conservatory in 1865, the Chicago Musical College, the Cincinnati Conservatory, and the New England Conservatory in 1867, the Institute of Music Art in New York in 1905. But American musical institutions did not become internationally competitive until the 1920s, when three great music schools were endowed by the munificence of private patrons—the Juilliard School in New York, the Curtis Institute in Philadelphia, and the Eastman School in Rochester. Today, New York and Philadelphia are magnets for aspiring violinists from all over the world. This development, begun half a century ago, has accelerated since the end of World War II.

Contributing to this growth of American music study are the music schools attached to major universities. Contrary to European universities, the American universities have recognized the importance of the

494

performing arts in the musical culture of a country. While European universities have clung to the narrow concept of musicology, American universities have expanded into funding schools of music endowed with an academic aura. The results are gratifying: standards of professional musicians have improved, and many have earned college degrees without impairing their professional accomplishments. Outstanding in this country are the music schools of Indiana University and of the universities of Michigan, Iowa, and California, among others.

Much valuable work in the performing arts is also done at summer schools and music centers operating during the summer months. Internationally famous are Tanglewood (Massachusetts), Aspen (Colorado), Marlboro (Vermont), Interlochen (Michigan); in fact, the American landscape is dotted with excellent summer programs for young musicians.

Surveying the list of prize winners at the 1978 Tchaikovsky Competition in Moscow, the chairman of the violin jury, Igor Oistrakh, praised the achievements of the American-trained violinists. There were more Americans among the finalists than ever before.

Maud Powell

Maud Powell was a remarkable personality. At a time when a woman's career as a violinist was fraught with obstacles, she won recognition in America and in Europe for her accomplished performances and her musical initiative. The long list of first performances she gave testifies to her venturesome spirit. She introduced to American audiences such major works as the concertos of Tchaikovsky (1889), Dvořák (1894), and Sibelius (1906), as well as those by Tor Aulin, Arensky, Bruch, Saint-Saëns, and Coleridge-Taylor. She began to record for the Victor Talking Machine as early as 1904, and anyone able to hear one of the old recordings can testify to her bell-like intonation and the firmness of her bowing. Vienna called her the Jeanne d'Arc of music, and with obvious justification.

Maud Powell was born in 1868 in Peru, Illinois, into an academic family. Her musical talent was discovered when she was four, and she played both violin and piano. At the age of twelve she was taken to Leipzig to work with Schradieck at the conservatory. A performance of the Bruch G-minor Concerto with the famed Gewandhaus Orchestra in

1882 completed her Leipzig period. Her next step was to win admission to the Paris Conservatoire. She was assigned to the class of Charles Dancla, once a student of Baillot. Dancla taught her to be an artist, she said. She proved her artistry by a successful tour of England, during which she played for the royal family. Joachim heard her in London and invited her to join his class at the Berlin Hochschule. At the end of one year she appeared as soloist with the Berlin Philharmonic under Joachim's baton. "He taught me to be a musician," she reminisced.

In 1885 it was time to return to her native America. She made her debut with the New York Philharmonic under Theodore Thomas, performing the Bruch concerto. According to one critic, "She deserves to rank among the great violinists of the day." Dvořák was in the audience when she played his new Violin Concerto with the New York Philharmonic and was delighted with her performance. Turning to chamber music, Miss Powell was the first woman in America to lead a professional string quartet, and she toured with that ensemble in 1894–95.

Around 1900, Miss Powell lived in England, where she became extremely popular. England was the ancestral country of her family and she felt very much at home there. In a way, she was considered the successor to that eminent violinist, Lady Hallé (Wilma Neruda), who had left England. Miss Powell's debut in Manchester under Hans Richter with the Tchaikovsky concerto brought her the accolade "The most sensational player we have ever heard" (Manchester *Guardian*). Saint-Saëns heard her play his Third Concerto and was happy with her performance. In 1903 she went on tour with John Philip Sousa and his band; they gave 362 concerts in thirty weeks (of which 217 were in England—52 in London alone). Far from making concessions to the public, Miss Powell performed a repertoire of Mendelssohn, Bach, Sarasate, and Saint-Saëns. She organized a piano trio under her name and toured England, South Africa, and America with the group in 1907–8, to great acclaim. In 1912 she premiered the Violin Concerto of the Afro-English composer Samuel Coleridge-Taylor. During World War I she took pride in performing good music for servicemen, convinced that America was "striding ahead in music appreciation." Even *Grove's Dictionary* commented, "This disclosed a gratifying preference on the part of the men for a better class of music than had at first been prescribed."[1] Maud Powell had a crusading spirit on behalf of good music, even early in her career, when she took up the cause of women in music. As early as 1893, at the Chicago World Exposition, she gave a lecture, "Women and the Violin," and performed a piece by the American composer Mrs.

H. H. A. Beach, who accompanied her at the piano. Later, in 1911, she stated in *Musical America*, "Women are making our music wheels turn." Many American composers, men and women, owed a debt of gratitude to Powell's performances, among them Foote, Burleigh, Cadman, Kramer, Hartmann, Herbert, and Grace White.

Maud Powell died, rather unexpectedly, in 1920, during a concert tour in Pennsylvania, at the age of fifty-one. A memorial concert was given by the New York Philharmonic on March 13, 1920, and glowing tributes were paid. Her favorite violin, a J. B. Guadagnini, is preserved in the Henry Ford Museum in Detroit. She also owned at one time the ex-Mayseder Guarnerius.

Albert Spalding

The first American-born violinist to win worldwide recognition was Albert Spalding. Born in Chicago in 1888 into a wealthy family, Albert was educated in Florence, where his family spent the winter months. His mother, a gifted singer and pianist, kept open house, and all the great artists who visited the Italian city were invited, among them Casals, Joachim, Sarasate, d'Albert, Busoni, César Thomson. Young Albert heard them all, and his musical taste was formed early.

He studied the violin in Florence and New York with teachers of little fame. In 1902, young Spalding entered an examination at the Liceo Musicale in Bologna to obtain a diploma; the difficult tests included not only violin but also piano and theory. The fourteen-year-old candidate passed with honors.

Although his success received wide publicity, Spalding was sent to Paris to continue his violin studies with Lefort of the Conservatoire. His debut in Paris at the age of sixteen—he played Saint-Saëns's Third Concerto—was not too promising. A year later he played the same concerto in Florence under the baton of the composer, then seventy-one, and they won much acclaim.

Spalding had some success in London, where he played under the formidable Hans Richter, who advised him never to read concert reviews. The great Joachim in Berlin granted him an audition and was complimentary, but Spalding was too advanced to enter the Hochschule, and Joachim gave no private lessons. Joachim impressed young Spalding by showing him how to enliven the Finale of the Bruch concerto with extra fire and sweep.

In 1908 Spalding returned to his native country for a debut at Carnegie Hall under Walter Damrosch. On the program was, once again, the well-tested Saint-Saëns concerto. Damrosch, having heard the soloist play privately, declared that Spalding was "the first great instrumentalist this country has produced." Unluckily, the stern critic of the *Tribune*, Krehbiel, disagreed: he found Spalding's playing full of "rasping, raucous, snarling, unmusical sounds." A month later, the New York critics exuberantly praised another debut—the seventeen-year-old Russian violinist Mischa Elman. Spalding, with his characteristic modesty, agreed: "I heard him, and I cheered him with all the rest. . . . It was such a success as I hoped for, would work for." [1]

Obviously, Spalding had not yet reached his peak, but his career developed steadily, with many concerts in the States and abroad. In January 1910 he visited Russia, and Prince Volkonsky said to him, "There is in your playing a distinctive quality that makes it quite different from any I have previously enjoyed." Spalding returned to Russia several times. On his last visit before World War I, he heard a "little wizard" violinist in Auer's class—it was Jascha Heifetz, still a child.

As soon as the United States entered the war, Spalding enlisted in the army and was sent overseas as a cadet pilot. His commanding officer was Captain Fiorello LaGuardia, a member of Congress (and later mayor of New York City). With his fluent command of Italian and French, Spalding was useful as LaGuardia's adjutant in Italy. In February 1919 Spalding was demobilized and reentered the musical world. He noticed one change about himself: he had lost the stage fright that had plagued him all his life.

Spalding played a tour of twenty concerts in Europe, then returned to travel extensively in the United States. Audiences were growing, new orchestras were formed, there was an enormous rise in public interest in good music. In the spring of 1920, Walter Damrosch took the New York Symphony on a European tour, and he invited two American soloists to join him—Albert Spalding and the composer-pianist John Powell. Pro-American sentiments ran high in western Europe immediately after World War I, and the American visitors were feted enthusiastically.

During the 1920s, the Spaldings lived in New York on East 67th Street. They kept open house for all their musician friends who assembled to play chamber music, including Thibaud, Heifetz, Kochanski, Elman, and Gabrilowitsch. Spalding did a good deal of composing, and one of his violin pieces, *Etchings*, was performed by Elman. The pianist Gabrilowitsch, a superb musician, became Spalding's sonata partner—

an ensemble that came to an end with the pianist's unexpected death in 1936. During summers, Spalding played tennis assiduously, not surprising for a member of the ball-manufacturing family. He is one of the few violinists who dared swing a racket without fear of ruining his bow arm. (Table tennis, however, is permissible, and both Heifetz and Milstein are masters at that.)

From his travels in Europe, Spalding brought with him a violin concerto as yet unknown in the United States, by the Hungarian Ernst von Dohnányi. He introduced it in Boston, Chicago, and New York, under the composer's baton. The following year he visited Hungary and played sonata recitals with Dohnányi, a splendid pianist.

Spalding's autobiography, A Rise to Follow, breaks off in the mid-1930s. He continued to play in public until about 1950, some three years before his death at the age of sixty-five.

Around 1950 Spalding recorded the Brahms concerto with a provincial Austrian orchestra. His tempos are more deliberate than usual, but it is Spalding's very personal interpretation, showing his sincere musicality and concentration.

I heard Spalding when he was at the height of his career, in a recital in Paris around 1926 and one in Berlin somewhat later. My recollection is that of a dignified artist with an attractive tone, musical discipline, and nobility. His performance of Bach's Solo Sonata in G minor was stylish. There was a certain lack of spontaneity and fire, but it was compensated for by his honesty and sincerity. In a world that admired the temperament of Elman and the virtuosity of Heifetz, Spalding's straightforward playing was refreshingly different and unmannered. Spalding himself quoted a jingle from the periodical Vanity Fair, which seemed to please him:[2]

> Said Spalding to Elman
> "You play very well, man!"
> "Your humor is scalding,"
> Said Elman to Spalding.

Franz Kneisel

As teacher and quartet player, Franz Kneisel contributed decisively to American musical life. He arrived in the 1880s, a time when the United States was emerging from a certain musical provincialism, and he contributed to that process of maturing.

Kneisel was born in Bucharest of German parents in 1865. He studied at the Vienna Conservatory with Grün and Hellmesberger and made his debut in 1882 with the difficult *Hungarian Concerto* by Joachim. Two years later, at the age of nineteen, he became concertmaster of the Bilse Orchestra in Berlin (later the Philharmonic), a post once occupied by Ysaÿe. In 1885 Kneisel made a major decision: he moved to Boston as concertmaster of the symphony and remained in America for the rest of his life. His Boston debut with the Beethoven concerto was highly successful; that same year he founded his own quartet, which remained active until 1917. The Kneisel Quartet played in every part of the United States and "it spread appreciation of chamber music from the Atlantic to the Pacific Oceans." Recently, a few recordings made by the Kneisel Quartet in 1913 have been reissued. "The playing is surprisingly modern . . . the performances have structure, strength, and dignity," wrote Harold Schonberg admiringly in 1976. Another New York *Times* critic, Richard Aldrich, who heard the Kneisel Quartet concertize for many years, is full of praise:

> Such playing was a new revelation here, where quartet playing had generally been a by-product. . . . With Kneisel it was . . . a chief end. He spent an enormous amount of time and labor in rehearsal, of thought, knowledge, mastery of style, and infinite attention to detail.[1]

To make the American public understand and appreciate the late Beethoven quartets was Kneisel's special concern. The Kneisel Quartet also gave first performances of Dvořák (including the *American Quartet*, Op. 96) and of Brahms, who was Kneisel's personal friend.

In 1903 Kneisel left the Boston Symphony and two years later joined the newly established Institute of Musical Art in New York. The summers were spent at Blue Hill, Maine, which developed into a music colony attended by students, music lovers, and fellow musicians who gathered for informal concerts. Great artists like Kreisler, Josef Hofmann, and Gabrilowitsch liked to participate in impromptu readings of chamber music. The Kneisel Quartet was dissolved in 1917; for one season the remaining three members gave a few concerts with Fritz Kreisler as first violinist. Kneisel received honorary doctorates from Yale and Princeton Universities. He died in New York in 1926.

While enrolled at the Vienna Conservatory, Kneisel was a fellow student of Flesch in Grün's class. Decades later they met again in New York on rather friendly terms. Flesch heard Kneisel only once, playing quartets, and said, "I was struck by his beautiful tone production, but thought his playing somewhat effeminate and superficial, of small scale." But Flesch fully recognized Kneisel's significance as a quartet player "blazing a trail for this branch of music" in America; he also considered him an excellent teacher guiding "a core of a purely American stock of violinists."[2]

Among Kneisel's students were several outstanding quartet leaders—Jacques Gordon, Sascha Jacobsen, and William Kroll, as well as Joseph Fuchs, still active as soloist and teacher.

David Mannes

David Mannes was a musician of rare idealism and integrity, who spent his long life in the cause of good music. He was a violinist, a teacher, and a conductor; in the broadest sense, he was an educator, believing in music as a means of self-expression, not to be limited to professionals, but to be shared by old and young alike, whether by playing or mere listening. His own career was a model of this unselfish devotion to these ideals. Born in lower Manhattan in 1866, the son of poor immigrant parents of German-Polish background, he struggled through childhood, unable to afford decent music lessons. As a teenager, he earned a bit of money playing in honky-tonks, dance halls, theater orchestras, summer resorts—wherever there was need for an extra violinist. He was finally admitted to the Musicians' Union, which, in turn, entitled him to stand on a certain street corner waiting to be hired. He came to know the seamy side of Broadway, but he kept up his quest for self-improvement.

In 1891, Mannes attracted the attention of Walter Damrosch, who was organizing a permanent Symphony Orchestra for the new Music Hall built by Andrew Carnegie. Mannes was engaged for the first violin section, feeling very inadequate among all the foreign-trained musicians (the rehearsal language was German!). He did not participate in the inaugural season in May 1891 (partly conducted by Tchaikovsky), but decided to go to Berlin for further studies. After working with de Ahna and Halir (both Joachim disciples), Mannes crowned his apprentice years with a six-month study period in Brussels under Ysaÿe. These European studies compensated for the deficiencies in his early training. Having gained self-confidence, Mannes eventually moved up to the concertmaster chair in the New York Symphony, which he kept until 1912; he also participated in the Wagner Opera Tours organized by Damrosch. At the same time, he began teaching in the Music School Settlement for disadvantaged children on Third Street and became a leader in the settlement movement. He extended help to Negro musicians, took music to Harlem, and organized music in Sing-Sing Prison.

With his wife Clara, an accomplished pianist (and a niece of Walter Damrosch), Mannes formed a sonata team which became quite successful. For a time they toured the country, giving as many as forty concerts a season. Their extensive repertoire included new works by Enesco, Lekeu, Carpenter, and Daniel Gregory Mason; they liked to present historical series of programs arranged chronologically; they were particularly known for championing Brahms and Franck. In June–July 1913 the Mannes Duo made a successful debut in London with a three-concert sonata series, but the war made further European plans impossible. For a few seasons, Mannes also led his own string quartet; at one concert, Richard Strauss, on a visit to New York, played the piano in a performance of his own Piano Quartet, a less than satisfying performance.

In 1916, David and Clara Mannes founded their own music school based on their principles and beliefs. It was to be a school of high standards but without pressures, for professionals and nonprofessionals, kept deliberately small so that students and teachers would know each other. Children were an important part of the enrollment. The faculty was chosen with great care. By 1920 the Mannes School could move into its own building on East 74th Street, where it functioned (since 1953 as Mannes College) until moving to West 85th early in 1984. Despite many vicissitudes, the Mannes School has survived and still bears the imprint of the humanitarianism of its founder.

An important phase in Mannes's remarkable career opened in February 1918, when he persuaded the Metropolitan Museum of Art to let him give orchestral concerts in the big entrance hall, primarily for servicemen. Admission was free; some two thousand portable chairs were set up, the others sat on the floor. When the attendance reached five thousand per concert, the frightened custodians shut the doors. But eventually as many as 15,000 people crowded in. Mannes conducted these concerts, usually given from January to April on a weekly basis, for thirty years, 1918–47. During that time, some two million people attended. The symphonic programs were well chosen; the orchestra had to play with one rehearsal. The cost was underwritten by philanthropic trustees of the museum. Mannes was the greatest philanthropist of all—he contributed his art and his initiative for the sake of music, for the good of people. He never forgot his own humble beginnings, his own thirst for great music and for encouragement. There was about him a luminous quality which he communicated to others. Until his last years (he lived to be ninety-three) he could be seen walking through *his* school, listening to children play, sharing impressions with the students, imparting his dedication to teachers. Fellow artists came to visit the school—Casals, Ernest Bloch, Schnabel, Enesco. On his ninetieth birthday in 1956, he was honored by a concert at the Metropolitan Museum.

Louis Persinger

"In his good and dedicated way, Persinger has done perhaps more than anyone else to establish a genuine American school of violin playing." With these words, Yehudi Menuhin paid tribute to the memory of his old teacher.[1]

Louis Persinger had a rich and varied career. Born in Rochester, Illinois, in 1887, he grew up in Colorado, where he began violin lessons. By the time he was twelve he was able to play in public. The following year he was sent to Germany: from 1900 to 1904 he was enrolled at the venerable Leipzig Conservatory and became equally proficient on violin and piano; he also took conducting courses with the famed Arthur Nikisch. Nikisch described Persinger on his graduation as "one of the most talented students the Leipzig Conservatory ever had."[2]

For three years Persinger settled in Brussels, where he combined studies under Ysaÿe with some concertizing in northern Europe. In addition, he coached with Thibaud for two summers. These years gave Persinger's violin playing the French orientation that came to characterize his performance and teaching.

In 1912, Persinger returned to the United States and made his solo debut with the Philadelphia Orchestra under Stokowski; it was followed by many concerts throughout the country. Two years later Nikisch invited him to become concertmaster of the Berlin Philharmonic, one of the most prestigious orchestras in Europe. The outbreak of World War I persuaded Persinger to return home; by 1915 he was concertmaster of the San Francisco Orchestra. But he was not cut out for orchestral work; two years later he resigned and formed his own string quartet, which acquired an excellent reputation. He also directed the Chamber Music Society of San Francisco from 1916 to 1928. While in San Francisco,

Persinger began his teaching career; one of his students was a five-year-old boy who came to him in 1921, Yehudi Menuhin. There was warmth and affection between teacher and student. When Persinger moved to New York in 1925, the Menuhin family moved, too, so that Yehudi would not be deprived of his lessons.

While guiding Menuhin through his first public appearances, Persinger's expertise as a pianist enabled him to be the boy's accompanist at his first New York recital in January 1926 and also during his first American tour in 1928–29.

In 1930 Persinger was appointed to the faculty of the Juilliard School in New York as successor to Leopold Auer, who had died that year. He remained with the Juilliard for thirty-six years, teaching violin and coaching chamber music. On his seventy-fifth birthday he gave a concert at the Juilliard, playing one half of the program as a pianist, the other half as a violinist—quite an accomplishment!

Persinger had a special gift of teaching talented children, and he explained, "Any success I've had has been based on keeping a child's interest, in sensing what might be amusing or arresting to him, and in using as few pedantic words as possible. I teach through the sound of the instrument. . . ."[3] This is how Menuhin remembered his very first lesson: Persinger played for him the Adagio from Bach's Solo Sonata in G minor with his "inimitable sweet tone," and left the child with an "unforgettable and inspiring sound." Other students remembered his manner of explanation: "he speaks in word-pictures, carefully avoiding the use of technical terms or of analysis." Obviously, such unorthodox methods were suitable only for unusually gifted children. Those who needed drilling with scales and etudes were not for Persinger. "He demonstrated and I imitated," remembers Menuhin; "what he gave me . . . was insight into music."[4] Insight, yes—but no firm foundation to build on. Admittedly, this caused Menuhin much distress in later years; the fact that he succeeded to "beget his own method" does not mean that others, less gifted, succeeded. Persinger's approach was predicated on getting hold of the student at a very young age. It worked less well with the teenage students at the Juilliard School, who would have profited from a stiffer, more authoritative and more demanding treatment. Be this as it may, he was generally beloved for his gentleness, patience, and subtle humor, as well as admired for his wide-reaching musicianship.

Besides Menuhin, Ruggiero Ricci, and Guila Bustabo, Persinger taught (among others) Frances Magnes, Fredell Lack, Sonya Monosoff, Miriam Soloviev, Arnold Eidus, Camilla Wicks, and, for a brief time,

Isaac Stern. For whatever reason, that mysterious chemistry needed for a happy student-teacher relationship did not work out for Stern, who returned to his old teacher Blinder.

Persinger enjoyed an international reputation to his death in 1966, and was called upon in later years to serve on the jury of various international competitions, where his fellow-judge was his former student Menuhin.

More American Violinists

The turn of the century saw quite a few meritorious American violinists, now barely remembered. They contributed to the growth of music in America and to the raising of musical standards, perhaps more so than the much publicized visits of foreign virtuosos. The developmental pattern was usually the same as that of Mannes and Persinger: years of basic studies in America, a few years of "finishing" work abroad, and a return to the United States to share new-found knowledge. To win recognition in their native country was not always easy, but they persevered and often succeeded. The following names deserve to be remembered.

Sam Franko was a remarkable musician by any standards. Born in 1857 in New Orleans, he was taken as a child to Germany and received a broad musical education, first with Joachim in Berlin, then with Vieuxtemps in Paris. After his return to New York in 1880, he became a leading member of the orchestras conducted by Theodore Thomas and Leopold Damrosch. In those days, most orchestral musicians came from Germany, and the rehearsal language was German. To disprove the prejudice against native talent, Franko founded the American Symphony, consisting of sixty-five American-born musicians, in 1894, and conducted it for five years. Many of the same musicians were used for his Concerts of Old Music, with innovative programs of mostly eighteenth-century music, which flourished in New York from 1900 to 1910 under Franko's able direction. He searched European libraries for old and forgotten music, which he edited and performed. He engaged artists from abroad, like the Dolmetsch family of England, to perform on old instruments, and was a pioneer in the revival of early music. Franko's editions of older music were published and often used by such conductors as Toscanini, Mengelberg, and Stokowski. His adaptation of a Vivaldi concerto was in the repertoire of Menuhin.

In 1910 Franko shifted his activities to Berlin, where he established similar concerts of old music. He also taught an advanced violin class

at the Stern Conservatory. When World War I broke out, he decided
to return to America. From 1915 to his death in 1937, New York became his base of operations, though he visited Europe every year. In
New York he built a large class of private students, and also taught in
Philadelphia. He was extremely demanding, a perfectionist and a purist,
a relentless critic respected and feared by musicians. Franko once said
that from Wieniawski to Menuhin there was no violinist of rank he had
not heard or personally known.

In 1936, Franko presented his valuable collection of old manuscripts to the New York Public Library, which honored him on his
eightieth birthday. He died a few months later, in May 1937, as a result
of an accident. His memoirs, *Chords and Discords*, were published posthumously.

Theodore Spiering (1871–1925), born in St. Louis, played an important role in American musical life. He studied at the Cincinnati
Conservatory under Schradieck (previously professor at Leipzig), followed by four years in Berlin with Joachim. In 1893 he returned to his
native America and made his debut with the Thomas Orchestra in the
Schumann *Fantasy*. For three years he was a member of the orchestra;
at the same time, he was leader of the Spiering String Quartet, which
gave over four hundred concerts in the United States and Canada during
the time of its existence (1893–1905). During those years he also taught in
Chicago, at the conservatory and the Musical College. At one time he
headed his own Spiering Violin School (1899–1902).

In 1905 Spiering moved to Berlin and made his debut with the
Philharmonic the following year; he also taught a class at the Stern
Conservatory. In 1909, he accepted Gustav Mahler's invitation to become concertmaster of the New York Philharmonic. His solo debut
with the orchestra took place at the first of the Historical Concerts on
November 10, 1909, in Bach's E major Concerto. How highly Mahler
valued Spiering can be seen from a letter dated June 21, 1910:

My dear Spiering,
So here I am in Munich, rehearsing my Eighth [Sym-
phony] with might and main.—*You* are just the person I need.
The leader is tolerably good, but his understanding does not
go very deep and he does not really lead the orchestra.[1]

When Mahler fell ill in the spring of 1911, Spiering replaced him
and conducted seventeen concerts of the New York Philharmonic. After

Mahler's death, Spiering returned to Berlin and was active as violinist and conductor. In 1914, he returned to New York. Aside from teaching and performing, he became well known as editor for the publishing house of Carl Fischer, specializing in violin repertory.

The Kneisel School

Between the two world wars, Sascha Jacobsen and Jacques Gordon played an important role in the musical life of America. In his memoirs, Flesch singles them out for particular praise: "The Kneisel school, too, has provided America with several excellent violinists, amongst whom I liked Jacques Gordon best. Sascha Jacobsen could likewise claim to be one of America's most outstanding fiddlers. . . ."[1] Kneisel was originally a pupil of Grün in Vienna, as was Flesch; one can almost feel a certain pride in Flesch's comment that two such excellent violinists as Jacobsen and Gordon could be traced to Grün rather than to Auer.

The lives and careers of Jacobsen and Gordon ran somewhat parallel: both were about the same age, of Russian parentage, both studied with the same teacher in New York and eventually became known as quartet leaders. But while Gordon's activity centered at first on Chicago, Jacobsen remained in New York.

Sascha Jacobsen, born around 1897, was, in fact, a native New Yorker, though his manager tried to make him into a Russian fiddler because it was the rage of the day. Kneisel took him as a student when he was eleven. He graduated from the Institute of Musical Art in New York in the summer of 1915 with the highest honor, the Loeb Prize. On November 27 of that year he made his official recital debut in New York and received exceptional reviews: "One of the most promising young violinists . . . marvellous technique . . . luscious tone . . . fire and abandon . . . tumultuous applause . . ."[2] Within a few years he had acquired such a following that he could make three consecutive appearances in New York's biggest halls—the Metropolitan Opera, Aeolian Hall, and Hippodrome—within three weeks (spring 1918). There were also prestigious orchestral engagements, including the New York Philharmonic and the New York Symphony. Henderson of the New York *Sun* called him "one of the foremost generation of violinists."[3] But his nemesis was the arrival of seventeen-year-old Heifetz, whose debut on October 27, 1917, eclipsed all the competition. Heifetz's name began to creep into reviews of Jacobsen's performances: "To find his superior one would have to look to no less a phenomenon than Jascha Heifetz." Or, "If Jacobsen's violin lacks the utter divinity of Heifetz, it sings with no meaner a tone." These are left-handed compliments. Some critics tried to defend Jacobsen, saying, "If Jacobsen had been born in Europe and presented himself as an Auer student, he would have gained instant recognition." (No wonder his manager tried to make him into a Russian!) A little patriotism was displayed, too: "Verily, Jacobsen is the stuff of which great violinists are made. Well may we Americans be proud of this boy."[4] But it was no use—his solo career was overshadowed, not only by Heifetz, but by the avalanche of excellent Russian violinists of the Auer school. By 1926 Jacobsen made an important decision: he accepted a teaching post at the Institute of Musical Art, as successor to his teacher Kneisel, who had just died; and he founded the Musical Art Quartet. For almost twenty years this quartet, with Jacobsen as leader, played an all-important role in the growing appreciation of chamber music, particularly in New York. The music patron Felix Warburg bought four Stradivari instruments for the exclusive use of the quartet. They had the support of a faithful subscription audience. The programs were mostly classical, interspersed with a few contemporary works, for example the Ernest Bloch Piano Quintet, or an all-American program in 1938 "of prevailing mediocrity" (according to the *Times*), which attracted a smaller-than-usual audience. The Musical Art Quartet quietly disbanded, and in 1945 Jacobsen resigned from his position at the Juilliard School and moved to California. Beginning with the 1946 season he was concertmaster of the Los Angeles Philharmonic under Wallenstein and joined the faculty of the Los Angeles Conservatory to conduct classes in violin and chamber music.

Jacques Gordon was born in Odessa in 1899 and began to study the violin at the Odessa Conservatory, where he was considered a prodigy. He came to the United States as a very young man and studied at the Institute of Musical Art under Kneisel. From 1917 to 1920 he was a member of the Berkshire Quartet. In 1921 he was appointed concertmaster of the Chicago Symphony and served until 1930; at the same time he was head of the violin department at the American Conservatory. In addition, in 1921 he had organized his own string quartet and in 1930 decided to devote all his time to his concert activities. That year he founded the Gordon Music Association at Falls Village, Connecticut, which sponsored the concerts of the Gordon Quartet. From 1936 to 1939 he conducted the WPA Orchestra at Hartford, Connecticut. In 1942 he became head of the violin department at the Eastman

School in Rochester, while continuing his quartet playing. In 1947 he suffered a stroke and resigned from the quartet; the following year he died of a cerebral hemorrhage, after returning from an informal music session spent at the home of Albert Spalding in the company of Fritz Kreisler. He owned a rare Stradivari violin of 1732, reportedly used during the nineteenth century by Paganini, Spohr, and Joachim.

Joseph Fuchs was born in New York City in 1900 and continues to be active in 1983, teaching at the Juilliard School and playing recital programs with undiminished mastery. He studied at the Institute of Musical Art with Kneisel (whom he remembers fondly) and graduated with several awards, enabling him to make a New York debut in 1920 and to undertake a European concert tour. He became concertmaster of the Cleveland Orchestra in 1929, but resigned in 1941 to pursue a solo career. A successful reappearance in New York in 1943 led to the founding of the Musicians Guild, a group offering varied chamber music programs. Fuchs directed the Guild until 1956, appearing frequently with his sister, the outstanding violist Lillian Fuchs. He toured Europe and South America in the 1950s, the Soviet Union in 1965, and was also heard in Japan and Israel. In 1953 and 1954 he was invited to participate in the Casals Festival in Prades.

Fuchs has always shown interest in modern music, though not of the avant-garde type. In 1960 he commissioned (through the Ford Foundation) a violin concerto from the eminent composer Walter Piston; the premiere was given in May 1961. He also gave the first performances of concertos by Ben Weber and Nikolai Lopatnikoff. The Czech composer Bohuslav Martinů dedicated his *Madrigals* for violin and viola to Joseph and Lillian Fuchs. Fuchs also introduced to New York the revised version of the Vaughan Williams Sonata in A minor.

Teaching at the Juilliard School since 1946, Fuchs has trained excellent violinists, though few of them have become prominent.

Fuchs is a superb technician with a truly masterful command of all intricacies of left- and right-hand techniques. His playing is vigorous and large-scaled, with a warm, rich tone. However, in moments of stress there is a certain harshness in his bow attack. His musical concepts are virile but at times lack grace and charm. His many recordings attest to both his technical excellence and his impressive interpretative powers. He plays a Stradivari, the "Cadiz," of 1722.

To the same generation as Fuchs belonged William Kroll (1901–1980), also a native New Yorker. While Fuchs was entirely American-

Joseph Fuchs, now an octogenarian, is still performing vigorously.

Benno Rabinof, the last to study with Professor Auer in New York, shown with his teacher in 1928.

The violinist Samuel Dushkin collaborated closely with Igor Stravinsky during the 1930s.

trained, Kroll was taken to Berlin as a child, where he studied at the Hochschule with Marteau from 1911 to 1914. Though he made a successful debut in New York upon his return in 1915, he felt the need for further study and entered the Institute for Musical Art to work with Kneisel, as well as with the theorist Goetschius. Kroll graduated with high honors in 1922 and decided to concentrate on chamber music, without entirely abandoning a solo career. He was leader of various ensembles, such as the Elshuco Trio (1922–29), the Coolidge Quartet (1936–44), and the Kroll Quartet (1944–69). Kroll and his ensemble groups have toured extensively in the United States, Canada, Mexico, and Europe. In 1958 and 1959 he formed a sonata team with the pianist Arthur Balsam. For his services to the cause of chamber music, Kroll was awarded the Coolidge Medal at the Library of Congress in 1942.

As a teacher, Kroll was mainly active at the Institute of Musical Art (1922–38) and at the Mannes College of Music (after 1943). He was also on the faculty of the Berkshire Tanglewood Festival from 1949 on and held guest teaching posts at the Peabody Conservatory, the Cleveland Institute, and Queens College. He was also known as a gifted composer; he published music for string quartet, chamber orchestra, and solo violin. His short piece *Banjo and Fiddle* was recorded by Jascha Heifetz. But Kroll's idol as a violinist was Kreisler, to such a degree that his friends nicknamed him "Fritz."

Kroll played with an extraordinary ease and elegance, unfailing intonation and bow control. His musicianship had depth and insight, and he led his quartet with authority, vigor, and much temperament. He played a Guadagnini violin until 1950, when he acquired the Stradivarius "ex-Ernst" of 1709.

The Last Three Auer Students

The last Auer disciples, who studied with the old master in New York during the 1920s, were Rabinof, Shumsky, and Dushkin. All three were of Russian parentage, but Rabinof and Shumsky were American-born, while Dushkin was brought to the United States as a child.

Benno Rabinof (1908–75) was born on Manhattan's Lower East Side. He grew up under the image of Mischa Elman's violin. Elman's emotional approach to music and his golden tone had a magical appeal for the Jewish population of New York, far more than the polished perfection of Heifetz. Once it was determined that young Benno was gifted for the violin—he started at the age of three and a half—it was clear that he had to emulate Elman. Between the ages of six and ten, he had several teachers, including the noted Franz Kneisel. But when, in 1918, the legendary Leopold Auer settled in New York, it became certain that only he would qualify as Benno's teacher. For the next nine years, he worked under the guidance of Auer, who reportedly said that "Benno was the most gifted of all the students he had taught in America."[1] On November 18, 1927, Auer proudly sponsored Rabinof's debut at Carnegie Hall by conducting the accompanying orchestra, sixty members of the New York Philharmonic. Rabinof played two concertos with the orchestra— the Elgar and the Tchaikovsky—and a critic remarked that the eighty-two-year-old Auer conducted "with youthful enthusiasm and vigor." After intermission came a group of shorter pieces with piano, by Glazunov, Debussy, Beethoven-Auer, and Paganini. Under such auspices, Rabinof's debut should have been a sensation—but it was not, though the critics were encouraging. They found the nineteen-year-old Rabinof to be "a decidedly accomplished performer" with a "modest and musicianly manner," but not yet a "commanding individuality." He received consistently good reviews; ten years later, in 1937, Olin Downes wrote in the *Times*, "A violinist of exceptional attributes, including a fluent and even spectacular technique and a tone prevailingly warm and brilliant."[2] By then, Rabinof had played from coast to coast as well as in Europe. He also explored the comparatively new medium of radio: in 1929 he was heard on a national network (NBC), and during the 1930s he played twenty-eight violin concertos under Alfred Wallenstein in a weekly broadcast series. But Rabinof's career did not really expand, and he was forced to rely more and more on radio performances. During the war, he gave many performances for the Armed Forces; afterwards began his collaboration with his wife Sylvia, a gifted pianist-composer. As a piano-violin duo, Benno and Sylvia Rabinof became quite popular on the American concert circuit. They also played in Europe in 1956. One of their specialties became the Beethoven sonata cycle—all ten works played in one day, divided between afternoon and evening sessions. In 1955 the Rabinofs commissioned a Double Concerto from Bohuslav Martinů and played it with the Philadelphia Orchestra under Ormandy. Rabinof continued to perform until his unexpected death in 1975; he died of a heart attack just prior to a concert at the Brevard Music Center in North Carolina.

Rabinof left a few excellent recordings which show the warmth of his tone and the brilliance of his technique. One of his best performances was of the Glazunov Violin Concerto with the Boston Symphony under the baton of the composer during the latter's American tour in 1930. Because Rabinof was endowed with all the qualities of a virtuoso violinist, it is difficult to say why he did not attain a big career. Perhaps he never developed that "commanding individuality" that was found missing at his debut, but he could be exciting in a repertoire that appealed to his warm and outgoing temperament. He was a born violinist rather than an intellectual musician. His human qualities matched his musical achievements, and he is remembered fondly by his many friends and admirers.

Oscar Shumsky was also an Auer student in the late 1920s, but Auer died before he could complete his studies; it was Efrem Zimbalist who guided young Oscar until his graduation from the Curtis Institute in 1938. Born in 1917 in Philadelphia, Shumsky started to play the violin at age four; his early teacher was the Russian-born Albert Meiff. At the age of eight the boy was sufficiently advanced to perform as soloist at a children's concert of the Philadelphia Orchestra under Stokowski. About the same time, he began working with Auer and continued until the master died in 1930. While still nominally a student, Oscar toured South Africa in 1932 and played the Brahms and Elgar concertos with the Philadelphia Orchestra, quite an accomplishment for a boy of fifteen.

In 1934 he gave his first New York recital, followed by a second concert the next year. The critics praised his generous and firm tone, as well as his technical skill. He was described as dependable and resourceful but not exciting. In 1936 he made his debut in Vienna and was warmly applauded. To broaden his musical experience, Shumsky entered the NBC-Toscanini Orchestra in 1939; a fellow member, the eminent violist William Primrose, invited Shumsky to become first violinist in the Primrose String Quartet. The new ensemble was highly acclaimed. During the war, Shumsky served as musician in the U.S. Navy Band. His return to the concert scene in 1946 was not an unqualified success; in his appearance at Carnegie Hall with Arthur Balsam at the piano, one critic found him "ill at ease and diffident," lacking fire and lift.[3] At that time, he acquired a beautiful violin, the "Duke of Cambridge" Stradivari; it had once belonged to Pierre Rode. Pursuing an active solo career, Shumsky was heard with many of the leading American orchestras, and his Carnegie Hall recital in 1954 was described as "an evening of most impressive violin playing."[4] In the late 1950s he branched out into conducting, and has since appeared in the dual role of conductor and soloist. He was honored as an "outstanding American artist" by the Ford Foundation in 1963, which enabled him to commission a work for violin and piano from the American composer Quincy Porter. In 1972 Shumsky revealed his talent for the viola and successfully presented a program playing both violin and viola.

Shumsky enjoys enormous esteem among discriminating music lovers and professionals. Yet he has not been able to build a real following with the broad concertgoing public. He has all the qualities expected of an important artist: strong technique, a warm tone, and sterling musicianship. He is not a "heroic" violinist, but a "remarkably satisfactory musician," wrote Harold Schonberg in the *Times* as far back as 1955, and he concluded that "a lack of personality, of inner strength and musical profile kept Shumsky from achieving . . . communication with the audience."[5] Undeterred, Shumsky continues his activities as a concert and recording artist; his cycles of Bach solo works and Mozart sonatas on the Musical Heritage label are highly rated by connoisseurs. A concert at Tully Hall in February 1981 showed him once again as a master musician of great versatility.

Samuel Dushkin was born around 1894 in Suwalki (Russian Poland) and began to play the violin as a child. At the age of eight or nine, he was brought to America, where the composer Blair Fairchild took charge of his musical education. He made it possible for young Dushkin to study in Paris with Rémy, a professor at the Conservatoire, before World War I. He had some additional coaching with Leopold Auer after the latter settled in New York in 1918.

Dushkin began his career in Europe with concerts in London and Paris in 1918. His New York debut was delayed until 1924, when he played with the New York Symphony under Walter Damrosch.

In the 1930s, Dushkin attracted international attention through his musical association with Igor Stravinsky, beginning with Stravinsky's Violin Concerto, which Dushkin commissioned in 1931. Stravinsky accepted on condition that Dushkin be available for continuous consultation while the work was in progress. This collaboration proved to be successful beyond expectation: not only was the concerto acclaimed in all the European capitals under the composer's baton with Dushkin as soloist, but the printed version bears a flattering testimonial (in French):

> This work was premiered under my direction . . . by Samuel Dushkin, to whom I profess a profound gratitude and a great admiration for the highly artistic excellence of his playing.

On the violin part is printed, "Violin part in collaboration with Samuel Dushkin." *

Dushkin's partnership with Stravinsky reached beyond the concerto. Plans were made to go on tour with an all-Stravinsky program for violin and piano. For this purpose, Stravinsky created a repertoire that he and Dushkin could play together, partly new works, partly arrangements, in which Stravinsky gave generous credit to his coworker Dushkin. The actual process of composition was, of course, Stravinsky's responsibility, while Dushkin's contribution extended to the idiomatic shaping of the solo violin part. This unique partnership produced the *Duo concertant*, the *Divertimento* (a free adaptation of Stravinsky's ballet *Le Baiser de la Fée* after Tchaikovsky), and the *Suite italienne* (based on music by Pergolesi, after Stravinsky's ballet *Pulcinella*). In addition, Stravinsky and Dushkin arranged a half-dozen short pieces for violin and piano drawn from such well-known works as *The Firebird*, *Petrushka*, and *Le Rossignol*. This repertoire for violin and piano formed a well-balanced recital program, with which Stravinsky and Dushkin toured Europe in 1932-34. They brought a similar program to America in 1937, opening with a festive evening at New York's Town Hall on January 27. Olin Downes wrote in the New York *Times* after their joint concert, "Mr. Stravinsky . . . had never played the piano so smoothly and clearly . . . with polish, almost with zest. . . . Mr. Dushkin was efficient and authoritative. The ensemble was excellently adjusted." [6]

The ten years that Dushkin spent in close—at times daily—contact with Stravinsky represent the high point of his artistic career. Never before and never since was he as successful as when he performed with Stravinsky as pianist or conductor. Fully immersed in Stravinsky's idiom, his performances acquired particular authority in collaboration with the composer.

In 1941, George Balanchine choreographed the ballet *Balustrade* based on the music of Stravinsky's Violin Concerto. Stravinsky liked the version and agreed to conduct the ballet orchestra at the New York premiere, with Dushkin as soloist. As concertmaster of the ballet orchestra at the time, I remember the occasion vividly. While rehearsing, Stravinsky lost a beat during a tricky change of meter in the first movement and found himself waving his hands in the wrong direction, mut-

---

* Before meeting Dushkin, Stravinsky had had another favorite violinist—Paul Kochanski, an extraordinary virtuoso and fine musician of Russian-Polish background. Kochanski had received several dedications of Stravinsky's earlier violin pieces, but there is no indication that Kochanski was ever asked to collaborate.

tering in French under his breath, "*Mais qu'est-ce qu'ils font? mais qu'est-ce qu'il y a?*" (What are they doing, what's the matter?). In the evening, the performance went without a hitch and Dushkin gave a polished reading, but the public's attention was focused on the stage.

Years later, in 1949, Dushkin wrote an essay, "Working with Stravinsky," an affectionate retrospective view of their collaboration. He said,

> My function was to advise Stravinsky how his ideas could best be adapted to the exigencies of the violin as a concert display instrument. At various intervals he would show me what he had just written. . . . Then we discussed whatever suggestions I was able to make.[7]

Stravinsky was a meticulous worker; he wrote and rewrote. Whether he accepted many (or any) of Dushkin's suggestions is difficult to tell. He once said, "When I show Sam a new passage, he is deeply moved, very excited—then a few days later he asks me to make changes."[8]

Working on transcriptions, Dushkin was given much latitude:

> My role was to extract from the original scores of former works we were transcribing, a violin part which I thought appropriate for the violin as a virtuoso instrument and characteristic of his musical intentions. After I had written out the violin part, we would meet, and Stravinsky then wrote the piano part which very often resulted in something different from the original composition. Stravinsky sometimes also altered details of the violin part which I had extracted.

In fact, he did not hesitate to reject the entire first version (prepared by Dushkin) of the Berceuse from *Firebird*, because it sounded like a Kreisler arrangement of Rimsky-Korsakov!

The active collaboration between Dushkin and Stravinsky came to an end when Stravinsky moved to California in 1941, though their friendship lasted a lifetime. During the 1940s, Stravinsky played and recorded with other violinists, among them Joseph Szigeti and Isaac Stern, while Dushkin tried to build a concert career independent of Stravinsky.

Actually, Dushkin was at his best when performing new music. In a more conventional repertoire he seemed nervous and unsure of his technique. The critic Paul Bowles characterized him as "a strange and gifted artist, a better musician than technician."[9] On another occasion, the *Herald Tribune* reported, "The performance combined technical unevenness with exhibitions of persuasive interpretative musicianship." Among contemporary composers performed by Dushkin were William Schuman, Copland, Virgil Thomson, Bohuslav Martinů, Vittorio Rieti, and Maurice Ravel, whose *Tzigane* he introduced to America.

Dushkin's recital programs aimed at certain intellectual standards: he chose works rarely played, and he found an accomplished pianist-partner in Erich Itor Kahn, himself a composer. In 1942–43 they gave a series of three programs at Town Hall in New York, "Profiles of Three Centuries of Music." Dushkin and Kahn played at Town Hall again in 1944 and 1946.

After 1950 Dushkin gradually retired from active concert life, though he maintained his interest in New York's musical events. He died in 1976 in New York. His beautiful Guarnerius is now played by Pinchas Zukerman.

Louis Krasner and
the Concertos of Alban Berg and Arnold Schoenberg

Louis Krasner deserves a place of honor among violinists for having been the first (and, for a time, the only!) interpreter of the concertos by Alban Berg and Arnold Schoenberg. It is ironic that it was Krasner, the Russian-born American, and not a European violinist, who thought of commissioning Berg to write a violin concerto. And it was a sign of mutual confidence that Schoenberg asked Krasner to introduce his new concerto and that Krasner accepted the difficult task without hesitation, all during the 1930s, when public acceptance of Berg and Schoenberg was severely limited.

Louis Krasner was born in Russia in 1903 and came with his parents to the United States when he was five. The family settled in Providence, Rhode Island, where the boy began to play the violin. A patron enabled him to study in Boston, where he graduated from the New England Conservatory in 1922 with high honors.

In 1923, Krasner went to Europe for further studies, and his teachers were Flesch, Capet, and Sevčik, certainly the best that Europe had to offer. He remained in Europe to give concerts, with an interest in contemporary music shown by his choice of repertoire: he played the European premiere of the Joseph Achron Violin Concerto in Vienna in 1928; the same year he performed the new concerto by Alfredo Casella in Siena and in Rome.

After hearing the opera *Wozzeck*, Krasner was so impressed that he approached Berg for a violin concerto. It happened that Krasner's offer, extended in 1934, came at an opportune moment, for the composer was hard pressed for money: vilified as "cultural bolshevik" by the Nazis, Berg was blacklisted in Germany. He accepted the commission in the spring of 1935; by July 15 the composition was completed in short score, and less than a month later the orchestration was finished. The speed was amazing, particularly in view of the otherwise slow process of Berg's work. Did the composer have a premonition of his imminent death? He had interrupted work on his opera *Lulu* to write the concerto, which was to be his last completed work. *Lulu* remained unfinished: Berg died the same year, on December 24, 1935.

During the genesis of the concerto, Berg and Krasner kept in touch. In mid-June of 1935, Krasner visited Berg in Carinthia and reminisced,

> We spent a full day together in music-making and fascinating discussion. The first part of his Violin Concerto was taking shape beautifully, but he was anxiously searching, he explained, for a fitting Bach chorale to embody in his work.[1]

But Krasner also remembers that in Berg's attitude "there was always a feeling of sadness which could not be dispelled. I have often wondered whether Berg did not sense that here was his own Requiem."

A few months after Berg's tragic death, Krasner played the world premiere of the concerto at the International Society for Contemporary Music Festival in Barcelona on April 19, 1936. Anton Webern was scheduled to conduct but withdrew unexpectedly, and Hermann Scherchen agreed to take over at the last moment. According to Slonimsky, "Webern, in his dogmatic insistence on perfection, spent several hours rehearsing the introductory measures of the work, and had to resign from his task."[2] Nevertheless, the endangered premiere was a great success, and Krasner played a number of repeat performances throughout Europe. He introduced the Berg concerto in Boston and New York under Serge Koussevitzky's direction. Everywhere, Krasner's perceptive performance won much acclaim. The New York *Herald Tribune* reported in March 1937,

> Mr. Krasner's playing was extraordinarily sensitive. The phrasing of this difficult work was executed with the greatest refinement. The tone was also beautiful. Indeed, Mr. Krasner deserved much more applause than he got. . . . The applause for the Concerto was uneven, showing the sharply divided opinion.[3]

Arnold Schoenberg was aware of Krasner's affinity for modern music when he wrote him in February 1938 about giving the premiere of his new Violin Concerto. He warned him, "The difficulties of this work are different ones and greater than those of the Berg Concerto."[4] He was right; aside from its uncompromising musical idiom, Schoenberg's Violin Concerto has horrendous technical difficulties—it requires "a violinist with six fingers," as musicians joked. In asking Krasner to play his concerto, Schoenberg relied on the recommendations of the violinist Kolisch and the conductor Klemperer, both of whom thought highly of Krasner. "I would be very happy if you were the man to play the work," wrote Schoenberg.

Krasner accepted the challenge: he studied and memorized the concerto and played it under Stokowski with the Philadelphia Orchestra on December 6 and 7, 1940. Musicians and management were antagonistic; the Philadelphians were not eager for the premiere and refused to budget Krasner's fee, which was ultimately paid with Stokowski's personal check. Schoenberg did not attend, but heard favorable reports and congratulated Krasner:

> It is a great pleasure to me to thank you for your great achievement: to play my Violin Concerto in such a perfect and convincing manner and so shortly after . . . it has been called unplayable. . . . You have achieved something which must be called "a historical fact."[5]

But despite the heroic performance, there were few requests for repeat hearings: the work was considered too forbidding. Five years elapsed before a second performance took place, by Krasner and Mitropoulos in Minneapolis in November 1945. Schoenberg's intent to come was frustrated by wartime difficulties, but he kept in touch with Krasner by letter, sending him detailed questions about the concerto.

By that time, Krasner was appointed concertmaster of the Minneapolis Orchestra, a position he held until 1949. He then moved to Syracuse University as professor of violin and founded the Krasner Chamber Music Ensemble. In 1971 he retired as professor emeritus but continued teaching. Since 1976 he has taught in Boston, at the New England Conservatory, his *alma mater*.

During the 1950s, Krasner continued his battle on behalf of the Schoenberg concerto. He played it with the New York Philharmonic under Mitropoulos in 1952, which was recorded. The first European performance took place in Munich on September 7, 1954, again with Mitropoulos, repeated a few days later in Cologne. By now the Schoenberg concerto is played by numerous violinists, though it is by no means a repertoire piece.

THE AMERICAN SCHOOL:
THE MIDDLE GENERATION

Yehudi Menuhin

Berlin, Philharmonic Hall, April 12, 1929. I remember sitting in a capacity audience, awaiting the appearance of a boy prodigy to play the three most challenging concertos in the violin repertoire—Bach, Beethoven, Brahms. The boy appears, blond and chubby, with a cherubic smile, looking younger than his age in his short trousers. He hands his violin to the concertmaster to be tuned. A ripple of surprise runs through the audience—he cannot even tune the violin by himself! (Many people are unaware that violin tuning is a physical job, requiring strength to manipulate the pegs.) But the first vigorous notes of Bach's E major Concerto dispel all doubts. The sounds that come out of that violin are as pure as gold, inspired by an angelic naturalness of phrasing and musicality, and without a trace of childishness. "Now I know that there is a God in heaven," was Albert Einstein's simple comment after he heard the boy.[1]

Thirty-odd years later, when I first met Menuhin personally, I told him that I was present at that historic concert. He looked at me and said with a wry smile, "Would you be surprised if I told you that you could fill Philharmonic Hall twice over with all the people who told me they were there?" I felt deflated, but still—I *was* there. And the memory is as much visual as it is aural: the image of the boy, totally immersed in music, with a concentration bordering on trance. This immersion has not changed over the years.

When Menuhin made his Berlin debut in 1929, he was already a veteran of the concert stage. His first concert in New York took place

Louis Persinger in his San Francisco studio with his prodigy student, Yehudi Menuhin, eight years old (1925).
Yehudi Menuhin is considered one of the truly great violinists of our century, besides being a profound humanitarian and a personality of enormous versatility and intellectual scope.

three years earlier, on January 17, 1926. The time seemed ripe for another prodigy: almost ten years had passed since the legendary debut of seventeen-year-old Heifetz in 1917. Since then, other young violinists had tried their luck—Seidel, Max Rosen, Poliakin, Eddy Brown, Erica Morini—all fine players, but no one a real sensation. To be truthful, neither was Menuhin in 1926, judging by the opinion of the second-string critics who attended the debut at the Manhattan Opera House. The critical praise was mild and cautious. One reporter remarked that three elderly gentlemen sat in the first row, the fathers of Elman, Heifetz, and Rosen. The implication was that they were scouting the new prodigy to evaluate the threat to their own progenies. Yehudi played an ambitious program with his teacher Persinger at the piano: Handel's Sonata in E major, Lalo's *Symphonie espagnole*, and Paganini's Concerto in D (the first-movement edition). In his autobiography *Unfinished Journey*, Menuhin belittles this first appearance and prefers November 1927 as his historic Carnegie Hall debut, about which more later.

Actually, Menuhin's tender age worked to his disadvantage. American critics were ill disposed toward prodigies: they gave short shrift to Huberman, Kreisler, Vecsey, and Josef Hofmann when they first arrived on these shores as children. There was always the suspicion that the children were exploited and denied a normal growth. By the time they were seventeen, as in the case of Elman or Heifetz, the danger seemed to have passed; but no children, please!

Yehudi was born in New York City in 1916 and grew up in San Francisco, where his Russian-Jewish immigrant parents moved shortly following his birth. After some initial violin lessons at age five revealed the boy's extraordinary musical gifts, he was entrusted to the care of Louis Persinger, an accomplished musician and a man of great sensitivity. "He demonstrated and I imitated," is Yehudi's description of the method used.[2] But the boy with the cherubic smile had a streak of intractability, as he himself admits, and to enforce any technical discipline would have been counterproductive. After a year of two lessons a week with Persinger, Yehudi made his first public appearance in Oakland in 1924, at the age of seven. One critic wrote, "This is not talent, this is genius."[3] The piece he played on that occasion was Bériot's *Scènes de ballet*, a melodious salon confection requiring a bit of showmanship, but there was something special about the playing of the chubby blond boy totally absorbed by the music. There seemed nothing studied or artificial about his performance; every inflection was Yehudi's own, reflecting his soul, unsullied by the world around him. This purity remained his hallmark long after he was grown.

Early in 1925, Yehudi played, for the first time with orchestra, Lalo's *Symphonie espagnole* accompanied by the San Francisco Symphony. This was followed, on March 25, 1925, by his first full-length recital. These appearances were considered by his parents not as steps toward a career, but as part of a learning process.

In the autumn of 1925, the Menuhin family followed Persinger to New York in order not to disrupt Yehudi's lessons. This stay in the East ended with the Manhattan Opera House recital in January 1926.

Although Yehudi had by no means outgrown Persinger's teaching, it was decided that he would go to Europe, possibly to study with Ysaÿe, Persinger's old master. With the help of a patron, the entire Menuhin family of five (including his two little sisters Hephzibah and Yaltah) set out for Paris late in 1926. Yehudi had his heart set on studying with Enesco, whom he had heard and met in San Francisco; but first the appointment with Ysaÿe in Brussels had to be kept.

This meeting did not turn out as happily as had been expected. Ysaÿe listened with obvious pleasure to Yehudi's playing of the *Symphonie espagnole*. Then he asked him to play a scale. Yehudi, obviously flustered, "groped all over the fingerboard like a blind mouse" (his own description). Embarrassed, he begged his mother to take him back to Paris on the first train.

By sheer persistence he obtained an audition with Enesco, and this meeting changed his life. There began a beautiful, creative friendship between two kindred souls. Enesco was forty-six, Yehudi eleven; yet it was an exchange: "Yehudi has as much to offer me as I can give him," said Enesco, and he refused any pay for the lessons.[4] Yehudi was fascinated by Enesco's personality and for a time imitated his free, improvisational style of interpretation.

While waiting to begin his studies with Enesco, Yehudi made his Paris debut with the Lamoureux Orchestra under Paul Paray (February 6, 1927) and won immediate acclaim. The summer of 1927 was spent in Rumania, near Enesco's summer home, where the master opened up a new world of music to his young disciple.

When the time came for the Menuhin family to return to America, an important engagement awaited Yehudi—an appearance with the New York Symphony Orchestra. The German maestro Fritz Busch had requested Mozart's A major Concerto, but Yehudi had his heart set on playing the Beethoven. Busch was adamant; "one doesn't hire Jackie Coogan to play Hamlet," was his rebuff. But he agreed to an audition, and later reminisced, "Yehudi played so gloriously and with such complete mastery that by the second tutti I was already won over. . . . That was perfection."[5]

This Carnegie Hall appearance, on November 25, 1927, marked the beginning of Menuhin's world fame. The performance was greeted with a wild ovation. Experts noted that he had used the most difficult of all cadenzas, the one by Joachim, but this was not the main point. He was, as Olin Downes (the *Times* critic) privately conceded, not an infant prodigy but a great artist who began at an early age. And Lawrence Gilman of the *Herald Tribune* wrote, "What you hear . . . takes away the breath and leaves you groping helplessly among the mysteries of the human spirit."[6] Yehudi was eleven at the time, but looking younger and indeed very small next to the towering Busch.

A few weeks later, on December 12, 1927, Yehudi gave a Carnegie Hall recital before a packed house. With Persinger at the piano he played a big program: Mozart's Concerto No. 7 (a rediscovered work he had studied with Enesco), Bach's Chaconne, Tartini's *Devil's Trill Sonata*, Chausson's *Poème*, and Wieniawski's *Souvenirs de Moscou*. Amidst all the acclaim, one cautionary paragraph stood out in a review. Despite the "technical armor of a virtuoso," the critic Richard Stokes observed,

> The method of playing appears to me faulty, in that the violin is permitted to slope down from his shoulder, instead of being flung aloft as in the American system; while the tone is dependent wholly on strength of bowing, instead of partly on the pressure of the fingers of the left hand.[7]

But this was a minority voice in a chorus of praise. For the time being, the "technical armament" seemed in perfect order, though tiny cracks began to surface in the coming years.

In 1928, Yehudi returned to the West Coast and to Persinger's musical care. That year, Persinger and his quartet were teaching at Santa Barbara in southern California. Once a week, Persinger drove overnight to San Francisco to work with Yehudi on new repertoire, covering a great deal of ground, from Vivaldi to Glazunov. Early in 1928, Yehudi made his first recordings, with Persinger at the piano: the selections, by Fiocco, Franz Ries, and similarly obscure composers, were chosen because they were unfamiliar. Engineers from RCA headquarters in New Jersey were dispatched to Oakland, California, to

handle the technical details. That year also saw Yehudi's first trans-
continental concert tour, again with Persinger at the piano. In order not
to overburden the boy, it was decided that he give one concert a week,
for about fifteen weeks, moving eastward from San Francisco to New
York, interspersing orchestral appearances with recitals. Persinger
worked with him every morning and was present at every concert, while
father Menuhin represented the family. The tour ended in New York
in January 1929, when Yehudi played the Tchaikovsky concerto at
Carnegie Hall. A generous music patron, Henry Goldman, heard him
on that occasion and presented him with a Stradivari violin, the "Prince
Khevenhüller." It was the violin of Yehudi's dreams—he had seen and
tried it a year earlier, but knew that he could not afford it. This is the
violin he took on his second tour to Europe and which he used for that
memorable debut in Berlin.

For Menuhin, 1929 was a "Busch year." The conductor Fritz Busch
introduced him to German audiences in the spring of 1929 and to
London on November 10 of that year. During the intervening summer,
Yehudi studied with the violinist Adolf Busch (Fritz's brother), considered the guardian of German violin tradition, and he returned for a
second summer the following year.

It was on Enesco's advice that Menuhin chose Busch as mentor
for the German repertoire, a kind of "compensating influence" to make
him understand the workings of a German musical mind—uncompromising, puritanical, idealistic. Busch embodied all this, and more—he
was a musician first, a violinist second. There was nothing in terms of
violin playing he could teach Menuhin, who in truth did not need a
violin teacher. But Menuhin profited from Busch's sterling musicianship, his strict adherence to the *Urtext* (the literal observance of the
composer's original text), his unswerving devotion to tradition. The
musical and human affinity that existed between Menuhin and Enesco
never grew between him and Busch, but there was respect and affection.
Menuhin obviously enjoyed his stay in Basel, where the Busch family
lived, where disciples shared the life of the master in daily musical
communion.* It speaks for Menuhin's resilient personality that he was
able to absorb the often conflicting advice of strong-willed teachers, yet
chose instinctively what suited his own musical vision.

From 1930 to 1935, the Menuhin family, always a close-knit unit,
lived in Ville d'Avray near Paris. Many musicians and artists came to

* One such disciple was young Rudolf Serkin, who became Busch's piano partner and
eventually his son-in-law.

visit; chamber-music sessions with Thibaud, Enesco, Cortot, Ciampi, and Nadia Boulanger were a regular occurrence. Horowitz and Piatigorsky entered the circle of friends. The ambiance was artistic, but well organized and regulated. Teachers and tutors took charge of the general education of the "children." Hephzibah and Yaltah were developing into accomplished pianists. Enesco, having heard Yehudi and Hephzibah play a Beethoven sonata, urged that the brother-and-sister team be heard in public. They made a recording of the Mozart Sonata in A (K. 526) early in 1934, which received the Prix Candide as best disc of the year. Later that year, on October 13, they gave a sonata recital in Paris, performing Mozart, Schumann, and Beethoven. Their unanimity of music making deepened over the years, until Hephzibah's lamented death in 1981.

During the summers, Yehudi retained regular contact with Enesco, exploring with that great musician the innermost secrets of great music. The winters were divided between Europe and America. Yehudi traveled with his father, while Mrs. Menuhin stayed with her daughters.

Important concerts of those years included the 150th Jubilee of the Leipzig Gewandhaus, where Menuhin played the Mendelssohn Concerto in 1931, and his historic collaboration with Sir Edward Elgar in 1932. Under the baton of the seventy-five-year-old composer, Menuhin recorded Elgar's Violin Concerto in London. "The recording was not only successful, but good" is Menuhin's own evaluation. So convinced was Elgar that his sixteen-year-old soloist would do a superb job that he was reluctant to rehearse; he preferred to go to the races! A few months later, a special concert was arranged at Albert Hall: in the first half, Menuhin played concertos by Bach and Mozart, with Sir Thomas Beecham as conductor; in the second half, Sir Edward took over the baton to accompany his own concerto. They repeated the Elgar concerto in Paris, where it was received politely. A plan to do the same in the United States was thwarted by the composer's death. Fifty years later I heard Menuhin give an inspired performance of the Elgar concerto with Mehta and the New York Philharmonic; his is the definitive interpretation of this magnificent score.

The culmination of Menuhin's early career was his appearance with the Beethoven concerto under the baton of Toscanini at the New York Philharmonic in January 1934. The following year he embarked on a world tour, including New Zealand, Australia, and South Africa, visiting thirteen countries and seventy-three cities, playing 110 concerts. It was a superhuman effort, leaving him "tired, indifferent, and sad" when friends saw him in March 1936. It was decided that he take a year off from concert work.

After eighteen months of rest, contemplation, and renewed study of violin repertoire, Menuhin reappeared on the stage, taller, slimmer, in white tie, looking handsome and romantic. He used the occasion to introduce a musical discovery—the "lost" Violin Concerto of Robert Schumann, rejected since a single try-out in 1854 by the composer and Joachim. Menuhin has an insatiable curiosity for music that is forgotten, neglected, or new, be it Vivaldi or Bartók; other rediscoveries of his are Mozart's *"Adelaide"* Concerto and Mendelssohn's Concerto in D minor.

The outbreak of World War II interrupted all normal travel. Menuhin volunteered his art freely for concerts in army camps and hospitals and for charitable purposes. In doing so, he traveled ceaselessly, covered tens of thousands of miles, made over five hundred concert appearances, and endured various hardships. Worst of all, he had no practice time to keep up his technique, and the mechanics of playing were affected. His ability as performer, once matchless, showed a decline.

It was not fatigue alone that made him lose ground—it was a delayed realization that he had played subconsciously most of his life. Kreisler once said, "Because the young Menuhin had anticipated so early and so much of what nature had given him, I foresaw that he would have great difficulties." [8] In fact, all child prodigies eventually go through a similar period of readjustment, but in Menuhin's case it came later and harder. He said candidly, "Just as I had married without being prepared for marriage, so I played the violin without being prepared for violin playing." [9] He had fallen into bad habits. Having learned to play by instinct, he never was forced to explore the basic mechanics. His teachers, Persinger, Enesco, and Busch, marveled at his "God-given" technique and saw no need to tamper with it. Now he was forced to retool, to rebuild his technical perception of the violin and the playing functions of his body. Eventually he succeeded in reconstructing consciously what he had mastered subconsciously as a child.

It was during that difficult period of his life that Menuhin became intensely interested in the music of Béla Bartók. At that time, the Hungarian composer lived in voluntary exile in the United States, ill and impoverished, little known by the public, neglected by orchestras and critics. His spiritual support came from fellow Hungarians like Szigeti and Dorati, who firmly believed in his greatness, and from forward-looking conductors like Koussevitzky and Mitropoulos. They were joined by Menuhin, who, in 1943, added the recent Violin Concerto (1939) and the early Violin Sonata No. 1 (1921) to his repertoire. Prior to the Carnegie Hall performance of the sonata (with Adolph Baller at the piano) in November 1943, a meeting with the composer was arranged at the home of mutual friends in New York. Bartók, a man of few words, was enchanted with the performance and said, "I did not think music could be played like that until long after the composer was dead." Menuhin took advantage of the composer's mellow mood and asked him to write a violin work for him. The result of this commission was the monumental Solo Sonata, which Menuhin received in March 1944. "I admit I was shaken. It seemed to me almost unplayable," was Menuhin's first and (as he now admits) "ill-judged" impression. An accompanying letter showed the composer's concern:

> I am rather worried about the "playability" of some of the double-stops, etc. On the last page I give you some of the alternatives. In any case, I should like to have your advice. I sent you two copies. Would you be so kind as to introduce in one of them the necessary changes in bowing, and perhaps the absolutely necessary fingering and other suggestions, and return it to me? And also indicate the impracticable difficulties? I would try to change them.[10]

The tone of this letter is very reminiscent of the one Brahms wrote to Joachim in 1878, wondering about the playability of his half-finished violin concerto. Like Joachim, Menuhin was reluctant to make suggestions, finding what Bartók had written "possible if difficult." The premiere of the Solo Sonata took place at Carnegie Hall on November 26, 1944, with the composer present. It was one of Bartók's last joys: he died less than a year later, on September 26, 1945. In January 1946, Menuhin recorded Bartók's Violin Concerto with Dorati and the Dallas Symphony: a noble and dedicated performance.

After the end of World War II—the shooting had barely stopped—Menuhin became the first foreign artist to perform in Moscow. David Oistrakh was there to meet him and they became friends. "I loved him immediately," wrote Menuhin in retrospect. Two years later, in May 1947, they met again in Prague and played Bach's Double Concerto. They found that their styles meshed well, and they played together many times.

Other war-torn countries Menuhin visited in 1945 were France, Holland, and Czechoslovakia. He also brought his violin to the DP

camps in Germany and intervened with American authorities on behalf
of the displaced persons. With his innate sense of justice, Menuhin led
the way toward official rehabilitation of Wilhelm Furtwängler, the German conductor who had remained in Hitler's Germany and was suspected of collaboration with the Nazis. Menuhin did not act on instinct
alone: he had evidence that Furtwängler had been helpful to Jewish
musicians in his orchestra and to other friends. Nevertheless, it was a
courageous act to appear with Furtwängler as conductor, one which
brought him a great deal of animosity, in America as well as in Israel,
a country he visited in 1950. There are great musicians, among them
Arthur Rubinstein and Isaac Stern, who refused to play in Germany,
mindful of the Nazi Holocaust. But Menuhin has never been afraid to
espouse unpopular causes and to act according to his beliefs.

Important events were yet to come in Menuhin's life. Accepting
an invitation from Prime Minister Nehru, he visited India in 1952 and
was captivated by its people, tradition, wisdom. He discovered yoga,
which contributed to his understanding of the mechanics of violin
playing, and studied Indian music, bringing about an exchange of
Western and Indian musicians and dancers. He introduced Ravi Shan-
kar, the master of the sitar, to the Bath Festival of 1966 and gave a joint
concert—actually an extended improvisation—with the Indian musicians. Menuhin's amazing versatility shows itself also in his performances and recordings with Stephane Grappelli, the great French jazz
violinist.

In 1958, Menuhin expanded his manifold musical activities to include orchestral conducting. The ambition to lead an orchestra had
been with him for a long time, and in fact he had conducted occasionally. But in 1958, in a combination of playing and leading, he recorded
the six *Brandenburg Concertos*, playing the solo violin. As his ambition and his repertoire expanded, he did more and more conducting.
The Bath Festival was an ideal proving ground: here he assembled a
chamber orchestra with Robert Masters as his trusted concertmaster.
With disarming candor Menuhin tells us that he learned the basics of
conducting from his players. But primarily Menuhin became a conductor by doing it with growing enthusiasm. "What activity can match
conducting in fulfillment?" he asks. He may not be a born conductor
by temperament (lacking the authoritarian ingredient) but he provides
a kind of inspirational guidance by force of his musical vision. Baton
technique becomes subordinate to the grand concept of a musical
masterpiece. Menuhin's luminous musicality proves to be effective in

front of an orchestra. Recently he has been named principal conductor of the London Royal Philharmonic and undoubtedly will devote more of his time to conducting.

A word about Menuhin as teacher. His music school at Stoke d'Abernon, established in 1963, is an experiment in practical idealism, and it works. Having grown up as a "loner," out of touch with children his own age, Menuhin envisaged a happy community of gifted children, sharing their musical experiences with sympathetic teachers and with each other. "We must guide not only fingers, but minds and hearts, for music is a way of being." The three or four dozen children, fortunate enough to be accepted at the boarding school, are carefully selected for talent, promise, and ethnic variety. The emphasis is on music, but actually all school subjects are taught here. The surroundings are rural, set in the most beautiful English countryside; the schedules are flexible, the discipline natural, without repression. It is not a breeding ground for prodigies, for precocious virtuosos, but a place where the musical mind can grow and expand according to its own God-given timetable, gently guided but never channeled.

Russia has schools for the gifted—the Central Music Schools attached to conservatories. These are ten-year schools for pupils age seven to seventeen, combining a normal school curriculum with strong emphasis on musical performance. I happened to be in Moscow as an exchange scholar when Menuhin visited in 1962, and we were invited to observe how such a school functioned. Several children played for us—serious, unsmiling, perhaps intimidated by the famous visitor—among them a ten-year-old boy named Pavel Kogan, the son of Leonid Kogan and today a violinist-conductor of growing fame. The children played very well, with beautiful schooling, clean intonation, and no virtuoso mannerisms. Menuhin was pleased by what he saw, by the repertoire the children played, by the balance of curriculum and the obvious care not to overburden the young minds. Behind the smooth exterior is much more discipline, I suspect, than Menuhin would tolerate in his own school. Essentially, it is Menuhin's concept of humanism and idealism that pervades Stoke d'Abernon, a luminous quality that emanates from everything he says and does. For children of talent, it is an ideal environment.

I have also observed Menuhin with older students. His critical remarks show much insight and sensitivity. He advocates exercises stressing mobility and relaxation of the left hand all across the fingerboard.

To his many accomplishments, Menuhin has lately added those of author. There are several books that bear his name—instructional, philosophical, musical, autobiographical. He has an exquisite command of the English language (especially noticeable in *Unfinished Journey*, in which he seeks to disentangle the complex web of his life).

He is always motivated by high idealism and a moral rectitude. When embroiled in controversies, he has felt that he was misunderstood and misjudged. He was not prepared for the storm of indignation aroused by the Furtwängler affair and his concerts in post-Hitler Germany. He was taken aback by the hostility shown in Israel in 1950 because of the German incidents. Most intriguing is his relationship with the Soviet Union. Instinctively—being partly of Russian origin—he always had a warm feeling toward Russia. When he went there immediately after the war had ended, he was full of good will and was received with open arms. His visit with Hephzibah in 1962 was also filled with expressions of mutual admiration. Their concerts were received with unbelievable manifestations of enthusiasm and affection, while Yehudi and Hephzibah were fascinated by what they saw in music, education, medical advances, and social progress. The mutual disenchantment came in 1971, during the Seventh Congress of the International Music Council held in Moscow. Menuhin, elected president of the IMC in 1969, arrived with certain reservations about Soviet policies toward dissidents and he expressed them in an honest speech (he spoke in Russian, which should have mollified his Soviet listeners). The fact that he mentioned the name of Solzhenitsyn among the heroes of Soviet culture was alone sufficient to create an aura of official distrust and disfavor. Although he was reelected for another two-year term, the Soviets cold-shouldered him; they refused to print his speech (it appeared on the editorial page of the New York *Times*) and he departed in an atmosphere of bitterness. Since then, Menuhin has continued to champion the cause of Soviet artists and dissidents, and he speaks out quite openly against Soviet intellectual oppression.

To describe Menuhin's playing is not easy. First of all—which Menuhin? Over the years, his playing has changed several times. As a child, he was unique. He did not have Elman's elemental fire or Heifetz's razor-sharp perfection, but music flowed out of his violin in flawless purity. Seemingly, it was not *he* who was making music, it was music that possessed him and used him as a subconscious conduit. He was in semi-trance when he played—Persinger relates the irate look of the five-year-old boy when he was interrupted at the first audition. He had all the technique he needed to play Lalo and Paganini, but was at his best playing the best music—Bach, Mozart, Beethoven, Brahms. There was no other child prodigy who, at Yehudi's age, could have played this music with comparable intuitive understanding. By the time he was fifteen, one could assume some of that innocence to have become tarnished, but this was not the case, according to at least one ardent listener, the English publisher Victor Gollancz:

> He was a revelation, not as a prodigy but as a musician. We heard him whenever we could: playing . . . the Beethoven in 1931; and it was on this last occasion that what I prefer to call not a miracle but an inevitability happened. He was nearing the end of the first movement, and had played the cadenza with extreme but not unsurpassable brilliance; and then, as the second subject returned, there came a purity from his violin that was at once childlike and divine. I rank this moment with the very greatest of my musical experience.[11]

Gollancz then speaks of "perfect tone, perfect time, and perfect phrasing" and continues: "by these qualities, combined with a total lack of self-awareness and total surrender to what is on hand, the divinity of great music is itself immaculately revealed."

But that "lack of self-awareness" could not last forever. It began to falter in the 1930s and reached its nadir in the early 1940s. After much travail, "the sureness of childhood has been regained, with added intellectual stiffening," to his "lasting satisfaction."[12]

Before performing, Menuhin needs to limber up. "Given a half hour to warm up, I know that I can play," he says. He also needs a short period of psychological adjustment on the stage to test the resonance of the hall. Under these optimum conditions, he plays as superbly as ever—and even better! Today, Menuhin's performance is a spiritual experience. His involvement in the music is total, he becomes one with the spirit of the composer, and we, the listeners, are privileged in hearing this fusion of creator and re-creator. I know of no artist before the public today who, like Menuhin, has that self-effacing quality. "Here is the essence of the music," he seems to say; "take it as it is, take it as the composer communicated it to me." He does not seem to interpose his own personality, though this impression is, of course, fallacious: the music is filtered through his personality to reach those who listen. But it is a clear, luminous filter, and the music emerges intact. As I listen to him in 1983, I think back to 1929 when I first heard him, and

I must confess that his artistry has retained for me its inspired message.

Menuhin the artist is inseparable from Menuhin the man. There is an innate nobility and goodness in everything he does, a lack of ostentation, a self-assured modesty, yet a remarkable firmness in the face of challenge, a determination to stand up for his beliefs. He is the most human among humans, guided as much by intuition as by conviction, a true humanist with deep concern about our ailing world, always generous and willing to be helpful.

On stage, he is a model of concentration and modesty. He enters with a smile but approaches the music with seriousness. His face is turned toward the violin while playing, very rarely toward the audience. With his classic profile and closed eyes, he is the image of an artist immersed in his music, oblivious to his surroundings.

When playing with piano, he prefers to stand in the curve of the grand piano (just as singers do); he explains that he has better eye contact with his partner. When performing with Hephzibah, he really did not need that eye contact; their ensemble was unrivaled, attuned to the slightest fluctuation of nuance. Though brother and sister were temperamentally quite different, their musical personalities fused into one. In his memoirs, Menuhin spoke at length about the uniqueness of his collaboration with her; "we had a Siamese soul."[13] When she died in January 1981 we all felt the pain of irreparable loss.

I heard Yehudi and Hephzibah together for the last time in March 1980. At the end of a demanding program stood the sonata by César Franck, a work in their repertoire since childhood, but I have never heard a more springlike, spontaneous performance. Before that, she was Yehudi's partner at his fiftieth anniversary concert on January 15, 1978, at Carnegie Hall, and the performances of the sonatas by Elgar and Beethoven (Op. 47) were played in the true spirit of piano-violin collaboration. Menuhin has played and recorded with other pianists, among them Balsam, Baller, Kentner, and Kempff, but his playing with Hephzibah had a very personal and inimitable ring.

Ruggiero Ricci

Ruggiero Ricci was born in San Francisco in 1918. Two years younger than Menuhin, he was the victim of a craze that swept San Francisco in the 1920s, similar to the one that swept Odessa in Mischa

Elman's time: every parent thought he had a child genius on hand. "Yehudi got everyone thinking about prodigies," said Ricci recently, "but believe me, when you find a prodigy, you find an ambitious parent in the background."[1]

Ricci was speaking from experience. He describes his father as "some kind of musical maniac—he had all seven children playing an instrument. . . . I wanted to be a pianist, but my parents got me off that jig. They bribed me with fiddles." On the whole, Ricci had an unhappy childhood. His father did not hesitate to put pressure on the boy. At the age of ten (though he was publicized as being eight), Ricci made his debut in San Francisco, with his teacher Louis Persinger at the piano. The program included the Mendelssohn concerto and virtuoso music by Vieuxtemps, Saint-Saëns, and Wieniawski. The success was so encouraging that a New York concert was arranged in October 1929, this time with orchestra. Young Ricci played a Mozart concerto, repeated the Mendelssohn, and showed off in Vieuxtemps's *Fantasia appassionata*. The critic of the New York *Telegraph* described him as "the greatest genius of our time in the world of interpretative music." This came only two years after Menuhin was extolled by New York critics in similar superlatives.

Shortly thereafter, a court battle erupted: it seems that father Ricci had signed Ruggiero's custody over to an assistant of Persinger, but then regretted the deal and won him back through the courts. The courtroom details filled the gossip columns of the papers and left a mark on the adolescent boy. He felt that he was treated like a marketable commodity: "When I was nine or ten, it was beautiful fiddle playing. By the time I was twelve I was a fiasco. They took me and they changed me. Persinger was of the Belgian school and when I was taken from him they sent me to Mishel Piastro."

Piastro was one of Auer's most accomplished students and had just moved to New York as newly appointed concertmaster of the New York Philharmonic. But he was apparently not a very perceptive teacher, according to Ricci:

> He thought I was a genius or something, so he threw the Brahms Concerto at me. There was no discipline, and I was playing on a large-model Strad that was too big for me. So of course I didn't play so well. People started criticizing me and it was hard. I was used to adoration.

Somehow, Ricci overcame that crisis and embarked on a European tour that was very successful. I remember his concert in Berlin at that

MUSICAL AMERICA

Another famous prodigy of the 1920s, Ruggiero Ricci, is shown as a boy and today, half a century later.

CHRISTIAN STEINER

time. He was small for his age and, though fourteen, was advertised as twelve. Every effort was made to duplicate Menuhin's success, even to the point of bringing Albert Einstein to the concert and extracting a statement from him. But Menuhin's campaign was handled more cleverly, with more understanding for the German concept of musical "depth." Ricci had to be satisfied with being recognized as a mere technical phenomenon.

Since Menuhin, Ricci's chief competitor, was entrusted to the care of the German violinist Adolf Busch, it was decided that Ricci work with Georg Kulenkampff. The choice was good, for Kulenkampff, the best of the younger German violinists, had a more modern approach than Busch. But Ricci was neither an intellectual nor a stylist: his strength was technique, and the German school confused him. Forty-five years later, in 1976, a reporter asked Ricci how his playing had changed over the years, and he answered with remarkable candor:

> I've been through three periods, and I'm still changing. My early playing was spontaneous—I liked it. I don't like concocted performances. Next comes a time when you try to be more profound. You study, you make decisions. You don't really get turned on, you tend to be programmed. With me, this middle stage—well, I don't say it was a disaster but I was too understated because I was afraid of bad taste . . .* Now after 45 years I say I'm going to play like I want, and if they don't like it they can go to hell. It's better to be a prostitute than a nun.

Obviously, in the 1930s Ricci was not yet ready for the great international career comparable to that of Menuhin. In fact, he returned to America in 1933 and resumed his studies, first with Paul Stassevich (a Russian-born Auer student), then with his first teacher Persinger.

The outbreak of World War II interrupted Ricci's growing career. After serving in the U.S. Army, he made a successful comeback in the late 1940s. He had always been a formidable technician; now he played and recorded all Twenty-four Caprices of Paganini as well as other pieces of extreme virtuosity by Ernst and Wieniawski, things few dared to play: "I forced myself in that direction because nobody had taken that road. . . . My first New York recital after the army was a program of unaccompanied works." On that occasion he played Bach's Partita in A minor, Ysaÿe's Sonata Op. 27, No. 4, Hindemith's Solo

---

* This must have been the period in Germany where "spontaneity is *verboten*," as Ricci remarked sarcastically.

Sonata Op. 31, No. 2, and pieces by Paganini, Wieniawski, and Kreisler. "Mischa Elman said I was crazy, but it put me back in business."

From then on Ricci rose to the rank of world violinists. His style stresses virtuosity, the slashing attack, the daredevil approach. Though he has a beautiful tone (perhaps overvibrated at times and with a tendency to bear down heavily on the strings), there is little repose or lyricism in his playing. But it is grand-style fiddle playing without plumbing great depths. The brio and fire make up for a lack of charm and sensitivity.

Ricci's playing mechanism is extraordinary. He has preserved his technique over the years so that today, though past sixty, he has lost none of his dexterity. He is the born fiddler: he can play supremely well on any violin, day or night, the master of an enormous repertoire. His adaptability was shown on a recording (and duplicated on a television show) when he used fifteen different Cremona violins for fifteen different violin compositions. The wonder was not that he could handle the idiosyncrasy of each violin but that essentially they all sounded like Ricci; his personal tone production erased the differences. He owns a Guarnerius del Gesù violin of 1734 but he occasionally substitutes a modern violin without noticeable difference in sound.

His repertoire, much of it recorded, includes the six Bach solo sonatas and partitas, the ten Beethoven sonatas (with Friedrich Gulda at the piano), and the entire Classical and Romantic concerto literature. His Paganini catalogue lists the Twenty-four Caprices and several violin concertos, including the rediscovered No. 4 in D minor, as well as shorter pieces like I palpiti and Le streghe. Ricci resurrected virtuoso compositions by Ernst and Wieniawski that border on circus stunts (one of his records is entitled The Virtuoso Violin). But he has also put his immense ability in the service of recent music—the solo sonatas of Hindemith, Bartók, and Ysaÿe, the concertos of Ginastera (premiere 1963), von Einem (premiere 1970), Benjamin Lees, and Alexander Goehr.

Ricci has done some teaching—at Indiana University, at the Juilliard School, and elsewhere—but his interest in teaching is peripheral. Nevertheless, he knows a good teacher from a bad one, as he explained:

> Teachers are ruining a lot of kids. Parents love to say "my kid plays the Mendelssohn Concerto," so they take their child away from a teacher who knows better and give him to one who will push him. . . . They are the criminals in this business.

Having been a victim, he knows what he's talking about!

Isaac Stern

In October of 1937, I went to New York's Town Hall to hear the debut recital of a new violinist from the West Coast. By the time he had finished his first piece, Tartini's *Devil's Trill Sonata*, I knew that I was hearing a major new violinist. His name was Isaac Stern; he was seventeen years old at the time, short, chubby, and open-faced. Today, he ranks among the greatest violinists of the world, a place he has held for some twenty-five years.

Isaac Stern was born in 1920 in a small town in the Ukraine and moved to San Francisco with his parents when he was one year old. He received his entire education in California, starting with violin lessons at the age of eight at the San Francisco Conservatory. For a brief time he studied with Persinger, who enjoyed much fame because of his student Yehudi Menuhin, but this was a transitory phase for Stern: his principal teacher was Naum Blinder, with whom he worked from 1932 to 1937. "He taught me how to teach myself—which is the sign of a good teacher," says Stern with gratitude.[1]

Blinder, born in 1889 in Russia, was a student of Brodsky at the Moscow Conservatory. Active as a performer and teacher in Odessa and Moscow, he settled in San Francisco in the late 1920s and was named concertmaster of the San Francisco Symphony, like Persinger and Piastro before him. By studying with Blinder, Stern absorbed the tradition of the Moscow and Odessa schools, a background rather similar to that of David Oistrakh. In fact, there is an audible relationship between Stern and Oistrakh, most convincing on their joint recording of music for two violins by Bach and Vivaldi. This Russian strain in Stern's violinistic "pedigree" must be contrasted to the Franco-German background of Menuhin through Persinger, Enesco, and Busch. Unlike Menuhin, Stern did not go abroad to study and received his entire training in America.

Without matching Menuhin's spectacular precociousness, Stern was considered ready at the age of fifteen to make his debut with the San Francisco Symphony: he and Blinder played Bach's Double Concerto. The following year he appeared with the Los Angeles Symphony under Klemperer playing the Tchaikovsky concerto. The New York debut of October 11, 1937, followed. Though the notices were favorable, Stern decided to return home for further studies. His second musical attack on New York, on February 18, 1939, was a tremendous success. In the intervening two years he had achieved remarkable artistic growth and was acclaimed immediately as one of the top-ranking young American violinists.

Stern made his career without the benefit of any contests. His rise to eminence was steady and continuous, slowed only by World War II. Affiliations he made early in life lasted for decades: his piano partner, the excellent Russian pianist Alexander Zakin; his impresario, the resourceful Sol Hurok, who managed his rise to stardom; and Columbia Masterworks, for which he has recorded since 1945. Under these auspices, Stern's career developed with remarkable consistency.

During World War II, Stern performed for the Allied troops in Greenland, Iceland, and the South Pacific. He also found time for some concerts, each of which contributed to his growing fame—the Carnegie Hall recital in January 1943 with a sonata program of Mozart, Brahms, and solo Bach, and the two performances with the New York Philharmonic in 1944, of the Sibelius concerto under Mitropoulos and the Tchaikovsky concerto under Rodzinski. His first recording for Columbia, made in 1945, was Beethoven's Sonata in C minor, Op. 30, No. 2, with Zakin. Stern speaks with particular warmth of the decades of collaboration with Zakin.

Stern's European career began in 1948 with a debut at the Lucerne Festival. Since then, he has returned to Europe every year; among the memorable dates are the Casals Festivals in 1950 and 1953 (which produced some marvelous chamber music recordings), the Edinburgh Festival in 1953, a tour of the Soviet Union in 1956. He has also played in Australia, Japan, and South America. However, Stern refuses to play in Germany as a protest against past Nazi atrocities.

A special relationship exists between Stern and the State of Israel. He has done more than any one artist for the cultural growth of the young state. (One is reminded of the achievements of Bronislaw Huberman on behalf of the Palestine Orchestra before the state was established.) Several times a year, Stern visits Israel for prolonged periods, not only to perform but to inspire a multitude of young Israeli musicians to raise their standards and their sights ever higher. In Jerusalem, he helped establish the Mishkenot, a center for creative artists and scholars, and the Jerusalem Music Centre, an archive of past accomplishments and a focal point for young musicians. Stern is the driving force behind the America-Israel Cultural Foundation, which supports gifted young artists during their studies at home and abroad. Among the many scholarship recipients of the past are the violinists Itzhak Perlman, Pinchas Zukerman, Sergiu Luca, Miriam Fried, and Shlomo Mintz.

In the spirit of concerned citizenship, Stern was the mastermind behind the 1960 Save Carnegie Hall campaign; the venerable hall was indeed saved through his active involvement. Carnegie Hall, with its unique acoustics and its tradition of great music and musicians since 1881, continues to be a focal point of music in New York City. One shudders to think how close to demolition it was, had it not been for the efforts of Stern, now president of the Carnegie Hall Foundation, and his associates.

In 1964, Stern helped establish the National Endowment for the Arts and was appointed as advisory member by President Lyndon Johnson. In fact, Stern has performed at the White House for every president since John F. Kennedy.

Stern's distinctive playing style reflects his vibrant personality—a total involvement in music and intense communication with his audience. He uses his virtuoso command of the instrument only in the service of music, never for technical display. His motto is, "To use the violin to make music, never to use music just to play the violin." He never plays "down" to his audience, nor does he have to: those who come to listen to Stern expect the best music interpreted in the best style.

Stern was one of the first to move away from the standard violin recital program by building programs of quality around chamber music. He invites colleagues to join him, and the concerts "Isaac Stern and Friends" are filled with musical treasures from violin duets to octets, with and without piano. Whether he plays solo or chamber music, everything he touches is filled with vitality and exuberance, balancing technical bravura and lyric introspection. He projects warmth without sentimentality; he has virtually eliminated the portamento from his expressive vocabulary. Listening to Stern, one feels that he plays only music he deeply believes in. This applies to his choice of modern music, too: he does not pay lip service to the latest fashion, but selects modern works which make the listener understand his identification with the composer, his artistic involvement with the new piece, and his feeling of responsibility for its quality. This was particularly evident when he recently championed two new concertos, by George Rochberg (premiere 1976) and Krzysztof Penderecki (premiere 1977). There seemed to be a give-and-take between performer and composer: while Stern adjusted his violin style to the demands of the modern idiom, the composers (perhaps subconsciously) let their inspiration be influenced by Stern's violin personality. When Stern plays, be it old or new music, he has to be emotionally involved, because nothing purely cerebral appeals to him. His repertoire includes a surprising number of twentieth-century works—by Sibelius, Stravinsky, Prokofiev, Hindemith, Shostakovich, Berg, Bloch, Bartók, Copland, Leonard Bernstein (the *Serenade* was written for him). His recorded repertoire is immense: there is hardly a piece in the violin literature that he has not put on a disc.

In 1960 Stern founded a trio with the pianist Eugene Istomin and the cellist Leonard Rose. Their performances of the great trio literature are virile and exuberant. During the Beethoven Bicentennial 1970 they gave cycles of eight Beethoven programs in various musical centers, including Paris, London, and New York, which were recorded and televised.

Stern does not teach individual students, yet he is a guide and fatherly friend to all young violinists who come from Israel to study in New York, as well as those who work in Israel. He has espoused and aided the careers of numerous young artists, many of them now internationally famous. His judgment, considered perceptive and incorruptible, carries enormous weight and is accepted everywhere with confidence. He has also organized string orchestras for the performance of Baroque and pre-Classical music, and his emphatic style of playing lends itself particularly well to the role of leader-conductor.

In celebration of Isaac Stern's sixtieth birthday in 1980, there was an outpouring of affection and admiration from Paris, London, and Jerusalem to New York and San Francisco. It lasted for months, and the artist responded by thanking with music—concert after concert, series after series—performing alone, with friends, and with orchestras. It was a torrent of music, and he had never played better; he gave generously of himself, with unquenchable enthusiasm, certainly inspired by the occasion and the love that flowed toward him from audiences all over. There was in particular one concert at Avery Fisher Hall (September 24, 1980) where he never left the stage: music for two violins, for three violins, for violin and viola, topped by the Brahms concerto. His playing was unsurpassable, his communicativeness irresistible. Those who joined him on that historic occasion—Perlman, Zukerman, Zubin Mehta, the New York Philharmonic—were caught up in that surge of music making, fortunately televised and recorded for posterity.

In 1981, a delightful documentary film, *From Mao to Mozart* (subtitled *Isaac Stern in China*), was released—a report on Stern's 1979

ICM ARTISTS, LTD.

A characteristic photo of Isaac Stern at rehearsal, one of the world's greatest violin personalities.
Guila Bustabo, like Menuhin and Ricci a student of Persinger, was a successful young performer in the 1930s.

MUSICAL AMERICA

trip to China. With him we discovered quite a few talented Chinese violinists and cellists performing surprisingly well; we also admired Stern's ability to function and to communicate as an artist and a human being on various levels and under different circumstances. The hour-long film was an enchanting experience and deserved the Academy Award later bestowed on it.

Another celebration—more restrained but no less significant—was Stern's Carnegie Hall recital on January 12, 1983, observing the fortieth anniversary of his debut at the same hall. It was a proud evening of dedicated mastery, where technique was taken for granted and only music spoke.

More Persinger Students

After the phenomenal success of Menuhin and Ricci, Persinger was recognized as the "trainer extraordinary of youthful talent," in the words of one critic.[1] Established in New York at the Juilliard School, he inherited the mantle of Leopold Auer, and every gifted child violinist was brought to him. He knew not only how to train the young violinists but also how to launch their careers: being an accomplished pianist, Persinger played the accompanist's role at important debut recitals and guided his fledgling artist into the world. His presence on the stage must have been greatly reassuring to the young violinist facing the ordeal of a New York debut.

During the 1930s and '40s, Persinger presented quite a few gifted young artists, but the "Menuhin miracle" did not repeat itself. (Something similar happened to Auer with his "inimitable" students Elman and Heifetz.) But it would be unfair to belittle the string of talented violinists trained by Persinger: he taught them all that is teachable and sent them out into the world.

Guila Bustabo enjoyed an early meteoric career that fizzled for no apparent reason. She came to Persinger when she was eleven or twelve, already with a reputation as a prodigy. Persinger listened to her and said, "Very good," but then shook his head sadly and muttered, "but too old." Though this story was told as a joke, it has a kernel of truth: it is more difficult to reshape a talent than to guide it from the very beginning. Guila, born in Wisconsin in 1917 of an Italian father and a Bohemian mother, started to play the violin at four as a student of Leon Sametini in Chicago and began her career at age nine. Her New York debut took place in November 1931, with Persinger at the piano. Her age was given as fourteen (later she became a bit younger) and her attractive photo, with her black hair cut in a page boy, was in all the papers. "The technical difficulties were overcome with surprising aplomb, if the young artist's tone was not always of great warmth," wrote one critic.[2] There was an illustrious audience—Toscanini, Kleiber, Schelling. Two years later she played the Brahms concerto "with breadth of style and emotional warmth."[3] She was presented with a valuable violin selected by Kreisler. In September 1934 she sailed for London, where she had a tremendous success, followed by many European engagements. In 1938 and 1939 she reappeared in New York, as soloist with the New York Philharmonic and in several recitals, and she gave "poised and expressive performances."[4] Suddenly, her career came to a halt. One German author speculates that there may have been a boycott directed against her because of suspected Nazi and Fascist sympathies: she was indeed a favorite artist in Germany and Italy in the late 1930s, when many of her colleagues were banished. For whatever reason, she disappeared from the world scene of music, though her memory remained alive through several impeccable recordings revealing an intense tone with a rapid and narrow vibrato. An attempted return to the concert stage in Germany in the mid-1960s brought critical acclaim but no renewed career. Miss Bustabo taught at the Conservatory of Innsbruck (Austria) from 1964 to 1970.

Another talented Persinger student, Arnold Eidus, did a disappearing act of his own. In 1938, at the age of thirteen, young Arnold was presented on the radio program "Rising Musical Stars" as one of the future great violinists; Mischa Elman personally handed him the award. Thirty years later, a headline in the *Times* read, "Advertising Man Conducts a Chamber Group. Eidus of Ted Bates Leads Stradivari at Carnegie."[5] One wonders what prompted him to abandon a promising career in order to become an advertising executive. Nor was Eidus's talent unrecognized; in 1946, he had created an international sensation by winning first prize in the Jacques Thibaud Contest in Paris, which included a European tour of thirty-eight concerts. His 1968 concert at Carnegie Hall was an attempt to prove that an artist-turned-businessman could still function as an artist. The results were honorable, but only a few old recordings remain as a reminder of Eidus's true potential.

Two fine Persinger students, Camilla Wicks and Frances Magnes, were forced to choose between family and career. Miss Wicks, born around 1929 in California of Norwegian parentage, was a blond-curled "Shirley Temple" child violinist when she first played publicly at the age of eight. At nine she performed with the Los Angeles Philharmonic. By the time she was thirteen, she gave her New York recital debut with her teacher Persinger at the piano. The *Sun* reported, "An unusually talented but not a sensational child violinist."[6] Four years later, at seventeen, she played the Sibelius concerto with the New York Philharmonic under Rodzinski "with a degree of control and poise that was indeed remarkable for her youth. . . . Her tone was pleasant, though it inclined at times toward a wide vibrato. . . ."[7] She returned to the Philharmonic with the Beethoven concerto under Walter in 1953 and again in 1957 with a new concerto by the Norwegian Klaus Egge. For a New York recital in 1955 she was joined at the piano by her old teacher Persinger, a rather touching sight, and was acclaimed by the *Times* as "one of America's outstanding young instrumentalists of concert stature."[8] But her career simmered down and (until recently on the West Coast) nothing much has been heard of her.

Family obligations also curtailed the career of Frances Magnes, who came into prominence in the 1940s and early '50s. Born around 1920 in Cleveland, she made her debut at fourteen with the Cleveland Orchestra and later came to New York to study with Persinger. Her Carnegie Hall debut in 1946 revealed "gifts of uncommonly high order."[9] I remember her as a big-style violinist, with an energetic approach and impassioned temperament. Under the influence of Adolf Busch, who became her mentor, she acquired more classical discipline and appeared often as soloist with the Busch Chamber Players. She also displayed praiseworthy interest in modern music, giving premieres of music by Tibor Serly, Stefan Wolpe, and Dohnányi. In fact, Dohnányi dedicated his Second Violin Concerto, Op. 43, to her, and she played the premiere with the New York Philharmonic under Mitropoulos in 1952. Her performance was found "expressively persuasive as well as technically dextrous," though at times "a slightly greater volume of tone would have been suitable."[10] It is with this Dohnányi concerto that Miss Magnes decided to reenter the concert field in 1981, after having been rather inactive for years. Dohnányi's rhapsodic style suits her talent to perfection, and she gave the work a splendid performance at Carnegie Hall.

Fredell Lack removed herself from the New York scene after a highly acclaimed beginning. Born in Oklahoma around 1924, she was a prodigy at eight, winning many prizes as she grew up. After coming to

New York, she became a student of Persinger at Juilliard; she also did some postgraduate work with Galamian. Her New York recital debut in 1943, at the age of nineteen, was criticized for a badly chosen program; but her "warmth and sustained lyricism" and her "rare sense of poise" were admired.[11] For a time, she was affiliated with the Little Orchestra Society in New York as concertmaster and occasional soloist. In 1959 she played in various European capitals on a two-month tour and then returned to Houston. She is an artist-in-residence at the university, teaching and performing with her own Lyric Art String Quartet. Her appearances in New York are widely spaced but of sufficient impact to show that she has lost none of her "sure command of instrument and music."[12] Her programs are challenging, with noteworthy attention to twentieth-century music. Perhaps she is "not a violinist of the smoldering-passion type,"[13] but her playing is eminently competent, self-assured, and sincere.

Sonya Monosoff—also a Persinger student—has carved a niche for herself as a specialist in the authentic performance of early violin music. Born in Cleveland in 1927, she went through the regular Juilliard curriculum. Her initiation into old music came when she joined the New York Pro Musica under the late Noah Greenberg in the 1950s. She founded her own Baroque Players in 1963, but did not limit herself exclusively to old music. Her concerts with the pianist Irene Jacobi and the violist Louise Rood contained a varied repertoire—"music-making without ostentation," one critic called it.[14] More and more she has become known not only as a stylish performer of Baroque music, but as a violinist willing to experiment with instruments in their original state of preservation, namely violins with short neck, fitted with a flat bridge and gut strings, tuned at a low pitch, and played with bows of different shapes and weights. She has also mastered the playing of *scordatura* violins (i.e., with strings tuned other than in the customary fifths); thus she has recorded the *Biblical Sonatas* by Biber written in twelve different tunings, a remarkable achievement. She often plays and records on original instruments at the Smithsonian Institution in Washington. Appointed to Cornell University in 1972, Monosoff plays old chamber music with Malcolm Bilson (fortepiano) and John Hsu (cello and gamba) under the name of Amadé Trio.

THE GREAT AMERICAN TEACHERS

Ivan Galamian

On the evening after Thanksgiving in 1977, a festive party marked an advance celebration of the seventy-fifth birthday of Ivan Galamian, the legendary violin pedagogue. It took place at the New York home of a former Galamian student, Itzhak Perlman, who tried to keep the guest list down to fifty. But how can you keep down a list that was to include every past Galamian student around New York? (In fact, the roster of Galamian's students—most of them with distinguished careers—is quite extraordinary and is comparable to that of Auer.) Ultimately, the guest list read like a *Who's Who* of violin playing, including one prominent "outsider," Isaac Stern.

Less than four years later, a saddened group of colleagues and friends assembled to pay their last respects to the master who had died on April 14, 1981. "Someone will replace him, but no one can ever take his place," were the words of his long-time associate and friend, Josef Gingold.[1] The void created by Galamian's death was indeed incalculable, though his method lives on.

Galamian's early career was not marked by particular distinction. He was born in 1903 in Tabriz, Persia, of Armenian parentage, and brought to Russia as an infant. From 1916 to 1922 he studied the violin at the Moscow Philharmonic School under the distinguished teacher Konstantin Mostras, who was a disciple of the Auer school.

After his graduation in 1922, Galamian emigrated to Paris. Here he became interested in the bowing theories of the eminent Lucien

547

Capet and studied with him in 1922–23. Following a debut concert in Paris in 1924, Galamian concertized briefly, but soon concentrated on teaching. He came to New York in 1937 and opened a private studio. Soon his reputation as an outstanding teacher spread; parents brought their would-be prodigies, teachers sent their problem students to his studio. In 1944 Galamian was named to the faculty of the Curtis Institute in Philadelphia, in 1946 he was appointed to the Juilliard School in New York. He kept both positions until the end of his life, but did most of his teaching at his private studio on West 73rd Street in New York. He used to teach from eight in the morning until six at night, with only one interruption for lunch. He was meticulously organized and totally dedicated to his work, a man of few words, with the razor-sharp ability to analyze and correct his students' violinistic ailments and to guide them on the road to optimum achievement. "His lessons were always intense work, with no time for small talk," reminisced a former student turned writer. After a few warm-up scales in an adjoining room, the intimidated student would face the stern professor at exactly the appointed time while the previous "victim" was dismissed. Those who could not endure the strict discipline or needed more "tender love and care" were better off with another teacher.

Yet Galamian was very much concerned about his students—their studies, their careers, their work habits. He was known to have called some of his "lazy" students early in the morning to tell them, "I'm glad I woke you up. Why aren't you practicing?" He believed in hard work. "Go home and practice!" was his standard remark. But he also believed that careers are not made in heaven: they are built with effort. "I tell them over and over: You have to push. You have to grow calluses on your head from pushing." A career does not have to be as a soloist; in fact, Galamian considered the virtuoso field saturated. But there is a widening field for fine performers through the expansion of chamber-music activities, a phenomenon particularly strong in North America. Galamian took pride in having trained so many quartet players, in addition to soloists, concertmasters, and teachers, proving the versatility of his teaching method.

Galamian's approach to violin playing was analytical and rational, with minute attention to every technical detail. His method was based on a personal amalgam of Russian and French traditions, with occasional hints of Flesch's ideas. Galamian's method of holding the bow is definitely not the so-called Russian grip, nor is it purely Capet's: it combines the best elements of both. He was not rigid in his approach: he dealt with every student in an individualized manner and stressed naturalness as guiding principle. Mental control over physical movement is the key to technical mastery. The secret of Galamian's success was his ability to develop the innate potential of every student without forcing him into a mold. But the method is unmistakable: one can always recognize a Galamian student by his bow grip (the typical extension of the index finger), by the intensity of sound, and by the fastidious technical preparation.

Galamian published a book about his method, entitled *Principles of Violin Playing and Teaching* (with Elizabeth A. H. Green, 1962) and he edited many standard violin works providing his fingerings and bowings. But it was his personal magnetism as a teacher that brought out the best in his students. He believed in hard work, discipline, preparedness. He thought that the task of a violinist was becoming harder every year because of the constantly expanding repertoire. He explained, "When I studied with Capet, there were perhaps a dozen violin concerti you had to know. Now it's what? A hundred?"

Asked who of his students was the most outstandingly gifted, Galamian hesitated at first but then confided to Donal Henahan, "Oh, I must say it was Michael Rabin. There was almost extraordinary talent— no weaknesses, never! Itzhak Perlman was like that, too. But Michael Rabin . . ." and his voice trailed off in nostalgia.[2] (Rabin's career ended tragically at thirty-five.)

In 1944, Galamian established a summer school for string players at Meadowmount in upstate New York. In these lovely rural surroundings, far removed from the distractions of the city, students worked and made music together under the watchful eye of the professor and a staff of assistants, among them Margaret Pardee and Sally Thomas. Eventually, chamber music was added to the curriculum, for which the help of Josef Gingold and the cellist Leonard Rose was enlisted. As a teenager, Itzhak Perlman was at Meadowmount for eight summers and remembers, "I loved every minute. The atmosphere was such that you were totally moved into achieving. Everybody around you was practicing and showing off. . . ." A different tune from Arnold Steinhardt (now first violinist of the Guarneri Quartet): "It was slave labor. It was terrible. You had to get up and practice all day long, and he demanded an almost monk-like existence. We all moaned and groaned and vowed we'd never go back, but somewhere we all loved it."

Not all of Galamian's students profited from his type of teaching to an equal degree. Says Isaac Stern, "You had to bring something of your own to him. The stronger your own personality, the more you could gain from him."

Today, winning international contests is a shortcut to making a career. Galamian encouraged his best students to enter important contests, and the list of his prizewinners confirms the quality of his teaching. Here is a partial listing.*

LEVENTRITT COMPETITION (New York)
    Itzhak Perlman, Pinchas Zukerman, David Nadien, Kyung Wha Chung, Arnold Steinhardt, Betty Jean Hagen, Sergiu Luca

TCHAIKOVSKY COMPETITION (Moscow)
    Eugene Fodor, Glenn Dicterow, Erick Friedman, Daniel Heifetz

QUEEN ELISABETH COMPETITION (Brussels)
    Miriam Fried, Jaime Laredo, Berl Senofsky, Charles Castleman, Peter Zazofsky

MERRIWEATHER POST (Washington)
    James Buswell, Young Uck Kim, Glenn Dicterow, Eugene Fodor

WIENIAWSKI COMPETITION (Poland)
    Charles Treger

MONTREAL COMPETITION (Canada)
    Miriam Fried, Peter Zazofsky

PAGANINI COMPETITION (Genoa)
    Stuart Canin, Miriam Fried, Eugene Fodor

CARL FLESCH COMPETITION (London)
    Eugene Sarbu, Dong-Suk Kang

AVERY FISHER AWARD (New York)
    Ani Kavafian

PHILADELPHIA ORCHESTRA (Youth Auditions)
    Sergiu Luca, Arnold Steinhardt

NATIONAL FEDERATION OF MUSIC CLUBS
    Michael Rabin, Charles Castleman

WALTER W. NAUMBURG AWARD
    Berl Senofsky

INDIANAPOLIS INTERNATIONAL VIOLIN COMPETITION
    Ida Kavafian

ROCKEFELLER/AMERICAN MUSIC COMPETITION
    Gregory Fulkerson

YOUNG CONCERT ARTISTS AWARD
    Ani Kavafian, Ida Kavafian, Daniel Phillips

---

* "Prizewinner" does not always mean "first prize."

Dorothy DeLay

Dorothy DeLay joined Ivan Galamian as his assistant in 1948 and remained in that position for some twenty years. When she wanted to pursue some of her own ideas on playing and teaching, they separated. Several very gifted students followed her, and her contact with Galamian was broken. It is not a question of who is the better teacher: both are highly qualified and dedicated to their profession. But the successful relationship between teacher and student depends on many intangible factors, many of them personal: some students require discipline, others rebel against it. Some teachers are deliberately impersonal, even harsh; others show personal concern for the student's needs. There can be no doubt that Galamian is an authoritarian teacher, of the type usually associated with the Old World, while DeLay has an infinite capacity for understanding the student's problems without being less demanding professionally. The advice "Go home and practice!" is not a cure-all for the emotional or practical needs of a young artist.

Before joining Galamian, DeLay had a varied musical background. Born in 1917 in a small town in the state of Kansas, she had music-oriented parents. She participated in high-school musical activities and led the violin section of her school orchestra. In 1933 she entered Oberlin College, but transferred after a year to Michigan State University, where she worked with Michael Press, an excellent Moscow-trained violinist.

After graduating in 1937, she moved to New York and entered the Juilliard Graduate Division to obtain an Artist's Diploma; among her teachers were Louis Persinger and Raphael Bronstein. While studying, DeLay was also active as a performer and founded the Stuyvesant Trio.

Circumstances interrupted her career during the war years, but in 1946 she returned to her musical activities. About that time she became interested in the method of Galamian, who had just joined the Juilliard faculty. Eventually, she was appointed his assistant.

For twenty years, DeLay was an indispensable part of Galamian's expanding domination of the violin-teaching field. Undoubtedly, she absorbed much of his experience, to which she added her intuitive understanding of a student's needs. Their relationship lasted until she became convinced that she could contribute something decisively personal to a student's development. The fact that Itzhak Perlman stayed with her testifies to the pull of her personality. "She has incredible understanding of the science of violin playing and a willingness to treat

Ivan Galamian, who arrived in New York around 1940, became the most successful violin teacher of the next forty years.
Below left, Josef Gingold, the foremost violin teacher at Indiana University.
Below right, Dorothy DeLay, once an assistant to Galamian, built her own class and is considered one of the world's foremost teachers.

students as individual artists. . . . She teaches you to be your own best teacher," said one of her gifted students.[1]

Part of DeLay's success with her students is psychological: there is a give-and-take relationship; she does not impose her will, but makes the student feel that he participates in the decision-making process. She is a very good listener, both when the student plays and when he talks. She unmistakably cares, a feeling that is gratefully reciprocated by the student. She is concerned with his total personality, with his musical and extramusical problems, with jobs and career opportunities and impresarios and contests. Her commitment to her students is total and she emanates an aura of warmth and helpfulness, balanced by experience and authority. It is no wonder that students rally around her as a tower of strength.

All this, however, would not have been enough to explain her reputation as a teacher. Her advice goes beyond fingerings and bowings, though she has a very practical mind; she teaches her students how to pace themselves, how to project on the stage, how to shape the interpretation. She is an inveterate listener, and after a day's hard work one can find her sitting in a student's violin recital to get a more objective view, or at a concert of other violinists to keep abreast of musical developments. She invites famous soloists to visit her class and speak on violinistic problems, and she herself is the most interested listener. I remember one such occasion, when Yehudi Menuhin came to her Juilliard class to demonstrate some of his unorthodox exercises. Miss DeLay's face lit up while watching Menuhin's violin acrobatics and she immediately drew parallels to her own approach. It is this broadmindedness, the openness to new ideas, which keeps her viewpoint fresh and up-to-date.

In addition to some sixty-five students at Juilliard, and summer sessions at the Aspen Institute in Colorado, she gives master classes in Boston, Cincinnati, and elsewhere. I have seen her in action at the Jerusalem Music Centre, calm and concentrated, violin in hand, ready to demonstrate a point or to give verbal criticism. Recently she visited South Africa, Japan, and the People's Republic of China.

Miss DeLay is not keen on contests ("Contests are nonsense in general," she is known to have said), which does not prevent her students from winning them right and left. Among her latest phalanx of rising stars are Shlomo Mintz, Mark Kaplan, Mark Peskanov, Joseph Swensen, Cho-Liang Lin, Nigel Kennedy, Christian Altenberger, Ida Levin, Nadja Salerno-Sonnenberg, and Dmitri Sitkovetsky.

Josef Gingold

In a quiet and unobtrusive way, Josef Gingold has made a most significant contribution to the art of violin teaching in America. Today he enjoys an international reputation, and his studio at Indiana University is filled with young, talented violinists from all over the country and from overseas. He is in demand as visiting professor and has taught in Colorado, Utah, and Tennessee. He was invited to give master classes at the Paris Conservatoire and the Toho School in Tokyo. He has served as jury member at virtually all prestigious violin contests. (When Igor Oistrakh praised the American violin school at a recent Tchaikovsky Competition, Gingold could claim part of the praise.)

Gingold was born in Brest-Litovsk (Russia) in 1909 and came to New York at the age of eleven, where he studied with Vladimir Graffman, an old Auer student, from 1922 to 1927. While still nominally a student, he gave a debut recital in New York's Aeolian Hall in 1926. Feeling a need to broaden his experience, he went to Brussels to receive the guidance of Eugène Ysaÿe. He stayed in Belgium for three years (1927–30), made his debut in Brussels in 1928, and concertized in northern Europe.

After his return to the United States, Gingold held several important orchestral positions. From 1937 to 1943 he was first violinist in the famed NBC Orchestra under Toscanini; at the same time, he was a member of the Primrose Quartet (named after the noted violist of the group), then of the NBC String Quartet. I met Gingold in 1937, when we were both members of the Toscanini Orchestra, and I found his cultured and refined playing most attractive. Somewhat later, he gave a sonata recital with Liza Elman, the pianist-sister of the famous violinist. His style was unmistakably French, stressing elegance and finesse, with an impressive command of the instrument; his interpretation had a particular sweetness and sincerity.

In 1943, Gingold's career took a new turn: he was appointed concertmaster of the Detroit Symphony, followed in 1947 by the same position with the Cleveland Orchestra. These were the years when Szell built the Cleveland Orchestra into one of the most polished ensembles in the country, and Gingold's contribution was an important one. In thirteen years, he made eighteen solo appearances with the orchestra, a sure sign of Szell's esteem, and he was a hard man to please. At the same time, Gingold taught at Western Reserve University in Cleveland.

Summers were spent coaching chamber music at Galamian's Meadow-mount School.

The decisive change came in 1960: a full-time appointment as professor of violin at Indiana University in Bloomington. The Indiana Music School was building a reputation as the finest in the country, where students were taught by artist-teachers, to which Gingold was perfectly suited. His ability to demonstrate anything with violin in hand makes his teaching utterly convincing. He is indefatigable in his work, and his ingratiating personality, helpfulness, and patience are much appreciated by his students. His knowledge of the repertoire (solo, chamber music, orchestral), based on personal experience, is inexhaustible. He has also edited a number of repertoire pieces and orchestral studies, which testify to the intelligence of his approach.

Gingold's merits were recognized in 1968, when he was named Teacher of the Year by the American String Teacher Association. He plays a 1683 Stradivarius, "The Martinelli."

Among the violinists who, at one time or another, have studied with Gingold are Joseph Silverstein, Jaime Laredo, Miriam Fried, Isidor Saslav, Dylana Jenson, and Ulf Hoelscher. Being very unselfish, Gingold often encouraged his best students to seek additional guidance from some prominent master like Galamian or Milstein.

Alexander Schneider

Alexander Schneider ("Sascha" to his innumerable friends) happens to be a violinist, but he can best be described as a musical activist. He has been involved in music all his life—organizing, initiating, energizing. His vision has made things happen; nothing was impossible, once his imagination took hold of it. His versatility and perseverance are unbelievable; but above all he is an artist to whom music means everything. He has enjoyed the trust and affection of many fellow artists, among them Isaac Stern.

"Sascha" was born on October 21, 1908, in Vilna, then part of the Russian Empire. His older brother Mischa played the cello, so it was only natural that Sascha should choose the violin. After lessons with Ilya Malkin (who once taught Heifetz), sixteen-year-old Sascha went to Germany to study with Rebner and Flesch. I remember meeting him in the summer of 1929 in Baden-Baden, where Flesch was holding his master class. At the time he was concertmaster in a west German city. In 1932 he joined the Budapest String Quartet as second violinist, taking the place of Roisman, who moved up to first chair; brother Mischa was already cellist of the group. By 1938, the quartet had settled in the United States and was appointed quartet-in-residence at the Library of Congress in Washington, using the four rare Stradivari instruments entrusted to the Library.

In 1944 Sascha made a difficult decision—he left the Budapest Quartet to strike out on his own. He founded the Albeneri Trio, with the cellist Benar Heifetz and the pianist Erich Itor Kahn; he formed a duo with the harpsichordist Ralph Kirkpatrick; he organized his own string quartet, primarily to record many of Haydn's quartets. He also worked to reshape his playing with an eye to more solo work. As a result he presented the six solo sonatas and partitas of Bach in two evenings, to much acclaim.

These Bach evenings were the result of Sascha's studies with Pablo Casals in 1947 at Prades. The two became close friends, and Sascha persuaded Casals to let him organize the first Casals Festival in Prades in 1950. It was a significant step: since Casals, for ideological reasons, refused to travel and concertize, the music world came to pay him homage in his village in the Pyrenées. Sascha was deeply involved in the festivals at Prades, which were transferred to Puerto Rico in 1957.

In the meantime, he became "one of New York's great civilizing influences."[1] He developed a fresh approach in presenting chamber music, reaching a new and receptive public of young people. In 1953 he inaugurated the outdoor chamber concerts at Washington Square, and offered such innovations as "Christmas Eve at Carnegie" and "Bach at Midnight," filling Carnegie Hall to overflow. He developed the String Seminars held during Christmas Week at Carnegie Hall, which attract young players from all over the country; after intense workshops and rehearsals this group gives concerts that can rival the best. Sascha conducts these concerts with violin in hand, in the old pre-Classical tradition, playing the solos or reinforcing the first violins, and his infectious enthusiasm inspires players and audiences alike. He once said,

> For me, my purpose is to get young people to learn how to make music. When you make music, it has to come from your heart, from your soul, or it has no meaning. It's an extraordinary experience when I see the results. They produce a sound a professional orchestra couldn't—a love of music.[2]

His energizing force is equally successful with professionals. When the Mostly Mozart Festival began modestly in 1966–67, he was there to conduct. When he felt the need for a new chamber orchestra, he organized the Brandenburg Ensemble in the early 1970s, which gives stylish performances of Baroque music.

In 1955 Sascha rejoined the Budapest Quartet. This did not keep him from establishing, in 1956, a concert series at the New School for Social Research. Here he tries out novel programs and gives young artists their first chance to face a public.

Sascha's ability to discover and develop young, talented musicians is nowhere more in evidence than at Marlboro, where he works with Rudolf Serkin, Felix Galimir, and other experienced masters to build young professional ensemble players. "Music from Marlboro" has become a hallmark for excellence. The students are young professionals ready for a career, but in need of chamber-music experience. Prizewinning soloists like Laredo and Steinhardt became modest participants in a common musical experience and discovered new outlets for their talents. In fact, the Guarneri Quartet was formed at Marlboro. Next to Sascha's countless admirers are a few dissenters, who feel that his interpretations overstress energy, vitality, and dynamism at the expense of subtlety, elegance, and refinement. Although his playing can sound a bit rough at times, his zestfulness is infectious.

THE AMERICAN SCHOOL:
THE YOUNGER GENERATION

MUSICAL CONTESTS are not an invention of our competitive age. There were contests in antiquity, as well as in the time of Bach and Mozart. Paganini competed against Lafont, Liszt was pitted against Thalberg. But these were usually contests between individual artists who were challenged to prove their superiority. The organized international contest among dozens of competitors is indeed an innovation of the twentieth century.*

Following the example of the Anton Rubinstein competition for pianists (1890 and later), a violin competition in honor of Leopold Auer was established in St. Petersburg in 1911 (won by Mishel Piastro) and a similar one in Moscow in the name of Jan Hřimaly (won by Michael Press). The Soviet Union has remained the most contest-conscious country; young performers have to run the gauntlet of regional, statewide, and national competitions before their names can be entered in international contests. It is a screening process which has worked well for Soviet artists, and the experience accumulated during such tests has prepared them for the international arena, where a preponderance of Soviet musicians can be found among the prizewinners.

A few important violin contests were established between the two world wars, particularly the Ysaÿe in Brussels (now renamed after Queen Elisabeth) and the Wieniawski in Poland. More contests began to proliferate, named after Thibaud (Paris), Flesch (London), Paganini (Genoa), Enesco (Rumania), Tchaikovsky (Moscow), Sibelius (Finland), Kubelik (Prague), Kreisler (Vienna), Menuhin (Folkestone). In the New World there are contests in New York (Leventritt, Naum-

* We are not speaking here of the competitive auditions to win a first prize at the Paris Conservatoire, for example, tough as they were.

burg, Rockefeller, Avery Fisher), Washington (Merriweather Post), Indianapolis, Montreal.

Some prominent musicians reject the whole idea of musical contests as inartistic. Others feel that such competition is good preparation for the rigors of a concert career. Steady nerves, absolute technical control, and the ability to function under pressure are the prerequisites. And the pressures are immense; Oistrakh's letters written in 1937 during the Ysaÿe Contest describe the agony, the self-doubt, the physical and mental exhaustion during that week in Brussels. Listening to one's rivals can become demoralizing. The winners are not necessarily the most sensitive, but the steadiest players. Ultimately, so much depends on the objectivity and taste of the jury and on certain extramusical considerations such as national, racial, or ideological prejudices. Members of the jury are often the teachers of certain contestants; nevertheless, they are not disqualified from judging. Even if a teacher wishes to be objective, he can argue the case of his student. After each of the big contests, there are "horror stories" about the backstage disputes among jurors. But injustices are usually erased, once the winner or loser steps before the international concert public: that is the true test.

Encouraged by Galamian's positive attitude toward competitions, young American violinists have entered national and international contests in growing number and with increasing success. It is a calculated risk: winning a gold medal does not guarantee a career, and winding up among the runners-up can actually be damaging. But looking at the list of American prizewinners, one must admit that there is solid accomplishment behind each name, though it is reassuring that careers are still made without contests.

Robert Mann

One is tempted to call Robert Mann the intellectual among American violinists. His intellect controls but does not shackle his emotion. In many ways he reminds one of Szigeti, whose innate artistry was shaped by a penetrating mind. But in Mann, as in Szigeti, the prime impulse comes from an emotional response to the music.

Robert Mann was born in 1920 in Portland, Oregon, into a family that was in no way connected with music. He began music lessons at the age of nine and chose the violin. In retrospect he muses "how a person born in Oregon, in a culture that was—in every good and bad

way—provincial, can make a journey and end up in the most sophisticated part of the discipline of music."[1] But there was a group of young
people in Portland interested in chamber music, and he joined them
during his teens.

At eighteen, Mann won a scholarship to the Institute of Musical
Art in New York and transferred to Juilliard the following year. He
became the student of Edouard Déthier, a fine violinist of the Belgian
school and a dedicated chamber music player. Though not strong in
teaching technique, Déthier instilled in Mann his own ardent love for
chamber music. It was he who taught Mann to come "to grips with
the essence of music. The point was to get inside a phrase, to make
that phrase really exist, and that has been a lifelong involvement for
me."[2]

Mann made his New York debut as a solo violinist in December
of 1941, after winning the Naumburg Prize earlier that year. Violin in
hand, he entered the U.S. Army in 1943 and served until 1946. Returning to Juilliard, he found that the new president, the composer
William Schuman, had made great changes. One of his goals was to
involve faculty and students in active music making, to banish dry
academicism and educational routine. It was Schuman's project to have
the spirit of the "new" Juilliard represented by a string quartet, and he
had the foresight to choose Robert Mann to lead it. Mann and the
young members of the newly founded Juilliard Quartet developed a
distinctive profile. Their playing was ebullient, intense, driving, extrovert; they chose fast tempos and strong dynamics, and built a repertoire
which included many twentieth-century works. It was an approach very
different from that of the Budapest String Quartet, whose suave and
elegant interpretations were considered the standard of perfection at
that time. True, there were raised eyebrows when the Juilliard Quartet
would attack Mozart with red-hot intensity; one had the impression that
they were intent on removing the cobwebs from an approach which
had become stale. The first major triumph of Robert Mann and his
quartet was an unsurpassed, integral performance of the six Bartók
quartets in the late 1940s, which they recorded in 1949. (They re-
recorded the Bartók cycle in 1963 and again in 1982, each time revealing new aspects of the works.)

Today, Mann is the last active member of the original Juilliard
Quartet. Remarkably, however, the style of the quartet has changed
very little in the thirty-five years of its existence. Obviously, the characteristics of the quartet—its immense vitality, its searching musicality—

are really the image of Robert Mann, who was able to shape the ensemble in accordance with his own vision. Yet at the beginning he was very much *primus inter pares*. Once the composite personality of the Juilliard Quartet was established, it remained constant over the years. At present there is a generation gap within the quartet, and Mann, recently turned sixty though ever youthful, leads a group of players considerably younger than he. But the spirit has remained unchanged.* When the Juilliard Quartet entered the musical scene in the 1940s, their exuberant and even aggressive style was hailed as a new prototype of quartet playing. The astonishing growth of chamber music in the United States can be attributed in part to the new interest their forceful and spirited interpretations sparked. "We would play old music as if it were composed today, and new music as if it were written a long time ago," says Mann. But having started the chamber-music revolution, he is almost frightened by the results all around. "The bigger the audiences become, the more they are going to want 'entertainment.' That's all I'm afraid of." As for the performers, "Unfortunately, those who are successful today strive primarily for sound and virtuosity. I adhere to a more Zen-like approach; in chamber music the virtuoso approach does not work."[3]

But Mann has provided his own safeguards: he has coached and taught a number of rising string quartet ensembles who will uphold the ideals of the Juilliard Quartet. Some are already widely known— the La Salle, the Tokyo, the Emerson, the Concord; others, like the Sequoia, the American, the New World, are in the process of winning recognition. Some are brand new and already prize-winning, like the Mendelssohn and the Colorado Quartets. Coaching by the members of the Juilliard Quartet is done not only in New York, but also at Michigan State University at East Lansing. In addition, Mann conducts an ensemble workshop at Baca, Colorado, during the summer months.

In 1962 the Juilliard Quartet reached the pinnacle of recognition in the United States: the group was named quartet-in-residence at the Library of Congress in Washington, succeeding the Budapest Quartet. This involved regular performances at the Coolidge Auditorium on the four Stradivari instruments bequeathed to the library on condition that they not be taken out of the library building. Thus, the quartet rehearsals must take place inside the building, and the instruments are collected at the end of each concert. There is one disadvantage: the

---

* The other members are presently Earl Carlyss (violin), Samuel Rhodes (viola), and Joel Krosnick (cello).

players can never become fully accustomed to the instruments they play, though over the years each has come to know the idiosyncrasies of his instrument.

When the Juilliard Quartet first appeared in Europe, its vigorous, ebullient, and often nontraditional style was considered characteristically American, typifying a new, young culture. They were not afraid to play Debussy in Paris, Beethoven in Vienna, Mozart in Salzburg, Russian music in Moscow. It worked.

> The Juilliard Quartet was the first major American string quartet that made a wholly convincing case to the world abroad that an American group could meet any standards. Of course, as a young quartet we were criticized for certain attributes. But we were accepted in Europe, and the Europeans felt that we identified with their music. . . . We proved that Americans could do this and not be considered dumb or nutty.[4]

At home, the Juilliard Quartet continues to be a vital part of the American scene. Robert Mann can be proud of his achievement.

Berl Senofsky

Berl Senofsky is typical of the American artist who, in spite of success and recognition abroad, finds it difficult to break through the neglect and indifference of the New York establishment—critics, managers, conductors, and in general the powers that control a career. In 1958, when reviewing a Senofsky concert, Howard Taubman wrote in the *Times*,

> The reproach falls on all of us—managers, board of directors, public, critics. Mr. Senofsky is not the only American musician who, despite the winning of impressive prizes, has failed to be treated with sufficient honor at home. It is an old American habit to minimize our own. Let us, by all means, be hospitable to the pre-eminent artists from abroad. But if there is any justice, we will wake up to the fact that we have young musicians of great gifts and will give them the same opportunities we reserve for their foreign peers.[1]

Berl Senofsky was born in 1926 in Philadelphia. His parents, both violinists, had immigrated from the Ukraine. The boy started to play the violin at age three, guided by his father. Among his later teachers were Stassevitch, Persinger, and Galamian at the Juilliard School. His budding career was interrupted by the war, when he served three years in the infantry. After his discharge he accepted a post as assistant concertmaster of the Cleveland Orchestra. In 1947 he won the Naumburg Award, which led to a New York debut in October of that year.

In 1955 Senofsky entered the Queen Elisabeth Competition in Brussels and won first prize, the first American-born violinist to have achieved this distinction.* Among the judges were Menuhin, Oistrakh, and Francescatti. Menuhin wrote, "As Mr. Senofsky is at one and the same time a mature musician and a brilliant violinist, I feel that he fully deserved this prize."

Returning to the United States, Senofsky found less of a demand for his art than he expected. True, he had a number of orchestral engagements, including Chicago, San Francisco, Minneapolis, St. Louis, Cincinnati. But the all-important New York Philharmonic waited three years, until January 1958, to present him to its subscribers.

That summer of 1958, Senofsky played with the Boston Symphony at Tanglewood under Monteux. Harold Schonberg of the *Times* had to admit that Senofsky had not been "too active on the New York scene." His review was mixed: "thoughtful, lyric manner, a beautiful tone . . . considerable virtuosity in the Kreisler cadenza."[2] But there were flaws: intonation occasionally insecure, vibrato sometimes excessive; also the reviewer wished for "just a shade more temperament."

For whatever reason, Senofsky's solo career did not unfold. He was heard in sonata programs with Gary Graffman and Brooks Smith. At present he is a highly respected violin professor at the Peabody Conservatory in Baltimore, and served on the jury of the 1980 Rockefeller Contest for violinists specializing in American repertoire.

Sidney Harth

Sidney Harth's career is so versatile in its various aspects that it is difficult to stress one angle without slighting another. He is a soloist and chamber musician of distinction, conductor and concertmaster, a teacher and academic chairman. At the center of everything he does is music of both the past and the present, without favoring one or the other. "That is a luxury a performing artist cannot afford," he once said; "I love all the works I am called to play." But he has realized an obligation toward contemporary composers by commissioning and performing new works.

* The runner-up, incidentally, was Julian Sitkovetsky, a fine Soviet violinist.

Robert Mann, *far left*, the outstanding leader of the Juilliard Quartet.
Below left, Sidney Harth, versatile soloist, concertmaster, and conductor in America.
Below right, Michael Rabin, magnificently gifted as a boy of fifteen, studied with Ivan Galamian but died young before his career could fully develop.

SHELDON SOFFER MANAGEMENT

MUSICAL AMERICA

Born in 1929 in Cleveland, Harth studied at the Cleveland Institute of Music with Joseph Knitzer from 1945 to 1949. After winning the Naumburg Award in 1949, he made his New York debut the same year. Yet he felt the need for further artistic stimulation and had coaching sessions with Mishel Piastro and Georges Enesco (1949–51), followed by his Paris debut in 1952. In 1957 Harth attracted international attention by being "nosed out" at the Wieniawski Competition in Poland by a student of Oistrakh, Rosa Fain.* The suspicion that musical politics had something to do with his second prize lingered on, but the Poles are known to be fair in running this contest. Harth, however, had the moral satisfaction of receiving the Wieniawski Medal struck *post factum* in his honor in 1965.

In addition to an active concert career, Harth was concertmaster and assistant conductor of the Louisville Orchestra in 1953–59, a progressive ensemble sponsoring contemporary music. There followed three years as concertmaster of the Chicago Symphony under Fritz Reiner, perhaps the most prestigious position in the country—certainly the most demanding.

In 1963 came the decisive move: Harth left orchestral playing for a time and became music chairman at Carnegie-Mellon University in Pittsburgh. It meant more time for solo appearances. But he also branched out into chamber music by founding his own string quartet. To keep active as conductor, he was in charge of the Carnegie College/Community Orchestra.

Harth was good for Pittsburgh, and the city responded with gratitude, voting him Man of the Year in Music. He brought Pablo Casals as visiting professor to the University, conducted Casals's oratorio *El Pessebre* on Easter Day, and collaborated with Casals in an integral performance of Bach's six *Brandenburg Concertos*.

But the lure to get involved, once again, with a great symphony orchestra was too strong: in 1973 Harth accepted Zubin Mehta's offer to become concertmaster and associate conductor of the Los Angeles Philharmonic. When Mehta went to the New York Philharmonic in 1978, Harth lost interest and asked to be released. The two were briefly reunited in 1980, when Harth agreed to serve as guest concertmaster of the New York Philharmonic during the European tour under Mehta. Apparently he was not interested in a permanent concertmaster post.

---

* Rosa Fain, now an emigré living in West Germany, made her belated New York debut with the New York Philharmonic in June 1981 and proved to be a highly accomplished—though not sensational—violinist.

While Harth's ultimate ambition seems to be conducting, he is primarily a master of the violin. His technical skill is accomplished, his musicianship solid. His beautiful tone is enhanced by the sound of his Stradivarius of 1731, the "Comte Armaiville." He is a thoroughgoing professional, a born violinist who plays Bach as well as Wieniawski, with all the right instincts. A man of massive build with a no-nonsense expression on his round face, he is not the image of the "romantic virtuoso." The critic Winthrop Sargent found his stance reminiscent of the great Eugène Ysaÿe and was particularly impressed by the variation movement of the *Kreutzer Sonata:*

> I do not remember hearing [it] played with more understanding or more sheer beauty of statement since the peak days of Joseph Szigeti. . . . If finer violin playing is being done nowadays anywhere, I have not heard it. Mr. Harth is more than a violinist; he is an artist.[1]

It remains to be seen whether Harth's ambition as violinist or as conductor will take precedence. His present post as music director of the Mannes College Orchestra in New York is not commensurate with his talent. Since 1982 he has also held a professorship in violin at Yale University.

Michael Rabin

In January 1972 the musical world was stunned and saddened by the unexpected death, at the age of thirty-five, of Michael Rabin, a violinist of immense talent. The glowing obituaries spoke of his years of success—he had made his Carnegie Hall debut at thirteen, had covered 700,000 miles on six continents, had been applauded by millions of enraptured listeners. But no one mentioned the tragic crisis that befell young Rabin during his growing-up years, when he was trying to make the transition from child prodigy to grown artist, and nearly faltered in the process. There were times when Rabin canceled engagements simply because he felt unable to perform, struck by feelings of inadequacy or insecurity he could not overcome.

Rabin was born in New York City on May 2, 1936. His father was a violinist and long-time member of the New York Philharmonic who had once studied with Kneisel, his mother a pianist. Michael gave evidence of a perfect ear when he was three, and at age five his lessons began. He came to the attention of Ivan Galamian—recently arrived from Europe—who accepted the nine-year-old boy as a pupil. He played his first engagement in 1947, at the age of eleven, and in 1949 he won a contest of the National Federation of Music Clubs. His debut at Carnegie Hall took place early in 1950 with the National Orchestral Association, followed by a reengagement a few months later. The choice of concertos stressed virtuosity: Vieuxtemps's No. 5 in A minor and Wieniawski's No. 1 in F-sharp minor, the latter a fiendishly difficult piece. The review in the New York *Times* was glowing, and Rabin's career was launched. Even more important were the favorable comments of leading conductors who had worked with him. Mitropoulos called him "the genius violinist of tomorrow, already equipped with all that is necessary to be a great artist." George Szell considered him "the greatest violin talent that has come to my attention during the past two or three decades." Rodzinski was impressed that young Rabin was different from the "usual musical prodigy story. . . . He was not overprotected and shut off from the world, but managed to enjoy a perfectly normal American boyhood."[1]

Michael's "normalcy" extended to the Professional Children's School in New York, where he received his general education while studying with Galamian. Of all the gifted students he taught over the years, Galamian considered Rabin the greatest: an "almost extraordinary talent—no weaknesses, never!"[2]

In May of 1951, the fifteen-year-old Rabin made his first appearance with the New York Philharmonic, though at an unusual place—the Roxy Theater, a Broadway movie house where the full orchestra gave four performances a day (forty-five minutes each) between the screenings of a feature film. Young Rabin seemed just right for such a venture into mass appeal. But there was no doubt that he was good enough to appear during the regular subscription series: later that year the Philharmonic Orchestra presented him as guest soloist in Philadelphia, followed by four regular solo performances at Carnegie Hall with Mitropoulos. Again, Rabin's repertoire was virtuosic—concertos by Paganini and Wieniawski's First (the latter never before played at the Philharmonic).

In 1954, Rabin appeared again with the Philharmonic; this time he gave the premiere of a violin concerto by Richard Mohaupt, followed by the Glazunov concerto. Two years later, in February 1956, he played the Brahms concerto: one can see the ascending line of musical quality. But in truth, Rabin really excelled in the virtuoso repertoire. His recordings of Paganini's Twenty-four Caprices and Wieniawski's Concerto No. 1 have remained historic documents of an immense technical mastery and a lovely sensuous tone. These qualities can also be heard in a recording of the Glazunov concerto, which sounds more luscious in the cantabile sections than is usual in the Russian tradition—and perhaps all the more attractive.

Around 1960 there was a noticeable decline in Rabin's performances. Engaged to play at the inauguration of Philharmonic Hall on September 26, 1962, he was totally incapable of functioning and had to be replaced at the last minute. That year he gave a violin recital in Berlin and played in such an indifferent and undisciplined manner that the public became unruly. Only a year earlier he had earned a big success with the Berlin Philharmonic. One critic noticed a somnolent behavior and a shuffling gait walking on and off stage. There were rumors that he was under the influence of drugs and that there was some mental instability. His death was attributed to an accident. In Galamian's words, "He did not die of drugs. By that time he had stopped the drugs and was playing better than ever. He slipped on a rug and hit his head on a table."[8]

This was the official version of his accidental death. Some speculated that there was too much pressure, too much responsibility thrown at him during his adolescence. Be this as it may, young Rabin seems to have been a victim of his early fame, and the world of music suffered a grievous loss.

Aaron Rosand

Aaron Rosand is better known abroad than in his native country. He is a first-rate violinist with effortless technical control, a ravishing tone, and a romantic dash that colors all his performances. Lately he has been typed as a "Romantic virtuoso," mainly because he has given incomparable performances of nineteenth-century violin music at the annual Romantic Festival in Indianapolis. Doing research in this field, he has revived a surprising number of forgotten or neglected violin works, which, beyond sheer virtuosity, require elegant phrasing and dashing brio to be fully effective. Rosand has a collection of such works in his repertoire: the *Hungarian Concerto* by Joachim, the *Concerto romantique* by Godard, the *Concerto russe* by Lalo, and rediscovered concertos by Ries, Hubay, and Saint-Saëns (No. 1), as well as the virtuosic Ernst in F-sharp. He has no rival in this field.

Rosand has a genuinely violinistic imagination, taking flight from the style of a Paganini or Ernst; no longer are the passages merely difficult to execute; they are tossed off with ease and insouciance, to reveal their sparkling imagery. To watch Rosand in his daredevil exploits on the violin is an aesthetic pleasure.

Born in Indiana in 1927, Rosand studied the violin in Chicago with Leon Sametini (once a student of Sevčik and Ysaÿe) and finished his education at the Curtis Institute with Efrem Zimbalist. He made his debut in New York in 1948 and spaced his recitals in New York rather far apart—1951, 1955, 1958. The critics were a bit slow in realizing the unusual accomplishments of this young man. Yet in 1951 the *Herald Tribune* praised his violinistic command, his steady bow, his uncommonly good intonation. The *Times* ran a headline about his 1955 concert, "Surging to Top." His program was challenging—the Walton sonata, the Prokofiev solo sonata, among others. In October 1960 I heard his debut with the New York Philharmonic under Bernstein, when he played the Samuel Barber concerto, which produced a rather pale and ineffectual impression.

Finally, a decade later, came the breakthrough—Rosand's "Romantic Recital" at Carnegie Hall caught the ear of Schonberg, who wrote a sizzling review in the *Times:* "He is one of the romantic violinists supreme, a tremendous virtuoso with extraordinary control over bow and fingers. . . . In its way, it is absolutely flawless playing. . . . Romanticism on the violin had a rebirth at Carnegie Hall."[1] Schonberg's only objection was that Rosand's dynamic scale was limited. This, however, was remedied when he acquired a magnificent Guarnerius of 1741, once owned by Paul Kochanski.

Winthrop Sargent wrote interesting details in *The New Yorker* about Rosand's approach to the violin. He spoke of Rosand's "violinistic *machismo*" and continued,

> He stands with his feet wide apart, hurling his bow at the strings, sometimes crouching over his instrument as Paganini did, sometimes weaving like a boxer. . . . He is a perfectly splendid violinist, with fantastic agility of the left hand and a bow technique that encompasses remarkable pianissimos, cascading spiccatos, and everything else that one expects of a true virtuoso.[2]

And Paul Hume of Washington, much feared for his sarcasm, surrendered to Rosand's musical prowess:

> Rosand in the Godard Concerto did something I would not have thought possible after hearing him in the Hubay Concerto at the opening concert. He surpassed the fantastic degree

of absolutely gorgeous playing. . . . There is not a violinist today who possesses a finer, more subtle command of his instrument. . . . He delivered what I cannot think was anything less than the greatest performance I have ever heard of the last, most famous Paganini Caprice [No. 24].[3]

Rosand has made a number of recordings (mostly on foreign labels), which capture the sparkle and elegance of his style. His long-awaited reappearance at Carnegie Hall in April 1982, with the Tchaikovsky concerto under the baton of Mstislav Rostropovich, produced a lukewarm response from the *Times* critic, but those who heard the performance recognized the same sterling qualities of tone and technique, in addition to a more refined projection of Tchaikovsky's extroverted music. Perhaps the time has come for Rosand to throw off the mantle of Romanticism and to give us Mozart and Beethoven with crystalline nobility; in fact he claimed in a recent interview that these two masters were his real specialty.

Carroll Glenn

Carroll Glenn was born in a small town in South Carolina around 1919. She received her earliest instruction from her mother, an ardent amateur; every Saturday mother and daughter traveled sixty-five miles to have violin lessons with a teacher in Columbia. At the age of twelve Carroll received a Juilliard scholarship to study with Edouard Déthier, with whom she worked for seven years. In the next years she won every award available to a young violinist—the Naumburg Award in 1938, the Town Hall Endowment Award in 1939, and two years later the National Federation of Music Clubs and Schubert Memorial Awards. The latter carried with them engagements with the New York Philharmonic and Philadelphia Orchestras, while Town Hall sponsored her recital debut in February 1940. Her lovely girlish appearance belied the strength and determination of her playing style; she chose nothing less than the Sibelius concerto for her debut with the New York Philharmonic under Rodzinski in December 1941. She tackled it "with the courage of youth and the assurance of a considerable technique. . . . The result was something less than completely satisfactory, but it was an impressive exhibition by one of the most talented of the younger violinists." Her Carnegie Hall recital of 1944 brought "fine playing of eminently lyrical passages. . . . Rather than a virtuoso, Miss Glenn is predominantly an

Aaron Rosand is a fine American violinist who has won recognition at home and in Europe.

Once a child prodigy, James Buswell is rising steadily in the estimation of music lovers because of his versatility as a soloist and chamber music performer.

Jaime Laredo was at eighteen the youngest winner ever of the Queen Elisabeth prize. He is highly regarded as a soloist and chamber musician.

interpreter of lyrical feelings. . . ."[1] In the meantime, she married the pianist Eugene List and they appeared often as a duo or as co-soloists. Thus, in 1948 and again in 1949, they drew capacity audiences at the Lewisohn Stadium with the New York Philharmonic, each playing a concerto. Glenn and List rediscovered neglected works, like the forgotten manuscript of a piano and violin duo by Franz Liszt or the Double Concerto for piano, violin, and orchestra by Viotti. Glenn also revived the Sonata for Two Violins by Ysaÿe, composed in 1915 but not played in New York until 1980 by Glenn and her student Clive Armor. For a number of years Glenn resided in Rochester, where she was professor at the Eastman School of Music, but she returned to New York City during the 1970s, enabling her to be more active on the concert scene while teaching at the Manhattan School and at Queens College. Glenn was trained in the Franco-Belgian school by Déthier, but did some postgraduate studies with Galamian in order to acquaint herself with his method. Her students in turn profit greatly from the versatility of her approach. In 1960, Glenn received a second Naumburg Award, this one to study and record a new work, the Violin Concerto by Andrew Imbrie. She founded the Southern Vermont Music Festival in Manchester, Vermont, which became a center for the study and performance of chamber music. She was fully active as performer and teacher, visiting China on a concert tour in the summer of 1981, and her death on April 26, 1983, came with shocking suddenness.[2]

Joseph Silverstein

Whenever I hear Joseph Silverstein, I am convinced that there is no more fastidious violinist around. His playing is so finely chiseled, his tone so warm, his interpretation in such good taste, that he has few rivals. What he seems to lack is dash and temperament, which limits his communicative powers. He is at his best in a repertoire of classical lines and noble dignity, equally accomplished as soloist and chamber musician.

Joseph Silverstein was born in Detroit in 1932. From 1945 to 1950 he studied at the Curtis Institute in Philadelphia where his teachers were Veda Reynolds and Efrem Zimbalist. Later he was coached by Josef Gingold and Mischa Mischakoff. Silverstein joined the Boston Symphony in 1955 at the age of twenty-three, at the time its youngest member. He came to international attention as a prizewinner at the

Queen Elisabeth Competition in Brussels in 1959. The following year he won the Naumburg Award, which led to his New York debut at Town Hall in 1961. Nevertheless, he maintained his connection with the Boston Symphony: he was named concertmaster in 1962 and assistant conductor in 1971. He also became leader of the Boston Symphony Chamber Players, as well as the Symphony String Quartet.

The Boston Symphony makes full use of the extraordinary performance talent of its concertmaster: not only does Silverstein appear often as soloist at concerts, but he has also recorded the concertos of Bartók and Stravinsky with that orchestra under Erich Leinsdorf.

Linked with his position is the summer activity at the Berkshire Music Center in Tanglewood: here he teaches, performs, and conducts; for a time he was the chairman of the music faculty. In 1972, he added the position as associate professor of music at Yale University to his many activities.

The Boston Symphony is the most patrician and tradition-minded of all American symphony orchestras. Being second in command in Boston is a job for which Silverstein is ideally suited, as an artist who can deal with any musical problem and whose quiet dignity commands respect and admiration. But his fame is by no means localized: in 1967 he led the Boston Symphony Chamber Players on their tour to the Soviet Union, Germany, and England. He is also much admired for his programs for unaccompanied violin, one of the hardest tests for any violinist. Silverstein plays a violin made by J. B. Guadagnini in 1773, formerly owned by Grumiaux, and recently acquired a Guarnerius del Gèsu of 1742 known as "ex-Camilla Urso."

Charles Treger

Charles Treger gained instant fame when he won first prize in the 1962 Wieniawski Competition. The odds were against him: the decision against Harth (biased, as some thought) in the 1957 contest was still remembered, and the Soviets prepared their contestants in 1962 with the tenacity of sports coaches. I happened to be in Moscow as an exchange scholar in the fall of 1962. Invited to attend a concert of advanced violin students at the conservatory, I remember hearing a very long program of mostly Wieniawski and Szymanowski. The next day I inquired, "Why so much Polish music?" "Oh, don't you know, professor, this is our brigade preparing for the Wieniawski contest." In my opinion, there was only one outstanding player among the many, a lanky fellow named Oleg Krysa. Great was my surprise (and everyone else's in Moscow) when it became known that an obscure violinist from Iowa had beaten Krysa, who placed second.

Actually, the winner came only indirectly from Iowa. Charles Treger was born in Detroit in 1935. The information about his early years is somewhat sparse: his teachers are listed as Szymon Goldberg, Adolf Busch, and Hugo Kortschak, though not necessarily in that order. Young Treger is known to have been soloist with the Detroit Symphony at the age of sixteen. In 1959 he gave a very successful recital in New York at the Metropolitan Museum of Art. At age twenty-seven, he was appointed head of the string department at the University of Iowa, known for the excellence of its music program. In 1962 came Treger's victory in Poland, the first American winner in the Wieniawski Competition. It resulted in an immediate stream of concerts. He played in fourteen countries sponsored by the U.S. State Department, which saw in Treger an ambassador of American achievement in the arts. He toured as soloist with the Pittsburgh Symphony; he appeared with the orchestras of Philadelphia, Washington, Detroit, and the New York Philharmonic. For New York he chose the rarely heard Second Concerto by Karol Szymanowski, balancing it with a concerto by Mozart.

After ten years in Iowa, Treger finally made the move to New York in 1969 by accepting the important position of first violinist with the Lincoln Center Chamber Music Society. It enhanced his stature in the musical world, but did little to further his solo career. To remedy this lag, he arranged a series of three concerts in 1972 entitled "The Romantic Revival." Schonberg of the *Times* described the playing as "unfailingly beautiful, tidy, accurate, and a shade reserved."[1] I attended one of the concerts and was impressed by Treger's accomplished playing, though the tone was overvibrated and not large, and the romantic boldness hardly in evidence. But what fastidious playing, what perfect double stops! Yet I heard him in a flawed performance of Joachim's *Hungarian Concerto*, where he skimmed over technical passages and made ill-advised cuts in the score. In 1973 Treger resigned from the Lincoln Center position because of pressures of outside engagements.

Treger's latest musical partnership was with the outstanding American pianist André Watts. During the Schubert year 1978 (and in fact into 1980), they formed a duo to perform Schubert programs all over the country. The Schubert repertoire for violin is deceptively gentle, yet very difficult to play, and Treger acquitted himself extremely well. At present, Treger and Watts are continuing their musical partnership.

Treger's career seems to be at a crossroad. He does some teaching at the Hartt College of Music in Hartford. Will his solo career gain new momentum, or will he return to chamber music? He certainly deserves wider recognition.

Arnold Steinhardt

Arnold Steinhardt turned his lagging career into a success by switching from solo playing to chamber music. At the age of twenty-seven he realized that, despite prizes and awards, the "Heifetz ambition" was unattainable. He also discovered the satisfaction and fulfillment one can derive in playing the greatest music ever conceived, the string quartet literature. In 1964, he and three like-minded musicians formed a new string quartet. Their "godfathers" were three members of the Budapest Quartet—the brothers Schneider and the violist Kroyt—the violist who suggested the name "Guarneri." The rest is history: within a few years, the new Guarneri Quartet reached the top of the profession.

Prior to becoming leader of the Guarneri Quartet, Steinhardt had been active in many fields. Born in 1937 in Los Angeles, he started to study the violin at seven and became a student of Toscha Seidel, the legendary disciple of Leopold Auer. At fourteen, Steinhardt made his debut with the Los Angeles Philharmonic, and at seventeen he won a scholarship to the Curtis Institute in Philadelphia to study with Galamian. In 1958, a good year for him, he won the Philadelphia Youth Auditions and played as soloist under Ormandy, and he emerged as unanimous winner of the Leventritt Competition. The prize included several engagements with major orchestras, among them the New York Philharmonic. However, Steinhardt's appearance under Schippers in the Wieniawski concerto was less than a complete success. The *Times* critic, while recognizing the qualities of tone and technique, found it "a workmanlike performance," lacking the necessary "dashing virtuosity."[1] There followed a number of solo performances with orchestra in 1959, but for some reason he decided to accept the position of assistant concertmaster with the Cleveland Orchestra. The opportunity of working closely with a great musician like Szell must have been tempting. Indeed, during the following years, Steinhardt played frequently as soloist under Szell and assistant conductor Louis Lane.

In February 1962 Steinhardt gave a debut recital in New York with a varied program consisting of Bach, Brahms, Schubert, and the *Sonata concertante* by Leon Kirchner. The *Herald Tribune* critic found "solid musicianship . . . handicapped by . . . a somewhat limited expressive range."[2] Feeling in need of new musical ideas, Steinhardt embarked for Europe to study for a few months with Joseph Szigeti, who encouraged him to enter the Queen Elisabeth Competition in 1963. Steinhardt won a third prize (a bronze medal) behind two Russians.

The summer of 1964 found Steinhardt in Marlboro, Serkin's summer institute for chamber music. It was a turning point for him. He teamed up with three equally gifted instrumentalists and they began to rehearse under the watchful eye and ear of Sascha Schneider and others on the senior faculty. They remember fondly Sascha's criticism voiced in "fractured Lithuanian": "I may not know from good, but that is terrible!" It was Sascha who launched their debut in March 1965. According to the New York *Times*, "The group's tone is like satin. The vibratos are warm and matched. The rhythm is solid, the intonation exemplary, and the sense of style masterly."[3] The acclaim grew with each appearance. By 1970 the Guarneri Quartet had moved to the top, filling in part the void created by the demise of the Budapest Quartet. The Tenth Anniversary Concert, given in February 1975 at Tully Hall, found them "as good as any quartet playing today."[4]

In the 1970s, Steinhardt formed sonata teams with Peter Serkin (1974) and with Misha Dichter (1978). His partnership with Serkin drew praise in a concert of "exceptional quality." But there is no doubt that Steinhardt is at his best as a quartet player: his playing assumes a commanding quality, which is less apparent when he performs as soloist.

Erick Friedman

How an undeservedly low placement in a competition can hurt a career is evident in the case of Erick Friedman.* He entered the 1966 Tchaikovsky Competition and shared a sixth prize, which shattered his self-confidence. Friedman had studied with Galamian, Milstein, and Jascha Heifetz. He seemed to be a favorite of Heifetz, who showed his esteem for his student by recording the Bach Double Concerto with him. Born in 1939, Friedman had a very promising career before embarking for Moscow; he had a big technique, a sweeping style, and seemed destined for success even under the pressure of a competition. What happened in Moscow is difficult to understand, particularly since a prominent

---

* At the suggestion of Heifetz, who is superstitious, Friedman added the final "k" to his first name so that the letters in his name would total thirteen, as in Jascha Heifetz.

Soviet member of the jury praised Friedman's talent while criticizing his rendition of the Tchaikovsky concerto. Be that as it may, Friedman was so shocked by the disappointing outcome that he considered suspending his violin career. Fortunately, the discouragement was only temporary.

I heard Friedman during the 1977–78 season, when he gave three sonata recitals with three different pianists in New York. Even when playing chamber music, he leans toward a "showy" brilliance, a remnant of his virtuoso days. Gradually, the early Heifetz influence seems to be giving way to a more balanced and restrained interpretative style, and this process of maturing will undoubtedly help Friedman achieve wider recognition. "He is not only a master violinist but also one with a distinctly personal and identifiable style of playing," wrote Henahan in the *Times* on December 9, 1979. His recent appointment as professor and chairman of the string department at Southern Methodist University in Dallas will widen significantly the scope of Friedman's musical activities.

Jaime Laredo

In May of 1959, a jury of fourteen experts, including such eminent violinists as Szigeti, Oistrakh, Menuhin, Stern, and Francescatti, awarded a first prize at the Queen Elisabeth Contest in Brussels to Jaime Laredo. He was seventeen, the youngest ever to win this award.

Born on June 7, 1941, in Bolivia, Jaime had begun lessons at age five. In 1948, he was taken to the United States to develop his unusual talent, studying first in San Francisco, then in Cleveland with Josef Gingold. In 1955 he entered the Curtis Institute in Philadelphia to complete his studies with the renowned Galamian and graduated *in absentia* while competing in Brussels.

All during his student years, young Laredo gave occasional concerts. In 1956 he played a ten-concert tour of Puerto Rico, Peru, and his native Bolivia. A recital in Washington in 1959 preceded his entry into the Brussels competition.

His success in Brussels resulted in a string of important solo engagements with orchestra and a European tour. But the most severe test was to face New York critics at his Carnegie Hall recital on October 19, 1959. Suddenly, Laredo discovered that winning a competition was no guarantee of instant acclaim. His program was conservative but well-chosen—sonatas by Vivaldi, Brahms, Debussy, and a solo partita by Bach. The critics were divided: while the *Times* pronounced him "a musician of remarkable gifts," the *Herald Tribune* found he had "much to learn."[1] Perhaps the critics expected too much from an eighteen-year-old. He reminisced, "That first year . . . the pressure was tremendous. I felt that I had to be flawless every time in order to survive. I was more nervous after I'd won the competition than before. . . ."[2]

At home in Bolivia, Laredo was received like a conquering hero. The government issued a postage stamp in his honor, spelling his name in musical notes (*la-re-do*) next to his picture. The City of New York presented him with the Handel Medal.

During the following year, Laredo worked diligently to broaden his musicianship. In 1961 he entered Serkin's Marlboro group, where the emphasis was on chamber music, against the advice of his manager who thought it would ruin his chances for a solo career. Subsequently he performed with the Music from Marlboro ensemble on tour. His marriage to a fine pianist, Ruth Meckler, in 1960 (now dissolved) caused him to focus on the sonata literature. His growth as a musician while preserving his virtuosity was obvious to the critics after his recitals in 1962 and 1969.

In 1973 Laredo replaced Treger as leading violinist of the Chamber Music Society of Lincoln Center. Eventually he organized his own chamber-music series, and his varied programs presented at New York's Kaufmann Auditorium attract large and loyal audiences. After marrying the gifted cellist Sharon Robinson in 1976, he formed a trio with her and Joseph Kalichstein, which is steadily gaining in popularity. Occasionally, Laredo performs on the viola as well, appearing, for example, with Isaac Stern in Mozart's *Symphonie concertante*. Recently he has taken over the Scottish Chamber Orchestra, which he leads violin in hand, and while he disclaims any ambitions to become a conductor, he derives obvious pleasure in further expanding his musical horizons.

In view of all these activities, Laredo's solo playing might suffer. At least that was the opinion of the New York *Times* critic after his solo recital in 1979:

> Jaime Laredo is a violinist of such sweetness of tone, temperament, and deportment that it is hard to imagine him sounding anything but benign. This is a cherishable quality . . . but can pose limitations as well. And so Mr. Laredo's recital December 15 . . . was an ingratiating but uneven affair.[3]

Be this as it may, Laredo is playing an increasingly important role on the New York musical scene, where versatility and initiative are highly prized. Having tempered his virtuoso instincts, he has become a mature and beautifully balanced musician who enjoys a large following.

Paul Zukofsky

A violinist with an interesting profile, Paul Zukofsky switched in his mid-twenties from a conventional career to become the "Fiddler (and Drumbeater) of the New, New Music . . . the master violinist of contemporary performance—without peer in America, perhaps in the world. . . ."[1] It all happened during the 1968–69 season, when Zukofsky, then twenty-five, gave a series of three concerts in New York entitled "Music for the Twentieth-Century Violin." Asserting that neither Kreisler nor Heifetz did much to further violin repertoire,* he explained, "I got very tired of the musical mentality of my contemporaries. I have a name for them—necrophiliacs."[2]

Zukofsky, born in Brooklyn in 1943, had lessons with Galamian beginning at age seven. He never went to a public school, his parents having obtained permission from the Board of Education to teach him at home.† When he was thirteen, young Zukofsky made his recital debut at Carnegie Hall, a bold stroke considering the disinclination of New York critics to encourage prodigies. Schonberg's curiosity was sufficiently aroused to review the concert for the *Times;* he called him

> a deadpan bundle of talent. . . . The playing was remarkably accurate and remarkably lifeless. . . . Never once . . . a smile or a shadow of any emotion. . . . One had the uncomfortable feeling that a little automaton was on stage. . . . He is the material of which great violinists are made. But about his musical capabilities there remained some doubt.[3]

By the time he was seventeen, Zukofsky had reached his third Carnegie Hall recital. This time the *Times* critic displayed polite impatience:

> Tall, gangling, unsmiling, diffident. . . . Played with an ease and fluency that seemed inborn. . . . Until Mr. Zukofsky begins to grow in musical understanding, it seems futile to keep putting him before the public. Technique alone has never been enough for the performing artist.[4]

---

* This is only partially true: Kreisler premiered the Elgar concerto, while Heifetz commissioned concertos from Walton, Gruenberg, Korngold, and Rózsa.
† His father was the well-known author and poet Louis Zukofsky.

His program followed mostly conventional lines—Bach, Brahms, and Saint-Saëns—but as an inkling of things to come the Piston Sonatina, Webern's *Four Pieces,* and a selection by Eric Satie were included. Zukofsky went back to Juilliard and obtained a master's degree at twenty-one. Then came the total conversion to modern music or to a repertory neglected by other violinists. He played the Busoni concerto (the only performance aside from that of Szigeti, who had sponsored its revival). He recorded the awesome concerto of Roger Sessions and the four violin sonatas of Charles Ives, long gathering dust. He played works by Wuorinen, Penderecki, Perle, Rochberg, paid attention to the minimalist composers Philip Glass (*Strung Out*) and Steve Reich (*Violin Phase*), and revived the concertos of Szymanowski and William Schuman. He became an "activist of apparently unlimited stamina," teaching, performing, always pioneering the new music. "Paul Zukofsky is to the contemporary violin literature what Joan of Arc was to the Dauphin," wrote Henahan of the *Times.*[5] To prove that he was as good a violinist as ever, Zukofsky also recorded the Twenty-four Caprices of Paganini. In 1982 he applied his intellectual scrutiny to Beethoven's ten violin sonatas, which he reinterpreted in terms of the "authentic" tempo. I heard the first of three concerts and found the rendition generally too fast and breathlessly inexpressive. Zukovsky applied Beethoven's late metronome markings to his early sonatas:* such mechanical transferals are treacherous, and the artistic results, in this case, were disappointing.

James Oliver Buswell

A Presbyterian minister for a great-grandfather, a theologian for a grandfather, an anthropologist for a father makes an interesting genealogy for a professional musician. But with a pianist and organist for a mother, the early musical talent of James Buswell IV is more understandable. Born in Fort Wayne, Indiana, in 1946, the boy began to play the piano and the violin at the age of five. At seven he was the youngest violin soloist with the New York Philharmonic Children's Concerts, and performed in the children's series of Chicago and Fort Wayne at age eight. He studied with Joseph Knitzer of the Eastman School, with Paul Stassevich at De Paul University, and finally with Ivan Galamian at Juilliard. Upholding the academic tradition of his family, Buswell entered Harvard, where he majored in fifteenth-century Italian art.

---

* The metronome was invented around 1815 and was occasionally used by Beethoven in later years; his violin sonatas were composed mostly in the years 1798–1803.

But his musical career came first. At the age of fifteen, he won first prize in the Merriweather Post Contest in Washington, leading to an appearance with the National Symphony. The critic Paul Hume found in him ". . . maturity and assurance and the technique of a veteran."[1] By 1965, Buswell was ready to face New York: he appeared as soloist with the visiting Pittsburgh Orchestra under Steinberg, playing the Mendelssohn concerto, and with the New York Philharmonic under Bernstein with the Stravinsky concerto. Harold Schonberg of the *Times* was impressed:

> He is fairly tall, 18 years old, blond—an all-American, milk-and-cornfields boy. And he can also play the violin. He came out with immense aplomb, confidence, and authority. . . . He plays with ease and relaxation, is in tune, draws forth a good volume of clear-sounding tone, and goes about his work with a good deal of temperament.[2]

Buswell's recital debut in New York in 1967 produced divided critical opinions. There could be no doubt about his violinistic ability, as the *Times* wrote: "The quality of naturalness, of thoughtfulness and authority, is astounding to find in a twenty-year-old debut artist. He has a virtuoso's equipment and a genuine musical mind."[3] Yet the same critic found some of the interpretations "a bit encapsulated." A similar reserved quality was criticized by Miles Kastendieck who called Buswell "a placid violinist" and continued, "The persistent trait in his performances was restriction of communication beyond a well-defined point."

As the years went by, Buswell broke out of this mold. He deepened his musicianship by the study of Bach, in collaboration with the harpsichordist Fernando Valenti, with whom he recorded all six sonatas for violin and keyboard. A recital in 1974, with a mixed program involving harpsichord and piano accompaniments as well as solo Bach, was favorably reviewed by Henahan: "[It] must be described among the finest musical events of any kind that New York will hear this season."[4]

The New York public has heard Buswell repeatedly as leading violinist of the Lincoln Center Chamber Music Society. He spends part of his time as professor of music at Indiana University, teaching violin and conducting an excellent chamber orchestra. His solo performances have become more rare; his performances in New York in 1980–82 have shown him as a stylish violinist with considerable temperament and authority, as well as a wide-ranging repertoire.

From the very beginning of his career, Buswell struck a healthy balance between art and life. A baseball fan, tennis player, and bowler (he considered bowling "useful for relaxing the bow arm and thereby improving the tone"), he was the delight of "talk shows" and inquisitive reporters. But Buswell is also an opera lover and has a large collection of recordings. There is something decidedly wholesome in both his playing and his views on life and art.

Glenn Dicterow

With his appointment to the concertmaster chair of the New York Philharmonic in September 1980, Glenn Dicterow, age thirty-one, was catapulted into one of the most visible positions in the United States. Not that he was unknown before: he was concertmaster of the Los Angeles Philharmonic before being brought to New York by Zubin Mehta, and he was among the prize winners of the Tchaikovsky Competition in Moscow in 1970. It was a year of tough rivalry, with the leading Soviet violinists, Kremer and Spivakov, the top winners. Dicterow placed fifth, an honorable showing considering his youth and the quality of his competitors. What attracted attention in Moscow was his choice of some American music for his elective program, the Suite by Paul Creston and the *Carmen Fantasy* by Franz Waxman. It must be mentioned that young Dicterow was experienced in competitions: as a teenager he had won the Merriweather Post Award in Washington, as well as a National Federation of Musicians Award.

Born around 1949 in California, Dicterow was heard at age eleven, as soloist with the Los Angeles Philharmonic, playing the Bach Double Concerto with his brother. Important were his two years of study with the Russian-born Naum Blinder (the teacher of Isaac Stern) between the ages of fourteen and sixteen. During his four years at the Juilliard School in New York, Dicterow studied with Galamian, who gave him the essential direction; he also coached with Jascha Heifetz. Shortly before he went to the competition in Moscow, a performance of the Tchaikovsky concerto at the New York Philharmonic Promenade Concerts brought the eighteen-year-old Dicterow to the attention of the New York critics.

Dicterow's successful debut as concertmaster-soloist of the New York Philharmonic took place early in October 1980, with Vieuxtemps's Concerto No. 4 in D minor, a somewhat faded virtuoso piece; he also won acclaim with Strauss's *Ein Heldenleben*, which has one of the most intricate violin solos ever written. Since then he has repeatedly proven his musicianly qualities. Particularly impressive was his idiomatic interpretation of the Shostakovich Concerto No. 1, working closely with the composer's son Maxim, who conducted the New York Philharmonic in his debut (October 7, 1982).

Ani and Ida Kavafian

The violin-playing sisters Ani and Ida Kavafian have enlivened the New York musical scene since the 1970s. Born in Istanbul of Armenian parentage, they were brought to America at an early age. The older, Ani (born around 1948), studied principally with Mischa Mischakoff and Ivan Galamian at the Juilliard School, where she received a master's degree, winning top honors. Her career began in 1971–72, when she went on tour with the Music from Marlboro ensemble. The Concert Artist Guild awarded her a solo recital at Carnegie Recital Hall in January 1972. She placed second in the 1975 Naumburg Competition (behind Oliveira), but won the Avery Fisher Prize in 1976 and the Young Concert Artists Award in 1977. That September, she played the Beethoven concerto with the New York Philharmonic under Leinsdorf to an excellent review by Harold Schonberg; her solo recital at Tully Hall in March 1978 was equally successful. Her playing has an introspective intensity, great refinement, and impeccable style. Her tone is warm and has a burnished quality, bringing out all the beauty of her 1736 Stradivarius.

Ida Kavafian's playing, on the other hand, is more outgoing and fiery, assertive and uninhibited. Her tone is sensuous, with quite a few slides and swoops, which she probably considers romantic. Born around 1953, she also studied with Mischakoff and Galamian and received a master's degree at the Juilliard School.

Her participation in the chamber group Tashi testifies to her wide experience in chamber music. She made her solo debut with Peter Serkin at the piano in November 1978 in a challenging program and was reviewed as "an uncommonly polished violinist who needs only to give her appealingly warm temperament a bit more elbow room."[1] When I heard her in the summer of 1980, she gave herself so much elbow room in a chamber music program that she overshadowed everyone around. Her choice of repertoire shows strong interest in music of the twentieth century. Ida has had her share of prizes, including the Young Concert Artists Award in 1978 and the Indianapolis International Violin Competition (silver medal) in 1982.

HERBERT BARRETT MANAGEMENT/PHOTO: KENN DUNCAN

YOUNG CONCERT ARTISTS/PHOTO: CHRISTIAN STEINER

The sisters Ani and Ida Kavafian enliven the New York music scene with their talented and colorful performances, and are equally adept at solo and chamber music.

Eugene Fodor won a top distinction at the Tchaikovsky Competition in Moscow and is lately winning wider recognition.

SHAW CONCERTS, INC.

The happy mixture of a career as soloist and chamber-music player, considered incompatible in the past, is demonstrated by the Kavafian sisters and, in fact, by other young instrumentalists: it seems to be a trend nowadays to be able to function in both worlds. Both Ani and Ida have appeared as soloists with many orchestras, in America and Europe, but they seem at their best in chamber music, where the vibrancy of their personalities enhances the vitality of the entire ensemble.

Eugene Fodor

When Eugene Fodor won a silver medal at the 1974 Tchaikovsky Competition in Moscow, there was celebration and surprise in American music circles. Twenty-four-year-old Fodor was virtually unknown in the East, though he had previously won several lesser contests—the Merriweather Post Contest in Washington, D.C., in 1967, and the Paganini Competition in Genoa in 1972. True, the victory in Moscow was not complete: no first prize was given that year, and Fodor had to share the second prize with two other contestants, both Soviet violinists; the usual mutterings were heard about unfair deals. But Fodor's career at the time seemed assured. Today, that assurance is somewhat tarnished.

Eugene Fodor was born in 1950 in Colorado to violin-playing parents. Like his older brother John (now a violinist with the Denver Symphony), Eugene started the violin early, at the age of seven. At nine he was heard publicly for the first time, and made his debut at eleven with the Denver Symphony. At the time, his teacher was Harold Wippler, concertmaster of the symphony, and he practiced about two hours a day. The young violin-playing Fodor brothers became known for their duo recitals.

After graduating from high school in 1967, Eugene received a scholarship to the Juilliard School in New York, where the eminent Galamian became his teacher. That year he appeared as soloist with the National Symphony in Washington, with the Glazunov concerto. After Juilliard, Fodor spent two semesters as a student of Heifetz at the University of Southern California. Heifetz is his idol—"That's whom I owe everything to. . . . From him I learned a lifestyle, a way of living with music . . . I practiced my tail off. . . ."[1]

The results of this hard work soon became evident: by unanimous decision of the judges, Fodor received first prize in the 1972 Paganini

Competition. The Tchaikovsky Competition, however, was a more difficult test, the demands more sophisticated. Though the Moscow public
clearly liked Fodor's playing, the jury, under the chairmanship of Oistrakh, disagreed; not only was no first prize given, but the second prize
was divided by Fodor and two others. Nonetheless, it was the highest
honor ever won by an American string player in Moscow, and the publicity made Fodor into a top prize winner.

Returning to the United States with considerable fanfare, Fodor
played at the White House for President Ford, at New York's City Hall
for Mayor Abraham Beame, and recorded for RCA. He discarded his old
violin, a Vuillaume of 1860, and began using a Guarnerius del Gesù of
1736 valued at $300,000, lent to him by an American admirer. He ap-
peared on talk shows, endorsed a brand of whisky, and became a matinee
idol with his handsome face, his flashing smile, and his "normal" hob-
bies. It was an American success story; all that was needed was the
approval of the New York critics.

Fodor's first American appearance after his return from Moscow
took place at the summer Caramoor Festival and was turned into a
media event. He acquitted himself well and was received with cautious
critical approval. But it was his New York debut recital (in November
1974) that damaged his career. He chose a program consisting almost
entirely of showy virtuoso pieces. Taken aback by such poor judgment,
Schonberg of the *Times* wrote, "His program was not only curious, it
was actually stunning in a reverse kind of way. . . . He plays like the
extremely talented student he is. . . ." There was "lack of real character
to Mr. Fodor's playing." Everything was done skilfully enough but the
interpretation was that of a "still unformed musician."[2]

Such a review was devastating: Fodor had failed, not as a violinist
but as a thinking musician. He responded like a pouting child, saying
that he would continue to play the virtuoso selections he liked. "I'm not
going to cater to anybody . . . I'm just there to make music." And a
reporter added, "He believes in giving his audience the programs that
they want."[3] Which audience? Johnny Carson's television audience was
certainly frenetic in its approval.

Nevertheless, Fodor's second recital program, in December 1975,
was more substantial: there was unaccompanied Bach, the Prokofiev
Sonata No. 2, and even some Penderecki, counterbalanced by Kreisler
and Paganini. But the damage was done: there was again criticism of
his musicianship. The "establishment" was distrustful of his qualifica-
tions as an interpreter of great music. The New York Philharmonic

failed to invite him as a soloist. A January 1980 recital was canceled because of family complications. Since then, efforts have been made to improve his image as a musician, particularly with sophisticated audiences. He builds more substantial programs, his approach is more mature and gaining in depth. Yet when he chose to play the Brahms concerto as guest soloist with the Prague Symphony at Carnegie Hall in November 1982, his performance was clean but small-scaled and modest in tone, somewhat hasty, lacking depth and true commitment. Eventually, Fodor will find the repertoire that is best suited to his mercurial temperament.

Elmar Oliveira

American string players enjoyed a banner year in 1978. The Tchaikovsky Competition in Moscow, which is not generous with awards to Western violinists and cellists, discovered the merits of American string players and rewarded several with prizes. Among the Gold Medal winners were the violinist Elmar Oliveira and the cellist Nathaniel Rosen. Second and fourth violin prizes went respectively to Dylana Jenson and Daniel Heifetz. In fact, Igor Oistrakh, chairman of the jury, singled out the Americans and their schooling for special praise. When Oliveira decided (rather late, in fact) to enter the Tchaikovsky Competition, he was by no means an unrecognized artist in his own country: he had won the prestigious Naumburg Prize in 1975 and had received favorable reviews, but the success in Moscow gave his career a decisive lift.

Elmar Oliveira was born in 1950 in Waterbury, Connecticut, the son of an immigrant Portuguese carpenter. When Elmar was five years old, his father carved a little violin for him after reading a book on the life of Stradivarius. It was an effort well spent, for it sparked the boy's interest in the instrument. His older brother John, an aspiring professional violinist, taught him the rudiments. At the age of eleven Elmar won a scholarship to study with Ariana Bronne and continued under the guidance of her father, the noted pedagogue Raphael Bronstein, at the Manhattan School of Music. Bronstein himself had been an Auer student at the St. Petersburg Conservatory (1916), and Oliveira absorbed the Russian tradition while studying in New York.

His career began when he was fourteen, as soloist with the Hartford Symphony Orchestra. Two years later he won a Young People's audition of the New York Philharmonic and appeared at one of its youth concerts.

Oliveira's recital debut in New York took place on March 18, 1973. The well-planned program consisted of music by Vitali, Bach, Beethoven, Paganini, Schoenberg, and Ravel. He played on a borrowed Stradivari of 1708, the so-called "Empress of Russia." The New York *Times* reported that, during the first half of the program, "his tone was sweet and small-scaled, and his performances were restrained—so well behaved indeed that they failed to convey the inherent elegance of Vitali and the full drama of Beethoven." Later his sound improved; the control and intensity in the Bach were "masterly" and the Paganini Caprices "glittered with quicksilver fingerwork."[1] Obviously there was great promise and room for progress.

The next opportunity came in 1975, when Oliveira won the Naumburg Prize, granting him two New York recitals at Tully Hall, which brought him acclaim as a "strong musical personality" and a "major young artist."[2] At this point, his entry in the Tchaikovsky Contest was a major gamble, for a mediocre rating could have endangered the progress of his career. But the risk paid off. He made his biggest hit in Moscow with his elective concerto, Vieuxtemps's Concerto No. 5, a highly romantic work composed in 1861 as a contest piece for the Brussels Conservatory, which condenses all violinistic potentials of cantilena and technique into one elegant movement. Oliveira played it glowingly.

Upon his return to the United States, he was given a hero's welcome at the White House. More critical was the reentry before the New York audiences, who expected much (perhaps too much) from the winner. It occurred in December 1978 in a medium-sized hall filled to the rafters with fellow violinists and self-appointed experts. One heard polished, note-perfect performances that lacked a strong profile, a somewhat wiry tone that did not project too well (he was said to be playing on a borrowed violin not quite to his liking). Far more successful was his second recital four months later at Carnegie Hall, when he used a Stradivarius beautifully attuned to the large hall. Nevertheless, the critics still had reservations. Wrote Harold Schonberg in the *Times*, "Mr. Oliveira is a very accomplished violinist, and if he can get just a shade more personality into his playing he will be in the very top international echelon."[3]

Whether Oliveira, at the age of thirty, will acquire "just a shade more personality" is an open question; in fact, one might ask whether personality is an acquirable commodity. It may well be that his artistic profile is that of an impeccable technician and aristocratic interpreter, a shade reserved, perhaps, but musically expressive nonetheless. (I am reminded of Franz von Vecsey, whose music making was equally flawless but slightly distant.) Oliveira's Carnegie Hall recital in January 1983 revealed no new facets of his personality, but all the superb qualities of his violin mastery were in evidence.

Like others before him, Oliveira reveals a tinge of disillusionment when speaking of the competition business, even belittling its value:

> A lot of skepticism surrounds competition winners now, because history has shown that winning's not necessarily such a good thing. . . . You come back . . . and the emphasis in certain reviews is that it was a *negative* thing to have won the Tchaikovsky, the feeling being "Oh, here's another competition winner."[4]

Be this as it may, Oliveira has done well in the five years since he won the Gold Medal in Moscow. He plays some one hundred concerts each year around the world, mostly as soloist with orchestra. He still lives in upstate New York, just outside Binghamton, where he taught at Harpur College until a few years ago. His colleague on that faculty was the composer Ezra Laderman, who wrote a violin concerto for him, premiered in December 1980 with the Philadelphia Orchestra. This is one of the few contemporary works in his repertoire. In 1983 he was awarded the prestigious Avery Fisher Prize.

Dylana Jenson

Dylana Jenson, the seventeen-year-old winner of a Silver Medal at the 1978 Tchaikovsky Competition in Moscow, is entering upon a major career. Strangely enough, she came home after this significant achievement to find herself ignored by major American concert managers because hers was "only" a second prize. For ten months she battled the general indifference and finally stopped playing for several months out of sheer discouragement. Then, hearing a recording made in Moscow of her rendition of the Sibelius concerto, Irving Kolodin predicted, "She will be one of the famous violinists of our time."[1] Since then, she has played the Sibelius concerto with the Philadelphia Orchestra under Eugene Ormandy (Carnegie Hall, December 9, 1980), which was later recorded and released. Her performance at Carnegie Hall was very impressive: her warm, rich tone filled the large hall without effort, and her ability to communicate with the audience is complemented by a very reliable technique. She showed lyricism and dramatic flair in the first two movements; only the Finale lacked a certain rhythmic incisive-

The American-born Elmar Oliveira won a gold medal at the Tchaikovsky Competition and is winning international acclaim.

Dylana Jenson recently won a silver medal at Moscow's Tchaikovsky contest.

Joseph Swensen is among the youngest violinists now beginning a major career after having been trained at the Juilliard School.

ness in the craggy second theme. The public responded with an ovation, and the *Times* was full of praise. She approaches the classical repertoire with youthful exuberance, and her performance of a Mozart concerto in July 1982 was a joy.

Dylana's background shows the usual tension between a normal childhood and the musical challenge. Born in California in 1961, she began to "play with the fiddle" at age two and a half. Manuel Compinsky became her teacher, later Josef Gingold. For three summers she attended master classes with Nathan Milstein in Zurich, where she made her recital debut. Throughout her student years she performed publicly, though not too often; at age twelve she played as soloist with the Cincinnati Symphony (under Thomas Schippers) and the New York Philharmonic (with André Kostelanetz). At thirteen she left school to give her full attention to music, following Milstein's advice.

While competing in Moscow, Dylana was very much a public favorite, and she was invited back to the Soviet Union for a six-city concert tour. By now she has overcome the initial upset of losing the big prize, but being a silver medalist in Moscow at the age of seventeen is an extraordinary achievement, and she has grown as an artist since then. An international success is within her grasp.

Gregory Fulkerson and Curtis Macomber

The latest addition to the roster of American competitions has a very elaborate name—Kennedy Center–Rockefeller Foundation International Competition for excellence in the performance of American music.* Pianists, vocalists, and violinists alternate in three-year cycles; 1980 was devoted to violinists. The first prize went to Gregory Fulkerson, the second to Curtis Macomber, the third to Robert Davidovici. Since the cash awards and "fringe benefits" are the highest in the field, this new contest is bound to attract many participants. On the other hand, the emphasis on American repertoire will discourage those who will have to learn an array of unfamiliar works. After hearing the three finalists and seeing the list of submitted compositions, I was amazed at the variety of American violin compositions available to a soloist willing to search and experiment. The question remains as to how many of these works will enter into the mainstream of concert programs.

For his final program, Fulkerson chose works by five Pulitzer prize winners: Aaron Copland, Richard Wernick, George Crumb, Charles

* Starting in 1982, the contest has been held at Carnegie Hall in New York.

Wuorinen, and Charles Ives. The sonatas of Copland and Ives (No. 2) were quite engaging and framed the experimentations of the other three. Fulkerson brought an enormous amount of enthusiasm and conviction to every work he played and kept the program consistently interesting. His purely violinistic qualities were never in doubt. Whether he will sound as convincing in Beethoven remains to be seen.

Fulkerson grew up in Louisville, Kentucky, and started the violin at the age of five. He had no thought of becoming a professional violinist until entering Oberlin College, where he concentrated on music and mathematics, graduating in 1971 with honors in both. For three years he served in the Cleveland Orchestra, but decided that there was more to life than sitting in a violin section. He entered the Juilliard School in New York and studied for an additional four years, this time under Galamian's guidance. "He accomplished miracles," Fulkerson reminisced; "somehow he managed to make me into a soloist. I don't know how he did it. The process was very slow, very gradual."[1]

Because it was slow, it also was solid. Fulkerson brought his own maturity to his studies and intellect to his approach. He considers himself "a player who expresses ideas. To play this music well it makes no sense just to pump out a series of pitches. The performer is under an obligation to go behind the notes and project the underlying ideas."[2]

When he won the competition, Fulkerson was concertmaster of the Honolulu Symphony Orchestra. He played on a borrowed instrument belonging to the Juilliard School, the same violin that Perlman used for winning the Leventritt Award. Fulkerson felt that it brought him luck; but clearly more was involved!

Curtis Macomber was particularly impressive in his rendition of the complex Solo Sonata of Roger Sessions. He opened the program with Beethoven's *Spring Sonata*, played in a somewhat clipped way, which probably cost him the first prize. But Macomber, a worthy finalist too, is a violinist to be watched—elegant, self-assured, and technically accomplished. He recently joined the New World String Quartet as first violinist.

Peter Zazofsky

A comparative newcomer to the concert scene is the Boston-born Peter Zazofsky, who made his recital debut in New York in November 1982. His unusual program included two contemporary works—the

Sonata in F minor by Prokofiev and a Capriccio for violin and two tapes by the Dutch composer Henk Badings—framed by some classical and virtuoso music. He was at his best in Prokofiev—incisive, colorful, and technically immaculate. The New York *Times* critic described Zazofsky as a "young and fully formed musician displaying the poise, technical proficiency, tonal sheen and concentration of a seasoned and sensitive professional."[1] A recent broadcast from Holland featured Zazofsky's performance of Prokofiev's Violin Concerto No. 2, which was played with beautiful tone, technical control, and all the required humor and verve.

Zazofsky received his first violin lessons from his father, a member of the Boston Symphony, who prepared him for study with Joseph Silverstein, the orchestra's noted concertmaster. He completed his musical education at the Curtis Institute with Dorothy DeLay and Ivan Galamian.

Determined to enter into the fray of competitions, Zazofsky did quite well: in 1977 he won third prize in the Wieniawski Contest, in 1979 he was first-prize winner in Montreal, and in 1980 he received the second prize at the Queen Elisabeth Competition in Brussels. Zazofsky's performance in Brussels attracted much attention and brought him a number of important European engagements. All indications point toward an international career in the making.

Others

In 1981–82, several very young and superbly gifted violinists stepped before the public and attracted wide attention. In November 1981, Ida Levin was selected for a special performance at the White House, and the eighteen-year-old violinist was partnered at the piano by the seventy-eight-year-old grandmaster of the keyboard, Rudolf Serkin. The musical collaboration was remarkably poised and balanced. Early in 1982, Nadja Salerno-Sonnenberg, Italian-born and New York-trained, won a Naumburg Award and made her debut in New York both with orchestra and in recital. Her playing, though in need of more discipline, is distinguished by great intensity and propulsive temperament; undoubtedly, she possesses a major talent. In March 1982, Joseph Swensen (born in 1960) gave a remarkably successful debut recital in New York and seems destined for a major career; he has both abundant technique and musical communicativeness. All three young artists studied with Dorothy DeLay at

Juilliard. Finally, Stephanie Chase, in her early twenties, competed in the 1982 Tchaikovsky Competition and returned with the Bronze Medal (third prize), which confirmed the excellent reputation she had gained as a teenage performer. Her teacher was Sally Thomas (one of Galamian's former assistants), and she also coached with the Belgian master Grumiaux.

Among the postwar generation of German violinists, my favorite is the youngest, the enchanting violinist Anne-Sophie Mutter. Born in southwest Germany around 1964, she had the good fortune of coming to the attention of Herbert von Karajan, who guided her in the choice of repertoire appropriate to her feminine style and temperament. There is a beguiling purity in her interpretation of Mozart: the tone production is unforced, the violin sings out without being prodded, yet the sound fills Carnegie Hall. I have not heard Miss Mutter play Mendelssohn or Beethoven, and have read some criticism of her placidity in works demanding more passion; but I cannot remember a more beautiful, more idiomatic interpretation of Mozart since the days of Morini and Thibaud. She has a great future if her personal involvement with the music will grow with age.

Recent Contests

A new International Violin Competition has been launched in Indianapolis, and the first contest took place in September 1982. The jury was chaired by the distinguished professor from Indiana University, Josef Gingold. The level of the contestants was very high and the three winners are extremely well qualified for a career: Mihaela Martin of Rumania, Ida Kavafian of New York, and Yuval Yaron of Israel, all in their twenties. The gold-medal winner, Miss Martin, was introduced at Carnegie Hall on May 1, 1983, in "one of the most exciting debut concerts of the year."[1] She interpreted Classical music with style and refinement while her earthy temperament and glittering technique were displayed in the concluding Stravinsky *Divertimento*.

Since age is a factor, the latest violin contest, organized by Yehudi Menuhin in Folkestone (England), admits no one older than twenty and has a special category for "junior" contestants under fifteen, with a repertory adjusted to their age. It took place from April 2 to 9, 1983, and brought a strong showing of violinists from the Orient, with Leland Chen of Taiwan, age eighteen, the senior winner, and Xiao-Dong Wang, of the

People's Republic of China, age thirteen, the junior winner.* But above all the age limit demonstrated the soundness of Menuhin's idea that contests should encourage developing talent as much as reward achievement. Certainly the Menuhin Competition was a valuable learning experience for the fifty teenage contestants from Europe, India, the Far East, and America.

* See pp. 619–20.

VIOLINISTS OF ISRAEL

A NEW GROUP of violinists has emerged from Israel to continue the long line of distinguished nineteenth-century violinists of Jewish origin. Some of this "new breed" were born in Palestine or in the State of Israel (established in 1948), others arrived there as infants or youthful immigrants. They were given musical training at the Rubin Academies of Tel Aviv and Jerusalem, where they achieved a high level of proficiency under the guidance of experienced violin teachers, among them Alice Fenyves, Ilona Feher, and Yair Kless. A constructive force in string teaching and chamber music was Rami Shevelov, who organized his own workshops. In 1982 Shevelov accepted a position at the Juilliard School in New York, succeeding his late teacher Galamian.

The most gifted among the young violinists received scholarships to complete their education abroad, in Europe or, more often, in America. It seems that New York and Philadelphia, Boston and Indiana University have displaced the old European capitals as the most desirable places to acquire violin mastery, because of the excellence and innovative spirit of American music schools and the presence of internationally famous master teachers. The musical ambiance of a metropolis like New York exerted an added attraction. Another important factor was the scholarship program of the America-Israel Cultural Foundation, among whose recipients were Fried, Perlman, Zukerman, Luca, and Mintz.

596

Ivry Gitlis

Ivry Gitlis was born in Haifa in 1922, a generation older than the new crop of Israeli virtuosos, to Russian-Jewish parents. Ivry began to play the violin at the age of five and gave his first concert three years later. Huberman heard the boy when he was ten and recommended that he be sent to Paris for further studies. He entered the École Normale de Musique to work with Marcel Chailley and won a *premier prix* after three years. Apparently, young Gitlis was a restless and ever-dissatisfied student, for among his next teachers were Enesco, Thibaud, and Flesch. He spent World War II in England, working in a factory and playing for the troops. His career began in earnest after the war, when he made his London debut with the London Philharmonic and various appearances with major British orchestras. In 1951 he won first prize in the Thibaud Competition in Paris. Shortly thereafter, he made a recording of the Alban Berg concerto, which earned him the Grand Prix du Disque. He performed in the United States in 1955, but did not return until 1980. In the meantime he built an excellent reputation in Europe, Soviet Russia, Canada, and South America. Particularly his interpretations of contemporary music—Bartók, Prokofiev, Sibelius, Berg—have aroused much admiration. He approaches the music with powerful intensity and *élan*; his total involvement in the music communicates itself to the listener. At times he seems a bit eccentric and undisciplined, but his artistic sincerity is beyond doubt. His sensuous vibrato can produce infinite shadings of tone color; his technique is confident and strong.

Shmuel Ashkenasi and Rony Rogoff

Not all Israeli violinists are destined for immediate great careers, witness the slow rise of Shmuel Ashkenasi and Rony Rogoff, both born in Palestine in the early 1940s. Ashkenasi studied with Ilona Feher in Tel Aviv, until a scholarship enabled him to enter the Curtis Institute in Philadelphia under Efrem Zimbalist. In 1962 he won a second prize at the Tchaikovsky Competition in Moscow (he had previously been a finalist at the Queen Elisabeth Contest in Brussels), but it did not lead to a solo career. Ashkenasi joined the faculty of the University of Iowa and developed the excellent Iowa String Quartet. Recently he became first violinist of the Vermeer String Quartet in Chicago. He is an ex-

Anne-Sophie Mutter, a
beautifully gifted young
German violinist

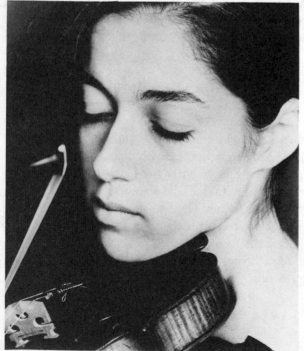

Miriam Fried, winner of the
Queen Elisabeth Prize, a performer of great intensity

quisite chamber-music player, with a lovely tone and perfect intonation, providing firm leadership without being overly assertive. His appearances in New York in 1981 and 1983 with the Vermeer Quartet received much praise in the New York *Times*.

Rony Rogoff, on the other hand, strives toward a big solo career, which so far has eluded him. His violin teacher in Israel was Rami Shevelov. Rogoff also studied at the Juilliard School with Galamian and Dorothy DeLay, in addition to some coaching with Joseph Szigeti in Switzerland. His appearances under Mehta and Celibidache were very successful, as were his recitals in New York in 1980 and 1981; his career now extends through Europe to the Far East. Performing on the famous 1715 Stradivari known as "Alard-Baron Knoop," Rogoff specializes in programs for unaccompanied violin, performing not only the complete cycle of Bach sonatas but also modern works by Stockhausen and Stravinsky. His playing is experienced and disciplined.

Edna Michell and Zvi Zeitlin

Edna Michell studied the violin in her native Tel Aviv with Alice Fenyves and Oedoen Partos. Yehudi Menuhin heard her when she was thirteen and recommended that she continue her studies abroad. At fifteen she entered the Guildhall School of Music in London, working with Rostal and coaching with Menuhin. Her successful debut at seventeen led to engagements in Europe, Israel, and America. Since 1965 she has lived in New York, where, in 1972, she organized the Cantilena Players; they have given authoritative performances of compositions especially written for them, by Avni, Foss, Orgad, Starer, and Tal, among others.

Also active in the United States is the excellent Zvi Zeitlin, born in 1923 in Russia and raised in Israel. He received most of his musical education in New York at Juilliard, with Sascha Jacobsen and Ivan Galamian. In 1940 he made his debut with the Palestine Orchestra and was first heard in New York in 1951 and London in 1961. He is known for his strong interest in contemporary music and has premiered works by Ben-Haim, Orgad, Rochberg, Schuller, and others. One of the few violinists to study the Schoenberg concerto, he introduced it to Israel in 1970, creating a heated controversy. (He recorded it with Rafael Kubelik in 1971.) In 1968, Zeitlin joined the violin faculty of the Eastman School of Music in Rochester where he is a member of the Eastman Trio.

Miriam Fried

Miriam Fried has a very personal style. She plays with utmost concentration and an introverted intensity, seemingly oblivious to the audience, and yet projecting convincingly. Her tone is warm but not cloying, her bow firm and elastic, her intonation impeccable. She is at her best in her rather severe repertoire—Beethoven, Brahms, Sibelius, Bach. I have also heard her play a few Paganini Caprices extremely well but without much display. She can handle anything, but will not stoop to "show off." This, perhaps, has made her ascent slower than she deserved.

Born in Rumania in 1946, Fried came to Israel with her family when she was two. Her mother, a piano teacher, started her on the piano when she was five, but she was attracted to the violin. At eight, she became a student of Alice Fenyves at the Tel Aviv Academy and stayed with her for a number of years. Obviously very talented, Miriam became the pride of the academy, playing for all the visiting celebrities. Among them was Isaac Stern, who recommended that she go abroad to study. After a year at the Conservatory at Geneva spent with Lorand Fenyves (a brother of her first teacher), she joined Gingold's class at Indiana University. It was a decisive turn, and she spent two years under his guidance:

> Gingold was a very big influence. When I came to him I didn't have a love affair with the violin. He adored the instrument. I didn't have a relationship with it. He taught me ways of looking for color in sound, and I've been doing it ever since. It opened up a completely new world.[1]

This is a remarkable confession. There are many gifted children who grow up playing the violin well without really enjoying it—it's too much of a daily drudgery. But Miriam seems to have overcome this under Gingold's influence. Moreover, Gingold gave her a solid technical foundation and a more self-critical attitude, beyond the fawning stance of a prodigy.

Her next step was New York and Galamian. She said, "Galamian was fabulous—particularly for me, because after 97 percent preparation I'd tend to quit working. . . . He persisted and would not let go, whether it took another week or another month, until I'd learn a work a hundred percent."[2]

While still Galamian's student at Juilliard, Fried won her first major competition—the Paganini Contest in Genoa in 1968. In the meantime she was under contract with Jeunesse Musicale, an international organization furthering young careers, on a modest scale. "I played under every tree on the Gaspé Peninsula," she reminisced.[3] In 1971 came the breakthrough—first prize in the Queen Elisabeth Competition in Brussels; in fact, she became the first woman to win the *grand prix*. Within a week, she had sixty-five engagements, and was now in the front rank of young violinists competing for public attention and concert engagements.

While still enrolled at Indiana University, Miriam Fried met her future husband, the violinist Paul Biss. She seems to thrive on a busy career attending to tours, motherhood, and a two-violinist home, not only personally but also as an artist. Her playing, once a bit on the severe side, has acquired a warmth and expansiveness, which shows her growth as an interpreter. In contrast to some virtuosos who like to repeat a few programs throughout a season, Miss Fried fears that this induces staleness. Still, her best repertoire piece seems to be the Sibelius concerto; here, Miriam Fried gives a performance that is hard to surpass.

Itzhak Perlman

Itzhak Perlman represents the perfect synthesis of artist and person: he plays as he is—warm, communicative, radiant, full of vitality and joy. His interpretations reveal thoughtfulness without brooding and an inner glow that communicates the innermost spirit of music to his listeners. Music is a natural way of self-expression for him—he speaks clearly and without affectation. But behind that apparent ease and simplicity there is much disciplined work, as well as a unique talent for music and a particular affinity for the violin.

The events of his life read like fiction. Born in Tel Aviv in 1945 to immigrant parents from eastern Europe, his perfect ear was discovered when he was two and a half years old. A year later he asked for a violin, whose sound he had heard on the radio. At age four he was stricken with polio; he recovered, but his legs remained paralyzed. Now that he was cut off from so many childhood joys, the violin became ever more meaningful to him. He had lessons at the Tel Aviv Academy of Music with Rivka Goldgart. Whenever famous artists visited the Academy, the curly-haired boy who moved on crutches and played the violin sitting down

Itzhak Perlman is at present the most accomplished violinist of his generation. The Israeli-born artist lives in New York.

was the center of attraction. He practiced three hours a day and covered the regular tedious curriculum of scales and exercises, but he also built up a repertoire of Vieuxtemps, Kreisler, and other "little things," and played occasionally with the Jerusalem Broadcast Orchestra. His career was pushed gently but not aggressively, because a large-scale solo career was thought to be impossible in view of his physical handicap.

The big change came in 1958: the thirteen-year-old Itzhak was chosen to represent Israel on the "Ed Sullivan Show" and to travel with Sullivan's Caravan of Stars through America. The two-month tour was an incredible experience for the boy who had never been outside his small native land. Eventually, the Perlman family settled in New York's Upper West Side so that Itzhak could continue his studies. The adjustment was not easy; he was homesick for his friends and his normal milieu. He supported his family by playing small engagements, usually at Jewish charity functions. But the main purpose of his being in New York was to perfect his violin playing under the guidance of Ivan Galamian and Dorothy DeLay. Isaac Stern, too, kept a fatherly eye on him. Miss DeLay took a personal hand in broadening the boy's artistic interests, as well as teaching him such practical matters as driving a hand-controlled car. Officially, he was enrolled as a student at the Juilliard School; the summers were spent at Meadowmount, Galamian's summer colony of violinists, where he met his future wife, Toby, also a violinist.

The decisive event that projected him into prominence was the Leventritt Award in 1964. It was followed, in 1965–66, by a coast-to-coast tour of thirty cities, by concerts in Europe, Australia, South America, and the Far East, and, of course, his native Israel. Since then, there has been no major orchestra, no major conductor with whom he has not appeared; he and Zubin Mehta have a particular musical affinity. Other musicians with whom Perlman performs frequently are his sonata partner Vladimir Ashkenazy and the cellist Lynn Harrell. Perlman and Pinchas Zukerman, who plays the violin and the viola with equal mastery, have toured Europe and America in special programs for two violins and for violin-viola duets. Born in the same country, brought up in a similar milieu, trained by the same teacher, and virtually the same age, they can blend their playing as no other two string players can. Perlman has also performed with the pianist-conductor André Previn (with whom he has recorded some jazz and Scott Joplin rags) and his constant piano collaborator Samuel Sanders.

Perlman's repertoire, expanded slowly over the years, is by now amazing in its breadth. At first, he was most comfortable in the Ro-

mantic and the virtuoso repertoire: "You can tell your age by the repertory you are asked to play. At 19, I had Paganini, Tchaikovsky, Wieniawski coming out of my ears. Now I play Mozart, Beethoven, Brahms,
Bartók, Stravinsky, I'm getting old!" He now finds the Classical repertoire more challenging: "It's just you and the music. Timing and pac-
ing are much more critical." Late Beethoven, according to Perlman, is
"like learning a new language, totally hermetic and sealed."[1] It speaks
for Perlman's musical inquisitiveness that he learned that language by
playing Beethoven's late string quartets. It helped mature his Beethoven
interpretation: the Beethoven sonata cycle which he recorded with
Ashkenazy must be counted among his greatest achievements, next to
the cycle of the six Bach solo sonatas and partitas, which astounded
and captivated connoisseurs and laymen alike. The polyphonic richness
of sound that he extracted from his Stradivari was unbelievable. After
such gigantic achievements, he can play with obvious fun-loving enjoyment such ditties as *Yankee Doodle* by Vieuxtemps, or his arrangements of Scott Joplin, or a Kreisler encore. He has also expanded into the
twentieth century, playing the concertos of Stravinsky, Berg, and Bartók,
to name but a few.

Good as Perlman was at the beginning of his career, the rise to
greatness came through work, experience, self-criticism, and listening to
the criticism of his peers. Though heeding what Isaac Stern and Robert
Mann have to say, he basically listens to himself. When he was young,
there was, of course, an imitative period, when he tried to emulate his
violinistic idols. "There was the Heifetz period, when I used a lot of
fast vibrato and fast tempi; the Oistrakh period, when I tried wide vibrato and sensuous rich tone, and the Stern period—when I didn't
vibrate for a whole year."[2] The last statement is, of course, facetious,
but it indicates an intellectual approach to sound which should not be
invariably "beautiful," but should be adapted to the character and style
of the piece performed. Ultimately, a young artist sheds all imitation,
discards all influences, and fuses everything into his own personal style.
If the result is unmistakably *his*, as in the case of Perlman, then greatness is achieved.

Anybody who has ever been to a Perlman concert will remember
forever the first impression. The lights go down, and across the stage
walks a young man on crutches, with a radiant smile, followed by either
the pianist or the conductor carrying his violin. Perlman bows briefly,
then settles down on the chair provided for him, and lays the crutches
on the floor within reach. He is given the violin, he tunes ever so briefly,

The versatile Pinchas Zukerman is a violinist, violist, and conductor, and does everything with equal mastery.
Shlomo Mintz has risen rapidly into the forefront of the young generation of superb performers. He is still in his twenties.

and suddenly that violin has become part of him. He begins to play, and he bares his soul. Swept away by the music, he sweeps his listeners along as well. It is his ability to take a mass of people into his musical confidence, to make them share his personal experience, that is the secret of his communicativeness.

Pinchas Zukerman

Pinchas Zukerman is not just a violinist: his name appears increasingly with the designation "conductor." In fact, he has a permanent post as musical director of the St. Paul Chamber Orchestra. He follows a tradition of violinists from the Baroque era to the nineteenth century who led an orchestra from the first-violin desk, violin in hand.* When Zukerman or Menuhin, Szeryng or Schneider, stand in front of a chamber orchestra, playing and conducting at the same time, they merely revive centuries of tradition. Care must be taken, however, lest what is gained by unity of approach—dispensing with the "middle man," the baton conductor—be lost by a less polished solo performance, a diminished concentration of the soloist on his instrumental control. Judging by the results that Zukerman obtains with the St. Paul Chamber Orchestra, he not only plays with greater intensity, but is able to impart some of his insights to the string players.

A "born" violinist, with enormous innate facility for the instrument, Zukerman gives the deceptive impression that violin playing is not really all that difficult. There is nothing labored, nothing studied about the way he handles the violin, though, of course, this inborn facility had to be developed, polished, directed.

Even as a youngster, Zukerman was supremely self-confident, not to say "cocky." Stern remembers his first encounter with the boy Pinky, already a "prodigy": "I remember the first time I heard them both [Perlman and Zukerman]. Pinky was a brassy kid. He put his two feet down, stared you in the eye and dared you not to like it. He had such marvelous impudence."[1]

Three years younger than Perlman, Zukerman was born in 1948— also in Tel Aviv, also of immigrant east European parents. But "Pinky" had a healthy and untroubled childhood. His father, a musician too, gave him the first violin lessons, and at the age of eight he entered the

* Louis Spohr, in 1820, was the first to put aside violin and bow, replacing them with a baton, to the consternation of the orchestra.

Tel Aviv Music Academy as student of Ilona Feher. His talent was immediately recognized and attracted the attention of visiting dignitaries. Isaac Stern first heard him in 1960 and arranged for him to study at Juilliard with Galamian. Transplanted to New York in 1961, he had a difficult time adjusting to a new language and a strange milieu. Living with a foster family, growing up without the guidance of parents, was a sad and lonely experience. He dropped out of high school because of language problems. At Juilliard, it took all of Galamian's enormous authority to keep the rebellious youngster attending to his work. But there were compensations: here he met Eugenia Rich, first flutist of the Juilliard Orchestra. As she describes the courtship, "he was an eighteen-year-old kid who kept staring at me and sending me notes." They were married in 1968 and are a successful duo, appearing in joint concerts in America and abroad.

In May 1967, Zukerman was cowinner of the Leventritt Award, which he shared with the Korean violinist Kyung-Wha Chung. This marked the beginning of his career: contracts with Sol Hurok and Columbia Records, a Carnegie Hall debut and rave notices. He still records for Columbia, both as violinist and as conductor, and the variety of his repertoire is astounding, from the Baroque music of Vivaldi to the concertos of Elgar and Bartók. There is also an attractive recording of jazz music played with the pianist-composer Claude Bolling. A set of recordings of the complete Beethoven trios, with the pianist Daniel Barenboim and the cellist Jacqueline DuPré, is by now a collector's item: radiant performances of three young artists completely attuned to each other.

Zukerman's musical activities are extremely multifaceted: solo recitals (usually with the pianist Marc Neikrug), sonata cycles with Daniel Barenboim, appearances as soloist with orchestra, performances as violinist-conductor with chamber orchestra, chamber-music concerts with colleagues like Stern, Perlman, and his wife Eugenia, and finally his expanding conducting career. Moreover, on many of these occasions he plays viola as well as violin, switching from one instrument to the other within one evening. Yet he always appears totally unruffled, totally in control. In fact, sometimes he seems too much in control, giving the impression of detachment, as if he were not fully committed, a kind of noble, blasé indifference. He seems more involved when playing the viola—his dark, burnished tone takes on an intensity that at times surpasses his violin playing. When he conducts, he is absorbed by the technical aspects of an art that is new to him, leaving no time or place for routine.

Some close to Zukerman worry lest that new activity will diminish his powers as a violinist, but conversely it might add new insight to his interpretations. He himself sees only the positive aspects, an extension rather than a replacement of his earlier career:

I was born to play the fiddle. It's so natural for me. But music is an extraordinary, intense ideal, and we musicians are constantly learning, preparing, changing. I am rarely satisfied when I play. The ideal disappears and I try for the best possible performance. Since I've been conducting, I hear so much more when I play with orchestra. I wonder how I didn't hear it four or five years ago.[2]

At this time, Zukerman divides his time about equally between conducting and violin or viola performances. Within the next few years, the problem will arise whether one will encroach on the other. The violin is a jealous taskmaster; it will not tolerate neglect. But Pinky's vital optimism does not foresee any such tragedy; he cannot stop playing the violin, just as he cannot stop breathing. "I'm living music all the time. To live your life with that as a guideline is a tremendous blessing."[3]

Sergiu Luca

The name of Sergiu Luca is not often mentioned among the top-flight violinists of the Israeli school. He deserves far more attention, because he has branched out into a field of specialization ignored by most virtuosos—authentic performances of eighteenth-century violin music using historically accurate equipment. This involves a violin with old fittings (gut strings, lower pitch, flatter bridge, shorter neck) and the use of several eighteenth-century bows, which are different in weight and tension from the modern Tourte bow in use since 1790. After having made a thorough study of historic performance practices, Luca has evolved a system of using three basic bows: a "Baroque" bow of about 1650 for the repertoire of Bach and his contemporaries, a "transitional" bow of the period before 1770 for Haydn, Mozart, and their Italian and French contemporaries, and a modern-style Tourte bow of around 1800. His two violins are a Nicolò Amati of 1669 with original fittings and a Carlo Bergonzi of 1733 with modernized fittings.

Luca's ability to switch from one piece of equipment to the other is remarkable. Within one evening's program, I have heard him play Bach and Tartini with the Baroque bow, Nardini and Mozart with the transitional bow (all on the Amati violin), then Schubert and Paganini with the Tourte bow on the Bergonzi violin. Needless to say, the entire performance style had to be adjusted from one period to the other.

Among the professional violinists struggling with such problems, Sergiu Luca is among the best. Born in Bucharest, Rumania, in 1944, Luca had his first violin lessons at the age of four from a gypsy. When he was seven, his family moved to Israel, where he continued his studies. At thirteen, he became a student of Max Rostal, at first in London, then at the Bern Conservatory. In 1960, Luca played an audition for Isaac Stern, who was appearing in Lucerne. It changed his life. Stern arranged for young Luca (then sixteen) to come to Philadelphia in order to study at the Curtis Institute with Galamian. Four years later, Luca won the Philadelphia Orchestra Youth Auditions and performed the Sibelius concerto with that orchestra. In 1965 he played the same concerto with the New York Philharmonic under Leonard Bernstein.

At that time, Luca was recognized as one of the most gifted of the young crop of concert violinists, with technique to burn and a fiery temperament. He began to make a career with the standard repertoire. It was only later that his interest in old music led him to an investigation as to *how* this old music ought to be played. He received much valuable advice from the scholar and violin historian David Boyden, who, in turn, became an avid admirer of Luca's experiments with old bows and old fittings. At present, Luca is recognized as a foremost performer in authentic eighteenth-century playing style, while continuing a conventional career with a repertoire from Beethoven to the present, and teaching at the University of Illinois.

Shlomo Mintz

The fair-haired boy of the Israeli group is Shlomo Mintz, who is rapidly rising into prominence. Born in 1957 in Russia, he was two years old when he was brought to Israel. He studied the violin with Ilona Feher and at age fifteen astonished everyone when he played the Paganini Concerto in D major with Mehta and the Israel Philharmonic, replacing the indisposed Perlman at short notice. The following year he made his Carnegie Hall debut in the Bruch concerto and "played with the poise and technical assurance of a veteran performer."[1] Mintz was brought to New York by Stern and the America-Israel Cultural Foundation to complete his studies at Juilliard with Dorothy DeLay. Since his debut in 1973 he has grown and matured as an artist. Without entering any contests, he has won recognition as one of the outstanding young virtuosos of the day. His adaptability is remarkable for one so young—a refined style when playing Mozart, a brilliant one for Paganini. He has all the equipment for a big career—beautiful tone, impeccable technique, noble musicality. His interpretations are not yet very personal, but this will change with age. After his debut in London, the *Times* wrote, "He must soon be recognized as a violinist worth hearing as often as possible."[2] He was also successful in Berlin and Vienna. His international career is assured: he is playing one hundred twenty concerts a year.

Others

Israel provided a haven for many Soviet and east European musicians emigrating during the 1970s. Among them were finished professionals, who were integrated into the musical life of the country as soloists, chamber musicians, orchestral players, teachers, composers, scholars. Established orchestras accepted the best of the string players, while smaller groups gained new strength by the influx. Performers of solo calibre were eager for a world career and tried their luck in Europe and America, with varying success. Philip Hirshhorn, a graduate of the Leningrad Conservatory under M. Vaiman, won first prize at the 1967 Queen Elisabeth Competition in Brussels as a Soviet representative; after some time spent in Israel (where I heard him in 1973) he now lives in Brussels. Dora Schwarzberg, born in Tashkent, studied at the Stolyarsky school in Odessa and with Yankelevich at the Moscow Conservatory; after settling in Israel in 1973 she made her debut with the Israel Philharmonic Orchestra and won first prize in the 1976 Carl Flesch Competition in London, leading to engagements in Europe and America. Concertizing widely is Silvia Marcovici, who emigrated from Rumania. Sergiu Schwartz arrived in Israel from the same country as a teenager in 1973; after completing his army service, he went to London and New York for study and performances, making his New York debut under the auspices of Artists International. The Soviet-born Liba Shacht won her first prize at the age of eleven in her native Lithuania. After emigrating to Israel, she continued her studies in Tel Aviv and recently in New York, where she was a winner of the 1983 Town Hall Select Debut series.

There is a present trend in Israeli educational circles to teach prodi-

gies at home rather than to send them abroad too soon. At the recent
Huberman Centennial (December 1982) two young Israeli violinists performed side by side with the celebrities assembled for the festive occasion—Shira Ravin (born 1969) and Roy Shiloah (born 1970), both
studying with the concertmaster of the Israel Philharmonic, Chaim
Taub. With master Isaac Stern in the lead, they gave a joyous performance of a Vivaldi concerto.

VIOLINISTS
OF THE ORIENT

MUSICIANS FROM THE ORIENT attaining high positions in the Western world are a comparative novelty. Since World War II, the United States has become a magnet for gifted musicians from the Orient, replacing Vienna as the most desirable place for study. Tradition could still be learned in Vienna, but the juices of new ideas were flowing in the New World. Some violinists turned to Soviet Russia, to the conservatories of Moscow and Leningrad, where the legendary Auer method was still taught. Otherwise, war-afflicted Europe had no counterparts to schools such as Juilliard, Curtis, Tanglewood, or Aspen. So they came to the States from Japan, South Korea, Taiwan—well-prepared youngsters, used to parental authority, attentive, disciplined, eager, motivated, and above all talented. A wise reservation comes from Isaac Stern: "The Asian respect for teacher, for art, for music, is both a help and a hindrance. Sometimes you have to show disrespect in order to find your way."[1] Likewise, the Japanese violinist Katsuko Esaki recognizes certain inhibitions built into the Oriental psyche—"It is painful for Orientals, particularly for the Japanese, to show deep feelings. It goes against everything we were taught."[2] But obviously these are not insurmountable difficulties. True, Galamian has found his pupils from the Orient more disciplined; it must indeed be flattering to a teacher to be "feared like people fear God" (to quote his student Kyung-Wha Chung). Even with a mild-mannered teacher like Dorothy DeLay, Oriental students have felt inhibited: "It's been an education for me, expressing myself, finding the courage to question a musical idea of Miss DeLay's," said the young Taiwanese Cho-Liang Lin. The phenomenal cellist Yo-Yo Ma, who grew up in Paris under the tutelage of his Chinese-born father, remembers having been "terrified of my father, who could never be contradicted." Apparently, under the influence of the "permissive" society in America, many of these ingrained inhibitions disappear, and we see the blossoming of young, talented musicians who combine the best of two worlds.

Slowly disappearing is the prejudice of the Western world—"Can Orientals really feel and interpret Western music"—as one after another Oriental violinists take prizes in international competitions, win coveted engagements, and charm audiences everywhere. The flood of students coming from the Orient to Europe and particularly to the United States (in the Juilliard Preparatory Department—ages eight to eighteen—Asians account for almost forty percent of the total enrollment) is steadily increasing and will undoubtedly be swelled further by applicants from the People's Republic of China, which until now did not encourage study abroad.

Japan

Japanese violin playing came to international attention when the Suzuki method, named after its founder Shinichi Suzuki (born 1898), became known in the West. The son of a violin builder, Suzuki studied the violin first in Japan, then in Berlin during the 1920s with Karl Klingler, one of Joachim's finest students. Beginning in 1933, he developed his philosophy of education and its application to violin teaching. Just as small children learn to speak their mother tongue regardless of native intelligence, so could children acquire the ability to play the violin "by rote" if environment and conditions were conducive to develop this latent ability. Although Suzuki does not rule out hereditary factors of innate musicality, he believes that any child can develop a considerable level of achievement if guided according to his concepts. Two years after he founded his own institute in 1950, 196 pupils graduated; twenty years later, in 1972, the graduates numbered 2321. At the annual meeting of his institute, one can hear three thousand children, aged three and older, play a Classical minuet or gavotte in unison; older children might perform a Mozart concerto as a group. Suzuki began touring the United States in 1964, demonstrating his method with groups of small children. At present many classes are held in various cities by teachers trained in the Suzuki method; it is an accepted (though not always approved) approach to teaching the violin to small children. It must be remembered that the child does not learn to read music until later; the handling of the instrument, the playing by ear and repetition come first. An important factor is that one parent must learn the violin alongside the child so that they can play and develop their ability together.

One of Suzuki's first pupils—before he developed the group method—was Toshiya Eto (born Tokyo, 1927). At the age of twelve, young Eto won a national competition and continued his studies at the Academy of Music in Tokyo. After World War II, he came to Philadelphia to work with Zimbalist at the Curtis Institute.

Eto made his highly successful Carnegie Hall debut in 1952. From 1953 to 1961 he taught at the Curtis Institute, but decided to return to Japan to teach. (It is interesting to note that Eto disagrees with the Suzuki method.) At the same time he continued his international concert career, characterized by an "expressive approach to the established Romantic repertory . . . balanced by wit and agility in more recent music."[1]

Another Suzuki student is Ekko Sato. She must have studied with him as a small child, for I met her in Leonid Kogan's Moscow Conservatory class in 1962, when she seemed to be in her early teens. Her playing of Lalo's *Symphonie espagnole* and a solo sonata by Ysaÿe in class was note-perfect, but she was as yet unformed as a musical personality. Later that year she made her debut with orchestra, but the stolid accompaniment obscured much of her childish charm. In 1966 she won the third prize at the Tchaikovsky Competition. Among the postcontest statements of the jury were those of Professor Tsyganov of the U.S.S.R.—"She is an enormous talent with a brilliant, confident, artistically free style. She masters the whole arsenal of performance technique with unusual brilliance"—and Philip Newman of England—"Whatever she played was full of brilliance."[2] However, little has been heard of Miss Sato since then.

The same 1966 Tchaikovsky Contest produced another Japanese prizewinner, Masuko Ushioda, who placed second. Szigeti mentions her as one of his advanced students, but before that she had studied for several years with Mikhail Vaiman at the Leningrad Conservatory. According to Professor Tsyganov,

> One of the discoveries of this contest was the performance of the talented Japanese violinist Masuko Ushioda. . . . Her

playing is marked by musical maturity and finished artistry. At each round of the contest Miss Ushioda convinced us invariably that she was a performer of unusual concentration, a bold creative personality deeply dedicated to music. Here one could feel the beneficial influence of J. Szigeti with whom she is working at the present time.[3]

Undoubtedly, Miss Ushioda had studied the Bartók concerto with Szigeti, who could convey to her the personal tradition of the composer. Since then she has made a recording of that concerto and other repertoire works, including the complete cycle of Bach's solo sonatas.

Miss Ushioda was born in Tokyo in 1942 and began studying the violin at an early age. At thirteen she made her debut with the Tokyo Symphony and at fifteen won the Mainichi Competition in Tokyo. She was also among the prizewinners at the 1963 Queen Elisabeth Competition in Brussels. Despite the prizes, her career moves slowly.

At the Tchaikovsky Contest of 1970 (the year Kremer won first prize), the second prize was divided between Vladimir Spivakov and the Japanese Mayumi Fujikawa, at that time twenty-four years old. While Kremer and Spivakov have since then achieved enviable reputations in Europe and America, Miss Fujikawa's recognition is still lagging behind, though her time will undoubtedly come. Rarely have I read such praise about any young contestant as appeared in the *Soviet Music Journal* about Miss Fujikawa: "She is one of the rarest talents. . . . Everything about her is attractive—such technical freedom, such charm, such purity coming from the heart, such freshness. . . ." Another member of the jury called her "a marvelous phenomenon, full of harmony and unparalleled plasticity . . . [combining] the charm and spiritual purity of Japanese art with the fundamentals of European musical culture. . . ."[4] A complete cycle of Mozart concertos, recorded by Miss Fujikawa in London, reveals an artistry of great finesse and impeccable style.

An extremely fine and polished violinist is Yoko Matsuda. I first heard her in 1961—a slim, determined girl of about nineteen, who was studying with Broadus Erle at Yale University. She played the Brahms concerto with such intensity and grandeur, coupled with technical control, that a great career seemed in store for her. But only gradually did she win the recognition she deserved. At present, she is the leader of the Sequoia String Quartet, which recently won the Walter Naumburg Award in New York and is on the way of gaining national attention. Miss Matsuda and her quartet are on the faculty of the California Arts Institute.

The latest violin prodigy from Japan is a ten-year-old girl, Mi Dori, who created a sensation when Zubin Mehta presented her unannounced at a Young People's Concert of the New York Philharmonic on December 30, 1982. Little Mi, in a bright red dress and black shoes, played Paganini's Concerto No. 1 with the aplomb of a veteran (which one critic found disturbing)[5] and received a standing ovation. One cannot dismiss a performance like that as pure mimicry, and the natural musicality of a child may well respond to the sweet melodiousness of Paganini's tunes.

South Korea

Korea, having endured occupation and annexation through half of this century, followed by a fratricidal war, is only beginning to emerge on the world musical scene.

South Korea has become a strong rival to the Japanese school. Among the artists that country has recently produced are the Chung family, who created quite a stir at the Juilliard School in New York: the violinist Kyung-Wha, her older sister, the cellist Myung-Wha, and their pianist-brother Myung-Whun, who recently added conducting to his accomplishments. While in general pursuing separate careers, the Chung Trio combined its talents in a beautiful chamber-music concert at Carnegie Hall in December 1982.

The violinist Kyung-Wha Chung was nine years old when she made her debut with orchestra in her native city of Seoul and twelve when she arrived in New York in 1961 to study with Ivan Galamian. She had many "Oriental complexes," as she calls them: she was too timid to speak English, was terrified of her teacher, felt pressured by obligations to her family and her country, always afraid to disappoint them. She was studious and obviously superbly gifted for the violin, despite her small, delicate hands. In 1967 she entered the Leventritt Contest in New York and divided the first prize with Pinchas Zukerman. Her international career began with a splendid success in London in 1970, when she played the Tchaikovsky concerto with the London Symphony Orchestra under André Previn. The orchestra was so impressed that Miss Chung was invited to join as soloist in a Far Eastern tour. Offers of engagements came from all over Britain, which has become, in her words, "the base of my career." In New York her reputation is steadily growing; after her Carnegie Hall recital in 1980 she was

The gifted Kyung-Wha Chung is a fiery and colorful performer of music both old and new. She is from South Korea but studied in New York.

The young Taiwanese Cho-Liang Lin is rising fast as a brilliantly gifted performer. He studied in New York at Juilliard.

COLUMBIA ARTISTS MANAGEMENT

Thirteen-year-old Xiao-Dong Wang from the People's Republic of China was first-prize winner in the junior division of the Yehudi Menuhin Violin Competition, 1983 in Folkestone.

called by the New York *Times* "certainly one of the most distinguished among today's younger generation of violinists."[1] Miss Chung is a many-faceted young artist; sometimes she appears cool, controlled, and objective; at other times she is full of fire and temperament, communicating her own intensity and a special suppleness of phrasing. This was particularly apparent when she played the Mendelssohn concerto with the Chicago Symphony under Sir Georg Solti: instead of rushing into the *molto appassionato* of the first movement, she gave it a pensive, introspective reading, shaping each lyric phrase with sensitive insight. Her recording of the Beethoven concerto also stresses the lyric aspects and moderate tempos, while modern concertos (Walton, Stravinsky) elicit springy interpretations. She seems to be discovering her own soul as the memories of Galamian's strict discipline wear off. Watching her play, one senses that her body, her violin, and the music are all fused into one inseparable entity—an utterly enchanting experience. At present she plays some 120 performances a year all over the world, and one can only hope that she preserves that springlike spontaneity.

Also a student of Galamian is Young-Uck Kim (born 1948). He made his orchestral debut in New York during the 1966–67 season, but waited to give a New York recital until February 1976. By then he was twenty-eight and an experienced performer. Playing a big program consisting of a Bach partita, Beethoven's *Kreutzer Sonata*, Stravinsky's *Duo concertante*, and some shorter pieces, he won the praise of Shirley Fleming, who wrote in *Musical America*,

> He [is] a patrician fiddler, commanding a silvery, pure-spun tone, an electric sense of rhythm, and the ability to calibrate dynamics and the placement of phrase against phrase to a fine measure. He is not a big-toned splashy, colorful player, but a fine-etched, neatly drawn one, sensitive to nuance and to structure within the framework of a carefully projected palette.[2]

He speaks for all of his colleagues when he says, "When I play music, it never occurs to me that I am a Korean. I am a musician."

Two other emerging Korean violinists are Dong-Suk Kang (born 1954), winner in 1974 of the second prize in the Carl Flesch Competition in London, and the precocious Sung-Ju Lee, who played as soloist with the Seoul Philharmonic at the age of nine. Later, she won prizes at the Sibelius Competition and the 1975 Kosciuszko Foundation and has appeared with the orchestras of St. Louis and Seattle.

Isaac Stern has said of Korean musicians,

They are called the Italians of the Orient—they are cruder, warmer, more loutish, but also more human. I think it is because their society is less codified than the others. The freedom, turbulence, and passion show in their music making.[3]

Taiwan

Modern independent Taiwan is barely thirty years old, and though it has an old, indigenous culture, there has not been enough time to produce musicians schooled in the style of Western music.

The latest musical sensation from Taiwan is a young violinist named Cho-Liang Lin (born 1960). His father was a physicist, his mother a teacher of English. Cho-Liang was encouraged to try the violin at the age of five, and won the Taiwan National Youth Competition at the age of twelve. He was sent to live with relatives in Australia and continued his violin studies. After winning a concerto contest in 1975, he came to America to study with Dorothy DeLay at the Juilliard School. Lin, too, is upset when people doubt his ability to interpret Mozart or Brahms because he is Oriental. His debut in a Mozart concerto at the Mostly Mozart Festival in August 1979 was a resounding success: "it was a mature interpretation imbued with the freshness of youth."[1] Since then, both Lin's playing and his career have developed with giant steps. His recent performance of the Saint-Saëns Concerto No. 3 with the Baltimore Symphony proved that his tone, once considered small, can now fill Carnegie Hall with glorious sound, and he plays with much passion and involvement. Stern's prediction of Lin as one of the three great Oriental musicians is coming true.[2]

Also a native of Taiwan, though a few years younger, is Leland Chen (born 1965), who won first prize in the senior division of the 1983 International Menuhin Competition in Folkestone. What made his performance so impressive was his musical versatility: he seemed to master every style from Bach to Bartók and at the end dazzled the listeners with Vieuxtemps's Fifth Concerto. Chen's technique is impeccable, his tone is warm and sensuous, his musicianship serious and probing. Since the age of thirteen he has studied at Stoke d'Abernon with Robert Masters and enjoyed the artistic guidance of Yehudi Menuhin. Chen is a major talent destined for an international career.

The People's Republic of China

In February 1981 the documentary film *From Mao to Mozart: Isaac Stern in China* was shown in New York. It afforded fascinating glimpses into the musical life of Peking and Shanghai—far too brief, yet very revealing. The young pianists, violinists, and cellists seemed talented and intensely musical. The violinists, playing difficult pieces like the concertos of Brahms and Sibelius, the *Rondo capriccioso* of Saint-Saëns, were quite accomplished. There can be no doubt that, once the cultural barriers are lowered, we shall witness a whole generation of emerging Chinese musicians.

Yehudi Menuhin, who also visited the People's Republic of China, has four Chinese students who are studying at his schools in Stoke d'Abernon and in Gstaad. Menuhin is very optimistic about the future development of musical ties between China and the Western world. The Peking government sent several contestants to participate in Menuhin's International Violin Competition in Folkestone in April 1983. The young Chinese violinists, all trained at the conservatories of Peking or Shanghai, were successful beyond expectations. In the junior division they won the three top prizes: first, Xiao-Dong Wang (age thirteen), second, Zheng-Rong Wang (age fifteen), third, Le Zhang (age fifteen). Among the seniors, the talented Hong-Ying He placed fourth. Remarkable was the official care surrounding the young contestants: they were accompanied by two pianists and a violin teacher and housed at the Chinese Embassy while in London. All the young contestants were beautifully schooled and impeccably prepared, yet there was nothing "drilled" about their playing; in fact, each of them had a distinct personality. Off stage they were happy and relaxed, on stage they were serious and showed experience in playing in public (all had won at least one contest in their native country). Hearing the young Chinese violinists was a joyous experience. It will be interesting to watch their future development; indeed, the next decades will show the unfolding of the enormous musical potential of the People's Republic of China.

NOTES

PART ONE: *The Distant Past: 1530–1600*

THE EMERGENCE OF THE VIOLIN AS A NEW INSTRUMENT

1. Gerald R. Hayes, *Musical Instruments*, 2:160.
2. Quoted in David Boyden, *History of Violin Playing*, 25, 28, 29 n. 4.
3. Quoted in Hayes, *Instruments*, 164–65.
4. Quoted in Boyden, *History*, 31–32.

PART TWO: *The Age of Experimentation: 1600–1700*

NORTHERN EUROPE

English Violinists
1. Anthony Wood, quoted in Ernst Meyer, *English Chamber Music*, 209.
2. Charles Burney, *General History*, 2:338.
3. Ibid., 366–67.
4. Meyer, *English Chamber Music*, 206.
5. Jack Westrup, *Purcell*, 48.
6. Roger North, quoted ibid., 236.

Austria and Germany
1. Charles Burney, *General History*, 2:462.

FRANCE
1. David Boyden, *History of Violin Playing*, 137.
2. E. van der Straeten, *History of the Violin*, 1:75.

PART THREE: *The Classics of the Violin: 1700–1800*

ITALY

Arcangelo Corelli
1. Quoted in Oliver Strunk, *Source Readings*, 449.
2. Charles Burney, *General History*, 2:443.
3. John Hawkins, *A General History of Music*, 2:676; Marc Pincherle, *Corelli*, 52.
4. Author of these passages is the English translator J. E. Galliard (1709). See *The Musical Quarterly* (July 1946):419, n. 15, and 419–20.
5. Burney, *General History*, 2:442.
6. Ibid., 446.

Antonio Vivaldi
1. Charles de Brosses, *Lettres familières*, quoted in Marc Pincherle, *Vivaldi, Genius of the Baroque*, 19.
2. P. Molmenti, *La vie privée en Venise*, quoted in Pincherle, ibid., 21.
3. Pincherle, ibid., 16–17.
4. J. J. Quantz, *Lebenslauf*, quoted in Pincherle, ibid., 47.
5. Quoted in Pincherle, ibid., 51.
6. Pincherle, ibid., 41.
7. Ibid.
8. March 6, 1715. Pincherle, ibid., 42.
9. Walter Kolneder, *Vivaldi*, 146, and Plate XV.
10. Pincherle, *Vivaldi*, 89. See Michael Talbot, "The Path to Rediscovery," in *Vivaldi*, 1–13.
11. J. J. Quantz, *Versuch einer Anweisung*, 309–10. Quoted in Kolneder, *Vivaldi*, 104.

Giuseppe Tartini
1. J. A. Hiller, *Lebensbeschreibungen*, quoted in Andreas Moser, *Geschichte des Violinspiels*, 2:226.
2. Charles Burney, *Music in France and Italy*, 129.
3. J. J. Quantz, *Lebenslauf*, quoted in Moser, *Geschichte des Violinspiels*, 1:227.
4. Quantz, *Versuch einer Anweisung*, 310.
5. Quoted in Minos Dounias, *Violinkonzerte Tartinis*, 199.
6. Quoted in Paul Brainard, *Violinsonaten Tartinis*, 1:66.
7. Opinions in this paragraph quoted in Dounias, *Violinkonzerte*, 196, 213.
8. Brosses, quoted in Dounias, ibid., 193.
9. La Laurencie, *L'école française de violon*, 2:505.
10. Title of Italian manuscript, published in French as *Traité des Agréments de la musique*, Paris, 1771.
11. Burney, *Music in France and Italy*, 126.
12. Ibid., 131.
13. Burney, *General History*, 2:449–50.
14. Lalande, *Voyage d'Italie*, quoted in A. Capri, *Tartini*, 19–20.

Francesco Geminiani

1. Charles Burney, *General History*, 2:991 (based on second-hand information).
2. Ibid., 992.
3. John Hawkins, *General History*, 2:848.
4. Ibid., 850.
5. Burney, *General History*, 2:991.
6. Hawkins, *General History*, 2:903.
7. Burney, *General History*, 2:993.
8. Nonesuch H 71151; Newell Jenkins, conductor.
9. W. H. G. Flood, "Geminiani in England and Ireland," *Sammelbände der Internationalen Musikgesellschaft* 12 (1910–11):111.
10. Hawkins, *General History*, 2:904.
11. Burney, *General History*, 2:993.
12. Leopold Mozart, *Versuch einer gründlichen Violinschule*, and Abbé le fils, *Principes du violon*.
13. Geminiani, *The Art of Playing the Violin*. Facsimile edition, London, 1952, with introduction by David Boyden.

Francesco Veracini

1. Charles Burney, *General History*, 2:990.
2. November 25, 1735. Quoted in O. E. Deutsch, *Handel: A Documentary Biography*, 395–96.
3. Charles de Brosses, *Lettres familières* (see *The New Grove*, 19:628).
4. Burney, *General History*, 2:451.
5. Ibid., 450.
6. Luigi Torchi, *La musica instrumentale in Italia*, 179f.

Pietro Locatelli

1. Told in Albert Dunning, *Locatelli*, 1:112–13.
2. Ibid., 118–19, from Dutch translation of Charles Burney, *Music in the Netherlands*.
3. Arend Koole, *Leven van Locatelli*, 17.
4. Burney, *Music in the Netherlands*, 2:290.
5. Quoted in Dunning, *Locatelli*, 1:204.
6. Luigi Torchi, *La musica istrumentale in Italia*, 179f.
7. This and the following three quotations from Dunning, *Locatelli*, 1:203–5, 118.
8. Koole, *Leven van Locatelli*, 60.
9. Burney, *Music in the Netherlands*, 2:291.
10. Burney, *General History*, 2:454.
11. Dunning, *Locatelli*, 1:279.
12. Dittersdorf, *Lebensbeschreibung*, quoted in Dunning, ibid., 178.
13. Fétis, "Paganini," in G. de Courcy, *Paganini the Genoese*, 1:46.

Gaetano Pugnani

1. Charles de Brosses, *Lettres familières*, quoted in *Die Musik in Geschichte und Gegenwart*, "Somis," 12, col. 863.
2. *Mercure de France*, March 1754, quoted in E. Zschinsky-Troxler, *Pugnani*, 40–41.

Pietro Nardini

1. Letter to Padre Martini, May 8, 1761, quoted in M. Dounias, *Violinkonzerte Tartinis*, 201.
2. Charles Burney, *Music in Italy*, 129.

3. Letter of Leopold Mozart, July 11, 1763, in E. Anderson, trans., *Letters of Mozart and His Family*, 1:33–34.
4. G. B. Rangoni, *Essai sur le goût dans la musique*, 38.
5. C. F. D. Schubart, *Aesthetik der Tonkunst*, 35f.
6. Burney, *Music in Italy*, 258–59.
7. Adalbert Gyrowetz, *Selbst-Biographie*, 19.
8. The spurious Concerto in E minor was arranged by Miska Hauser (c. 1880), who based his version on an obscure viola sonata by Nardini arranged after several violin sonatas by L. A. Zellner (1877). See A. Moser, *Geschichte des Violinspiels*, 1st ed., 259–60.
9. Flesch edition of Sonata No. 2, C. F. Peters, New York; *Six Sonatas*, ed. Paul Doktor, G. Schirmer, New York.

GERMANY AND AUSTRIA

Violinists Around Johann Sebastian Bach
1. The Bach Fugue in C major was first published in Cartier, *L'Art du violon*, 1798.
2. *Denkmäler Deutscher Tonkunst*, Vols. 29–30 (1906), Preface, p. xii.
3. Schubart, quoted in *Die Musik in Geschichte und Gegenwart*, "Benda," 1, col. 1623.
4. Burney, *Music in Germany*, 2:128–29.

Leopold and Wolfgang Mozart
1. *The Letters of Mozart*, trans. E. Anderson, 1:191–92.
2. *The New Grove*, "Linley," 11:10.
3. O. E. Deutsch, *Mozart: A Documentary Biography*, 530.
4. *Letters of Mozart*, 1:438; 2:495.
5. Ibid., 2:909.
6. Ibid., 2:787.
7. *Letters of Mozart*, 2:825.
8. Ibid., 3:1304.
9. Bauer-Deutsch, *Mozart Briefe (Gesamtausgabe)*, 3:467.

THE FRENCH SCHOOL

Leclair and His Time
1. Nicolas Slonimsky, "The Murder of Leclair," *A Thing or Two about Music*, 86–90.
2. Ancelet, in La Laurencie, *L'école française de violon*, 1:313.
3. La Dixmerie, ibid., 313.
4. Ibid.
5. Prefaces by Leclair, see La Laurencie, ibid., 1:297, 315–17.
6. De Rozoi in ibid., 1:312.

Pierre Gaviniès
1. Mercure de France, May 1759, in La Laurencie, *L'école française de violon*, 2:282.

French Contemporaries of Leclair and Gaviniès
1. Marpurg, "Beyträge," in La Laurencie, *L'école française de violon*, 2:15.
2. Daquin, "Hommes célèbres," La Laurencie, ibid.
3. Burney, *Music in France*, 44.
4. La Laurencie, *L'école française de violon*, 2:181.
5. Franklin's letter to Mme. Brillon, ibid., 182.

6. Ibid., 414.
7. Barry S. Brook, *La Symphonie française*, 1:289.
8. Ibid., 268–69 (from *Journal de Paris*, February 1777).

GIOVANNI BATTISTA VIOTTI

1. Remo Giazotto, *Viotti*, 26.
2. *Berliner Musikzeitung* (1794), quoted in W. J. v. Wasielewski, *Die Violine*, 170.
3. *Morning Chronicle*, March 12 and 26, 1794, in H. C. Robbins Landon, *Symphonies of Haydn*, 514–15, 517.
4. *Oracle*, February 11, 1794, ibid., 509.
5. Baillot, *Notice sur Viotti* (1825), quoted in A. Pougin, *Viotti*, 81.
6. Letter, quoted in Giazotto, *Viotti*, 162.
7. Baillot, *Notice*, in Pougin, *Viotti*, 86.
8. Ibid., 88.
9. Recent publications:
    Viotti, *Four Violin Concertos* (Nos. 7, 13, 18, 27), ed. Chappell White (Madison, Wis.: A-R Editions, 1976).
    Viotti, *Symphonies concertantes*, ed. C. White (New York: Garland, in prep.).
    Viotti, Concerto No. 2, ed. W. Lebermann (Mainz: Schott, 1974).
    Important recording: Viotti, Concertos Nos. 16 (arr. Mozart) and 24, Andreas Röhn, violin, English Chamber Orch., cond. Charles Mackerras (Archive Production 2533 122 Stereo, 1971).
10. Quoted in A. Moser, *Joseph Joachim*, 2:241–42.
11. *Morning Chronicle* (1794), quoted in Landon, *Symphonies of Haydn*, 511.

PART FOUR: *The Nineteenth Century*

FRANCE: THE HEIRS OF VIOTTI

1. *Les Tablettes de Polymnie*, April 1810, quoted in Pougin, *Viotti*, 126–27n.
2. Letter to Prof. Zelter, February 15, 1832. Mendelssohn, *Letters*, ed. G. Selden-Goth, 191.

Pierre Rode
1. Quoted in Pougin, *Notice sur Rode*, 10.
2. *Allgemeine musikalische Zeitung*, 1800, No. 41.
3. Ibid., 1803, 5:484, quoted in Moser, *Geschichte des Violinspiels*, 2:110.
4. Ibid., 1809, 11:601, quoted in Wasielewski, *Die Violine*, 379.
5. *Letters of Beethoven*, Emily Anderson, trans., No. 392 (December 1812).
6. *Glöggl's Musikzeitung*, quoted in Wasielewski, *Beethoven*, 1:330.
7. Spohr, *Autobiography*, 1:165.
8. Mendelssohn, *Letters* (April 20, 1825), 33.
9. J. F. Reichardt, *Vertraute Briefe aus Paris*, 1:389–90, 448–49.

Rodolphe Kreutzer
1. *Letters of Beethoven*, No. 99.
2. Gerber, *Neues historisch-biographisches Lexikon*, 3:118.
3. *Allgemeine musikalische Zeitung*, 1800, No. 41, quoted in *Die Musik in Geschichte und Gegenwart* 7, col. 1782.

4. Quoted in J. Hardy, *Kreutzer*, 57. See Fetis, "Kreutzer," *Biographie universelle*.
5. Joachim and Moser, *Violinschule*, 3:104.
6. Examples in Boris Schwarz, "Beethoven and the French Violin School," *The Musical Quarterly* 44, 4 (October 1958):440–46.

Pierre (Marie François de Sales) Baillot

1. Fétis, "Baillot," *Biographie universelle*, 1:219.
2. Letter in Thayer-Deiters-Riemann, *Beethoven*, 3rd ed., 3:502.
3. *Allgemeine musikalische Zeitung* (February 1810), 12:331.
4. *Wiener Musikzeitung*, 1817, 212, quoted in Wasielewski, *Violine*, 389–90.
5. Quoted in Jacques Barzun, *Berlioz*, 1:99.
6. Quoted in Berlioz, *Evenings with the Orchestra*, ed. Barzun, 244n.
7. Mendelssohn, *Reisebriefe*, 10 (letter of April 20, 1825).
8. Mendelssohn, *Briefe 1830–47*, 1:227 and 258–59 (December 20, 1831, and March 17, 1832).
9. Spohr, *Autobiography*, 2:129–30.
10. *Gazette musicale* (1834) 1:327.

François Habeneck

1. See Harold Schonberg, *The Great Conductors*, 99–106, for a vivid description of Habeneck's conducting career.
2. Berlioz, *Memoirs*, ed. Cairns, 104–5.
3. Jeffrey Pulver, *Paganini: The Romantic Virtuoso*, 223.
4. M. Pincherle, *Feuillets d'histoire du violon*, 172–81.
5. Henry Chorley, quoted in Schonberg, *The Great Conductors*, 102.

Charles Lafont

1. Fétis, *Notice sur Paganini*, 23; also "Lafont," in *Biographie universelle*.
2. Reichardt, *Vertraute Briefe*, 2:410.
3. F. Hiller, *Künstlerleben*, 2:53, quoted in Wasielewski, *Die Violine*, 413.
4. J. Schottky, *Paganini*, 300–301; trans. in Courcy, *Paganini*, 1:148.
5. Courcy, ibid., 150 (*Allgemeine musikalische Zeitung*, 1816; see Schottky, ibid., 303n).
6. *Harmonicon*, London, 1830, 177, quoted in Courcy, ibid., 149–50.
7. Spohr, *Autobiography*, 2:128–29.

NICOLÒ PAGANINI

1. Paganini's reminiscences, in J. Schottky, *Paganini*, 254.
2. Schottky, ibid., 368; trans. in Courcy, *Paganini*, 1:99.
3. Schottky, ibid., 369; trans. in Courcy, ibid., 100.
4. Quoted in Courcy, ibid., 113; see also 123.
5. *Allgemeine musikalische Zeitung*, trans. in Courcy, ibid., 125.
6. Spohr, *Autobiography*, 1:280; see also 283.
7. Letter of Rahel Varnhagen von Ense, quoted in Courcy, *Paganini*, 1:316.
8. H. Heine, "Musikalische Saison in Paris," *Zeitungsberichte über Musik*, 140.
9. *Berliner musikalische Zeitung*, trans. Courcy, *Paganini*, 1:317.
10. *Vossische Zeitung*, trans. in Courcy, ibid., 318.
11. *Autobiography*, 2:168.
12. J. Pulver, *Paganini: The Romantic Virtuoso*, 209.
13. All three quotations, ibid., 214–15.
14. Ibid., 217.
15. Ibid., 218.

16. Ibid., 240–41.
17. Courcy, *Paganini*, 2:101, n. 10.
18. Berlioz, *Memoirs*, ed. E. Newman, 201.
19. A. Heller, *H. W. Ernst*, 14, letter to his family, April 15, 1837.
20. Excerpts from a letter, March 20, 1839, in Courcy, *Paganini*, 2:294–95.
21. Quoted in Pulver, *Paganini*, 302.
22. Sivori's account quoted in Courcy, *Paganini*, 1:219.
23. B. Litzmann, *Clara Schumann: ein Künstlerleben*, 1:16.
24. Schottky, *Paganini*, 274–75.
25. Carl Guhr, *Paganini's Art of Playing the Violin*, see Courcy, *Paganini*, 1:375–78.
26. Schumann, *On Music and Musicians*, 248.
27. Pulver, *Paganini*, 316.
28. Moser, *Geschichte des Violinspiels*, 2:139–40.

AFTER PAGANINI: THE AGE OF VIRTUOSITY

Paganini's Impact on the Viennese School

1. Moser, *Geschichte des Violinspiels*, 2:243.
2. Quoted in Courcy, *Paganini*, 1:262, n. 13.
3. Moser, *Geschichte des Violinspiels*, 2:244.
4. Ibid., 140.
5. Ibid., 251.
6. *The Musical World* 19, no. 16 (1844).
7. Letter to F. David, April 12, 1847, in *Letters from and to Joachim*, 3.
8. Moser, *Geschichte des Violinspiels*, 2:251.
9. Schindler, *Tagebuch*, 51, in Heine, *Zeitungsberichte über Musik*, 225.
10. Moser, *Geschichte des Violinspiels*, 2:251.
11. Heine, *Zeitungsberichte über Musik*, 119.

Henry Vieuxtemps

1. *Journal des Debats*, April 21, 1851, quoted in Radoux, *Vieuxtemps*, 81.
2. *Revue musicale* 5 (1829):164, quoted in Radoux, ibid., 19.
3. Radoux, ibid., 26.
4. Ibid., 33–34; the following quotation is from p. 36.
5. Three excerpts from Vieuxtemps's autobiography, in M. Kufferath, *Vieuxtemps*, 19.
6. E. Hanslick, *Vienna's Golden Years of Music*, 37, 77.
7. Schindler, *Tagebuch*, 66–67, in Heine, *Zeitungsberichte über Musik*, 225.
8. T. L. Phipson, *Famous Violinists*, 244, 247.
9. A. Moser, *Joseph Joachim*, 2:292.

Henryk Wieniawski

1. Quoted in I. Yampolsky, *Wieniawski*, 15–16.
2. Letter, January 19, 1864, quoted in ibid., 17.
3. Lev Ginzburg, "Wieniawski in Russia," in *Russko-Polskiye Musikalnye Svyasi*, 272.
4. Ibid., 265.
5. Ibid., 271 and n. 48.
6. Anton Rubinstein, *Autobiography*, 116.
7. Moser, *Geschichte des Violinspiels*, 1st ed., 267 n. 1; following quotation is from p. 471.
8. Leopold Auer, *My Long Life in Music*, 242.
9. Sam Franko, *Chords and Discords*, 46.

Ole Bull

1. Sara Chapman Bull, *Ole Bull: A Memoir*, 330.
2. Albert Schweitzer, *J. S. Bach*, 1:390.
3. Quoted in Mortimer Smith, *Life of Ole Bull*, 28.
4. Spohr, *Autobiography*, 2:213.
5. *Letters from and to Joachim*, 214–15.
6. Moser, *Geschichte des Violinspiels*, 2:159.
7. Mikhail Glinka, *Memoirs*, 206.
8. Quoted in Lev Raaben, *Zhizn zamechatelnykh skripachei*, 95–96.
9. Hanslick, *Vienna's Golden Years*, 66.
10. Grieg, *Artikler og taler*, 100.

Pablo de Sarasate

1. Flesch, *Memoirs*, 38.
2. Moser, *Geschichte des Violinspiels*, 2:179.
3. George Henschel, *Musings and Memories of a Musician*, 169.
4. G. B. Shaw, *London Music in 1888–89*, 132.
5. *Szigeti on the Violin*, 169–70.
6. Auer, *My Long Life in Music*, 175, 179; also in *Violin Playing*, 37, 118; see also Raaben, *Zhizn zamechatelnykh skripachei*, 131–32.
7. Flesch, *Memoirs*, 38, 39.
8. Ibid., 43.
9. Spalding, *A Rise to Follow*, 36.
10. Flesch, *Memoirs*, 38.
11. Wasielewski, *Die Violine*, 574.

COUNTERCURRENTS

Louis Spohr

1. This and the following extract from *Autobiography*, 1:62, 63, 75.
2. Ibid., 167–68. Körner's remark in Spohr, *Lebenserinnerungen*, 1:360, n. 31.
3. Remarks on Beethoven in *Autobiography*, 1:185, 187f.
4. Moser, *Joachim*, 2:291; footnote on cadenza in Spohr, *Autobiography*, 2:318.
5. A. W. Thayer, *Beethoven*, 3:203.
6. Spohr, *Autobiography*, 1:264.
7. *Allgemeine musikalische Zeitung* (1816), col. 883, in Spohr, *Lebenserinnerungen*, 1:383, n. 28; also 386, n. 16.
8. Letter to W. Speyer, in *Music & Letters* 31 (1950):314 n.
9. *Music & Letters*, ibid., 316. Other notices, p. 314.
10. *Autobiography*, 2:81–82. See Arthur Jacobs, "Spohr and the Baton," *Music & Letters* 31 (1950):307–17, for a thorough discussion.
11. *Lebenserinnerungen*, 2:240, n. 33 (letter to Speyer).
12. *Autobiography*, 2:119–20. For other Paris quotes see pp. 113, 114, 123.
13. Quoted in F. Göthel, *Das Violinspiel L. Spohrs*, 92.
14. *Lebenserinnerungen*, 2:206–7.
15. Göthel, *Das Violinspiel L. Spohrs*, 14 (quoting H. Schletterer).
16. Ibid., 60 (quoting *Allgemeine musikalische Zeitung*, 1808).
17. Ibid., 90 (quoting *Allgemeine musikalische Zeitung*, 1818).
18. Letter to his wife, Dorette, February 7, 1822 (Spohr, *Briefwechsel*, 43).

Joseph Joachim

1. Moser, *Joachim*, 1:45 (shortened).
2. Ibid., 54–55.
3. Ibid., 82.

4. B. Litzmann, *Clara Schumann*, 2:111–12.
5. Ibid., 2:278.
6. Moser, *Joachim*, 1:159.
7. Letter to conductor Golschmann, in R. Magidoff, *Yehudi Menuhin*, 203–4.
8. Moser, *Joachim*, 2:305.
9. Hanslick, *Vienna's Golden Years*, 76, 77, 80.
10. Raaben, *Zhizn zamechatelnykh skripachei*, 152.
11. Auer, *My Long Life in Music*, 22–23.
12. Franko, *Chords and Discords*, 19–20.
13. J. Szigeti, *With Strings Attached*, 54–55.
14. Flesch, *Memoirs*, 34.
15. Shaw, *London Music in 1888–89*, 331–32.
16. Sir Henry Wood, *My Life of Music*, 183–84.
17. Letter to Frau v. Herzogenberg, in Florence May, *Brahms*, 2:197.
18. Letter No. 477 (April 25, 1888), in *Johannes Brahms in Briefwechsel*. Refers to Double Concerto, but can be applied to the Violin Concerto.
19. See A. Holde, "Suppressed Passages in the Brahms-Joachim Correspondence," *The Musical Quarterly* 45, no. 3 (July 1959):312–24.

PART FIVE: *The Twentieth Century*

A New Breed of Virtuoso

Eugène Ysaÿe

1. Flesch, *Memoirs*, 79.
2. E. Christen, *Ysaÿe*, 35.
3. Antoine Ysaÿe, *Eugène Ysaÿe*, 55. See also Lev Ginsburg, *Ysaÿe*, trans. Danko, 367 and 31.
4. Original in Ginsburg, *Isai* (Russian ed.), 132; see trans. by Danko, ibid., 359.
5. Ibid., 156 (Russian), 391 (English).
6. Spalding, *Rise to Follow*, 158.
7. A. Ysaÿe, *Eugène Ysaÿe*, 172.
8. Ibid., 472.
9. Flesch, *Memoirs*, 78–79.
10. Franko, *Chords and Discords*, 31–32.
11. Louis Lochner, *Kreisler*, 21 (italics added).
12. A. Ysaÿe, *Eugène Ysaÿe*, 431.
13. Flesch, *Memoirs*, 80.
14. A. Ysaÿe, *Eugène Ysaÿe*, 183–84.
15. Lochner, *Kreisler*, 111.
16. A. Ysaÿe, *Eugène Ysaÿe*, 185.
17. Shaw, *How to Become a Music Critic*, 143–45, 194–95; *Music in London 1888–89*, 359.
18. Sir Henry Wood, *My Life of Music*, 130.
19. Ibid., 128.
20. Ibid.; see also 252 and 286.
21. A. Ysaÿe, *Eugène Ysaÿe*, 382.
22. Ibid., 382–83.
23. Ibid., 393–94.
24. Ibid., 382.

Fritz Kreisler

1. Louis Lochner, *Fritz Kreisler*, 60.
2. Ibid., 20–21.
3. Ibid., 28.
4. Flesch, *Memoirs*, 118.
5. Lochner, *Fritz Kreisler*, 78.
6. R. Elkin, *Royal Philharmonic*, 104.
7. *Sunday Times*, May 1921, quoted in Lochner, *Fritz Kreisler*, 192.
8. Lochner, ibid., 164.
9. Ibid., 248.
10. J. Hartnack, *Grosse Geiger unserer Zeit*, 114. Kreisler's letter in Lochner, ibid., 281.
11. Lochner, ibid., 277.
12. I. Yampolsky, *D. Oistrakh*, 2d ed., 53 (in Russian).
13. M. Pincherle, "Fritz Kreisler tel que j'ai connu," *Musica disque*, 97 (April 1962): 45.
14. Lochner, *Fritz Kreisler*, 90.
15. Samuel Applebaum, *The Way They Play*, 1:98.
16. Flesch, *Memoirs*, 118–22.

Bronislaw Huberman

1. Menuhin, *Unfinished Journey*, 97.
2. Ludwig Speidel, *Wiener Fremdenblatt*, January 23, 1895.
3. Max Kalbeck, *Johannes Brahms*, 4, pt. 2, 430.
4. Eduard Hanslick, *Neue freie Presse*, 1895.
5. New York reviews in *The Critic* (December 5, 1896), *The Sun*, *The Times* (November 15, 1896).
6. Hartnack, *Grosse Geiger*, 114–15; The New York *Times*, September 14, 1933.
7. B. Huberman, *Aus der Werkstatt des Virtuosen*.
8. Flesch, *Memoirs*, 176–78; Keller's reply, 367–68. See also Hartnack, *Grosse Geiger*, 100, 105–6.

GERMAN ANTIPODES TO JOACHIM

August Wilhelmj

1. Joachim's letter to his wife, in Moser, *Geschichte des Violinspiels*, 2:212–13.

BERLIN AFTER THE DEATH OF JOACHIM

1. Flesch, *Memoirs*, 250.

Henri Marteau

1. Both quotations in this paragraph from Flesch, *Memoirs*, 90.
2. Ibid., 91.

Adolf Busch

1. Szigeti, *With Strings Attached*, 109.
2. Donald Brook, *Violinists of Today*, 16.
3. Flesch, *Memoirs*, 265.
4. Joseph Wulf, *Musik im Dritten Reich*, 133–34.
5. Magidoff, *Menuhin*, 143–44.
6. Menuhin, *Unfinished Journey*, 101–2, 94.

Georg Kulenkampff

1. Flesch, *Memoirs*, 267.

Carl Flesch

1. Flesch, *Memoirs*, 66.
2. Ibid., 145–46.
3. Ibid., 173; see also p. 66.
4. Ibid., 371–72 (facsimile on pp. 338–39).
5. Walter Kolneder, *Das Buch der Violine*, 530–31.

The Flesch School

1. Flesch, *Memoirs*, 274.
2. Ibid., 316–17.
3. Donald Brook, *Violinists of Today*, 139.

THE PARIS CONSERVATOIRE AFTER 100 YEARS

1. Flesch, *Memoirs*, 68.

Jacques Thibaud

1. J. Thibaud, *Un violon parle*, ed. J. P. Dorian, 122.
2. Irving Kolodin, The New York *Sun*, February 18, 1947.
3. Enesco, *Les souvenirs de Georges Enesco*, ed. B. Gavoty, 74.
4. J. P. Dorian (see note 1), 12 (Preface).
5. Flesch, *Memoirs*, 196–97.
6. *Sovietskoye Iskusstvo*, April 17, 1936, in Raaben, *Zhizn zamechatelnykh skripachei*, 206.
7. *Sovietskaya Muzyka*, 11 (1953):68, in Raaben, ibid., 199–200.

Georges Enesco

1. J. M. Corredor, *Conversations with Casals*, 190.
2. B. Gavoty, *Yehudi Menuhin and Georges Enesco*, 10.
3. This and the following quotation are from Enesco, *Les souvenirs d'Enesco*, ed. Gavoty, 105, 106–7.
4. Enesco, *Souvenirs*, 65–66.
5. Flesch, *Memoirs*, 179.
6. Menuhin, *Unfinished Journey*, 56–57.
7. Menuhin, in *The Score*, September 1955, no. 13, p. 39.
8. Pincherle, *World of the Virtuoso*, 106.
9. Flesch, *Memoirs*, 180.
10. Menuhin, *Unfinished Journey*, 72.
11. Pincherle, *World of the Virtuoso*, 106–7.
12. Flesch, *Memoirs*, 179.
13. Menuhin, *Unfinished Journey*, 72.
14. Quoted in Raaben, *Zhizn zamechatelnykh skripachei*, 217.
15. Menuhin, *Unfinished Journey*, 71.
16. Corredor, *Conversations with Casals*, 189.
17. George Manoliu, "Violinistica enesciana," *Musica* 9 (1960):11–18, quoted in Raaben, *Zhizn zamechatelnykh skripachei*, 211.
18. Magidoff, *Menuhin*, 75–76.
19. Pincherle, *World of the Virtuoso*, 108.
20. Magidoff, *Menuhin*, 74. Last sentence in Menuhin, *Unfinished Journey*, 70.

Lucien Capet

1. Flesch, *Memoirs*, 94.
2. Ibid.

3. Moser, *Geschichte des Violinspiels*, 1st ed., 467.
4. Flesch, *Memoirs*, 94.
5. Menuhin, *Unfinished Journey*, 321.
6. Lucien Capet, *La technique supérieure de l'archet*, preface, 7.

THE NEW FRENCH SCHOOL

Ginette Neveu
1. New York *Times*, March 13, 1937 (also *The Sun*).
2. Quoted in Szigeti, *With Strings Attached*, 90–91.
3. Quoted in M.-J. Ronze-Neveu, *Ginette Neveu*, 149.

THE HUNGARIAN SCHOOL

1. Flesch, *Memoirs*, 153.

Jenö Hubay
1. Radoux, *Vieuxtemps*, 139–40.
2. Sir Henry Wood, *My Life of Music*, 234.

Franz von Vecsey
1. Kolneder, *Das Buch der Violine*, 491.
2. Flesch, *Memoirs*, 251–52.

Joseph Szigeti
1. Szigeti, *With Strings Attached*, 35; also, pp. 48, 76–77, 250.
2. Ibid., 2nd ed., 360.
3. Béla Bartók, *Letters*, ed. J. Demény, 329.
4. A. Ysaÿe, *Eugène Ysaÿe*, 414.

THE BOHEMIAN SCHOOL

1. Flesch, *Memoirs*, 181.

Otakar Sevčik
1. Schneiderhan, Opening address, *International Violin Congress*, Graz 1972, 7.

Jan Kubelik
1. Flesch, *Memoirs*, 175–76.

THE NEW VIENNESE SCHOOL

1. Flesch, *Memoirs*, 52.

THE RUSSIAN SCHOOL

Early History
1. I. Yampolsky, *Russkoye skripichnoye iskusstvo*, 218, n.2 (letter to Moscheles, June 17, 1840).
2. Schumann, *Gesammelte Schriften* 3:16.
3. Moser, *Geschichte des Violinspiels*, 2:217.

Leopold Auer
1. Auer, *My Long Life in Music*, 63–64.
2. Raaben, *L. Auer*, 22–23.
3. Auer, *My Long Life in Music*, 209.
4. Modest Tchaikovsky, *P. I. Tchaikovsky*, trans. R. Newmarch, 415.

5. Auer, *Violin Playing*, 46.
6. Kolneder, *Das Buch der Violine*, 545.
7. Auer, *Violin Playing*, 60, 62.
8. Auer, *My Long Life in Music*, 345.

THE GREAT AUER DISCIPLES

Mischa Elman
1. Saul Elman, *Memoirs*, 1.
2. Auer, *My Long Life in Music*, 320–23.
3. Elman, *Memoirs*, 191f. (press excerpts).
4. Ibid., 105.
5. Raaben, *L. Auer*, 120.
6. Flesch, *Memoirs*, 255.
7. Hartnack, *Grosse Geiger*, 92.

Efrem Zimbalist
1. Raaben, *L. Auer*, 136–37.
2. Flesch, *Memoirs*, 255.

Jascha Heifetz
1. Flesch, *Memoirs*, 337–38.
2. Spalding, *Rise to Follow*, 202–3.
3. Hugo Rasch, in *Allgemeine Musikzeitung* 39, no. 23 (June 7, 1912):638.
4. Otto Lessmann, ibid., 44 (November 1, 1912):1147.
5. *Signale für die musikalische Welt* 45 (November 6, 1912):1484.
6. Auer, *My Long Life in Music*, 339–40.
7. Ibid., 352f.
8. Herbert Axelrod, ed., *Heifetz*, 223.
9. This and the following quotations from ibid., 231, 244, 65, and 280.
10. Ibid., 434–36.
11. Ibid., 129–31.

Nathan Milstein
1. Auer, *My Long Life in Music*, 343–44.
2. This and the following quotation from an interview in *High Fidelity*, November 1977, 84, 86.
3. Pavel Kogan, *Vmeste s muzykantami*, 14–20.
4. *High Fidelity*, November 1977, 86.

More Auer Students and a Few Muscovites
1. Flesch, *Memoirs*, 338.

THE SOVIET SCHOOL

Leningrad and Moscow: Miron Poliakin
1. Raaben, "M. Poliakin," *Zhizn zamechatelnykh skripachei*, 251.
2. J. Jelagin, *Taming of the Arts*, 202.
3. Ibid., 205.
4. Szigeti, *With Strings Attached*, 91f.

Odessa: Piotr Stolyarsky
1. Jelagin, *Taming of the Arts*, 204.
2. Ibid., 203.

David Oistrakh
1. I. Yampolsky, *D. Oistrakh*, 2nd ed., 18.
2. Ibid., 21.
3. Ibid., 27.
4. Ibid., 24.
5. Flesch, quoted in Szigeti, *With Strings Attached*, 92.
6. The New York *Times*, Obituary, October 24, 1974, 32.
7. Menuhin, *Unfinished Journey*, 191.
8. Yampolsky, *D. Oistrakh*, 96.
9. Ibid., 98.
10. Jelagin, *Taming of the Arts*, 201.

Leonid Kogan
1. Szigeti, *With Strings Attached*, 2nd ed., 360.

Younger Soviet Violinists
1. *Music Journal*, September 1966, 72f.
2. The New York *Times*, April 24, 1979.
3. *Time*, January 24, 1977.

Soviet Emigré Violinists
1. Joseph Horowitz, "The Sound of Russian Music in the West," *New York Times Magazine*, June 11, 1978.

THE BRITISH SCHOOL

1. Radoux, *Vieuxtemps*, 143.
2. *Letters from and to Joachim*, 385.
3. Watson Forbes, "Catterall," *The New Grove*.
4. *The Strad*, April 1980, 903–6, and May 1980, 22–24.
5. E. Fenby, *Menuhin's House of Music*, 118.

VIOLIN PLAYING IN AMERICA: THE OLDER GENERATION

Maud Powell
1. *Grove's Dictionary*, American Supplement (1942), 331. See also *The Strad*, August 1980, 237–41.

Albert Spalding
1. Spalding, *Rise to Follow*, 99.
2. Ibid., 287.

Franz Kneisel
1. New York *Times*, September 12, 1976.
2. Flesch, *Memoirs*, 281–82.

Louis Persinger
1. Menuhin, *The Juilliard Review Annual* (1966–67), 16.
2. Margaret C. Hart, *The Juilliard Review* (Winter 1961–2), 5.
3. This and the following quotation: ibid., 8.
4. Menuhin, *Unfinished Journey*, 32.

More American Violinists
1. Gustav Mahler, *Selected Letters*, 358.

The Kneisel School
1. Flesch, *Memoirs*, 339.

2. Excerpts from *The Sun, The Press, Musical Courier*, after his debut on November 27, 1915.
3. Henderson, in New York *Sun*, March 10, 1919.
4. Max Smith, in New York *American*, March 10, 1919.

The Last Three Auer Students
1. Press release at time of Rabinof's debut, November 1927.
2. New York *Times*, February 10, 1937.
3. Ibid., October 16, 1946.
4. Ibid., November 6, 1954.
5. Ibid., November 12, 1955.
6. Ibid., January 28, 1937 (Stravinsky and Dushkin).
7. "Working with Stravinsky," in *Stravinsky*, ed. E. Corle, 186.
8. This and the following quotation from ibid., 187, 190.
9. New York *Herald Tribune*, February 9, 1943.

Louis Krasner and the Concertos of Alban Berg and Arnold Schoenberg
1. *Journal of the A. Schoenberg Institute* 2, no. 2 (February 1978):86.
2. Slonimsky, *Music since 1900*, 4th ed., 625.
3. New York *Herald Tribune*, March 6, 1937.
4. Schoenberg letter, February 11, 1938, *Journal of the A. Schoenberg Institute* 2, no. 2 (February 1978):88.
5. Schoenberg letter, December 17, 1940, ibid., 93.

THE AMERICAN SCHOOL: THE MIDDLE GENERATION

Yehudi Menuhin
1. Magidoff, *Menuhin*, 137.
2. Menuhin, *Unfinished Journey*, 32.
3. Magidoff, *Menuhin*, 51.
4. Ibid., 68.
5. Quoted ibid., 90.
6. Both quoted ibid., 95.
7. Ibid., 97.
8. Ibid., 249.
9. Menuhin, *Unfinished Journey*, 163–64.
10. Ibid., 167, 168–69. See also Bartók's letter to Menuhin, June 30, 1944, in Bartók, *Letters*, 332–33.
11. V. Gollancz, *Journey towards Music*, 213–14.
12. Menuhin, *Unfinished Journey*, 255.
13. Ibid., 110.

Ruggiero Ricci
1. This and all other quotations of Ricci from New York *Times*, Sunday, January 18, 1976 (section 2), ". . . Child Prodigy who Survived," by Shirley Fleming.

Isaac Stern
1. Personal conversation with the author.

More Persinger Students
1. New York *Times*, February 21, 1942.
2. *Musical America*, December 10, 1931.
3. New York *Herald Tribune*, November 22, 1933.
4. February 19, 1938 (clipping file)

5. New York *Times*, December 17, 1968.
6. *Sun*, February 21, 1942.
7. April 8, 1946.
8. New York *Times*, March 14, 1955.
9. New York *Times*, October 7, 1946.
10. New York *Herald Tribune*, February 15, 1952.
11. New York *World Telegram*, February 13, 1943.
12. New York *Times*, October 20, 1962.
13. New York *Times*, October 30, 1970.
14. New York *Times*, May 7, 1961.

THE GREAT AMERICAN TEACHERS

Ivan Galamian

1. All quotations in this section are from New York *Times*, April 26, 1981, "Galamian—a great violin teacher," by Judith Karp.
2. New York *Times*, November 23, 1977, "All his kids have such talent," by Donal Henahan.

Dorothy DeLay

1. New York *Times*, June 22, 1980, "She teaches Violin the American Way," by Joseph Deitch.

Alexander Schneider

1. Alan Rich, New York *Herald Tribune*, April 28, 1964.
2. *Current Biography*, March 1976.

THE AMERICAN SCHOOL: THE YOUNGER GENERATION

Robert Mann

1. Shirley Fleming, in *Musical America*, June 1980.
2. Ibid.
3. Joan Peyser, in New York *Times*, July 6, 1980.
4. *Musical America*, June 1980.

Berl Senofsky

1. New York *Times*, February 1, 1958.
2. New York *Times*, August 11, 1958.

Sidney Harth

1. *The New Yorker* (press clipping, not dated).

Michael Rabin

1. All three quotes in Obituary, New York *Times*, January 20, 1972.
2. Ibid., November 23, 1977.
3. Ibid.

Aaron Rosand

1. New York *Times*, April 29, 1970.
2. *The New Yorker* (press book, not dated).
3. Washington *Post* (press book, not dated).

Carroll Glenn

1. New York Public Library at Lincoln Center, clipping file (one review dated December 15, 1941, the second December 4, 1944, New York *Herald Tribune*).
2. Obituary, New York *Times*, April 26, 1983.

Charles Treger
1. New York *Times*, October 19, 1972.

Arnold Steinhardt
1. New York *Times*, November 10, 1958.
2. New York *Herald Tribune*, February 24, 1962.
3. New York *Times*, March 1, 1965.
4. Ibid., February 28, 1975.

Jaime Laredo
1. New York *Times*, October 20, 1959 (Taubman); New York *Herald Tribune*, October 20, 1959 (Harrison).
2. *Current Biography*, September 1967.
3. New York *Times*, December 23, 1979 (Horowitz).

Paul Zukofsky
1. *New York Times Magazine*, March 23, 1969 (R. Kostelanetz).
2. *Musical America*: Musician of the Month, March 1969 (Shirley Fleming).
3. New York *Times*, December 1, 1956 (H. Schonberg).
4. Ibid., February 4, 1961 (R. Ericson).
5. Ibid., February 13, 1969 (D. Henahan).

James Oliver Buswell
1. Washington *Post*, 1962.
2. New York *Times*, October 20, 1965 (Schonberg).
3. Ibid., April 20, 1967. See also New York *World Journal*, April 20, 1967.
4. New York *Times*, December 9, 1974 (Henahan).

Ani and Ida Kavafian
1. New York *Times*, November 9, 1978.

Eugene Fodor
1. Interview, *Current Biography*, April 1976, p. 12.
2. New York *Times*, November 4, 1974.
3. *Current Biography*, ibid., p. 13.

Elmar Oliveira
1. New York *Times*, March 20, 1973 (R. Sherman).
2. Ibid., February 14, 1977 (Ericson).
3. Ibid., May 1, 1979 (Schonberg).
4. Ibid., Sunday, January 30, 1983, section 2 (A. Adler).

Dylana Jenson
1. Press release; reworded in *Musical America*, December 1980, 24.

Gregory Fulkerson and Curtis Macomber
1. Washington *Post*, September 29, 1980.
2. Ibid.

Peter Zazofsky
1. New York *Times*, November 21, 1982 (Rothstein).

Others (Mihaela Martin)
1. New York *Times*, May 8, 1983.

Violinists of Israel

Miriam Fried
1. New York *Times*, March 2, 1980 (Raymond Ericson).
2. Ibid.
3. *Musical America:* Musician of the Month, July 1977 (Shirley Fleming).

Itzhak Perlman
1. *Newsweek*, August 14, 1980 (A. Swan).
2. Ibid.

Pinchas Zukerman
1. New York *Times*, Sunday, March 11, 1979 (section 2), "Pinky and Itzhak . . ." by Eugenia Zukerman.
2. *Musical America:* Musician of the Month, August 1978 (B. Paolucci).
3. Ibid.

Shlomo Mintz
1. New York *Times*, November 30, 1973.
2. London, *The Times*, no date available

Violinists of the Orient

1. Leslie Rubinstein, "Oriental Musicians Come of Age," *New York Times Magazine*, November 23, 1980.
2. Ibid.

Japan
1. *The New Grove*, 6, 287 (Noël Goodwin).
2. *Sovietskaya Muzyka*, 9 (1966).
3. Ibid.
4. Ibid., 10 (1970) :no. 10, 61.
5. New York *Times*, January 2, 1983 (Bernard Holland).

South Korea
1. New York *Times*, February 3, 1980.
2. *Musical America*, June 1976.
3. Leslie Rubinstein, ibid., p. 92.

Taiwan
1. New York *Times*, August 12, 1979 (Allen Hughes).
2. Leslie Rubinstein, ibid., p. 30.

BIBLIOGRAPHY

Applebaum, Samuel and Sada. *The Way They Play*. Neptune, N.J.: Paganiniana Publications, 1960f.

Auer, Leopold. *My Long Life in Music*. New York: Frederick A. Stokes, 1923.

———. *Violin Playing as I Teach It*. New York: Frederick A. Stokes, 1921. 2d ed. Philadelphia: Lippincott; London: Duckworth, 1960.

Axelrod, Herbert R., ed. *Heifetz*. Neptune City, N.J.: Paganiniana Publications, 1976. 2d ed. enl. 1981.

Bachmann, Alberto. *An Encyclopedia of the Violin*. New York, 1925. Reprint. New York: Da Capo, 1966, 1975.

———. *Les grands violonistes du passé*. Paris: Fischbacher, 1913.

Bartók, Béla. *Letters*. Ed. János Demény. London: Faber & Faber; New York: St. Martin's Press, 1971.

Barzun, Jacques. *Berlioz and the Romantic Century*. 3rd ed. Boston: Little, Brown & Co., 1969.

Beethoven, Ludwig van. *The Letters of Beethoven*. Trans. and ed. Emily Anderson. London: Macmillan & Co.; New York: St. Martin's Press, 1961.

Berlioz, Hector. *Evenings with the Orchestra*. Trans. and ed. Jacques Barzun. New York: Alfred A. Knopf, 1956.

———. *Memoirs*. Trans. Ernest Newman. New York: Alfred A. Knopf, 1932.

———. *Memoirs*. Trans. David Cairns. New York: W. W. Norton, 1975.

Boyden, David D. *The History of Violin Playing from its Origins to 1761*. London: Oxford University Press, 1965.

Brahms, Johannes. *Johannes Brahms im Briefwechsel mit Joseph Joachim*. Ed. Andreas Moser. 3rd enl. ed. Berlin: Deutsche Brahms-Gesellschaft, 1921.

————. *Concerto for Violin, Opus 77: A Facsimile of the Holograph Score.* Introduction by Yehudi Menuhin. Foreword by Jon Newsom. Washington, D.C.: Library of Congress, 1979.

————. *Letters of Clara Schumann and Johannes Brahms, 1853–1896.* Ed. Berthold Litzmann. New York: Longmans, Green & Co., 1927. Reprint. New York: Vienna House, 1971.

Brainard, Paul. *Le sonate per violino di Giuseppe Tartini. Catalogo tematico.* Milan: Carisch, 1975.

————. "Die Violinsonaten Giuseppe Tartinis." Dissertation, University of Göttingen, 1959.

Brodsky, A. *Recollections of a Russian Home: A Musician's Experience.* 2d ed. London: Sherratt & Hughes, 1914.

Brook, Barry S. *La symphonie française dans la seconde moitié du XVIII siècle.* Paris: Institut de Musicologie de l'Université de Paris, 1962.

Brook, Donald. *Violinists of Today.* London: Rockliff, 1948.

Brosses, Charles de. *Lettres familières sur l'Italie.* Paris: Didier, 1858. Reprint. Paris, 1931.

Bull, Sara Chapman. *Ole Bull: A Memoir.* Boston: Houghton, Mifflin & Co., 1882. Reprint. New York: Da Capo, 1981.

Burmester, Willy. *50 Jahre Künstlerleben.* Berlin: Scherl, 1926.

Burney, Charles. *A General History of Music.* London, 1776–89. Reprint. Ed. Frank Mercer. London, 1935. New York: Dover, 1957.

————. *The Present State of Music in France and Italy.* London, 1775. Facsimile reprint. New York: Broude Brothers, 1969.

————. *The Present State of Music in Germany, The Netherlands, and United Provinces.* London, 1775. Facsimile reprint. New York: Broude Brothers, 1969.

Busch, Fritz. *Pages from a Musician's Life.* Trans. Marjorie Strachey. London: Hogarth Press, 1953.

Capet, Lucien. *La technique supérieure de l'archet.* Preface by Henri Expert. Paris: Maurice Senart, 1925.

Capri, Antonio. *Giuseppe Tartini.* Milan: Garzanti, 1945.

Cartier, Jean-Baptiste. *L'art du violon.* Facsimile reprint of 3rd (1803) ed. New York: Broude Brothers, 1973.

Choron and Fayolle. *Dictionnaire historique des musiciens.* Paris, 1817.

Christen, Ernest. *Eugène Ysaÿe.* Geneva, 1946.

Corredor, J. M. *Conversations with Casals.* New York: E. P. Dutton, 1958.

Courcy, G. I. C. de. *Paganini the Genoese.* Norman: University of Oklahoma Press, 1957. Reprint. New York: Da Capo, 1977.

Deutsch, Otto Erich. *Handel: A Documentary Biography.* New York: W. W. Norton, 1955. Reprint. New York: Da Capo, 1974.

————. *Mozart: A Documentary Biography.* London: A. & C. Black, 1965.

————. *The Schubert Reader.* New York: W. W. Norton, 1947.

Dittersdorf, Karl Ditters von. *Lebensbeschreibung.* Leipzig, 1801. New ed. by B. Loets. Leipzig: Staackmann, 1940.

Dounias, Minos. *Die Violinkonzerte Giuseppe Tartinis* (with thematic catalogue). Wolfenbüttel and Berlin: Kallmeyer, 1935. Reprint. 1966.

Dunning, Albert. *Pietro Antonio Locatelli, der Virtuose und seine Welt.* Buren, Holland: F. Knuf, 1981.

Dushkin, Samuel. "Working with Stravinsky." In *Igor Stravinsky,* ed. Edwin Corle. New York: Duell, Sloan & Pearce, 1949.

Elkin, Robert. *Royal Philharmonic,* Foreword by Pablo Casals. London: Rider & Co., 1946. [Contains programs 1912–45; see Foster for earlier programs.]

Elman, Saul. *Memoirs of Mischa Elman's Father.* New York: By the Author, 1933.

Elwart, Antoine A. *Histoire de la Société des Concerts du Conservatoire.* Paris: S. Castel, 1860.

Enesco, Georges. *Les souvenirs de Georges Enesco.* Ed. Bernard Gavoty. Paris: Flammarion, 1955.

Engel, Hans. *Das Instrumentalkonzert: eine musikgeschichtliche Darstellung.* Wiesbaden: Breitkopf & Härtel, 1971.

Eppelsheim, Jürgen, *Das Orchester Lullys.* Tutzing: Schneider, 1961.

Fanna, Antonio. *Antonio Vivaldi: catalogo numerico-tematico delle opere instrumentali.* Milan: Ricordi, 1968.

Farisch, Margaret K. *String Music in Print.* 2d ed. New York and London: R. R. Bowker, 1973.

Fayolle, François M. *Notices sur Corelli, Tartini, Gaviniès, Pugnani et Viotti.* Paris, 1810.

Fenby, Eric. *Menuhin's House of Music.* Photographs by Nicholas Fisk. London: Icon, 1969.

Fétis, François-Joseph. *Biographie universelle des musiciens et bibliographie générale de la musique.* 2d ed. Paris: Firmin-Didot, 1875–78. *Supplément.* Ed. A. Pougin. 1878–80.

———. *Notice sur Paganini.* Paris: Schönenberger, 1851.

Flesch, Carl. *The Art of Violin Playing.* 2 vols. Trans. Frederick Martens. New York: Carl Fischer, 1924, 1930.

———. *Memoirs.* Trans. Hans Keller. London: Rockliff, 1957. Reprint. New York: Da Capo, 1979.

Foster, Miles B. *History of the Philharmonic Society of London.* London: J. Lane, 1912. [For later programs see Elkin.]

Franko, Sam. *Chords and Discords.* New York: Viking Press, 1938.

Galamian, Ivan. *Principles of Violin Playing and Teaching.* Englewood Cliffs, N.J.: Prentice-Hall; London: Faber & Faber, 1962.

Gavoty, Bernard. *Yehudi Menuhin and Georges Enesco.* Portraits by Roger Hauert. Geneva: Kister, 1955.

Geminiani, Francesco. *The Art of Playing on the Violin.* Facsimile ed., with an introduction by David D. Boyden. London: Oxford University Press, 1952.

Gerber, Ernst Ludwig. *Neues historisch-biographisches Lexikon der Tonkünstler.* Leipzig: Kühnel, 1812–14.

Giazotto, Remo. *Gianbattista Viotti.* Milan: Curci, 1956.

Ginsburg [Ginzburg], Lev. *Eugène Ysaÿe.* Trans. X. M. Danko. Neptune, N.J.: Paganiniana Publications, 1980.

———. *Giuseppe Tartini.* Trans. into German by A. Palm. Zürich: Eulenburg, 1976.

———. "Henryk Wieniawski in Russia." In *Russko-Polskiye Muzykalnye Svyasi* [Russian-Polish musical relations], ed. Igor Boelza. Moscow, 1963.

Glinka, Mikhail. *Memoirs.* Trans. Richard Mudge. Norman: University of Oklahoma Press, 1963.

Gollancz, Victor. *Journey towards Music.* New York: Dutton & Co., 1965.

Göthel, Folker. "Das Violinspiel Ludwig Spohrs." Dissertation: Berlin, 1935.

Greenwood, Neva Garner. "Maud Powell," *The Strad* (August 1980).

Grieg, Edvard. *Artikler og taler.* Oslo, 1957.

Grove's Dictionary of Music and Musicians. 6th ed. [*The New Grove.*] Ed. Stanley Sadie. London: Macmillan, 1980.

———. *American Supplement.* Ed. Waldo S. Pratt and Charles N. Boyd. New York: Macmillan Co., 1942.

Gutmann, Albert. *Aus dem Wiener Musikleben, Künstler-Erinnerungen 1873–1908.* Vienna: A. J. Gutmann, 1914.

Gyrowetz, Adalbert. *Selbst-Biographie.* Vienna, 1848. Reprint in *Lebensläufe deutscher Musiker,* ed. Alfred Einstein. Leipzig: Siegel, 1915.

Haendel, Ida. *Woman with Violin.* London: Victor Gollancz, 1970.

Hanslick, Eduard. *Vienna's Golden Years of Music 1850–1900.* Trans. and ed. Henry Pleasants III. New York: Simon and Schuster, 1950.

Hardy, Joseph. *Rodolphe Kreutzer: sa jeunesse à Versailles, 1766–1789.* Paris: Fischbacher, 1910.

Hartnack, Joachim. *Grosse Geiger unserer Zeit.* Gütersloh: Bertelsmann, 1968.

Hawkins, [Sir] John. *A General History of the Science and Practice of Music.* London, 1776. The J. Alfred Novello edition of 1853 reprinted New York: Dover, 1963, with new introduction by Charles Cudworth.

Hayes, Gerald R. *Musical Instruments and Their Music.* Vol. 2. London: Oxford University Press, 1930.

Heine, Heinrich. *Zeitungsberichte über Musik und Malerei.* Ed. Michael Mann. Frankfurt am Main: Insel-Verlag, 1964.

Heller, Amely. *H. W. Ernst im Urteile seiner Zeitgenossen.* Wien/Brünn/ Berlin: By the Author, 1905.

Henschel, [Sir] George. *Musings and Memories of a Musician.* London: Macmillan & Co., 1918.

Hiller, Ferdinand. *Ein Künstlerleben.* Cologne: Dumont-Schauberg, 1880.

Hiller, Johann Adam. *Lebensbeschreibungen berühmter Musikgelehrten und Tonkünstler.* Leipzig, 1784.

Holde, Arthur. "Suppressed Passages in the Brahms-Joachim Correspondence." *The Musical Quarterly* 45, no. 3 (July 1959):312–24.

Horowitz, Joseph. "The Sound of Russian Music in the West." *New York Times Magazine,* June 11, 1978.

Huberman, Bronislaw. *Aus der Werkstatt des Virtuosen.* Vienna: H. Heller & Cie, 1912.

Hutchings, Arthur J. B. *The Baroque Concerto.* London: Faber & Faber, 1961.

Jacobs, Arthur. "Spohr and the Baton." *Music and Letters* 31 (1950): 307–17.

Jelagin, Juri. *Taming of the Arts*. Trans. N. Wreden. New York: Dutton, 1951.

Joachim, Joseph, and Andreas Moser. *Violinschule*. Vol. 3, with prefaces of both editors. Berlin: N. Simrock, 1905.

———, eds. *Letters from and to Joseph Joachim*. Trans. Nora Bickley. London: Macmillan, 1914. Reprint. New York: Vienna House, 1972.

Jusefovich, Viktor. *David Oistrakh: Conversations with Igor Oistrakh*. Trans. N. de Pfeiffer. London: Cassell & Co., 1979.

Kalbeck, Max. *Johannes Brahms*. Berlin: Deutsche Brahms-Gesellschaft, 1908–14.

Kapp, Julius. *Paganini*. Berlin and Leipzig: Schuster & Loeffler, 1920.

Kogan, Pavel. *Vmeste s musykantami* [Together with musicians: memoirs of a concert manager in the U.S.S.R.; chapters on Milstein, Oistrakh, Stolyarsky]. Moscow, 1964.

Kolneder, Walter. *Antonio Vivaldi*. Wiesbaden: Breitkopf & Härtel, 1965. Trans. Bill Hopkins, London, 1970.

———. *Antonio Vivaldi, Documents of his Life and Works*. New York: Heinrichshofen Edition, 1982.

———. *Das Buch der Violine*. Zurich and Freiburg: Atlantis, 1972.

Koole, Arend. *Leven en werken van Pietro Antonio Locatelli da Bergamo*. Amsterdam, 1949.

———. *Pietro Antonio Locatelli: conferenza tenuta al Lions Club*. Bergamo: Collegium musicum, 1969.

Krasner, Louis. "A Performance History of Schoenberg's Violin Concerto Op. 36." *Journal of the Arnold Schoenberg Institute* 2, no. 2 (February 1978):84–98. (Also on Alban Berg Concerto.)

Kufferath, Maurice. *H. Vieuxtemps, sa vie et son oeuvre*. Brussels: Rozez, 1882.

Kulenkampff, Georg. *Geigerische Betrachtungen*. Regensburg: Rozez, 1952.

Lalande, Joseph-Gérome de. *Voyage d'un Français en Italie, fait dans les années 1755 et 1766*. Paris, 1769. (See vol. 8, pp. 293–94 about Tartini.)

La Laurencie, Lionel de. *L'école française de violon de Lully à Viotti*. Paris: Delagrave, 1922–24. Reprint 1971.

Landon, H. C. Robbins. *The Symphonies of Joseph Haydn*. London: Universal Edition & Rockliff, 1955.

Litzmann, Berthold. *Clara Schumann: ein Künstlerleben*. Leipzig: Breitkopf & Härtel, 1906. English trans. (abridged), 1913; reprint 1972, 1979.

Lochner, Louis P. *Fritz Kreisler*. New York: Macmillan, 1950. New ed., ill. Neptune City, N.J.: Paganiniana Publications, 1981.

Loft, Abram. *Violin and Keyboard: The Duo Repertoire*. New York: Grossman, 1973.

Magidoff, Robert. *Yehudi Menuhin*. New York: Doubleday & Co., 1955. 2d ed. 1973.

Mahler, Gustav. *Selected Letters*. Ed. Knud Martner. London: Faber & Faber; New York: Farrar, Straus & Giroux, 1979.

Mannes, David. *Music Is My Faith: An Autobiography.* New York: W. W. Norton, 1938.

May, Florence. *The Life of Johannes Brahms.* London: E. Arnold, 1905. 2d ed. rev. London: W. Reeves, 1948.

Melkus, Eduard. *Die Violine, eine Einführung in die Geschichte der Violine und des Violinspiels.* Bern and Stuttgart: Hallwag, 1973.

Mendelssohn, Felix. *Briefe, 1830–1847.* Leipzig: Hermann Mendelssohn, 1875.

———. *Letters.* Ed. G. Selden-Goth. New York: Pantheon, 1945.

———. *Reisebriefe, 1825–1832.* Munich: Piper & Co., 1947.

Menuhin, Yehudi. "Louis Persinger." *The Juilliard Review Annual* (1966–67):16.

———. *Unfinished Journey.* New York: Alfred A. Knopf, 1977.

Meyer, Ernst H. *English Chamber Music: The History of a Great Art. From the Middle Ages to Purcell.* London: Lawrence & Wishart, 1946.

Moser, Andreas. *Geschichte des Violinspiels.* Berlin: Max Hesses Verlag, 1923. 2d ed. enl. and rev. by H. J. Nösselt. Tutzing: Hans Schneider, 1966–67.

———. *Joseph Joachim, ein Lebensbild.* 2d ed. Berlin: Deutsche Brahms-Gesellschaft, 1908–10. English trans. of first ed., 1900.

Mozart, Leopold. *Versuch einer gründlichen Violinschule.* Augsburg: 1756. 2nd ed., 1770. 3rd ed., 1787. Facsimile eds. Ed. H. J. Moser. Leipzig: Breitkopf & Härtel: 1922 (1st ed.); 1956 (3rd ed.). Trans. Editha Knocker: *A Treatise on the Fundamental Principles of Violin Playing.* Preface by Alfred Einstein. London: Oxford University Press, 1948.

Mozart, Wolfgang Amadeus. *The Letters of Mozart and His Family.* Trans. and ed. Emily Anderson. 2nd ed. London: Macmillan & Co., 1966.

———. Briefe und Aufzeichnungen: Gesamtausgabe, eds. Wilhelm A. Bauer and Otto Erich Deutsch. Kassel: Bärenreiter, 1962–75.

Müry, Albert. "Die Instrumentalwerke Gaetano Pugnanis." Dissertation: Basel, 1941.

Die Musik in Geschichte und Gegenwart. Ed. Friedrich Blume. 14 vols. plus two supplementary vols., Kassel: Bärenreiter, 1949–79.

Newman, William S. *The Sonata in the Baroque Era.* Chapel Hill: University of North Carolina Press, 1959. Reprint. New York: W. W. Norton, 1972.

North, Roger. *Roger North on Music.* Ed. John Wilson. London: Novello & Co., 1959.

Petrobelli, Pierluigi. *Giuseppe Tartini: Le Fonte biographiche.* Universal Edition, 1968.

Pfäfflin, Clara. "Pietro Nardini. Sein Leben und seine Werke." Dissertation with thematic catalogue. Stuttgart, 1936.

Phipson, T. L. *Famous Violinists and Fine Violins.* 2d ed. London: Chatto & Windus; Philadelphia: Lippincott, 1903.

Pierre, Constant. *Le conservatoire nationale de musique et de déclamation. Documents historiques et administratifs.* Paris, 1900.

———. *Histoire du Concert spirituel, 1725–1790.* Ed. François Lesure. Paris: Heugel et Cie, 1975.

Pincherle, Marc. *Antonio Vivaldi et la musique instrumentale*. [With thematic index.] Paris: Floury, 1948. Reprint 1968.

———. *Corelli: His Life, His Work*. Trans. Hubert Russell. New York: W. W. Norton, 1956.

———. *Feuillets d'histoire du violon*. Paris: Legouix, 1927.

———. *Jean-Marie Leclair*. Paris: La Colombe, 1952.

———. *Les violonistes compositeurs et virtuoses*. Paris: Henri Laurens, 1922.

———. *Vivaldi, Genius of the Baroque*. Trans. Christopher Hatch. New York: W. W. Norton, 1957; London: Gollancz, 1958.

———. *The World of the Virtuoso*. Trans. Lucile H. Brockway. London: Victor Gollancz, 1964.

Pougin, Arthur. *Notice sur Rode*. Paris: Pottier de Lalaine, 1874.

———. *Viotti et l'école moderne de violon*. Paris: Schott, 1888.

Preussner, Eberhard, ed. *Die musikalischen Reisen des Herrn von Uffenbach* (1715). Kassel and Basel: Bärenreiter, 1949.

Pulver, Jeffrey. *Paganini: The Romantic Virtuoso*. London: Herbert Joseph, 1936. Reprint, with new bibliography by Frederick Freedman. New York: Da Capo, 1970.

Quantz, Johann Joachim. *Lebenslauf*. In F. W. Marpurg, *Historisch-kritische Beyträge*. Berlin, 1755. See Paul Nettl, *Forgotten Musicians*, New York: Philosophical Library, 1951.

———. *Versuch einer Anweisung, die Flöte traversière zu spielen*. Berlin, 1752. Facsimile of 3rd (1789) ed., ed. H. P. Schmitz. Kassel and Basel: Bärenreiter, 1953. English trans. *On Playing the Flute*. London, 1966.

Raaben, Lev. *Leopold Semyonovich Auer: ocherk zhizni i deyatelnosti* [Leopold S. Auer: life and activity]. Leningrad, 1962.

———. *Zhizn zamechatelnykh skripachei* [Lives of famous violinists]. Leningrad, 1967.

———. *Zhizn zamechatelnykh skripachei i violoncelistov* [Lives of famous violinists and cellists]. Leningrad, 1969.

Radoux, Théodore. *Henry Vieuxtemps*. Liège: Benard, 1891.

Raguenet, Abbé François. "Parallèle des Italiens et des Français en ce qui concerne la musique" (1702). English trans. (1709) attributed to J. E. Galliard. *The Musical Quarterly* 32, no. 3 (July 1946):411–36.

Rangoni, Giovanni Battista. *Saggio sul gusto della musica col carattere de' tre celebri sonatori di violino Nardini, Lolli e Pugnani*. Livorno: T. Masi, 1790. Facsimile Milan: Bolletino bibliografico musicale, 1932 (in French and Italian).

Reeser, H. Eduard. *De Klaviersonate met Vioolbegeleiding* [The keyboard sonata with violin accompaniment]. Rotterdam: Brusse's, 1939.

Reichardt, Johann Friedrich. *Vertraute Briefe aus Paris*. Hamburg: B. G. Hoffmann, 1804.

Reiss, Józef W. *Wieniawski*. Cracow: Polskie Wydawnictwo Muzyczne, 1970.

Riemann Musik Lexikon. 12th ed. Ed. Wilibald Gurlitt. Mainz: Schott, 1959.

Ronze-Neveu, M. J. *Ginette Neveu.* Paris, 1952; London: Barrie & Rockliff, 1957.

Rubinstein, Anton. *Autobiography.* Trans. Aline Delano. Boston: Little, Brown & Co., 1892. Reprint 1969.

Rubinstein, Leslie. "Oriental Musicians Come of Age," *New York Times Magazine,* November 23, 1980. Replies, ibid., December 28, 1980.

Ryom, Peter. *Verzeichnis der Werke Antonio Vivaldis. Kleine Ausgabe.* 2d ed. Leipzig: VEB, 1974.

Schemann, Ludwig. *Cherubini.* Stuttgart: Deutsche Verlagsanstalt, 1925.

Schering, Arnold. *Geschichte des Instrumental-Konzerts.* Leipzig: Breitkopf & Härtel, 1905. 2d ed. 1927. Reprint 1965.

———. Preface to Violin Concerto by Pisendel in *Denkmäler Deutscher Tonkunst,* vols. 29–30, p. xii. Leipzig, 1907.

Schneiderhan, Wolfgang. Opening address, *International Violin Congress, Graz 1972, Kongress-Bericht.* Ed. Vera Schwarz. Vienna: Universal-Edition, 1975.

Schonberg, Harold C. *The Great Conductors.* New York: Simon & Schuster, 1967.

Schottky, Julius M. *Paganini's Leben und Treiben als Künstler und als Mensch.* Prague: Taussig & Taussig, 1830. Facsimile reprint 1909. Reprint 1973.

Schubart, C. F. D. *Ideen zu einer Aesthetik der Tonkunst.* Vienna, 1806. Ed. P. A. Merbach. Leipzig: Wolkenwanderer-Verlag, 1924. Reprint 1969.

Schumann, Robert. *Gesammelte Schriften über Musik und Musiker.* 1854. Ed. Heinrich Simon. Leipzig: Reclam, 1888. 5th ed. Leipzig: Breitkopf & Härtel, 1914. Reprint (4th ed.) 1968. English trans. 1877.

———. *On Music and Musicians.* Ed. Konrad Wolff. Trans. Paul Rosenfeld. New York: Pantheon, 1946.

Schwarz, Boris. "Beethoven and the French Violin School." *The Musical Quarterly* 44, no. 4 (October 1958):431–47.

———. *French Instrumental Music between the Revolutions, 1789–1830.* 2nd rev. ed. New York: Da Capo Press, 1983.

———. *Music and Musical Life in Soviet Russia, 1917–1981.* 2d enl. ed. Bloomington: Indiana University Press, 1983.

Schweitzer, Albert. *Johann Sebastian Bach.* Leipzig: Breitkopf & Härtel, 1905. English trans. Ernest Newman, Leipzig, 1911; London: Black, 1923.

Shaw, George Bernard. *How to Become a Music Critic.* Ed. Dan H. Laurence. New York: Hill & Wang, 1961.

———. *London Music in 1888–89 as Heard by Corno di Bassetto.* London: Constable & Co., 1937.

Slonimsky, Nicolas. *Music since 1900.* 4th ed. New York: Charles Scribner's, 1971.

———. "The Murder of Leclair." In *A Thing or Two about Music.* New York: Allen, Towne & Heath, 1948.

Smith, Mortimer B. *The Life of Ole Bull.* Princeton: Princeton University Press, 1943.

Spalding, Albert. *A Rise to Follow.* New York: Holt & Co., 1943. Reprint. New York: Da Capo, 1977.

Spohr, Louis. *Autobiography.* London: Reeves & Turner, 1878. Reprint. New York: Da Capo, 1969.

———. *Briefwechsel mit seiner Frau Dorette.* Ed. F. Göthel. Kassel: Bärenreiter, 1957.

———. *Lebenserinnerungen.* Ed. Folker Göthel. Tutzing: Schneider, 1968.

———. *The Musical Journeys.* Trans. and ed. by Henry Pleasants. Norman: University of Oklahoma Press, 1961.

Straeten, Edmund van der. *The History of the Violin.* London: Cassell & Co., 1933. Reprint. New York: Da Capo, 1968.

Strunk, Oliver. *Source Readings in Music History.* New York: W. W. Norton, 1950.

Szigeti, Joseph. *Szigeti on the Violin.* New York: Frederick Praeger, 1970.

———. *With Strings Attached. Reminiscences and Reflections.* New York: Alfred A. Knopf, 1947. 2d ed., rev. and enl. New York, 1967.

Talbot, Michael. *Vivaldi.* London: Dent, 1978.

Tartini, Giuseppe. *Le Opere di Giuseppe Tartini.* Ed. Edoardo Farina. Milan: Carisch, 1971– (in progress).

———. *Traité des Agréments de la musique.* Paris 1771. New ed. by Erwin R. Jacobi (in German, French, English, Italian facs.). Celle & New York: Hermann Moeck Verlag, 1961. (Contains Tartini's letter to Maddalena Lombardini in three languages, including Dr. Burney's English trans.)

Tawaststjerna, Erik. *Sibelius.* Vol. 1, 1865–1905. Trans. Robert Layton. London: Faber & Faber; Berkeley: University of California Press, 1976.

Tchaikovsky, Modest. *The Life and Letters of P. I. Tchaikovsky.* Trans. and ed. Rosa Newmarch. London: John Lane, 1906.

Thayer, Alexander Wheelock. *The Life of Ludwig van Beethoven.* Ed. Henry Krehbiel. Rev. and ed. Elliot Forbes. Princeton: Princeton University Press, 1964.

———. *Ludwig van Beethovens Leben.* Ed. and trans. Hermann Deiters. Vols. 1–3. Berlin, 1866–79. Vols. 4–5. Ed. Hugo Riemann. 1907–8.

Thibaud, Jacques. *Un violon parle.* Ed. Jean-Pierre Dorian. Paris: Editions du Blé qui Lève, 1947.

Torchi, Luigi. *La musica instrumentale in Italia nei secoli XVI, XVII, XVIII.* Torino: Bocca, 1901.

———, ed. *L'arte musicale in Italia.* 7 vols. Milan: Ricordi, 1897–1907.

Veinus, Abraham. *The Concerto.* London: Cassell, 1948; New York: Doubleday, 1949. 2d ed. rev. 1964.

Walker, Alan, ed. *Robert Schumann: The Man and his Music.* London: Barrie & Jenkins, 1972.

Wasielewski, Wilhelm Joseph von. *Ludwig van Beethoven.* Leipzig: List & Francke, 1888.

———. *Die Violine und ihre Meister.* Leipzig: Breitkopf & Härtel, 1869. 5th ed. rev. 1910.

Westrup, [Sir] Jack Allan. *Purcell.* London: J. M. Dent & Sons, 1937. 3rd ed. rev. 1947.

Wieniawski, Henryk, Kronika życia [Chronicle of Life; pictorial chronicle, Polish captions]. Ed. Wladyslaw Duleba. Cracow: Polskie Wydawnictwo Muzyczne, 1967.

Wood, [Sir] Henry J. *My Life of Music.* London: Victor Gollancz, 1938.

Wulf, Joseph. *Musik im Dritten Reich.* Gütersloh: Rowohlt, 1963.

Yampolsky, Israil. *David Oistrakh.* Moscow, 1958. 2d enl. ed. 1968.

————. *Genrik Wieniawski.* Moscow, 1955.

————. *Russkoye skripichnoye iskusstvo* [Russian violin art]. Vol. 1, from the beginnings until the 1860s. Moscow and Leningrad, 1951.

Ysaÿe, Antoine. *Eugène Ysaÿe.* Brussels: Editions Ysaÿe, 1974.

————. *Eugène Ysaÿe: sa vie, son oeuvre, son influence.* Preface by Yehudi Menuhin. Brussels: Editions L'Écran du monde, 1948.

————, and Bertram Ratcliffe. *Ysaÿe, His Life, Work and Influence.* Preface by Yehudi Menuhin. London: W. Heinemann, 1947. (Revised English version of previous book.)

Zschinsky-Troxler, Elsa von. *Gaetano Pugnani.* Berlin: Atlantis, 1939.

INDEX